Also by David King

Finding Atlantis:
A True Story of Genius, Madness, and an Extraordinary
Quest for a Lost World

Vienna, 1814

How the Conquerors of Napoleon Made Love, War, and Peace at the Congress of Vienna

David King

Broadway Paperbacks
New York

Published in the United States by Broadway Paperbacks, an imprint of the
Crown Publishing Group, a division of Random House, Inc., New York.
www.crownpublishing.com

Broadway Paperbacks and its logo, a letter B bisected on the diagonal,
are trademarks of Random House, Inc.

Originally published in hardcover in the United States by Harmony Books,
an imprint of the Crown Publishing Group, a division of
Random House, Inc., New York, in 2008.

Library of Congress Cataloging-in-Publication Data

King, David, 1970–
Vienna, 1814 : how the conquerors of Napoleon made love, war, and peace
at the Congress of Vienna / David King.—1st ed.
Includes bibliographical references and index.

1. Congress of Vienna (1814–1815)   2. Napoleonic Wars 1800–1815—Treaties.
3. Europe—Politics and government—1789–1815.   4. Statesmen—Europe—
History—19th century.   I. Title.
DC249.K46 2008
940.2'714—dc22   2007024680

ISBN 978-0-307-33717-7

Design by Lauren Dong

First Broadway Paperbacks Edition
146122990

To my parents

Contents

You have come at the right moment. If you like fêtes and balls you will have enough of them; the Congress does not move forward, it dances.

—Prince de Ligne

Vienna, 1814

PREFACE

May 4, 1814

The tall, sleek frigate HMS *Undaunted* slowly made its way toward the tiny fishing harbor. Two dozen exhausted rowers helped steer the graceful vessel to the hastily constructed wooden quay. Assembled crowds cheered themselves hoarse, and bouquets of flowers floated on the water to welcome the strangers. For on board was the new emperor of Elba, absolute sovereign of every bit of the sixteen-mile-long island.

Everyone was curious, straining to catch a glimpse of the short man in the old green coat, white breeches, and bright red top boots. He was instantly known by his walk, head down, body somewhat stooped forward, hands clasped behind his back, frantically pacing like some "wild animal in a cage." Flakes of snuff frequently dangled from his lips, completing the ruffled, disheveled impression.

Only two weeks before, he had attempted suicide, downing a poisonous concoction of opium, belladonna, and white hellebore carried in a heart-shaped vial worn around his neck. The dose was certainly enough to be fatal, but its strength had been sapped during the brutal Russian winter. Now all the bitter memories of that disastrous time seemed worlds away. Certainly, the island at the other end of his spyglass was no Corsica. But the emperor was resigned to his fate, imagining what lay ahead on his sunny yet confined new home.

For Napoleon Bonaparte, that brilliant maniac, had been stopped after conquering most of the continent. Territory after territory had succumbed with astonishing rapidity to the bold "man of destiny." The

French tricolor had been raised everywhere from Madrid to Moscow; proud members of the Bonaparte clan had been placed on thrones all over the sprawling empire. By 1814, however, overextension, exhaustion, and too many military fiascoes had sent the monstrous edifice crashing down. Napoleon had been defeated, his empire shattered, and the entire web of international relations thrown into utter disarray. It was time to rebuild.

Kings, queens, princes, and diplomats would all pour into the city of Vienna in the autumn of 1814 for the highly anticipated peace conference. More than 200 states and princely houses would send delegates to settle the many unresolved issues. How were the victors to reconstruct the war-torn continent? How were they going to make restitution to the millions who had lost family members or suffered the horrors of Napoleonic domination? The Vienna Congress offered a chance to correct the wrongs of the past and, many hoped, create the "best of all possible worlds."

Reasoned opinion predicted that all negotiations would be wrapped up in three or four weeks. Even the most seasoned diplomats expected no more than six. But the delegates, thrilled by the prospects of a lasting peace, indulged in unrestrained celebrations. The Vienna peace conference soon degenerated into a glittering vanity fair: masked balls, medieval-style jousts, and grand formal banquets—a "sparkling chaos" that would light up the banks of the Danube.

Indeed, while the peacemakers enjoyed themselves, hopes for a timely resolution were quickly fading. Secret intrigues, personal animosities, bitter hatreds, and a host of other unexpected obstacles would prevent the dazzling entourage from agreeing on just about anything. Waging peace, the delegates learned, would be as difficult as defeating Napoleon.

Suddenly, six months into the "happy, unfettered confusion," a courier reached Vienna with a letter marked URGENT. It was slightly past 6 a.m., and the Austrian foreign minister, Prince Klemens von Metternich, was too tired to be bothered with yet another matter claiming immediate attention. He put the letter on his nightstand and went back to bed. An hour and a half later, he opened the dispatch, sent from an imperial and royal consulate general in Genoa (actually, it was Livorno). It read in full:

> The English commissioner Campbell has just entered the harbor to inquire whether anyone has seen Napoleon at [Livorno], in light of

the fact that he has disappeared from the island of Elba. The answer being in the negative, the English frigate put to sea again without delay.

To his horror, the truth dawned on the dazed insomniac. Napoleon Bonaparte had escaped and no one had any idea where he was headed. The Austrian minister scrambled out of bed, dressed "in a flash," and broke the news to the congress. By the time the curtain fell at the Redoutensaal theater that evening, the hunt was on for the "most feared warlord since Genghis Khan."

THE CONGRESS OF Vienna was indeed quite unlike any other peace conference in history. It was to be the first large peacemaking venture in almost 175 years, and it has been controversial ever since. In addition to the many issues and tensions, one of its most fascinating features is the explosive mix of delegates sent to the decadent Habsburg capital.

Representing the Austrian hosts was the elegant, sophisticated, and vain Prince Metternich, a "Don Juan" who excelled in the arts of seduction. With Napoleon's defeat and exile, France sent a diplomat every bit as polished and devious: Prince Charles-Maurice de Talleyrand-Périgord. Almost all the scandalous accusations about him were true, Madame de la Tour du Pin acknowledged, but Talleyrand was still the most enchanting man she had ever known. His powdered wig, velvet coat, and red heels made him look like the last survivor of the ancien régime. "Shit in silk stockings" was Napoleon's verdict.

The most volatile and hot-tempered of the delegations, however, was undoubtedly Prussia, the north German state that was, at this time, too strong to be a minor power, and yet not quite strong enough to be a great one. Their king, Frederick William III, came in person, bringing one of the largest, most educated, and hardworking delegations to town. The Prussians demanded compensation after their country had been unceremoniously carved up at the whims of the French invaders.

As for Great Britain, Foreign Secretary Robert Stewart, Viscount Castlereagh, made the journey himself. He was an aloof and eccentric gentleman, who had previously caused a scandal in London when, as a member of Parliament, he had hoped to end malicious political intrigues by challenging a rival cabinet minister to a duel. Now Castlereagh had turned his energies to strategy, all too aware that he represented an economic powerhouse with a royal navy in a league of its own.

Finally, the last of the great powers were the Russians, and they produced the greatest celebrity of the conference, at least at the beginning: the Tsar Alexander. Tall, blond, and sporting a dark-green uniform with a wide hat cocked to the side, Alexander was a man of sudden impulse and excess. His sexual appetites were insatiable, already rivaling those of his grandmother Catherine the Great. In addition, the tsar was growing increasingly mystical and unpredictable. "If he were a woman," Napoleon once said, "I think I would make him my mistress."

Such were the distinguished and worldly leaders who would come together for the unforgettable nine-month drama of the Vienna Congress—the greatest and most lavish party in history. They would plot, scheme, jockey for position, and, in short, infuriate each other as they competed in affairs of state and the heart. One participant, the young songwriter Count Auguste de La Garde-Chambonas, described the spectacle:

> A kingdom was cut into bits or enlarged at a ball; an indemnity was granted in the course of a dinner; a constitution was planned during a hunt . . . Everyone was engrossed with pleasure.

Yet despite the unabashed frivolity, world maps were redrawn, the neutrality of Switzerland guaranteed, the freedom of the seas and international rivers proclaimed, diplomatic procedures established, and priceless works of art restored, along with many other achievements. And by the end of this historic gathering, the delegates accomplished what they had hoped to do—the peace was signed on June 9, 1815.

Set in ballrooms, bedrooms, and palaces, *Vienna, 1814* tells the story of how these unlikely revelers created what Henry Kissinger called the longest period of peace Europe has ever known.

Chapter 1

BREAD AND CIRCUSES

There is literally a royal mob here. Everybody is crying out:
Peace! Justice! Balance of power! Indemnity!
As for me, I am a looker-on. All the indemnity I ask for is a new hat.

—PRINCE DE LIGNE

Ornate rococo carriages rumbled through a landscape scorched by twentysome years of revolution and warfare. Dangers lurked everywhere on the poor, unlit roadways. Cutthroat highwaymen preyed on isolated travelers, and inns were hardly safe havens, either, often little better than "murderer's dens." Venturing out into the bleak postwar world was for "the fearless, the foolish, or the suicidal." During the autumn of 1814, it was also for the idealistic and the idle. Hordes of pleasure-seekers would flock to Vienna for an unprecedented pageant.

The occasion was the Congress of Vienna, the long-awaited peace conference to decide the future of Europe. Kings, queens, princes, princesses, dukes, duchesses, diplomats, and about a hundred thousand other visitors would make their way to the central European city, swelling the population by as much as a third. No one, though, it must be said, really had an idea of what to expect. The invitation for the congress had been sent by way of an announcement in the newspaper.

The Revolutionary and Napoleonic Wars had ripped Europe apart. For the first time in history, enormous armies based on universal conscription had marched across the continent to wage a "total war." France had set the standard for this comprehensive mobilization of the people with the famous decree of August 1793:

The young shall fight; married men shall forge weapons and transport supplies; the women will make tents and clothes and will serve
in the hospitals; the children will make old linen into lint; the old
men will have themselves carried into the public squares to rouse
the courage of fighting men.

By the end of the war in the spring of 1814, the suffering had been
immense—a terrible ordeal that ruined states, wrecked economies, and
ravaged families. As many as 5 million people were dead, and many more
had been permanently or seriously disabled. Entire villages had been
wiped off the map. Lands had been devastated, laws trammeled, and
atrocities committed on a horrific scale.

The many issues arising out of this wreckage were, to be sure, tangled,
thorny, and controversial. During the war, the Allied powers had under-
standably hoped to postpone the many difficult decisions until after victory. Now that Napoleon had been defeated, the only matter that had been
officially decided was the question of France, which had been settled back
in May 1814, after two months of wrangling following the capture of the
capital.

According to the terms of the Treaty of Paris, France's frontiers were
redrawn as they had been on the first of January 1792. This meant that
France would have to surrender the vast majority of its conquests, but
not, in fact, all of them. Any territory that France had seized by that date
twenty-two years before would be retained, including communities in the
northeast, Chambéry in Savoy, the former papal enclave of Avignon, and
even some colonies in the new world. Thanks to the treaty, France would
actually possess more territory and a greater population than it had
under Louis XIV, Louis XV, or Louis XVI.

The Allies had hoped that such generous terms would help the new
king, Louis XVIII, establish himself on the throne, and at the same time,
reintegrate his country peacefully into the international community.
That's also why the victors spared France many of the usual penalties
inflicted on a defeated power. There was no indemnity to pay, no foreign
occupation army to endure, and no limitation, in any way, on the size of
the army. This was, in many ways, a remarkably lenient agreement.

Everything else, however, remained unresolved. The Vienna Congress would have to make some hard decisions about the former empire and its many satellite kingdoms. At stake was virtually all of western Europe, vast realms east of the Rhine, and some highly coveted islands from the Caribbean to the East Indies.

The most difficult of these questions, at least at the beginning, was the fate of Poland. Napoleon had called this country the "key to the vault," and the so-called enlightened despots of the eighteenth century had tried to seize as much of its strategic territory as possible, carving it up no fewer than three times. By 1795, Poland had completely disappeared from the map, devoured, as Frederick the Great had said, "like an artichoke, leaf by leaf."

Russia had ended up with the lion's share of Polish territory, including Lithuania, Ukraine, Belarus, and eastern Poland. Austria had taken the ancient capital of Kraków, along with the rich agricultural region of eastern Galicia and the salt mines of Tarnopol. Prussia had seized Warsaw, Gdánsk, and the strip of territory running north to the sea later known as the "Polish Corridor." For many, such a cynical and ruthless display of power politics was simply indefensible.

During the war, Napoleon had played on these sentiments, blasting the Polish partitions as "unforgivable, immoral, and impolitic." He promised the Poles that if they could prove to him that they were "worthy of being a nation," he would restore their country. But despite the many Polish sacrifices, Napoleon never did more than create the tiny Duchy of Warsaw, and exploit it ruthlessly. The Vienna Congress seemed an excellent opportunity finally to restore Poland, though finding a solution was not going to be easy.

Napoleon, moreover, had been a fertile kingmaker, placing family and friends on thrones all over the continent, from Italy to Holland to Spain. Napoleon had also created brand-new kingdoms in Germany, such as the Kingdom of Bavaria, Württemberg, and Saxony. What were the victors going to do with all the newly minted monarchs desperately clutching their crowns? What, for that matter, was going to happen to the older ruling families who had been ousted in the Napoleonic whirlwind and were now lobbying for a return to their kingdoms? The Vienna Congress was gearing up for an unusual battle royal for the thrones of Europe.

In addition, there was also a controversy brewing about the works of art that had been stolen. In only a few years, Napoleon and his Grande Armée had earned a reputation as history's most audacious thieves. Countless masterpieces from Michelangelo, Raphael, Titian, and Rembrandt were carted up and carried off by Napoleon's henchmen. The emperor's goal was simple: to make the city of Paris, as he put it, "the most beautiful that could ever exist." The Frenchman in charge of the art confiscations, Dominique-Vivant Denon, acted with a merciless efficiency, and transformed his museum, the Louvre, into an artistic "wonder of the world."

Now all these sculptures, paintings, jewels, tapestries, and other stolen treasures were once again up for grabs. The French, of course, insisted on retaining their war trophies, and the Allied powers had tentatively agreed, adding a clause to the Treaty of Paris allowing France to keep its loot. But in the autumn of 1814 there was a new call to return the art to its previous owners, and this motion was particularly popular among the heavily despoiled lands such as Italy and the Netherlands.

Indeed along with the official delegations, there were many informal and unofficial representatives, often self-appointed, that came to press their own hopes and projects. As the form of the congress had been vague, many believed that they had a right to participate in the decision making and arrived fully expecting to do so. These private delegations would be selling everything from constitutions to songs. One American entrepreneur, Dr. Justus Bollmann, arrived with a whole portfolio of projects, including a plan to create the first steamship company on the Danube.

There were delegations coming from Frankfurt, Lübeck, and Prague to protect the rights of Jewish minorities, so recently granted under Napoleon and now at risk of being repealed. One group wanted the congress to launch a crusade against piracy around the world, from the corsairs infesting the Mediterranean to the buccaneers raiding the Caribbean. Representatives of publishing firms came to Vienna to address another kind of piracy, "the gang of robbers known as literary pirates" who unscrupulously preyed "with impunity against authors and publishers." The hope was to create an international copyright to protect intellectual property.

Everyone, it seemed, had a vision of how the postwar world should best be reconstructed. The problem, however, was that the peacemakers were far more divided than it was imagined. And all the underlying differences, which had been so successfully suppressed in the life-and-death struggle against Napoleon, would now reemerge in Vienna with a vengeance.

THE HABSBURG CAPITAL was a good choice for the world meeting. Geographically and culturally, Vienna was the heart of Europe. Until as late as August 1806, Vienna had been the center of the Holy Roman Empire, the gigantic, ramshackle realm that had been dismantled by Napoleon. After nearly a thousand-year run, looming over central Europe at times with a menacing and other times tottering presence, the Holy Roman Empire was no more. Imperial majesty and grandeur, however, had far from faded.

"The city proper," one traveler noted on entering Vienna's gates, "seems like a royal palace." Grand baroque mansions lined the narrow, twisting lanes that snaked their way through the old medieval center. Spires, domes, towers, and neoclassical columns carved in bright white stone, each roof and facade looked more sumptuous and elaborately adorned than the next. Rows of large bay windows predominated, overlooking one of the greenest capitals in Europe, a fact that was due at least partly to the foresight of the eighteenth-century emperor Joseph II, who had decreed that a tree must be planted for every one cut down.

Vienna had indeed an aristocratic flair that many other cities like London lacked, or like Paris had lost since the revolution. Austrian, Hungarian, and Bohemian aristocrats lived there, often in mansions with their own ballrooms, riding schools, and sometimes even private opera houses. Many French émigrés fleeing the revolution had also settled there, though most were considerably poorer now, and lived in cheaper third- and fourth-floor apartments.

The merchant class, if that term can be used about such a small group, was not that visible in Vienna, and the town's artisans overwhelmingly geared their production to meeting the demands of court and society, making saddles, harnesses, carriages, clocks, musical instruments, and other luxuries. The biggest source of production was still wine, which always found a ready market in a town where residents, as one historian put it, "lunched until dinner, and then dined until supper."

The vast majority of the events at the peace congress would take place in the old town, still encircled by its city walls, which ran roughly along the lines of today's sweeping boulevard, the Ringstrasse. According to legend, the thick stone walls had been constructed using ransom money for King Richard I, "the Lion-Hearted," who was captured in 1193 on his way to the Second Crusade. In reality, the walls were built and rebuilt almost incessantly over the centuries, as they withstood various sieges, including two particularly frightful ones from the Turks. After the last attack from the French in 1809, the city walls were not being reconstructed, and the remaining bastions would serve at the congress mainly as a fashionable walkway affording some excellent views of the town.

Vienna was built on a large plain where the Danube divides and can be easily forded, as the Romans who founded a camp there in the first century discovered. During the Middle Ages, the small town lay on the exposed eastern rim of Charlemagne's empire, a fact that survives in the German name for Austria, Österreich. Historically, Vienna has long served as a crossroads between east and west. Crusaders, merchants, friars, and many other travelers would pass through the town, traveling east along its river—the mighty, muddy Danube, flowing on its two-thousand-mile journey from the Black Forest to the Black Sea.

With a population reaching some quarter of a million, and ranked third in size behind London and Paris, Vienna enjoyed a reputation for being a joyous and sensuous, if also irritable and somewhat cranky, place. "Vienna is the city of the world where the most uncommon raptures are experienced," as the French émigré Baronne du Montet put it. Another admirer, the songwriter Count Auguste de La Garde-Chambonas, who had traveled extensively in his search for adventure, called Vienna enthusiastically "the homeland of happiness." That autumn, the visitors to the peace conference would see exactly what he meant.

Hosting the congress officially was the emperor of Austria, Francis I, the last person ever to be crowned Holy Roman Emperor. Born in Florence, Italy, Francis was head of the Habsburg family, Europe's oldest and arguably most illustrious dynasty, occupying the throne in virtual unbroken succession since the thirteenth century. The single exception to this six-hundred-year dominance was Charles VII of the Wittelsbach family, who ruled briefly in the early 1740s, before the crown reverted to the Habsburgs (or more correctly, as they were known, from then on, the House of Habsburg-Lorraine).

Emperor Francis stood about medium height with high, sharply chiseled cheekbones, snow-white hair, and the infamous Habsburg jaw that jutted out from his bony face. He was only forty-six years old, though he looked considerably older. He had already weathered twenty-two stormy years on the throne, facing first the French Revolution and then Napoleon. Indeed, Emperor Francis looked tired and worn-out, or as one put it, "If you blew hard, you'd blow him to the ground."

As insiders knew, Francis was popular among the people and the court. He was called "Papa Franz" and "the father of his country," and was celebrated in music, including Joseph Haydn's "God Save Emperor Franz!" (the melody still used for the German national anthem). Some family members called the white-haired emperor Venus, the goddess of love. This was admittedly something of a Habsburg eccentricity, though the emperor was a well-known lover of statues, seals, and antiquities, and he looked out with a gaze as dreamy and blank as any ancient sculpture.

When the emperor was not trying to make order out of the managed chaos of the administration, which far too often seemed to run in circles after yet another rubber stamp, Francis enjoyed the music of this great *Musikstadt*. The emperor played the violin in the family string quartet, sometimes accompanied by his foreign minister, Metternich, on the cello. Francis also liked to make candy, tend to his plants in the palace hothouses, and study the large collection of maps in his library. The emperor possessed a knowledge of continental geography that, among the sovereigns coming to the congress, was unmatched. His large book collection, which at his death reached forty thousand volumes, would form the core of the Austrian National Library.

The headquarters for the social maelstrom of the Vienna Congress would be Emperor Francis's palace, the Hofburg, or as it was known, the Burg. Originally a functional four-tower fortress built into the old city wall as part of the city's defenses in the late thirteenth century, the rambling palace had grown to occupy several blocks in the city center as the Habsburg rulers continually added new wings and courts.

Emperor Francis had decided to open up this palace to his fellow sovereigns. After some consideration about rank and status, in order not to ruffle any royal feathers, the emperor had offered the Russian tsar the fanciful white and gold paneled rococo suites on the third floor of the

Amalienburg, a late-sixteenth-century addition to the palace named after the wife of Emperor Joseph I, and recently renovated. It was a superb suite with extravagant gilded mirrors, crystal chandeliers, and damask-covered chairs atop shining parquet floors.

The king of Prussia was to have a suite on the third floor of the Schweizerhof, the old medieval center of the castle, the courtyard of which had originally been intended for jousts. At its entrance stood the sixteenth-century Renaissance "Gate of Virtue" with a crowned Habsburg eagle flanked by two large resting lions. This wing had served as the favorite dwelling of the Austrian empress, Maria Ludovika, who moved to another part of the palace in order to make room for this royal guest.

Three other kings, two empresses, a queen, and many princes would also be housed in the palace. The king of Denmark, the tall, thin, and talkative Frederick VI, would also be lodged in the Schweizerhof, and the large, stern, melancholy king of Württemberg on the second floor of the Amalienburg. By the end of the month, the king of Bavaria, Maximilian I Joseph, the popular "Good King Max" and the founder of the Oktoberfest celebration, would take over suites in the early eighteenth-century wing known as the Reichskanzlei, or the Imperial Court Chancellery.

Every night at the palace, some forty or fifty banquet tables would be set at a cost that, it was whispered, ran to wildly exorbitant amounts. They were certainly elaborate affairs, sometimes involving as many as eight courses. The first was usually soup and hors d'oeuvres, brought out in large tureens and platters by wigged and liveried servants, and placed on tables adorned with court silver, crystal, and often gigantic gilded bronze centerpieces that incorporated many flowers and candles.

Guests progressed through a number of other dishes, usually including beef, ham, venison, pheasant, partridge, or some other meat. Years later, the choice of wine and entrée became much more standardized: oysters with Chablis, boiled beef with Rhenish wine, roast meat with Bordeaux or perhaps Tokay, the delicate dessert wine from imperial vineyards in Hungary. Fruits, sweets, cakes, and a wide variety of pies, cheeses, or jellies often followed. Ice cream was served only when Emperor Francis was present, and some six hundred rations of coffee, in mammoth kettles, were set aside daily for the sleep-deprived guests.

The kitchens that turned out such feasts for the congress were a sight unto themselves. In the main kitchen, accessed by a staircase underneath the court chapel, there was a giant spit, large enough to roast an ox, and joined with several other spits that could turn a few geese, ducks, hares, or pheasants. Cauldrons and copper pots and charcoal fumes dominated in the scorching heat—the fire on the largest spit so large, one said, it seemed a vision of hell. In other smaller rooms, a team of chefs, under-chefs, cooks, and other kitchen staff chopped, spiced, and diced on "the poor animals like the devil treats the soul of the damned."

To make sure that his elegant guests were entertained in style, the emperor had appointed a Festivals Committee, and made it responsible for planning, promoting, and managing all the official entertainment. The committee would set the busy social calendar that, as the emperor insisted, should be lively and fresh. The Festivals Committee would be continually challenged to find new or more interesting ways to enhance the "pursuit of pleasure" and make sure that the mood of "universal rejoicing" did not falter—all this for an elite crowd used to the very best and sharply critical when their high standards were not met.

The Festivals Committee was, by most accounts, one of the hardest-working committees at the congress. It would organize a series of lavish balls, banquets, masquerades, hunts, and the whole "preposterous extrav-agance" that later, more sober generations would come to associate with the Congress of Vienna.

Catering to the whims of their houseguests for an uncertain length of time would sometimes be exasperating. Vienna wits soon put these diffi-culties in perspective, while also poking fun at the early impressions made by the celebrated guests who would so readily accept Emperor Francis's generosity.

The Emperor of Russia:	*He makes love for everyone.*
The King of Prussia:	*He thinks for everyone.*
The King of Denmark:	*He speaks for everyone.*
The King of Bavaria:	*He drinks for everyone.*
The King of Württemberg:	*He eats for everyone.*
The Emperor of Austria:	*He pays for everyone.*

For a short time, indeed, Vienna would be the capital of Europe, the site of a massive victory celebration, and home to the most glamorous gathering since the fall of the Roman Empire. Palaces and parks, opera houses and ballrooms—the entire town would turn into a shimmering baroque playground. There had been large peace conferences before, but never anything like this. The Vienna Congress was to be the most spectacular peace conference in history. It was also, with its extravagance and decadence, going to be one of the most controversial.

Chapter 2

Two Princes

Good heavens, Madame. Who could resist loving a man with so many vices?

— COUNT FRANÇOIS-CASIMIR MOURET DE MONTROND,
DESCRIBING HIS FRIEND TALLEYRAND TO ONE OF HIS MISTRESSES

ilverware was hastily polished, white tablecloths were pressed, and napkins starched and folded. The wine cellars were stocked with the region's finest wines, including some bottles of Tokay, one hundred years old, costing about a year's salary for a junior lecturer at the University of Vienna. Many distinguished arrivals would soon pour into town, as one put it, "like peasants to a country fair."

Imperial carriages received a fresh coat of paint, dark green with a yellow coat of arms on the door, and their coachmen were outfitted in matching yellow livery. All three hundred of the carriages, soon to be placed at the disposal of the guests, would sport a uniform appearance, which would hopefully help avoid unpleasant squabbles over precedence. This was a wise decision, though at least one member of the Naples delegation, Signor Castelli, would have preferred more glitz, comparing his carriage to a "slow-rolling maid's chamber."

In the center of the bustle was Austria's foreign minister, Prince Klemens von Metternich. He was forty-one years old with curly blond hair, pale blue eyes, and the slender toned physique of a fencer. He stood above medium height, and had a handsome, delicate face and a gift for sparkling conversation. Metternich was hailed as the "Adonis of the Drawing Room."

It was hard to believe that this elegant and sophisticated man who had spun so many webs of intrigue for the Austrian Foreign Ministry had not been born in the country whose policy he was now crafting. He had not even seen Vienna itself until after his twenty-first birthday. Metternich was a Rhinelander. He was a native of the city of Koblenz, located on the bank of the Rhine in a region renowned for its towering cathedrals, its terraced vineyards, and its creative blend of Franco-Germanic culture that fostered such an easygoing lifestyle.

Metternich's real name was a tongue-twisting mouthful: Klemens Wenzel Nepomuk Lothar von Metternich-Winneburg-Beilstein, each designation harkening back to a distinguished ancestor or an extensive family estate somewhere in central Europe. Metternich's father, Franz Georg Karl, had been an imperial count of the Holy Roman Empire, one of only four hundred families that enjoyed a privileged status. His mother, Maria Beatrix von Kagenegg, had been a lady-in-waiting for Empress Maria Theresa. Yet by the standards of the time, the Metternichs barely ranked among the elite. There was a definite pecking order, and a number of princes, margraves, dukes, and electors all floated on a social plane high above the count. For many years, Vienna's crème de la crème would not let Metternich forget this tenuous status.

He had gained a social boost, however, when he married into one of Vienna's most distinguished families. His wife, Countess Eleanor von Kaunitz—or Laure, as he called her—was a granddaughter of Prince Wenzel Kaunitz, the famous Austrian minister who guided foreign policy for some forty years in the eighteenth century. "I cannot understand at all how any woman can resist him," she had said of Metternich, swept away by his charm. After overcoming her family's considerable resistance to the match, they had married in September 1795. By most standards, this was not a happy marriage.

Metternich, a notorious harlequin, would have many love affairs over the years, including one with Napoleon's younger sister Caroline, and another with the wife of the French marshal Jean-Andoche Junot. Metternich, indeed, never overcame his weakness for romantic liaisons, those "secret dashes in hired cabs, rendezvous in ghostly grottoes, and moonlight scampering in and out of upper-storey windows." Laure had to settle for amiable compatibility.

While this arrangement was certainly not uncommon among aristocratic families, Metternich was considerably more affectionate with their children. The oldest, seventeen-year-old Marie, was his favorite, with her wit, charm, and good looks that already reminded many of her father. Victor, aged fourteen, was the only surviving son in the family, an excellent student already tapped for a career in the Austrian bureaucracy (two other boys had died in infancy). The two youngest were ten-year-old Clementine and three-year-old Leontine. "If I had not been a minister of state," he said, "I would have been a nursery governess."

What had brought Metternich to Vienna for the first time, in November 1794, was the turmoil of the French Revolution. Fanatical armies had swarmed into the Rhineland on a rampage of destruction, intent to wage war on the aristocracy and its sleek, lacy decadence. The Metternichs, epitomizing this target, were forced to flee for their lives. The family estate on the Rhine was ruined, and their property plundered.

No surprise, Metternich would long be horrified of war, "that hateful invention" that released humanity's most savage urges and almost invariably ended with all sorts of barbaric crimes. Later experience only confirmed these early impressions. In 1809, when the time had seemed right to attack Napoleon, Austria was quickly squashed and almost annihilated as a power. Next time, Metternich knew, Austria might not survive.

It was during that same year of defeat that Metternich was given his chance to manage foreign policy. After a grand tour through the embassies of Dresden, Berlin, and then Paris, Metternich had been named Austrian foreign minister. His career in the five years before the congress had certainly been controversial.

Metternich had arranged the marriage of the Austrian emperor's oldest daughter, Archduchess Marie Louise, to Napoleon, a move highly unpopular in many Viennese circles, which still regarded Napoleon as the devil incarnate and the match as a bitter humiliation. For Metternich, this was a necessary evil that would strengthen Austria, ally it to the continent's strongest power, and allow more time to heal her wounds. Equally controversial, when the French empire started to unravel, Metternich seemed slow to abandon Napoleon and the alliance that, he believed, had kept Austria alive.

Critics were indeed quick to point out Metternich's many shortcomings. He seemed a flippant and frivolous lightweight. One year's essential priority in his foreign office might be discarded the next with an astonishing ease, suddenly dismissed as "antediluvian," as the prince referred to outdated concerns. His policy had a tendency to fluctuate and infuriate, with Metternich bouncing back and forth between colleagues, flittering about like a "butterfly minister."

All the while, Metternich displayed an unshakable confidence in his own abilities—a shocking and annoying arrogance that, as a colleague said, confused "haughtiness for dignity." How easily he brushed aside criticisms, and how little, really, he seemed troubled by the magnitude of the problems he often faced. For many, Metternich was a sly, superficial, and shallow fop, hopelessly out of his league.

Metternich's admirers, on the other hand, were unmoved by this criticism. Sure, there was a kernel of truth in each charge. Metternich seemed lazy, vain, and irreverent, but it was also true that he deliberately cultivated his image of gentlemanly nonchalance. He liked to pose as a playful and idle dabbler, while at the same time he waged diplomacy like a game of chess and did whatever it took to win. His rivals, continuing to underrate his abilities, went right on being checkmated.

In his five years as foreign minister, Metternich had carefully and skillfully guided Austrian diplomacy through a maze of challenges, advancing stage by stage from Austria's utter defeat and subservience to Napoleon in 1809 to becoming an ally of significance, and then, finally, at the right moment, in August 1813, defecting to the Allied coalition that would eventually defeat Napoleon. Austria had helped tip the balance. One historian has called this subtle craftsmanship one of the most remarkable feats in the history of diplomacy.

It was certainly dangerous to underestimate this charming foreign minister with his less than scrupulous means—he himself once summed up his approach as "hedging, evasion and flattery." Austria had benefited tremendously from Metternich's diplomacy, and, on the eve of the congress, seemed poised to do so again.

THE IDEA OF holding a peace conference in Vienna dated back one year to the middle of October 1813, when the Allies achieved a monumental victory over Napoleon at the Battle of Leipzig, the largest single battle in the Napoleonic Wars. Historians call the three-day slaughter the "Battle of Nations"; Metternich called it the "Battle of the World." It was there, at Leipzig, that the Russian tsar Alexander first proposed Vienna as the location for the future gathering. The Austrian emperor immediately agreed, before the unpredictable tsar changed his mind.

Originally, the intention was to invite only the sovereigns of the victorious powers. But in the spring of 1814, the British foreign secretary, Lord Castlereagh, had urged that the conference be expanded to include the representatives of all the states who had fought in the war. Article XXXII of the Treaty of Paris specifically adopted this interpretation, calling for a "general conference" of "all the participating nations" to open in Vienna no later than the fifteenth of July. This date, however, had been pushed back over the summer in response to the tsar's wishes to return first to his capital at St. Petersburg, where he had long been absent. The new opening date for the congress was set for the first of October.

Austria, of course, realized it would be expensive to host a peace conference and celebration worthy of the Allied victory, and it would certainly strain the government's already shaky finances. Austria had, only three years before, declared bankruptcy. Its new banknotes, issued in 1811, had already lost four-fifths of their value, and the government was heavily in debt. Austria had fought France more constantly, since 1792, than any other power except Great Britain, and its governmental income had been severely reduced during the war.

Twice, Vienna had been captured and occupied by Napoleon; twice, the aristocracy and the court had been forced to pack up their valuables and flee the capital. From Ulm to Wagram, the sweeping plains of central Europe seemed to be dotted with names of villages commemorating some defeat or another. Vienna wits had adapted the motto emblazoned on Julius Caesar's chariot to fit Emperor Francis's army: *Venit, Videt, Perdit* ("he comes, he sees, he loses").

Each time after a defeat—1797, 1801, 1805, and 1809—Napoleon had inflicted humiliating terms on the Austrians, demanding enormous cash payments and large amounts of territory. Austria had lost Belgium, Lombardy, Tuscany, Venice, Trieste, Tyrol, Vorarlberg, Croatia, Istria, Dalmatia, and Kraków, along with other former Polish lands and many princely dependencies on the left bank of the Rhine. The 1809 treaty alone had removed 3.5 million Habsburg subjects, sliced off forty-two thousand square miles, and imposed a harsh penalty of 85 million francs. The emperor had been forced to melt down much of the court plate and silverware to pay the sums demanded by Napoleon.

Realistically, Austria had little hope of regaining all of this lost territory, and, actually, the Austrians did not want it all back. They were content to abandon Belgium because of its distance and its proximity to France, and they were also resigned to relinquishing the crown of the Holy Roman Empire, deemed too cumbersome with its limitations on the emperor's power. But Austria did want northern Italy, along with Dalmatia and other territory on the Adriatic coast, which had been completely removed by Napoleon.

So a country whose fortunes had fallen low in the war had been selected to host the peace conference. Despite their country's much-reduced state, and the fact that it was still dangerously close to bankruptcy, Emperor Francis and Prince Metternich were happy to accept responsibility for the congress. The reasoning was clear. As host, Austria hoped to take advantage of its well-deserved reputation for hospitality, and gain as much as possible from the goodwill of its guests.

SEVERAL BLOCKS AWAY from the Hofburg Palace, France's chief delegate, Prince Charles-Maurice de Talleyrand, had slipped into town around midnight on September 23. After a six-hundred-mile journey from Paris completed in only seven days, the traveling carriage dropped him off at the stately and stylish yellow-gray Kaunitz Palace, centrally placed at 1029 Johannesgasse, right off the busy Kärntnerstrasse and down from St. Stephen's Cathedral. This was to be the headquarters of the French embassy at the Vienna Congress.

Despite the excellent address, with its spectacular limestone staircase and its stocked wine cellar, the house had needed a thorough whipping into shape. Indeed, the French staff, which arrived one week before, was appalled. White sheets still covered furniture in the drawing rooms, and dark cloth shielded the portraits from the sun. The red damask hangings had long faded from their original splendor. Crystal chandeliers, still encased in their protective dust bags, needed polishing. Every room, it seemed, needed a good cleaning and airing out, right down to removing the moths from the mattresses.

The mansion was named after Prince Kaunitz, the most versatile Austrian diplomat of the eighteenth century, and the man who had played a major role in achieving the "diplomatic revolution" of 1756 that brought the bitter enemies Austria and France together for the first time in centuries. Talleyrand liked the thought of working in the house of a man who had accomplished such a dramatic reconciliation, and he hoped to achieve his own miracles. But, at the same time, he was very much aware of the challenges that his embassy faced.

"I shall probably play a wretched role," Talleyrand sighed, as he imagined his prospects at the peace conference. He was asked to represent a country that had both launched and lost the war that left Europe in a mess, and many were sure to blame France. Yet despite his concerns for his country's diplomatic position, which he labeled "singularly difficult," Talleyrand was well suited for this mission. He had the talent, the connections, the charisma, and the reputation, not to mention the razor-sharp instincts that had been honed working with nearly every leading figure of the Napoleonic age. In diplomacy as well as society, Talleyrand was a living legend.

Approaching his sixty-first birthday, he stood about five feet eight inches and had a mop of wavy light brown hair tucked under his powdered wig. His face was thin, delicate, and unscarred, despite a dangerous bout of smallpox as a child. He had a slight snub nose, a high forehead, thickset eyebrows, and blue eyes that often fell half closed in boredom. His lips seemed locked in a perpetual smirk. His face, otherwise, was almost expressionless. One might kick him twenty times in the backside, it was said, and not a single muscle on his face would flinch.

Talleyrand looked like he had stepped right out of an eighteenth-century salon, complete with silk stockings, tight knee breeches, diamond buckled shoes, and velvet coats, often in purple, scarlet, or apple green. His starched satin cravat was impeccably tied, and the lace at the end of his cuffs exquisite. His movements were slow and deliberate, as he dragged his lame right foot across the floor. He was known for his elegance, his sophistication, and his immense charm. "If Talleyrand's conversation could be purchased," one admirer said, "I would gladly go into bankruptcy."

But in many ways the limping French minister was the ultimate survivor. In the previous thirty years, he had served everyone from the Church to the Revolution, the upstart Bonaparte to the restored Bourbon king, Louis XVIII. He certainly had an uncanny ability to make himself indispensable, and he also had a way of leaving his mark on every regime that he had served.

Indeed, some in Vienna had never forgiven Talleyrand for his past. He had been a witty and worldly priest who had left a trail of admirers, lovers, and, in some cases, even illegitimate children (including probably the romantic painter Eugène Delacroix). He had scandalized further when, after his consecration as bishop of Autun, he had resigned, and even married. His bride, the beautiful Catherine Grand, had also had a notorious past; it was, as some wits quipped, the former bishop who married the former courtesan.

Additionally, Talleyrand was notorious for having turned his position in the foreign ministry into a highly lucrative enterprise. He routinely collected diamond rings and large payments for his services—gifts, bribes, "user's fees," or whatever one wanted to call them. When France sold the Louisiana Territory to the United States in 1803, for example, Talleyrand had personally pocketed as much as one-third of President Thomas Jefferson's $15 million purchase price.

What troubled his Vienna colleagues most, of course, was not his financial affairs, his romantic liaisons, or even his string of broken oaths. It was instead his relationship with Napoleon. It was Talleyrand, after all, who had helped mastermind Napoleon's seizure of power in the coup of 1799. It was Talleyrand, too, who had helped guide the young, inexperienced, and tactless general through the quagmire of French politics. "Talleyrand is an extraordinarily intelligent man," Napoleon once acknowledged. "He gives me excellent advice."

But it was also Talleyrand who, as everyone knew, had helped bring down Napoleon. By 1805, Talleyrand had realized that the general's many military triumphs had clouded his judgment and rendered him incapable of listening to advice. Again and again, Talleyrand had protested against Napoleon's actions—his blind aggression, his harsh authoritarian rule, and his appalling humiliation of conquered peoples. Repeatedly, Talleyrand had pressed in vain for a more just and humane approach that, he argued, would also better serve France's national interests. By August 1807, Talleyrand had had enough. "I do not wish to become the executioner of Europe," he said, and resigned from office.

Talleyrand had come to realize that Napoleon, despite all his raw charisma, was a frightening figure with an inability to stop waging war. Napoleon had come to power illegitimately, and he could only maintain his authority by extraordinary measures, or, in his case, by waging constant warfare. If France or Europe were ever to know peace any time soon, Napoleon would simply have to be stopped. Of course, with a tyrant, legal opposition was out of the question, and the only effective means of resistance, Talleyrand concluded, was to help Napoleon's enemies. Indeed, over the next few years, he would do just that.

Most prominently, Talleyrand had sent a secret message back in the spring of 1814 to Allied supreme headquarters, encouraging its hesitant leaders to march on Paris at once. Napoleon's regime was tottering, he said, and this was the time to act: "You are walking on crutches, when you should be running." The note, written with his invisible ink and smuggled by an accomplice through the war zone, arrived at the Allied camp at just the right time. Tsar Alexander ordered the army to march, and within a few days, they had captured Napoleon's capital. For Bonapartists, Talleyrand's action was treason. For others, it was a heroic act that saved many lives.

Now, in the autumn of 1814, Talleyrand's arrival in Vienna was causing some concern. To be sure, few diplomats at the congress had not applauded Talleyrand for his services to the Allied cause, and most wanted the newly restored king of France, Louis XVIII, to succeed. But at the same time, many remembered the French minister's checkered past and showed a marked reluctance to deal with him too closely. Talleyrand was a "double-edged sword," Metternich warned; "it was extremely dangerous to toy with him." He was a master of manipulation, a helpful friend who might also turn into a dangerous foe. France's delegate must be treated with great caution.

Chapter 3

ILLUSTRIOUS STRANGERS

That's right, those poor kings ought to have a holiday.

—PRINCE DE LIGNE

In the late morning of September 25, while church bells clanged and cannons thundered, crowds poured onto the streets and peered out of upper-story windows with great excitement for the arrival of Vienna's most anticipated guest: the Russian tsar Alexander. He was celebrated as a modern Alexander the Great. If Napoleon had been the "Conqueror of Europe," then Alexander was enjoying his reputation as the foremost conqueror of the Conqueror of Europe. Napoleon's invasion of Russia and the burning of Moscow had set his soul on fire, the tsar said to awestruck audiences. Arriving in Vienna, Alexander was ready for the time of his life.

Evidently, the Festivals Committee had been eager to welcome the tsar. That morning, at dawn, cannons had woken the town with news that Alexander had just departed from a nearby village and would arrive in Vienna in just over two hours. How ridiculous this salute was, Metternich noted; it just proved "that nobody has any common sense any more, for never did anyone wake up a whole city with cannon shots to inform them that a sovereign is still forty leagues away."

The weather was beautiful that morning, sunny and warm with a light breeze. The timing was also good, as the tsar's arrival fell on a Sunday, when a large part of the town could turn out to watch the spectacle. Obviously, the crowds were anxious to see the famous tsar in person, and this was particularly the case for many younger women, who adored him like "maniacs at full moon."

The tsar, riding on a white Lipizzaner stallion trained in the Austrian emperor's stables, tipped his hat and waved his large hand, looking and acting like someone accustomed to the cheering crowds. Witty, handsome, and urbane, he stood about six feet tall. Wavy light-brown hair curled around the top of his high forehead, and thick whiskers wrapped around his face. He had a straight nose, a small mouth, very white teeth, and the blue eyes of his grandmother, Catherine the Great. Alexander's cheeks were so rosy that they were often confused with a blush.

Riding at his side on another white stallion was the king of Prussia, Frederick William III, a forty-four-year-old man with dark brown hair and eyes as blue as his uniform. The two were entering Vienna together, just as they had entered Paris in triumph at the end of the war. They were joined by a third monarch, the host, Emperor Francis of Austria, who had ridden through town and crossed the Tabor Bridge to greet his guests.

It was certainly a grand entrance into the emperor's capital. The three victorious monarchs were followed by archdukes, generals, former princes of the Holy Roman Empire, and an escort of soldiers that sported a dazzling array of uniforms from the Napoleonic Wars. The procession passed under the chestnut trees of the Prater, through the Red Tower Gate in the northeast, and then along the narrow streets of the town, ending about an hour later in one of the inner courtyards of the imperial palace. The parade was full of "brilliance and pomp," one police agent in the crowds noted. "Perfect order," he added. "No incident or accident to report."

Later that morning, the tsar and the king of Prussia sat down to a large formal breakfast at the palace, joined by the king of Denmark, the king of Württemberg, and the emperor of Austria. Only the king of Bavaria, who would arrive three days later, was absent. It was rare to see so many monarchs together at the same table—a sight that would soon be almost commonplace in Vienna that autumn.

TSAR ALEXANDER WAS, in many ways, one of the most puzzling and complex figures at the congress. On one hand, he was praised by Thomas Jefferson as a beacon of enlightenment: "A more virtuous man, I believe, does not exist, nor one who is more enthusiastically devoted to better the condition of mankind." Others thought this saint was really a terrible sinner with blood on his hands.

Alexander had grown up in difficult and rather unusual circumstances. His grandmother, Catherine the Great, had fawned on him as her obvious favorite. He was raised in the spirit of the enlightenment, with an upbringing that emphasized the importance of reason, liberty, the happiness of the people, and the value of a written constitution. This education was somewhat strange, some thought, for an apprentice tsar who would one day rule over one of the most autocratic realms on earth.

Catherine's indulgence and obvious preference for her grandson displeased Alexander's father, Catherine's own son and successor, Grand Duke Paul. Intensely jealous by nature, Paul reacted to his rival in his own brutally simple way. He took every opportunity to humiliate his son, and the abuse was mental as well as physical. When Paul became tsar in 1796 (despite Catherine's direct orders to pass the throne to her grandson), life had not gotten any easier for Alexander. Paul's unpredictable outbursts of cruelty gave him the name "the mad tsar" and the bullying only ended in March 1801, when he was violently murdered. A gang of conspirators, including a commander of the elite guard, the Semeonovsky Regiment, stormed the castle, forced their way into the tsar's rooms, and strangled him to death.

It was this murder that placed the young, idealistic Alexander on the throne. The twenty-three-year-old's role in the assassination has long been debated. Some contemporaries, as well as historians, have accused him of outright complicity; others have suggested that he knew of the plot, though made no attempt to prevent it. He certainly did not prosecute or punish the murderers, many of whom would later be at his side. At the very least, Alexander was severely shaken, burdened with a sense of guilt that, by all accounts, only grew worse. He would long be tortured in his sleep, hearing his father's awful screams over and over in his head.

His marriage was not a source of comfort, either. Alexander was married unhappily to Elizabeth of Baden, a German princess with ash blonde hair and sparkling eyes, who was described by one as "certainly one of the most beautiful women in the world." The two looked like angels together—Cupid and Psyche, Catherine the Great had said. But they were not well matched, and ended up living almost separate lives. Elizabeth, for her part, was stuck in a foreign country, feeling, as she put it, "alone, alone, absolutely alone."

Both were certainly having affairs on each other: the tsar with his mistress, Maria Narishkiva, and some speculated even his sister, Grand Duchess Catherine; and Elizabeth with a number of people, ranging from soldiers to a certain "ambiguous intimacy" with a lovely countess. Empress Elizabeth also had an affair with one of the tsar's advisers, Prince Adam Czartoryski, the Polish patriot who had come to Russia as a hostage after the destruction of Poland and won Alexander's trust. The tsar, however, never seemed disturbed by his wife's relationship with his adviser, and in fact, by most accounts, encouraged it as only fair, given the liberties he was taking himself.

When Alexander came to Vienna for the peace conference, he had ruled for thirteen taxing years. During this time, Russia had been invaded by Napoleon and well over six hundred thousand troops, at that time the largest army the world had ever seen. Villages had been destroyed, the countryside devastated, several hundred thousand people killed, and the city of Moscow burned to the ground. Surely Russia should be compensated for its sacrifices in the war against Napoleon. At the very least, its concerns should not be ignored. Under no circumstances would the tsar compromise on an issue as important to him as Poland.

Alexander had yet to specify his exact plans for the region, though privately he had promised to re-create the Kingdom of Poland—that is, he would combine the slice of Poland he had inherited from Catherine the Great with the lands of the Napoleonic Duchy of Warsaw, which his army had occupied since the end of the war. The tsar seemed genuine enough, and many Polish patriots took him at his word. But there was a nagging concern that he might not be able to deliver on these grand promises. Even if he had the best intentions, would the tsar, in the end, allow this creation to be free and independent?

Certainly, no one was comfortable having Russia's enormous realm stretching so far to the west with this satellite kingdom of Poland, and the touchy, unpredictable tsar as a neighbor. Castlereagh and Metternich alike feared the implications. Would this not make Russia the new unrivaled power, potentially enjoying a dominance that not even Napoleon had commanded?

Alexander already had the support of his traveling companion and old friend, the king of Prussia. The tsar and the king had developed a close working relationship, which had been sealed with a melodramatic act, even for that melodramatic age. When Alexander had visited Berlin in 1805, the tsar and the king had descended into the crypt of the enlightened despot Frederick the Great, and, beside the tomb of the dead king, they had sworn oaths of eternal friendship.

Of course, during the stress of the war, the emotional scene had been forgotten, and the two powers had betrayed each other. But later, when the tide had turned in their favor, both had acknowledged their mistakes. This time, they swore that they would stick together, and cemented their renewed alliance with a deal: Russia would gain a free hand in Poland, and Prussia, in return for its support (and surrender of its Polish territory), would receive a part of central and eastern Germany known as Saxony. They had written their promises, in the secret Treaty of Kalisch, signed back in February 1813, and pledged to support each other no matter what.

"YOU CANNOT BELIEVE how beautiful my rooms are when the sun shines through them," Metternich had once said, admiring the tall, well-designed oriental windows of his office study at the Foreign Ministry. The challenge, he knew, was finding the time to enjoy them properly.

By late September 1814, the congress had not yet opened and the foreign minister was appalled to see the staggering amount of work already piling up. There were dispatches to read, protocols to draft, and agendas to juggle, never mind the endless logistical matters of launching the peace conference, for which Metternich was already serving, unofficially, as president. "Interminable chores," it all seemed to the foreign minister in one of his weak moments.

Just as he had feared, visitors were beating down a path to the white stone Chancellery building, home of the Foreign Ministry, a large, early eighteenth-century structure adorned with Corinthian columns and facing out onto the northern end of the Hofburg Palace. The Chancellery was also known as the Ballhaus, after its previous use as a Habsburg tennis court. This was only appropriate, Metternich's critics pointed out, given the foreign minister's frivolous gamelike approach to diplomacy.

Metternich's offices with the lovely large windows were on the second floor. Green damask covered the walls in the main negotiating room, from the parquet floor to the new stucco ceiling. There were dark woodwork, oil paintings in gilt frames, and white marble busts resting on pedestals. The room had been redecorated with a new marble fireplace and many new pieces of furniture that Metternich had purchased a few months before in Paris. He had given the matter some thought, Metternich said, because he feared he would probably be spending a lot of time there.

The large anteroom, with its high, eighteen-foot ceilings, was regularly filled up to capacity. Petitioners hoping to have a word with Metternich found themselves facing what seemed like an interminable wait, and passed the time the best they could, exchanging stories or just staring at the walls, which were lined with mahogany bookshelves holding handsome volumes in red morocco.

One morning that month, for example, Metternich found this room packed yet again with people eager to press some case or other. Prussia's chancellor, Karl August von Hardenberg, who had arrived in Vienna a few days before, had come to request an audience. He was already complaining about the difficulty of gaining a meeting with Metternich the Invisible, as he dubbed him. A representative of the king of Bavaria, Field Marshal Prince Karl Wrede, was also there waiting, probably with his trusty maps in hand. Four officials in long black robes with a shining silver Maltese cross also stood out, representing the Knights of Malta, an elite chivalric order that dated back to the twelfth century.

No doubt the knights wanted to have their treasures returned after Napoleon's plundering in 1798. He had sacked their island, running off with gold and silver chalices, goblets, and jewels from a treasure vault that had been accumulated since the thirteenth century. The knights also wanted their island, Malta, returned. The British had promised a prompt restoration after they liberated it from Napoleon, but they had not yet complied and, in the opinion of the Grand Master of the Order, showed no signs of doing so. The Grand Master was correct. The British had grown attached to the beautiful strategic island with the excellent naval base, and they had secured it in the Treaty of Paris.

Countless other people filled the crowded room, including two or three dozen German noblemen, all former knights of the now defunct Holy Roman Empire. Many of these aristocrats had lost ancient privileges, and often also family property, when Napoleon dismantled the empire and parceled out its western edges, awarding territory to his vassal kingdoms of Bavaria, Württemberg, and Westphalia. Some of the knights would press for restoration of their rights and property, and others went further, hoping for nothing less than the revival of the Holy Roman Empire itself.

"I found all of Europe in my anteroom," Metternich said with vanity and frustration, as he eyed the many petitioners with their bulging leather portfolios and the endless amount of work that they represented. Metternich was not looking forward to the hard wrangling ahead. It was sure to be, he predicted, "four or six weeks of hell."

WHEN THE SHEER magnitude of the problems seemed overwhelming, Metternich could shuffle down a private staircase, cross a cobbled lane, and escape into an eighteenth-century mansion at 54 Schenkengasse.

This was the Palm Palace, and for the past year Metternich had been drawing on all his finesse in arranging a love affair with a woman who occupied one of its large suites: Wilhelmine, the Duchess of Sagan. Metternich had had many liaisons in the past, but this one was different. The duchess was one of the most desirable matches of the day, and Metternich was clearly succumbing to her charms.

The Duchess of Sagan was a slim and petite thirty-three-year-old with dark-blonde hair and deep brown eyes—a ravishing and restless beauty who also happened to be heiress to one of the largest fortunes in Europe. She owned castles all over eastern and central Europe, including Sagan, built by the mercenary of the Thirty Years War, Count Wallenstein, and located a hundred miles south of Berlin.

When Metternich met the duchess, through a mutual friend during his carefree days as a diplomat in Dresden, he had been intrigued. She had grown up in Courland in the Baltic (today's Latvia), traveled all over Europe, and spoke half a dozen languages fluently. She was in her second unhappy marriage, and soon to be her second divorce. "I am ruining myself with husbands," she was said to have quipped.

The duchess had kept her own name, and managed her own estates, a somewhat daunting prospect given her extensive property. She had used some of her fortune for charity, even financing a private hospital for wounded soldiers. At one time, when a maid in her household went into premature labor, Wilhelmine had stepped in as an emergency midwife and helped deliver a healthy baby girl.

The relationship between Metternich and the Duchess of Sagan had first started to heat up in the summer of 1813 when he was working on arranging a peace with Napoleon. The peace at that time failed, but the romance thrived. Metternich saw the duchess as much as he could, and in the midst of the crisis, wrote his first long love letter to her:

> I watched you for years. I found you beautiful; my heart remained silent; why has that sweet peace deserted me? Why out of nothing have you become for me everything?

The duchess was surprised and frankly flattered by the attentions of this dashing statesman, but she had not been won over, at least not yet. Metternich, however, had persisted. One month later, he wrote:

> I am writing because I shall not see you this morning, and I must tell you that I love you more than my life—that my happiness is nothing unless you are very much a part of it.

The duchess could fill a room in her palace with all the gifts Metternich would send, everything from books bound in red morocco to lamps made of lava. Metternich, in turn, cherished every gift that he received. On one shelf in his study was a special black box that had a lock of her hair.

Metternich liked her mind, her judgment, her generosity. He liked how beautiful she looked in her formal gown that sparkled in the ballroom, and he liked the baggy flannels that she wore when she was only lounging around her suite, including her personal favorite, an old "wadded gown with holes in the elbows." Metternich liked the little things, such as the way she drank her cognac, balancing a sugar cube onto the small silver spoon, gently dipping it into the amber drink, and then, at the end, slurping down the rest. "What," he once wrote to her, "don't I like about you."

By the end of that summer, the duchess had finally come around, and confessed her love for Metternich as well: "I do not know how I love you, but I love you very much, and with my whole heart." Metternich had been thrilled with the news—making love was one thing, confessing it was another. He wrote back immediately, feeling like he had been suddenly "transported into the loveliest, most blessed spot on earth."

> You have made me drunk with happiness. I love you, I love you a hundred times more than my life. I do not live, I shall not live except for you.

Their relationship was impossible to keep completely secret, and the Palm Palace was certainly going to be a fascinating place that autumn. With the Duchess of Sagan hosting her fashionable salon on its second floor, there was another woman, in a parallel wing, just as intelligent, witty, rich, beautiful, and it must be said, controversial. This was Princess Catherine Bagration, the thirty-one-year-old widow of Pyotr Ivanovich Bagration, a Russian general and war hero who had fallen at Borodino. She was blonde with light blue eyes and pinkish white skin that one admirer compared to alabaster. Her scandalous evening gowns, very low cut, earned her the nickname "the beautiful naked angel."

For many years now, Princess Catherine Bagration and the Duchess of Sagan had been sworn enemies. The reasons for the hostility were many, buried under many layers of gossip, intrigue, and counterintrigue, though no small part of this animosity stemmed from a long rivalry for honor and influence in high society. They certainly had a lot in common.

Nearly the same age, both had come from the Baltic, and both were the oldest daughters of rich, high aristocratic families, who had traveled and lived all over the continent. Both, after marrying young, were now single and surrounded by many admirers. Both had now ended up in Vienna at the time of the congress, and by "a curious and fatal chance," as one salon regular put it, the two young divas had ended up in the same palace, immediately opposite each other. The windows, in fact, overlooked a shared courtyard.

All throughout the autumn, eyes would peer out from behind silk curtains, keeping careful tabs on the carriages coming and going, and who went to which salon. The two women would compete for everything, from the most prized guests to the greatest social esteem for their evening soirees. They were two queen bees, trying to share the same hive, and their rivalry would both enliven and embitter relations at the congress.

Many intrigues would be spun in the corridors, staircases, and drawing rooms of this palace.

Vienna society would effectively have to make a choice, either taking the left staircase up to Princess Bagration, the "Russian siren," or the right staircase to the Duchess of Sagan, "the Cleopatra of Courland." As for the outcome of the competition between the two women of the north, one society watcher reported, "the bets were open."

But there was something else the two ladies shared: Both had been Metternich's lover. And now, both women, it seemed, were attracting the attentions of Russia's flamboyant tsar.

Chapter 4

DOROTHÉE'S CHOICE

It is essential to make the French embassy a pleasant place.

—TALLEYRAND

Despite the distance of the journey, the British had been one of the first official delegations to roll into town. The leader was Lord Castlereagh, tall, blond, and looking twenty years younger than his actual age of forty-five. His thin, almost frail frame was usually draped in black; his somber choice in clothes, it was said, often matched his mood. His long, angular face gave the impression of aristocratic detachment, or, as some dryly noted, made him appear to be in a state of perpetual boredom. It was certainly a champion poker face, which would serve him well both at Vienna's diplomacy and gambling tables.

Castlereagh and his team had reached the Austrian capital back on the thirteenth of September, and immediately hunted down their designated headquarters, a house tucked away in the narrow Milchgasse. The rooms had actually been rented some years before to a young musician named Wolfgang Amadeus Mozart. While living there in the early 1780s, Mozart had worked on his first full German opera, *Die Entführung aus dem Serail (The Abduction from the Seraglio),* and carried on an affair with the landlady's daughter, Constanze, whom he married in 1782. The cozy flat may have proven a happy place for Mozart and his opera, but its cramped size hardly suited the delegation representing Great Britain, proud financier of Allied victory.

Castlereagh would indeed seek out a new place to stay, and within a week move into a twenty-two-room suite on the Minoritenplatz, an elegant cobbled square lined with aristocratic mansions and the fourteenth-century Church of the Friars Minor. The British delegation was now just a few steps away from both Metternich's offices on the Ballhausplatz and the Hofburg Palace itself. Castlereagh and his wife, Lady Emily, were housed on the top floor, the diplomatic staff on the first floor, and the ground floor was reserved for entertainment. The Castlereaghs would enjoy setting the mood for some evening soirees with the hauntingly ethereal sounds of the glass harmonium, a musical instrument invented by Benjamin Franklin.

Unlike the other major delegations at the peace conference, Britain was actually still at war, fighting across the ocean against the young republic of the United States. In American history, this is known as the War of 1812; in British history, it has not received its own name, generally submerged into the wider conflict with Napoleon. Battles still raged across a number of fronts in Canada, on the Great Lakes, and on the Atlantic. Indeed, just a few weeks before Castlereagh arrived in Vienna, British troops had landed at Chesapeake and burned Washington to the ground, destroying the Treasury, the Library of Congress, and even the President's Palace. James and Dolley Madison had fled, and the war showed no signs of abating.

While this meant that their attention would be divided between America and Europe, Britain clearly prioritized the conference at Vienna, and felt confident in its position. Castlereagh's country had earned immense prestige as the only power that had hung on for the entire struggle against Napoleon, sometimes facing the foe all alone. They had the world's largest navy, its richest economy, and colonial possessions already dotting the globe from South Africa to India. During the war, they had scooped up other colonies from the French and their allies. All of this would, they figured, translate into a strong negotiating position.

National hopes were centered on securing freedom of the seas, so important to the Royal Navy, and one of the many issues in the war with the States. Castlereagh also wanted to make sure that the flatlands and coasts of the area known today as Belgium would not, under any circumstances, fall again into the hands of a hostile country. This meant, above all, that it should be kept away from France. The port of Antwerp was a potential launching pad for an invasion—"the loaded pistol held to England's head."

Castlereagh was pushing for handing over this port, and in fact all of Belgium, to the newly created Kingdom of the Netherlands, whose monarch, William I of the House of Orange, was a good ally of Britain. Actually, Castlereagh had already been assured of success on this point. The handover of territory had been decided as part of a secret clause attached to the Treaty of Paris, and the British foreign minister fully expected that the signing would be a mere formality, no matter how spirited Belgian opposition might turn out to be.

Otherwise, as far as Britain's goals were concerned, Castlereagh was content to promote the general balance of power, a policy that he felt would best serve the interests of world peace. This policy would also, he knew, serve Britain's own commercial interests, the island power already well on its way to becoming the "workshop of the world."

As he saw it, following in a line of politicians including his mentor, former prime minister William Pitt, no single power, or group of powers, should be allowed to dominate the continent, and if any seemed on the verge of surpassing the others, Britain would interfere to restore the "just equilibrium." Traditionally, the biggest threat to this balance had come from France, which had off and on challenged it for the last 150 years. Now, though, with the defeat of Napoleon, there was a potential new menace.

This was Russia, which had been Britain's ally in the last years of the war. While several countries had pretensions of being a Great Power, Great Britain and Russia were the only countries in a league of their own. Russia, of course, was a giant, boasting the continent's largest landmass, equal to some seventy times the size of Great Britain. It had the largest army in the world, and it was now occupying much of the former French empire, including Poland, Saxony, and Holstein, bordering on Denmark. Castlereagh, for one, was worried about the quick rise of Russia—a country whose prestige had been enhanced by its smashing victories, and whose ruler was not exactly known for his moderation.

Prior to his career as foreign minister, Castlereagh had studied at St. John's College at Cambridge, though he left before receiving a degree. He had returned instead to his home in Ireland, Standford Lough in the heart of County Down in the northwest, where he had been elected to the Irish Parliament at age twenty-one. He rose quickly. At every stage in his ascent, as minister of trade, minister of war, and then, in 1812, foreign secretary, Castlereagh had shown himself to be confident, and rather brave in facing stiff opposition. He was dogged in a Churchillian way, and about as stubborn as one might find in the political arena.

Lord Castlereagh had played a pivotal role in founding the modern British Foreign Office. When he had assumed responsibilities two years before, Britain had six diplomatic missions, and only one of them was *not* ruled by a government in exile, prison, or some other greatly reduced state. As Napoleon's empire started to crumble, however, Britain could again establish embassies in the liberated countries. Castlereagh had been in the right place at the right time; he had appointed almost the entire Diplomatic Service of Great Britain.

Castlereagh had also been the first British foreign secretary ever to visit the Continent on an official mission—back in January 1814, during the last stages of the war. Now on his second trip, Castlereagh was bringing one of the larger teams to the peace conference. There were fourteen assistants, including the indefatigable Lord Clancarty, who had previously served as minister to the Hague and would advise on many matters, including the Netherlands, and Lord Cathcart, the former soldier and specialist on Russia, brought along for his good relationship with the tsar. There was also the undersecretary of state, Edward Cooke, and Castlereagh's private secretary, Joseph Planta, both of whom were hardworking assistants loyal to their leader.

Clearly, the most notorious resident of the British embassy was Sir Charles Stewart, a thirty-six-year-old ambassador to Vienna and a veteran of the Spanish campaigns. Loud and obnoxious, Lord Stewart had an outlandish sense of humor better suited to the barrack rooms than the salons, and many critics doubted his diplomatic abilities, to say the least. Far too often, it seemed, after a few drinks, Stewart would stalk around "out to kick everybody in the teeth." His bright yellow boots and extravagant mannerisms would earn him a new nickname, Lord Pumpernickel. Stewart was only there, many thought, because he was Castlereagh's half brother.

UPON HIS ARRIVAL at Kaunitz Palace, Talleyrand began paying his courtesy visits to the embassies scattered around town. He had a new title on his calling card, Prince de Talleyrand, an honor awarded by King Louis

XVIII just before his departure from Paris. The French foreign minister no longer had to use the title Prince de Bénévent, which had been granted by Napoleon. Talleyrand needed to distance himself and his country as far away from Bonaparte as possible.

Although France had happily, as he put it, "escaped destruction" in the Treaty of Paris, Talleyrand knew that the Allied powers had been severely criticized for not being a great deal more demanding. For many, France was still the same reckless and dangerous power full of crusading fanatics simply incapable of allowing their neighbors to live in peace. The congress would run more smoothly without its participation.

Such a negative image, of course, threatened to undermine the efforts of French diplomacy, and this was unfortunate because Talleyrand had many objectives that he hoped to obtain. For one, just as Louis XVIII had been restored as king of France, he wanted to see another member of the Bourbon family, Ferdinand IV, returned to the throne in Naples, which had been lost in 1808 and was now occupied by one of Napoleon's flamboyant marshals, Joachim Murat. As Talleyrand would argue, the Bourbon was the legitimate king, and the best hope for any peace on that peninsula.

Another high priority was saving the king of Saxony, Frederick Augustus, who was in danger of losing both his crown and his country. The king was a cousin of Louis XVIII, an ally of France, and, most important, a counterweight to the rising power of Prussia, which, Talleyrand feared, wanted to dominate all of Germany. Prussian ambitions must be curbed, Talleyrand argued, or that kingdom "would in a few years form a militarist monarchy that would be very dangerous for her neighbors."

That first week in town, Talleyrand would lay the basis for his diplomatic campaign, attending fashionable salons, and calling upon Emperor Francis, the imperial family, the Great Powers, and many of the smaller delegations that were often neglected. He had a good eight or ten days of visits ahead, and it was a task that, he mused, "would weary better legs than mine."

To help achieve his goals, Talleyrand had selected a team of diplomats, experts, and support staff to join him in Vienna. One of the most prominent was an old friend, Emmerich, the Duke of Dalberg, a young man who came from one of the oldest aristocratic families in Germany with considerable property in the Rhineland, especially between Speyer and Worms. Dalberg could be unscrupulous and untrustworthy, not to mention an indiscreet boaster. Talleyrand was not unaware of this fact: Dalberg was chosen, he said, "so that he might broadcast those of my secrets that I want everyone to know."

Talleyrand brought along two other prominent plenipotentiaries, as the chief delegates were called (from the Latin word meaning "someone invested with full authority"). The first was his old friend Gouvernet, the Marquis de la Tour du Pin, a former ambassador to Holland and a handsome and harmless pleasure-seeker who would not be saddled with too many responsibilities. "He will do," Talleyrand said, "for stamping the passports." The second, Comte Alexis de Noailles, an extreme royalist, was selected primarily because he was a well-known informer for the royal family, particularly the king's brother. "If one must be spied upon," Talleyrand explained, "it's best to be surveyed by an agent I have chosen myself."

While these three appointments might not sound the most qualified for complex international negotiations, they had strengths as measured by the standards of early nineteenth-century diplomacy. Each was a nobleman, familiar with the intricacies of drawing-room politics, and boasted many social connections within Europe's cosmopolitan aristocracy, all of which would come in handy at the Vienna Congress.

The best choice for dealing with the hard foreign policy questions was Jean-Baptiste de Gouey, Comte de la Besnardière, a forty-nine-year-old plucked from the Ministry of Foreign Affairs. According to Talleyrand, he had earned a reputation as the department's most promising talent. Besnardière would certainly help with the workload, serving as the unsung coauthor of many of the French delegation's papers.

In addition to these selections, Talleyrand also brought along a team of valets, barbers, hairdressers, cooks, and other staff who would keep the embassy running. Among them was the thirty-six-year-old personal assistant and piano player Sigismund Neukomm. An Austrian from Salzburg and a former student of Joseph Haydn, Neukomm's soft, dreamy keys would help Talleyrand focus, relax, or just escape into his own world of plots and counterplots.

Talleyrand's greatest success in the tricky area of staff selection, however, was arguably his choice of hostesses. He picked a twenty-one-year-old niece by marriage, Dorothée de Talleyrand-Périgord, an intelligent, beautiful woman who, it turns out, was also the Duchess of Sagan's younger sister.

DOROTHÉE WAS A young lady with striking black hair and flashing dark eyes—they were so dark blue that they seemed black, burning, as one admirer put it, "with an infernal fire which turned night into day." Her skin was pale, offset by dabs of rouge, and she had a very thin waistline. By the time of the peace congress, Dorothée was painfully unhappy and very much alone.

Some thirteen years younger than her sister Wilhelmine, Dorothée could not have been more different. Wilhelmine, the oldest in the family, was clearly her father's favorite, adored, indulged, and reared with a stellar education. Dorothée, by contrast, was largely neglected. Her childhood was, in her own words, "sad and miserable." Whereas Wilhelmine could, as a young girl, recite Virgil in Latin, guests at castle were shocked to see the seven-year-old Dorothée unable to read or recognize the letters of the alphabet.

There is some uncertainty about the identity of her biological father. Dorothée always called Peter, the Duke of Courland, her father, though biographers have long noted that it was very likely an impoverished Polish nobleman and captain of a mercenary regiment, Count Olek Batowski, who had briefly stayed at the family castle. At any rate, Duke Peter was almost seventy years old at the time of her birth, and very sick.

Dorothée had never had the chance to know either man. The Polish nobleman had left the castle soon after her birth, and the Duke of Courland died when she was seven. Her mother, Anna-Dorothea, the Duchess of Courland, was also distant, often busy with her own active social life. Dorothée did not grow up close to her three sisters, either; the nearest one in age was ten years older. Dorothée had very few playmates her own age, and, for the most part, she had been left on her own.

Years later, Dorothée described herself and how she had felt as a child:

> Small, skinny, yellow in complexion, always ill from the moment of my birth. My eyes were so dark and huge that they were out of all proportion to the rest of my face and seemed to dwarf the other fea-

tures . . . Sad almost to the point of melancholia, I remember perfectly how I longed to die.

It was one of her mother's lovers, Count Gustav Armfelt, a Swedish
guest, who first took an interest in Dorothée's upbringing. He had
decided to teach Dorothée personally, and, much to his surprise, he discovered that she was a very quick learner. In fact, he soon became convinced that Dorothée was an unusually gifted child.

All of a sudden, with his prompting, nothing was too much for the
family's talented youngest daughter. The Duchess of Courland hired two
full-time tutors, one of them being Abbé Piattoli, the former secretary to
the last king of Poland. He in turn would take her on excursions that
suited her newfound interests, such as many trips to the theater, complete
with lessons from the queen of the Berlin stage, Madame Unzelmann. For
Dorothée's interest in astronomy, the abbé arranged lessons from the
royal astronomer at the Berlin Observatory.

With the help of her encouraging and stimulating teachers, Dorothée
was soon showing signs of an exceptionally sharp mind, and the ability
to grasp sophisticated subjects quickly. All the while, she was enjoying her
new love of reading. She would dash into the family library, scale the lad-
der to the top, and sit there, under the high ceiling, with a book in her lap.

But by the age of fifteen, Dorothée was under considerable pressure to
marry. Despite being promised the freedom to choose a husband herself,
she was now being pressured to marry the man of her mother's choice—
or rather Tsar Alexander's choice, or more exactly, Talleyrand's choice.
Her future had been plotted like an international intrigue.

The French minister had heard of the beautiful heiress Dorothée, and
wanted her for his nephew, the twenty-old-year-old Edmond de Talleyrand-
Périgord. As Dorothée was a subject of the Russian tsar, Talleyrand had
asked Alexander to talk with Dorothée's mother, and persuade her to
arrange this marriage. The tsar, being grateful to Talleyrand for his support against Napoleon, agreed. In October 1808, at a visit to their castle,
the tsar made his wishes abundantly clear: "My dear Duchess, I refuse to
accept any excuse. I have given my word. I ask for yours."

When the duchess approached her daughter about Edmond,
Dorothée had flatly refused. She preferred to choose her own husband,
and that was going to be the Polish patriot Prince Adam Czartoryski,

whom she had heard about from her tutor. Sure, he was twenty-three years older, and they had barely exchanged a word, but for a budding romantic like Dorothée, this was irrelevant. She was determined to make the match work, and no one, including the Tsar of All the Russias, was going to stop her.

At this point, when her mother realized the intensity of her conviction, she resorted to an elaborate scheme to trick Dorothée out of her teenage infatuation with an idealized prince of her imagination.

First, her tutor was threatened and forced to declare, falsely, that the Polish prince had just been engaged to another woman. As Dorothée still held out, her mother arranged for Polish friends to arrive at the castle with confirmation of the lie. All Warsaw was talking of the prince's engagement, they claimed, and in the end, a sad Dorothée agreed to marry this Frenchman she hardly knew.

Edmond was an excellent soldier and cavalry officer who had been decorated several times for his bravery, but he was not a good husband. He was a notorious philanderer, squandering a fortune on his extramarital lovers and his losses at the gaming tables. He racked up considerable debts, too, splurging on his lavish uniforms, adorned with "gold braid, spangles and gems." Worse still, Edmond could not stimulate Dorothée's mind, and the married couple had almost nothing to talk about.

"It was impossible to predict his temperament or his thoughts," Dorothée complained, because "no one has ever relied so heavily . . . on silence." Edmond was only home long enough, it seems, for the couple to have three children: Napoleon-Louis, or Louis since the emperor's downfall; Dorothea-Charlotte-Emily; and the infant Alexander-Edmond. Other than her children, whom she loved dearly, it was a sad and dreary marriage.

Then, that summer of 1814, on the eve of the congress, tragedy struck. Dorothée's daughter had fallen ill to the measles, a frightening situation in the early nineteenth century. Sadly, after an apparent recovery, the little girl had a sudden setback and died.

Dorothée was devastated, and, unfortunately, had to bear most of her suffering alone. Edmond was still away at war—he had not been home for more than a few months of the girl's life. The rest of her family was away in Berlin, Courland, or the spas of central Europe. The only person who came to see her was Talleyrand. He found time from his busy schedule at the foreign ministry to console the poor mother in her grief.

Clearly, Dorothée needed a change of environment, and one day that summer, Talleyrand asked if she would like to accompany him to Vienna for the upcoming peace conference. She could be hostess at the embassy.

Dorothée, for her part, accepted the offer. There was nothing left to hold her back in Paris. She would miss her children, of course, but they could stay with her mother. After all, the congress was only supposed to last a few weeks.

So with a new activity to occupy her mind, Dorothée started selecting dresses, gowns, gloves, fans, masks, stockings, jewels, and many different kinds of shoes, all of which were packed into large trunks and then loaded by footmen onto the traveling carriages. On September 16, the preparations were ready. Dorothée and the chief delegate would travel to Vienna together.

Talleyrand had indeed come to admire her abilities. She was beautiful, graceful, charming, and, above all, very intelligent. She had a love of reading, a talent for the art of conversation, and a knack for putting people at ease. Other salon hostesses might be more worldly or sophisticated, but Dorothée, with her youthful and unstudied innocence, would carve out a niche of her own.

THE BIG FOUR

With so many royalty, statesmen, and other celebrities making their way to the congress, Vienna's street performers were busy honing their acts. New marionette shows appeared in puppet theaters around town, and animal shows flourished as well, including one where the entertainer boasted a monkey, an owl, and what he claimed was a shark that he had fished out of the sea at Trieste. A wider selection of exotic animals could be found at the Schönbrunn Palace Zoo, such as rare birds, bears, buffalo, two camels, and a small collection of kangaroos from New Holland, in what is now Australia.

The giant park known as the Prater, the former royal hunting ground north of the city center, was especially lively. There were cafés, restaurants, dance halls, gambling rooms, some buildings shaped exotically as Chinese pavilions, Indian kiosks, Swiss chalets, and "savage huts." There were good places for fireworks, carriage rides, and pleasant walks. The tall trees of its "magnificent forest" and great lawn, as one visitor, Cadet de Gassicourt, said, "cast shadows that cover the earth with a green carpet that the sun never yellows."

One entertainer in the park had opened his own "mechanical optical theater" to show scenes of the awful war, including "The Fire of Moscow" and "The Battle of Leipzig," to name some of his attractions. He also had a new act depicting the Allied march into Paris, complete with "more than one thousand popular moving figures."

Curious sightseers strolled through the narrow winding streets around St. Stephen's Cathedral and filled the intimate market squares of the inner city. Even Castlereagh's wife, Emily, who was used to the delights of London's West End, was pleased at what she saw. "*Mon Dieu*," she exclaimed to her husband. "What a fine city! What shops! We almost broke our necks looking."

All around the town, merchants were looking forward to a golden age of business. Innkeepers, restaurateurs, café owners, and theater managers were just some of the entrepreneurs positioning themselves to house, feed, and entertain Europe's richest and most powerful figures, many of whom would also bring their own large retinues. Hatmakers, wigmakers, glove makers, tailors, seamstresses, hairdressers, bakers, butchers, florists, and toymakers were likewise hoping for a good season.

Landlords were calculating their likely profits as the congress dignitaries thronged into the city and competed for housing that was scarce in the best of times. Sometimes mansions were leased to the lucky delegations, such as the Spanish, who moved in near the British on the Minoritenplatz. More often, though, the delegates would have to make do with suites, single rooms, or even just attics.

When Prussian ambassador Wilhelm von Humboldt had arrived in August, he complained that already, at this early date, he could not find anything other than a drab "hole in the wall." Rents had soared. Proprietors of the best real estate near the Hofburg speculated, happily, that if the congress lasted slightly longer than the three to six weeks that most diplomats suspected, then rental intake alone might very well pay for the entire property.

Prices were spiraling higher for many other basic goods. The cost of meat shot up to several times its level just a few months before, and many Viennese blamed the butchers for raising prices arbitrarily. Quality firewood was already hitting 50 gulden a cord, not including additional charges for "cartage, sawing, and splitting." Candles were likewise on the rise, given the demand to fill all the chandeliers and candelabra for all the balls, banquets, and other late-night activities. Soap went up, too, because, someone joked, "the Congress is going to have a heap of dirty laundry to wash."

Winegrowers of the fertile valleys surrounding Vienna were bottling their best vintage, and rushing new ones onto the market, too. Bakers, not to be outdone, had created a special Vienna Congress roll, though some critics complained that a powerful pair of glasses was needed to find the slice of meat on the inside.

Already that autumn, as Metternich pranced, the tsar strutted, and Talleyrand limped, the crowds came to gawk. Notice was taken of the smallest detail—who went to which café, inn, or tavern, and who left the "monstrous tip." Even the most insignificant gesture could attract the curious onlooker. As one observer, Friedrich Anton von Schönholz put it, "Wherever a scaffold went up, equipment was carried in and out, a glass carriage washed, a rug beaten, the pushing crowd was sure to gather."

Indeed, the advertisement about the holding of a congress to decide the future of Europe had stimulated imaginations and brought a whole stream of delegates into town, even from the tiniest principality and the smallest Swiss canton. The pope was sending his secretary of state, Cardinal Consalvi, and the sultan of the Ottoman Empire his adviser, Mavrojény. Even Napoleon's marshals sent an agent to bargain on their behalf for their right to maintain the generous property endowments that the former French emperor had given them, before almost all of them had betrayed him.

Napoleon's stepson, Prince Eugène de Beauharnais, the former viceroy of Italy still in his Napoleonic uniform, had come to safeguard his interests—he had been promised a state by the Treaty of Paris, though it had not yet been specified where it would be. Among the countless German princes, there was Karl August, the Duke of Weimar, the generous patron of Goethe, Schiller, Herder, Wieland, and many other poets and writers who made his small duchy a literary Arcadia.

There were also several members of the Reuss family, whose ancestors had ruled the tiny principality of Reuss since the eleventh century. Every male had been named Henry (at first Henry the Tall, Henry the Short, Henry the Brave, and so on, though by the seventeenth century they had started using numerals, planning to continue until one hundred and then start over again). The family had also split into an elder branch, represented at the congress by Prince Henry Reuss XIX, and a younger branch, by Prince Henry Reuss XXII. Other members of the family who came to Vienna for the congress included Henry LII and Henry LXIV.

Far less conspicuous, of course, was a young erudite twenty-nine-year-old representing the small delegation of Hesse-Cassel named Jacob Grimm. He and his brother Wilhelm had just published, two years before, the *Kinder- und Hausmärchen,* better known as *Grimm's Fairy Tales,* and Jacob Grimm would use his free time in Vienna to work on another collection of folktales that would be published after the congress.

Excitement was indeed in the air, and there was a scramble to participate in the lavish peace conference in any way possible. Vienna's most distinguished families angled to secure a place, as Schönholz noted with surprise, even offering "to don servants' garb only to be close to the wondrous events to come." Prince de Ligne had said that he would not have missed the Vienna Congress for 100,000 florins.

MINGLING, TOO, AMONG these throngs were some spectators with a special mission. Vienna's chief of police, the fifty-four-year-old Baron Franz von Hager, was running an extensive, intrusive, if sometimes highly inept espionage service. He had many agents already watching, following, and befriending the visitors streaming into Vienna. Hager answered directly to the Austrian emperor, Francis, who, like many enlightened despots before him, was particularly keen to stay enlightened about what his people were doing, saying, and thinking.

Austria had considerable experience in the art of surveillance, letter snatching, cipher breaking, and snooping in general. Habsburg agents had honed their skills under the watchful eyes of Joseph II. Emperor Francis would take up where his uncle had left off, increasing the cloak-and-dagger budget by a staggering 500 percent and vastly expanding its activities. An energetic class of agents was recruited, showing the emperor's talent for selecting officers who were, in the words of one well-placed archduke, "repulsive to all decent-minded people."

Stationed in the Hofburg Palace, in a suite of offices in the Imperial Court Chancellery wing of the palace, placed, conveniently, next to the emperor, the Vienna spies would need much more than repulsive qualities to meet the expectations placed upon them. There was indeed a great sense of urgency as the police system finalized its preparations for a large peace conference.

Spies had in fact just uncovered a ring of disaffected Italian patriots who had plotted to open the Vienna Congress by assassinating the Austrian emperor. The suspects were not happy that their homeland would once again fall under foreign rule—passing, as one put it, from the purgatory of Napoleon to the hell of Austria. By the middle of August, however, the police had quietly foiled this conspiracy and expelled the suspects.

Regardless of how dangerous the threat of an assassination actually was, the police acted with quick diligence, and seized upon this occasion to bargain for additional resources to prevent tragedy at the peace conference. It was imperative, they argued, to keep a close eye on the activities of everyone and provide real security for their many royal guests. The emperor agreed.

The official instructions, promulgated at the end of August 1814, suggest the growing ambitions of this revamped espionage network:

> Since a certain number of representatives of the different powers attending the Congress have already arrived in Vienna and the rest will be following them in a steady stream, you should not only keep me informed of the arrival and address of each one, but by virtue of a secret watch intelligently maintained you should also make it your business neither to lose track of their whereabouts nor of the company they keep.

Daily reports, it was added, were to be written and delivered to the emperor's office. Francis would read them closely every morning.

Baron Franz von Hager had entered police administration after his promising career as a cavalry officer, leading a regiment of dragoons, had been cut short by a riding injury. He had been president of the Ministry of Police and Censorship since 1812, and he had hounded rebels, radicals, secret societies, and many other threats to the government, real or suspected. But he would now face a series of challenges in providing security and intelligence that would enervate the most intrepid and dedicated spymaster.

How was he, for instance, to infiltrate the many foreign delegations—French, British, Russian, Prussian, and probably about two hundred sizable others—with all their exotic languages and customs? Even before he could deal with this issue, which he would soon do with zeal, there was another concern. All of Baron Hager's tireless efforts would further be complicated by the fact that the emperor sometimes issued orders and made decisions that quite frankly obstructed the tasks already assigned.

The Austrian emperor had opened up his palace to many sovereigns, a hospitable gesture that brought many guests into close proximity, but it also created a number of problems for the spy baron. For one thing, the royal palaces were technically off limits to his team's prying activities. For another, even assuming that they could overcome this situation with some creative infiltration, there were still serious problems posed by the palace itself.

The Hofburg was a meandering, labyrinthine structure with many back doors, side entrances, and secret passageways—a nightmare situation for even the most skilled surveillance team. Worse still for the information-hungry agents, much of the action at the Congress of Vienna would take place in just these locations—that is, sealed off in the bedrooms where the young delegates would soon, as some grumbled, turn Emperor Venus's palace into a gilded brothel.

As VIENNA PREPARED to stage an unprecedented house party for the royal mob, Talleyrand found the lack of discussion frustrating and disturbing. He had good reason to worry.

Talleyrand had arrived a week before the congress was scheduled to open, but he discovered, just as he had feared, that Prince Metternich had already been busy arranging secret meetings around the green-baize-covered table in his office at the Chancellery. Only a few countries had been invited. "The Big Four," as they were called, were Austria and its major allies at the end of the war: Great Britain, Prussia, and Russia.

In these meetings, Metternich represented Austria and Castlereagh Great Britain. Russia sent Count Karl Nesselrode, a German by birth who had risen spectacularly from a sailor in the Russian navy to the tsar's trusted adviser. Representing Prussia was the state chancellor, Prince Karl von Hardenberg, a sixty-four-year-old who had a head of white hair and was nearly completely deaf. He was joined by the Prussian ambassador to Vienna, Wilhelm von Humboldt, an exemplary classical scholar and linguist who had previously redesigned the Prussian educational system and founded Berlin University. His brother Alexander was a famous explorer and naturalist.

Article XXXII of the Treaty of Paris had called for a "general congress" consisting of representatives from "all the powers that have been engaged on either side in the present war." But in a secret article attached to this treaty, the Big Four had given themselves the authority to organize the peace conference and establish the rules for the deliberations. This had proved more difficult than expected, and the group struggled to agree.

Ever since their first secret meeting, a five-hour affair on September 15, Metternich had emphasized the problems of a congress in the usual sense of a parliament-style assembly. First of all, it would be too large and unwieldy. Too many states with too many demands would hopelessly complicate the negotiations and cause the whole affair to degenerate into a sorry spectacle of disorder. They could, as Metternich put it, poison diplomacy by rekindling "all the maneuvers, intrigues, and plots, which had so great a share in causing the misfortunes of late years."

It was much better, Metternich argued, to adopt a more confidential style of diplomacy, with the four powers making all the decisions themselves, as a cabinet meeting behind closed doors. Compromise-friendly exchange would be much better than a wild free-for-all diplomatic bazaar. The Prussians and the Russians agreed completely. Castlereagh, on the other hand, was skeptical.

While the British foreign secretary also wanted to maintain control over the actual decision making, he advocated establishing a congress of states that would ratify or sanction their decisions. This was more in line with the public articles of the Treaty of Paris, and besides, was not all of Vienna being filled with delegates, who had come on this pretense, and expected to see the congress open soon, presumably in one of the large ballrooms of the imperial palace?

Yes, Metternich conceded, but there were messy problems. Who exactly would be allowed to participate in such an assembly? Take Naples, for example. Would the representative of the current king, Joachim Murat, a former Bonaparte marshal who received his crown from Napoleon, be recognized as the official delegate, or would it be the representative of the exiled King Ferdinand IV, who claimed his throne on the grounds of legitimacy? What about all the princes and knights of the former Holy

Roman Empire? There were hundreds of them—or "millions of them," as someone scoffed—and each had a representative. Would every self-proclaimed delegate in Vienna be permitted in the congress?

On September 22, the day before Talleyrand's arrival in Vienna, the four powers had finally agreed on the organization of the conference. Castlereagh had been outvoted. The Vienna Congress was not in fact going to be a congress. It was no parliament of equal sovereign states, and certainly not any kind of a "deliberate assembly of Europe." Rather, the congress was simply the "site of many individual negotiations." It was only a "Europe without distances."

As for the management of the diplomacy, the Great Powers had agreed simply to take it upon themselves to appoint the Central Committee, or Directing Committee, that would facilitate all the negotiations. More exactly, this committee would control everything from selecting the agendas to making the final decisions:

> This committee is the core of the congress; the congress exists only when the committee is in being, and it is terminated when the committee dissolves itself.

This central committee, further, would be staffed only with members of the four Great Powers—the idea of a "Great Power" enjoying its own special privileges was about to be born in this secret protocol.

This arrangement was only fair, they reasoned. The Big Four were the ones who had carried the brunt of the fight against Napoleon, and, as a result, earned the right to decide Europe's future. All the other states could, of course, voice their opinion, but this would only take place *after* a "final decision" had been reached and the Allied powers had arrived at "a perfect agreement among themselves." The consulting powers could only give "comment and approval." They would have no power to initiate or change anything. Decision making was about to be sealed up in the hands of the Big Four alone.

But there was one glaring obstacle to this plan: How would they inform all the people who had arrived to deliberate in the assembly, or watch its proceedings from the gallery? The French minister, for one, was not likely to respond favorably to this idea of "a congress that was not a congress."

Castlereagh had been pressing his colleagues to include France in their discussions, or at least inform the embassy of their plans. It was not long before Metternich realized that Castlereagh had a point. According to gossip, both in salons and in the spy dossiers, Talleyrand had spent his first week in town whipping up discontent and alarm among the many states about to be shut out of this scheme. Reports also suggested that many were listening.

Why not call him aside and win him over to this plan? Surely as the representative of a defeated country, Talleyrand would go out of his way to be accommodating, if only for the hopes of making gains for his country, or himself. This was, of course, possible. It was also possible that the plan would backfire.

Chapter 6

BARTERING DESTINY

What took twenty years to destroy can't be rebuilt in thirty days.

—TALLEYRAND

On the morning of September 30, Metternich sent a note over to Kaunitz Palace curtly inviting Talleyrand to a "private conference" later that afternoon. The invitation arrived between nine and ten in the morning, long before Talleyrand was usually out of the bed.

Getting ready for the day ahead, Talleyrand entered his dressing room and took his seat by the porcelain stove. Three valets waited on him, one supervisor and two assistants dressed in gray livery, covered with long aprons. The team began removing his flannel and stockings from the night before, and placed them in a bucket of eau de cologne. One handed him a cup of camomile tea, and the others set about taking away the rest of the night garments, the "drawers, vests, dressing gowns, with all sorts of odds and ends flopping about."

After the nightcap, a cambric bonnet tied with lace ribbon around his neck, was removed, two valets attacked his hair, "combing, curling, pomading, and powdering him." In the meantime, Talleyrand refreshed himself with a glass or two of warm water, which he then emptied into a silver basin, as one eyewitness described the maneuver, "sucked in through the nose and spit out, much the way the elephant uses his trunk."

A warm cloth was applied to his face, and his feet were washed in unpleasant, medicinal eau de barèges, dried, and then perfumed. His valets put on his white silk stockings, his breeches, and his shoes. As he stood up, the valets skillfully removed the last dressing gowns and maneuvered the shirt over his head—everything was done modestly, as he often entertained guests at the same time. By the end of the lengthy ritual, usually just under two hours, Talleyrand was immaculately dressed in velvet, silk, and satin. He was ready for his first showdown.

Early that afternoon, with the beautiful summer weather still holding, Talleyrand's dark-green coach clattered and clanked its way down the narrow Johannesgasse, lined with impressive palaces. It was a twenty-minute carriage ride out to Metternich's summer villa, a sprawling, rather than towering, classical Italianate structure located on the Rennweg, a main road that passed through another area full of aristocratic palaces.

On the way to the meeting, the French minister met a colleague, Don Pedro Gomez Havela de Labrador, the Spanish envoy, who also found himself unhappily excluded from Metternich's secret meetings. Like Talleyrand, Labrador had received an invitation to the meeting at the summer villa as one of the signatories of the Treaty of Paris.

Spain had played a major role in defeating Napoleon, Labrador could say with justice. Napoleon's invasion of Spain, back in 1808, had been catastrophic. The French army had found itself mired in a long bitter struggle that drained resources, eroded morale, and kept them spread out over a great distance, unable to concentrate effectively in a single arena. As a result, Spain rightly expected to participate at the Vienna peace conference. And its role, Labrador said, would not be simply rubber-stamping the decisions of others. "We are not going to play the role of marionettes."

Talleyrand had a long history of working with his neighbor to the west. Even if the two delegates did not always get along well, they shared several traits: They were aristocratic, haughty, and resourceful when it came to finding ways to attain their own goals. Not everyone, however, had been impressed with the Spanish envoy. "Never have I met a more stupid man," the Duke of Wellington had said after meeting him. Labrador was certainly a dogged and extravagant fellow with a volatile temper.

Arriving early at Metternich's mansion, which was in the final stages of its refurbishment for the congress, including the installation of a brand-new ballroom, the French and Spanish delegates climbed the granite steps, passed through the spacious halls, and entered a large room. It was about two o'clock in the afternoon, and they were right on time. When they crossed the threshold, however, they found other ministers already seated comfortably around a long table. Austria, Russia, Prussia, and Britain were the only powers present, just as they had heard.

Talleyrand calmly took his seat, in the empty high-backed chair between Prince Metternich and Lord Castlereagh, and Labrador sat down on the opposite side near the two Prussian ministers. Britain's foreign secretary, sitting at one end of the table, seemed to be in charge, running the meeting, despite his poor French. At the far end of the table sat Metternich's assistant, Friedrich von Gentz, who had just been appointed secretary for the Vienna Congress.

Glancing around the room and sizing up the handful of men around the table, Talleyrand asked suspiciously: Why was he the only member of the French embassy who had been invited to this meeting?

"It was wished to bring together only the heads of the Cabinets at the preliminary conferences," Castlereagh declared.

"But Count de Labrador is not a head of Cabinet, and he has also been invited," Talleyrand rightly objected, pointing to the Spaniard who accompanied him.

"That is because the Secretary of State of Spain is not in Vienna," Metternich explained in his nasal drawl.

"Even so," Talleyrand countered, looking over at two members of the Prussian delegation. "I see that Herr von Humboldt is here in addition to Prince von Hardenberg, and he is not a Secretary of State."

"This is an exception to the rule," someone said, politely referring to Hardenberg, who used a hearing horn. This exception was "made necessary by the infirmity with which, as you know, Prince Hardenberg is afflicted."

"Oh, well then, if it's a question of infirmities, each of us has one of his own, and we can all claim an exception on that basis," Talleyrand retorted, referring to his limp.

Cantankerous in his disarmingly becoming style, Talleyrand was not one to act like he represented a defeated country, even though he did. His confident approach was already working. In the future, it was agreed that a French diplomatic assistant would also be welcome at the meetings. More important than winning this small point, Talleyrand was demanding equality with the other powers.

Calling the meeting to order, Lord Castlereagh began by reading a letter from the representative of Portugal, the Comte de Palmella, who was disturbed at being excluded from the meetings. His country, after all, had also signed the Treaty of Paris. Why had he not been invited to these meetings, he asked, and why was Vienna's Big Four insulting the crown of Portugal in this way?

When Castlereagh finished reading the letter, both Talleyrand and Labrador voiced their support of the Portuguese count. The other ministers listened politely, and then promptly decided to postpone a decision about who should be invited to the organizational meetings until a later date.

"The object of today's conference," Castlereagh droned in a dry monotone voice, "is to acquaint you with what the four Powers have done since we have been here." He glanced over to Prince Metternich, who on cue handed Talleyrand the protocol. (The protocol, an official summary of policy or a decision, just coming into greater use, remains one legacy of the Vienna Congress.)

The French minister started reading the document, already signed at the bottom by the four powers, and found it sprinkled freely with the term *allies*. Talleyrand stopped reading at once. Allies? "Allies against whom?" Talleyrand asked with displeasure:

> Not against Napoleon, he's on Elba. Not against France, peace has been made. Surely not against the King of France. He guarantees the durability of this peace.

"Gentlemen, let's speak frankly," he added. "If there are still Allied Powers, then I don't belong here."

Talleyrand was hitting upon a potential public relations problem— public opinion becoming an increasingly important force in a close-knit, gossip-ridden town like Vienna. The war was over, and the tasks ahead were daunting. It served no purpose to maintain such divisive vocabulary.

No harm was intended, the leaders explained, trying to brush aside the objection. The word was simply convenient, "chosen only for the sake of brevity."

"Brevity," Talleyrand objected, "should not be purchased at the price of accuracy."

The point evidently hit home, and Talleyrand returned to the protocol, making his way through the dense prose.

"I don't understand," Talleyrand muttered.

The articles were read over again. "I do not understand any better," Talleyrand said. The blank look was deliberately overplayed, he later admitted, to highlight the absolute inappropriateness of the secret meetings. Decision after decision had already been made, even before the other diplomats had had a chance to arrive in town.

Talleyrand was being handed a summary of their conclusions and basically being asked to consent. He was not, however, willing to play along as easily as they had hoped. Talleyrand took a direct shot at the legality of decisions coming from secret, unauthorized meetings:

> For me there are two dates and between them there is nothing—the 30 May, when it was agreed to hold a Congress, and the 1st of October, when the Congress is to open. Nothing that has taken place in the interval exists so far as I am concerned.

Talleyrand's words were greeted with an oppressive silence. Remarkably, when Metternich spoke up, the protocol was immediately withdrawn, and Talleyrand had won another point. How pliable the conquerors of Napoleon seemed before the representative of the defeated power.

No sooner had Metternich retrieved the protocol than he pulled out a second one for consideration, placing it on the table as smoothly as if he were playing a card in a game of whist.

This protocol was more complicated, though, Talleyrand noticed, it hardly seemed any less suspect. This plan proposed dividing every possible issue or territorial question at the Vienna Congress into two categories: general (concerning Europe as a whole) and particular (deemed relevant only on a local or regional basis). But both categories would still be dealt with by committees, appointed by the Great Powers. After the two committees had deliberated and reached their conclusions, the Congress would *then* be assembled. This was proposing, Talleyrand later said, "to finish where I had thought it would be necessary to begin."

Besides, this protocol would also effectively make the four Great Powers, as Talleyrand pointed out, "absolute masters of all the operations of the Congress."

Thinking quickly on his feet, as he was known to do, Talleyrand knew that he had to stall for time. "A first reading," he said, "was not sufficient for the formation of an opinion upon a project of this nature." He would need some time for reflection. "We have assembled to consecrate and secure the rights of each of the powers," he said. After the anarchy of the last war, it would be unfortunate indeed if Vienna's diplomats violated the very rights that they should protect. Working out all the details "before convening the Congress," he added, was new to him.

It was a question of practicality, Castlereagh answered calmly. The smaller number of powers could work with haste and fairness.

Talleyrand also shared these goals, but proved his impatience with his next question: "When is the general Congress going to open?" Why can't it open right now?

Listening to Talleyrand defend the rights of all the states who deserved a voice at the conference, Prussia's Hardenberg blurted out that he would not be dictated to by a bevy of petty princes, such as the Prince of Leyen and the Prince of Liechtenstein. At this point, Castlereagh quickly adjourned the meeting. He did not want to give Talleyrand the chance to score another point.

Talleyrand's opposition was threatening to upset the designs of the Great Powers for transforming the congress into an elite club meeting behind closed doors. That night, Friedrich von Gentz confided in his diary the severity of the crisis. Talleyrand had "savagely upset our plans, and torn them to shreds."

After the meeting, a good two-hour event in which the French delegate had "rated them soundly," Gentz and Metternich cooled down with a casual stroll through the villa's gardens. Austria's foreign minister was showing the preparations that were well under way for an upcoming celebration in honor of Allied victory the previous year at Leipzig. What particularly surprised Gentz, however, was Metternich's attitude. He seemed strangely oblivious to "the embarrassment and the dreadful state of our position."

LEAVING THE SUMMER villa, Prussian ambassador Wilhelm von Humboldt made his way back to the Spielmann mansion on the Graben, a central street lined with boutiques, cafés, and restaurants. Routine business for the embassy would be conducted there on the mansion's second floor. This was a much better environment for concentrating on work than his first temporary lodgings, which were in a room adjacent to Princess Bagration's lively suites in the Palm Palace, where Vienna's beau monde was already gathering.

Forty-seven years old with light hair prematurely turning white, Humboldt was regarded as one of the hardest-working delegates in town. Diplomatic dispatches, memoranda, and drafts of protocols jostled haphazardly on his desk, next to many other projects in progress. When he was not working on another memorandum outlining Prussian policy, Humboldt relaxed by polishing his massive study of Basque languages, already a good decade into the work.

Humboldt was also busy translating the ancient Greek playwright Aeschylus's tragedy *Agamemnon*. He would tinker with the text almost every day of the congress, and, at this point, he was almost happy with the prologue. The challenges of ancient Greek would help Humboldt relieve stress from the day's work around the diplomacy table. "Wars and peace come and go," Humboldt once said, "but a good verse lasts forever."

It is no surprise that Humboldt had made many enemies in the course of his career. His negotiation style was aggressive, and he was blunt for a diplomat. Erudite and intellectually sharp, Humboldt also had a high-handed approach that often manifested itself in a stubborn and inflexible disposition. He was also criticized for appearing overambitious, a tad elitist, and far too much concerned about showing he was right. As he put it himself, he lived for ideas. To many of his colleagues, Humboldt was too enamored by his own "subtleties and paradoxes," which, however delightful to himself, soon wearied them ad nauseam.

Indeed, some wondered if Humboldt, with his scholarly air, would have been better suited to a university, like Berlin University, which he had earlier founded, than the manic high-stakes intrigues that he would encounter at the Vienna Congress. Worse than his pedantic tendencies, which stood out at that worldly conference, some noted a shocking, even chilling detachment to his personality. How could he tour the grim battlefields, strewn with the aftermath of slaughter, and still calmly carry on a discussion of Aristotle's *Poetics?* Like a calculating abstractician, one colleague said, Humboldt only "toys with the world and with human beings as though it were a game."

But the Prussian delegation was in no mood for toys or games in the autumn of 1814. By far the weakest of the Big Four, Prussia was usually viewed as a dangerous and probably the most unsettling delegation at the congress, armed with ambitious, hardworking, and brilliant minds like Humboldt. They seemed aggressive, and they had a formidable scholarly apparatus to back up their belligerency.

No major power had lost such a high percentage of its own territory as Prussia, and, with the exception of Austria, no other power had suffered as many humiliations at the hands of the French. But unlike other victors, who had already made gains during the war, or in the Treaty of Paris, the Kingdom of Prussia remained only a shell of its former self, a "parceled-out territory" that was barely half the size it was on the eve of the war.

Besides that, there was an acute sense of vulnerability that had dogged Prussian rulers for centuries. Flatlands of pine forests, sand dunes, and marshy coastlands in the north afforded no obstacle whatsoever to a determined invader. There were no mountains, oceans, or other natural frontiers demarcating its territory, and this lack of natural defenses only increased the militaristic bent of the kingdom in the exposed center of the Continent. Long before the current king, Frederick William III, Prussian rulers had been notorious for putting their trust in the army.

For several years now, and especially after the embarrassing defeats at Auerstedt and Jena in 1806, Prussia had been reforming its institutions. The army copied French tactics, drill, and conscription, and the government centralized its administration—no longer, as Metternich joked, "a conspiracy of mediocrities held together by the fear of taking a single step." Peasants had been emancipated, education revamped, and the whole tax system made more efficient. Prussia was determined to play a greater role in central Europe.

Like its soldiers, who were feared for looting and destroying more than other armies on campaign, Prussia's diplomats were earning a reputation for their intensity in the conference room. They were the "lions of diplomacy." Humboldt and Hardenberg were among a select few diplomats who would earn a coveted Iron Cross, the famous military honor that had been instituted a few years before by Frederick William III. In fact, both were awarded an Iron Cross First Class with a white band, and they were the only ones ever to receive this honor.

What Prussia wanted most of all at the Vienna Congress was to annex a region that many, including Lord Castlereagh, literally had trouble placing on the map. This was the Kingdom of Saxony, located right in the middle of the Continent. Draw two straight lines, one north-south from Copenhagen to Rome and the other east-west from Warsaw to Paris, and they intersect in Saxony. Castlereagh was no master of geography and the issue of Saxony sounded pretty obscure, but it was soon to be hugely important to the peace conference, and also to the future of the continent.

In the early nineteenth century, Saxony had been a thriving region of towns, farms, and mining, including silver and jade. The capital of the kingdom, Dresden, straddled the Elbe River, and boasted many fine palaces, some "the size of towns," which earned it the distinction of being the "Florence of the Elbe," renowned for its beautiful Renaissance and baroque architecture.

Now this Saxony was under great threat at the Vienna Congress— and that is why the king of Saxony appears in a caricature of the "dancing congress" as the figure desperately "clutching his crown." The problem with Saxony, as far as the Prussians were concerned, was that it had fought on the wrong side of the war. While the Russians, the Austrians, and even the Prussians had also supported Napoleon at one time or another, they had all eventually rallied to the Allies and helped the coalition obtain its victory. The Saxon king, however, had rejoined Napoleon in 1813 after a brief attempt at neutrality, and now many members of the victorious alliance wanted his throne.

Prussia was demanding the entire region, claiming it by right of its sacrifices in the war. Chancellor Karl von Hardenberg asked simply: "Has not Prussia, who made the greatest efforts and the greatest sacrifices in the common cause, the right to claim acquisitions proportionate to those of her neighbors?"

But others were not so sure. Although Prussia had certainly sacrificed, many like Talleyrand feared that this annexation of lands in its immediate south would give Prussia too much influence and upset the balance of power in central Europe. Besides, what right did the Prussians have to dethrone a king and annex an entire kingdom, including Dresden and Leipzig? The king of Saxony was outraged, sending ministers to Vienna to plead his case. He was unfortunately not able to come himself because the Prussians had captured him in October 1813 and locked him away in the Schloss Friedrichsfeld, a fortress prison outside Berlin. As the congress set out to debate his future, the king was still a prisoner of war.

"ᴇUROPE, ᴜNHAPPY ᴇUROPE"

Politics is the art of making war without killing anyone.

—Prince de Ligne

ll throughout September, Prince Metternich was spending as much time as possible with the Duchess of Sagan. He was as deeply in love with her as he had ever been. Emperor Francis was not merely humoring him when he had said, "I consider her one of the most essential ingredients of the Congress." The duchess was becoming an indispensable part of Metternich's life.

The foreign minister looked forward to each meeting with the duchess, every morning at eleven—"our hour," as he called it—when he came into her pink and white salon in the Palm Palace and they discussed affairs over a cup of chocolate. Metternich was not discreet, and they talked about everything. He respected her opinion so much that he wanted to make her his "secret advisor." "You know—and understand—our problems far better than any of [my] Ministers," he had once confessed to her.

When they were not together, and that was unfortunately too often as far as Metternich was concerned, he would yearn to see her. He would retire to his desk, and late at night, by candlelight, he would plead, in arching swirls: "If the love of my heart grants me another night I shall be repaid for the pains of a lifetime." Wilhelmine would write back, saying that she would be waiting for him, and thinking only of him.

Yet the Duchess of Sagan had many other things on her mind. Behind her glamorous facade, she sometimes seemed melancholy, even depressed. Congress gossipers—and historians, too—had long believed that she was very much concerned about losing properties or income in the territories ruled by the tsar. The duchess was anxious about them, of course, but she had another, much deeper concern that almost no one at the Vienna Congress knew, not even the baron's spies.

Her secret was revealed only in 1949 when the Czech scholar Maria Ullrichová was visiting an old Cistercian abbey at Plass, one of Metternich's Bohemian estates. Underneath the abbey's brewery was a wall—a fake wall, it turned out, that blocked the entrance to a hidden cellar. When Ullrichová noticed the decoy and managed to push it aside, she found a number of blue cardboard boxes marked "Acta Clementina," and among them a small black box with gilded edges. On its side were the words, in Metternich's clear handwriting, "Letters of the Duchess of Sagan."

Metternich scholars knew, of course, of his affair with the duchess, but no one realized that the letters had survived, or had any idea of how close the two lovers had been. The letters tied with a small white ribbon had been hidden by Metternich's descendants sometime in the mid to late 1930s, just before the Nazi seizure of Czechoslovakia. Fortunately, they survived intact, all 616 letters, and they reveal a great deal about the private life of Metternich, the duchess, and her salon at the center of the congress.

What few realized was that fourteen years before, the Duchess of Sagan had given birth to a daughter, and then, under pressure from her mother, given her away. Wilhelmine had only been eighteen years old at the time. Her difficult pregnancy and heartbreaking surrender of her child were explained to her younger sisters as a recuperation from a carriage accident.

The father of the child was unfortunate. It had been the Swedish nobleman and former cavalry officer Gustav Armfelt, who had been forced out of his country in the early 1790s (and the same man who had encouraged Dorothée in her studies). Armfelt had drifted down to the duchess's estate, Sagan, and stayed on as a guest of the family. He looked like a cavalry officer, and his conversation was as glittering as the medals on his uniform. The Swedish gentleman was charming, dashing, and, at that time, regrettably also the lover of Wilhelmine's mother.

Wilhelmine's affair had been discovered in a cruel way. One night before going to bed, her mother, the Duchess of Courland, noticed that a candlestick had been taken from its holder, and wondered who would be stirring at that hour. Following the trail, she entered a room in the large castle, and found the forty-two-year-old man and her teenage daughter in a compromising situation. Shocked, she had slapped her daughter across the face, the sharp edges of her sapphire ring scratching into her skin.

Over the following months, Wilhelmine was forced by her mother into a marriage to Prince Louis de Rohan, a high aristocrat who had fled France during the revolution. Ruined by large debts, he cared little about his rich fiancée who happened to be pregnant with another man's child.

Under further pressure from her mother, Wilhelmine had then handed over her baby, born Adelaide-Gustava, or "Vava," to be raised by Armfelt's cousins back in Finland. The duchess would make sure her daughter had every monetary need fulfilled. Vava's true identity was to be concealed until she turned fifteen, which, by the autumn of 1814, was only months away.

But the duchess had come to regret that decision, and she wanted her daughter returned immediately. How she hated that she had handed over the baby to her lover's family, and how she despised herself for yielding to her mother's demands. Her remorse would at times be all-consuming. She tried to escape by losing herself in the world of the salon, or waltzing "like a lost soul." Yet she suffered increasingly from bouts of depression and intense migraine headaches that lasted three to four days.

There was one person in Vienna who knew her secret, and that was Prince Metternich. The duchess had told him, some ten months before, around Christmas 1813, when she had asked for his help. Could the Austrian foreign minister, she had hoped, use his finesse and influence to help her regain her daughter? Could he perhaps talk with the Russian tsar?

Little Vava was in Finland, a country the tsar had conquered in 1809 and now controlled; he had also appointed the girl's father as its governor. Perhaps Metternich could convince Alexander to intervene—after all, the tsar had done it before, when he had visited Wilhelmine's mother and won Dorothée for Talleyrand's nephew.

Thrilled to be able to help, and confident of his own success, Metternich had at once given his word. He would ask the tsar for this favor immediately, and he added, "I shall make the safety of Russia depend on it."

ACROSS THE CORRIDOR in the Palm Palace, Princess Bagration was making a stir, hosting salons attended by the elite of the congress, particularly from the Russian and Prussian delegations. Prince Hardenberg and Count Nesselrode were regulars, and the salon would sometimes seem like a tiny St. Petersburg in the middle of Vienna. Years later, one admirer left a vivid description of the "lovely princess" who attracted attention wherever she went: "The Princess never wore anything but white India muslin, clinging to her form and revealing it in all its perfection."

As one of Baron Hager's agents pointed out, Bagration had not entirely lost her wild "foolishness of youth." She had had many love affairs over the years, including one, thirteen years before, with none other than Metternich. At that time, both of them had been living in Dresden, then regarded as an opulent, if decadent, backwater. Metternich was a young twenty-eight-year-old ambassador on his first diplomatic mission; Bagration, the beautiful nineteen-year-old wife of a much older Russian general, who was almost always somewhere else. By 1802, the princess had given birth to a daughter and boldly named her Clementine, after the man who almost certainly was the father, Klemens Metternich.

This extramarital affair did not last long, but it had left its scars. Although little remains of the end of this relationship beyond gossip and rumor, there is no sign that the two former lovers parted on anything other than difficult terms. Yet by the summer of 1814, Metternich was again visiting Bagration's salon. Both found themselves in the spa town of Baden bei Wien, nestled in the Vienna Woods, some two hours away by carriage. Metternich was preparing for the congress, and coming over regularly to the princess's fashionable salon for cards, drinks, and the latest gossip. He was enjoying himself so much that he even toyed with the idea of hosting the entire peace conference in this pleasant spa town.

Now, at the Vienna Congress, Bagration seemed interested again in her old lover, "her" Metternich, and seemed determined to win him back. Even if Metternich apparently seemed more interested in the woman across the wing of the Palm Palace, Princess Bagration was not one to sit idly and concede defeat, especially not to the Duchess of Sagan. What's more, if she could not have him herself, then Metternich would suffer the consequences.

ON THE DAY after his initial meeting challenging the Big Four at the summer villa, Talleyrand went over to the Hofburg for an audience with the Russian tsar. Alexander had let it be known that he wished to speak with Talleyrand. The French minister then, in the etiquette of the day, politely requested an audience. This was their first meeting in Vienna, and the first time they had seen each other in months.

Talleyrand and the tsar had come to know each other during the Napoleonic Wars. In September 1808, they had plotted together against Napoleon at Erfurt and collaborated on arranging Dorothée's marriage. The tsar had become a great admirer of Talleyrand's ability. In fact, when the Allies captured Paris, Alexander honored Talleyrand by staying at his house, instead of the royal palace (it was rumored that the palace had been mined, and more than a few historians have wondered about Talleyrand's role in spreading this rumor).

But their relationship had deteriorated greatly in the intervening months. For one thing, the tsar blamed Talleyrand for the king of France's failure to live up to his promises of establishing a genuine constitutional monarchy. This was all the more frustrating for the tsar because he also blamed Talleyrand for convincing him to support the king's restoration in the first place. Alexander had personally been unimpressed with Louis and had preferred placing many other alternatives on the throne, including the former Bonaparte marshal Bernadotte and a younger Bourbon like the duc d'Orléans. Alexander had even considered establishing a republic. Talleyrand, however, had persuaded him to accept Louis, and now that French affairs seemed to be struggling, the tsar was not pleased.

The tension was palpable as the French minister arrived at the Hofburg. After a preliminary discussion about the situation back in France, the conversation switched to diplomacy at Vienna, particularly Russia's intentions in Poland, and immediately took a more menacing turn.

"Now let us talk of our affairs," the tsar said impatiently, "we must finish them here."

"That depends on Your Majesty," Talleyrand replied. "They will be promptly and happily terminated if Your Majesty brings to bear on them the same nobility and greatness of soul as in the affairs of France."

"But each must find what suits it here," the tsar countered.

"And what is right."

"I shall keep what I hold," the tsar affirmed bluntly, referring to the Russian armies in occupation of Poland.

"Your Majesty would only wish to keep that which is legitimately yours," the cunning minister responded provocatively, in his deep guttural.

"I am in accord with the Great Powers."

"I do not know whether Your Majesty reckons France among those Powers."

"Yes, certainly; but if you will not allow each to look after his own interests, what do you propose?" Alexander asked.

"I place right first, and self-interest second," Talleyrand said.

"The self-interest of Europe is what's right," the tsar snapped.

"This language, Sire, is not yours; it is foreign to you, and your heart disowns it."

"No, I repeat it; the self-interest of Europe is what's right,"

As Talleyrand described it, he turned to the wall, and exasperated, rested his head on the fine paneling and muttered, "Europe, unhappy Europe!" After this display of frustration, fearing that the "might is right" mentality would only plunge the Continent into more war and suffering, the French minister turned again to the tsar about the future peace. "Shall it be said that you have destroyed it?"

"Rather war than that I should renounce what I hold," Alexander blurted out.

Talleyrand said nothing, his body language showing, he said later, a combination of displeasure, opposition, and resignation to resumed hostilities, if necessary,

"Yes, rather war," the tsar repeated, breaking the uncomfortable silence.

Then, as the clock struck in the corner, the Tsar of All the Russias beamed. "Ah! It is time for the play; I must go. I promised the Emperor; they are waiting for me."

With these words the tsar abruptly left, nonchalantly dismissing the fate of 2.5 million souls in Russian-occupied Poland, never mind the anxieties of his fellow peacemakers.

$\mathcal{S}$PIES $\mathcal{A}$RE $\mathcal{E}$VERYWHERE!

My children cannot sneeze but that Prince Metternich is sure to hear about it.

— ONE VISITOR DESCRIBING VIENNA'S ESPIONAGE NETWORK

$\mathcal{C}$andles were already burning late into the night at the Secret Cipher Office in the Hofburg Palace. The minister of police, Baron Hager, was well aware that even with the recent budget increases, Vienna's espionage service was woefully inadequate to cope with the task of keeping track of all the arrivals in town.

Baron Hager was frantically recruiting a large network of agents and underlings to infiltrate foreign missions, maintain surveillance, and trail important dignitaries through town, carefully noting the places they visited, the people they met, and anything that happened out of the ordinary. Special attention was paid to dinner parties and evening entertainments, where a great deal of the Vienna Congress would take place. Every morning, with his café au lait, Emperor Francis would devour the thick dossiers of police reports. He would soon be one of the best-informed people in town.

The spy baron already had some high-placed people on his payroll. Confidants would range from the poet Giuseppe Carpani, Mozart's old friend, to the celebrated Viennese courtesan Josephine Wolters. The identity of the agents was always closely protected, and some of the most active spies have in fact never been identified, known only by their code names, like the prolific agent known as ∞, or the sophisticated, enigmatic informer who signed his daily reports **. The latter was certainly an aristocrat who moved at the highest levels of society, even addressed by Baron von Hager as "Your Highness."

Some would attend the fashionable salons—Mondays at Metternich's, Tuesdays at Castlereagh's, and Fridays either at the Duchess of Sagan's or Princess Bagration's. Talleyrand, who usually dined later than the other hosts, was also a high priority, though he was not attracting Vienna's most powerful guests. Society reflected diplomacy: France was isolated.

Spies were instructed to observe all important happenings with "maximum zeal and vigilance" as they sipped champagne, chatted over tea, or played cards at the small round tables. They were to frequent the cafés and the candlelit taverns in the inner city. They were also to mill about the crowds that invariably gathered around the boutiques of the Graben, the parks of the Prater, and the promenades along the old city walls.

With the help of postal lodges across the empire, many official letters were also intercepted and sent over to the Secret Cipher Office in the imperial palace. There, in this "Cabinet Noir," talented agents pried open the top secret dispatches with a bone knife, copied their contents, and then carefully resealed the envelopes over a smokeless candle. Another team decoded the messages, when necessary, and the spies were always adding to their collection of ciphers.

In addition to tapping into the courier system and covering the ballrooms, drawing rooms, and other meeting places of the plenipotentiaries, Baron Hager was working on extending the reach of his information network around town. Coachmen driving the three hundred imperial carriages were instructed to relay anything they overheard from their distinguished passengers. Porters standing outside the embassies and mansions, staffs in hand, kept tabs on the visitors received and their length of stay. Even some landlords would report on their tenants, such as an editor for the newspaper *Wiener Zeitung,* who would communicate on the activities of Count Anstett of the Russian delegation, who had moved in with him at Weihburgasse 983.

Ideally, the Vienna police would succeed in planting agents inside the main embassies, and, of course, some of the best sources were the servants. Liveried footmen standing behind the chairs at dinner, lackeys carrying the three-branched candlesticks through darkened mansions, observers inside an honor guard attached to a sovereign, and sometimes an assistant to a valet, or even a valet, could be successfully placed near a main delegate.

Some of the most valuable agents of all were the chambermaids, who perused the contents of desks, rummaged through wastepaper baskets, and peered into porcelain stoves and fireplaces looking for any scraps of paper that had not been sufficiently destroyed. These scraps—known in spy parlance as *chiffrons*—were then forwarded to the baron's office and, when possible, painstakingly reassembled. No one knew if some little piece of paper, however meaningless it might seem, did in fact hold a clue that unlocked a secret that puzzled analysts at headquarters.

Astute delegations, however, were soon taking measures to resist unwanted intrusions. "We have enough proofs of the dishonorable passion for opening letters," Prussia's Humboldt wrote back to Berlin, notifying that his delegation was seeking safer channels of communication. One member of his embassy, the influential military strategist General Antoine-Henri Jomini, went further in taking precautions. He had started locking up his papers, and made sure that after changing all his locks, he did not leave the office without taking the set of keys with him.

Castlereagh's own secretiveness was likewise paying off—his annoying "excess of prudence," as one spy complained. The British foreign secretary had insisted on hiring his own staff, including doorkeepers, chambermaids, and kitchen hands. The men and women sent over by the police looking for jobs kept being rejected. Castlereagh was also making sure that all stray documents, however bland and unimportant, were collected and methodically destroyed.

Like the British, Talleyrand was also making it difficult for the eavesdroppers. Anyone who knew Talleyrand, one frustrated agent reported, would not fail to understand the difficulties in gaining information from his headquarters. The spies would have to escalate their efforts. Talleyrand was turning Kaunitz Palace into a veritable fortress.

KINGS AND QUEENS at the Vienna Congress were not exactly used to living in such close proximity with other sovereigns, and, according to police agents, frustrations were mounting at the Hofburg Palace. Some apparently resented it when one of them gained more attention than the others, and in the eyes of many, the Russian tsar was receiving the most attention of all.

Stories circulated that emphasized his narcissistic behavior: how he ordered a block of ice delivered to his room every morning, rumored to improve his rosy complexion, though in fact it might well have been used to treat a skin disease that he already showed signs of developing. It was also said that he thought only of his uniform, and as he had gained weight over of the summer, he could no longer squeeze into it comfortably, and had been forced to order a replacement wardrobe from St. Petersburg. His delegation did not escape gossip, either, accused of boasting irresponsibly of Russian power, spitting on parquet floors, and, in general, behaving as if they were not "housebroken."

The tsar had brought a whole team of advisers to Vienna, and of the Great Powers, they were undoubtedly the most diverse and international delegation in town. Of the tsar's nine most prominent advisers, four came from Germany: Count Nesselrode, Baron Heinrich Friedrich Karl vom Stein, Count Gustav von Stackelberg, and Count Jean Anstett. There was also one from Poland, Prince Adam Czartoryski, and one from Switzerland, Alexander's former tutor, Frédéric-César de La Harpe. There was also one from Corfu, Iōannēs Antōniou Kapodistrias, and one from Corsica, Carlo Andrea Pozzo di Borgo. The tsar had only one prominent Russian adviser at the Congress, and he was Ukrainian: the former Ambassador to Vienna, Count Andrei Kirilovich Razumovsky.

This cosmopolitan set of advisers was certainly puzzling, and some feared that the tsar had only brought them to find ways to increase Russian influence in their home countries. Others feared their pet projects. Would the tsar, for instance, listen to his advisers who wanted him to encourage national sentiments in Germany, or pressed him to undertake a more active policy toward the Ottoman Empire and the eastern Mediterranean? Some wondered, too, if the tsar would take up the cause of oppressed national minorities in the Balkans. So if Alexander's behavior was not difficult enough to predict, Vienna diplomats would also have to gauge which adviser currently had the ear of the impressionable tsar.

Like other monarchs visiting the congress, the tsar did not bother with any special security as he walked the streets—at least not yet. He was spotted slipping into a tavern, ordering a beer, gulping it down, and, then, most unusually, paying for it himself. The tsar was seen, on another occasion, talking to a young Viennese girl he met at a recent ball. Spies were immediately placed on the case. The girl was tracked down, identified, and an agent placed outside her house. Sometimes, indeed, the spies were sent on a wild-goose chase. Nothing else was noted from that address in the bulging dossiers.

The baron's agents had begun in earnest following other sovereigns on their daily excursions and intercepting letters from the foreign missions—royal mail was no exception. Correspondence of the king of Denmark, Frederick VI, was pilfered unmercifully. The Danish king was also often recognized by his green cape, gold-tipped cane, and almost scholarly air, and easily followed. The king liked to visit a young Viennese flower girl, who would soon cause a scandal when she started calling herself the "Queen of Denmark."

One of the best places for gathering information was on the busy Graben, a central street that was once the moat for medieval Vienna. Many delegates were staying in rooms or houses there, which was then, as now, an excellent place for rendezvous or impromptu discussions. It was the home of the "open-air club," as one agent called it, where "loafers, idlers, spouters and disputants" watched the congress go by.

For many people-watchers, the highlight was seeing Prince de Ligne, a delightful seventy-nine-year-old former field marshal from Flanders who, in his long career, had served Frederick the Great, Joseph II, and Catherine the Great. His nickname in Paris salons had been "Prince Charming." With a million stories, and a "delicately malicious wit," he was the Oscar Wilde of his day, having known everybody from Voltaire to Rousseau to Casanova. He was one of the first, for instance, to read Casanova's scandalous memoirs literally as they were written, and one of the last to see the adventurer before his death in 1798.

Prince de Ligne's latest quips were eagerly devoured. It was this prince who gave the congress its lasting memorial: "The congress does not move forward, it dances." He should have known, because he did not miss many of the occasions.

Now, however, he was impoverished. He had lost a fortune when the French revolutionaries seized the vast majority of his landed estates, and he had squandered the rest with his lifestyle. At the time of the congress, he lived in a very small apartment near the old city walls. It was one room wide, with the bedroom doubling as his salon; de Ligne called it his "birdcage." But as its many visitors testified, the pauper prince was still very much the dandy.

The walls were as pink as his cheeks . . . [and his cheeks were as pink] as his humor which was as pink as his talk. Pink as his talk was his stationery, pink as this was his livery, everything in pink.

His cramped quarters had long hosted Vienna's elite; everyone wanted to meet the legendary prince, and hear his stories, anecdotes, and repartee, uttered, as he was known to do, with his eyes "nearly shut." He still drove his old clanky carriage that would have been the height of style a half century before under Louis XV, led by a thin white horse also past its prime. The prince was "the man that time had forgotten."

Another favorite sighting, though rare, was Anna Protassoff, who had, many years before, served Catherine the Great and rendered her invaluable assistance as her "tester," that is, the woman who would try out the guardsmen selected for the empress's bedroom. She was now almost seventy years old and considerably heavier. Prince de Ligne took his protégé, the songwriter Auguste de La Garde-Chambonas, to meet her in her small flat. The young man described his first impressions on meeting this legend: "a huge shape on a sofa" that, when speaking or moving, jingled with jewelry.

On her head, around her neck, covering her arms there was a veritable waterfall of glittering diamonds, bracelets, necklaces, ruby-studded medallions, tremendous earrings that reached down to her very shoulders.

As he looked on, Anna Protassoff and Prince de Ligne conversed, as if they had been magically transported some fifty years into the past—appropriately enough for a congress that would itself sometimes seem anachronistic, and be accused of trying to turn back the clock, as if Napoleon, the French Revolution, and the last two decades of history had only been a bad dream.

WHILE TALLEYRAND WAS displeased with the Big Four and their plans for controlling the congress, he was at least satisfied with the early success of the French embassy. The Duke of Dalberg, the Marquis de la Tour du Pin, Comte Alexis de Noailles, and Comte de la Besnardière had been performing as he hoped, keeping him informed, and spreading news that he wished around town. The French chefs were serving up excellent fare, and the musician Neukomm was playing well, too, though he was under close surveillance by the baron's police, who refused to believe that he was brought along only to play the piano. But Talleyrand was especially pleased with Dorothée.

By her family connections alone, Dorothée had close links to the main delegations. She knew the Russians through her mother, and the Austrians through her sister, Wilhelmine. As for the Prussians, Dorothée was influential in her own right, on account of her own extensive properties in their kingdom. Her mansion in Berlin, built originally by Frederick the Great for his sister and located at 7 Unter den Linden right near the Brandenburg Gate, was one of the most impressive in the capital; in the twentieth century, it would be used as the Soviet embassy.

When Talleyrand had not been invited to the highly sought Monday night soirees at the Metternichs', he had asked Dorothée to appeal to her older sister, the Duchess of Sagan. One simple request was all that it took. The Austrian foreign minister replied immediately that Dorothée and Talleyrand would of course be welcome. They should also, Metternich added, consider themselves as having a standing invitation to the intimate suppers.

This was, of course, a major breakthrough. Salons were ideal settings for diplomacy as Talleyrand preferred to practice it, subtly and informally advancing his interests in a place, like Metternich's, that was sure to be crowded with the people who ruled Europe. At such a gathering, it was really a stroke of bad luck, one salon regular put it, "not to encounter an emperor, a king, a reigning prince, or not to knock into a crown prince, a great general, a famous diplomat, a celebrated minister." On some memorable occasions, too, Metternich would serve on the fine Sèvres china that Napoleon had given him for arranging his marriage to Marie Louise. At Metternich's, diplomats could wrangle over the spoils of Napoleon's empire by day, and then dine on his china at night.

Dorothée was indeed proving herself valuable, not least as an excellent hostess at the French embassy. She ran the salon, presided at the table, and generally lit up the room like a magic lantern. She helped everyone feel welcome and stimulated conversation, guiding it skillfully. If someone harped on a subject too controversial, serious, or just unpleasant, she could gracefully redirect it. The songwriter La Garde-Chambonas, who visited the French embassy that autumn, praised her social skills. Even if France was not at this point attracting the most prominent figures to its salon, Dorothée was performing masterfully: She "did the honors of her drawing-room with an enchanting grace."

Behind the scenes, too, Dorothée was beginning to help Talleyrand in many other ways, apparently even in drafting key documents. In a style reminiscent of the eighteenth century, Talleyrand preferred to avoid the strain of composing his letters and dispatches himself. He would rather dictate as he paced up and down the room, while Dorothée, lying on the bed or sitting at the mahogany desk, scratched away with her quill. Together the two then went over the memorandum or dispatch, line by line, waging "the battle of the words."

Working with Talleyrand must have been an extraordinarily valuable experience, especially for someone as intelligent and observant as Dorothée. She had come to admire his "cool-headed courage"; he had "a presence of mind, a bold temperament, [and] an instinctive type of defiance," all of which, she added, "rendered danger so seductive."

While Talleyrand and Dorothée were trying to lure the congress over to Kaunitz Palace, Metternich was consumed by his affair with Dorothée's older sister, the Duchess of Sagan. To his critics, Metternich's work as foreign minister and host of ceremonies sometimes looked neglected, and now this was getting worse because the Big Four had just voted him "President of the Congress." The Prussian ambassador, Humboldt, for one, complained that "Metternich was mad with love, pride and vanity . . . wasting all his mornings getting up only at ten and then running off to sigh at the feet of Sagan . . ."

Metternich looked forward to seeing the duchess at their morning meetings and everywhere else, from her box at the theater to her commanding presence in a hot, crowded drawing room. He was glad to be able to help the duchess obtain her daughter, and he had put some of his best assistants on the case, including even Gentz, the secretary of the Congress. Metternich continued pouring out his heart to her by night:

> If ever the world were lost and you remained to me, I would need nothing more; but if I lose you, I would not know what to do with the world—except for the [plot of land] they'd need to bury me.

With Metternich's regular visits to her salon in the Palm Palace, other leading members of the Austrian Foreign Ministry followed suit. So did the British, who were clearly finding common ground with the Austrians in opposing the Russians. In fact, the duchess's salon was called "Austrian headquarters," and Princess Bagration's, across the way, "Russian headquarters," frequented, as it was, by so many Russian and Prussian well-wishers.

The duchess's salon on Friday night, September 30–October 1, was particularly lively, and Metternich thoroughly enjoyed himself. As the carriages waiting outside in the courtyard gradually took the last lingering guests away, there was no sign that Metternich had left. He was not seen again until the afternoon of the following day, when he arrived at the Chancellery. Almost certainly Metternich spent the night with the duchess. It was then, he later confessed, that he had experienced "the greatest happiness of [his] life."

At the opposite end of the Palm Palace, the same night, Tsar Alexander was also distracted by matters of the heart. He was seen with Princess Catherine Bagration, barely dressed, at his side. The princess had been sending callers away all evening, her servants apologizing that she had a terrible headache. Then the servants themselves were sent away. If this was to quiet rumors, it was not successful.

Vienna heard the stories of the tsar's visit: how he arrived at the palace, rang the bell four times, and the princess descended the staircase in only her negligee. Some also heard of one tense moment: When the tsar had entered her bedroom, he found, to his surprise, a man's hat. Nonplussed, the princess smiled and answered, "Oh, that's the hat of the decorator Moreau. He's the one who is decorating my house for the party tomorrow."

Perhaps the princess was telling the truth, as she did in fact have a ball planned for the next day, and Karl von Moreau, being on the Festivals Committee, was one of the most active decorators in town. The tsar, at least, accepted the explanation, and they laughed at his "unfounded assumptions." The spy who related the gossip remarked ironically, "Evil to him who evil thinks."

The tsar's late-night visit to the princess set Vienna ablaze. "No one," one spy reported, "is talking of anything else."

Chapter 9

Dancing with the World
in Their Hands

*Truly, the ruins of a ball are as interesting to contemplate
as the ruins of monuments and empires.*

— Count Z at the Roman Emperor Hotel
one night in the autumn of 1814

The congress was scheduled to begin on October 1, 1814. But that day had arrived, and there still had not been any official word about the peace conference. The opening masked ball at the imperial palace the following day, however, was proceeding as planned. Emperor Francis and Empress Maria Ludovika wanted to make sure it was a success, and as one countess recalled years later, it was "a truly magnificent affair."

Large crystal chandeliers and an estimated eight thousand candles produced a "blinding almost dizzy effect" in the white and gilt paneled ballroom. The central staircase, adorned with a wide array of flowers and plants, led to the upper galleries and balconies, which were draped in red and gold velvet, and overlooked rows of chairs arranged symmetrically on the fine parquet floors below. Some ten to twelve thousand guests had filled the spacious ballroom, spilling over into the smaller ballroom, the Kleiner Redoutensaal, and the indoor arena of the Spanish Riding School. Some of the side rooms had been transformed into a lush orange grove scented with loans from the emperor's greenhouses.

The Grand Ball had been vastly oversold, thanks in part to enterprising counterfeiters who had superbly forged the invitations. Even more responsible for swelling the event beyond capacity were a few doorkeepers, who had apparently adopted a simpler method of cashing in on the enthusiasm: They would take the admission tickets from the guests and then resell them to the crowds eager to experience, if only for an evening, the revelry of emperors and kings.

The waiters, a "broad and noisy phalanx," struggled with the "murderous crush" of the masked guests and gate-crashers. It is not known what exactly the Festivals Committee served that night, but a catering record survives for a similar grand ball for the same number of guests at the congress that called for some 300 hams, 200 partridges, 200 pigeons, 150 pheasants, 60 hares, 48 *boeuf à la mode,* 40 rabbits, 20 large white young turkeys, and 12 "medium-sized wild boar." Among many other things, there was also an assortment of roasted, baked, and cold meats, and other delicacies, including 600 pickled and salted tongues.

The confectionary supplied a range of pies and pastries, as well as almond, pistachio, chocolate, Seville orange, and French puff-pastry gateaux. There were between 2,500 and 3,000 liters of olla soup, 2,500 assorted biscuits, 1,000 Mandl-Wandl (oval-shaped pastries with an almond filling), 60 Gugelhupf (sponge cakes), and other cakes and sweets. Almond milk, lemonade, chocolate, tea, and many kinds of wine were also available, including Tokay and Meneser. Filling the empty wineglasses and replenishing the dishes on the buffet tables must have seemed a never-ending task.

Suddenly, resounding trumpet blasts signaled the arrival of congress royalty. The emperor, the tsar, and many kings entered, with empresses, queens, and archduchesses on their arms. All eyes turned to the glittering promenade that circled the room and ended at their seats on an honored platform, adorned with large white silk hangings "fringed with silver." The empress of Austria sat in the front, along with the empress of Russia; behind them were the queen of Bavaria and the Russian grand duchess Catherine, Alexander's sister. The dignitaries were flanked with elegant women "as beautiful as statues."

Most of the leading diplomats and ladies attended, with a few prominent exceptions, such as Prussian ambassador Wilhelm von Humboldt. He had been to a party the night before, and had evidently had enough of trying to squeeze into a hot room packed elbow to elbow, where he could not move and the sweat poured down his face. He had been so miserable that he found himself somewhat jealous of the delegate of Hanover, Count Münster, who had broken a rib in a recent carriage accident and had a good excuse for staying home.

The young songwriter August de La Garde-Chambonas found his way to the ball that night, and he was thrilled with everything he saw. What impressed this happy adventurer most was not, of course, the leaders of the world:

> You should have seen those ravishing women, all sparkling with flowers and diamonds, carried away by the irresistible harmonies, leaning back into the arms of their partners.

Many of these women would have worn elegantly simple gowns with deep décolletage. The outer dress was usually in petinet or crepe, the underdress in satin of the same color, white being the most popular, followed by light blue, yellow, pink, or pastels. Sleeves were usually long, tight, and edged in lace, embroidery, or satin. Some preferred short sleeves, or combined them with long white gloves. Flowers and ribbons were often fixed into the hair, along with diamonds, pearls, and other precious stones that glittered marvelously from the light of thousands of candles. When dancing, the women looked like "brilliant meteors" lighting up the heavens.

Orchestras had started with a polonaise, the long procession, like a rhythmic march, through the giant room. Alternatively, in one of the smaller rooms, the minuet was danced, it seemed, with a stiff "Teutonic gravity" that drew snickers from young, fashionable wags. The favorite for the younger generation was, of course, the waltz, the graceful gliding and twirling across the floor, as if the first chords of the orchestra sent an electric current through the happy dancers.

The waltz in the autumn of 1814 was not yet the waltz of later Vienna fame, such as Johan Strauss the Younger's "The Blue Danube," "Tales from the Vienna Woods," and "The Emperor Waltz." It was slower and closer to its origins as a southern German or Austrian country dance. Still, it was a "revolving dance," or *Walzer*, that was every bit as controversial. The waltz, after all, divided the dancers into couples, not groups, and involved much more touching than any previous dance in modern history.

It was perhaps only appropriate the congress would be captivated by this intimate dance. Lord Byron described the waltz in a famous ode:

> *Round all the confines of the yielded waist*
> *The strangest hand may wander undisplaced;*
> *The lady's, in return, may grasp as much*
> *As princely paunches offer to her touch . . .*

Just like the waltz, the masquerade was also a central feature of the entertainment in Vienna during the congress. The ballroom, teeming with revelers in mask, became the "the living image of a society devoted to pleasure, to flirting, and seductive pastimes of every description." Elaborate, at times oppressive protocol easily collapsed, on those occasions, behind the mask, which added a rare freedom, not to mention the allure and enchantment of the unknown. The person behind the mask could, in Vienna of 1814, be literally almost anyone at all.

The dresses, the diamonds, and the dances—La Garde-Chambonas was dazzled. He rhapsodized further on the ladies he saw, with their "shimmering silks and light gauzes of their gowns floating and swaying in graceful undulations."

> The continuous music, the mystery of the disguises, the intrigues with which I was surrounded, the general incognito, the unbridled gaiety . . . in a word, the magic of the whole vast tableau turned my head.

"Older and stronger heads than mine," the young man continued, "found it equally irresistible." Unfortunately for Austria's Festivals Committee, many guests found other things irresistible as well. Almost three thousand of the imperial silver tea spoons disappeared that night.

THE DAILY ROUTINE was already emerging at the Vienna Congress. While the delegates of the Big Four worked in their offices, attended meetings, or tried to schedule appointments, the sovereigns generally spent the mornings on hunts, reviews of troops on parade grounds, or some other activity with their fellow monarchs or favorite companions. Afternoons were usually devoted to meetings and sessions, though by no means, as some complained, simply undoing what the diplomats had done during the day. By the evening, they were in dress uniform again, "sparkling in the truly magical festivities given by the Emperor of Austria."

Among the many activities scheduled for the first week of the congress, there was a concert conducted by Vienna's *Hofkapellmeister*, Antonio Salieri, the opera composer who taught Beethoven, and later Schubert and Liszt. The rumor that Salieri had poisoned Mozart was already circulating at the congress, despite the lack of evidence (one of the police agents, Giuseppe Carpani, would later write a defense of Salieri). Salieri would be active in the musical life of the Vienna Congress that autumn, even directing one "monster concert" of some hundred pianos—apparently an arrangement more experimental and innovative than pleasing to the ear.

In accordance with courtesies of the day, the monarchs were busy bestowing honors and awards upon each other. Britain inducted the leaders into its Order of the Bath and the Order of the Garter with the "Diamond George" pendant. The king of Denmark awarded his fellow sovereigns his state's highest prize, the Order of the Elephant, and the king of Prussia the Black Eagle. The emperor of Austria conferred perhaps the most coveted of all, the Order of the Golden Fleece. All of these ribbons, stars, crosses, and collars, along with many others, were slipped around necks or pinned on breasts that first week.

The Festivals Committee was not the only one planning events. Every night there was entertainment at an embassy, salon, tavern, or somewhere else around town. On Tuesday evenings, for example, the Castlereaghs hosted their soiree at the Minoritenplatz, complete with supper, violin and guitar music, and dance. Despite being well attended and usually difficult to gain entrance to before 10 p.m., Agent ** complained of their tediousness. Guests were poorly greeted and often ignored. The room was dimly lit and poorly furnished, and many women who could not find a seat had to stand. Indeed, without the presiding hand of a talented hostess, this drawing room sometimes seemed more like a café than a salon.

When the British delegates ventured out into other salons in town, many seemed awkward and clumsy. "Either they try to impress us," one police agent overheard, "or they skulk like beasts in a cave." Others smiled at their odd selection of clothes, deemed eccentric at best. The effects of being an island power, so insulated from the Continent, seemed evident to more than a few observers that autumn.

One member of the British embassy, Ambassador Lord Stewart, had already gotten involved in a traffic dispute with the driver of another carriage—a common enough hazard in a town with many horse-drawn vehicles racing through the narrow streets. The event made the rounds in Vienna's salons. According to one rumor, the British ambassador almost ended up tossing the coachman into the Danube. Police agents also followed the case, though they learned that it was actually the coachman who was close to pummeling the ambassador.

What had happened was that after the near accident, Lord Stewart, who had apparently "emptied some bottles of Bordeaux," shouted obscenities, clenched his fists, boasted at his record as a boxer, and challenged the other man to a fistfight. The cabdriver, who evidently did not understand English, grabbed the whip and cracked him in the face. Bystanders broke up the scuffle, and police arrived on the scene before it turned worse, though the officers refused at first to believe that the loud drunk was really a high-ranking member of the British delegation.

Lord Stewart was already cropping up in police reports, too, for the vast amount of time he was spending in the company of what the spies called "ladies of easy virtue." He was a regular customer at local brothels, many of them housed in the Leopoldstadt district, a mostly seventeenth-century development in what had once been the city's thriving Jewish quarter. Stewart and his buddies had also discovered the merits of Hungarian wine, and, in the first week in Vienna, the British ambassador had several times been carried to his carriage.

Perhaps the liveliest topic buzzing in the salons the week of the scheduled opening was the reputed imminent arrival of Napoleon's wife, Marie Louise. Since the fall of the empire, the twenty-three-year-old woman had been torn in her allegiance, vacillating between joining her husband on Elba or returning to her father, Emperor Francis, and the family in Vienna. She had spent a great deal of time pondering her choices and had, in the end, decided to return to Vienna. She was supposed to arrive at any moment, and speculation raged on how she would react to the sight of Vienna carried away in its celebration of her husband's downfall.

WHILE ALL THE plenipotentiaries were preparing for the diplomatic duel
at the next meeting of the Big Four, Talleyrand decided to take matters
into his own hands. Fearing that his ostracization in the conference of the
Great Powers would deprive him of any real influence, the French minister played to his strength. Talleyrand was rightly convinced that his con-
ception of the congress as a parliament of states with equal power would
resonate with the vast majority of the delegates, who were destined to be
excluded from the proposed scheme.

On his own initiative, Talleyrand drafted, signed, and circulated an
account of the secret meeting—a maverick breach of diplomatic etiquette. The Great Powers, he announced, had "formed a league to make
themselves masters of everything." This was very much against the spirit
of the congress and the hopes of establishing a genuine peace. The Great
Powers had no right to sabotage the congress, and had set themselves up
instead as the "supreme arbiters of Europe."

This note was, needless to say, very unpopular among the Big Four.
Not only was the structure of the upcoming congress now out in the
open, introduced in an unbecoming and an untimely fashion by an outside party, but Talleyrand's version, in their eyes, blew everything out of
proportion. Russia grumbled, Austria took offense, and the Prussians
were absolutely furious.

In a meeting of the Big Four on October 2, Wilhelm von Humboldt
denounced the French document as a "firebrand flung into our midst."
The Prussian embassy, it seems, quickly countered with its own campaign
of propaganda, spreading rumors that the French were once again up to
their old habits. Talleyrand was accused of sowing discontent among the
Allies in order for his country to seize coveted regions of Belgium and the
left bank of the Rhine.

Castlereagh, on the other hand, opted for a more constructive
approach and went over to Kaunitz Palace, early that same morning, to
discuss matters with Talleyrand personally. He had come to respect the
French minister and his opinions, though the two men certainly did not
agree on everything. Many thought Castlereagh was the friendliest to the
French embassy, and among the Big Four, he no doubt was.

The British minister explained to Talleyrand in his calm, reassuring manner that the proceedings at the meeting at Metternich's summer villa were intended to be "entirely confidential." Talleyrand's unexpected publication of his note had "rather excited apprehension" among the Austrian and Prussian ministers. Talleyrand listened, but he did not recant, apologize, or otherwise give any sign of remorse. He only reminded him that Castlereagh had asked his opinion, and "[he] was bound to give it."

Talleyrand further explained that he could not participate in this ill-advised attempt to close off the congress. Napoleonic ideas of seizing power and acting unilaterally should be banished from international politics. Respecting principles of law and justice, on the other hand, was the best way forward. Castlereagh, unimpressed, returned to headquarters.

On October 3, Talleyrand wrote a second note, reiterating his main points, and this time he distributed it more widely. Sure enough, it had great impact. Many princes and delegates outside of the elite club of Great Powers shared Talleyrand's concerns, and they applauded his defiance. He was speaking up for the minor states, and the only one, it seemed, doing so. Indeed, by maneuvering into position to be able to champion law and justice, the foreign minister of a country that had only recently devoured small nations was now, remarkably, being praised as their protector.

THE GREAT POWERS knew that they had to work quickly to rein in the Frenchman. The person that Metternich wanted to draft the official response to Talleyrand's inflammatory paper was his assistant, Friedrich von Gentz, the secretary of the Congress, a short man with red hair and thick small-rimmed glasses. By a combination of talent and his own pushy efforts, he had managed to position himself right in the middle of everything.

In many ways, Gentz had a lot to prove. He was not a prince like Metternich, Talleyrand, or Hardenberg, all of whom had been raised to that title either during or immediately after the war. He was not even a count like his friend, the Russian adviser Karl Nesselrode, a man he had discovered and supported for years. Sure, Gentz had an aristocratic-sounding "von" in his name, but no one seemed to know where it had come from, and many suspected it was on his own initiative, as indeed it was.

A German by birth, the fifty-year-old Gentz had studied at the University of Königsberg under the philosopher Immanuel Kant, and this training showed. He was sharp in debate, adept at manipulating ideas and concepts, and so skillful in his questioning that he sometimes seemed like the Socrates of the Vienna Congress. Like the great philosopher, Gentz would also be unpopular with the people subjected to his painful tactics. He was a very hard worker, shunning many of the entertainments for a quiet evening in a salon discussing politics, which was his main passion. The Socratic comparison, of course, breaks down with Gentz's unabashed worldly streak. He had a love of chocolate, perfume, and flashy rings. "If you want to make him deliriously happy," Metternich said, "give him some bonbons."

Gentz had previously worked as a civil servant in Prussia, where he had edited the conservative *Historisches Journal* and translated political thought, including Edmund Burke's *Reflections on the Revolution in France*. In 1797, he went bankrupt; five years later, his marriage collapsed and he moved to Vienna. He joined the Austrian administration and eventually gained Metternich's attention, becoming one of his most influential assistants. It was Metternich who had given him entrée into the congress and its high society.

Asked to answer the charges made by Talleyrand, Gentz went to work immediately with characteristic intensity. The next day, he was finished. Every decision of the committee was legal, Gentz argued in a frontal assault on Talleyrand's accusations. Every decision, moreover, was shown to be completely in accord with the previous agreements, most importantly with the Treaty of Paris, the international document that legally gave rise to the Vienna Congress. As his colleagues had come to expect, Gentz was a wizard at finding just the right word for the occasion.

Gentz's document was readily accepted and signed by the Great Powers. That night, Tuesday, October 4, at a soiree held by the Duchess of Sagan, it was officially presented to the French delegation. Metternich waited for the right moment, then pranced up to the French minister and, in front of a packed room, made a big show of handing him the protocol.

Talleyrand, of course, was not ruffled in the least. Less than twenty-four hours later, he also had a response, another letter that defiantly stood its ground. The Great Powers had no right, Talleyrand reaffirmed, to "take it upon themselves to decide everything in advance" and leave everyone else outside their cabal. Trying to impose their will as law was no better than Napoleon's tactics and would only have the same result—more war and bloodshed.

When Talleyrand presented this paper at the next meeting of the Big Four at Metternich's summer villa on October 5, the result was another "very tumultuous and very memorable conference," as Gentz put it in his diary. Talleyrand's protest was passed around the table. Both Metternich and Nesselrode frivolously "glanced at it with the air of men who require only to look at a paper to lay hold of all its contents." Metternich turned to Talleyrand and asked him directly to withdraw the letter. He refused. Metternich tried again with more persuasion, but Talleyrand held firm. The French minister then added:

> I shall take no more part in your conferences . . . I shall be nothing here but a member of the Congress, and I shall wait until it is opened.

But Talleyrand was making too many waves in salons and drawing rooms around town, and gaining too large a following to be ignored. Clearly, the French minister was not behaving in the way the Great Powers had hoped when they summoned him to their conference.

Exasperated, Metternich blurted out that he would cancel the peace conference immediately—a threat, at this point, so wildly unrealistic that it did not faze anyone. Russia's Count Nesselrode came to Metternich's assistance, stating unequivocally that the decisions in Vienna needed to be wrapped up quickly because the tsar was leaving town by the end of the month. Talleyrand, still unmoved, only replied, "I am sorry to hear it, for he will not be here to see the end of things."

"How can the Congress be assembled," Metternich asked, "when nothing is ready to lay before it?"

"Well, then," Talleyrand replied in a planned burst of cordiality, "since nothing is ready as yet for the opening of the Congress, and since you wish to adjourn, let it be put off for a fortnight or three weeks. I consent to that." Provided, of course, he added significantly, that the leaders seated around the table accept two conditions. First, they set a firm date for the opening of the congress, and second, they specify the criteria for deciding who will be admitted to the proceedings. He scribbled the terms down immediately and handed the paper over to the Big Four.

This meeting had not gone well for the conquerors of Napoleon, and their disappointment was read in the way the conference ended. It was not adjourned in an orderly fashion, but instead seemed to evaporate, with ministers drifting off at will.

Castlereagh, the last to leave, walked down the wide stone steps afterward with Talleyrand. Like many in Vienna, he preferred to take the personal and informal approach whenever possible. He tried to persuade Talleyrand by hinting at his own help: "certain affairs that most interest [France] could be arranged to my satisfaction."

"It isn't at all a question of certain particular objects," Talleyrand replied, "but rather of the law which ought to serve to rule us all . . . How can we answer to Europe if we have not honored those rights, the loss of which caused all our troubles?"

Turning again to Castlereagh, Talleyrand emphasized the opportunity at hand, a chance to reestablish law, order, and peace:

The present epoch is one of those which hardly occur once in the course of several centuries. A fairer opportunity can never be offered to us. Why should we not place ourselves in a position to answer to it?

Chapter 10

THE PEOPLE'S FESTIVAL

I have made two mistakes with Talleyrand—first,
I did not take his good advice,
and second, I did not have him hanged when
I did not follow his ideas.

—NAPOLEON

astlereagh had found himself in an awkward and frustrating position. Besides the fact that he sympathized with Talleyrand's viewpoint, he had another reason for tolerating the sheer defiance of this defeated power. Castlereagh was concerned, more than ever, about the threat of Russia, and its ominously close relationship with Prussia.

In a council of only four powers, the grouping of these two was significant. Castlereagh was about to be left with only one potential ally: Austria, a notoriously ambiguous and tentative partner led by a foreign minister, as a common critique ran, "more polished than steeled." The British minister was worried about how his Austrian ally would stand up under pressure, and wondered if he might in the future need Talleyrand's assistance.

Castlereagh's ideal plan was not, of course, to work with France; he much preferred to win over the Prussians, and shift them away from their Russian ally. He believed that he had a good chance. He related well with the Prussian diplomatic team, and he wanted a strong Prussia anyway. As he saw it, a powerful Prussia would create a "stable foundation" for Germany and, at the same time, provide a valuable counterweight against the temptations of the "devouring powers" from the outside, either France in the west or Russia in the east.

Actually, Prussia's Chancellor Hardenberg and Humboldt shared many of Castlereagh's fears of a mammoth Russian power that could potentially dominate Germany and central Europe, if not also the entire continent. They could not voice these concerns openly, however, because Prussia was still closely allied with Russia. Yet both statesmen made it clear, behind closed doors, that they believed that Prussia had a better future working with Britain and Austria. The problem they faced was convincing their king, who was as determined as ever to stick with the Russian tsar.

Meanwhile, inside Kaunitz Palace, Talleyrand was waiting for an invitation, as promised, to discuss his criteria for admitting delegates to the congress. One day passed, and then another. There was still no word of the meeting. The only invitation in circulation, it seemed, was to the royal hunt in a wooded park outside Vienna.

On October 6, while Talleyrand was still waiting, there was another pageant planned for the vast green span of manicured lawns and shady walkways northwest of the inner town. This was the Augarten, a former royal playground and hunting field that had been opened to the public almost forty years before. It had the oldest baroque garden in Vienna, and an eighteenth-century palace that serves today as the home of the Vienna Boys' Choir. The Augarten also housed a center for porcelain making, and had long staged summer concerts, including Mozart and Beethoven. Now it would host the "People's Festival"—a celebration for the people who had done so much to achieve the Allied victory.

Organizers of the event had erected a grand amphitheater for the sovereigns, along with a large structure built with colored glass to resemble a rainbow. With flags and trophies prominently displayed, veterans of the Napoleonic Wars marched past the tents and crowds to drum and fife. There were footraces, horse races, and an "open-air circus." Acrobats tumbled, equestrian teams performed, and crossbowmen from the Tyrolean Alps competed in sharpshooting contests.

At the end of the games, a Vienna hot-air balloonist climbed into his canvas contraption, about the size of a four-story building, and soared "majestically over the heads of the crowd, waving flags of every nation." Then the honored veterans sat down at sixteen long banquet tables weighed down by food and drink, and enjoyed a feast to military music. They were toasted by fellow soldiers and leaders alike, including the Russian tsar, who stood, drink in hand, and announced in his excellent German, "The Emperor of Russia drinks to the health of you, old men!" Then he sealed the toast by hurling his crystal glass against a nearby garden urn.

Elsewhere in the park, spectators were treated to a group of dancers, in folk costumes, performing regional dances from different parts of the Austrian empire. The grand finale was entrusted to Vienna's fireworks master, Stuwer. His whistling rockets painted the flags of the victorious Allies in the sky.

Later that night, revelers walked through the streets of Vienna, admiring the palaces and mansions illuminated with candles in their windows. While many moved on to ballrooms such as the Apollo Saal and waltzed all night amid its indoor gardens with make-believe grottoes and moss-covered rocks, the sovereigns and their retinues continued to the theater. They saw the ballet *Flore et Zéphire,* which featured the star ballerina Emilia Bigottini, whose graceful dances held the audience in thrall.

The joy that surrounded the People's Festival was fueled, as one observer put it, by "the hope of a durable peace, the price of which had been paid by many years of constant sacrifices." The peacemakers indeed owed it to the people who had suffered so much in the war to make the best peace possible.

TWO DAYS LATER, on October 8, Metternich's invitation to the private meeting to set the terms for the opening of the congress finally arrived. Talleyrand was requested to be at the summer villa at eight o'clock that evening. He was asked to come a little early, if he liked, and Metternich would update him about some developments.

When Talleyrand arrived that evening, Metternich thanked him for his proposal on the opening of the congress, and added that he had taken the liberty of drawing up another plan that differed slightly, but he hoped it would be satisfactory. Talleyrand asked to read it.

"I do not have it yet," Metternich answered. "Gentz has carried it off to put on some finishing touches."

"Probably, it is being communicated to your *Allies*," Talleyrand snapped back sarcastically, referring to the divisive term that had earlier provoked his displeasure.

"Let us not speak any longer of Allies," Metternich reassured him. "There are no more Allies."

"But there are people here who ought to be Allies," Talleyrand added, wasting no time to remind the Austrian foreign minister that both of their countries had a lot in common, not least the desire to stop an aggressive Russia. The tsar wanted Poland, and should he be indulged in this whim, the situation could potentially be disastrous for Austria. Talleyrand hammered home the risks of a Russian Poland with a direct question: "How can you possibly contemplate placing Russia like a girdle all round your principal and most important possessions, Hungary and Bohemia?"

Metternich remarked coolly that the French minister obviously placed no trust in him, and Talleyrand replied, equally coolly, that so far he had not been given any reason to do so.

"Here are pen, ink, and paper," Talleyrand continued theatrically. "Will you write that France asks nothing, and even that she will accept nothing? I am ready to sign."

"But there is the affair of Naples, that is properly yours." Metternich reminded the French minister of his desire to place the Bourbon king Ferdinand IV back on the throne in southern Italy.

"Not mine, more than everybody else's," Talleyrand replied, implying that the restoration of law was in the interests of everyone.

> For me it is only a matter of principle. I ask that he who has a right to be at Naples should be at Naples; that is all. Now, that is just what everyone, as well as myself, ought to wish.

"Let principles be acted upon, and I shall be found easy to deal with in everything."

One of those principles that Talleyrand urged upon the congress was legitimacy. Although vague and undefined, the word was generally used to mean the rule of law, or the accepted "order of things" based on the sanction of time. As Talleyrand argued, this was "a necessary element of the peace and happiness of peoples, the most solid, or rather the only guarantee of their strength and continuance." Legitimacy, in other words, was "the safeguard of nations," and Talleyrand hoped it would serve as a guiding principle in restoring Europe.

Specifically, he wanted Vienna to maintain the king of Saxony as the *legitimate* ruler of a sovereign state, and restore Ferdinand IV as the *legitimate* king of Naples. As for France's aggressive neighbors, the Prussians, Talleyrand said that he would never consent to their outlandish demands for territory. Nor would he, for that matter, ever allow the Russian tsar to create a "phantom Poland" and thereby advance his empire all the way to the Vistula River in the center of Europe.

Sharing this fear of Russia, Metternich grasped Talleyrand's hand and reassured him: "We are much less divided than you think."

At that point, a footman announced that the other delegates had arrived for the conference, which was, in fact, the first meeting of a new committee, the Committee of Eight. This was actually the Big Four, joined by the four other powers who had signed the Treaty of Paris (France, Portugal, Sweden, and Spain). Reluctantly, the Great Powers had accepted Talleyrand's argument that they had no basis for simply making all decisions themselves, and they had retreated onto more solid ground with this committee. Everyone went into the large meeting room to hammer out the conditions for accepting delegates to the congress. After some negotiation, they agreed to open the congress on the first of November.

As for who exactly could participate, there were two plans for consideration, one drafted by Talleyrand and the other by Metternich. The two plans were similar. The main difference was that Talleyrand's plan, by definition, would not permit the delegate of the Bonapartist Murat to participate in the conference, while Metternich's was vague enough that it did not specify one way or the other. Metternich's plan won.

Talleyrand consented to this arrangement with one small change: The congress "shall then be conducted in conformity with the principles of public law," as international law was then called.

At these words, Prussia's Hardenberg stood up, banged his fists on the table, and shouted, "No, sir, public law is a useless phrase. Why say that we shall act according to public law? That is a matter of course."

"If it be a matter of course," Talleyrand responded, "it can do no harm to specify it."

"What has public law to do here?" Prussia's Humboldt asked.

It was public law, Talleyrand responded, "that sends you here."

The tensions were heating up, and Castlereagh, the force of moderation, called Talleyrand aside and discreetly asked him if his colleagues conceded on this point, would he "afterwards be more accommodating"? The French minister agreed.

But the trouble in convincing the Big Four to recognize the authority of law at the peace conference seemed a bad omen. Talleyrand, however, was hopeful that the force of law would help restrain the appetites of the more aggressive powers. Metternich was glad to win another postponement of the congress, and he planned to use the time to find a way to oppose the Russians. He went home to read some poetry, and, as he wrote, think about the Duchess of Sagan.

A FEW DAYS before that important meeting, Talleyrand had gone to a dinner party with Dorothée. It was in many ways typical of the dinners held every night in Vienna that autumn: lavish menus, excellent wine, sparkling conversation led by prominent and often fascinating guests. The Duchess of Sagan was hosting the party and putting her talents to use. But what was most surprising about that party was that the person at her side was not Prince Metternich.

In fact, it was an old lover, Prince Alfred von Windischgrätz, a twenty-seven-year-old from an Austrian aristocratic family who was a cavalry officer with a distinguished record in the war as a colonel in a regiment of cuirassiers, the O'Reilly Light Horse Regiment. He was a soldier's soldier, tall and strong, with a taste for smoking cigars, a habit he picked up in Brussels. Prince Alfred is often credited with popularizing this "Belgian habit," as it was called, among the Austrian aristocracy.

That evening, the two had carried on, evidently, with more than their usual flirtatious ways, and everyone present had left the party without any doubt that the duchess had rekindled this old flame. The duchess's relationship with Prince Alfred was on a different level than the one with Metternich. Whereas the foreign minister was a sophisticated, worldly charmer, very much at home in elegant drawing rooms and plush opera boxes, Windischgrätz preferred more simple pleasures.

Prince Alfred von Windischgrätz and the Duchess of Sagan had begun their affair in a way that was somewhat characteristic of their relationship. One afternoon, back in 1810, they had ridden out to a country inn in a beautiful wine district just outside Vienna. While they sat together, the duchess nursed her glass, and the prince, cigar in hand, noticed a ring on her finger. It was a giant, impressively cut ruby. The count asked about the gem, wondering no doubt if it had been given to her by a lover.

Actually, the duchess had purchased the ring herself. She had come across it on display at a Vienna jeweler's shop and just had to have it. But for a combination of motives—a sense of pride, mischief, and curiosity about what would happen—the duchess did not wish to say that outright. She was vague and noncommittal in her responses, and this promptly sent the decorated cavalry officer out of his mind with jealousy. At one point, the impulsive prince sprung across the table and snatched the ring from her finger.

As he started to look it over, hunting for an engraving or other sign of its sender, the duchess leaped up and quickly circled the table to take it back. A playful wrestling match ensued, like two teenagers in love, when the duchess, determined to win, sank her teeth into his arm. The prince reacted by locking his hold on her, and then with his free hand, for a prank, put the ring between his tobacco-stained teeth. The duchess broke free, and in the process, the prince accidentally swallowed the ruby. The ring was later recovered and returned to the duchess. Anything could happen on an outing with Prince Alfred.

Now, when word of the Duchess of Sagan's dinner companion made it back to Metternich, he was deeply disturbed. Though he was not unaware of their previous liaison, the thought of them together made him lose his usual cool. He could not stand the idea of anyone taking his place by her side, and wrote to the duchess asking for clarification. Surely, there must be some misunderstanding.

By the time of the emperor's ball at the Spanish Riding School on October 9, Metternich could still not shake the thought from his mind. He wrote to the duchess that day, in the middle of a meeting. He thought of their past, and how during their relationship he had cried "tears of joy." He could not wait to see her.

That evening, the duchess looked more beautiful than ever. She arrived with twenty-three other women, who, arranging themselves in four groups, dressed as the Four Elements. Six young ladies wearing blue and green dresses, adorned with pearls, coral, and other seashells, went as Water. Six others in blazing red silk dresses and carrying torches were Fire. Another group of young women wearing wings and the clearest "flimsiest veiling" was the Air. The Duchess of Sagan was with the group representing Earth, and wore a brown velvet dress and a headdress in the form of a "golden basket filled with jeweled fruit." To Metternich, she outshone everyone.

The ballroom was packed, and maneuvering through the throngs of dancers was challenging. Yet Metternich started to suspect that the duchess was avoiding him. Clearly, she had no time for him, and he never was alone with her. Prince Alfred, on the other hand, seemed to pull off the feat with no problem at all.

Had Metternich been with the duchess, he could have enjoyed the magnificent, glittering spectacle of kings and princes at play in the white stucco hall lit up by silver chandeliers and thousands of candles. The tsar danced, it was said, with fifty women, apparently doing his best to make sure the peace conference earned its reputation as the dancing congress.

Metternich was miserable. Late the following night, he penned a long letter to the Duchess of Sagan describing how he felt: "You have surely been loved, and you will be loved again, but you will never be more loved, and you have never been more loved, than by me." Metternich was even more unused to losing in love than in diplomacy.

Chapter 11

A LAWLESS SCRAMBLE?

Treason, Sire, that is a question of dates.

—TALLEYRAND

While Metternich brooded over the duchess and feared that she was slipping out of his life, Vienna's diplomats were again facing long waits in his anteroom. Two days after the masked ball, Geneva's delegates, Jean-Gabriel Eynard and Charles Pictet de Rochemont, appeared at the Chancellery for a meeting scheduled at one in the afternoon. They had been the first to arrive that day—it was a Tuesday, and Metternich's salons on Monday nights typically lasted until the early morning hours. While they waited for Metternich, a tall, elegant man with a red skullcap, long scarlet gloves, and silk habiliments approached and struck up a conversation.

This man, it turned out, was Cardinal Consalvi, the pope's secretary of state and delegate at the Vienna Congress. For the last fourteen years, he had guided both foreign policy and domestic affairs for the Vatican. He was known as a reformer, and had, among other things, led the excavation of the Forum and the restoration of the Colosseum. He had also ordered names placed onto streets, and numbers given to individual buildings. Above all, Consalvi was known for his work with Napoleon, including the landmark negotiation of the Concordat (1801) that brought about the reconciliation between the Catholic Church and France after the turmoil of the revolution.

It was also Consalvi who, in 1804, had persuaded the reluctant Pope Pius VII to travel to Paris for Napoleon's imperial coronation, the first time a pope had participated in such a ceremony in almost three hundred years, the last time being the coronation of Charles V at Bologna in 1530. Consalvi, meanwhile, back at the Vatican, served as the "Papal-Vicar," the only occasion of this office in the history of the papacy.

Consalvi was indeed a talented diplomat in the league of Metternich, Talleyrand, Castlereagh, and the other giants at the Vienna peace conference. According to the writer Stendhal, Consalvi was actually the greatest of them all because he was "the only honest one" in the lot. Besides his frankness, the pope's secretary of state had earned a reputation as a tough negotiator, as was shown on many occasions when relations between Napoleon and the Vatican later soured. Napoleon called Consalvi "a lion in sheep's clothing" and threatened several times to have him shot. (Consalvi, for instance, refused to recognize Napoleon's divorce from his first wife, Joséphine, and led a group of cardinals in a boycott of the wedding ceremony.)

During the Revolutionary and Napoleonic Wars, the papacy had fallen to one of its lowest points in modern history. The French army invaded the Papal States several times and seized vast amounts of property, including its richest territory, the Legations (Ferrara, Bologna, and Ravenna). The swampy Marches to the south of Rome had also been lost, along with many other places, including Avignon, which had been papal property since 1309, and Venaissin, since 1228.

Napoleon had also plundered the Vatican shamelessly, stealing some one hundred works of art, selected by French commissioners. One observer described the awful spectacle of French "doctrinaire cannibals running around, catalogues at hand," selecting the treasures to be brought back to Paris: the Apollo Belvedere, the Dying Gaul, Raphael's *Transfiguration,* Domenichino's *Last Communion of St. Jerome,* and *Laocoön and His Sons,* to name a few. The French had forced the pope to sign away ownership of these works of art in the Treaty of Tolentino (1797), and subsequent raids brought many more treasures. Two years later, when the pope refused to relinquish his rights as a ruler, Napoleon had him seized from the Vatican. Pius VI actually died in captivity as a French prisoner, and his successor, Pius VII, was only released in January 1814.

Like many others at the congress, the Vatican had strong arguments for regaining its territory and property, especially given the wide support of the principle of legitimacy. But the pope had signed the treaty, and there was no guarantee that congress dignitaries would accept Consalvi's argument that it was done under duress, no matter how self-evident it might appear. There were powerful interests at stake. The current holders of the Papal States wanted to keep them: Murat's army now in the Marches, and the Austrians in the Legations.

Eynard, Pictet de Rochemont, and Consalvi continued to wait on the Austrian foreign minister, who eventually arrived an hour and a half late. Consalvi received the first audience in honor of his position as the pope's delegate. The second meeting went to the Prussian ambassador, Humboldt, who had just arrived and immediately jumped to the front of the line. Urgent business, he said, though it must have seemed to many who now filled the room as just another instance of Prussian arrogance. By the late afternoon, after three hours of waiting, one of Metternich's valets de chambre entered and announced that the Austrian foreign minister could no longer see anyone, as he had a dinner appointment and he had not yet dressed for it. Somehow, though, the Swiss delegates managed to gain entrance, probably with the help of a handsome tip.

"It is impossible to have more agreeable manners than Metternich," Eynard wrote in his diary later that day, after the brief meeting. Metternich, of course, appeared to be on their side—he always seemed on the side of the person he was with. Although the foreign minister was affable and engaging with his usual touch of "lightness and unconcern," Eynard thought he looked "overwhelmed with fatigue." He noted the dark circles under Metternich's eyes, and how the foreign minister fought off yawns. He had no idea about Metternich's current preoccupations with the Duchess of Sagan.

No one knows for certain what Princess Bagration was doing at this time, either, though many rumors were circulating about the mischief she was making at Metternich's expense. Evidently, her attempts to win Metternich had not worked, and as several spy reports began to note, the princess was becoming much angrier at her former lover. She was actively pursuing "revenge for Metternich's neglect," one informed. Another agent reported that she was "openly revealing all she knows, or has heard, that might hurt Austria." Guests to her salon were shocked at her outspoken comments, though the details of her tantrums were discreetly omitted from the police reports.

The Russian tsar, too, was suspected of exploiting Princess Bagration's lingering resentment against the Austrian foreign minister. "Metternich never loved you," Alexander was overheard saying, according to Agent Nota. "Believe me," the tsar was said to have added, Metternich "is a cold fish who is quite incapable of love. Can't you see this plaster-of-Paris figure? He loves no one."

JUST AS GOSSIPERS predicted, Marie Louise had arrived in Vienna back on the seventh of October and moved into the west wing of Schönbrunn, the Habsburg summer palace located south of the town. It was a large residence with a facade in a shade of mustard yellow that the Viennese called "Maria Theresa Gold" after the eighteenth-century monarch who had redecorated the palace. Schönbrunn was originally intended to outshine Louis XIV's Versailles, though the Austrians had run out of money long before they achieved that goal.

Marie Louise had returned to Vienna without fanfare, arriving purposely late to avoid the opening ceremonies of the peace conference. She looked only slightly older now than she did when she had been forced, four years earlier, to marry Napoleon. She still had a youthful face, as one put it, "like peaches and cream," and a figure that looked crafted in a "turner's workshop." She also brought their son, the three-and-a-half-year-old Napoleon Francis, the former infant king of Rome and heir to the throne of France. This "little Napoleon," who resembled his mother with his fair complexion, spoke often of his father and showed a great curiosity about any Frenchman he met. Their carriage still bore Napoleonic emblems, and her servants still dressed in Napoleonic livery.

It had been a stressful six months since Napoleon's abdication, and eight months since Marie Louise had last seen her husband. They had parted in late January 1814, when Napoleon rode out for the brilliant though ultimately unsuccessful spring campaign. Marie Louise had remained in Paris presiding over a council of Napoleon's foremost advisers and administering what was left of his empire. By late March, however, the Allies were closing in on the capital, and Marie Louise had to decide whether to stay or leave for safer territory. Uncertain, though inclined to remain in Paris, she had put the question to the council.

After a long discussion, a vote, and a letter produced at the last minute from Napoleon emphasizing that his family was not, in any circumstances, to "fall into the hands of the enemy," Marie Louise had agreed to leave for temporary residence in Orléans. It was there, on April 12, that a bizarre race for the former empress took place: Napoleon had sent a cavalry escort to "liberate" Marie Louise, while some Austrian officers rode to "save" her and bring her back to her father. The Austrians arrived first.

"I am worried to death for you," Marie Louise wrote her husband as she was forced to accompany the Austrian officers to the castle of Rambouillet, nearly thirty miles southwest of Paris. But once she saw her father, Emperor Francis, she promised Napoleon to make it perfectly clear that she was to join him on Elba, and "nobody is going to prevent me from doing that." By most accounts, Marie Louise had meant every word.

Indeed, despite the politics that inspired their marriage, it is clear that Napoleon and Marie Louise had developed a loving relationship. This fact came as a surprise to most historians when a whole collection of Marie Louise's personal letters was discovered in the twentieth century. "There's no one in the world who loves you as much as your faithful Louise," Marie Louise had written to her husband in one of many affectionate letters composed during this time.

Yet Marie Louise's determination to join her husband on Elba had met some considerable opposition from her father. "He forbids me to come to you to see you," she informed Napoleon. "I told him outright that it was my duty to follow you." But her father had refused, and instead ordered her back to Austria, though he had assured her that she would soon have the freedom to choose her future herself.

Unhappily, Marie Louise had obeyed her father's wishes and returned to Vienna for some five or six weeks before spending the rest of the summer at the spas of Aix-en-Savoie, which were supposed to cure her anxieties. Her doctor had prescribed "absolute rest and tranquility in some suitable spot where she can follow a strict course of treatment." Still, as she left for the healing waters, she had assured Napoleon that she "loved him more tenderly than ever" and planned to come to Elba after that.

It was during that time apart that Marie Louise's resolution apparently began to waver. She had been promised the duchies of Parma, Piacenza, and Guastalla, and this had been written in the Treaty of Fontainebleau (confirmed, too, in the Treaty of Paris). To her great dismay, however, Marie Louise now learned that this might not be a guarantee after all. Her father and Metternich had both written to inform her that there was a movement to return those duchies to the Spanish Bourbon dynasty that had owned them before the war, and several states supported this view, including Bourbon Spain and France. Marie Louise's presence in Vienna would be vital, they emphasized, or no doubt overemphasized. She should make plans to return home to look after the interests of herself and her son, not to mention her duties as an Austrian archduchess.

So it was back to Vienna for the congress. "What a sad prospect," she had confessed to her secretary as she had made her slow, leisurely ride to a town filled with her husband's conquerors.

AMONG THE MANY unofficial delegates still arriving every day, Johann Georg Cotta and Carl Bertuch were representing some eighty-one publishing houses and book dealers in Germany. Cotta was head of a major publishing house in Stuttgart, which owned the newspaper *Allgemeine Zeitung,* and Bertuch was the son of a publisher in Weimar who printed the works of many literary giants. Together they hoped to persuade the Vienna Congress to correct many of the ills that plagued the publishing business. Specifically, they would petition against censorship and stifling governmental controls of the press, and, at the same time, appeal for more protection against rogue printers who pirated their work. The first problem damaged the quality of publication; the second ate substantially into the profits.

This was not an easy argument to make with monarchist governments comfortable with the control of the press, whether by censorship or the licensing of official printing houses. In Austria, for example, a government edict of September 1810 justified the need for "a cautious hand," as it called censorship, to protect the "heart and head of immature persons from the corrupting products of a depraved imagination, from the poisonous breath of self-seeking seducers, and from the dangerous phantoms of perverted minds." Besides this self-interested paternalism that very often squashed dissenting opinion, the state had other incentives to maintain the status quo. After all, the printers who forged and plagiarized works also paid taxes and fees.

But a great deal was at stake, Cotta and Bertuch argued. Without basic freedom and protection, few authors would undertake any serious work, and even fewer firms would be willing to risk publishing them. Only songbooks and prayer books would be published, they argued, with some exaggeration. At any rate, it would be a shame to miss an excellent opportunity for scholarship and commerce in the newly emerging Germany. There was a large population, growing wealth, and a common vernacular that transcended state boundaries—in short, a potentially large market of readers.

Vienna's police department was leery of many foreign delegations, but these publishers seemed particularly suspicious. Agent Goehausen believed that both Cotta and Bertuch belonged to a banned secret society, the Tugendbund, or "League of Virtue," that flourished amid the patriotism that swept Germany in the wars against France, and promoted unsettling patriotic aims like the unification of Germany. "Agent H"— almost certainly Wilhelm Hebenstreit, the theater critic and future editor of the fashion magazine *Wiener Modenzeitung*—was recruited to keep a close eye on their activities.

Agent H knew that the publishers already enjoyed support among major delegations. The Prussians, in particular, were favorable. Hardenberg and Humboldt had championed liberal and reform policies for years, and Bertuch gained a meeting with the latter, thanks to a friendly letter of introduction written by no less a person than Goethe. Baron vom Stein of Nassau, then serving the Russian delegation, was another easy sell. He saw copyright protections as part of a package of basic rights that he wanted enshrined in the new German constitution: equality of all citizens, the right to study at any university, the right to choose occupations, the right of emigration, and protection against crimes ex post facto, among others.

Both Cotta and Bertuch were engaging, well-rounded conversationalists who could make a strong case, all the while peppering their arguments with anecdotes about famous writers they knew, such as Goethe. They also dangled tempting offers of publishing contracts before some people in town, such as the Swiss strategist serving on the Prussian delegation, Henri Jomini. Cotta, in particular, was someone to watch, being, as Agent H put it, a rich man with many important and diverse contacts.

By the middle of October, the publishers had already secured an audience with Prince Metternich, which was no small feat given his preoccupations at that time. During the conference, held in the afternoon of the fourteenth, Metternich promised his support. He seemed sincere, as he often did. The question was, however, what exactly did his support mean? Metternich sometimes promised assistance, and then the matter went on to die a quiet, mysterious death. The publishing delegates would be well advised not to stop their lobbying.

Among other groups actively seeking support at this time were the Jewish delegations, which came from several cities in Germany and central Europe. During the French occupation, many old laws discriminating against Jews had been repealed, and new ones enacted that extended the rights of Jews. After the war, however, several German states and towns were rebelling against the French legislation, and some were on the verge of reenacting the old discriminatory regulations. The Jewish delegations were working to preserve their equality, which, however, incomplete, was still preferable to a return to repression.

There were several different Jewish delegations in town, each working largely independently of the others. Jakob Baruch and J. J. Gumprecht represented the Jews of Frankfurt, and the banker Simon Edler von Lämel represented the Jewish community in Prague. Dr. Carl August Buchholz, a Christian lawyer, worked on behalf of Jewish communities in Bremen, Hamburg, and his native Lübeck. Buchholz was also completing a 157-page booklet advocating Jewish rights, which would soon circulate among congress dignitaries. Fortunately, these delegations had valuable support networks in town, which included some of Vienna's most influential bankers: Nathan von Arnstein, Salomon Mayer Rothschild, and Leopold Edler von Herz.

But the Vienna police were suspicious of these delegations, ordering special surveillance in July 1814, even before the conference had begun. One official in the police bureau responsible for Jewish affairs had been asked to submit a list of names of prominent Jews in town, who were to be investigated; when the delegates began arriving in the autumn, they, too, were followed and their activities scrutinized. Police suspicions were not easily dispelled, and in late October, one agent discovered that Frankfurt's Jewish delegates were posing as "merchants" and tried to have them expelled from town.

It was long suspected that Metternich was behind the harassment, but as the distinguished scholar Enno Kraehe has shown, it was probably the Austrian foreign minister who intervened to prevent their expulsion. He was a friend of one of the delegates in question, Jakob Baruch, whom he had met at the coronation of Emperor Francis in 1792.

The police continued to follow the new arrivals closely, and the more prominent figures were announced in the court newspaper, *Wiener Zeitung*. By the beginning of October, the Grand Duke of Baden had arrived, and his dossier was soon filled with reports of nightly outings at the theater and his pursuit of women, including actresses, maids, and eventually a daughter of an orange and lemon seller. Prince Thurn und Taxis was here as well, hoping to secure a family monopoly on running the postal service in the Habsburg empire. The Prince of Piombino brought a portfolio of arguments explaining why he deserved the island of Elba, rather than its current occupant, Napoleon Bonaparte.

Some tiny rulers indeed had grand pretensions, and one of the most notorious was the Prince of Nassau-Weilburg. The Russian officer and "army historiographer" Alexander Ivanovich Mikhailovsky-Danilevsky described one such audience. Entering into the prince's suite, he had to pass many footmen and chamberlains in gold livery standing at the double doors. The prince, in a distant room, stood completely still, receiving his supplicants like the Sun King. "I nearly laughed out loud," he said, surprised by the ridiculous sight.

Many others slipped into town that autumn for profit and adventure: rogues, charlatans, courtesans, actors, and gamblers, including one of the Continent's most talented whist players, Mr. O'Bearn, and Mr. Raily, a notorious cardsharp, who would die impoverished. The salon run by Madame Frazer was said to be a favorite with many seasoned gamblers. Her gaming tables—"candle snuffers of conversation," as one young socialite said disapprovingly—were the draw, not the tea, which was cold. Two small barking dogs often greeted the guests who arrived hoping to make a fortune.

Meanwhile, on Thursday afternoon, October 13, three days after touring the battlefield at Aspern-Essling outside Vienna where the Austrians defeated Napoleon in the summer of 1809, the Russian tsar made the dramatic move of paying a visit to Castlereagh's headquarters. It was a breach of etiquette for a monarch to call upon the foreign minister of another power. But the matter was serious, and the tsar maneuvered around the formalities by officially visiting Emily Castlereagh. He then stayed on afterward for a chat with her husband—a tense hour-and-a-half talk.

The tsar was flabbergasted at Castlereagh's opposition to his plans for re-creating Poland. Alexander claimed that his interest was not a matter of power politics, but rather "public morality." The outrageous carving up of the country in the eighteenth century could now finally be corrected. He would, moreover, grant an enlightened constitution. Polish patriots were thrilled about the future, the tsar said, and he himself looked forward to the dawning of a new golden age for this ancient kingdom.

How could Great Britain possibly resist such an act of philanthropy, and besides, the tsar wondered, what business was it really of Castlereagh's what he did in Poland, something so far removed from British national interests? Castlereagh was indeed placed in a difficult position. He feared that this Russian plan would threaten the balance of power, and hence the future peace of Europe, yet he had to show his opposition in an accurate manner without further upsetting the tsar, or violating the complicated rules of protocol that governed relations between a sovereign and a foreign minister.

Russia, of course, had rights, Castlereagh acknowledged, though he was quick to point out that these rights must be limited to what does not harm anyone else, particularly "the security of the Emperor's neighbors." Russia's plan was liable to inspire the Poles who lived in neighboring countries, like Austria's East Galicia, to want independence, which in turn could create much unrest in the region.

When the tsar replied that there was only one possible solution for Poland because his army already occupied it, Castlereagh countered that the tsar's rights to territory must not be based on conquest alone.

It was becoming clear that Britain and Russia had serious differences of opinion, and personal diplomacy was not leading to any reconciliation. Later that day, Castlereagh handed the tsar a memorandum, a written summary of their discussion, which, like the protocol, remains another legacy of the Vienna Congress. He wrote that it was his "solemn conviction" that everything now depended on Alexander—that is, "whether the present Congress shall prove a blessing to mankind, or only exhibit a scene of discordant intrigue, and a lawless scramble for power."

Then, while the tsar went over to Princess Bagration's salon, staying until two in the morning, Castlereagh drew up a second memorandum. He reiterated his concerns that Russian policy in Poland "will plant the seeds of another war" and end by destroying "all hope, rest and real confidence and peace." After writing these words, Castlereagh sent his memo to his fellow allies—all of them, that is, except the Russians.

As MANY HAD predicted, Poland was clearly going to be a major stumbling block—the "aching tooth" of the peace conference. Russia and Britain had both refused to budge, and now the dispute was at a standstill. But there was something else that complicated the Polish question at the Vienna Congress. All discussion of Poland was closely tied to another bitter controversy: the future of the Kingdom of Saxony.

Geographically, the two regions were connected. The Polish plains rolled out into the south, merging without any clear or natural demarcation into the Saxon lowlands. Historically, the two territories had been united under the same ruling dynasty in the late seventeenth century. Although the links had been severed in the 1760s, Napoleon had rejoined them when he created both the Kingdom of Saxony and the Duchy of Warsaw—and then gave them both to the king of Saxony.

Diplomatically, too, there was a connection: If Poland were to be re-created as the tsar demanded, then the congress would have to remove territory from both Austria and Prussia. Now, quite simply, if Prussia lost its former Polish territories, it would then have to be compensated elsewhere to reach its population of 1805, as it had been promised, and the most obvious place was in Saxony. So, in other words, if the tsar would have his way in Poland, then the king of Prussia would most likely receive Saxony. That was the deal the two monarchs had struck and were now supporting with great vigor.

But, of course, many in Vienna were uncomfortable with this arrangement. For one, the king of Saxony refused to yield a single acre of his kingdom, though unfortunately for him, he was still locked up in a Prussian prison. The king of Saxony's representative in Vienna, Count Friedrich Albrecht von Schulenburg, was also protesting, though he, too, had been marginalized. The Prussians had refused to recognize his credentials as an official delegate, and they pressured everyone else to do the same.

It was Talleyrand, then, who had taken it upon himself to lead the defense of the Saxon underdogs. Characteristically, he acted with flair. When the Prussians argued that they deserved Saxony because of the king of Saxony's treachery to the Allied cause, Talleyrand replied simply: Was this not "a sin that we all have on our conscience?" Had not Austria, Russia, and Prussia all at one time or another sworn allegiance to Napoleon? Everyone in Vienna had at one point been loyal to the conqueror—everyone, that is, but a few exceptions like Castlereagh and the British. Why should the king of Saxony be singled out and punished?

From discussions in alcoves of salons to dinners at the embassy, Talleyrand was denouncing Prussian ambitions on seizing this region as a "breach of all public morality" and an "unspeakable crime." It was also, he added, a dangerous folly. If Prussia gained Saxony with its many fortresses, palaces, estates, and rich farmland, then Europe would be creating a powerful state in the center of the Continent that might, Talleyrand warned, be a menace to France and the peace of Europe.

Most of the other German states and princes, in fact, agreed with Talleyrand. One defender, the Duke of Saxe-Coburg-Saalfeld, put this argument well, succinctly dismantling the basis for Prussian claims for seizing Saxony. Did they have a right of conquest? Not by international law. Was it on the basis of surrender? "The king has not ceded and never will cede his rights." Was there a sentence or judgment from an international tribune or trial? No trial had been held, and the king should at least be allowed to defend himself.

What did the Saxon people want themselves? They wanted their king, their *legitimate* king, Frederick Augustus. Besides that, would the congress leaders really like to establish the precedent whereby an aggressive power could legally dethrone a fellow sovereign and seize his territory? How was this any different from Napoleon Bonaparte, and had they not learned anything from the violent chaos of the last twenty years?

But these arguments had almost no impact on the Prussians. They had, after all, not fought a terrible war and sacrificed blood and treasure only to be dictated to by the defeated enemy and some small princes under its influence. They also, for that matter, still had the support of the Russian tsar, who now seemed so frustrated at the diplomatic impasse that he had started threatening to take matters into his own hands. The Russian army had Saxony, Alexander reminded, and he might as well just hand it over to his Prussian ally.

Such a prospect was alarming, as the tsar was certainly not bluffing. Ironically, some of the most concerned were actually Prussia's own ministers Hardenberg and Humboldt. Even though they would have liked to have Saxony, to say the least, neither wanted to receive the realm this way—a simple seizure of territory that would put them in the debt of Russia, and eventually, they feared, also at its mercy.

So with this dilemma in mind, Hardenberg had penned an urgent letter to the foreign ministers of Britain and Austria, appealing to them to act immediately. Prussia would readily support them against the tsar on Poland, he promised, provided that they assure him that Prussia would still be given Saxony. He needed something tangible to take to his king.

Castlereagh had no problem at all making such a concession, as he put it, "for the future tranquility of Europe." Talleyrand, however, was appalled by Castlereagh's "weakness" and warned him that he was about to make a terrible mistake. There was a much better way to save both Poland *and* Saxony: Open the congress at once. Force the aggressive powers to state their claims in front of all Europe, and watch their project collapse under the weight of its own unsustainability.

But the British minister's mind was made up, and that left only one person in a position to resist, and that was Metternich, who was unfortunately very distracted at the moment. "Metternich is in love, he paints himself up, he writes notes, his Chancellery muddles along," Talleyrand observed. Gentz, unfortunately, had to agree. He visited Metternich several times during this Saxon crisis, only to find that Austria's foreign minister was consumed by the Duchess of Sagan, and that "unhappy liaison with Windischgraetz."

One thing was certain: Unless something was done immediately, the Russian tsar was simply going to hand over an entire kingdom to his Prussian allies—with or without the permission of the Vienna Congress.

Chapter 12

SIX WEEKS OF HELL

*Hiding behind velvet and purple robes, hostile spirits
fight one another with the daggers of intrigue.*

—KARL VON NOSTITZ, A SAXON SOLDIER IN
RUSSIAN SERVICE, LOOKING ON
WITH FRUSTRATION AT THE CONGRESS

ummer seemed to linger a little longer for Vienna's guests
that autumn. On October 18, yet another brilliant sunny
day, Metternich and the Festivals Committee staged the
spectacular Peace Festival to mark the first anniversary of the Allied victory at the Battle of Leipzig. Valets and maids were sent all over town
in search of the latest fashions. Hat shops, one said, "were mobbed like
bakeries in a famine."

Metternich had wanted this to be a celebration of peace with no military overtures—"No more soldiers!" he had insisted. But he had been
overruled. At the last minute, Emperor Francis had preferred to showcase
Austrian military strength and asked Field Marshal Prince Schwarzenberg to prepare something appropriate. Complaining in private about
the "furious turmoil" that he had been placed in at such short notice,
the aged field marshal nevertheless complied. The Vienna garrison, some
sixteen thousand men strong, was quickly drilled for the parade.

Almost certainly, it was the growing tensions with Russia that inspired
the emperor's decision to march his troops. A little sword rattling just
might convince the tsar to abandon his autocratic ways.

That afternoon, sovereigns, soldiers, and spectators assembled in the
giant public park, the Prater, for the celebration of peace that now had a

more martial air. Over the river, a branch of the Danube, the organizers had constructed a temporary bridge, complete with a rather unique handrailing: muskets captured from Napoleon's armies at the Battle of Leipzig and strewn together with branches of a willow tree.

The focus of attention was a large structure in the center known as the Peace Tent. Trophies and battle standards adorned its columns, and red damask carpets lined the steps up to its altar, covered with a blanket of flowers. Velvet chairs were on the platform for Europe's royalty.

With the crowds hushed into a respectful silence, and hats removed, the archbishop of Vienna led the monarchs, the soldiers, and the enormous throng of spectators in a public celebration of High Mass. The songwriter La Garde-Chambonas described the scene:

> At the moment of blessing the Bread and the Wine, the guns thundered forth a salute to the God of Hosts. Simultaneously, all those warriors, princes, kings, soldiers, and generals fell on their knees, prostrating themselves before Him in whose hands rests victory or defeat.

After the smoke of cannons and incense cleared, church bells rang and a large choir sang a German "hymn of peace." The sovereigns moved over to position near the Burg Gate. The soldiers marched past under their view, and afterward received medallions struck from melted-down cannons seized from Napoleon's Grande Armée.

There was another dinner served on tables arranged together in the shape of a gigantic star. Sergeants carried each soldier a bowl of soup, a plate of pork, another three-quarters of a pound of roast beef, rolls, and doughnuts filled with apricot jam, all washed down by a quart of wine. Despite the tensions behind the scenes, both the emperor of Austria and the Russian tsar toasted the soldiers in a public show of solidarity.

That night, invited guests were treated to a Peace Ball at Metternich's summer villa on the Rennweg, where the Austrian foreign minister had built an extension to his estate for this occasion. The building itself was shaped like a dome and ringed by classical pillars. It was made of wood, with walnut parquet floors. Everything was adorned with the new "colorful lights of Bengale," and with many red Turkish tents in the lobby, it seemed like a scene out of *The Book of 1001 Nights*.

As requested, women wore dresses in either blue or white, "the colors of peace," many embroidered in gold or silver, and adorned with diamonds. Several women also wore flower headdresses or wreaths of olive, oak, or laurel, symbolizing the peace. Other ladies preferred a tiara, which along with diamond earrings, pearl necklaces, and a vast array of jewels adorning the dresses made them sparkle from head to toe. The men glittered and clinked as well, with many medals and medallions.

When deciding on the seating arrangements for the feast, Metternich made sure the Duchess of Sagan had a good table. In fact, he sent her the plan beforehand and let her choose the seat herself. She was well placed for the show that evening. A hot-air balloon drifted overhead, to the delight of the eighteen hundred guests. Ballets were danced in his enormous garden, in and around faux temples in honor of the classical gods Apollo, Mars, and Athena, and orchestras hidden behind hedges serenaded the guests.

The evening concluded with a fireworks display that attempted to paint in the sky the horrors of war and then the pleasures of peace. To one guest, Metternich's party surpassed every celebration he had experienced in France, including the heyday of Napoleon's empire. In parties, too, it seemed, Metternich had defeated Napoleon.

THE NEXT MORNING, Gentz had come over to Metternich's for breakfast and to trade stories about the Peace Ball. But despite the apparent success, he found Metternich depressed. "What a sad morning after a festival," Gentz confided in his diary. Evidently, there had been a disturbing incident the night before.

The Russian tsar, who had devoured gossip spread by Princess Bagration, had been loudly bad-mouthing Metternich all evening. The atmosphere of the party had been spoiled, the tsar accused, by the presence of "too many diplomats." They make bad decisions and then "we soldiers," he said identifying himself with the troops, "have to get ourselves shot into cripples." Diplomats, he added, were categorically untrustworthy and he could not stand their falseness.

The tsar's behavior had embarrassed and humiliated Metternich, the host. Along with the tsar's insults, Metternich had also been upset because he had wanted to talk to the Duchess of Sagan that night, even if only for a moment. He had not succeeded. That morning after the ball, as Gentz noted, it had been a "very black scene."

Metternich was also disturbed about the lack of success so far in gaining little Vava for the duchess. He had promised not to let up for "all the treasures of the world," and success had seemed imminent, too, when he had learned that the child's father, Gustav Armfelt, had suffered a stroke and died the previous month. But, unfortunately, instead of helping, the tsar was proving highly uncooperative. At their last meeting, on October 15, when Metternich raised the question again, the tsar abruptly declared that he knew for a fact that Vava preferred to remain in Finland with the Armfelt family. And, indeed, after the last outburst at the Peace Ball, the tsar seemed even less likely to help.

Metternich hung on to the child case—"our child," as he called her. Perhaps his adamancy was his last desperate ploy to win the love of the duchess, as one historian wondered. Metternich certainly seemed to be grasping at any opportunity to have contact with his beloved duchess, no matter how businesslike it might be and how unlikely his chances of success now appeared. He swore he would keep his word, and work even harder on the custody case.

With these disturbing failures absorbing his mind, Metternich was not the most receptive when Talleyrand came over to warn him about relying on the Prussians. Metternich had still not answered Hardenberg's offer of support against Russia in exchange for Prussian gains in Saxony. Talleyrand was determined to prevent Metternich from accepting this proposition, and he thought that he had just the argument to suit the Austrian foreign minister.

If Metternich allowed Prussia to seize Saxony, Talleyrand pointed out, Prussia would surrender its Polish territory to the tsar. Metternich would then end up helping Alexander gain exactly what he wanted. Austria, on the other hand, would be stuck with a much stronger Russia *and* Prussia threatening its borders. Austria simply must resist Prussia, Talleyrand concluded. "Justice, propriety even safety require her to do so."

But Metternich brushed aside Talleyrand's arguments, hatching a plot of his own: He was considering accepting Prussian gains in Saxony, but he would attach so many strings to his consent that Prussia would either accept and serve Austrian interests, or decline and not have his approval at all.

One of these conditions would be that not only must Prussia oppose Russia, but it must also *succeed* in preventing the tsar from having his way in Poland. This way, Metternich would leave it to Prussia's own ministers to convince their king that the dangers of gaining Saxony from the hands of the unpredictable tsar were far greater than any possible benefit.

Metternich did not mention this plan at that time to Talleyrand, who, of course, would have strongly opposed it. After all, as far as the French foreign minister was concerned, it failed to solve the real problem of Prussian aggression, and it might well end by upsetting the fragile equilibrium and endangering the peace of Europe.

The Duchess of Sagan, meanwhile, was discouraged about the slow progress being made on regaining custody of her daughter. As hostess of one of the most informed salons in town, she knew that the peace conference might in fact erupt into war at any time. Something had to be done immediately. If Metternich could not convince the tsar, then perhaps she would have to do so herself.

On October 20, at a ball given by the Russian ambassador, Count Stackelberg, the duchess wore a sleek red dress, designed by the fashionable Paris designer Louis-Hippolite Leroy, and donned a family heirloom, a "pearl-shaped emerald" that had been set in a "delicate golden circlet" that sparkled from her forehead. She walked up to the tsar and politely requested an audience. The tsar's response was as cordial to her as it was cruel to Metternich, who was standing within earshot.

"My dear Wilhelmine, there is no question of an audience," the tsar said, grabbing her hand and raising her up from her curtsy. "Of course I shall come to see you!" he continued. "Only name the day and the hour—shall it be tomorrow at eleven?"

Eleven o'clock! The tsar had deliberately taken what used to be Metternich's hour with the duchess, and worse, she had allowed it without the slightest hesitation. Metternich's feelings of betrayal and rejection were immense. First she had gone back to Prince Alfred, and now this. Metternich, deeply wounded, left the ball immediately. It must have been a lonely carriage drive home that night.

When he arrived back at the Chancellery, he could not sleep. He went to his desk and poured out his thoughts in another desperate note to the duchess. It was four in the morning. "A relationship, a dream, the fairest of my life has vanished . . . I am punished for having entrusted my existence to a charm only too seductive."

Metternich felt that he was indeed losing the duchess. Heartbroken, the statesman continued:

> You have done me greater harm than can ever be compensated by the whole universe—you have broken the springs of my soul. You have endangered my existence at a moment when the fate of my life is bound up with questions that decide the future of whole generations . . . I have placed everything I have, this life, my trust, my future, all my hope, I have placed everything in the balance.

With this letter, which he did not yet send, Metternich was about to officially end their relationship. Deep down, though, he knew that she had ended it by her own preferences, and he was crushed. "I have lost my last illusion," he mourned, contemplating the implications of this rupture. Without her love, he was condemned to "a world without color and a life without charm."

From the very beginning, one of the main subjects in the salons was, of course, Napoleon Bonaparte. Many of the delegates in Vienna had known him personally, and others were curious about this ogre who had once terrorized the world.

Napoleon's successes, failures, and many controversial acts were discussed and debated around town. One delegate, the Duke of Rocca Romana, who represented King Joachim I of Naples (Murat), enlivened the conversations with his rousing tales from the Russian invasion of 1812. At the climax, this "Apollo of a man" would take off his glove and show his hand, where he had lost four fingers from the terrible frost. Listening to the many stories of Napoleon's accomplishments and shortcomings, some delegates seemed to miss his presence on the world stage, openly admitting that he had many more statesmanlike qualities than the victorious sovereigns who were making a royal mess out of the Vienna Congress.

"It's scandalous how the congress behaves," France's Duke of Dalberg told Agent **, launching into an outspoken critique of how the Great Powers conspired to shut out Talleyrand, the French embassy, and most of the other delegations in town. "We do not understand anything of Metternich's politics," he continued.

If he gives the crown of Poland to Russia, then in less than fifteen years Russia will hunt the Turks out of Europe, and Russia will be more dangerous to the liberty of Europe than Napoleon had ever been.

Dalberg, growing more animated as he went along, wanted to sound a general wake-up call. It was essential, he urged, to "oppose the colossus that is going to crush Austria and the other powers."

The tension between Russia and Austria was certainly one of the main problems of the congress. The two powers had been uneasy allies since the end of the Napoleonic Wars. They had often ended up on opposing sides on questions of strategy and tactics, most notably in early 1814, when the Austrian army invaded Napoleonic France through Switzer-land—in direct conflict with the tsar's wishes and his promises that the Allies would respect Swiss neutrality. The relationship between Austria and Russia had never recovered, Gentz later observed.

Indeed, a vibrant personal rivalry between Metternich and Tsar Alexander had exacerbated the political problems. As Gentz saw it, the tsar had come to regard Metternich as "a sworn enemy" and harbored an intense jealousy of Metternich's flair in the drawing room. He was witty, mannered, and very popular with women. The tsar had come to Vienna hoping, as Gentz said, "to be admired," and found it difficult to share the limelight, especially with a man he had come to detest.

Spies had likewise noticed the tsar's growing interests in Metternich's private life—his "morbid curiosity" as one agent put it. Alexander was still suspected of prying for information at the Palm Palace, where both the Duchess of Sagan and Princess Bagration, of course, were authorities on their former lover. Princess Bagration, in particular, was glad to comply. She still seemed upset at Metternich for neglecting her in favor of the Duchess of Sagan, and seemed happy to satisfy the tsar's appetites, spies reported, feeding him the most intimate details of their previous love affair.

It was at the congress, Gentz believed, that the tsar's resentment of

Metternich "reached the point of an implacable hatred," and this, in turn, fueled the tsar's "daily explosions of rage and frenzy." All of this, of course, may have delighted gossipers, but it was causing considerable strain on the negotiations. As Gentz concluded, it was Alexander's hatred for Metternich that served as "the key to most of the events of the Congress."

Now, Gentz was often biased in Metternich's favor, and this assessment certainly seems slanted. But Gentz actually no longer regarded Metternich as an infallible "Delphic Oracle," as he had earlier dubbed him. Far from it. At times, Gentz was already emerging as an outspoken critic of Metternich—blasting him not only in his diary, but also openly and indiscreetly at salons and dinner parties around town.

Police agents had noticed, too, that by the middle of October, Gentz was making many visits to Kaunitz Palace. Reportedly, he and Talleyrand were getting along well. They were dining together at the embassy, or with mutual acquaintances like the Duchess of Sagan. The French minister had, it seemed, discovered Gentz's well-known weakness for flattery, perfume, chocolate, and money, and he was increasingly gaining influence over Metternich's assistant.

On October 21, when Gentz arrived at ten in the morning, as usual, for breakfast (only a few hours after Metternich had finished his letter to the duchess), another, more interesting breakfast was about to take place a few blocks away at the Palm Palace. The tsar was coming to the so-called Austrian salon for his meeting with the duchess at Metternich's hour. Their conversation lasted about two hours, though what exactly happened is not known. Presumably, the tsar agreed to do everything he could to help the duchess regain custody of her child. He was certainly in no mood to disappoint her.

Immediately afterward, the ecstatic duchess took a carriage over to Kaunitz Palace to see her sister Dorothée, and rumors soon magnified the morning meeting in countless ways. It was reported and widely believed, for example, that the tsar had forced the duchess to break off her relations with Metternich. Baron Hager's spies thought that this had in fact happened. When Metternich had had an opportunity to ask her about the meeting, the duchess had been coy, replying evasively, "The tsar was at my house and behaved very well, at least with words."

On Saturday, October 22, Metternich was ready to lay his cards on the table. First, he delivered the note ending his relationship with the

Duchess of Sagan, and then, later that evening at a ball over at Count Zichy's mansion, he declared his stance on Saxony in a monumental letter to Hardenberg. He had decided to accept Prussia's offer of support in return for annexation of Saxony. But sure enough, Metternich attached some important conditions to his tentative acceptance: Prussia must give up all other claims to Germany, regard this annexation as part of the larger settlement, and, most important, must actually *succeed* in preventing the tsar from gaining Poland. Alexander, Metternich was now more convinced than ever, must be stopped.

It must have been a stressful night for Metternich. Emotionally, he was a wreck; diplomatically, he had just handed over a letter that would cause, in Gentz's words, "more grief in three months than he has had in all his life."

As AUSTRIA TENTATIVELY approved of Prussian gains, Metternich wasted no time in demanding that Hardenberg fulfill his end of the bargain. Prussia must join Austria at once, and, moreover, they had to act immediately. On October 24, just two days away, the Austrian emperor, the Russian tsar, and the king of Prussia would leave for a weeklong trip to Hungary. Metternich wanted to work out a common strategy before that trip—that is, before the Austrian emperor would be out of town and cooped up with these two close allies.

On the afternoon of October 23, the day before the departure, Metternich and Hardenberg had a rushed meeting. Castlereagh, fearful as ever of a strong Russia, joined them. By the end of their private session, held at Castlereagh's headquarters on the Minoritenplatz, the three ministers had decided to confront the tsar with a united stance and demand that he cooperate on Poland: Alexander would either have to agree to a fully independent Poland, or there would be no Poland at all. Russia, Prussia, and Austria would instead split the territory among them. But under no circumstances would the tsar be allowed simply to impose his will.

They would give Alexander five days from his return to Vienna to comply, or, as Castlereagh suggested, they would threaten to put the question of Poland before the entire community of powers. With this plan agreed upon, it was urgent for Metternich and Hardenberg to gain approval at once from their sovereigns.

The Russian tsar, meanwhile, was feeling his own sense of urgency to wrap up Poland before he went on his trip. He had heard how displeased the French delegation had become with the peace conference, and again let it be known that he wished to speak with Talleyrand. The French minister, obeying etiquette again, then requested an interview with the tsar.

Talleyrand was indeed unhappy. Prussia, his biggest fear, was still pressing its revolting principles, aiming to dethrone kings and destroy kingdoms. Metternich, oblivious to the dangers, was merely "the plaything of the intrigues that he believes he is directing." Castlereagh, worst of all, was fumbling about like a "schoolboy in diplomacy." Diplomats everywhere were moving like tortoises, as he put it, and Saxony, meanwhile, was about to be wiped off the map. Something had to be done.

So on the evening of October 23, Talleyrand and the Tsar of All the Russias had their second interview. After a short exchange of greetings, Alexander brought up Poland and asked where Talleyrand stood on this question. As Talleyrand's correspondence makes clear, he was hoping to barter his cooperation on Poland in return for the tsar's help in saving Saxony.

Talleyrand explained that he was "still the same" on Poland; that is, he favored a restored and independent kingdom. France's only concern, he added, was that the redrawn borders would not in any way endanger Russia's neighbors.

"They need not be alarmed," the tsar said. "Besides, I have two hundred thousand men in the duchy of Warsaw; let anyone try to chase me out."

As the conversation turned to Saxony, the tsar was not any more accommodating. Everything had been arranged, he said bluntly. He had given the territory to the king of Prussia, and Austria had consented.

"I do not know whether Austria does consent," Talleyrand responded. "I should find it difficult to believe that she does—it would be so much against her interest."

Then, raising the question to the level of law, Talleyrand asked if the "consent of Austria" could make Prussia "the proprietor of that which belongs to the King of Saxony."

"If the King of Saxony does not abdicate, he shall be taken to Russia. He will die there; another has already died there," the tsar responded, referring to the last king of Poland, Stanislaw II Augustus, who had been taken hostage by Russian troops in the 1790s and whisked away to finish his days outside St. Petersburg.

"Your Majesty will permit me not to believe that; the Congress has not been called together to witness such an outrage."

"How, an outrage?" the tsar replied. "Why should the King of Saxony not go to Russia?"

Talleyrand did not know where to begin in answering this question, and struggled, as he put it, to control his indignation. Before he could say anything, the tsar launched into a monologue about how much France owed him, and how meaningless all this talk of international law really was. "Your public law means nothing to me," the tsar said. "What do you suppose I care for all your parchments and all your treaties?"

Alexander continued to talk about how he had pledged his word to the king of Prussia to give him Saxony, and he intended to keep it. At this, Talleyrand saw an opportunity to remind the tsar that he had promised him a population of some nine or ten million. "Your Majesty could give them without destroying Saxony," Talleyrand said, handing over a piece of paper outlining some alternatives.

"The King of Saxony is a traitor," the tsar answered, referring to the king's loyalty to Napoleon and conveniently forgetting that he, too, had once been loyal to Napoleon. So had the king of Prussia, and, in fact, most of the leaders and delegates at the congress at one time or another.

Talleyrand had hoped to convince the tsar that he could obtain a satisfactory peace without having to destroy his reputation. He had not succeeded. Alexander was still committed to his policy of annihilating the Kingdom of Saxony and handing its territory over to Prussia. The interview ended, as it began, in irritation and frustration.

By the next morning, the day of the departure for Hungary, Metternich and Hardenberg had not yet gained sanction for their united stance against the tsar. Alexander, instead, had preempted their move and summoned Metternich alone over to his apartments. Their discussion in the white and gold paneled wing of the Hofburg was one of the most difficult of Metternich's entire career.

The tsar flat out demanded Metternich's compliance: "I intend to create an independent state of Poland. I want your agreement before I leave for Hungary today."

"Your Majesty," Metternich replied in a manner that sometimes came across as flippant, "if it is a question of creating an independent Poland, Austria too can create one."

At this, the tsar exploded. Metternich was the only man, he declared, who dared use such a tone with him. In Alexander's words, it was "a tone of revolt," as if the Austrian foreign minister were one of his subjects. The tsar then unleashed a barrage of "haughtiness and violence of language" that left Metternich stunned and visibly shaken.

Metternich compared the talk with the tsar to meeting Napoleon at his most irrational, and felt unsure whether he would end up leaving the palace through the door or through the window, as Alexander allegedly threatened. The Austrian minister never wanted to see the tsar in private again, he said, and predicted "the tsar will end up mad like his father."

Diplomatic relations had hit rock bottom. The tsar set off to Hungary with the emperor and the king, but he did not leave anyone in charge in his absence, and all the pressing problems of the peace conference remained unresolved.

Chapter 13

ROBINSON CRUSOE

I can never see a throne without being tempted to sit on it.

— NAPOLEON

All over Europe, governments were watching Vienna's victors lose themselves in celebrations and squabbles. One of the most curious observers, it turned out, was Napoleon Bonaparte.

He was, at this time, settling down in his new home on Elba, a rocky isle some seven miles off the northwestern coast of Italy. It is one of six main islands in the Tuscan Archipelago, a circle that also includes, in the south, the tiny, windswept Montecristo, immortalized in the Alexandre Dumas novel. To the north lies the barren Gorgona, which had served as the setting for another work of romantic fiction, *Clisson and Eugénie,* this one about a young Corsican rebel who commands an army only to be betrayed by a trusted friend. The author of the novella was none other than Napoleon himself, at age twenty-six.

The choice of Elba as Napoleon's new home had been made in the spring of 1814, when the Allies captured Paris and demanded his immediate, unconditional abdication. Tsar Alexander had promised, personally, that if Napoleon cooperated, the terms would be generous. Maps were scanned for a place of exile that would encourage the French emperor to vacate the throne without delay.

France, Italy, and other sites within the former continental empire were quickly ruled out as being unacceptable to the victors. As the historian Norman Mackenzie explained, Corsica was objectionable because it was Napoleon's birthplace, and also French property. Sardinia belonged to the House of Savoy, and Corfu was coveted by both England and Russia. Other places were considered, from the Canaries to the Caribbean. Some wanted Trinidad, others the Azores, or even Botany Bay in Australia. Talleyrand pressed for St. Helena in the South Atlantic. It was the Russian tsar who, in the end, proposed the island of Elba.

Actually, Alexander did more than propose the island—he simply refused to consider any other option. The reasons for this stance are open to question. For some, the tsar was relishing his new role as the magnanimous conqueror, an enlightened ruler who would be as forgiving in peace as he had been ferocious in war. Others saw the tiny island as a ridiculous choice intended to humiliate the fallen giant. Austria, however, had a very different explanation.

Behind the tsar's "theatrical generosity," Metternich saw only an attempt to antagonize Austria. The island of Elba was far too close to the Continent, and very near Austria's own interests in northern Italy, especially since it could not be ruled out that Napoleon might one day tire of this new home. He was, after all, only forty-five years old with a promising career ahead, and would likely prove a magnet for the Continent's discontented. Besides that, the island was not the tsar's to give: it belonged to the Habsburg family (as part of the restored Habsburg duchy of Tuscany). As Metternich suspected, the tsar's proposal could only be aimed at placing a source of turmoil in Austria's rear. The southern half of the sprawling Habsburg empire was left highly exposed to the threat of Napoleon's return.

Unfortunately for Austria, there had been very little discussion about sending Napoleon to Elba. The Russian tsar had reached Paris first and started working on his solution immediately. By the time the Austrian delegation made it through war-torn northeastern France in early April 1814, Alexander had already made his proposal and gained Napoleon's consent. The signing of the agreement had to be firmed up as quickly as possible, the tsar said, before Napoleon changed his mind.

But had the Austrians really been held up outside Paris, as they claimed, or were they deliberately holding back? Emperor Francis surely did not want to take part in officially dethroning his daughter Marie Louise, his son-in-law Napoleon, and his grandson, the king of Rome. As for Metternich's best ally, Castlereagh, he was not present, either, and he certainly didn't seem to be in a hurry, hoping perhaps to avoid the unpleasant appearance of imposing a regime change onto France. How long did the tsar have to wait on his Allies? Napoleon was already wavering in his abdication, and this restless man was, as everyone knew, prone to make rash, risky moves. The tsar had made his decision and pressed ahead.

According to the terms of the treaty, known at the time as "the Treaty of Abdication" (history remembers it as the Treaty of Fontainebleau, after Napoleon's palace, though it was not signed there), Napoleon was to maintain the official title "Emperor and Sovereign of the Island of Elba." He was granted this authority for the rest of his life, along with an annual pension of 2 million francs a year, to be paid from the French treasury. His wife, Marie Louise, was to be given the duchies of Parma, Piacenza, and Guastalla in northern Italy, and their son, little Napoleon, would be "the Prince of Parma." Article III of the treaty even incorporated the fiction that the abdication had been Napoleon's choice. As for Napoleon's family members, many of whom had lost thrones, they were also to share a yearly stipend of 2.5 million francs. Just as the tsar had promised, he had been generous indeed.

When Metternich and Castlereagh arrived in Paris, in early April, they had been shocked at the terms of this treaty. Castlereagh refused to sign it. Britain would in fact *never* sign this treaty guaranteeing Napoleon's rights to Elba. Austria was also very disappointed. Confronted with what was essentially the tsar's fait accompli, Metternich had angrily denounced this agreement as malicious and stupid. Within one year, he predicted, Napoleon would be back, and Europe would have to fight him all over again. His protests were in vain. No one was in a position to oppose the tsar, and so, without any more discussion, Napoleon was going to Elba.

WHEN NAPOLEON ARRIVED in early May 1814, some twelve thousand people lived on the small, sun-drenched island. The capital, Portoferraio, facing out onto a secluded bay on the southern shore, was home to about three thousand islanders. The roads were appalling, often mere goat and mule tracks, and the streets were hardly any better, usually little more than dusty stone steps rising steeply up the cliffside. There was a church, a tavern, and a café called Buono Gusto, serving up the island's local wine, *alciato*. The capital, at that time, has been summed up as "no more than a small and seedy Mediterranean port."

From the perspective of a vessel sailing into the island's chief harbor, Elba seemed all rugged mountains, red-tiled rooftops, and whitewashed walls. Relics of its storied past also stood out, like the old castle, built some twelve hundred feet atop a prominent cliff and attributed by local legend to awesome giants. Many legends, in fact, surrounded the isle. It was said, for instance, that Jason and the Argonauts had docked there in their quest for the Golden Fleece, and even the Trojan prince Aeneas had come on a mission to recruit stalwart Elbans for the Trojan War.

Colorful traditions aside, the small island packed a great deal of history within its eighty-six square miles. Much of it, unfortunately, was bloody and tragic. Elba had fallen prey to a long list of conquerors, including Etruscans, Romans, Visigoths, Ostrogoths, and Lombards. Later in the Middle Ages, the towns of Pisa and Genoa captured the exposed island. Then came the kingdom of Spain, which soon handed the island over to the Florentine dynasty of the Medici, who went on to dominate the island for some two hundred years. Others had ruled there at some point, too, including Germans, Turks, and, most recently, English and French.

Elba was, generally speaking, a very poor island. Its soil was rocky and its seasons extreme. Droughts and torrential, almost tropical, storms ravaged the fields and made famines all too common. Many years, Elba had to import as much as two-thirds of its grain, most of it from nearby Italy. But despite the agricultural challenges and the widespread poverty, the island had some valuable natural resources.

At Rio Marina, on the eastern side of the island, men with pickaxes and shovels gathered the iron ore that gave the island its largest source of revenue, and also lent the name to its capital, Portoferraio, literally the "port of iron." To the south, there were rich stone quarries, which shipped hard granite and marble to the mainland for use in the construction of buildings, including the cathedral of Pisa. There were also salt marshes, supplying the large warehouse in the Piazza della Granguardia behind the harbor. Oranges, olives, pomegranates, and grapes grew in abundance, and fishing nets yielded rich hauls, too, particularly tunny and anchovy.

For the most part, Elba had quickly accepted its new sovereign—a tribute, in part, to Napoleon's well-known charisma. He had arrived on the island at a most inauspicious time. After some wild swings of fortune the previous twenty years, ownership had flip-flopped from French to British rule, and then the French gained the upper hand, though the islanders were in revolt, and Elba seemed on the verge of chaos. In fact, guards at the coastal fortifications had fired on the approaching British frigate HMS *Undaunted* as it carried the emperor to his new island.

In all the confusion, however, one thing was certain: The little capital of Elba was unprepared, to say the least, for the strange saga that lay ahead. All the trappings of an imperial court would have to be found or created. As there was no imperial residence, Napoleon was to be housed in a makeshift palace—the unused upper floor of the town hall, which had once been a biscuit warehouse. Chairs, tables, desks, and other furniture were quickly borrowed for the improvised throne room. As for a throne itself, there was none to be found. "What is a throne" anyway, Napoleon had once said; "a bit of wood covered with velvet." On Elba, this was literally the case: Napoleon's throne was a borrowed sofa decorated with paper flowers.

WHILE NAPOLEON WAS playing Robinson Crusoe, as Prince de Ligne put it, Vienna was absorbed with its own gossip and speculation. Count Francis Palffy, it was whispered, was having an affair with the celebrated ballerina Bigottini, and now apparently she was pregnant. The count was said to have just offered her a 6,000-franc pension for life. Prince Eugène de Beauharnais was spotted ducking into a jeweler's shop and splurging on his latest mistress. According to an anonymous police report submitted to Baron Hager in late October, the bill was 32,000 ducats, and the prince paid in part by handing over a cavalry saber given to him by his stepfather, Napoleon.

The biggest source of gossip was still the Russian delegation. While the tsar insisted on making all the main diplomatic decisions himself, many members of his staff found that they had time on their hands, and some were finding their way to Vienna's red-light districts. One member of the delegation was even said to be in charge of inspecting the brothels and procuring for the tsar himself, though others dismissed this as empty gossip. Alexander, they said, needed no help in this regard.

Many high-ranking Russian military officers were also often spotted at the theater in the Leopoldstadt with well-known courtesans, and sometimes they brought them into their suites at the Hofburg Palace. The nineteen-year-old courtesan Josephine Wolters was making a name for herself, slipping past the guards at the palace almost every night, usually wearing the disguise of a man's clothes. Despite complaints from other delegations, police agents were not exactly inclined to put a stop to these escapades. The courtesan was also working for the spy chief.

Apparently, according to police reports, the Russians were upset with many things that autumn, and not just the intrigues of Austria. They did not "hide their discontent with England," particularly with Castlereagh, who was meddling, not mediating, on the question of Poland. They blamed France, too, for stirring up fears among the smaller states and trying to divide the Allies. Some members of the Russian delegation were also unhappy about the growing anti-Russian sentiments expressed around town. Two Viennese wigmakers, for instance, one near St. Stephen's Cathedral and the other on the Schwertgasse, were indecently and offensively using busts of Tsar Alexander as mannequins to display their latest wigs.

Spies were picking up many other signs of tension as they continued their surveillance, interception of letters, infiltration of embassies, and secret rummaging around offices in search of any papers or any scraps left behind. Two crown princes of rival kingdoms, Bavaria and Württemberg, had almost ended up in a duel. They had been playing a game of "blindman's buff" at the salon of Princess Thurn und Taxis when one accused the other of cheating. Fortunately, the duel was stopped in time, by an order from the king of Bavaria.

Remarkably little crime had been reported that autumn, considering how many of the world's richest were in town and that they were not exactly modest about displaying their wealth. Someone had stolen a rare gem from Princess Liechtenstein, and someone else had broken into the Spanish embassy, making off with papers from Labrador's office, but, on the whole, Vienna had so far experienced little criminal activity.

One event that did briefly capture the attention of the police department was an intrigue by the delegate of the Prince of Walachia in today's Rumania. The delegate, Prince Bellio, was responsible for forwarding the correspondence between his sovereign and Friedrich von Gentz. But evidently Bellio had been opening the confidential letters, copying their contents, and then resealing them with a counterfeit seal. By the middle of October, Bellio was trying to arrange a meeting with Princess Catherine Bagration to sell or pass on some of his discoveries to the Russian tsar. Before that transpired, however, police raided his rooms on the third floor of a mansion on the bustling Stock-im-Eisen-Platz and seized his papers. The prince was promptly escorted to the border.

Amid all the rumors, gossip, and intrigues being plotted all over town, the most tantalizing scoop during the first month came from a small scrap of paper retrieved from the French embassy by a chambermaid recently placed inside. The note was vague, enigmatic, and of uncertain reliability. It referred to a French consul in Livorno, the Chevalier Mariotti, who was working on a plan to kidnap Napoleon. The motive for this plot was unknown, and it seemed far-fetched, but, just in case, Baron Hager relayed the information immediately to the Austrian emperor.

AS LEAVES TURNED crimson and gold, the temperatures dropped and the sky clouded more frequently into a gray dreariness—weather not exactly suited to lifting Metternich's spirits. He had been desperate to know the duchess's response to his letter, and on October 23 he received it. She explained that she had in fact wanted to break off her relationship with Prince Alfred von Windischgrätz, but even though she realized he was not good for her, she had cared too much to stop seeing him. Bluntly, she added that she no longer regarded Metternich as a lover: "Beyond the enthusiasm of friendship, all remained calm within me."

Hearing that assessment had hardly soothed his nerves. Metternich was still overcome and distraught. "You have had the power to kill me," he wrote back that night. "I told you it would be so." Metternich once again poured out his heart to the duchess, comparing the agonizing last twenty-four hours to one hundred years:

I am no longer the man I was the day before yesterday . . . the old friend is dead and you have thrown his ashes to the wind.

His heart had been violently ripped out of him, he alleged. Rumors of the tsar prying in his private affairs also continued to bother him. Could she please let him know what exactly she "had promised the tsar"?

Alexander was certainly attacking Metternich's credibility, but could he really have put pressure on the duchess to break all contact with him, as gossipers claimed? The tsar had interfered in the private lives of other subjects in his realm in the past, including the time he virtually imposed a marriage on the duchess's younger sister, Dorothée. Baron Hager's informers were convinced that the tsar was doing so again, threatening his control over her estates and making it clear that "only a formal break with Metternich will satisfy him."

Perhaps the tsar had pressured the duchess—he could, of course, have done so with even more powerful leverage than what the spies suggested: her daughter in Russian-controlled Finland. At any rate, whether the rumors were true or not, Metternich believed that the tsar had ruthlessly used the duchess's daughter as a pawn in diplomacy, and then pressured the duchess to abandon him. "I am no longer astonished at anything, especially when it comes to that man," Metternich said. This belief would influence how he behaved toward his rival.

By the end of October, the emperor, the tsar, and the king had returned from their trip to Hungary. The three sovereigns had visited the cities on the Danube, the pearl of Buda, and the newer, more commercial Pest, which would later that century merge to form Budapest. They had toured the capital, picked grapes, and visited the tomb of Alexander's sister, Alexandra, who had married Archduke Joseph, Palatine of Hungary, and died there thirteen years before.

Despite the hope that a change of environment would ease tensions, the problems had simply moved 150 miles down the Danube. The Russian tsar continued his uncooperative behavior, at odds with prevailing diplomatic etiquette. Rude and crude, he exploded unpredictably, and spies reported a rage of door slamming in the Hungarian palace where they were staying. They also reported that he was insulting his fellow sovereigns by spending most of his time with "pretty women."

The tsar, it was also said, took every opportunity to disparage Metternich and the diplomats he so detested. Alexander told the Austrian emperor that he wanted the two of them, along with the king of Prussia, to band together, in a sort of sovereign's league, to reach solutions about Europe themselves. He wanted to begin by having Metternich removed from office.

But that would not happen, at least not yet. What saved Metternich was undoubtedly the support of Emperor Francis. The Austrian emperor liked his foreign minister and trusted his opinion, no matter what the tsar or Metternich's growing legion of critics had said. Besides, the tsar's domineering behavior showed, if the emperor needed a reminder, how difficult it could be to work with him.

In fact, during this trip to Hungary, Francis suggested that everyone would be better served if the monarchs left the complicated negotiations to their foreign ministers. As diplomats at later conferences would also learn, the differences in rank between a head of state and a foreign minister strained the normal give-and-take consensus-building procedures of the conference room.

So despite Alexander's efforts, Metternich would continue to have his emperor's support and would remain Austrian foreign minister. Emperor Francis, for his part, returned to Vienna, even more wary of the tsar, while the king of Prussia emerged from the royal trip more loyal to Alexander than ever, earning a new sobriquet: the tsar's valet de chambre.

ᴅɪɴɴᴇʀ ᴡɪᴛʜ ᴛʜᴇ ᴛsᴀʀ

It would be difficult to have more intelligence than Tsar Alexander, but there is a piece missing. I have never managed to discover what it is.

—Nᴀᴘᴏʟᴇᴏɴ

Public opinion about the Vienna Congress, meanwhile, was falling to a new low. "Our conference is not progressing at all," one member of the Bavarian delegation grumbled. "Nothing is decided, nothing is agreed on." The paralysis was blamed on a simple cause: "Far too few meetings are held; the whole time being consumed with these nauseating, never-ending fetes." Even the king of Prussia was overheard at a ball complaining, "We only seem to be here to amuse ourselves."

It was Metternich's fault, some said: He was devious, deceitful, and, above all, distracted with his love affair. How on earth could he be Austria's foreign minister, let alone president of the congress? Rumors circulated, too, that Metternich would soon resign, be sacked, or even succumb to a nervous breakdown. Others blamed the tsar and his bullying, boasting style of negotiation. Still others, however, traced the ultimate cause for all the discord back to salon intrigues orchestrated by the Duchess of Sagan and Princess Bagration, who, it was said, were playing the leaders of the world like chess pieces.

After the last postponement two weeks before, the congress's new opening date, November 1, was also quickly approaching, and once again there was no sign of an official opening. Many feared that the congress might not take place at all. The peacemakers had never seemed so far apart.

For most of the delegates outside the Big Four, all this wasted time was infuriating and intolerable. How ironic it seemed that the representative of the defeated power, Talleyrand, was emerging as the most prominent spokesman for an immediate opening of the peace congress.

True, Castlereagh, Metternich, and Hardenberg had secretly agreed to threaten the tsar by summoning the assembly of states and throwing the question of Poland before them. But this was Castlereagh's urging, and he really was the only minister inclined to look favorably on the opening of a congress. Talleyrand, of course, realized this fact and saw a potential ally in Castlereagh.

The two foreign ministers related fairly well, both professionally as diplomats and socially as cosmopolitan gentlemen. Both could look over the fact that their countries had been at war the past 20 years, which in turn was part of a larger pattern of hostility that stretched back almost 150 years. Britain and France were used to being enemies, and Talleyrand, at least, hoped to change that.

At Vienna, the biggest difference between the two delegates was a question of priorities. For Castlereagh, the main challenge lay in resisting the growth of Russia, led by a tsar who acted like "another Bonaparte." Talleyrand, on the other hand, was less concerned about an idiosyncratic tsar than angry and belligerent Prussians who might truly launch another war. As he saw it, Castlereagh's views were naive and rather simple-minded, based on the luxury of being a secure island power defended by a strong navy and a stormy English Channel.

Castlereagh, for his part, thought that Talleyrand was overreacting, consumed with unnecessary fears of his German neighbor. "France need never dread a German league," Castlereagh concluded, "it is in its nature inoffensive."

So once again Talleyrand's task, as he saw it, was to set Castlereagh straight and show how dangerous Prussia would become if it gained Saxony. At a private meeting at English headquarters on the Minoritenplatz in late October, Talleyrand limped over to the maps on the table and gave a history lesson to the British minister: "I pointed out to him how that, Saxony and Silesia being in the same [Prussian] hands, Bohemia might be taken in a few weeks."

This was something that Prussia had done three times previously in conflicts with Austria under Frederick the Great, and later that century Prussia would do so again under Otto von Bismarck. And should Bohemia be exposed, then "the heart of the Austrian monarchy would be laid bare and defenseless." As Talleyrand described it, an "astonished" look crept over Castlereagh's long face.

At this point, Talleyrand targeted his appeal more directly to British self-interest: Did they really want to hand over Saxony, with the rich trading city of Leipzig, home to great markets and fairs since the Middle Ages, to a country like Prussia, whose allegiance they could not count on for sure? This was robbing the friendly disposed state of Saxony in order to reward a power whose policy was uncertain at best.

Talleyrand had pounced on a basic problem in British foreign policy: Castlereagh's whole strategy was based on the assumption that Prussia would act as an independent sovereign power and not be subjected to any undue outside influence. But that was simply not the case. Given the king of Prussia's dependence on the tsar, Castlereagh was basically pursuing a policy that would likely end in what he feared most: a much stronger Russia.

Yet it would take more than a few arguments for Talleyrand to change Castlereagh's mind. By the end of the conversation, the French minister began to suspect that there must be another reason for Britain's support of Prussia. Castlereagh was not only preparing for a threat coming from Russia, but he also still harbored a fear of France. Talleyrand tried to assure him that his country posed no threat whatsoever. France would be insane, he argued, to launch another war.

As Castlereagh remained unconvinced, Talleyrand tried yet another line of argument. There was, of course, one way to stop Russian expansion once and for all: Open the Congress. Dare the tsar to make his outrageous demands in front of an assembly of all the delegates. He cherished his image as a war hero, a liberator, and an enlightened thinker too much for that.

There were difficulties in calling a congress, the British statesman said vaguely. When Talleyrand pressed him to specify what exactly those might be, Castlereagh urged him to talk to Metternich. "I conclude from this," Talleyrand wrote, "that something has been agreed to between them," and the two leaders "would not have kept [that agreement] secret from me if they had no reason to believe that I should object to it."

ON OCTOBER 30, as if on cue, Talleyrand received an invitation for a confidential interview with Prince Metternich that evening at eight o'clock. This was immediately before a meeting of the Committee of Eight, which now had to figure out what to do about the congress. Its proposed opening was, as promised, a mere two days away.

Clearly, Metternich was starting to wonder if opening a congress might not be such a bad idea after all. It was the lesser of evils, compared to the risks of a Russian empire creating a satellite Kingdom of Poland and extending its influence all the way to central Europe. His colleagues on the committee likewise felt such a great pressure that they had decided to ask Talleyrand to submit his ideas for the organization of the peace conference.

Ready for this request, Talleyrand brought along his plan to the meeting. His proposal called for a main directing committee that would organize all negotiations and also, interestingly, appoint a series of sub-committees to deal with the more specialized problems the diplomats faced. He proposed three such committees: one dealing with Saxony, another Italy, and the last with Switzerland. As for the tricky problem of who could participate, there would also be a "Commission of Verifica-tions" to examine credentials of the aspiring delegates. The congress of all the states, which would ratify everything, should open immediately.

Castlereagh supported this plan, of course, and now he was joined by Metternich. Russia's Count Nesselrode, however, protested that he could not vote for it because he was not yet well enough informed. The Prussian delegates were even more adamantly opposed; Chancellor Har-denberg, in particular, was said to have a special "horror" at the thought of a congress. By the end of the meeting, with Russia and Prussia sticking together, Talleyrand's proposal was tabled. On the eve of its opening, the congress was postponed once more. A few weeks later, it would be post-poned one last time, never in fact to open. The congress, in a sense, would never meet. The Directing Committee and the subcommittees, however, were not scrapped, and the real work of the Congress of Vienna was going to be done there, in small groups meeting behind closed doors.

It was during this minor crisis, when it seemed to many that the Great Powers could not agree on anything, that Metternich apparently received a curious, anonymous note. It was probably the same night of the meet-ing, October 30, at a masquerade in the Hofburg Palace. A masked figure had approached the Austrian foreign minister, handed him a folded paper, and then promptly disappeared into the crowded ballroom.

Opening the note, which was sent from an unnamed source identified only as "a person of the highest distinction" with whom he had recently quarreled, Prince Metternich was promised a handsome sum, if only he would be more cooperative on a certain matter. The rest of the offer must have been much more tempting. The unidentified sender claimed to be in a position to help Metternich solve his problems with "a woman of rank" in whom he was very much interested. All of this was admittedly vague, but the author of the note reassured Metternich: "Your Highness will understand."

Now, of course, Metternich understood perfectly well. The mystery "person of the highest distinction" that he had quarreled with was almost certainly the tsar, and there was only one "woman of rank," at that time, that he was interested in: the Duchess of Sagan. As one of Castlereagh's assistants described the episode, the Austrian foreign minister simply took the note, "tossed it aside [and] pretended not to understand." Later, Metternich regretted that he did not hang on to the paper as proof of the tsar's cheap tricks.

Talleyrand, about the same time, was also receiving some information that might prove useful in future negotiations. This concerned Britain's Castlereagh, who, however helpful with respect to the congress, was proving a tough nut to crack when it came to his Prussian policy. Perhaps that would soon change, Talleyrand hoped, with good reason.

According to Talleyrand's sources, Castlereagh was hiding a secret that, if disclosed, would leave him in a compromising position. Castlereagh apparently had no government sanction for his policy of supporting Prussia. In fact, it seemed that the British foreign secretary was acting in defiance of his own government's orders.

This timely discovery had come from a Saxon officer who had just arrived in Vienna from London bringing news of his recent meeting with the prince regent, who clearly shared Talleyrand's concerns. Other sources had confirmed this discovery, including one of King Louis' ministers in Paris, who had had a revealing conversation with the British ambassador to France, the Duke of Wellington. In other words, Castlereagh, at best, had no authorization for his actions, and quite likely could be exposed for disregarding the wishes of his own government.

While Talleyrand was figuring out how best to use this information, Castlereagh worked frantically with Prussian leaders in their plan to lure the Prussian king away from the Russian tsar.

Indeed, the whole tense and uncertain situation exploded at a dramatic dinner in early November in Tsar Alexander's private suites at the Hofburg Palace. The tsar and the king of Prussia were dining alone, and toward the end of the meal, Alexander turned the discussion to foreign policy, reminding his ally about the importance of reestablishing the Kingdom of Poland. Then, after swearing that he would never yield on this question, the tsar expressed his surprise, disappointment, and anger that the king of Prussia, his "dearest friend," had been scheming against him.

Startled at this accusation, the king uttered a "thousand protestations" and begged his complete innocence. He swore that he had supported the tsar, just as he had promised, and this went for Poland, or any other matter that his ally desired. They had declared their oaths of eternal friendship. Nothing had changed.

"It is not enough that you should be of this mind," Tsar Alexander replied. "Your ministers must agree to support me too!"

"But of course my ministers will support what I choose to support!" the king answered defensively.

At that point, the Prussian chancellor, Hardenberg, was summoned to the dinner table. The aged and sophisticated statesman, who "knew how to make time fly by his charming conversation," found himself in a most uncomfortable and unpleasant situation.

The tsar immediately bombarded him with a series of facts and questions. Russia and Prussia, Alexander said, had reached a "definite and unshakable" agreement about Poland. Will you or will you not listen to the orders of your king, the tsar demanded to know. The Prussian king just sat there, indifferent to his minister's plight.

When Hardenberg tried to explain, at one point, the importance of international consensus on Poland, the tsar said, bluntly, "Those are the arguments of Monsieur Metternich," and then, out of the blue, alleged that Metternich had offered to betray the Prussians. Hardenberg was rightly skeptical. Metternich might have been unpredictable, but this wild assertion was highly unlikely. The Austrian minister was far too upset with the tsar, while Alexander, on the other hand, appeared angry and desperate enough that he might just resort to any means at his disposal to have his way.

What right did the tsar have to treat another king's minister this way? Gentz said afterward that the Prussian chancellor was so shaken by the experience that some friends "feared for his health." When his colleagues on the British and Austrian staffs heard of the dinner, they hoped that he would resign in protest.

The Prussian chancellor was ordered to break off his "intrigues" with Britain and Austria immediately. He would now be bound to carrying out Prussian policy as determined by his king, and that meant, in practice, supporting a policy that he personally felt threatened his country and the stability of the entire continent.

Hardenberg was deeply upset, reportedly afterward denouncing the tsar as "the most perfidious, treacherous, usurping character, and infinitely more dangerous than Bonaparte." Yet he was uncertain about how exactly to proceed. He scribbled his impression in his diary: "Russia, supported by the King [of Prussia] on all points, is wrong. But what to do?"

When Metternich found out about the tsar's accusations, he immediately wrote to Hardenberg to affirm that the allegations were not true: "I deny not only the fact but I am also ready to maintain the opposite in the presence of the Tsar himself."

Another person particularly troubled by this development was Lord Castlereagh. He had been trying to establish a united front with Hardenberg for months—both of them, in fact, working against their own governments for something that they felt would better serve the future peace. Still, their cooperation was a deliberate act of disobedience, and, unfortunately for them, it had backfired. The Russian tsar and the king of Prussia had only been brought closer together.

On November 7, Hardenberg unhappily but officially notified his colleagues that Prussia would now have to support Russia. Castlereagh read this note with a great deal of concern and despondency. "Unless the Emperor of Russia can be brought to a more moderate and sound course of public conduct," Castlereagh sighed, "the peace which we have so dearly purchased will be of short duration."

Chapter 15

PURSUING PHANTOMS

The triumphal chariot of the congress is stuck in the mud.

— BARON FRANZ VON GÄRTNER, IN A LETTER TO COUNT ERBACH,
MAY 16, 1815, INTERCEPTED BY THE POLICE

Seven miles off the coast of northern Italy, Napoleon was still trying to adjust to his life as the emperor of Elba. After staying only one night on the island, he had realized that his current "palace" in the town hall was not working out. Sounds of the city square, with its lively chatter and strumming guitars, wafted up to Napoleon's window late into the night. For such a small capital, the residents of Portoferraio could make a lot of noise.

Rivaling the commotion of the square was the odor that stemmed from the unfortunate habit of simply tossing the trash into the streets. While many cities at that time relied on a similar approach, Elba had far too little rain for most of the year to sweep it away, and the garbage ended up rotting in the gutters. The stench could be overpowering. The first order of business, back in May, had been to find a new place to live.

Obviously, there was nothing on the island that could rival the Tuileries, Fontainebleau, Versailles, Saint-Cloud, or any of the other palaces Napoleon had known back in France. There wasn't anything close. After discounting a couple of possible residences, none of which was particularly enticing, Napoleon had settled for a house on the outskirts.

It was a modest single-story house with eight rooms, four of which had been added in a renovation some fifty years before. Its name, Casa il Mulini, derived from a pair of windmills that had turned there until their destruction in 1808. The house itself, about ninety years old, had originally served as the residence of a Medici gardener. The outside facade was strikingly pink and adorned with emerald green shutters.

What Napoleon particularly liked about the house was the location. On a remote cliff some one hundred feet above the sea, Napoleon could sit comfortably in the villa's breezy garden and scan the blue horizon for incoming ships. With the bay, the fort, and the reefs, no large ship arriving on his island could escape a trained spyglass.

Napoleon's interest in the horizon was not, of course, idle curiosity. He was concerned for his personal safety, and with good reason. During the last twenty years, Napoleon's policies of heavy taxation, forced conscription, mandated legal reforms, and undisguised looting had made many enemies in France and occupied Europe. Royalists, radicals, patriots, and even monks with daggers in their robes—there were many people who nursed grudges and wished to settle vendettas. In addition to aspiring assassins, there was the threat that pirates swarming the Mediterranean might try to kidnap the emperor and ransom him for the rumored treasures stored somewhere on his island. Napoleon was, in other words, potentially in a great deal of danger.

So while guards were posted to keep watch on incoming ships, Napoleon set about immediately to improve the island's dilapidated state of defenses. He was to rebuild the ruined watchtowers, fortify the walls protecting the harbor, and strengthen the firepower atop its ramparts. The best harbor, the only one for sizable ships, must be as secure as possible.

The emperor had been especially glad, too, when his faithful Imperial Guard had arrived safely in the early summer. Four hundred men had been permitted, though their number had already risen to over one thousand. These soldiers were the last remnants of his once invincible Grande Armée. Now they formed the core of his army on Elba, though their functions had to change with the circumstances. The Polish lancers, for instance, who would now have little opportunity for ferocious cavalry charges, were to be retrained for artillery duty.

Napoleon had surrounded himself with loyal followers. Antoine Drouot, a baker's son who had risen to the rank of general, was appointed minister of defense and governor of Elba. Nicknamed the "Wise Man of the Grande Armée," Drouot was looking forward to spending time on his studies. He was learning Italian, reading the Bible daily, and playing chess with Napoleon.

General Pierre-Jacques Cambronne, leader of the Guard, was far less content. "A desperate, uneducated ruffian" who had been wounded so many times that he looked "completely tattooed with scars," Cambronne was a restless soldier bored out of his mind. Another high-ranking loyalist who was frustrated with the lack of action was General Count Henri Bertrand. This engineer turned administrator was now the grand chamberlain at the Elban court, presiding over the etiquette that would be as elaborate as it had been back in imperial France. Bertrand's career advancement seemed to have come to a standstill since moving to Elba, and his wife, Fanny, who had joined him, felt that they had made a mistake.

As for the navy, Napoleon had the small sixteen-gun *Inconstant* (which he used as his flagship), the three-masted *Etoile,* and the twenty-six-ton *Caroline.* In addition, Napoleon was setting up another line of defense with a new police force. A fellow Corsican, Poggi di Talavo, was named chief of police and given the main responsibility for watching all traffic to and from Elba. Permits would be needed for travel, and all newcomers would have to register at the Star Fort, beside the harbor. Police officers piloting small, fast feluccas patrolled the island's isolated beaches. Strangers and suspicious characters were questioned thoroughly. Elba, small and exposed, would be turned into a fortress island.

There were, however, two people that Napoleon deeply wanted to see arrive on his shores: his wife, Marie Louise, and their three-year-old son, the former king of Rome. She had promised to join him on Elba, and Napoleon had been waiting since May, lamenting her absence, his "daily sorrow." At the beginning, he had written her almost every day. He had also started preparing a special wing for them in his palace, repainting and refurbishing it for the expected arrival. Napoleon had everything he needed in his little kingdom, he wrote. "Only you, my dear Louise, are missing, you and my son."

MEANWHILE, BACK IN Vienna, Marie Louise was avoiding the celebrations of the peace conference as much as possible. "Festivities go on every day, so they tell me," Marie Louise wrote to Napoleon, adding that she was "scarcely informed of them" and had no interest in them whatsoever.

All those parties hosted by her husband's conquerors must have seemed distasteful. They must also have highlighted the frustrating new uncertainties over the duchies that she had been promised by treaty. Rumors swirled about how eager some of the treaty's signatories were to break those agreements. "Each day there was a fresh story," her secretary, Baron Claude-François de Méneval, wrote. "To-day Parma was assured to her, on the morrow it had been given to somebody else." The result was that Marie Louise's mood swung rapidly between hope and fear, and all of this, in turn, only increased her anxieties and made her much more willing to submit to the wishes of her father.

While she waited for the congress to decide her future, Marie Louise filled her days by riding in the park, strolling in the gardens, learning Italian, dining with her suite, taking drawing lessons—anything that took her mind away from her worries. One favorite pastime was music, and there was increasingly a new man found at the piano in her salon, a newcomer with a beautiful tenor voice: the handsome and debonair general Count Adam Albert von Neipperg. He had a black silk patch over his right eye as a result of a saber blow received in battle, and a reputation as a ladies' man. Neipperg had been placed in her suite that summer by no less than Emperor Francis. Neipperg was supposed to prevent Marie Louise from going to Elba, and he was instructed to use "any means whatsoever." He had succeeded.

By all accounts, Marie Louise and Neipperg had become lovers on her way back to Vienna from the spas. Their affair had started perhaps by late August 1814, and almost certainly by late September, when they were staying at the inn, Zur Goldenner Sonne, in Küssnacht, just outside of Lucerne, Switzerland. This romantic liaison was, of course, carried on in utmost secrecy. Marie Louise's secretary, the loyal Bonapartist Baron Méneval, already had his suspicions, though. "I can no longer fool myself," he confessed, "that she is the pure and spotless angel whom I held above reproach."

The French members of her suite must also have wondered about Neipperg's growing influence over the former empress, and they, too, cold-shouldered the Austrian officer. The loyal Bonapartists were not inclined to receive him well, anyway. It was Neipperg, after all, who had helped negotiate the agreements that persuaded some of Napoleon's most prominent marshals to desert to the Allies, including no less than Murat, the king of Naples, and Bernadotte, the Crown Prince of Sweden. And now he was trying to steal Napoleon's wife.

Like many in Vienna, Marie Louise's son, the little Napoleon, had no idea how important Neipperg was becoming in his mother's life, of course. The young boy spent his time mainly with his governess, Madame de Montesquiou—"Mamam Q," as he called her. He did, however, pick up some talk from the strongly Bonapartist suite that looked after him at Schönbrunn. The little prince was heard complaining about Louis XVIII, who had taken his father's place back in Paris, and also all his toys. Louis had better return both at once, the little boy had demanded. Actually, the French king would soon send over some toys that had been left behind in the hurried retreat from the Tuileries the previous spring.

In truth, the little prince was lonely and bored. At this stage, few bothered to visit the family locked away in the palace, living symbols of French dominance and occupation. One of the few and, indeed, favorite guests that autumn, however, was Prince de Ligne, who put on his field marshal's uniform spangled with medals from decades of military service. Once on a visit to the palace, the prince was greeted by the king of Rome's obvious joy: The toddler jumped down from his chair, ran excitedly to the old man, and threw his arms around his frail, powdered neck. Separated by almost a century of history, the two played games on the floor with the miniature toy soldiers.

In the words of one observer, this little boy—"Napoleon II"—would tempt any painter with the "angelic cut of his face, the unblemished whiteness of his skin, his sparkling eyes, and the beautiful locks of his curly blond hair cascading down to his shoulders." One of the spies, however, put it slightly differently: "that young Napoleon is an extremely wicked, stubborn child." He must have inherited this quality from his father, many hastened to add.

The Austrian police were vigilant, reporting on all the activities of Marie Louise, Neipperg, little Napoleon Francis, and the French suite that surrounded them. They were also among the first to detect the new relationship between the former empress and Neipperg, whom the Austrian government had named as her lord chamberlain. The baron's spies would have much to report from the west wing of Schönbrunn Palace.

Apparently, Marie Louise was having second thoughts about having returned to Vienna, and all she wanted now was to leave town again, preferably to the Duchy of Parma, though those who did not know of

Neipperg thought she wanted to leave for Elba. But Emperor Francis now was refusing to allow her to go anywhere until the congress had wrapped up its affairs. In the meantime, both Marie Louise and her son, now called Franz to sound more Austrian, were being closely guarded. They were well on their way to becoming virtual prisoners in the palace.

The day of the masked ball at Metternich's summer villa, November 8, was now nearing, and Metternich was going out of his way to make this celebration memorable, as the congress might end abruptly at any time. While the sovereigns wore black, women were asked to appear in regional costumes. Countesses appeared in peasant garb—peasants, that is, with diamonds sewn into their silk dresses. Others dressed as Venetians, Persians, Native Americans, or peasants elsewhere on the Continent. The Duchess of Sagan opted for Carinthian attire. No one was sure about Lady Castlereagh's dress. Was it really supposed to be that of a vestal virgin?

The Prussian diplomat Humboldt had chosen to remain at home, buried in his work. He needed to draft a number of policy papers for the upcoming meetings, and that meant research, marshaling arguments, and putting the final touches on Prussian policy statements. Grand as Metternich's ball was, Humboldt was not sorry to have missed it. "I hate those social affairs unto death."

This time, however, Humboldt missed out. The masked ball had all the color, the excitement, and indeed the magic of many other masquerades— but it also had a special attraction. At midnight, many revelers had switched masks and enjoyed the mischief that followed in the delightful confusion of mistaken identities. At another point that evening, when the dignitaries lined up as usual to march off in the polonaise through the rooms of the villa, the stately promenade degenerated into drunken chaos. The head and tail of the march collided in one of the drawing rooms. The king of Denmark, for one, "laughed so hard he could barely stand up."

Most interesting, despite swearing to the contrary, the Russian tsar had in fact come to Metternich's villa. Alexander and the king of Prussia, together as usual, were seen enjoying themselves, like the fifteen hundred other guests that evening. Even Gentz came out, and did not return home until after four in the morning.

Yet however successful the ball had been, Metternich was almost at his wits' end, suffering what Gentz called a real "state of crisis." It was, of course, impossible for Metternich and the duchess to end their relationship as neatly as their letters claimed. Meetings were inevitable in the close-knit society of the congress, and they were often awkward. The duchess wrote to Metternich:

> Everything is so completely changed in us that it is not at all surprising that our thoughts and our feelings no longer meet in anything, and that we find ourselves in a situation more than strange to one another. I begin to believe that we never did know one another. We were both pursuing phantoms.

As she further explained, Metternich had only seen her as an idealized lady, "a model of perfection." She, in turn, had reciprocated, seeing Metternich before as representing "all there is of beauty and of intellectual grandeur, something well above honor." Metternich's false idealization was now swinging to the opposite extreme.

While the duchess denied that she had succumbed to outside pressure to abandon him, Metternich did not believe it. The tsar must have had a role in the breakup, and despite everything, Metternich still hoped to regain his lover. He was consumed as ever. Gentz found the whole situation exasperating. "Long conversation with Metternich," he wrote in his diary for the eleventh of November, "always more on that cursed woman than on business."

The exhaustion, physical strain, and sheer mental anguish were taking a toll on Metternich, and this at a time when the Congress of Vienna needed the full attention of its president. He confessed:

> As to my health, there is no question of it any longer! I am completely ill, my body attacked, my soul has not protected it for a long time. I am still needed for a few weeks more; those weeks will bring to an end the most painful years of my life, and if they finish my life, the world will lose only the sad remnants of an existence which I myself deserved to lose.

While the delegates wrangled over Poland and Saxony, teetering on the verge of war, another major dispute had been uncomfortably placed

on hold: the future of Italy. But it was now becoming increasingly difficult to avoid this delicate subject.

Napoleon had entered the peninsula back in 1796 promising to break
the people's "chains of bondage." But by the time the last French troops
straggled back across the Alps eighteen years later, the Italian states were
left in near chaos. The land had been stripped of valuables, treasure
vaults were looted, and countless masterpieces were carted off to Paris.

The extent of Napoleon's looting was shocking. Everything from the
Belvedere Apollo to the Medici Venus, the Dying Gaul to *Laocoön and
His Sons*—these were just some of the masterpieces in the 288 cartloads
of treasures that comprised Napoleon's *first* raid of Italy. They were soon
joined by other treasures, including Raphael's *Leo X*, Titian's *Death of
Saint Peter Martyr*, Veronese's gigantic *Marriage at Cana*, and the four
bronze horses atop St. Mark's Basilica in Venice. Every campaign had
added to the collection. As one critic put it, the French would have carried off the Colosseum and the Sistine Chapel, too, if they could have figured out how to do so.

Of all the questions regarding Italy—from old republics destroyed in
the war, such as Genoa and Venice, to magnificent art collections ruthlessly plundered, namely, in Florence and the Vatican—the most difficult
challenge at this point lay in the southern part of the peninsula. One of
Bonaparte's former marshals, Joachim Murat, still ruled as king of
Naples, having been placed on the throne in 1808 by Napoleon himself.
To allow King Joachim to remain in power was tantamount to "reward-
ing crime." Conquest, as Talleyrand argued, should not bestow any
rights. For the good of Europe, that notion had to be banished forever.

Another problem in allowing Murat to retain his crown was the fact
that his presence placed all the states of Italy at risk of another war.
Murat was one of the bravest and undoubtedly one of the most talented
cavalry officers alive. He was also an unpredictable hothead with the
touchiness of someone who had not a shred of legitimacy to his throne.
Like Napoleon, Murat would probably have to keep fighting in order to
maintain his authority.

Yet to deprive him of the throne would require military intervention,
and a large one at that. Murat would certainly not go down without a
fight, and after the long war, few wanted to take up arms again over this
issue, even if the money were to be readily available, which it was not.

Murat's main supporter at the congress was actually Prince Metternich. This was, by no means, a surprise to insiders at the congress. Salon gossip traced his support back to the fact that Metternich had earlier carried on a passionate affair with Murat's wife, Napoleon's sister Caroline. Many believed that he was still supporting his former mistress. Metternich had certainly had that affair, and he had stayed in contact with her over the years, but he also had many other reasons for hesitating to remove Murat.

Most notably, back in January 1814, during a critical stage in the war, Metternich had signed an agreement regarding Naples: If Murat would desert Napoleon, Metternich would guarantee his right to the throne. Murat had deserted, to the benefit of the Allies. Now Metternich was trying to stick to his end of the bargain, though he did not personally like Murat, and he was taking a lot of heat, from Talleyrand in particular.

In early November, the Committee of Eight had held its first meeting to discuss the fate of Italy. Talleyrand, representing France on this committee, had participated fully. His argument, no surprise, was to remove Murat the usurper, "the last excrement of the revolution," and replace him with the legitimate king, Ferdinand IV.

Metternich reminded him that it would require a bloody campaign. Peasants all over the region were rushing to Murat's support, and who knew what he might do. He could very well call for the unification of Italy, rally the people behind his banner, and end up causing a massive civil war.

"Organize Italy," Talleyrand responded, and Murat would no longer have any supporters. Restore the *legitimate* crown, and Murat would be "no more to Italy than a brigand."

The Austrian foreign minister continued to speak of "complications"—which Talleyrand interpreted as a stratagem employed to "keep up the vagueness which his weak policy requires."

By the end of the meeting, the committee had decided to approach the problems of Italy in a methodical fashion, or at least a geographical one. They would begin their discussions in the north with the fate of the old republic of Genoa, which had been destroyed in the revolution. They would proceed down the peninsula, through Rome and the papacy, until they reached the murky areas of the south, ending with the issue of Naples.

Both Metternich and Talleyrand were happy with this arrangement.

France's minister planned to use the time to gain support for his principles of legitimacy, and Austria's minister hoped to flatter, tack, hedge, and stall the whole uncomfortable subject right out of the congress.

ONE EVENING, A few days after this meeting, Talleyrand returned to Kaunitz Palace and found a troubled Saxon minister waiting impatiently. The guest, Count Schulenburg, held a dispatch straight from the king of Saxony. It was not the usual lament about being uninvited to the congress or imprisoned outside of Berlin. The king had some other disturbing news.

> We have just learnt with great sorrow that our Kingdom of Saxony
> is to be temporarily occupied by the troops of His Prussian Majesty.

According to this report in Talleyrand's hands, the governor-general of Russian-occupied Saxony, Prince Nicolas Grégoriévitch Repnin-Wolkonski, had ordered the army to pull out and hand over the entire kingdom to the king of Prussia. The Prussians were to assume control of Saxony, effective immediately.

Warnings of the tsar's tendency to act unilaterally seemed to have hit their mark with an alarming accuracy. But there was something else unsettling about this announcement. When the Prussian army marched into the region, it made the startling claim that it acted with "the consent of Austria and of England."

Metternich was furious; he had done nothing of the sort. As he put it in his official letter, Austria had promised to accept the seizure of Saxony if—and only if—the Prussians succeeded in preventing Russian gains in Poland. Failure in this question rendered the offer void. Metternich's conditional acceptance was printed as if it had been absolute. It was a complete misrepresentation, he claimed.

Castlereagh also protested against this distortion of the facts, and showed concern about the implications for his diplomatic mission. He had gambled on Prussia and lost. The king of Prussia was now closer to the tsar than ever before; moreover, when the Russian army moved out of Saxony, it marched straight into Poland, fortifying its hold on the disputed territory. Russia was simply acting like the dictator of Europe, imposing its views on the other states. Castlereagh's policy was in shambles.

Chapter 16

THE LAST JOUST

The Congress seemed like a theatrical performance
while the house was burning.

—COUNTESS ELISE VON BERNSTORFF

While the congress worked and danced, there was a peculiar forty-seven-year-old in a small flat on the fourth floor of a narrow building on the Mölker Bastei, hunched over a black Auster pianoforte. He was a stocky man of average height, with a mass of dark curly hair, thick eyebrows, and an intense gaze. His nose was "square like a lion," and he had the most "marvelous dimples, formed by two jawbones capable of cracking the hardest nuts." This was Ludwig van Beethoven, and he was composing music for the Congress of Vienna.

During the autumn of 1814, Beethoven was at the height of his popularity. He had moved to Habsburg capital twenty-two years before, from Bonn, where he had been born in 1770. Beethoven had never liked Vienna or its people: "From the Emperor to the bootblack, all the Viennese are worthless," he had generalized. He did, however, enjoy the strolls, particularly out on the slopes of the Kahlenberg at the edge of the Vienna Woods.

Here he walked daily, sometimes "muttering and howling" as thoughts passed through his head. He made sure to bring along paper and pencil for any impromptu jottings—after all, he believed, it is the "woods, trees and rocks [that] produce the echo which man desires to hear." When Beethoven arrived back at his flat, he was known, on a good day, to rush excitedly to his black stool and proceed to lose himself at the keyboard. Walking companions, if there had been any, were quickly forgotten.

His rooms overlooking the old city wall were just as cluttered and untidy as his clothes were shoddy and sloppy. One musician who paid a visit, just after the congress, described them as "dreary almost sordid . . . in the greatest disorder: music, money, clothes lay on the floor, linen in a heap on the unclean bed, the open grand piano was covered in thick dust, and broken coffee cups lay on the table."

Beethoven was one of the first of a new generation of artists, regarded less as a craftsman for hire than as a genius, who, it was believed, could make his own rules and live on his own terms. The concept of genius, influenced by the Romantic movement, was changing, from a particular talent that someone possessed to a description that applied to the whole person, and Beethoven personified this shift. His odd behavior and eccentricities were tolerated as a hallmark of his genius.

Indeed, when he went out to dine at inns or restaurants, Beethoven preferred a table in the far corner, and would often sit there brooding. Gloomy and sullen at times, the musician liked to complain about the endless problems caused by his lazy or scheming servants or friends. He might also, suddenly and unexpectedly, lash out at anyone nearby. He had only recently hurled a plate of food at a waiter.

For the last two years, Beethoven's hearing had been steadily growing worse, and his guests already had to shout. Along with the deterioration, caused, it seems, by a growth in his inner ear by the bone, Beethoven's idiosyncrasies became more marked. He was in pain, and losing contact with the world of sound was only increasing his own sense of isolation. With his rough edges and abruptness, he had already been called an "unlicked bear." He was paying even less attention now to social conventions.

At the moment, the grumpy genius was preparing for the upcoming concert at the Redoutensaal of the Hofburg. His compositions, he knew, should celebrate the Allied victory over Napoleon, and commemorate the Congress of Vienna, convened to reconstruct Europe.

WHEN THE MONARCHS were not acting like "spoiled children" or "playing soldiers," as Baronne du Montet put it, they spent many mornings hunting—often stag, boar, hare, or pheasant. The English physician Richard Bright witnessed one of the hunting parties at the Congress of

Vienna and thought it had all the "barbarity of a bullfight." The carnage, however, was often on a much larger scale.

On November 10, the court traveled to the Lainzer Tiergarten outside Vienna for one such hunt. Some twenty stands had been constructed for the occasion, like an amphitheater. No fewer than six hundred wild boar, and a number of other animals, had been rounded up from nearby forests and were then released, a few at a time, into the small makeshift arena. The monarchs, ready with gun at hand and assistants at their side to help load, shot according to rank. First the emperors fired and then the kings, followed by the princes, dukes, field marshals, and so on. The Swiss banker Jean-Gabriel Eynard was appalled; there was no skill, stamina, or even risk. It was pure slaughter.

Meanwhile, as the Committee of Eight started working its way through the affairs of Italy, proceeding in a geographical fashion, as planned, the first item on the agenda was resolving the fate of Genoa, a port on the northeastern coast that had been a commercial power since the Middle Ages. The ancient republic had been seized by Napoleon, incorporated into his empire in 1805, and transformed, as lamented famously in the first sentence of Tolstoy's *War and Peace,* into the "private estates of the Bonaparte family." Now, with the war over, Genoa was eager to be restored to its independence and regain its former status as a free republic. This was, after all, what the city had been promised.

In the spring of 1814, at the end of the war, Great Britain had assured Genoa that its republic would be revived "as it had been before the Revolution." All the city had to do was officially support the Allied army. The Genoese accepted these terms, and now sent a delegation to Vienna to oversee its promised restoration.

But there was a rude shock awaiting the city's chief delegate, the twenty-eight-year-old scion of a prominent banking family, the Marquis de Brignole-Sale. Britain was now claiming that the man who made the offer of restoring the republic, Lord William Bentinck, the commander of the Mediterranean and minister to Sicily, was not authorized to make such a claim, as indeed he was not. Worse still, rumors circulated that Britain had promised that Genoa itself would be handed over to the king of Sardinia. The rumors were true. Castlereagh had signed his name to that agreement, a secret article attached to the Treaty of Paris.

Castlereagh and the Allies had reasoned that Genoa, a small and relatively weak republic, would be a temptation to future French aggression; moreover, situated as the city was near strategic Alpine mountain passages, the loss of Genoa could threaten all of north Italy as well. The king of Sardinia (Piedmont-Sardinia) could defend the territory much more effectively. Genoa was then just another part of Castlereagh's strategy of building an "iron ring" around France: the greater Netherlands in the north, the stronger Prussia in the east, and now this enlarged Sardinia in the south.

So despite the protests of Genoa's delegate, not to mention the millions he was said to be dispensing to lobby support, the Committee of Eight remained unmoved. Previous promises to the city were now denied and shrugged aside. Arguments for restoring the republic, the legitimate form of government before the war, were made in vain. The delegates simply pointed to the words inked in a secret article of the treaty, "The King of Sardinia will receive an addition to his territory in the state of Genoa," and proceeded to do just that.

As the Great Powers planned to proceed down the peninsula on to the next Italian questions, they were also busy appointing a number of standing committees, not too different from what Talleyrand had proposed. The first of the special committees, the German Committee, had been established in the middle of October to create a federation and write a constitution, though the trouble of Saxony had embittered all its discussions. On the sixteenth of November, the German Committee had actually stopped meeting. It would be some five months before this committee would convene again.

The Great Powers would eventually appoint ten such specialized committees. There would be one, for example, to ensure the free navigation of rivers, and another to sort out the tangled questions that governed diplomatic etiquette. Others would be created as the need arose.

One new committee, appointed on the twelfth of November, was the Swiss Committee, which, like its counterparts, clearly faced some major challenges. Switzerland, at the time of the Vienna Congress, was a federal union of some twenty-two cantons that varied greatly in culture and history. Some spoke French as their official language, others German, and one Italian, not to mention a few places like Engadine and Graubünden, which had a large minority population speaking a fourth language, the Latin-based Romansh. More divisive still, some cantons were predominantly Catholic, others Protestant. Some were bastions of aristocracy, and others fiercely democratic.

The cantons could not agree on their vision for Switzerland. Some wanted closer cooperation between the cantons, and others wanted less; some wanted in the federation, others out. Two different diets—or directing bodies—had been created the past year, one around the aristocratic Bern, the other around the more democratic Zürich. Many feared that their country was headed toward civil war. The Swiss Committee, it was hoped, would find a satisfying solution. It would be difficult to secure peace in Europe as long as war raged in its center.

BY THE MIDDLE of November, as new committees met behind closed doors, two main topics appeared to dominate discussions in Vienna salons. The first was the fate of the king of Saxony, whose kingdom had been seized by the Prussians. The second, more pleasantly, was the upcoming Carousel at the Spanish Riding School, a full-scale attempt to re-create a medieval tournament. Of all the grand spectacles at the Congress of Vienna, many thought that this was the greatest.

Vienna had been eagerly looking forward to the pageant, scheduled for Wednesday evening, November 23. The Festivals Committee had pored over accounts of other elaborate carousels from history, hoping to understand their conventions and then "surpass them in splendor."

The Spanish Riding School, designed by Josef Emanuel Fischer von Erlach and completed in 1735, was a magical setting for the Carousel. Underneath the crystal chandeliers blazing with candles, the arena was shaped in a long rectangle well suited for equestrian maneuvers. At one end was the imperial grandstand, with rows of gilded armchairs waiting for the sovereigns. The balcony at the other end of the hall was reserved for the twenty-four ladies selected to be the tournament's *belles d'amour,* the "Queens of Love," for whom their champions would battle. Galleries ran along the sides connecting the two grandstands. The columns around the hall were hung with the armor, weapons, and mottoes of the knights scheduled to compete.

Crowds started to arrive in the early evening, and by about seven, when La Garde-Chambonas arrived with Prince de Ligne, the arena was nearly full. Counterfeiters had once again produced a number of bogus tickets for the occasion, and the baron's police were put on the case. They wanted to prevent too many uninvited guests from gate-crashing their imagined medieval tournament.

Some thousand to twelve hundred people, it was estimated, packed the good seats in the two main galleries. One section was reserved for the high nobility of the Austrian empire, and another for the ambassadors, diplomats, and ranking plenipotentiaries at the congress. Even Wilhelm von Humboldt had set aside his enormous stacks of paper to attend the Carousel. Talleyrand had run into him that evening, and could not resist teasing him: "Does Your Excellency prefer horse-riding to statistics?"

What a sight it must have been: "an almost unbroken line of glittering gold and diamonds in their Court dresses and uniforms disappearing beneath their orders and embroideries." Dresses had been selected with the greatest care, and jewel boxes ransacked for gems that, in many cases, had been hidden since the turmoil of the French Revolution. One goldsmith in attendance confessed that he could not begin to estimate the worth of all the jewels on display. Princess Esterházy's dress alone was probably valued at 6 million francs. "I do indeed believe," said Dorothée, swept away in the enthusiasm, "we shall wear every pearl and diamond to be found in Hungary, Bohemia, and Austria."

Standing out in the audience, too, with his scarlet hat and silk habiliments, was the pope's delegate, Cardinal Consalvi, along with the sultan's representative, Mavrojény, in his turban and caftan. Castlereagh's wife, Emily, was also conspicuous, once again wearing her husband's Order of the Garter "as a kind of tiara" in her hair.

At eight o'clock, heralds blasted their trumpets to announce the arrival of the Queens of Love. Prince Metternich's seventeen-year-old daughter Marie had been chosen, along with the Duchess of Sagan, her sister Dorothée, Sophie Zichy, and Princess Pauline Esterházy. Each "queen" wore an exquisite velvet dress, La Garde-Chambonas observed, "trimmed with priceless lace, and sparkling with precious stones." Diamonds, emeralds, rubies, and sapphires reflected the glow of the chandeliers with a dazzling brilliance.

"My God," one Prussian had exclaimed with surprise at the ostentation, "three campaigns could be fought with that."

After the ladies promenaded through the arena, their long gossamer veils flowing behind, and reached their seats, the heralds sounded their horns again for the arrival of the Austrian emperor, the empress, and the train of sovereigns. Everyone stood. The Queens of Love removed their veils and the riding school erupted with "a storm of applause."

Scanning the crowds that evening revealed a number of conspicuous absences. Despite persistent rumors that she would attend, Napoleon's wife, Marie Louise, did not show. Notably absent, too, was Metternich. He could not bear watching his beloved Duchess of Sagan, a Queen of Love in her striking green velvet dress with matching jewel-encrusted green velvet cap. Worse still, her champion in the tournament was Prince Alfred von Windischgrätz.

The most obvious no-show, however, was the Russian tsar. Officially, Alexander was sick, though some speculated that this was just a convenient excuse for him to boycott the Austrian-sponsored entertainment. To those gossipers, the tsar's absence suggested deep divisions among the Great Powers, and probably also a sign of the congress's imminent rupture.

But despite this interpretation, plausible enough given the tensions of the moment, it seems that the tsar was in fact sick that night. A few days before the tournament, Alexander had been dancing in one of the ballrooms at the popular Mehlgrube on the Neuer Markt, and then suddenly collapsed on the dance floor. The fall had been so unexpected that many started speculating that the tsar had been poisoned (and one cook in the Hofburg kitchens was fired for his alleged involvement in this plot). Instead, the tsar was probably just exhausted from his long hours, his lack of sleep, and the overall stress from the congress. He had reportedly danced some thirty nights in a row. The night of the Carousel, the tsar was in bed at the Hofburg.

As the orchestra on the top floor of the Spanish Riding School struck up a martial piece, the tournament's twenty-four knights trotted out on powerful black Hungarian chargers, hoofs stomping the matted sand, which had been poured onto the floor to help break the fall of any unseated knight.

To be selected a champion, as La Garde-Chambonas put it, was "tantamount to a diploma in grace and elegance." The champions were generally from the old landed families. There was Prince Vincent Esterházy, Prince Anton Radziwill, and the Duchess of Sagan's lover, Prince Alfred von Windischgrätz. Another knight selected was Prince Leopold of Saxe-Coburg-Saalfeld, the future king of Belgium.

The Carousel at the Vienna Congress was, of course, an imitation of chivalry as it had flourished in a late revival, long after its heyday. The knights looked closer, if anything, to the early sixteenth century than the high Middle Ages. Hence, there were more trunks, hose, and snug velvet doublets with puffed sleeves than hot and heavy plate armor. Instead of cumbersome helmets, too, each knight wore a large diamond-buckled, broad-reamed hat, complete with a "plume of feathers drooping from the side."

The whole procession of champions, joined by squires carrying shields and pages waving large unfurled banners, made its way around the arena, stopping just in front of the sovereigns. The knights did homage, standing in the stirrups, turning to bow to the assembled monarchs, and then "dipping their lances" respectfully to the queens and empresses in the gallery. Then, after paying homage to their Queens of Love at the other end of the hall, they prepared to begin the games.

The first challenge was the so-called *pas de lance,* a "tilting at the rings," which involved champions charging on horseback and lowering the lance to pierce rings hanging from ribbons. Among other events, the knights tossed javelins at fake Saracen heads, or charged forward, scimitar in hand, to slice an apple dangling by a ribbon from the ceiling.

Then it was time for the main event, the mock combat of a joust. This was not like the tournaments of the Middle Ages, when soldiers could and indeed did die on the field, like the unfortunate tournament in 1240 that ended with some eighty knights dead. The Carousel at the Congress, by contrast, was intended to be a highly stylized simulation. The knights were to ride in a gallop and try to unseat their opponent, but the judges had urged that they show the utmost civility. The event did, in fact, go well. The only incident was when Prince Liechtenstein was unhorsed and carried off the field unconscious.

After some further displays of horsemanship, the knights riding to "a kind of dance to the rhythm of the music," the sovereigns, the Queens of Love, and their champions then led the way out of the riding school and into the palace for a banquet. The sovereigns had their own special table, where everything was gilded, from the forks to the fruit baskets. In large rooms, circulating around the banquet tables, acrobats tumbled, jesters juggled, and minstrels, with harp in hand, serenaded the guests. The evening culminated in a grand ball for some three thousand guests.

The Festivals Committee had attempted to create "a never-to-be-forgotten feature of the brilliant" congress, and they had certainly put on a show. The organizers pledged to present another "precise replica" of the tournament for the absent tsar. The details might not have been strictly correct historically, but the sovereigns were happy. The committee had even created a special place for the large king of Württemberg, "five feet in height and six in girth." As few diaries fail to recount, the committee had cut a "large half-moon" shape from the dining table to "accommodate his fabulous paunch."

And so, as kings, queens, champions, and the revelers glided and twirled across the parquet floors, the "dazzling Carousel" drowned out the diplomatic difficulties of the moment.

Chapter 17

"THE GLORIOUS MOMENT"

We make but slow progress in our affairs and yet we are not idle.

—TALLEYRAND

No amount of glitter, however, could obscure the troubles, and the baron's informants detected considerable grumbling outside the palaces, ballrooms, and haunts of the exclusive society at play. The "thinkers and idlers" congregating on the Graben were loudly criticizing the congress for its unrestrained indulgence. Why couldn't the delegates put the same energies into ironing out a just peace as they did in organizing tournaments? Would diplomats ever really have an incentive to wrap up negotiations as long as Emperor Francis continued to open house so freely and set out fifty banquet tables almost every night?

Austrian patriots worried about the great expenses for this lavish entertainment, and wondered how the emperor would ever be able to pay for it all. They also disliked the glaring contrast between the generous Vienna hosts and the countless houseguests, who seemed ungrateful to say the least. Some of the allies from the war, like the Russian tsar, even behaved more like enemies. One spy reported the sentiment that Austria's generosity threatened to cripple its economy if not bankrupt the state: "This is a new way to wage war: eat your enemy."

All the frustration and resentment was only compounded by the exclusiveness of the club of diplomats meeting behind closed doors, and the apparent ridiculousness of some disputes. The leaders were bickering over who entered or left a room first, who sat where at a dinner, who signed a document first. There is a legend that Metternich had several extra doors cut into his office to allow the negotiators to enter and leave at the same time. This is not true, but the issues were real enough.

Protocol was a reflection of power and prestige, especially as diplomats at this time represented monarchs, rather than the state, and everyone could be highly sensitive to any slight. Famously, in September 1661, when a Swedish envoy arrived in London, the Spanish ambassador refused to follow France in the welcoming procession and raced ahead, nearly causing a riot, a scandal, and a declaration of war.

At the congress, business had literally stalled over such issues. The declaration of October 8, which postponed the opening of the congress until November 1, for instance, had been unsigned, in part, because the plenipotentiaries could not agree over the order of signatures. The German Committee experienced countless troubles as its members jostled for precedence—that is, until it stopped meeting entirely.

Perhaps standardizing the rules governing diplomatic transactions would help ease tensions that sometimes bedeviled negotiations. There was no consensus, however, on how to achieve this goal. How much, for instance, should protocol at a negotiation be based on a state's power? What distinctions, if any, should be drawn between representatives of a kingdom and representatives of a republic? What about between the Continent's oldest and most legitimate dynasties, and the newest creations spawned by the sword of Bonaparte? The Congress of Vienna's most recent committee, the Committee on Diplomatic Precedence, which would be meeting by the middle of December under the leadership of Spain's Labrador, was established to sort out those questions.

Still other concerns were heard in Vienna's drawing rooms. Some of the older generation believed that all this hobnobbing with kings would only damage royal prestige. How unbecoming it was, even Talleyrand remarked, "to meet three or four kings, and a still greater number of princes at balls and teas at the houses of private individuals." The situation had almost degenerated into a farce. The Geneva banker Jean-Gabriel Eynard confessed that one night at a party he saw the king of Prussia standing alone against the wall, and confused him with a waiter. He nearly asked the king to fetch him a glass of champagne.

For a number of reasons, many were unhappy with the conference, and the city's discontented sought out places to vent and exchange news. The tavern-inn Empress of Austria was a favorite for a cosmopolitan group of thinkers, who wanted to escape the rigors of court etiquette and speak more freely. Another spot, the Three White Lions Café, was popular especially with many young Germans who met for heated debate over wine and oysters.

Interestingly, some of the most popular centers for information and criticism were churches in the city. Many of the people in town crowded into wherever the energetic priest Zacharias Werner happened to be preaching his provocative and often highly unpredictable sermons. From the pulpit, this tall and thin man with long hair that had been compared to a lion's mane would consistently blast the Vienna Congress as a sorry spectacle of vanity and frivolity. This general theme could be elaborated and varied at will. Most recently, he had preached about how the mob of emperors, kings, and princes in town had clearly fallen under the spell of another ruler, the real ruler of the Vienna Congress: King Foolishness.

Prior to his conversion to Catholicism several years before, Werner had spent much of his career around a theater, and it showed. He had been a playwright who had composed a number of works, including the tragedy *The Twenty-fourth of February,* which had been staged by Goethe. At the age of forty-two, Werner had been overwhelmed by the experience of Mass, and converted. The former vagabond poet renounced his previous debauchery, and traded his activities in the brothel and the stage for the pulpit, and even, for a few years, a monastic cell in southern Italy.

It was during the peace conference that Werner had made his way to Vienna. In a city overflowing with theater, both on the stage and in the streets, Werner had attracted a considerable following. He boasted enthusiasm and passion, though some objected to the language of this fiery preacher, claiming it was as coarse as a coachman and probably better suited to the tavern.

On one Sunday, for example, when the pews were once again packed in the Franciscan church, Father Zacharias veered his sermon onto a discussion of a certain part of the human anatomy—"a tiny piece of flesh . . . on a man's body"—that often led to the most difficult temptations and the most flagrant transgressions. Its effects were evidenced every day at the congress. The audience must have wondered where this unpredictable priest was headed. Then, gripping the edge of the pulpit, Werner leaned his thin face toward the congregation and asked, "Shall I show you that tiny piece of flesh?"

The congregation was "deathly silent," and then, after an "agonizing pause," the priest answered: "Ladies and gentlemen behold the source of our sins." For those who looked up, Father Zacharias was standing there showing the organ in question: He had stuck out his tongue.

To the sound of "nervous giggling" and the relief of the congregation, the priest reminded how the tongue wagged in excess seriously damaged relationships. Gossip, however, was not to be vanquished so easily, and it would continue to rage, dividing the peacemakers until it seemed that it might succeed foolishness as the uncrowned king of the congress.

IN LATE NOVEMBER, the scheduled day for Ludwig van Beethoven's highly anticipated Gala Concert was nearing. The first date picked for the event, November 20, had been moved back a couple of days due to the unexpected illness of the Austrian emperor.

Indeed, as exhaustion seemed pervasive, a vicious flulike virus swept Vienna in late November. Just as the tsar and the emperor had been forced to spend several days at rest, Prince Metternich also succumbed, as did the king of Prussia, Prince Hardenberg, Princess Bagration, Dorothée, and a host of others. In a congress dominated by fashion, it suddenly seemed almost fashionable to be sick. Fortunately, though, this flu—the congress's "uninvited guest"—would leave town as quietly as it had arrived.

Two additional postponements of the concert followed that week, the last one because of English protests against holding a concert on a Sunday. Soon Beethoven's concert seemed uncannily like the Vienna Congress itself, riddled with delays, protests, and postponements.

On Tuesday, November 29, Beethoven was finally able to hold the Gala Concert at the Redoutensaal. The program promised a full afternoon of music, and tickets cost only 3 gulden, or 5 gulden for the better seats upstairs. A stellar audience filled the auditorium, including the Russian tsar, the king of Prussia, and many other princes and princesses.

The concert began with "Wellington's Victory" (also known as "The Battle Symphony"), a triumphant celebration of the Battle of Vitoria, with its creative sampling from "Rule Britannia" and "God Save the King," packed with drumrolls, trumpet fanfares, cymbal crashes, and veritable cannon blasts that re-created the "horrors of battle" and the joyous celebration of the victory over the Napoleonic beast. It was an explosive extravaganza quite unusual for classical music at the time.

Beethoven had originally written the music for an instrument called the panharmonicon, a small handheld box designed to reproduce mechanically the wind, brass, and string sections of a large orchestra. The device had been invented by Beethoven's collaborator, Johann Nepomuk Mälzel, the "Court Mechanician," whose inventions included an ear trumpet and a "Mechanical Trumpeter" that sounded military marches. He also claimed to have invented a mechanical chess player that had supposedly defeated Napoleon in a game of chess during his occupation of Vienna (actually, the real inventor was Wolfgang von Kempelen, and the trick, of course, was a man hidden inside the machine). Another one of his inventions that might have been useful at a congress swarming with spies was a desk with secret compartments guarded by a built-in mechanism that, if disturbed, released a deafening alarm and thick iron locks that automatically gripped the wrists of the transgressor.

It was this rogue inventor and showman who had suggested that Beethoven revamp "Wellington's Victory" for a real orchestra and launch the piece at a public concert packed with Vienna's virtuosos. And in the patriotism sweeping Vienna after the war, Beethoven's work was a hit. The audience in the Redoutensaal received it with rapturous applause.

The second work, the new cantata "The Glorious Moment," was named in honor of the Congress of Vienna. The text was written by a surgeon named Alois Weissenbach, who had come to Vienna for the peace conference, and Beethoven set the patriotic poem to music. This piece has not aged well, often dismissed by critics as "absurdly bombastic." Yet it, too, opened to huge applause. Neither composer, however, could hear this response. Like Beethoven, Weissenbach was deaf.

The concert concluded with the Seventh Symphony, billed as the "new large Symphony." This was, however, not literally new. Beethoven had completed this symphony back in the spring of 1812, and he had actually performed it publicly in December 1813. It was a notoriously difficult piece of music, and the musicians objected at first. Beethoven himself conducted, and was said to "crouch down at the soft passages" and then suddenly leap up for the louder ones. The audience loved it, and Vienna's newspaper, the *Wiener Zeitung*, raved about the performance.

Actually, it seems, Beethoven was not really directing the concert. He was on stage, of course, moving his baton, but the real director was his assistant, Ignaz Umlauf. As historian Ingrid Fuchs rightly shows, Beethoven was no longer capable of directing complicated pieces. Less than a month later, the musician, Ludwig Spohr, heard one of Beethoven's rehearsals and testified to the decline: Beethoven's pianoforte was "badly out of tune," and "the poor deaf musician hammered the keys so hard in forte that the strings rattled." Beethoven made countless mistakes, and the visitor left, as he put it, "gripped by profound sorrow at such a miserable fate."

Beethoven's patron, the Russian ambassador Count Razumovsky, looked on loyally with admiration, claiming that the "world is too small for him." Others were less impressed, prone to judge Beethoven's compositions as too loud, too long, and too heavy, "like Hercules using his club to kill flies." Indeed, just as the congress had split in Russian and Austrian factions, police spies reported that "anti- and pro-Beethoven factions [were] forming." Sure enough, since Beethoven had been supported by a Russian patron and the tsar, the Austrians stayed away from the concert, and the English were not much in evidence there, either. Entertainment, it seemed, was echoing diplomacy.

That night, Beethoven was exhausted, he confessed, by the many "fatiguing affairs, vexations, pleasure and delight, all intermingled and interflicted or bestowed upon me at once." He also complained about the measly tips he received. The king of Prussia, who left halfway through the concert, gave only a "very paltry" 10 ducats, whereas the Russian tsar generously paid some twenty times that.

As BEETHOVEN CONDUCTED "The Glorious Moment," the congress it celebrated was still no closer to resolving its disputes.

The Russian tsar was increasingly viewed as a villain. Besides his rude treatment of foreign ministers, he had arbitrarily handed over one kingdom to his allies, and ordered his army to occupy another. Everything seemed to confirm the worst fears of some diplomats—that he was a dangerous megalomaniac. Gentz summed up the sentiment: "The language of justice and truth is not one Russia understands."

At a ball, for instance, Alexander approached the beautiful Countess Széchenyi-Guilford and asked flirtatiously, "Madame, I note that your husband is not present; may I have the pleasure of occupying his place temporarily?" Her response expressed the frustrations of many: "Does Your Majesty take me for a province?"

Vienna's drawing rooms and makeshift embassy suites also buzzed with heated discussion of Prussia's controversial seizure of the kingdom of Saxony. Outside of the Prussian delegation and its few allies, opinion was overwhelming negative. Many complained of "the detestable Prussians" and denounced their occupation as an outrageous breach of international law.

In fact, many German states had started a petition to resist this aggression. Smaller and midsized states that felt threatened by Prussia signed to protect their "unfortunate brother," the king of Saxony, agreeing that they could not sanction such a dreadful and unjust "act of violence."

This petition against the Prussian annexation made its rounds, and was soon signed by almost every major prince or delegate in Germany. By the middle of December, however, the protest was dead. The reason was simple. The Prussians had made known, in no uncertain terms, that they would regard any state that signed the petition as an outright enemy. One by one, the weaker powers had asked to remove their signatures.

After the Prussian occupation and the intimidation that squashed the protest, tempers were flaring, and feelings of betrayal burned on all sides. Talleyrand took quill in hand and penned one of the more remarkable documents of the Vienna Congress. This paper, a letter addressed to Metternich dated the nineteenth of December, was an elegant combination of philosophy and policy that affirmed the importance of justice and the rights of states in the face of aggression in international affairs.

The French foreign minister first reminded Metternich that his country asked nothing for itself. France was satisfied with its borders and had no desire whatsoever for additional territory. What his embassy hoped instead was to persuade its fellow peacemakers to agree to one guiding principle, namely, "that everywhere and forever the spirit of revolt be quenched, that every legitimate right be made sacred."

France aspired, in other words, to create a situation whereby "every ambition and unjust enterprise [would] find both its condemnation and a perpetual obstacle." This might sound like a grand, unattainable ideal, he said, but Europe really had no choice. Without such principles in place, held firm and rigorously guarded, international affairs would soon degenerate into a reckless pursuit of self-interest and power—just as that reckless scramble had plunged the Continent into that "long and deadly horror" of the last quarter century.

Now that Napoleon was defeated, Europe must take this opportunity to crown justice as the "chief virtue" of international affairs. Leaders of states must pledge that they would never act nor acquiesce in any deed that could not be considered just, "whatever consideration [that] may arise," because only justice, he said, can produce a true state of harmony and stability. Anything short of that would create a misleading and meaningless false order, destined to collapse when the first powerful state decided to take advantage of its superior strength.

"Might does not make right," Talleyrand reminded. Has not Europe, he added, suffered enough from that doctrine, and paid for it "with so much blood and so many tears"? The golden age of peace could be right around the corner, if only every peacemaker would follow this course of action.

Talleyrand had pored over this statement, selecting every word with care, and he made sure it circulated in Vienna. He personally handed a copy of the letter to the tsar's minister, Adam Czartoryski, and sent another one to Castlereagh. Talleyrand's audience, he clearly hoped, was not only Metternich, but also Vienna and, ideally, eventually the Continent at large.

While many praised Talleyrand's masterpiece, as admirers already dubbed it, the Prussians were not so happy. For them, this was, of course, nothing more than another clever yet thinly veiled attempt on the part of France to sow discord among the Allies for her own gain, and the Prussian ministers lost no time trying to undermine and discredit this statement. This was Talleyrand, after all. Was this man, with his string of broken oaths, really to be taken seriously? Some in the Prussian embassy circulated stories that the French were trying to seize the left bank of the Rhine and Belgium, as they had done in the 1790s.

Besides that, Talleyrand's position was being undermined by another rumor, this one undoubtedly true.

News trickled into Vienna that France was becoming highly unstable. King Louis XVIII, after only six months on the throne, was very unpopular, and his whole government was as detested as the French government had been on the eve of the Revolution. Generals were restless. Soldiers missed Napoleon, and so did many veterans who had been reduced to half pay, or even unceremoniously dismissed at the end of the war, and now, in the postwar recession, were forced to beg or steal. A report reached Talleyrand in December from the War Office telling of a regiment of the king's infantry that had "burnt its [Napoleonic] eagles, collected the ashes, and each soldier swallowed a portion of them while drinking a cup of wine to the health of Bonaparte."

All of this made Talleyrand's life more difficult. He seemed to represent a king who was losing his grip on his country, where, unfortunately, "nothing but conspiracies, secret discontent and murmuring" reigned. No matter how confident Talleyrand appeared, and he was as calm as usual, it was easy for the Prussians to cast doubts on his credibility. As they put it, the French minister either did not know the true state of the crisis back home, or he was covering up. Clearly, Talleyrand would have to step up his own campaign, so he called for his chef.

Chapter 18

THE COOK, THE PAINTER, THE BALLERINA, AND THE DIPLOMAT

I was sleeping beside a volcano, without a thought for the lava that would pour out of it.

—METTERNICH ON THE FRENCH REVOLUTION

Flying from the towers on both sides of the island harbor was Elba's brand-new flag, a white banner with a diagonal red stripe adorned with three golden bees. Napoleon himself had designed it, back in May 1814, while still on board the *Undaunted*. A tailor on the ship borrowed some sailcloth and sewed the first two flags for the new empire.

The new palace was not exactly the Tuileries. Napoleon would not be surrounded by his familiar bronze gilt chairs with griffins' heads, or his favorite table, an hourglass-shaped piece of furniture that he had invented to facilitate close collaborative work. Absent, too, was the large oil painting of King Louis XIV, with the head of the Sun King wearing a red, white, and blue republican cockade. The luxurious environment may have changed, but Napoleon was still the same man, only a little older, thinner on top, and rounder in the middle.

The forty-five-year-old emperor would still wear out the floors with his rapid pacing up and down a room, all the while firing off dictation to a secretary who sat there "as silent as another piece of furniture." The faster Napoleon spoke, the quicker he paced, and his secretary hurried to keep up.

Once he had found his house, orders flew out of his mouth in a spirited and disjointed whirlwind. Masons, carpenters, and architects were hired and ordered to complete the renovation plans, which Napoleon had also designed himself. He was adding a second floor, accessed by new pink marble stairs and consisting of two four-room suites, linked by a grand spacious salon. One of the wings was for his wife, and the other his son, who had not arrived and showed no signs of doing so. The eight windows added light to the house's most majestic room. Shutters, however, were necessary. Napoleon's palace had a tendency, in the hot Elban sun, to heat up to a "veritable furnace."

Restless as ever, Napoleon had moved in, back in late May, amid a flurry of remodeling activity in the largely unfinished construction site. Scaffolding had still covered the front facade, and the inside reeked of fresh paint. White and gold armchairs were lugged up to the salon, the workers sidestepping the cement that had not yet dried. The dark wooden chairs with green silk were going to the study, along with his mahogany desk, glass-encased bookshelves, and a gray wooden couch adorned with gold lions and covered with yellow silk.

The ceiling of the bedroom was being painted to resemble a military tent. As for other furniture, he sent a ship to the mainland and raided his sister Élisa's abandoned palaces in Tuscany, now occupied by Austrian troops. Napoleon was still angry at her for deserting him for the Allies. Napoleon's villa was to be decorated with furniture literally stolen from her, including a desk, a clock, and even her famous gilded dark oak bed. It was a superb policy, he joked. He had raided Austria and punished his sister, all at the same time.

To keep up the palace, Napoleon was hiring staff to fill the newly created positions. There was a chief cook and a chief baker to oversee the team of thirteen people preparing meals in the kitchens. There were nineteen other servants in the house, as well as valets, gardeners, coachmen, grooms, harness makers, stablemen, locksmiths, tailors, and many others in their brand-new green coats with gold braids. If the salary was not great, the positions had other benefits. Some of the kitchen boys were so proud of being near the famous man that they strutted about town like "little Napoleons."

The emperor had hired an international group, including French, Italians, Elbans, and Corsicans. A pianist from Florence was recruited as the new director of music, and a woman from a local village selected as the mistress of the wardrobe. A fellow Corsican was named court hairdresser, and his work was cut out for him. Napoleon's hair had become so lumpy and shaggy in the humidity that it was compared to candlesticks.

But there was one other important figure on the island: a soldier from Great Britain who was asked to look after Napoleon and keep in close contact with London. This was Neil Campbell, a thirty-eight-year-old officer, a Highlander by birth, who had fought the French in the West Indies, Spain, and elsewhere. By the end of the war, Campbell was serving as military attaché to the Russian tsar. He had won respect with his bravery, and in fact had been severely wounded in battle, taking a saber blow to the head and a lance point in his back. As he set off for Elba, his head was still wrapped in bandages and his right arm cast in a sling.

That such a relatively unknown man was chosen to accompany the former ruler of the Continent may seem surprising, and many have wondered about the appointment, made by no less than Castlereagh. But the truth of the matter is that few were willing to take on this responsibility. More prominent figures had already declined the post, hardly relishing the prospects of being cooped up with Napoleon on some "little island half forgotten in the sea."

The position would certainly have its difficulties. For one thing, Castlereagh had not explained very clearly what Campbell was supposed to do. It wasn't that he received secret instructions or contradictory orders, but rather that he had had almost no guidance at all. Campbell had not been officially informed of the terms of Napoleon's abdication, or even been shown the treaty itself. What he knew came from reading the newspaper and using his own initiative.

The closest Campbell came to having clear instructions was Castlereagh's general directive to keep Napoleon free from "insult and attack" and not to address him as Your Highness—only "General Bonaparte." It was a vague task that left an enormous amount to his discretion. One historian well summarized Campbell's role as part bodyguard, part spy, and part ambassador. Campbell was effectively turned loose to sink or swim, but, above all, to do so in a way that would not reflect poorly on British leadership. For what was Britain doing there, anyway, a country that had not even signed the treaty?

So there they were, an obscure young officer and the former ruler of Europe. And yet this unlikely pair would get along fairly well. Napoleon seemed to enjoy the company, calling him, in his thick Corsican accent, "Combell." They would talk about everything from Scotland to warfare, and one day, in conversation, Napoleon confessed the greatest mistake of his career: He had not made peace back in 1813, when he had had the chance to save his throne and his empire. All he had to do was to come to Prague and negotiate a settlement in good faith. He refused. "I was wrong," Napoleon said, "but let any one imagine himself in my place." After so many victories, he had faith in his army and chose "to throw the dice once more."

"I lost," Napoleon concluded, "but those who blame me have never drunk of fortune's intoxicating cup."

BACK IN VIENNA, several reports from Elba reached the congress. Talleyrand had heard from many Swiss, Italian, and other travelers who all believed that Napoleon was getting restless. "Bonaparte will not remain in banishment at Elba," one informant bluntly predicted.

With cool, polished finesse honed by years of intrigue, Talleyrand lobbied to have Napoleon moved farther away from Europe. Few, this time, were listening. Napoleon, after all, had been defeated, and banished into exile with an army of only four hundred men. The British Royal Navy was patrolling the waters, as were several French warships. Napoleon might be restless and unhappy, but what exactly could he do? The Vienna Congress hardly seemed distressed by these rumors.

But the king of France knew something that many plenipotentiaries in Vienna did not. Prior to Napoleon's arrival on Elba, the French government had stripped the island's warehouses bare, removing everything from guns and ammunition to government treasuries. Captain Thomas Ussher, the commander of the HMS *Undaunted,* which ferried the emperor into exile, already observed Napoleon's "dismay," as he put it with characteristic understatement. Other insults and injuries had been inflicted on the emperor. None of the 2 million francs promised in the Treaty of Abdication had been paid; worse still, another 10 million francs of Napoleon's personal property had been seized by the king of France.

For many royalists, Napoleon's presence on Elba alone constituted a grave security threat for the restored Bourbon dynasty, whose popularity was plummeting, particularly among soldiers and artisans, many of whom openly mourned the emperor. Leaving Napoleon on Elba was, under the circumstances, risky at best.

While Talleyrand made appeals in Vienna's salons and drawing rooms, someone at the French embassy was apparently planning to take matters into his own hands. The evidence is sketchy, and there are many unanswered questions. But papers uncovered by chambermaids inside the embassy suggest that someone there was in fact working on a plan to kidnap Napoleon. The trail leads to Talleyrand's number two, the Duke of Dalberg, if not also to Talleyrand himself.

The plan was being coordinated with the help of the French consulate in Livorno, which Talleyrand, as foreign minister, had reestablished three months before. Talleyrand had personally selected the consul, Chevalier Mariotti, a Corsican who had once provided security for Napoleon's sister Élisa, and now, for some reason, held a grudge against the Bonaparte family. Mariotti had spent the autumn extending his network of agents and informants, recruiting heavily from nearby seaports. Gradually, he had built up a fairly accurate picture of Napoleon's life on Elba, including the times when he was most vulnerable. The emperor, for instance, often sailed to the neighboring island of Pianosa, traveling with only a fraction of the guard he used at his palace, and then sleeping on board one of his ships. "It will be easy," Mariotti had informed the French embassy in late September, "to kidnap him and take him to Ile Sainte Margueritte."

Apparently, Chevalier Mariotti had hired a young Italian adventurer to pose as an olive oil merchant, travel to Elba, and arrange the abduction. On the last day of November, the "olive oil merchant" arrived at the island capital. According to his passport, he was a thirty-three-year-old Italian patriot from Lucca named Alessandro Forli, though it is by no means certain that this was his real name. He registered with authorities at the Star Fort, and then slipped away amid a crowd of other arrivals, which Britain's Neil Campbell summed up as "mysterious adventurers and disaffected characters." The oil merchant had no difficulty extending his contacts in the capital. Soon he was selling oil at Napoleon's court and waiting to act.

EARLY DECEMBER MARKED the beginning of Advent season, the four weeks of contemplation and reflection that culminate in the celebration of Christmas. During this time, authorities frowned on Catholics who acted frivolously, and some hostesses feared that this might put their salons at a disadvantage, compared with rivals of a different confession. The Duchess of Sagan, a Protestant, and Princess Bagration, who was Russian Orthodox, could continue entertaining as they liked.

Banquets and masked balls would, indeed, take place throughout the season, and there was also a marked increase in intimate dinner parties. One of the favorite sites was Friedrich von Gentz's flat on the Seilergasse. Guests climbed the steep staircase, entered the small apartment on the fourth floor, and squeezed around the table, elbow room only, in the middle of the dining room. On many occasions, with so many at the table, footmen carrying plates had difficulty maneuvering in the narrow space between the chair and the wall. Metternich, Talleyrand, Humboldt, and Princess Bagration were regulars at his highly sought-after dinners.

At one such party, there were many distinguished guests huddled around Gentz's table. During the course of the meal, one of the guests, a German-born American citizen, Dr. Justus Bollmann, started a discourse on the merits of the United States. In particular, he raved about the virtues of a republican form of government—all this to a table of ministers who represented emperors, kings, and princes. Gentz, clearly troubled with the uncomfortable choice of subjects, was said to look "as though murder had been attempted in his presence."

Dr. Bollmann had arrived in Vienna that autumn, hoping to convince some rich patron to invest in his many projects. Among other things, he had drawn up a plan for creating an Austrian national bank and another one for putting a new coin, minted in platinum, into circulation. He also wanted to start a steamship company on the Danube, and increase trade links between Austria and the New World, particularly in quicksilver, linen, watches, and musical instruments. Dinners such as this one were among the best places to make contacts and informally pitch his ideas. So far, though, he was not having any luck.

At another dinner party, hosted by Count Zichy, guests traded ghost stories, very much in vogue in the flourishing Romanticism of the day. Sitting on the floor of a drawing room in the large mansion, to the light of a single candle, Prince Radziwill was telling of a haunted castle back in Poland. Then, all of a sudden, the salon door "creaked slowly open" and then slammed shut again. As one guest in attendance described it, "ladies screamed, gentlemen leapt to their feet," and then Count Zichy, smiling, confessed that he had tied a string to the door. Everyone laughed, particularly the king of Denmark.

It was at the Zichys' where the search for new and exciting ways to pass the time already took on innovative forms. Among other things, there were games of chess in which creatures of the salon, wearing the costumes of kings, queens, bishops, knights, and pawns, moved at command on the large black-and-white squared floor.

Dorothée, too, was relishing the many opportunities for enjoyment, and a new man was often at her side, a young Austro-Bohemian aristocrat and army officer, Count Karl Clam-Martinitz. He was only twenty-two years old and already a reputed favorite of the former Allied commander, Prince Schwarzenberg. It was this same Count Clam who had had the unusual experience of having saved Napoleon's life (eight months before, in April 1814, when he had helped escort the emperor to Elba, and then rescued him from some hostile crowds of southern France).

Dorothée had caught his eye at last month's Carousel, and it was their mutual acquaintance, Gentz, who had introduced them. Count Clam was soon paying visits to the French embassy; the two were seen riding together in the Prater, and dining in restaurants, such as the fashionable Roman Empress. In honor of Dorothée's new beau, Talleyrand's chef had created a new dessert, the divine "Clam-Martinitz Torte."

Talleyrand's chef had actually served several new dishes in honor of the delegates. There was, for instance, "Bombe à la Metternich" and "Nesselrode Pudding." The latter, named after the Russian foreign minister, was a feast of chestnuts, currants, raisins, and whipped cream—and if that weren't sweet enough, it was soaked overnight in Maraschino, and served in a pineapple-sized dome.

No wonder French embassy dinners were becoming increasingly popular and well attended. All the chef's meals—those towering culinary creations, fantastic cream sauces, and rich, sweet desserts—were doing wonders for French diplomacy. "I don't need secretaries, as much as saucepans," Talleyrand was said to have quipped when asked what he required in Vienna.

Someone else helping the French image in town was the ballerina Emilia Bigottini, whose breathtaking performances on stage did not hurt the popularity of the French. This was also true for the French painter

Jean-Baptiste Isabey, who had set up his studio near Café Jungling in the Leopoldstadt, where he was busy painting the portraits of congress dignitaries.

Every Monday, when the painter opened the doors to his studio, guests flocked there to see and be seen amid the half-finished and barely started oils of leading lights that crammed the room. Carriages were parked outside the entrance and lined the street, a testament to the popularity of his studio, "the rendezvous of crowned heads," as Isabey boasted. The painter, with his wit and delightful tales of the foibles of Napoleonic Paris, was a hit.

It was, of course, Talleyrand's idea to invite the cook, the ballerina, and the painter to Vienna—and each one, in his or her own way, was reminding the Vienna Congress that the real France was the civilized champion of sweetness and light, not the Bonapartes and their gang of usurpers.

ALONG WITH THE intimate dinners and the formal feasts, other forms of entertainment were in vogue during Advent, such as the *tableaux vivants,* or "living pictures," which consisted of actors appearing on stage frozen in certain poses that depicted a well-known painting or image. La Garde-Chambonas and Prince de Ligne attended one of these tableaux in December in the grand ballroom of the imperial palace.

Arriving early to an already packed auditorium, the two were taken to their reserved seats next to Princess Marie Esterházy. When everyone was seated, an orchestra of "horns and harps" began playing, and the sovereigns made their entrance. Candles in the white and gold rococo ballroom were extinguished, so as to better focus attention onto the stage.

Scenes of history and mythology were then performed by amateur actors at the congress. There was "Louis XIV kneeling at Madame de la Vallière's feet," and then the ill-starred "Hippolytus refuting Phaedra's accusation before Theseus." The orchestra helped set the atmosphere with the works of Mozart, Haydn, and others, including Napoleon's stepdaughter Hortense, who had briefly, under the empire, been queen of Holland.

The highlight of this particular show was the depiction of the classical gods atop Mount Olympus. Parts were assigned for Jupiter, Juno, Mars, Minerva, Mercury, and the other deities. The person most suited to play

Apollo, famous for his beauty, was the Comte de Wrbna. He was a good match, except for one small thing: his mustache.

The managers tried to convince him to shave in time for the performance—no one had ever seen "the god of light wearing a distinctive hallmark of a hussar." It was a patent absurdity, the stage manager tried to argue; the whiskers had to go. Yet he was having no success, and eventually the empress of Austria intervened, persuading Count Wrbna to remove his "inconvenient ornament." At least diplomacy was making progress somewhere in Vienna, even if it was only on the illusory Mount Olympus of the Hofburg stage.

After the final "loud bravos," the sovereigns and guests went back to the palace for a ball, the actors still in costume. Guests mingled in a crowd that included the tsar, the emperor, and several kings and queens, along with the god of war, the goddess of love, and Louis XIV. The tsar, as usual, opened with a polonaise around the ballrooms, and his train of dancers marched up and down and through nearby rooms of the palace.

They passed Talleyrand, lounging in an armchair, discussing the future of Naples. Spain's Labrador and Cardinal Consalvi, along with a number of other delegates, were standing together deep in conversation. Castlereagh, leaning against a mantelpiece, was talking to an unnamed king. His brother, Lord Stewart, was roaming the rooms aimlessly, like some "golden peacock." Off in a side drawing room, the tsar and his train of dancers marched past some other diplomats locked in silent battles at the whist table.

After another "magnificent supper" at midnight, the ball ended, and the emperor's guests sauntered off "to recruit their strength for the next day by much-needed sleep."

EVENINGS CONTINUED TO be full of opportunities for entertainment, but the excitement did not end, of course, in the early morning hours when the sovereigns went to bed. Often, in fact, it was just beginning.

One night that December, for example, when La Garde-Chambonas was walking home, he took his usual route along the city walls. There on the bastions, much to his surprise, he met his good friend, the aged Prince de Ligne.

"What in Heaven's name are you doing here, Prince, at this hour of the night and in the biting cold?" La Garde-Chambonas asked with concern.

The prince, however, was not his usual self. He muttered something about love affairs, their delightful beginnings, and, afterward, their many painful moments. He was waiting for a rendezvous that apparently was not going to happen. "At your age, though," the prince said, "it was I who kept them waiting; at mine they keep me waiting; and, what's worse, they don't come."

Shaken by his wounded pride, Prince de Ligne showed a new unexpected "tinge of melancholy," noting how all things, at the end, "flee as age approaches." He was, at his advanced age, about to lose his illusions.

At the dawn of life . . . one carries the cup of pleasure to one's lips; one imagines it's going to last for ever, but years come, time flies, and delivers its Parthian darts.

"From that moment," he added, "disenchantment attends everything, the colors fade out of one's existence. Ah me, I must get used to the idea."

The prince went on about how he was no longer "good for anything." It was all a painful contrast to the days he was welcomed by Marie-Antoinette, celebrated by Catherine the Great, and sought after by Casanova. "My time is past, my world is dead."

After bidding good night to the melancholy prince, with assurances that they would meet again soon, La Garde-Chambonas walked home. On the way, he encountered another old friend, a certain "Count Z," who was just returning to his temporary residence at the hotel called the Roman Emperor.

Count Z was a young man about twenty-one years old and rich. His father, who had been a favorite of Catherine the Great, had recently died and left him a fortune. (Was this Count Zavadovsky?) La Garde-Chambonas joined him in his room and, over a few glasses, the two discussed the evening and decided to meet again the next morning, at noon, for a ride in the Prater. But when La Garde-Chambonas returned at the appointed time, he got a surprise.

With curtains drawn, the room was dark and Count Z was still in bed asleep. "Up, up! The horses are waiting for us! Or are you ill?" The count sat up and, holding back tears, said, "I lost two million roubles last night!"

"Are you mad or joking? You are in bed as I left you when I put out the lights."

The count explained that some of his friends had come by shortly afterward, relit the candles, and challenged him to a game. They had played all night.

When La Garde-Chambonas pulled back the curtains, he could see that the floor was still "littered with cards." He was determined to set things right, and went to have a word with the gamblers. No avail. Then he tried the Russian delegation, which might put some pressure on the cardsharps who had despoiled his friend of his inheritance.

He encountered more resistance than he had expected. "Is it worthwhile to make so much ado about the loss of a few boumashkis-boumashkis?" the unnamed diplomat said, referring to the money.

"Europe in Vienna sits round a table covered with a green cloth; she is gambling for states and a cast of the diplomatic dice involves the loss or gain of a hundred thousand, nay, of a million of heads. Why should not I win a few bits of paper when luck favors me?"

Count Z, it seemed, would just be another person that autumn who had lost out in the high-stakes gambling in Vienna.

$\mathcal{I}$NDISCRETION

It is rumored that the congress will terminate on the 15th December.
Let the thought of the closing of the Congress be
with you every moment, as it is with me.

—PRINCE DE LIGNE ON HOW TO TAKE ADVANTAGE OF THE
LAST DAYS OF THE FESTIVE PEACE CONFERENCE

$\mathcal{A}$s the peacemakers struggled over Prussia's seizure of Saxony, Castlereagh was disillusioned with the apparent collapse of his strategy, stumbling around like "a traveler who has lost his way." On December 6, a dispatch from the prime minister's office in London arrived at his headquarters, and it only added to his discomfort.

The British government had learned of their minister's idiosyncratic, indeed disobedient, behavior from many sources, including both Austria and France. The prime minister, Lord Liverpool, ordered him to adhere strictly to British policy in the future. He had now to turn, volte-face, and support the Kingdom of Saxony.

Frustratingly, too, the English dispatch also ordered Castlereagh, in a sweeping and unqualified declaration, to stop antagonizing Britain's allies, meaning particularly, of course, Russia. Britain was still fighting a war across the Atlantic with the United States, Castlereagh was reminded, and the government did not want to risk another war in Europe, especially not over these issues deemed tangential to their interests. The letter clearly stated that this went for "any of the objects which have been hitherto under discussion in Vienna."

With new orders in hand, Castlereagh now faced the unpleasant task of confronting the Prussian chancellor. Uncomfortably yet firmly, Castlereagh stated that Britain's earlier acceptance of Prussian occupation would have to be withdrawn. Britain was no longer at liberty to condone this act.

Hardenberg, stunned at the abrupt change, protested against this "stab in the back." At least, the Prussian chancellor consoled himself, he still had Metternich's assent. But was Hardenberg conveniently forgetting how hedged and tentative this had been, or was he perhaps referring to an oral, off-the-record understanding?

Just a couple of days before, the Prussian chancellor had sent over a message to Metternich, affirming the importance of Prussian-Austrian relations. Hardenberg's means of communication was unusual for diplomacy, though perhaps not so out of place in this dancing congress. It was a poem, celebrating the benefits of their cooperation:

> *Away discord, vanish from our folk.*
> *Give way, thou monster with the snaky hair!*
> *A single perch atop a giant oak*
> *The double eagle and the black one share.*

> *From this time forth in all the German Reich*
> *One word, one thought, is uttered by this pair*
> *And where the lutes sound out in German tongue*
> *There blooms one Reich so mighty and so fair.*

On Saturday night, December 10, Hardenberg received Metternich's response: Despite the history of good relations between the two powers, which he recounted in the politest terms, Metternich notified Prussia that his country would join Britain, virtually all of Germany, and other civilized states to resist this seizure of Saxony.

Still claiming to have his friend's best interests at heart, Metternich enclosed a compromise counteroffer. Instead of granting Prussia all of Saxony, he proposed an alternative plan that involved handing over a small part of Saxony, with a population of about 330,000, and also territories farther west in the Rhineland. Together these lands would bring Prussia back up to its 1805 size, as promised, with a population of 10 million. A table of statistics was included in the proposal.

Hardenberg was outraged. One-fifth of Saxony! Prussia must have the entire region, as he still claimed that Metternich had promised. For the past several months, Hardenberg had been trying to rein in extremist Prussian generals who continually pressed their king to make even more vigorous demands. Now Hardenberg was being rewarded with this insult. Many other Prussians in town were equally angry, pouring wrath on Metternich. As Gentz put it, "All the Prussians and all their supporters cried murder."

In the meantime, steaming over the Austrian foreign minister's letter, Hardenberg proceeded to commit an act that Talleyrand would call "a most culpable indiscretion." If Metternich had decided to abandon previous agreements, then Hardenberg knew how to respond: He took all his confidential correspondence with Metternich, marched over to the Hofburg, and showed everything to the tsar.

Metternich's propensity for "tacking, hedging and flattery" was frightfully exposed. Worst of all was the letter Metternich had written in early November, defending himself against the tsar's absurd accusations—which in effect implied that the tsar was a liar. Reading these words, Alexander flew into a rage. He had been personally insulted, and demanded satisfaction. Allegedly, he slammed his sword down on the table and shouted that he would challenge Metternich to a duel.

MEANWHILE, IN HIS small flat on the Mölker Bastei, Prince de Ligne lay sick in bed. Having caught a cold in early December, he lay atop his torn mattress, surrounded by his favorite objects: his books, his etchings, and his paintings, most of which no longer had frames, only "fastened with pins to the walls." His family stayed by his bed, medicine in hand, and guests continued to pay their visits. People looked up to his third-floor window, hoping to see through the light-blue silk curtains for signs of a flickering candle.

"I know it is nature's way," the prince said to the people gathered around him. "We must leave our appointed place in the world to make room for others." After a pause, he continued, "Only leaving all those one loves, oh, this is what makes dying so painful." He muttered some final bits of gossip, and spoke of his plans to travel here and there. He asked about the affairs of the congress, and drifted off imagining himself leading troops into battle. According to one, the prince sighed from his bed, "Oh

I feel it, the soul has worn out its outer garment." Others said that he promised to give the Vienna Congress the spectacle of a field marshal's funeral. By the evening, his doctor was admitting that there was nothing more that he could do. The prince died the following morning, December 13, 1814.

Two days later, and on the day he had feared the congress would end, the prince's funeral took place at the Scottish Church on the Freyung. A large crowd gathered to pay their respects, in the church as well as outside in the square and the streets, while others looked on from balconies and upper-story windows. Marshals, generals, and officers led a long procession through town, past the palace, and out to the Kahlenburg for burial at the edge of the Vienna Woods.

Eight grenadiers pulled the coffin, on top of which were the prince's sword, his baton, his plumed hat, and an array of military orders. A horse followed, riderless and draped in black cloth "spangled with silver stars." At the back of the procession was a knight in black armor, his visor lowered, symbolizing the world of chivalry. The march was slow and silent, except for the sound of a beating drum.

IN DECEMBER, VIENNA was preparing for the Christmas season. The days were shorter, darker, and colder, with snow occasionally falling and whitening the trees. Vienna's residents, both the older and the newer adopted ones of the congress, strolled by markets, shuffled into boutiques in the inner town, and made plans for the celebration of the first Christmas without war in years.

When Agent ** entered the salon of Fanny von Arnstein, wife of a prominent banker in the firm of Arnstein and Eskeles, he had been surprised by what he found in the room: a tall fir tree, decorated with candles and gifts. This was apparently the first Christmas tree that he had ever seen, and he was not alone. Many historians have pointed out that December 1814 saw the first Christmas trees arrive in Vienna—this was called the "Berlin custom."

At the French embassy, Dorothée also convinced Talleyrand to celebrate Christmas "Berlin-style." This meant lots of marzipan, butter cookies, and, in the hallway, a giant fir tree decorated with "colorful garlands and lit candles." Another, even larger tree was placed near the famous stair-case. The French embassy hosted a party on Christmas Eve, and then cel-ebrated afterward, as Dorothée liked, in the German style, exchanging gifts that night, and not, as in Catholic France or Austria, on New Year's Eve.

Talleyrand gave Dorothée a cashmere shawl and some Meissen porce-lain, and she gave him a new Breguet watch, sent over specially from Paris. Inside was a miniature portrait of herself, by the painter Isabey. This watch, she said, would help him make it through the tedious confer-ences that sometimes seemed like they would never end.

Despite the failure of their liaison, Metternich was still thinking very much of Dorothée's older sister, Wilhelmine. That Christmas, he sent over a small jar of fancy English lemon salts that, he hoped, would help ease her migraines. "Little gifts preserve friendships," he added in a letter accompanying the package. "Bon soir, devote a good thought to me, and tell me you are mine!" he added. "I shall see you tomorrow evening."

On the Mölker Bastei, Ludwig van Beethoven continued his work on some new pieces of music, including the Polonaise in C Major (op. 89) which he dedicated to the empress of Russia and for which he received 50 ducats. Beethoven was also working on setting music for a patriotic tragedy written by the king of Prussia's private secretary, Johann Friedrich Leopold Duncker, as well as his previously written Three Violin Sonatas (op. 30), to be dedicated to the Russian tsar. Interestingly, too, Beethoven was polishing another piece that he intended to celebrate the Congress of Vienna. The title was going to be "The Choir for the Allied Princes." The congress, however, would end before he finished; the piece would, in fact, never be completed, and probably never performed—that is, until the 1990s.

On Christmas Day, Vienna's court composer Antonio Salieri conducted the music at High Mass at the palace chapel. Many Protestant delegations headed to Lutheran and Calvinist churches, and houses of worship all over town were packed. Later, Beethoven's concert featuring the Seventh Sym-phony, "The Glorious Moment," and, most popular of all, "Wellington's Victory" was repeated at the Redoutensaal, with proceeds benefiting a local hospital. This time, however, Beethoven neither conducted nor per-formed. Two days before, on the Russian tsar's birthday, he had given a concert, and, as it turned out, this would be the last time that Beethoven ever played the piano in public.

While Princess Bagration planned to host a Christmas dinner for the tsar and the Festivals Committee prepared a ball that evening in the palace, Castlereagh was entertaining at the British embassy on the Minoriten-platz. Guests included Cardinal Consalvi, Prince Eugène de Beauharnais, and the Crown Prince of Bavaria, who apparently spent the evening try-ing to speak in ancient Greek. It was only his fourth language, he boasted, and he needed to keep it fresh. It is unknown how many bottles of wine were consumed that night. When a tally was made of the wine stock in January, the British embassy had finished no fewer than ten thousand.

Baron Franz von Hager, meanwhile, was still at his office, reading the intercepted letters and working on his daily reports. It was business as usual. Some seventy pieces had been forwarded to his Cabinet Noir.

Talleyrand's embassy was no longer an impenetrable fortress. A door-man had been paid to hand over some bits of paper, and chambermaids, securely placed inside, were now roaming the embassy offices. Fortu-nately for the spies, Dalberg left many papers lying around, and not all of them were love letters or lists of his entertainment expenses, which included some 180 florins he had recently spent on the ballerina Bigot-tini. Agents also found it worthwhile to search the carriages used by the French. Comte Alexis de Noailles, in particular, was known to leave a letter or two behind.

Baron Hager had also succeeded in placing both a valet and a door-man with Humboldt, and other agents near the Russian advisers, at least those who were staying outside the Hofburg. As for Alexander, one anonymous agent was gaining valuable information from the tsar's physician, Jacob "James" Wassiliévitch Wylie. The spies even had success with the careful Castlereagh. The key there was finding out the couriers he used in sending his dispatches back to London. From here on in, Britain would be less of a stranger to the Austrian police.

On the day after Christmas, one of the most prominent guests at the congress, the king of Württemberg, left town—or, more accurately, stormed out. Frustrated by the lack of progress, the king had no desire to continue the charade. He had not gotten on well with many of his fellow sovereigns or the Viennese. He refused to tip his hat to crowds and sulked in salons after making only a token appearance. Gossipers called the huge, rude, melancholy king "the Monster," and indulged in tales of his escapades, including an alleged affair with a handsome young guardsman. Yet, as the king of Württemberg's carriage pulled out of the Hofburg early in the morning, palace servants soon had something else to talk about. The so-called Monster had dispensed snuffboxes, rings, and tips freely. His doorman received 300 florins, his hunting personnel 500, and another 1,000 went to the staff at his favorite theater, Theater an der Wien, and he did not forget the clerk in the ticket window.

DURING THE CHRISTMAS season, the humanitarian urge, for a moment, seemed to triumph over the usual squabbles and intrigues. Although it did not as yet lead to any official agreement, many leading sovereigns were coming together for a cause, a pioneering humanitarian fund-raising feast, held in the Augarten, to fight the awful problem of slavery.

The event was arranged by English admiral William Sidney Smith, who had come to the congress to represent the exiled Swedish king Gustav IV Adolf, who had been dethroned in the war, though he remained, Smith argued, the rightful king of Sweden. The English admiral was also hoping to achieve success in another cause dear to his heart: the plight of Europeans kidnapped and sold as slaves in northern Africa. He wanted the congress to abolish, once and for all, the slave trade, a stigma on the civilized world. He had seen the horrible cruelties up close during his time in the Royal Navy, and he would personally lead the crusade against these atrocities as head of a new military order that he proposed, the Knights Liberators of the Slaves in Africa.

Back in 1798, this English admiral had led resistance against Napoleon's siege at the crusader castle of Acre. "That demon Sidney Smith has made Dame Fortune jilt me!" Napoleon had said afterward. Smith had, in fact, a whole range of stories about Napoleon, or the time he escaped from a French prison, or the time, in 1807, when Smith ferried the Portuguese royal family to safety in Brazil. Many enjoyed his colorful stories, though some listeners proved less than patient when the admiral, not known for his succinct qualities, insisted on telling every detail.

Vienna society was inclined to indulge Smith, whose idiosyncrasies, for many, only added to his appeal. Crowds crammed into his apartment

for his Wednesday-night salons, spilling over into the hallways and staircases. Smith would often appear there, or at a ball, wearing not one
honorary order at a time, but proudly displaying his whole collection,
sometimes strung together onto his white silk sash. Alternatively, Smith
would select one order, wear it for a while, and then change later in the
evening, shuffling through his collection of stars, crosses, and insignia,
"so as not to insult any guest" or award he had received.

To raise awareness and drum up support for freeing slaves in North
Africa, Smith was organizing a series of events, and one of the first was a
remarkable banquet scheduled for December 29, 1814. It was a gigantic
picnic—a "humanitarian feast"—that would occur in the palace in the
Augarten. Guests would pay 3 ducats for the banquet, and an additional
10 guldens for the palace ball afterward, with all proceeds going toward
ransoming slaves.

No fewer than 150 kings, princes, generals, diplomats, and other
celebrities had accepted his invitation, including the Russian tsar, the
Prussian king, and many other leading figures at the congress. They were
certainly attracted to the cause. Part of the curiosity, too, it was said, was
the experience of paying for a meal themselves, "a novelty of such great
charm that not one of the crowned heads . . . would miss it."

Seated around a long table in the form of a horseshoe, the guests
enjoyed some of the finest delicacies of the Austrian empire. The food
had been catered by Vienna restaurant owner Herr Jann, and some of the
best wine from the Rhineland, Italy, and Hungary circulated liberally.
The walls of the palace were covered with flags of the assembled states,
and two orchestras entertained with national anthems. Royal entrances
were further celebrated with a trumpet fanfare, the heralds blowing their
horns on horseback and showing the admiral's flair for drama. As La
Garde-Chambonas said with admiration, it seemed like something from
"the theater of Shakespeare."

The only uncomfortable moment was when Herr Jann's waiter, carrying a silver plate with a bill on top, approached the king of Bavaria, Maximilian I Joseph. The king, well known for his generosity, reached down
into his waistcoat pocket to pay the donation. When he came up empty-
handed, he shifted his weight and fumbled around in other pockets, soon
realizing that he did not, in fact, have any money on him.

With the waiter still standing over his shoulder, "impatiently jingling his money against the dish," the king glanced at one of his courtiers, Count Charles Rechberg, down the table, hoping that he would come to the rescue. Rechberg, however, was deep in discussion with Wilhelm von Humboldt about a new book: his own, two-volume *Les peuples de la Russie*. Another nervous glance down the table, but Rechberg was still oblivious. The king's "torture reached a point where," as Count La Garde-Chambonas jokingly put it, "he would have liked to shout, Three ducats! Three ducats! A kingdom for three ducats!"

The farce ended when the Russian tsar came to the rescue and paid the king's fee. The waiter was "a better bill collector than a courtier," someone observed, and the whole table roared with laughter—the king of Bavaria, afterward, the loudest of all. Admiral Smith also had good reason to be happy. His philanthropic feast had netted several thousand for the cause of fighting slavery.

Chapter 20

KING OF THE SUBURBS

Too frightened to fight each other, too stupid to agree.

—TALLEYRAND ON THE GREAT POWERS AT THE CONGRESS OF VIENNA

With only a few days left in the year, the congress continued to take one step forward, two back, as Cardinal Consalvi noted. The delegates had reached a stalemate over Saxony. While Talleyrand advocated law and justice, Metternich was trying to solve the dispute by striking a bargain.

After the last outburst, when Hardenberg stormed over to the tsar with a portfolio of confidential letters, the Austrian foreign minister had not given up on finding another way whereby Prussia could reach its promised population of 10 million without having to commit the crime of seizing the whole of Saxony. There were, in fact, many possibilities, and Metternich hoped that Prussia would be intrigued enough at least to consider them.

Of these options, the plan that Metternich preferred would offer territory along the Rhine to return Prussia to its promised population size of 10 million "souls"—this was the word for population, the yardstick measure adopted by the congress in carving up the map. Metternich also threw in another five hundred thousand souls to sweeten the deal. This was an interesting proposal, Prussia admitted, but some of the population figures for the territories on the list seemed rather inflated, and given Metternich's track record, Prussia was not inclined to take him at his word.

For weeks, diplomats had pored over numbers, and, typically, they ended up rejecting the statistics claimed by the other side. Accuracy was not easy, even with the best of intentions, given all the loss of life and the vast movements of peoples in the war. For this reason, Metternich proposed another way to resolve the conflict: Why not create an Evaluations Committee to look more closely into the population figures in all the territories, and help obtain the best estimates possible?

Castlereagh also liked the idea of the committee, and he came over to Kaunitz Palace in late December to introduce the issue with Talleyrand. The French minister's support was crucial. Even if he was still outside the inner circle, Talleyrand enjoyed rising popularity for his defense of Saxony and commanded a veritable legion of admiring smaller states that looked to him for leadership. Fortunately, Castlereagh found, Talleyrand did not oppose the idea outright. On the contrary, he liked it, provided, of course, that the committee did not lose sight of the importance of principles in the labyrinth of numbers.

Talleyrand suggested that this new committee should begin, first of all, by recognizing the rights of the king of Saxony. The committee should also consider other factors in evaluating a territory than a simple head count. Peasants "without capital, land or industry," he said, ought not to be counted the same as the prosperous inhabitants of the Rhine, or some other relatively affluent part of Germany. Next, Talleyrand went further and proposed that he, Castlereagh, and Metternich make an agreement to support Saxony.

"An agreement?" Castlereagh asked, taken somewhat aback. "It is, then, an alliance that you are proposing?"

"This agreement can very well be made without an alliance; but it shall be an alliance if you wish," Talleyrand answered. "For my part, I have no objection."

"But an alliance supposes war, or may lead to it, and we ought to do everything to avoid war," Castlereagh said, mindful of his recent orders from London.

"I agree with you," Talleyrand replied. "We ought to do everything, except to sacrifice honor, justice, and the future of Europe."

"War would be regarded with disfavor among us," Castlereagh replied.

"War would be popular with you if it had a great object—one truly European."

Remarkably, when Talleyrand mentioned this idea of a possible British-French-Austrian alliance, Castlereagh, to his pleasure, had not refused outright. He had not even seemed startled. In fact, given his own frustrations with the deadlock, Castlereagh had also been considering the possibilities of working in closer collaboration with France.

The next day, Talleyrand was updated on the proposed Evaluations Committee. There was good news and bad news. The good news was that the idea of establishing it had been accepted; the bad news was that the committee had already been appointed and France had not been invited to participate.

Correctly predicting that this information would provoke an unpleasant scene, Castlereagh had not wanted to convey this message himself. Instead, he sent over his brother, Lord Stewart, who, though not exactly known for his tact or finesse, made a gallant effort to break the news gently.

When Talleyrand learned that the French had been blackballed, he demanded to know who opposed his membership.

"It is not my brother," Stewart replied.

"Who is it, then?"

Hesitating, Stewart started, "Well—it is." He paused before the words escaped his mouth: "the Allies."

At this point, Talleyrand lost his patience. Since the Big Four were still acting as if they were at war against France, he would just let them sort out the congress themselves. He had had enough.

"Europe shall learn what has occurred," Talleyrand threatened. He would make sure that everyone learned how Castlereagh had abandoned Saxony and Poland, and then "rejected the aid by which he might have saved them." All this was highly sensitive, given the recent criticism Castlereagh had received back home.

The conversation ended abruptly, and Stewart rushed back to the British embassy to inform his brother.

Talleyrand's outburst—threatening to call for his horses then and there and leave Vienna immediately, as one English embassy official described it—had made an impression. When the Evaluations Committee met a second time, in late December 1814, Talleyrand's colleague, the Duke of Dalberg, sat comfortably at the table as France's representative.

WHILE THE FOREIGN ministers disputed the number of people in a given province, the Great Powers decided to arrange one last set of meetings to resolve the Saxon crisis peacefully. This problem had, as Gentz put it, "eclipsed" all the others in importance. It was urgent to move quickly before either Prussia consolidated its hold over the seized territory or the congress ended in a fruitless stalemate.

During the meeting on December 30, the Russians proposed, yet again, that all of Saxony would go to Prussia. The tsar, by way of compromise, promised to free the king of Saxony and transfer him to a newly carved-out territory on the left bank of the Rhine. The Saxon king on the Rhine, with a proposed new capital of Bonn, would also receive Luxembourg, and many towns of the former archbishopric of Trier, including Cologne.

Austria was not pleased with these terms. The plan still involved destroying Saxony, handing over the entire territory to Prussia, and leaving its own realm exposed. As for the proposal about the Rhine, was it really a good idea to spirit away a legitimate king and set him up elsewhere in some newfangled kingdom? Why not wait and see what the newly appointed Evaluations Committee could find?

Three full months into the congress, the peacemakers were as divided as ever, and, in fact, they were still lining up in their original constellations. Russia and Prussia stood on one side, and Austria and Britain on the other.

Now, after hearing the Russian proposal, Britain and Austria countered with one of their own. As Saxony was a matter of European concern, why not ask other powers for their opinion? Why not, for that matter, consult the king of Saxony?

At this point, Hardenberg exclaimed that he would rather end the entire Congress of Vienna than allow such a scene to transpire. And should Prussia's temporary occupation be made permanent, then the Prussians would, he added, consider any further opposition as "tantamount to a declaration of war!"

Castlereagh was losing his patience. Such a threat might intimidate "a Power trembling for its existence," he replied, but it would have the opposite effect on a country that valued its dignity, like Great Britain. If that was the way Prussia wanted to conduct business, it might as well "break off the Congress" right now. The tension in the room, Gentz said, felt like "an enormous weight suspended over our heads." The last meeting of 1814 had ended in chaos.

LATER THAT EVENING, the Russian diplomat Count Andrei Razumovsky was throwing his eagerly anticipated end-of-the-year bash. The count was a former Russian ambassador to Vienna, renowned for his wit, good looks, cosmopolitan good manners, and, above all, his enormous fortune. He is remembered in music circles today for his love of the arts, patronizing such Viennese luminaries as Haydn and Mozart. At the time of the congress, he was a generous supporter of Beethoven (hence the "Razumovsky Quartets"), and one of the last noblemen to have his own private orchestra.

The count had, in fact, inherited two large fortunes, one from an uncle who had been the lover of Catherine the Great and a second from another uncle, the lover (and perhaps also secret husband) of Empress Elizabeth. Count Razumovsky had built a large mansion—or, more accurately, a palace—on the outskirts of Vienna. With parties during the congress attended by an array of royalty, the Russian host was earning his own honorary title: "King of the Suburbs."

Some seven hundred guests would make their way out to his palace in the Landstrasse on the thirtieth, where he had turned "a piece of wasteland" into "an Eden of a princely residence." Carriages passed along his own boulevard, manicured park, and bridge to Vienna's "new Winter Palace." Inside, guests marveled at its marble halls, mirrored office, mosaic floor, and library full of rare books and manuscripts, not to mention the hanging staircase. There were galleries of masterpieces, including works by Raphael, Rubens, and Van Dyck, and an entire room devoted to works of the Italian sculptor Antonio Canova. Razumovsky's palace seemed like "a temple erected to art."

The last party at the Razumovskys', three weeks before, had certainly been memorable. The tsar had himself hosted, and no expense was spared. Sturgeon were brought from the Volga, oysters from Ostend, truffles from France, oranges from Sicily, and strawberries from England. On each table was a bowl of cherries, transported that week across Europe from the tsar's greenhouses back in Russia. Guests also admired the pineapples, arranged in the form of a pyramid with exuberance "such as had never before been served on any board." The partygoers danced until dawn, and looked forward to the count's next bash. Little did they know it would end in tragedy.

Early in the morning hours of December 31, Razumovsky's palace caught fire, erupting like a "Vesuvius in full blast." As ringing church bells warned the town of the emergency, Vienna's fire department galloped out to the Landstrasse as quickly as possible. Smoke and flames were soon everywhere, the copper roof glowing a "fiery red."

Volunteers hacked their way through the count's manicured shrubberies to hasten the efforts to fight the fire. Hearing of the emergency, Emperor Francis had come at once, as did other congress members. Talleyrand hurried out as well, because Dorothée had gone to the party with her friend Count Karl Clam-Martinitz, and neither one had yet returned home.

Fortunately, the majority of the partygoers had already left the palace by the time the fire had spread and the "burning beams" began crashing down. But some people were still inside, and the whereabouts of others still unknown. Razumovsky himself could thank a loyal valet and his smelling spices for waking him out of his deep sleep.

Valets and friends alike were frantically tossing the count's belongings out the second-story windows, dropping "dozens of vests, trousers and coats, one after the other," down to the "muddy puddles." Desperate now to save anything, they hurled other goods out the windows. "Expensively bound books, chandeliers, marble tabletops, alabaster vases, silverware, bric-a-brac, paintings, even clocks" crashed down, many shattering on impact, while others were "carted away by the mobs."

Artistic treasures by the hundreds were lost forever, including those in the splendid Canova Hall, consisting solely of the sculptor's marble works. "That's the gallery that held the Dutch genre painting," Dorothée said, safely outside the palace, as she saw a wing crash down. "I sat in it for supper." Tragically, two men died that night, daring chimney sweeps who had entered the burning labyrinth with the hope of rescuing at least some of the embassy papers.

The search for the origins of the fire degenerated into a din of confused and animated speculation. Some believed that the blaze began in the kitchen, the bakery, or maybe with the straw in the stables. Others suggested that it was sabotage. Investigators eventually settled on a flaw in the heating system—or, as one fumed, "the *French* heating system"—installed the previous year. Count Razumovsky had added a wooden extension to his palace for the party, and the fire, it was believed, probably started there.

"One of the ducts concealed in the walls had become overheated by the huge fires maintained around the clock," Friedrich von Schönholz explained, and this "over-heated duct had first charred, then set fire to a wooden beam." The fire then spread ferociously among the combination of wood, wax, and cloth in so many rooms, and, further, the "tapestries and draperies now became the fuses that carried the fire . . . to the remotest corners of the palace."

The tsar had returned to the scene that morning, arriving, it was noted, after the other sovereigns. Walking past the ground, carved with deep ruts made by fire wagons and strewn with plumed hats in the mud, the tsar found Razumovsky, in sable coat and velvet hat, sitting alone under a tree, his head down and sobbing.

All that was left of two decades of the count's collecting and construction were charred, smoking ruins and a few blackened treasures that had been rescued. "This is truly a great misfortune, but we are all in God's hands," the tsar said, trying to comfort the count. But then, in the next breath, he was overheard adding, "This may happen to my knights' hall, also hot-air heated." Maybe it was diplomatic frustrations that solicited the next tactless remark: "That's what we get for aping the French!"

METTERNICH HAD CHOSEN not to attend the Razumovsky ball. He could not bear to participate in an event that was intended to celebrate Russia and its tsar. His relationship with Alexander was as tense as ever.

Happily, Alexander had at least backed down from challenging him to a duel, talked out of it, apparently, by Emperor Francis. The last thing the congress needed, the Austrian emperor had said, was the spectacle of a duel between the Tsar of All the Russias and the foreign minister of His Apostolic Majesty. But the argument that worked most effectively was that a duel would actually hurt Alexander's honor, as it implied a sense of equality between the combatants. The tsar replied that, in any case, he would have no further dealings with a minister "as untrustworthy as Metternich."

Having missed the Razumovsky ball, Metternich was pleading with the Duchess of Sagan for a meeting. He was still desperate to hear from her. He needed her company and her insight, especially given the strains he felt around the diplomacy table. "Write me a word," he said, "I am quite sad, and I certainly need all my strength at this moment!"

In yet another note from the Chancellery, Metternich begged for one last chance to see the duchess before the New Year. It was urgent, he emphasized with the desperation of someone with a superstitious reverence for symbolic dates, but he pleaded in vain. The duchess replied that she was "sick as a dog" and would probably not be well again for a few days.

Interestingly, however, Gentz had stopped by the Palm Palace that night and had a drink with the duchess, as he recorded in his diary. She seemed well enough, surrounded in her drawing room by her sister Dorothée, Count Clam-Martinitz, and many others, including Prince Alfred von Windischgrätz.

It must have been a lonely New Year's Eve for Prince Metternich. He tried a third time to arrange a meeting, adding that "I do not want the first day of the new year 1815 to pass without seeing you."

Indeed, before the champagne toasts were clinked that night, a package would arrive for the duchess from a Vienna jeweler's shop. When the duchess opened the small silk box, she found a handsome gold bracelet, an exquisite piece of craftsmanship, shining with a diamond, a ruby, an emerald, and an amethyst. Each stone symbolically conveyed a message in those romantic times: The diamond and the ruby stood for love and fidelity; the other two were their respective birthstones, amethyst for the duchess and emerald for himself. It had arrived, on Metternich's instructions, "at the stroke of midnight."

Metternich had written an accompanying letter, explaining another symbolism in his gift. Each stone had been engraved with the letter *G*, which stood for the words that, as he put it, "I had hoped to say as I fastened it on your wrist this evening: *Gott gebe Gnade, Glück, Gedeihen*" ("May God grant you Grace, Happiness, and Prosperity.")

What Metternich did that night, after finishing this letter, is not known. The songwriter La Garde-Chambonas claimed to have seen him at Count Zichy's New Year's Eve ball, and that is possible, though the young man was notoriously sketchy when it came to connecting people and places with specific dates. It was probably more likely that when the foreign minister laid down his goose pen at eleven o'clock that night, he rang out the end of the year all alone in the Chancellery office.

Chapter 21

REQUIEM

I agree with you that Talleyrand cannot be relied upon, and yet I know not on whom His Majesty can better depend.

— CASTLEREAGH

After the New Year celebrations, which marked the opening of the Carnival season, Vienna was eagerly anticipating the upcoming social calendar. There was a full schedule of events, including balls, hunts, feasts, plays, concerts, tableaux vivants, and a host of other entertainments to lighten the dark months of winter.

Early morning on New Year's Day, a cold and tired messenger arrived at Castlereagh's embassy on the Minoritenplatz. It had been a hard six-day journey through central Europe, the last leg through rain, snow, and ice. The courier was bringing news that Britain's war with the United States had now ended. On Christmas Eve in Ghent, British and American diplomats had finally agreed on peace.

This was extraordinary news for Castlereagh, who, bogged down with his own negotiations, was thrilled to be released from a difficult war on the other side of the world. Castlereagh sent a messenger over to Metternich and Talleyrand immediately. It was time for a meeting.

"I hastened to offer [Castlereagh] my congratulations," Talleyrand said on hearing the news of the treaty, and then he added, "I also congratulated myself on the event." He knew its importance right away.

With this war over, Great Britain no longer had to divide its attention over such a large amount of territory. Frigates, men-of-war, and ships of the line tied up in the New World would now be freed en masse, and, potentially, so would a large war chest of millions of pounds sterling. Should Prussia insist on pressing its demands, Great Britain could now devote the full might of the British war machine to supporting its diplomacy.

When the British foreign minister was congratulated on the peace agreement at a ball that evening at the Hofburg, Castlereagh enigmatically replied, "The golden age begins." Stories of this response swept through Vienna's salons and drawing rooms, along with speculation on what exactly the foreign secretary meant. Was he implying that the plenipotentiaries would soon reach agreement and avert war? Or was it, as one member of the English delegation sneered, only a reference to the likelihood of more English gold flowing to allies who promised to do his bidding? Castlereagh's words suddenly carried more meaning than before.

Good news had indeed rung in the New Year, but Talleyrand was glad to report, in a dispatch to the king of France, that the end of the war between Britain and the United States was in fact only "the precursor of a still more fortunate event." Enjoying the boost in confidence, Castlereagh had approached Talleyrand with a bold plan: Britain was now willing to offer an alliance with none other than its mortal enemy France.

Castlereagh had been upset at the Prussian and Russian behavior in the last meetings. Prussian arrogance seemed intolerable, and its delegation insisted on adopting a "very warlike" stance unsuitable for negotiation. Castlereagh felt that there was no other way to avoid an all-out war than this pact. The only problem was that it was unauthorized, and again, strictly speaking, against his government's orders.

The whole negotiation was conducted under the strictest secrecy, and the resulting treaty hurriedly written up and signed on January 3, 1815. According to its terms, Britain, Austria, and France pledged to support each other in the case of an attack from any other power, and contribute 150,000 troops, though Britain reserved the right to replace its quota of soldiers with additional financing. There was nothing in the treaty that bound the powers to join an ally in an attack. It was a purely defensive alliance.

That night, at a crowded soiree held at the British embassy, as two Italians strummed a guitar and fiddled on a violin, Talleyrand played cards as usual, Metternich surrounded himself with women, and Castlereagh danced a frantic Scottish reel. The three ministers were not seen together, even for a minute. Few could have imagined that they had just signed a secret agreement that would have a great impact on the negotiations.

Talleyrand, in particular, had reason to rejoice. After only three and a half months in town, representing a shunned, defeated power, he had maneuvered his way right into the council chamber of the Great Powers. The congress had reached such an impasse that Britain and Austria had preferred to work with an enemy they had fought for almost a quarter of a century, rather than with their own allies of the victorious coalition.

RUMORS OF SOME sort of secret pact were soon circulating throughout Vienna, though no one had any confirmation, and they were lost in a sea of other rumors: that war would break out at any moment; the widowed king of Prussia would soon remarry (and his next wife, some wildly predicted, would be Marie Louise!); the tsar had caught a venereal disease; almost every leading figure of the congress would be sacked, and a new team would be appointed to wrap up the negotiations.

Then, all of a sudden, at one of the first meetings of the Big Four in early January, Metternich, rather nonchalantly, proposed that Talleyrand be allowed to join in the deliberations. Castlereagh supported the motion. But while the Prussians fumed and fumbled, there was another surprise that day. The Russian delegation actually gave way and agreed to admit Talleyrand to the committee.

But why would Russia suddenly be so willing to cooperate with Britain and Austria? This is a difficult and important question, because the tsar was now, in many ways, unmistakably proving more accommodating. He was, as Metternich put it, experiencing one of his "periodic evolutions of the mind." The tsar was now even willing to discuss Poland, something that he had so far only adamantly refused. Why?

Certainly, the awareness that Britain was no longer restrained by a war across the seas had played a role in causing the tsar to begin to doubt the wisdom of fully supporting Prussia. Alexander had also suspected that some sort of deal had been struck between Britain, Austria, and France. When he met Castlereagh on January 7, for instance, he asked him directly about the rumored alliance, but Castlereagh neither acknowledged nor denied it. He said only that if the tsar "acted on pacifick [*sic*] principles he would have nothing to fear."

In addition, over the last few weeks, Alexander had seemed more serious and reflective, tired of the frivolous parties and endless bickering. Some historians claim that the tsar was returning to a full-fledged mysticism that had flourished back in 1812 when Napoleon invaded Russia. Alexander was receiving some remarkable letters from an admirer, and apparently he devoured their contents.

The author of these letters was Baroness Julie von Krüdener, a fifty-year-old widow from Latvia, who had preached a fiery apocalyptic mysticism nourished in cold Baltic winters. In letter after letter, Krüdener had instructed the tsar to remember his "divine mission," just as he had in the dark days of Napoleon's invasion. No matter what the tsar suffered at the congress, Krüdener assured him that she knew the "deep and striking beauties in the Emperor's soul."

The flattering letters were increasing in frequency and intensity that winter, reaching the tsar in Vienna with the help of one of Krüdener's well-placed admirers, Roxanne Stourdza, his wife's lady-in-waiting. Alexander had come to look forward to each new letter, and then discussing every shade of meaning with this lady-in-waiting. They would meet in private, away from his foreign policy advisers, and usually in her quarters, a tiny room on the fourth floor of the Hofburg. There they conversed, as the tsar saw it, as "spiritual husband and wife."

Sometimes the letters contained prophecies, or dark troubling visions that awaited the dancing congress: "You do not know what a terrible year 1815 is going to be," Krüdener had predicted that autumn.

Do you suppose that the Congress will finish its labors? Undeceive yourself. The emperor Napoleon will leave his island. He will be more powerful than ever, but those who support him will be pursued, persecuted and punished. They will not know where to lay their heads.

To the tsar, she was a "divine prophetess," and he hoped, one day, to meet her in person.

Yet even with this rekindled interest in mysticism, there is probably also another factor for the tsar's abrupt change in attitude: Alexander was more cooperative, it seems, because he was tiring of the Prussian alliance. When Hardenberg had shown Metternich's private letters to him a few weeks before, the Austrian foreign minister had retaliated by allowing the tsar to read one of Hardenberg's own letters. In this piece, the Prussian minister had written, in a striking indiscretion, that he was only supporting Russian policy in Poland because it was official Prussian policy, and also because "it would make Russia weaker."

As the tsar looked back over the last few months, he had cooperated with Prussian desire to gain territory, and now he was rewarded, he felt, by treachery from his so-called ally—an ally, the tsar was increasingly convinced, whose aggression would only drag Russia into an unwanted war over Saxony. Alexander, feeling like a man of peace once again, was disillusioned with the Prussians. He now had a reason, or at least a rationalization, for abandoning his ally.

So, indeed, there were many reasons for the tsar's sudden burst of cooperation with Britain and Austria at the congress. Unfortunately for Prussia, she would now suffer the consequences, and find herself an angry but isolated power. As for Talleyrand, he was ready to join the Directing Committee. The former Big Four was now going to be a Big Five, the real center of power and decision making at the Vienna Congress.

MEANWHILE, METTERNICH WAS trying to move on with his life and finally put closure on his ill-starred affair with the Duchess of Sagan. Despite his midnight gift on New Year's Eve, the duchess clearly still preferred Prince Alfred, and Metternich was trying to resign himself to this reality. The same day that he signed the secret treaty with Britain and France, Metternich wrote another letter to the duchess that tried to put the irrational into a meaningful perspective.

> I was your lover for two years. I loved you—I ended by adoring you. You ceased even wishing me well the day when I began to love you—natural enough course of human affairs! I was not disheartened; I did not ask you for love at all but only for some certainty— either refusal or hope. You did not cease giving me [hope]; you nourished that feeling in me that you saw as more than imperious; you encouraged it even while you saw it exhaust those faculties of which my honor demanded the full use.

"Called to lead twenty million men," he added, "I should have known how to conduct myself." Metternich was indeed trying to put the past behind him.

Metternich was also busy in January using the secret treaty to great advantage and recruiting other states to join the coalition against Prussia. Bavaria signed on, and so did many smaller German states that wanted a guarantee of their safety. Some were so frightened of Prussia and eager to join that they swore not to deal with any other state without first discussing the matter with Austria. The treaty was thus not only helping break the deadlock of the Vienna Congress, but also, in Metternich's hands, likely to pay rich dividends for Austrian influence in central Europe.

Esteem for Talleyrand had also been growing on the wake of his support for Saxony and his newfound position on the Directing Committee. The French foreign minister likewise knew how to seize this opportunity. The embassy at Kaunitz Palace would entertain even more flamboyantly than before.

One of his great successes that winter was actually a somber event: Talleyrand staged a requiem for the dethroned king of France, Louis XVI, who was guillotined in 1793. January 21, 1815, marked the twenty-second year since that "day of horror and eternal mourning." Talleyrand proposed that Vienna acknowledge the anniversary with a "solemn expiatory service."

When the emperor of Austria heard of Talleyrand's plans for a ceremony, he offered his help—Louis XVI was, after all, his uncle, and Marie-Antoinette his aunt. With the emperor's support, Talleyrand knew that he would now probably have his choice of locations for the service, and it would, moreover, be packed. Sure enough, Talleyrand was offered Vienna's largest and most stately church, the medieval Gothic masterpiece St. Stephen's.

With the emperor's blessing, too, Talleyrand had gained access to the Festivals Committee. Stalwarts of the committee would be turned loose and their "melancholy zeal" would adorn St. Stephen's for a day of public mourning. The cathedral itself was draped in black velvet. A pyramid was placed in the center, with four statues at its base, symbolizing "France sunk in grief, Europe shedding tears, Religion holding the Will of Louis XVI, and Hope raising her eyes to heaven." On every pillar in the church hung the Bourbon crest.

The emperor of Austria appeared, as promised, in mourning. Although the empress could not attend due to her poor health, the other sovereigns had appeared on their platform draped in black velvet and decorated with silver tassels. Members of the noble order Knights of the Golden Fleece and Vienna Congress participants were placed in the choir. Seats in the nave were reserved for other prominent figures, many of the ladies dressed in "flowing veils" and ushered to their pews by the handsome French ambassador, Marquis de la Tour du Pin. Seats open to the public were quickly taken, the crowds everywhere in thick fur and sable coats.

The emperor's confessor, the archbishop of Vienna, celebrated Mass. Antonio Salieri, Vienna's *Hofkapellmeister,* led the chorus of 250 voices, and Talleyrand's piano player, Sigismund Neukomm, composed the music. Another Frenchman in town, the parish priest of St. Anne's, Abbé de Zaignelins, delivered the address, neither a funeral oration nor a lecture nor a sermon. The theme was "The earth shall learn to hold the Lord's name in awe."

The French priest gave a stirring speech that touted the glorious fourteen-hundred-year history of the French monarchy—and the horrors the Revolution committed against the legitimate dynasty. It was a speech that Talleyrand, almost certainly, wrote or edited himself. True to form, Talleyrand had made sure that both the Russian tsar and the king of Prussia were seated prominently in the front of the cathedral. That way, they would not miss the lesson and, equally important, no one could avoid seeing their participation.

Twenty-two years after his execution, Louis XVI finally received his memorial service. Like many of Talleyrand's other projects, the requiem worked on several levels. It honored the past, championed the importance of legitimacy, and, at the same time, subtly though forcefully promoted causes dear to France—from preserving the *legitimate* king of Saxony to restoring the *legitimate* king of Naples. The post-requiem soiree and banquet offered further opportunities for gathering in remembrance of the guillotined king. Although it was an expensive day, indeed, Talleyrand had managed to have all of Vienna celebrate France and its royal dynasty. It was a marvelous success.

Chapter 22

THE GREAT SLEIGH RIDE

One must keep an eye on his allies, no less than on his enemy.

— METTERNICH

On the morning of January 22, Vienna's cold weather had finally created that magical combination of "heavy snowfall" and hard, "biting frost" necessary for the long-awaited sleigh ride. Thirtysome large sleighs were pulled into the Hofburg courtyard, Josefsplatz, each as gilded and grand as any Habsburg carriage. Congress dignitaries were scheduled to arrive in the early afternoon for a ride through the streets of Vienna, the cobblestones covered in snow. They would continue out to Schönbrunn Palace for a gigantic winter party.

The crowds had come to the central square, early in the morning, to take a look at the spectacular sleighs, shining with a bright gold set off by emerald-green velvet upholstery and fine silver bells. Each sleigh was pulled by a team of horses, "caparisoned in tiger skins and rich furs," and each sleigh spared nothing that "taste could imagine and money buy." "Silk, velvet, gold everywhere" was how one observer summed up these veritable winter chariots.

As in many other functions at the congress, the Festivals Committee had struggled with a way to solve the complicated protocol for a sleigh ride that included an emperor, an empress, a tsar, a tsarina, and many kings, princes, and other dignitaries. Who, for instance, would ride first? Who would share sleighs, and how could they allot partners and positions in the procession without offending tender sensibilities? In the end, the Festivals Committee had struck upon a simple solution to the intricate problems: lottery. Let fate decide.

Looking at the results of the draw, however, it seems that the mandate of fate had been tweaked by a committee eager to avoid diplomatic pitfalls. The tsar, who had expressed his displeasure with this sumptuous expedition, had miraculously drawn his current love interest, the salon celebrity Princess Gabrielle Auersperg. The king of Prussia, equally sour at the event, was paired with his favorite, Countess Julie Zichy.

A special cavalry squadron marched in front of the procession, followed by a "leviathan of a sled" containing a small band blasting trumpets and banging on kettledrums. The first of the congress dignitaries were the emperor of Austria and the empress of Russia, dressed in a fur "trimmed in ermine and green silk," a matching plumed green cap, and diamonds once worn by Catherine the Great. Purple, rose, and amaranth-blue fur coats were also all the rage at the sleigh ride; the gentlemen preferred warm Polish long coats also edged with "expensive furs."

Given the biting cold wind that day, some dignitaries had traded their place in the sleigh procession for a seat in a closed carriage. Empress Maria Ludovika, who had fallen ill again recently, opted for the carriage ride to the palace, as did the king and queen of Bavaria. That was fine, and actually probably a good thing, the Festivals Committee knew. A few sleighs should be pulled empty as reserves, in case a sleigh broke down out in the countryside. In the back of the procession was another monstrous sleigh, carrying a second band playing "war-like tunes."

About two o'clock, the emperors, kings, queens, musicians, and other guests climbed into the sleighs. After a grand trumpet fanfare, the Great Sleigh Ride was ready to begin.

Before the sleighs swished out of Josefsplatz, however, there was an unexpected delay. A carriage had slammed into the square and blocked the designated route. When the driver was politely asked to make way for the royal procession, he refused. Another request for the coachman to move his carriage was rebuffed. The court chamberlain then sent one of his trusted officials over to investigate. It turns out that the mysterious haughty coachman was none other than Britain's ambassador, Lord Stewart, and he was apparently drunk.

An order from the emperor did the trick, and off the royal sleighs went, gliding on the packed snow at a stately walking pace, which would allow the curious crowds to watch the parade of sovereigns and sleighs. Once the expedition passed out of the inner town, the drivers turned the horses loose and they galloped, at top speed, to Schönbrunn Palace for the banquet and the ball.

About halfway out of town, the procession stopped at a monument to the Polish king Jon III Sobieski, whose heroic ride with an army of reinforcements in September of 1683 had saved Vienna from the famous siege by the Turks. This was a good opportunity to repair some of the sleighs, whose delicate frames with golden sphinxes on their axles had suffered on the roads, and it was also, undoubtedly, a good opportunity for some subtle diplomacy. The Sobieski monument called to mind the many sacrifices and services that Poland had rendered Europe—a timely advertisement, no doubt, given that Vienna's dignitaries were then weighing the future of Poland.

When they arrived and parked their sleighs, the summer palace seemed a winter wonderland. The lake lay frozen like a "polished mirror." Some skaters entertained with acrobatic jumps, others performed dances on the ice, and one group, dressed as Venetian gondoliers, steered sleighs decked out as gondolas. Others pulled imaginative constructions, such as the "make-believe sleigh" in the form of a swan with silver wings. Enterprising merchants skated out onto the lake, hoping to sell some "fortifying refreshments."

While the guards at the palace tried to prevent the curious crowds from disturbing the festivities, a certain member of the British embassy stole the show with his flashy gliding and twirling, "whirls, loops, and figure-eights." Apparently he was a member of a London skating club, and he really drew admiration when he skated the initials of ladies on the ice. Particularly popular, too, were the women dressed as Dutch milkmaids who gracefully waltzed on the frozen lake.

The party continued at the palace theater with a performance of the opera *Cinderella*, complete with special ballets written for the occasion. Marie Louise and her son were believed to have left the palace earlier that morning, not wanting to witness the elaborate celebration. Another rumor was that she was there the whole time, peering through a specially cut "peephole." After all, some members of the sleigh party swore that they had seen her son, the little prince, on his sled, flying down the palace hillside. The party concluded in the drawing rooms, decorated with orange trees, myrtles, and plants from the emperor's greenhouse.

It was an extraordinary spectacle—surely the most grandiose sleigh ride in history. Count August de La Garde-Chambonas was, as usual, highly impressed, noting that "it was, indeed, a picture which for many centuries will not be repeated." His friend Comte de Witt agreed that it was a "beautiful, marvelous and elegant affair." His only complaint was that the Festivals Committee should have also built an ice palace on top of the lake.

After the "intoxicating pleasures" of Schönbrunn, the revelers returned to central Vienna in a jingling torchlit sleigh ride, racing to make it back for yet another masked ball at the Hofburg. There "they ride with our fifty percent and we must pay more each day," one Vienna resident was overheard complaining, referring to a controversial new tax levied earlier that month, a 50 percent increase needed to pay for this congress, which many thought should have been wrapped up by now.

INDEED, WITH A secret treaty, a more cooperative tsar, and a new majority on the expanded Directing Committee, it seemed that the congress could now finish its pressing business. Few things, however, were easy or simple at the Congress of Vienna.

Britain, Austria, and France had pledged to resist aggression with one voice, but admittedly that left a considerable amount of discretion in interpreting what was considered aggression and how much they should resist. Talleyrand was, of course, urging that they take a firm approach and force Prussia to back down from its demands, even it if meant war. Law, justice, and public opinion were on their side, Talleyrand argued, and a showdown would only rally the rest of Europe to their cause.

Castlereagh disagreed. He did not wish to provoke Prussia, and preferred instead to forge a compromise that he believed would produce a better peace for Britain and Europe. As he saw it, if Prussia wanted a big chunk of Saxony, including the town of Leipzig and the key fortresses of Erfurt and Torgau, why not give it to them? Why risk war over something that he called, at one point, "a mere question of details"? The British government had ordered him to preserve the Kingdom of Saxony, or, more precisely "a kernel of Saxony." He was planning to do just that, though if he had his way, that kernel would be small indeed.

Metternich was stuck in the middle, though now leaning toward Talleyrand. The disputes among the secret allies were growing increasingly acrimonious, and Castlereagh was again finding himself isolated among his partners. On January 24, as the debate about the size of Prussian gains raged, Castlereagh made another desperate gesture and told his allies that they would either have to accept his proposal for a small Saxony or England would leave the peace conference at once.

Actually, Castlereagh was not bluffing, no matter how far-fetched the threat might sound. Under great pressure from London, Castlereagh had just learned that he would soon be leaving Vienna anyway. British policy at the congress was proving highly unpopular, and the opposition party back home, the Whigs, was criticizing them more and more. Castlereagh would have to return to London to defend himself. A government order for his recall, he knew, would arrive at any time.

Desperate to accomplish something before he left, and feeling close to a breakthrough, Castlereagh had backed himself into a corner. If he could just solve the Poland-Saxony crisis, many of the other complicated negotiations would very likely fall into place. He could not imagine returning to London and a hostile House of Commons without anything tangible to show.

So while working frantically in a final diplomatic blitz, and once again finding himself outvoted in the alliance, Castlereagh was ready to make another unexpected move: He swallowed his pride and asked for help from the Russian tsar. Perhaps he could have a word with the king of Prussia and convince him to accept a compromise. So, ironically, the Russian colossus that he feared and worked so energetically to resist would now be his best hope for success.

IN *DE L'ALLEMAGNE,* PUBLISHED one year before the congress, Madame de Staël complained about all the time lost in Vienna's fashionable salons:

> Time is wasted on getting dressed for these parties, it's wasted on traveling to them, on the staircases waiting for one's carriage, on spending three hours at table; and in these innumerable gatherings one hears nothing beyond conventional phrases.

The whole experience, which could be repeated three, four, or even more times a week, simply devoured time, not to mention dulling the mind in an endless round of superficiality. The salon, Madame de Staël suspected, was "a clever invention by mediocrity to annul spiritual faculties."

By January 1815, Friedrich von Gentz was another who shared the disillusionment about the tedious follies that sometimes had to be endured in a salon or drawing room. At first, he had been captivated by the environment. He was overjoyed to be in the midst of the beautiful young people who, as he put it, "hold the world in their hands." He later paused and pondered, "Good God, how did I ever get in with this crowd?"

Four months into the Vienna Congress, however, his enthusiasm had begun to fade. Gentz had started to resent the talk about peace, legitimacy, and rule of law, which often seemed to ring hollow. It was all "fine-sounding nonsense," he concluded. The real purpose of the peace conference was only to divide the spoils. Hardened by the revelation, Gentz now laughed at the foibles of this diplomatic farce: "I enjoy the whole spectacle as though it were given for my own private entertainment."

Not all salons were simply glamorous and fashionable centers of intrigue. On Tuesday evenings, Fanny von Arnstein hosted a salon on the second floor of her mansion on the Hoher Markt, overlooking the stands of the fish, crab, herring and geese sellers below. Arnstein was a fifty-six-year-old Jewish woman who had settled in Vienna in the reign of Joseph II. As her friend Karl August Varnhagen, an assistant with the Prussian delegation, described her, she was "a tall, slim figure, radiant with beauty and grace." Her husband, Nathan, was a partner in the prominent firm Arnstein and Eskeles, which managed the accounts for several embassies during the congress; her father had been banker to the previous king of Prussia, Frederick William II.

The Arnstein salon enjoyed a reputation of being the most intellectually stimulating of the major salons. On any given night, guests might encounter the Prussian ambassador, Wilhelm von Humboldt, the pope's delegate, Cardinal Consalvi, or the young poet Friedrich von Schlegel, soon to be famous in Romantic circles and then serving in a minor capacity with the Austrian delegation. Famous physicians also made appearances, such as the opinionated magnetist David Koreff, and an early champion of the smallpox vaccine, Jean Carro, who was then known more for his chest of powders and perfumes as the "doctor of beauty."

Carl Bertuch, who represented German publishing firms and book dealers at the congress, particularly enjoyed the concerts at the Arnstein salon, which were invariably accompanied by generous supplies of "tea, lemonade, almond milk, ice cream, and light pastries." Another hit was Fanny von Arnstein's collection of wax figures. On one occasion that January, Arnstein opened her cabinet of wax figures, which depicted the gods of classical, Norse, and Egyptian mythology, along with Odysseus, Daedalus, the Queen of the Night, and the Four Seasons. The lighting was superb, and the wax figures looked lifelike as usual. But toward the end of the evening, the guests were startled when the wax figures suddenly stirred. Everyone marveled at the ability of the actors who posed as wax dolls.

One person who sometimes attended the Arnstein salon was a young assistant for the Hesse-Cassel delegation, the folklorist and philologist Jacob Grimm. Highly critical of the diplomacy and the drawing room, which he was experiencing up close from his apartment near the domes of the Karlskirche, south of the city center, Grimm described the Vienna Congress to his brother as a maze of rudeness and courtesy, recklessness and reserve, that, so far, had very little to show for its efforts.

In his memoirs, Grimm dismissed his stay at the congress as being "without usefulness." He found his work at the embassy frustrating and mind-numbing, especially the copying of mundane documents. Yet Grimm was also able to spend time hunting for lost manuscripts and pursuing his studies. He was learning Serbian, beginning Czech, and familiarizing himself with the rich traditions of Hungarian and Bohemian folklore. He enjoyed his Wednesday evenings with a group of like-minded writers, intellectuals, and booksellers at the tavern Zum Strobelkopf, where they discussed everything over "a passable roast beef and poor beer and wine."

Interestingly, in addition to preparing *The Spanish Romances* for publication and translating the Norse *Songs of the Elder Edda,* Grimm found an early manuscript of the medieval German epic *Nibelungenlied* ("the *Hohenems* codici") that differed from previous known versions. He was also busy extending his contacts among scholars and working to establish an international folklore society to collect, among other things, folk songs, legends, proverbs, jokes, games, superstitions, idioms, customs, nursery rhymes, ghost stories, and, as he put it, "children's tales about giants, dwarfs, monsters, princes, and princesses, enchanted and redeemed, devils, treasures and wishing-caps." Despite long hours in the office, Grimm was setting the basis for some highly productive years of scholarship that would follow his stay at the Congress of Vienna.

MEANWHILE, ON ELBA, Napoleon had not heard from his wife and son for months, and started to fear that they were being held against their will. He suspected that few of his letters were actually reaching them in Vienna. Although he sent multiple copies, with different messengers, and signed the envelopes with fake names, all his efforts to elude police spies continued to fail.

Napoleon first attributed the cruel obstruction of communications to a faceless Austrian bureaucracy. As time passed, however, Napoleon would blame instead his father-in-law, Emperor Francis, and the Austrian foreign minister, Metternich. Indeed, Marie Louise's secretary, Méneval, soon affirmed that Marie Louise was no longer at liberty to write or receive his letters.

In the meantime, other members of his family had arrived on Elba. His mother, Maria Letizia, had come in early autumn on board the *Grasshopper* and immediately made an impression on the islanders. "I have seen eminent people more intimidated in front of her than in front of the Emperor," one said of the sixty-four-year-old Corsican matron. Napoleon and his mother often played cards and dominoes, with Napoleon, of course, cheating as he tended to do.

Napoleon's favorite sister, thirty-four-year-old Pauline, also arrived on Elba, as she had promised. She brought along her reputation as the wild Bonaparte, having twice modeled nude or seminude for the sculptor Canova. One of the works, now at the Borghese Gallery, depicts her as the goddess Venus, reclining on a couch. By a mechanical device inside the base, the sculpture itself used to rotate to reveal her charms from many angles. Canova also added a thin layer of wax that, when the work was viewed by candlelight, added a more glistening lifelike appearance to the marble. Pauline would certainly enliven court festivities, not to mention the island's social life.

Visitors were coming more frequently to Napoleon's small empire. One day, back in September, rumors circulated that Marie Louise and the little prince had actually arrived on Elba, landing one night in a secluded olive grove at San Giovanni. Eyewitnesses had reportedly seen them travel with the emperor to a remote mountain hermitage, Madonna del Monte, on the western part of the island. A little boy was said to be calling Napoleon "Papa Emperor."

What the curious Elbans had witnessed was not the arrival of Marie Louise and the king of Rome, but in fact Napoleon's Polish mistress, Maria Walewska, and his illegitimate son Alexandre. It is not surprising that the rumors flourished. The two women were of similar age (Maria Walewska was two years older) and looked vaguely similar from a distance; Alexandre was about a year older than the former king of Rome.

Napoleon and Maria Walewska had first met seven years before, when the emperor passed through Warsaw and showed an obvious infatuation with the young Polish woman, then an eighteen-year-old newlywed. Her husband, an elderly patriot, had encouraged her to use Napoleon's interest to the advantage of Polish independence, and she had reluctantly agreed. They had carried on an affair intermittently ever since, and after Napoleon's abdication, Walewska had offered to join him on Elba. He had declined, still hoping, of course, that Marie Louise would arrive. Historians have long suspected that her trip had more than romantic or family purposes, and she was secretly carrying messages between Napoleon and Murat in Naples, though no direct evidence has yet surfaced to confirm that. At any rate, it was just a short weekend visit.

Napoleon was busy on many other projects—building roads, devising schemes for a fire brigade, and even building a kiln to fire bricks for future construction on the island. He was planning a new garbage service to remove the filth that rotted in the streets and to combat some nasty diseases, like typhus, that thrived on the island. In addition, Napoleon was planning a series of aqueducts to bring fresh water to the capital and planting mulberry trees along the sides of the road out to the nearby village of San Martino, hoping, in the long run, that they would furnish enough worms to create a new silk industry. Oaks, pines, and olive trees were also planted, as were chestnuts to stem the erosion on the mountainsides. Napoleon was even landscaping along Portoferraio's main road, striving to create an Elban equivalent of the elegant Champs-Élysées.

Indeed, Napoleon had been running his sixteen-mile-long island with the energy and authority with which he used to rule Europe. Ever since he had arrived, he had marched troops, performed daily maneuvers, and even, on one occasion back in May, brought some forty soldiers and invaded a nearby island. Pianosa, some fifteen miles to the southwest, had been conquered and incorporated into the Elban empire.

This "conquest" was admittedly only a small island, deserted except for its wild goats trampling about some ancient Roman ruins. The island was too dangerous to be settled, and, unlike Elba, it did not have natural defenses and was easily raided. The island was well-named: Pianosa means "flat land."

What it had was fertile soil. Napoleon intended to create a colony to supply grain to Elba. Also on Pianosa, Napoleon planned a hunting reserve, a stud farm to breed horses, and a retirement home for veterans who had served the state. Loyal Elbans had been sent over to start building the island he envisioned.

Pianosa had at least one other advantage that is often forgotten. Unlike Elba's harbor, Portoferraio, which lay in a bay that was easy to close and trap, Pianosa's harbor faced the open sea. If Napoleon were to ever find himself in danger, or wish to leave Elba in secret, he could escape to this island and from there set sail without anyone being too certain of his destination.

Chapter 23

"Odious and Criminal Traffick in Human Flesh"

*It is not the business of England to collect trophies
but to restore Europe to peaceful habits.*

— CASTLEREAGH

By early February, Vienna's Carnival season was in full swing. Every night, there was a dinner, ball, concert, play, or some other form of entertainment dreamed up by the Festivals Committee or an embassy around town. Congress dignitaries found themselves shuffling diplomatically from party to party, salon to salon. Big events were pushed later into the evening, to allow everyone to squeeze in as many events as possible, and seldom, it seemed, did any major celebration end before sunrise. It was like "living six weeks in a kettledrum."

The weather—like the spirits—was also improving. "Magnificent weather, spring temperature," Gentz scribbled in his diary that February, "the finest sun in the world; winter such as I've never seen." As the delegates bid farewell to their furs and Polish long coats, the strollers came out again in great numbers. The Graben, the Prater, the Bastions—all the main promenades were once again "positively swarming with people."

At the salon of Princess Bagration, the Russian tsar and Countess Flora Wrbna-Kageneck were in a discussion that somehow veered onto the issue of who could dress the fastest, men or women. The tsar said men were faster, and the countess disagreed. There was one way to find out. And so a few days later, a dressing duel took place at the fashionable salon of Countess Zichy. Both the tsar and the countess showed up in plain attire, giving proof that there were no tricks or cheating. Then, at the given signal, each went into a separate dressing room for the race, or behind a divider placed in the center of the room—eyewitness accounts do not agree.

Several minutes later, the tsar appeared proudly in his full gala uniform shining with "orders and decorations." Snickers were heard, and he looked around the room to see the countess, already there, looking like a vision of the ancien régime. She had not forgotten powder, perfume, rouge, bouquets, beauty spots, or anything else. The countess, it was clear, had won the wager.

"How clever and amusing all this is!" Humboldt snapped sarcastically, marveling how low the congress had fallen. "I am deadly tired of all this partying," he had long complained.

It was during the Carnival season, with its masks, costumes, and sophisticated debauchery, that Vienna received the news that Castlereagh's successor at the congress was to be one of the most popular men alive: the Duke of Wellington, the famous general with a string of victories to his credit in the Spanish campaign, and not a single loss in the war. Vienna society was thrilled.

Wellington was, like Castlereagh, a conservative Tory who had played a vital role in defeating Napoleon. After the war, he had been appointed British ambassador to France, not at first sight the most tactful choice. At any rate, Wellington was well informed. British dispatches between London and Vienna had passed through his office in Paris, the former home of Napoleon's sister Pauline, which Wellington had bought and turned into the British embassy, as it has remained ever since.

Only named a duke nine months before, Wellington was born Arthur Wesley, the third son and fourth surviving child in a large landowning family that belonged to the Anglo-Saxon Protestant Ascendancy of Ireland. His father, Garret Wesley, 1st Earl of Mornington, was professor of music at Trinity College, Dublin. Like Napoleon, born Napoleone Buonaparte, Arthur had changed his name, taking an old-fashioned form of Wellesley that had been his family's name for centuries. The duke always played down his origins. Born in Ireland, he once said, did not make one Irish any more than being born in a barn meant you were a horse.

He was tall and lean with broad shoulders, chestnut-brown hair, and blue eyes. When he appeared in his scarlet field marshal uniform, with its "gold-embroidered velvet collar" and his array of medals, Wellington looked like the "Iron Duke" of his later reputation (the nickname only appeared in the 1820s when he set up a new wrought-iron railing in front of his London house). One thing that did not fit the image, though, was his laugh. Wellington reportedly let out a slightly hysterical cackle like a "horse with whooping cough."

Wellington had been a quiet and introverted young boy who excelled at the violin. He had drifted into a military career after a lackluster record as a student, and after becoming a soldier, he destroyed his violin in 1793, never to play again. He advanced quickly in the military ranks, serving eight years in India, before the Spanish campaign that really won his reputation. Wellington had won big at Salamanca and Vitoria, and, in 1814, he drove Napoleon's army out of Spain.

Confident and distinguished, he could also be smug, brash, icy, and haughty. Few suggested that he was a budding philosopher. When one man asked his views about whether humanity creates the environment, or vice versa, Wellington merely replied, "It would take a volume to answer your question [and] I must go and take off my muddy boots." Others noted that Wellington was not the most engaging conversationalist. He was a stern "master of monosyllables."

Vienna salons were immediately competing for the honor of hosting the new celebrity in town, the excitement coming in part at least because this arrival "supplied something new, for which they were really at a loss." With the famous opera singer and society sweetheart Giuseppina Grassini on his arm, the duke entered Vienna as the "Victor of the World."

Talleyrand won the honor of holding an introductory dinner, Saturday night, February 4, at Kaunitz Palace. Sixty guests feasted on the chef's excellent meal, to the accompaniment of Neukomm's music. Most of the leading figures of the congress were there; in an embassy drawing room, decorated in white carnations and azaleas, the illustrious guests paid their respects to the Duke of Wellington, and, by implication, the host, Talleyrand, and his country, France.

A series of events for the new head of the British delegation followed. Metternich hosted him the next day with a dinner, and then a ball for a few hundred guests. Castlereagh, of course, hosted him at a reception, and then another one that evening, at a salon of the rich banking family the Herzes, "since nowadays," one disgruntled aristocrat observed, "the world's great ones gather at the homes of the moneymen."

With his replacement already in town, Castlereagh's days were numbered. Ironically, only a few months before, Castlereagh could not wait to leave Vienna. Now, with hopes of progress on several diplomatic fronts, Castlereagh wanted to finish the negotiations himself. But sure enough, the order came from London demanding his return. Castlereagh made plans to hand over the portfolios to his celebrated successor, though he stalled as much as he could.

THERE WAS ONE issue that Castlereagh was particularly anxious to address before returning to London: the terrible practice of African slavery. To the horror of an increasing number of reformers, there was an entire industry built on the buying, selling, and trading of human beings.

Conditions were brutal at every stage of the business—human beings seized, bound in chains, strapped together in a yoke, and then subjected to a perilous forced march to the coast. If they managed to survive this ordeal, fighting off extreme heat during the day and cold during the night, the captives were then loaded onto slave vessels, crammed below deck in dark cellar compartments, for a nightmare ocean voyage without sufficient water, air, or space. Sharp irons tore at the skin, and the smell made it difficult to breathe, the stench so bad that it often crept into the porous wood of the ship. Cries, shrieks, and groans further "rendered the whole a scene of horror almost inconceivable."

Once the survivors, often no more than about two-thirds of the cargo, arrived in the New World, whether the United States, Brazil, the Caribbean, or elsewhere, the vast majority would spend the rest of their lives laboring unfreely on large tobacco, rice, coffee, cotton, and especially difficult sugar plantations. They were at all times at the mercy of their masters.

Many reformers had hoped that the Congress of Vienna would abolish this practice entirely, and Castlereagh was one delegate who pushed for action. The problem was that he faced many special-interest groups that benefited from slavery and resisted any limits imposed on their lucrative business. Fortunes and indeed entire industries were built on "the Trade," as it was known, and outlawing it was not going to be easy.

Slave captains, plantation owners, and other defenders had come up with many arguments why they should be allowed to continue business as usual. There would be lost income, the deterioration of tax revenue, and even, some prophesied, the collapse of the British economy. One merchant declared hysterically that banning the trade would "render the City of London one scene of bankruptcy and ruin."

Others pointed out that should the slaves be freed, they would likely rise up, murder their former masters, and then set the entire British West Indies on fire. Recent riots in Jamaica and Haiti provided a chilling reminder, and self-styled pragmatists urged the eager reformers to move slowly on this issue.

Back in December, Talleyrand proposed that the Great Powers establish a committee to look into the question of the slave trade more closely, but this had been blocked by the protests of Spain and Portugal. In the middle of January, Castlereagh renewed the call for a committee, and this time one was appointed by the Committee of Eight. Abolitionists and vested interests alike were represented at the regular meetings, though Castlereagh sometimes felt as if he were the only real spokesman for abolition.

Specifically, one immediate problem that this Slavery Commission encountered was enforcement. If the Vienna Congress banned the slave trade, how would they make sure that this policy was obeyed? What would prevent renegade captains from smuggling contraband slaves, or other nations, for that matter, from trying to meet the enormous demand? Britain's answer—the Royal Navy—did not reassure its colleagues.

In Castlereagh's plan, naval officers would take it upon themselves to board vessels and search for transgressors, a particularly sensitive issue given the resentment this practice had long caused. Britain was the undisputed mistress of the sea, and opponents of the measure tried to position Castlereagh's countrymen as arrogant islanders trying to dominate even more. Wasn't the right to board and search *any* trading vessel all that the British really wanted, some asked, and wasn't it shameful how they cloaked these ambitions under the idealistic pretext of championing the abolition of slavery?

Another argument that opponents of any restriction on the slave trade used was that Britain, already well stocked with slaves in its colonies, wanted to impose a ban to cement its hold over the lucrative colonial trade. To agree to this abolition was then to submit to losing, permanently, to the British.

While trying to overcome this resistance, the British delegation was also constantly being pressed from the government back home to advance further and faster. Around the country, speeches were made, petitions signed, and many letters written, all demanding that the abomination be ended and pressuring the British government to achieve something in Vienna. In Castlereagh's view, all these efforts, no matter how well-meaning, were actually hampering his ability to make progress.

The word was out that England was desperate, and Castlereagh found himself forced to bargain for each and every concession, no matter how small. States were dangling out hints of possible support—for a price, that is. Talleyrand was not immune to this temptation. Castlereagh offered France the beautiful island of Trinidad in return for his support, but Talleyrand did not at first bother to answer, and when he did, one month later, it was a refusal. The French minister held out for what he really wanted: help in restoring the Bourbon dynasty to Naples. Castlereagh eventually agreed.

It was frustrating and tiresome business wringing out concessions from other powers, and Castlereagh's experiences made him seriously consider employing other tactics. For instance, should the Vienna peacemakers be unwilling to cooperate on banning the slave trade, Castlereagh was looking into the possibility of employing economic sanctions—probably the first ever in peacetime. He did, in fact, threaten, as a last resort, to lay an embargo against the very lucrative colonial products of any country that persisted in this "immoral and pernicious" activity.

With the hope of avoiding such a drastic move and most likely igniting a chain of escalating retaliations, Castlereagh went about his diplomacy with verve, making concession after concession. Countries in southern Europe proved to be most difficult to win over. Portugal finally agreed to end the trade in eight years, in return for 300,000 pounds. Spain, too, showed willingness to agree, though Spain's price seemed odd. In return for banning the slave trade, Spain's diplomats demanded Louisiana.

As Spain's argument went, the U.S. purchase of Louisiana in 1803 was illegal. President Thomas Jefferson had bought the enormous region that comprises some thirteen states today from Napoleon, and, at one stroke, more than doubled the size of the United States. But Napoleon did not have a clean lease to sell, Spain argued. He had only acquired Louisiana three years before from Spain, which had sold it under duress. Besides, Napoleon had promised never to part with the territory until he had first offered Spain the chance to buy it back. He had not done that, either. The Vienna Congress should, the Spanish legal team argued, correct this injustice.

In other words, Spain was arguing that over half of the United States was held inappropriately, if not also illegally. If Britain would support Spain on regaining its rightful territory, then Spain would return the good measure and ban the slave trade.

Such were the challenges that Castlereagh had to face in fighting against this "odious and criminal Traffick in Human flesh." Whatever the merits of Spain's arguments—and its legal advisers, of course, claimed that they had a strong case—this was hardly a realistic proposal at that time. Britain had, only weeks before, ended a war with the United States and had no desire to renew one, especially over the Louisiana Purchase. Castlereagh politely turned down Spain's proposal and offered instead a tidy 400,000 pounds. Spain accepted.

On February 8, 1815, just days before his expected departure, Castlereagh could finally point to some success. France, Portugal, Spain, and others had come on board, and the Great Powers issued a joint declaration condemning the practice as "repugnant to the principles of humanity and universal morality." They further agreed in the importance of putting an end to a scourge that had so long "desolated Africa, degraded Europe and afflicted humanity." The slave trade should be abolished as soon as possible; France promised to do so in five years, Spain and Portugal agreed on eight years. Admittedly, this was slow and tentative, an abolition of neither slavery nor even of the trade itself. Yet it was a start, and human rights, for the first time, had been made a subject of a peace conference.

Chapter 24

BEFORE THE CAKE WAS CUT

Everything is over or nearly over. All the clouds are dispersed.
Europe owes the happy issue of the negotiations to
the departure of Lord Castlereagh.

— CONVERSATION OVERHEARD AT A BALL IN EARLY 1815

The arrival of the Duke of Wellington had not only affected Vienna's diplomatic activity and social calendar; it was also posing a problem to the painter Jean-Baptiste Isabey, who was trying to capture the congress on canvas. He had been working for some time, and he had finally found a way to balance all the strong personalities, many of them patrons, into one single painting, and yet not offend national sensibilities or fragile egos.

The painting, which depicted the delegates gathered in a conference room, turned out to be a compromise in the best spirit of Vienna diplomacy. Metternich, the president of the Congress, draws the eye, as the only standing figure in the foreground. Castlereagh, though, commands the center, sitting with his legs gracefully crossed and elbow resting on the table. The light shining through the window, however, falls onto Talleyrand, sitting across the table with his dress sword at his side. An empty chair on both his right and left make him further stand out, as do the nearby figures who look to him, just as many of the smaller powers had sought his leadership the last few months.

As Isabey was putting the finishing touches to his composition, he had to figure out what to do about the fact that the Duke of Wellington was now also in town. Starting over was out of the question. Omitting a man of his stature was equally impossible. Yet it was not easy to incorporate him into a canvas on which all the best places had already been taken. The painter's solution was simple and elegant: Why not make the painting commemorate the Duke of Wellington's arrival in Vienna?

That way, the duke could simply be inserted on the far left side of the painting, without any insult to his position. As for the duke's reluctance to be painted from a side angle (he was self-conscious about his nose), Isabey had overcome that with a well-targeted compliment: Didn't Wellington look like the handsome and chivalric Henry IV? Pleased with this comparison, Wellington accepted, joking that Isabey was a "good enough diplomat to take part in the Congress."

The painter also had to apply his finesse to convince Humboldt to enter the studio. The Prussian ambassador hated to have his portrait made, and, sure enough, he first declined, claiming that he had "too ugly a face ever to spend a penny" on a portrait. With this statement, Isabey saw his opportunity and emphasized that he would not "ask the slightest recompense for the pleasant trouble I am going to take." Isabey only wanted "the favor of a few sittings."

"Oh, is that all?" Humboldt quickly came around when he realized it would not cost him anything. "You can have as many sittings as you like."

Later, many congratulated Isabey on his portrait, particularly the fine job with Humboldt. The Prussian did not pay anything, as agreed, and Isabey got his revenge, Humboldt joked, by painting "an excellent likeness of me."

Few could complain of the treatment received from Isabey's flattering brush. This famous painting of the Congress of Vienna was pleasing to all, though typical of this peace conference, the scene was purely imaginary. The group of twenty-three delegates had never met in exactly this way before. Isabey had painted the portraits of each figure individually, and then later assembled the whole group together. And so, symbolically, this simulated image would commemorate a congress that never was.

OVER THE COURSE of the next few weeks, the foreign ministers of all the Great Powers worked hard to finish the negotiations, and their efforts, in turn, showed how misleading it was to imply that the congress only danced. They danced, of course, but they also carried substantial workloads. In an attempt to reach an agreement in early February, Castlereagh was toiling "day and night." Prussia's Hardenberg was working himself to exhaustion, often collapsing in his chair, falling asleep at his desk, and, at times, breaking down into tears. Metternich, too, felt glued to his desk, "like a convict on his chain." The same, of course, went for their assistants.

That February, the Great Powers had finally reached an agreement on Poland: A kingdom was, in fact, to be established. Its territory was to come mostly from the former Duchy of Warsaw, though Austria kept Galicia, while Prussia retained Posen and Gdánsk, and Russia most of its share of eastern Poland. Kraków was to remain outside as a "free, independent and strictly neutral" city. The new Kingdom of Poland was indeed much smaller than the tsar had promised (only 3.2 million people, instead of 10 or 11 million). Its new constitution, moreover, still made Poland "irrevocably attached to Russia" and its king was to be Tsar Alexander. While this compromise left many unhappy, the discontent was not spread equally, and many Polish patriots felt greatly disillusioned.

On February 11, three days after the condemnation of the slave trade, some real results were finally seen on Saxony as well. Despite all the Prussian claims the last several months, the Kingdom of Saxony would in fact be saved. Frederick Augustus would remain its king, and Dresden its capital. Remarkably, too, Saxony would hang on to the thriving town of Leipzig and retain about three-fifths of its kingdom, including lands in the east and south, which were actually its richest and most populous regions.

Prussia would have to settle for the remaining two-fifths of Saxon territory, and one-third of its population, a far cry from its demands for the entire kingdom, which only months before had looked so certain. Prussia would not gain any of the largest towns, or the strategic mountain passageways into Bohemia, but instead it would receive a string of fortresses commanding the waterways of eastern Germany. (These included Erfurt, Torgau on the upper Elbe, and also the historic fortress town of Wittenberg, birthplace of the Protestant Reformation.)

To help ease the pain of this deal, the Russian tsar offered some additional territory from his share of Poland, including the fortress town of Thorn, straddling the Vistula River. The Great Powers had also awarded Prussia Westphalia, which had recently been ruled by Napoleon's younger brother Jérôme, and they added Swedish Pomerania, in the north. Former lands of the archbishop of Trier were also transferred to Prussia, as well as areas from neighboring Hanover and the Netherlands ceded in a last-minute offer made on Castlereagh's initiative. Most important, the Allies handed over a sizable chunk of the Rhineland from the old Holy Roman Empire, including the city of Cologne, with its beautiful soaring medieval cathedral and its prime location on a major central European trade route. Prussia had received its promised 10 million population, and Britain had succeeded in getting a strong Prussia.

Significantly, in one of the most important results of the congress, Prussia had shifted from being a state centered in the east to one pointing to the west—and this, in fact, very much against its own wishes. Significantly, too, Prussia was brought into much closer contact with France. So while the Congress had buried the centuries-old Bourbon-Habsburg rivalry, it had also, by bringing Prussia into the Rhineland, helped create another one that would soon haunt European history.

Few Prussians at the time, however, saw any reason to celebrate. Many were furious. "Where is Germany going to get its security in the future," Humboldt's wife asked him pointedly, if they did not gain Saxony? The army had been promised this region, and they had occupied it, only to be turned out without any significant resistance. No true soldier, Field Marshal Gebhard von Blücher had said, could ever again wear the Prussian uniform with any honor. When the news was announced, Hardenberg's windows back in Berlin were smashed by an angry mob.

Yet while many accused the Prussian delegation of being tricked, corrupted, or simply too weak to resist the "siren charms" of Metternich and the allies, Humboldt realized that there was another side to this story. Despite his formal protests and complaints, he wrote to his wife that Prussia was actually benefiting more by gaining the Rhineland, rather than Saxony. This region was more populous, more productive, and, on the whole, much more valuable. "Prussia is now the greatest German power," he boasted. He was right about the value of the Rhineland, but no one at that time knew the full extent of the wealth, in iron and coal, that would be found in that territory. Fifty years later, the region that they had accepted so reluctantly would be a powerful engine of Prussian industrial might.

For the moment, there would be "two Prussias," as Humboldt saw it, the eastern and the western, separated by sharp cultural and historical differences. Geographically, Prussia would not even be linked together, but sprawled out over and around other independent states, such as Hanover. It was an odd-shaped country. But Humboldt was not too concerned. This unnatural state of affairs would not last long. "With the first war that comes," he added ominously, "Prussia will fill in the gaps."

AS DIPLOMATS DISCUSSED affairs in the middle of a ballroom, or the corner of a salon, conversations often ended abruptly, or quickly shifted onto other subjects when someone approached. Spies were still everywhere, and often ended up observing, reporting on, and even following each other.

In this environment, with work and pleasure intermingling in intrigue-rich salons, many agents were working overtime. The police dossiers give an insight into a day in the life of an agent in early February. After a night at the theater, Agent ** paid a visit to the tsar's physician, always a good source for understanding the mood of the Russian embassy, and then he topped it off at a palace ball. Afterward, he went from "one salon to another" in search of entertainment and information, arriving back home at five in the morning.

As Agent ** circulated in high society, or tried to catch a carriage ride with someone well placed, other agents were finding valuable information in the taverns and restaurants. The delicatessen Jean de Paris on Herrengasse was one popular place to swap gossip as the guests "titillated their palate and ruined their stomach." Spies also continued their work posing as servants, or purchasing information from them. Chambermaids, footmen, porters, and coachmen remained the eyes and ears of the Austrian police.

"I am the victim of the lowest kind of espionage," Marie Louise's secretary, Baron Méneval, complained. "A swarm of ignoble spies crawl around me and study my gestures, my steps, and my face." The Prussian adviser General Jomini was still warning of the letter opening and advising his correspondents: "Write only what you would like to see in the newspapers." Knowledge of this advice, of course, comes from one of his intercepted letters.

By early February, Vienna had moved into the season of Lent and the forty days of reflection and contemplation that culminate in the celebration of Easter. Many delegates and guests lined up to see Zacharias Werner deliver his colorful sermons in his flamboyant style, dropping onto his knees, springing up into the air, shouting, and then falling silent.

Lotteries were another form of entertainment that flourished at the congress, never more than during Lent, when the masquerade balls stopped. At one of these occasions, each invitee would bring a gift and then draw a lot for one of the other presents in the salon. "Everyone contributes and everyone wins" was how Talleyrand described it. Guests might walk home with a jewel case, a mosaic box, a fine Persian rug, a set of porcelain vases, or virtually anything at all.

Castlereagh was probably, at least in part, glad to be leaving this vanity fair behind. He had stalled as long as possible—two grueling weeks that witnessed the resolution of the Poland-Saxony crisis and the condemnation of the slave trade. Before he packed his bags and officially handed over all responsibility to the Duke of Wellington, however, the foreign secretary would make one last initiative. He was working on a plan to resolve the Russian-Turkish conflict that sometimes raged and sometimes smoldered over the Black Sea, the Danube, the Balkans, and virtually anywhere the two empires came into contact.

The British foreign secretary wanted the congress to agree to guarantee peace on the basis of the status quo in this turbulent area that would soon be known as the "powder keg of Europe." This would in turn keep Turkey alive, and at the same time help constrain the appetites of an expansionist tsar poised to pick up gains from the crumbling empire. But to Castlereagh's dismay, his plan was being opposed by the sultan of Turkey. Castlereagh spent one of his last meetings in Vienna, literally on his last day in town, pressing unsuccessfully for an agreement. The question was thus left unresolved, and would unfortunately cause a great deal of tension and bloodshed over the next century.

On February 15, after leaving behind parting gifts to his colleagues, among other things a jeweled snuffbox with a handsome miniature portrait of himself on the inside, Castlereagh's carriage clanked its way out of the Minoritenplatz and headed out of Vienna. He was disappointed with the overall results of the conference and feared that the peace that they had worked so hard to settle would not last more than two years. Moreover, he was returning to London, where he would have to answer for his actions before a hostile Parliament.

WITH POLAND AND Saxony solved at last, the congress would surely now finish "cutting up the cake," as some had termed the efforts. Decisions were, in fact, soon reached on other pending issues as well. One of the first was the Netherlands. As the deal was worked out, Holland was to be re-created as a kingdom, and given Belgium, Luxembourg, and other nearby territories. It was a larger kingdom than some had expected or wanted.

Many Belgians resented being shuffled around against their wishes, preferring either their own rule, Austrian rule as in the eighteenth century, or the French as during the happier moments of the Revolution. Indeed, many wanted anything except the Dutch, who had a different religion, language, culture, and historical traditions. But Great Britain had pushed for an enlarged Kingdom of the Netherlands to safeguard the territory from a renewed French attack, and to create a buffer for itself. And Britain had succeeded.

At the same time, Metternich was working to resolve a border dispute with Bavaria over Salzburg, the birthplace of Wolfgang Amadeus Mozart and the home of lucrative salt mines. There was a conflict over the ownership of Berchtesgaden, the mountain resort later notorious as a retreat for Nazi leadership, which had been Austrian before Napoleon took it away and gave it to his ally at the time, Bavaria. The two countries were working on finding some agreement over these territories, a difficult negotiation that showed little sign of progress and would not in fact be completed until after the congress, when Austria gained Salzburg; and Bavaria, Berchtesgaden.

Boosted by the progress on so many fronts, Talleyrand now shifted his attentions to focus on the pressing question of Naples. King Joachim I (Murat) was still in power there, and while no one particularly liked the fact, few were willing to do anything about it. Talleyrand was using all his arguments to rally support, emphasizing the importance of legitimacy for the postwar order, and the vital necessity of removing this unpredictable warrior from the throne. Peace could never be assured, he argued, as long as the last usurper ruled in Europe.

It was important to reach a favorable conclusion on this matter immediately, Talleyrand felt, because the congress seemed to be winding down. Rumors abounded everywhere of imminent departures. Tsar Alexander had already announced his intention to return home by the middle of the month, though the date of departure had been postponed a couple of times. He pledged, at all events, to be back in St. Petersburg in time for the celebration of Easter, which in the Russian Orthodox calendar fell that year on the last day of April.

Following the tsar's lead, other sovereigns had also expressed their desire to return home. Even the host, Emperor Francis, was restless. Officially, he wanted to leave town to make a tour of the banking city of Milan, the ruined marvel of Venice, and other gems of northern Italy that were being restored to Austria. Indeed, after months of putting on a never-ending round of banquets, masked balls, and other forms of entertainment, the emperor was growing weary of his permanent houseguests.

"This desire on the part of every one to go away," Talleyrand predicted, "will expedite the conclusion of affairs." If he had any chance to restore the Bourbon king to Naples, he knew that he had to act quickly.

One morning in mid-February, Talleyrand went over to meet with the tsar, hoping to recruit his assistance on removing Murat. The tsar, however, was more interested in finding out why exactly the king of France had not paid the 2 million francs that he had promised Napoleon.

"As I have been absent from Paris for five months," Talleyrand answered, "I do not know what has been done in this respect."

"The treaty has not been executed; we ought to insist on its execution," the tsar assured him. "Our honor is at stake; we cannot possibly draw back." Alexander added that the emperor of Austria agreed completely.

"Sire, I will report all that you have done me the honor of saying to me," Talleyrand answered politely, and then tried to turn the discussion back onto the subject of Naples. He argued as best he could, but the tsar had a valid point, as would soon be painfully clear.

IT WAS INDEED true that King Louis XVIII had not paid any of the 2 million francs in pension promised to him. Napoleon's own funds, meanwhile, were dwindling. He had to support about a thousand guards, maintain his palace, and pay many other expenses, not to mention the cost of the court life he had wanted as emperor of Elba.

Napoleon had heard rumors about the squabbling heads of state in

Vienna, and, worse, his own informers reported that some delegates were lobbying to have him moved farther away from the Continent. Story after story had also arrived emphasizing the chaos that reigned in France. The army was on half pay, if paid at all. Many had been discharged from service, or relegated to the sidelines to make way for the king's favorites, fit only for the parade ground. The government seemed stuck in a "malevolent muddle," and many openly expressed their regret for the loss of their former emperor.

Napoleon, too, seemed frustrated and bored. On the surface, he had settled down into a modest domestic routine. Evenings ended early, about nine, when Napoleon would stand, walk over to the piano, and, with a single finger, tap the first fourteen chords of Haydn's Symphony no. 94 *(Surprise)*. Then he "bowed and left the room." But those near him knew how much Napoleon resented the way the Allies had treated him, and he feared more treachery. Above all, he regretted that he had abdicated without a fight. Why had he listened to his advisers and not his own inclinations? Just the thought of that made him sick.

In this discontent, a mysterious visitor arrived at Elba that February: Fleury de Chaboulon, a thirty-year-old out-of-work bureaucrat, a former subprefect in Burgundy. Traveling incognito, this man brought reminders of Napoleon's popularity, and, more important, news that a plot was being hatched to overthrow King Louis XVIII and replace him with the king's more popular cousin, the duc d'Orléans. The significance was clear. Napoleon could not sit back on this tiny island while someone else captured the throne of France.

In all likelihood, Napoleon had been planning to leave Elba for some time. But this visit probably convinced him that the time for action had come. In addition, in mid-February, Neil Campbell announced that he was leaving for a trip to the mainland for a cure of his wounds (and a visit with his mistress). Campbell would not be back for two weeks, and Napoleon realized his opportunity.

It was his audacious moves, after all, that had crowned his greatest achievements. A bold strike to seize power had succeeded back in 1799 when many others had plotted and failed. He had crowned himself emperor in 1804, and succeeded, despite the protests of others. A daring decoy maneuver had helped him win big at Austerlitz. Again and again, it was the gutsy moves that had worked best, pushed at breathtaking speed and catching his opponents off guard (of course, they had also failed spectacularly sometimes, like the Russian invasion).

Fed up with the string of broken promises and determined to strike before something worse happened to him, or someone else capitalized on the turmoil back in France, Napoleon had made up his mind. It was time to return to France.

All the energy he had invested in conquering and controlling Europe was now brought to this enterprise. As always, he was careful not to reveal his true intentions. The ship *Inconstant,* which had mysteriously crashed into a roadstead on a routine sail around Elba a few weeks before, was now being refurbished without too much undue attention. He strengthened the masts, revamped the hull, and added a layer of paint that, on inspection, made the brig look remarkably close to an English warship.

On February 26, 1815, the very day of his departure, Napoleon had made sure that everything seemed normal. The soldiers had been planting trees, working in the garden, and carrying out other standard duties, as they had done for months. Napoleon went to Mass in the morning, dined with his mother and sister in the evening, and then rode down to the harbor, passing many curious cheering and waving Elbans. Everything had been loaded onto the sixteen-gun brig *Inconstant.* After nine months and twenty-two days, Napoleon and his crew were ready to set sail.

Napoleon had earned a reputation for daring enterprises, but this one was to be his riskiest venture yet. He was invading one of the most powerful countries on earth, and he had about 1,100 men, seven small boats, and four cannons. The emperor liked the odds. "I shall reach Paris," he announced, "without firing a shot."

Chapter 25

TIME TO SAVE THE WORLD AGAIN

The events are so extraordinary, so unexpected, so magical . . .
it seems that 1,001 Nights is coming true, and everything
happens by the wand of some invisible magician.

— JEAN-GABRIEL EYNARD IN HIS DIARY, MARCH 1815

On Tuesday, March 7, after three in the morning, Metternich climbed the marble steps to his private rooms on the third floor of the Chancellery, where he crawled into bed for a well-deserved sleep. Another lengthy meeting of the Committee of Five had finally ended, and he was exhausted. "I had forbidden my valet to disturb my rest," he said.

Only a few hours later, his valet entered the chamber with a dispatch marked "URGENT." Metternich took the envelope, glanced at the far-away sender, and then promptly set it on his nightstand. He then tried to go back to sleep, but as he put it, "sleep once disturbed, would not return." About half past seven, he gave up his tossing and turning, and opened the dispatch. It was a letter that he would never forget.

The commissioner on Elba, Neil Campbell, reported that Napoleon was nowhere to be found and wondered if anyone had seen him. The Austrian foreign minister sprang out of bed, threw on his clothes, and raced over to the Hofburg to inform Emperor Francis. By eight in the morning, they were deep in discussion.

"Napoleon apparently wants to play the adventurer; that is his business," the emperor told Metternich. He continued:

Our business is to secure for the world that peace which he has troubled all these years. Go at once to the Emperor of Russia and the King of Prussia; tell them that I am prepared to order my army once again to march back into France. I have no doubt that the two Sovereigns will join me.

As Metternich described the historic morning, he had a meeting with the tsar over in the Amalia wing of the palace at 8:15 and then hurried across the inner court to meet with the king of Prussia. By nine that morning, he was back at the Chancellery for a meeting with Austrian field marshal Prince Schwarzenberg. "It was in less than an hour," he boasted with some exaggeration, "that war was declared."

Meanwhile, a few blocks away at Kaunitz Palace, Talleyrand was still in bed. Dorothée was seated next to her uncle, drinking chocolate and looking forward to her dress rehearsal later in the day for a theater production that opened that evening. A white-wigged footman in gray livery brought in a note from Prince Metternich.

"It is probably to tell me what time today's meeting of the Congress is to begin," Talleyrand predicted without much concern, as he handed the note to Dorothée. She opened it and read its contents. "Bonaparte has escaped from Elba. Oh, Uncle, what about my rehearsal?"

"Your rehearsal, Madame, will take place all the same," Talleyrand replied with an unruffled composure. Equally calm, he rose from the bed, summoned his assistants, hurried through his ritual levee, and then headed over to the Austrian Chancellery.

BY TEN O'CLOCK, the Allies were already gathering in Metternich's study for an emergency meeting.

Talleyrand was the first to arrive at the Chancellery, and Metternich took the opportunity to read the dispatch.

"Do you know where Napoleon is headed?" Talleyrand asked.

"The report does not say anything about it."

"He will land somewhere on the Italian coast and fling himself into Switzerland," Talleyrand predicted.

"No," Metternich answered, "he will go straight to Paris."

This viewpoint was by no means obvious at the time. The road to

Paris would mean progressing through many parts of southern France that had been bastions of royal support and scenes of bitter opposition to Napoleon. Given his unpopularity there, a French destination seemed unlikely, to say the least. If Napoleon "sets foot there," Russia's Corsican adviser, Pozzo di Borgo, would soon predict, "he will be seized the moment he lands, and hanged from the nearest tree."

At this point, Prince Hardenberg and Count Nesselrode entered Metternich's study. The Duke of Wellington also arrived, having quickly changed his plans upon hearing the news. He had hoped to spend the morning hunting in the park.

When the ministers began discussing the dispatch, it was clear that they had no idea of Napoleon's intentions. One thing that they did agree on, however, was the importance of keeping everything quiet, as they did not want to alarm the town. Napoleon's escape would not appear in the next morning's newspapers, *Wiener Zeitung* and the *Österreichischer Beobachter*. On the following day, there was only a small notice in the latter paper, buried in the "Foreign News" section under the headline for Italy.

Even Metternich's assistant, Friedrich von Gentz, who had shouldered so many duties as secretary of the Congress, was not informed. Gentz would come by Metternich's office that same morning, as usual, where the two discussed congress business, though there was no hint of Napoleon being on the loose. Gentz would not find out until later that day, when his old friend Wilhelm von Humboldt told him.

NEWS OF THIS kind could not be hushed up for long in a town buzzing with gossip. Once leaked, it spread rapidly, and, typically for the congress, this happened later that night at the theater.

It was during an amateur production of Kotzebue's *Old Love Affairs* in the Redoutensaal. The tsar, the king of Prussia, and all the leading figures were in the audience, trying to act as if nothing had happened. They did not want to cause panic, nor spoil the performance. After all, Metternich's daughter Marie, Talleyrand's niece Dorothée, and the tsar's "celestial beauty," Gabrielle Auersperg, would all be appearing onstage that night.

Just before the heavy curtain rose, the delegates in their plush red velvet-and-gold-trimmed seats were seen whispering, and then, not long afterward, so were the audience and the actors backstage. It was there at the theater that Countess Bernstorff first learned of the news, and also Countess Lulu Thürheim, the diarist. She described how the dignitaries tried valiantly to keep their opera glasses fixed on the stage. The feigned nonchalance, however, was in vain. Fear could be "read on their faces," as Countess Bernstorff noticed.

As everyone knew, Napoleon was a dangerous threat, and even if he did not yet have an army, that would probably not last long. He was still wildly popular with the soldiers, who remembered with pride how the warlord had triumphed over great odds, humbled kings, and led them to many victories. It was Napoleon who had given France honor and glory, only, in the end, to be unceremoniously betrayed by his marshals. What a miserable sight King Louis and his cronies made in comparison.

There were indeed many angry people in France—the question was how many soldiers and citizens were upset enough to abandon their king and join Napoleon. Also, as the Vienna Congress had alienated many factions the last several months, some feared that Napoleon might attract more international support than originally thought. For example, Joachim Murat, the former Bonaparte marshal, was still ruling as king in Naples, despite all Talleyrand's opposition, and he could potentially rally to Napoleon's side.

There were also many Poles disillusioned with the Russian project for their country. One spy reported that "the Poles overflow with delight" on the news of Napoleon's departure, as many sensed a chance, finally, to realize dreams of a restored kingdom. Napoleon had promised them a kingdom long before, and many believed that unlike the tsar, he might actually fulfill his promise this time.

What if Tsar Alexander, for that matter, had another one of his "periodic evolutions of the mind" and decided to desert his allies at the Vienna Congress? This was a real concern for the Allies; he had already gotten everything that they were going to give him, but Napoleon might soon have a more tempting offer for him.

Indeed, once the shock of Napoleon's voyage wore off, the gravity of the situation settled in, and the Allies began to blame one another. Many accused the English of sloppy work, bungling their vigilance. Where had those famous Royal Navy cruisers been when Napoleon was leaving

Elba? Why did Britain's governor, Neil Campbell, leave the island so mysteriously on the eve of Napoleon's departure? Talleyrand articulated this position when he remarked that "the English, whose duty it was to watch his movements, were guilty of a negligence which they will find it difficult to excuse."

"Are we Napoleon's keepers?" Lord Stewart asked, defensively shrugging off Britain's critics. "What right do we have to keep him under guard?"

Stewart had a point, to an extent. Napoleon was a sovereign ruler of an independent power, and there was, in fact, nothing in the treaty of abdication that prohibited him from leaving Elba. And Britain had never signed the treaty that placed him so close to the Continent. They had, in other words, never recognized Napoleon's right to the island, much less his retention of the title *emperor*. Why exactly was it Britain's responsibility that Napoleon chose to leave Elba?

The French might be quick to point fingers, but matters might have been different if the French government had only fulfilled its obligations. King Louis XVIII had never paid, as promised, the 2 million francs. Many had reminded France of this fact, only to be ignored. To Talleyrand's endless frustration, the king's government had made many blunders. As the Danish foreign minister put it in his journal, the French were acting "as if they had put a dangerous man in prison, refused him bread and then left the door open"—and now complained when he left.

Prussia's Humboldt, for his part, wanted to know where Napoleon had received financing for his departure. Obviously, it was not from the French king, and Napoleon's own funds were supposed to be running low. Rumors of an Austrian general, Franz Freiherr von Koller, making a secretive trip to Elba prior to Napoleon's departure were circulating, and, indeed, it was true. But what exactly was he doing on Elba? The Austrians claimed it was to negotiate a divorce between Napoleon and Marie Louise, though some were skeptical. Would it not be in Austria's interest to have an Austrian archduchess as empress of France, and her son as heir to the French throne? Did Austria have a hand in Napoleon's extraordinary departure?

Then there was the tsar, whose "sentimental politics" had caused Napoleon to be sent to Elba in the first place, over the protests of his allies. Just like the British, Metternich had tried to warn about the close proximity, and during the congress, Talleyrand had attempted several times to have Napoleon moved off Elba. Islands from the Azores to St. Helena in the South Atlantic had all been proposed as a better place for his exile, but nothing had been done.

Of course, with Napoleon's rash actions, everything had changed at the peace conference, and the planned departures that spring would have to be temporarily postponed. Urgent matters were, once again, thrust onto the agenda for the Vienna Congress.

Looking around at his harried colleagues, the British diplomat Lord Clancarty observed how everyone made heroic efforts "to conceal apprehension under the masque of unconcern." Yet, he added, "It was not difficult to perceive that fear was predominant in all the Imperial and Royal personages." Napoleon had to be stopped, it was clear, before he "could set the world on fire again."

Chapter 26

His Majesty, the Outlaw

All that may be only an illusion, but what in our days is real?

—Duchess of Sagan, spring of 1815

Back in Paris, the French government pretended not to be overly concerned with the new threat. King Louis XVIII noted that he was sleeping better than ever, and complained more about his gout than the man of Elba. The official newspaper, the *Moniteur,* summed up Napoleon's enterprise as an "act of madness" that would be squashed by "a few rural policemen."

Yet the fact remained that the king's army was deserting in droves, and so were government officials. Given the challenge that Napoleon posed, it was necessary for Vienna's peacemakers to act quickly. But what exactly should they do? One of the French embassy officials, Alexis de Noailles, had no trouble reaching a conclusion about Napoleon: "Now he had escaped, we must hang him!"

"We can't hang him until we've caught him," the king of Prussia responded, "and that won't be so very easy."

In fact, the plenipotentiaries were limited in what they could do until they knew, for certain, where Napoleon was headed. In the meantime, they had to wrap up the remaining disputes of the peace congress. The first order of business was to finish the Saxony affair—that is, convince the king of Saxony to accept last month's solution that he yield two-fifths of his territory and about one-third of his population.

Recently released from prison, the king of Saxony was staying in the old fortress in the nearby town of Pressburg, today's Bratislava, Slovakia. He had no desire to enter Vienna in the presence of his spoliators, and many at the congress returned the sentiment. The congress would send a distinguished delegation to him: Talleyrand, Metternich, and Wellington.

When the leaders arrived at the court of the king on the eighth of March, they were greeted with a cool reception. After a preliminary dinner and general meeting, the king of Saxony received each one individually, and haughtily. The king's men raised objection after objection to the congress's plans for Saxony. "They seemed to nourish a hope," Talleyrand said, "that the terms which have been agreed upon were still open to negotiation."

But the king of Saxony did not change his tune, no more inclined to yield now than he had been earlier, when he had held out as one of the last loyal rulers to Napoleon. No doubt, the king figured that he had more to gain from the emperor than these polished gentlemen, and decided to gamble on better terms in the future. The congress's delegation returned to Vienna without any success.

All over town, people were discussing—and speculating wildly—about Napoleon's actions. In an anonymous police report submitted to Baron Hager, one agent reported that many people now believed that the English had played a role in Napoleon's escape. They had allowed, if not also encouraged and supported, his enterprise. Napoleon had been lured out, it was surmised, so that the congress would have a "pretext to treat him with more severity."

Napoleon's departure from Elba was the topic of every conversation, the Russian soldier Alexander Ivanovich Mikhailovsky-Danilevsky remembered, "if not the only topic of conversation." He had heard it everywhere, on "walks, at gatherings, and meetings in private houses and in cafés." Baronne du Montet recalled, too, how the frightening news caused a great deal of distress. The king of Bavaria, for instance, "walked around for days as if he were deranged." Others were more detached. As spies reported, several people were placing bets on what Napoleon would do next and how far he would go.

On March 10, a messenger arrived with the first real news about Napoleon's destination. He had not, as many suspected, crossed over to Italy, either to seize Genoa or land farther south. He had instead opted for the far more difficult option of France. Moreover, against all odds, he had landed safely at Golfe-Juan, about one mile west of Cannes.

According to La Garde-Chambonas, the shocking news came at a ball over at the Metternichs', and spread like wildfire among the happy waltz-ing couples. Metternich's orchestra struggled, in vain, to maintain the dreamy graceful swirls, but the dancers had merely stopped and stared at each other in disbelief. Who could really believe that Napoleon was back in France? "Thousands of candles," La Garde-Chambonas added, "seemed to have gone out simultaneously."

The songwriter paints a vivid scene. The Russian tsar turned to Tal-leyrand and snapped, "I told you that it would not last." The French minister did not say a word in reply, but only bowed politely. The king of Prussia and the Duke of Wellington hurried out of the ballroom together, followed by the Austrian emperor and the Russian tsar. "Napoleon, not wishing to finish by a tragedy, will finish by a farce," Talleyrand pre-dicted to Prince Metternich, who, not responding, "excused himself" and joined the congress dignitaries who had just left the floor. The French minister left that evening arm in arm with Dorothée. The crowded ball-room was very soon emptied.

This scene almost certainly never happened. For one thing, Vienna was still in Lent, and there were no balls then. Yet the scene, despite the lack of literal truthfulness, is true to the personalities and the tensions of the time. Talleyrand, for example, faced a whole new set of challenges now that France was at risk from Napoleon, civil war, and an invasion from the powers at the congress. The French foreign minister would no longer be welcome in the deliberations. Having worked his way into the inner circle, Talleyrand was finding himself at risk of being pushed out-side again.

As for the grand balls, where "the quivering violins alternated with serious negotiations," as Countess Thürheim remembered, they were occurring much less frequently now. The Carnival season had ended three weeks before, many sovereigns planned to return home, and the Austrian emperor had started looking for ways to curtail the expensive entertain-ment. In a letter dated March 21, Emperor Francis would specifically instruct his lord chamberlain to decrease expenses and reduce "the num-ber of servants employed." The court was also "to follow the general guidelines that extraordinary celebrations should no longer be arranged or given." So despite the make-believe surrounding La Garde-Chambonas's scene, Vienna's ballrooms were soon to be emptied indeed.

ON HIS WAY from Elba, Napoleon had enjoyed good fortune in eluding several ships patrolling the waters. The *Inconstant* passed the French frigates *Melpomène* and *Fleur-de-Lys* without incident, and then, rounding Corsica, Napoleon passed yet another enemy warship, the *Zéphir,* without any difficulties. Even the British vessel carrying Campbell back to Elba, the *Partridge,* was sighted on the horizon. No one had stopped him. Conspiracy theories would proliferate for years. Had the winds blown differently, others have speculated, Napoleon might easily have been seized or sunk.

By the first of March, when Napoleon's brig had approached Golfe-Juan, people at first thought it was a small band of pirates about to make a raid. Learning the true identity of the crew, however, did not seem to please them any more. Some scoffed at the ragtag gang that had just been "vomited up from the sea."

But Napoleon had safely disembarked, and managed to pass through the streets without harm. To the thrill of his supporters, at first mainly soldiers and peasants, the initial surprise and cold reception was beginning to thaw. Gradually, there were more cheers and shouts of *"Vive l'Empereur!"*

At this beautiful medieval town, Napoleon faced another major decision. Examining his map sprawled out on a table in the middle of an olive garden, Napoleon calculated his chances either way. He could continue through southern France, a hotbed of royal support, or chance a dangerous mountain path through the French Alps into Grenoble. It was steep and narrow, hardly fit for his cumbersome baggage trains and cannon pieces, and it was covered with ice. Still, that one was deemed the least risky route.

Southern France had suffered tremendously during his empire. Ports like Marseille had been crippled under Napoleon's unsuccessful attempt to boycott English goods, and their shipping business decimated. Taxes had been crushing, and extended to all sorts of items, including alcohol and tobacco. Farmers there, and elsewhere, complained of being forced to furnish the army with supplies, their fields stripped down to the "last kernel of corn and the last forkful of fodder." And, of course, like so many others, they resented the conscriptions into the army and the heavy loss of life in his wars, all of which seemed a high price to pay for Napoleon's so-called glory.

While preparing for the mountain passageway, and abandoning his cannons, which he figured he would not need, anyway, Napoleon finished his own proclamations, one to the French people and another to his soldiers. Both sounded like rallying speeches straight out of those stirring addresses of his early campaigns: "Frenchmen, in my exile, I heard your plaints and prayers; I have crossed the sea amid perils of every kind; I [have] come to you to assert my rights, which are ours."

To the soldiers, he reminded them that they had been not defeated, but rather betrayed by a few marshals who sold out the country, the army, and its glory. He had been summoned back to France by the will of the people, and his symbol, the eagle, would soon "fly steeple to steeple all over the country to Notre Dame."

The emperor's progress was, in fact, astounding. His soldiers marched some fifteen to twenty miles, and often many more, each day under exhausting and very difficult conditions. It was necessary to move quickly, before the Bourbons had a chance to realize what had happened.

King Louis XVIII and the French government were, of course, taking measures to resist Bonaparte. The minister of war, Marshal Nicolas Jean Soult, the former Bonapartist, had some 60,000 troops in the south waiting for deployment, and supposedly another 120,000 on reserve at Melun, south of Paris, that could cover the main roads to the capital. Another marshal working for the king, André Masséna, was marching troops after the invaders. Orders were also made to blow up strategic bridges, such as Ponhaut, and block the way to Grenoble.

On March 7, at Laffrey, some fifteen miles outside Grenoble, Napoleon had the famous confrontation with the Fifth Infantry Regiment. The commander had orders to stop "Bonaparte's brigands," and he was determined to obey. Napoleon's army approached, led by his Polish Lancers and the Old Guard to the rallying anthem of "La Marseillaise." Napoleon himself rode to the front of his troops, dismounted, and advanced straight ahead in the line of fire of the king's soldiers. "There he is, fire," the royalist commander ordered. Napoleon then shouted, "Soldiers of the fifth, I am your Emperor."

"If there is any one among you who would kill his Emperor," Napoleon continued as he opened his greatcoat, "here I am." The tense silence was broken with shouts, *"Vive l'Empereur!"* The soldiers deserted and joined him.

Later that day, only hours after Vienna learned of his escape, Napoleon had already reached Grenoble, some two hundred miles north of his landing. "The inhabitants of Grenoble [were] proud to have the conqueror of Europe within their walls." Five army regiments had come over to his side, and he also gained a large cache of artillery, guns, gunpowder, and other military supplies. No major bridge had been destroyed to slow the advance.

Few orders were, in fact, carried out. Bonapartists in the king's army often refused to obey them, or sabotaged their execution, if they did not desert outright to Napoleon. Other Frenchmen, divided in their loyalties, hedged their bets and waited on the outcome.

Louis XVIII had committed so many mistakes since his restoration that he had effectively obliterated the memories of the worst excesses of the Napoleonic regime. When Napoleon arrived in a town, many rushed to greet him as a liberator. His sympathizers swarmed the popular cafés, looking for supporters and returning encouraged by what they saw. Townsmen stopped their daily activities and talked quietly in their own private enclaves, and street vendors even paused from their tireless railing to observe the astonishing events.

Back in Vienna, the news from France was bad and getting worse. Napoleon was marching with great momentum, and the king's soldiers were rapidly flocking to his side. Fewer symbols of the king, such as lilies and white handkerchiefs, were seen. In fact, when they appeared, the flowers were often trampled, the flags torn to shreds, and the Bourbon coats of arms smashed. Only ten days after his landing, France's second city, Lyon, had fallen. Louis XVIII was having to come to grips with betrayal, desertion, and incompetence on a grand scale.

Vienna's stock exchange had plummeted on this news, and the momentous events surrounding Napoleon's march north were clearly raising the specters of war all over again. The Swiss banker Eynard gave the odds of Napoleon's success, first at 1,000 to 1, and then, a few days later, at 10 to 1. Two additional days, and the bet was even. How on earth could this have happened? Had Napoleon, some asked, made a pact with the devil?

While many of Vienna's diplomats worked with zeal to oppose Napoleon, there were others visibly delighted by Napoleon's success, particularly the many disenchanted, disillusioned, and disenfranchised delegations that deeply resented the way the congress had acted.

The Prussians, for example, seemed happier than they had been for a long time. Extreme opinion not only wanted war, but also hoped to wipe France off the map, carving it up into small states such as Burgundy, Champagne, Auvergne, Brittany, Aquitaine, and others. Territories in the east, like Alsace and Lorraine, would promptly return to a German home. French property would be granted outright to the Allies, or, at the least, used to offset the costs of the new war. Prussian generals looked forward to accomplishing with the sword what the diplomats had failed to secure with the pen.

FOR TALLEYRAND, NAPOLEON'S success caused a lot of concerns. The last thing he had wanted was another Allied invasion of France, and hundreds of thousands of soldiers marching across the country, some undoubtedly preying upon the people again like "ferocious beasts." In this scenario, Talleyrand knew that the suffering would be great, and the chances were slim that France would enjoy such a lenient peace a second time.

Faced with this challenge, Talleyrand had hatched a plan that he hoped would ensure that Vienna's plenipotentiaries made an important distinction between France and Napoleon, and kept the two entities separate. He would draw up a declaration that would specifically name Napoleon, not France, as the enemy. Perhaps, then, all the inevitable anger unleashed in war would be confined to that single person and his supporters and not be projected onto the entire country.

Talleyrand had written a draft, and prepared to present it at a meeting on March 13. The stakes were high. Before his carriage left Kaunitz Palace, he advised his fellow diplomats:

> Watch for my return from the palace windows. If I succeed, you will see me in the carriage window holding up the treaty on which hangs the fate of France and Europe.

As Talleyrand worded it, Napoleon was denounced as a "wild beast" and all of Europe was called upon to rid the world of this "bandit." As he put it, "every measure permissible against brigands should be permissible against him."

Historians have often depicted the outlawing measure as inevitable, but it hardly seemed that way at the time. When Metternich read the draft at the meeting, he was skeptical. Should such words as "wild beast" and "bandit" really be used for Emperor Francis's son-in-law? Wellington also found the terminology inappropriate. Although he had no love for Napoleon, he did not wish to be seen as encouraging outright murder.

Debate raged throughout the night on this declaration that Talleyrand urged on the congress, and it reached a climax—a loud climax—around midnight, when, according to Humboldt, twenty voices were all shouting at once. In the end, Metternich offered a more moderate formulation, and this one was adopted.

In this declaration, drafted by the indefatigable Gentz, Napoleon Bonaparte was in fact declared an outlaw and denounced for his reckless violation of his previous agreement. Napoleon had also, the document continued, "deprived himself of the protection of the law and demonstrated before the world that there can be neither peace nor a truce with him."

However much it was moderated, this solemn document would still cause a scandal. In Vienna, only eight powers were allowed to sign the declaration—the same members of the Committee of Eight. The rest were excluded completely. The king of Denmark and the king of Bavaria, among many others, had not been invited to the meetings, or even consulted on the matter.

Outside Vienna, two passages in the declaration particularly came under fire, one claiming that Napoleon had lost "his sole lawful right to exist," and the other:

> The Powers declare that Napoleon Buonaparte has placed himself outside all human relations and that, as the enemy and disturber of the peace of the world, he has delivered himself up to public justice. *(vindicte publique)*

Some newspapers, when reporting the story of the declaration, translated the phrase *vindicte publique* as "public vengeance," and not, as

Metternich had insisted with his better grasp of French, only as "public justice" or "prosecution." As for the words about Napoleon forfeiting his "sole lawful right to exist," this only referred to legal status, though that was too subtle a distinction for some newspapers' editors. The damage was done. Mistranslations were in print, and critics now had another accusation to hurl at the Vienna Congress: the peacemakers were trying "to deliver Buonaparte over to the dagger of the assassin."

It was Wellington and the British delegation, of course, who would be most criticized for this declaration; after all, they came from a land with a Parliament, an active opposition party, and a relatively free press. One opposition leader, Samuel Whitbread, spoke for many when he criticized this vindictive and "abhorrent" declaration, which branded Napoleon an outlaw and encouraged his murder, when it was the Bourbons who had failed to fulfill their obligations to him. Wellington would be criticized almost daily. Talleyrand, on the other hand, would not have to worry that much. His critics had long accused him of worse.

Indeed, Talleyrand was pleased to put his graceful signature at the bottom of the document. He had obtained his main objective. Declaring Napoleon an outlaw would focus the animosity on him, not the French people, and, moreover, it would serve to "deprive traitors of confidence and to give courage to the loyal." In his letter to King Louis, Talleyrand praised the wording of the document: "It is very strong; there has never been a document of so much power and importance signed by all the sovereigns of Europe."

This was, in fact, the first time in history that states had effectively declared war on a single person. Talleyrand returned to the embassy late that night, waving a copy of the document, signed and stamped with red and black seals. His diplomatic team at Kaunitz Palace was thrilled. "I do not think," Talleyrand concluded in his letter back to Paris, "that we could have done better here."

ONE PERSON INTIMATELY affected by the news of Napoleon's actions was, of course, his estranged wife, Marie Louise. Despite her promises to join him on Elba, she had not done so. She had instead stopped writing, or even answering his letters, and at the same time continued her love affair with General Count Neipperg.

Marie Louise had not immediately been informed of her husband's escape. She only learned the news on Wednesday, March 8, when her son's governess, Madame de Montesquiou, forwarded the information in a letter, before someone else told her. Marie Louise did not take it well. According to agents in the palace, the young former empress "burst into tears," ran to her room, and cried uncontrollably, "sobbing [heard] all the way out in the anteroom."

Only a few days before, after months of uncertainty, Marie Louise had finally been assured the Duchy of Parma as promised. She had been thrilled by the prospects of moving there with her lover, Count Neipperg, and leaving behind the bad memories of the Vienna Congress. Unfortunately, however, Napoleon's flight was threatening to upset her life again. Wouldn't this act of desperation be interpreted by some as breaking the treaty that guaranteed her right to Parma? Her opponents now had another excuse for handing the territory over to the Spanish Bourbons. "My poor Louise, how sorry I feel for you!" her uncle, Johan, Archduke of Austria, said. "For your sake and ours, I hope that he breaks his neck!"

With Bonaparte the outlaw on the loose and advancing closer to the French capital, it was more important than ever to keep the little Napoleon under close surveillance. The four-year-old boy playing on the parquet floors of Schönbrunn Palace was potentially, once again, heir to the French throne, and the link that could solidify Napoleon's dynasty.

The French embassy reported hearing a rumor that someone would soon attempt to kidnap the little prince. Vienna's police chief, Baron Hager, was also worried about this threat. Bonapartist agents were allegedly already in town, and many suspicious people had been seen in the neighborhood of the palace.

By the middle of March, Baron Hager had increased the number of guards patrolling the grounds, and he had planted more policemen in the castle, disguised as servants. In case of emergency, Hager sent a detailed description of the boy to "police stations and customs houses" in the area. Agents were told to be on the lookout for a four-year-old male, tall for his age, with blue eyes, curly blond hair, and a distinctive nose "tip-tilted with wide nostrils." He spoke French and German, and gesticulated greatly.

On March 19, the night before Napoleon's son's fourth birthday, there was allegedly an attempt to kidnap him from his nursery. Rumors of this alleged abduction made their rounds, despite official denials. Soon the culprit was identified as his nurse, Madame de Montesquiou, an ardent Bonapartist. Her son Anatole, who had arrived from Paris just before, was also suspected, and promptly arrested.

It is by no means evident that either one was actually involved, and both would always proclaim their innocence. Madame de Montesquiou was fired the next day, as were many others around her. Spies also stepped up security against another Bonapartist attempt—or even, for that matter, a royalist plot—to seize the heir for their own purposes. Little Napoleon was moved out of Schönbrunn Palace and placed under tight security in the Hofburg.

1. Twenty-three delegates in the negotiation room of the Austrian Chancellery. Standing, from left to right: Wellington, Lobo da Silveira, Saldanha da Gama, Löwenhielm, Noailles, Metternich, La Tour du Pin, Nesselrode, Dalberg, Razumovsky, Stewart, Clancarty, Wacken, Gentz, Humboldt, and Cathcart. Seated, from left to right: Hardenberg, Palmella, Castlereagh, Wessenberg, Labrador, Talleyrand, and Stackelberg.

2. Kings, queens, and princes, as well as rogues, renegades, adventurers, gamblers, and courtesans flocked to Vienna for the congress—"every person a novel," the Prince de Ligne said.

3. Austrian foreign minister and president of the Congress, Prince Metternich—handsome, flirtatious, and seemingly frivolous master of diplomacy.

4. France's foreign minister, the brilliant, unscrupulous "prince of diplomats," Charles-Maurice de Talleyrand.

5. Francis I, the last Holy Roman Emperor and the first Emperor of Austria. He had once wanted a special clock that would slow down in times of pleasure and speed up in times of trial—a device that would have helped him cope with a palace full of houseguests who never seemed to agree, or leave.

6. Russian Tsar Alexander I, the foremost conqueror of Napoleon, whose sexual escapades and mystical experiences fascinated, wearied and alarmed Vienna. Alexander took offense at the Prince de Ligne's famous quip about the "dancing congress," believing that it was aimed primarily at him.

7. King of Prussia, Frederick William III, lived in the shadow of his famous great uncle, Frederick the Great. While he lacked his predecessor's flair for military strategy, he certainly loved uniforms. "How do you manage to button so many buttons?" Napoleon had once teased him.

8. British Foreign Secretary Lord Castlereagh pressed for a balance of power (except, of course, on the seas). He spoke little, smiled less, it was said, though in private, he could be quite charming.

9. The oldest and one of the ablest of the delegates, Prussia's Chancellor Hardenberg, strongly disagreed with many policies that he was forced to carry out.

10. Philologist, scholar, administrator, and ambassador to Vienna, Wilhelm von Humboldt, served Prussia with the same energy that he had used when he had reformed the Prussian educational system and founded Berlin University.

11. The Duke of Wellington was one of the most popular men alive. His arrival in February 1815 raised expectations: peace or war in fourteen days, it was widely believed.

Women had never before and have never since played a more influential role at a peace conference.

12. Hostess of a lively salon and center of intrigue in the Palm Palace, Princess Bagration the "beautiful naked angel" who wore scandalously revealing dresses. She was immortalized in a Balzac novel, as well as *le potage Bagration* and *la salade Bagration*, both coined by Talleyrand's chef.

13. Hostess of a rival salon in the Palm Palace, the glamorous Duchess of Sagan, who, like her archenemy Princess Bagration, seduced Vienna, becoming a major source of tension between Metternich and the tsar.

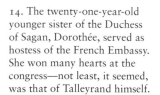

14. The twenty-one-year-old younger sister of the Duchess of Sagan, Dorothée, served as hostess of the French Embassy. She won many hearts at the congress—not least, it seemed, was that of Talleyrand himself.

15. View of Vienna as seen by many travelers who approached by land. Others arrived on the Danube, which appeared to Jacob Grimm one moonlit night in September 1814 as neither blue nor muddy, but "melting silver."

16. Vienna was one of the most sophisticated cities in Europe. It had welcomed French aristocrats who had fled the French Revolution, and former princes of the Holy Roman Empire who had been dispossessed by Napoleon. The Congress of Vienna added even more luster, leaving a legacy of chic elegance that survives today.

17. On September 25, 1814, the Emperor of Austria (center) met the Russian tsar (right) and the king of Prussia (left), just north of Vienna, prior to their arrival for the congress.

18. During the Congress of Vienna, the Hofburg Palace contained more royalty under one roof at one time than any other place in history. Guards were posted outside entrances to each royal suite, and troop maneuvers were a daily sight. One day in September, a visitor counted no fewer than fifty-three calls to arms.

19. Celebration at the Peace Festival on the anniversary of the Allied Victory at the Battle of Leipzig, October 18, 1814.

20. "Quivering violins alternated with serious negotiations, court intrigues alternated with delicate romantic adventures," said Countess Thürheim, describing the charged atmosphere of Vienna's ballrooms. A later rendering of a ball at Prince Metternich's.

21. One of the many masked balls, or *redouten*, held in the spacious ballrooms of the Hofburg during the Congress of Vienna.

22. Grand Carousel held on November 23, 1814, in the Spanish Riding School.

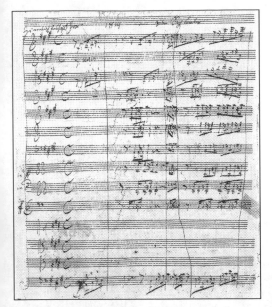

23. This is a page from the score of Beethoven's unfinished celebration of the Vienna Congress, "The Choir of the Allied Princes."

24. On Twelfth Night, the Congress of Vienna cuts up the cake of Europe. Alexander receives Poland, and the King of Prussia Saxony. Austria will take Germany, or at least as much of it as possible. Castlereagh, knife and fork in hand, prepares to serve his colleagues. In the background, marginalized and excluded powers beg in vain for a few scraps. Others watch from the box seats as the orchestra plays, and Justice, overhead, appears wounded, with a bandage over an eye and her scales broken.

25. For the many distinguished guests in town, congress planners had compiled a short list of sightseeing opportunities, ranging from Napoleonic battlefields to a lunatic asylum. The historic abbey on the Danube, Klosterneuberg, was one of the sights, and the print comes from the collection of the king of Denmark, who proved to be the most avid royal sightseer in town.

26. Vienna was one of the greenest cities in Europe, thanks to its many former royal, princely, and aristocratic parks, and the progressive tree-planting policies of Joseph II. The Belvedere Palace, depicted here, also boasted several art exhibits.

27. The Razumovsky Palace, owned by the fabulously rich Count Razumovsky of the Russian delegation, was destroyed by fire on the night of December 30–31, 1814, after one last grand party.

28. The seventy-nine-year-old Prince de Ligne had known everyone from Voltaire to Casanova. His small salon attracted the most distinguished and glamorous guests, and the prince's anecdotes and bons mots circulated in drawing rooms across town.

29. The tsar, the emperor, the kings, queens, and princes—along with an escort of musicians, police, and servants—embarked on a magnificent sleigh ride to Schönbrunn Palace for a banquet and ballet. They returned that evening to the Hofburg for another masked ball.

30. Once ruler of a vast continental empire, Napoleon was now emperor only of the tiny island of Elba. When the original print was held to the light, Napoleon no longer appeared alone, but surrounded by crowds of enthusiastic supporters.

31. After landing at the Golfe Juan in southern France, Napoleon camped in an olive grove outside Antibes (likely near or on the spot of today's railway station). Napoleon had to move quickly, he knew, before news of his arrival spread, along with knowledge of just how small his army actually was.

32. News of Napoleon's flight from Elba struck Vienna, as one put it, "like a flash of lightning and thunder." Painting captures the excitement of Napoleon's march to Paris in March 1815.

33. On March 19, only three days after promising to die in defense of his country, King Louis XVIII left the Tuileries for northern France and then slipped across the border into Belgium.

34. Famous ball, hosted by the Duchess of Richmond, on the eve of the Battle of Waterloo, was less grand than the one celebrated in literature. It took place in a coach house or carriage workshop.

35. "Nothing except a battle lost can be half so melancholy as a battle won," the Duke of Wellington said, surveying the scene of slaughter after the Battle of Waterloo. He hoped that he would never have to fight another battle, and he had his wish.

36. The Congress of Vienna, carving up Europe, trades countries like snuffboxes. The large man to the left was the king of Württemberg, the brash "monster" who stormed out of the conference in December 1814.

LE CONGRÈS.

37. The congress dances. Britain's Castlereagh serves as the dancing master, while Talleyrand, at the far left, observes from the sidelines no doubt awaiting his entry. The jumping figure represents the unhappy Marquis de Brignole, the delegate from Genoa, who protested the fate of his city. On the far right, the king of Saxony, who was in danger of losing his throne, clutches his crown. The "dancing congress" would be a lasting image of the Congress of Vienna.

Chapter 27

With the Spring Violets

*The fact is, France is a den of thieves and brigands, and
they can only be governed by criminals like themselves.*

— Castlereagh

Napoleon's confidence in his success, already high, was growing as he advanced toward the French capital. With expectations of an imminent return to power, he had started appointing his new government: General Armand de Caulaincourt, his former foreign minister, was to be recalled. General Lazare Carnot, "the organizer of victory" in the Revolution, would supervise the Ministry of the Interior, and he wanted his top commander, Marshal Louis-Nicolas Davout, to head the Ministry of War. Fleury de Chaboulon, who had visited him on Elba, was also to find a place as Napoleon's new secretary.

In contrast to Bonaparte's spirited veterans, many in their blue coats, red epaulettes, and tall bearskin hats of the Old Guard, King Louis's men seemed demoralized. Marshal Michel Ney—"the bravest of the brave"—swore to bring Napoleon back in an iron cage. But even he had switched sides. The Paris stock exchange continued its nosedive, the printing of newspapers ground to a halt, and government ministers fled the capital in embarrassingly disorganized retreats.

King Louis XVIII tried to rally his supporters, reaffirming his promise to confront the outlaw Bonaparte. "Can I, at the age of sixty," the king proudly claimed to the French legislature, the Chamber of Deputies, "better end my career than by dying in defense of my country?" Many cheered the brave words, but three days later, just after midnight on

March 19–20, Louis boarded a royal carriage and rumbled away from his capital.

For the sake of safety, six identical carriages left the palace at the same time, separating at the Place de la Concord in different directions. The one with the king headed north. The crown jewels, several millions in the government treasury, and another stash of funds followed in the royal caravan. The king could not be too careful. He did not want to share the fate of his older brother, Louis XVI, whose flight from Paris back in 1791 had ended disastrously with his capture, imprisonment, and eventual execution.

As the king sped away, the palace no longer flew the white flag of Bourbon France, and instead showed an unmistakable "gloomy appearance of its being deserted, with a straggling sentry here and there." Paris itself, as Napoleon approached, looked like "a great city which feels itself to be on the eve of a catastrophe."

Peacemakers in Vienna were clearly facing the prospects of another war. But what was the best way to defeat Napoleon? Where should the armies be placed, and who was to command them?

Appearing to enjoy the challenge again, the tsar volunteered to take personal charge of the Allied troops. Wellington, a far better strategist and tactician, wisely hesitated at the offer. Metternich also balked, having seen the tsar, with all his shortcomings, a little too closely the last six months. With polite firmness, Alexander was persuaded to accept another supreme war council that would include, like last time, himself, the king of Prussia, and the Austrian field marshal Schwarzenberg. Wellington declined to join them, preferring instead "to carry a musket," and the Allies certainly needed his presence on the battlefield.

For the moment, it seemed, the British and the Prussians would take charge in the north, probably somewhere in the Low Countries; the Austrian army would be in the center and south, on the Rhine. The Russian army, still in Poland, was far away from the conflict and would have to hurry to reach the likely battleground, somewhere near France. That, of course, raised an additional concern: Given all the recent tensions with Russia over its claims to occupied Poland, did anyone really want to see the Russian army march across Germany and western Europe?

One of the most important decisions in the series of strategy sessions that followed took place on March 25, when the Great Powers renewed an agreement made at Chaumont at the end of war, and officially created the so-called Seventh Coalition. Each power pledged not to make a separate peace with Napoleon and furnish 150,000 troops for the campaign, with Britain reserving the right to pay additional funds in lieu of its quota. This agreement, moreover, would last for twenty years, or "until Bonaparte should have been rendered absolutely incapable of stirring up further trouble."

BY MARCH, THE Duchess of Sagan had spent months hosting parties in her salon at the Palm Palace, where everything was said to be "debauched, dissolute, unconcerned, extravagant, and racked with debts and blunders." Her personal debts were enormous, and she was having to find ways to raise money to pay off her creditors.

As Metternich had earlier expressed interest in a particular sapphire necklace, the duchess bundled it up in a piece of silk and sent it over to his office. She hoped the jewels would fetch a reasonable price, and asked for his assistance in selling them. Metternich, for his part, was eager to help. "You have not wanted to share the throne with me," Metternich had written before, "but you do not rule less in my realm."

Sure enough, two days later, Metternich had managed to scrounge up a buyer for the duchess's sapphires. The gems were going to Madame de Montesquiou, the former governess of Napoleon's son, who had just been sacked in the alleged kidnapping plot. The price was a solid 3,000 ducats, and the tab was picked up by Emperor Francis. Metternich had convinced the Austrian emperor to buy the sapphires as a farewell gift for Montesquiou's years of services looking after the energetic boy. The necklace traded hands, a small example of Metternich's dexterity, smoothly juggling issues and sometimes managing to have everything fall in the right place.

That Easter weekend, Talleyrand also had to do some juggling of his own. At midnight on Good Friday, the French embassy received an unexpected visitor: the Duchess of Courland, Dorothée's mother and also Talleyrand's mistress.

Like many aristocrats, the fifty-four-year-old duchess had fled Paris in a hurry, and decided to come to Vienna, which had welcomed many French émigrés over the last quarter of a century. The arrival of the duchess, however, must have been awkward, to say the least. A woman of her sophistication could hardly have failed to sense that Talleyrand had come to appreciate her daughter as someone more than a successful embassy hostess.

What a bizarre weekend it must have been, even for Talleyrand, who had seen his share of the unusual. The prospect of the mother and daughter, already suffering a strained relationship, competing for the attentions of the wily Frenchman was simply too much for gossipers. Even Dorothée's older sister, the Duchess of Sagan, could not resist commenting on Talleyrand's rumored affections for her sister: "The great man is at least kept in the family."

ACCORDING TO TRADITION, Napoleon had promised at his abdication to return to France with the spring violets. On Tuesday, March 28, Vienna learned that Napoleon had indeed returned to power. It had taken twenty-three days. Moreover, just as he promised, he had succeeded without firing a shot. The flight from Elba was, in many ways, the most audacious and reckless undertaking in his long career of monumental achievements and colossal blunders. The beautiful flower would be adopted by Bonapartists as a symbol for their hero.

Symbolically, too, Napoleon had returned on March 20, his son's fourth birthday. His supporters went wild with joy. Inside the palace courtyard, cheering enthusiasts swarmed the coach, and, as one put it, "seeing that he could advance no further, the Emperor descended in the midst of the immense crowd, which quickly engulfed him." Eyewitness accounts do not agree on all the details, but give a vivid impression of the euphoria. Some describe the emperor being carried halfway up the palace steps; others claim that he calmly strode them on his own, preceded by a supporter walking backward, repeating in disbelief, "It's you! It's you! It's finally you!"

After Louis XVIII's flight, Napoleon's supporters had prepared the palace for the return of their emperor. Royal emblems were removed from carpets and curtains—in many cases, the fleur-de-lis had only been sewn hastily over the Napoleonic golden bees from the last restoration. "The explosion of feelings was irresistible," one soldier described the enthusiasm, and Napoleon was no less thrilled, calling these days "the happiest period of [his] life."

Street vendors were now hawking small portraits of Napoleon, Marie Louise, and the little prince. A newspaper account in the *Königsberger Zeitung* reported that tailors were gearing up for the task of supplying many new imperial uniforms. Bonapartist cafés and restaurants enjoyed a brisk trade, full of celebrants whose "carousing, feasting, drinking, singing never cease."

As Napoleon's stunning triumph became apparent, Metternich was returning to some old habits, including regular visits to Wilhelmine's salon in the Palm Palace. The duchess was actually delighted, congratulating the foreign minister for having "at last broken the chains that kept you away from my house." Then she added her wish that in the times of uncertainty and the threat of war, they could once again "enjoy peacefully the charms of a friendship and of an agreeable relationship."

But friendship was, of course, not what Metternich wanted. Underneath his cheerful smile, Metternich had not ceased loving her, and it probably seemed at the time that he never would. He had cried a great deal, he confessed, and he had sought help from friends, though without success. Without the duchess, he was only a wanderer adrift in a cruel world—"a man who sees cast up on the shore the wreck of the vessel carrying his whole fortune."

With the news that Napoleon had reached Paris, March 28 was to be the Duke of Wellington's last night in Vienna. "I am going into the Low Countries to take command of the army," he announced. The Duchess of Sagan hosted a farewell party for him that evening, the duke "kissing each lady good-bye and arranging a rendezvous in Paris with one and all."

Britain would once again have new leadership at the embassy. This time, the responsibility would be shared by Lord Clancarty and Lord Cathcart, who had come originally as Castlereagh's advisers. The peace conference was still unfinished, but war was about to begin.

AFTER ANOTHER TENSE late-night session, Friedrich von Gentz, the congress's secretary, woke up and found, at his bedside, a cup of coffee and the morning newspaper *Wiener Zeitung*. As he picked up the paper,

Gentz was struck by an announcement on the front page: "Reward. 10,000 ducats. To whosoever delivers Friedrich von Gentz, the well-known publicist, dead or alive, or simply produces proof of his murder." The manifesto was signed Napoleon.

What a shock it must have been to read his own death warrant. Nervous and high-strung, Gentz already suffered from insomnia for fear that Napoleon would seek revenge on him for drafting the document that branded him an outlaw. Now, presumably with a price on his head, any assassin, mercenary, or bounty hunter eager to make a quick fortune could track him down in his flat on Seilergasse. Everyone knew where he lived. How could he walk home on the narrow dark streets at night, after a salon or late diplomacy session? Would he ever be safe again?

Later that morning, Dorothée and Count Clam-Martinitz came by Gentz's apartment and found him in a terrible state—a wreck amid the half-stuffed suitcases that suggested he was about to leave town in a hurry. "Look at the front page," Gentz explained, flinging the copy of the newspaper to them. "I've got to get out of town." He poured more of his powders into a cup, jerkily stirred them around, and then managed a drink, requiring "both shaking hands to raise it to his lips."

Dorothée could not watch Gentz suffer any longer, and advised him to look at the date of the newspaper. It was the first of April. Prince Metternich had thought it would be amusing to orchestrate an April Fools' prank, and he had overseen its execution, right down to having the paper printed especially for this occasion. That night, at a dinner hosted by Bavaria's Prince Wrede, Gentz had boasted that he had not, in the least, been fooled by the phony paper. People near him, however, knew otherwise. The prince's prank had "almost paralyzed the unfortunate secretary."

Pranks may have helped Metternich cope with the enormous stress, but, unfortunately, what Talleyrand faced was no laughing matter. After seizing power, Napoleon had ordered an immediate halt to the transmission of funds to Vienna. He had also canceled the French embassy's account at the Bank of France, along with its standing credit. In addition, Talleyrand's personal property, worth millions, had been impounded, as had the assets of many other employees at the embassy.

At this time, too, Talleyrand inquired about the state of all his confidential correspondence with the king and the Foreign Ministry since he had arrived in Vienna. "I trust that your Majesty has taken with you all the letters I had the honor of addressing to your Majesty," along with all the other papers sent to the Foreign Ministry, Talleyrand wrote. The reason for his concern was simple: There were many things in his correspondence that Talleyrand feared might upset his new allies, and he did not want it to fall into the wrong hands.

The response came from the acting foreign minister then in the king's temporary headquarters in Brussels, and it was not at all comforting. A few dispatches had been burned, including the secret reports sent from Elba and presumably the documents surrounding the alleged kidnapping and assassination attempts. But, unfortunately, the government had been in a hurry to leave. "I did not take with me, Prince, any important papers," one of the king's officials confessed sadly. None of the other ministers, regrettably, had done so either.

And so the vast majority of Talleyrand's private correspondence during the Vienna Congress, not to mention the secret treaty signed with Britain and Austria, were now lying openly in the ministry offices, just waiting for Napoleon.

Chapter 28

CRIERS OF VIVE LE ROI! DOERS OF NOTHING

Let us embrace and let all be forgotten.

—Tsar Alexander to Metternich

With the return of Napoleon, the Vienna Congress was now forced to confront the unpleasant fact that the emperor's former marshal, Joachim Murat, was still king of Naples. Murat was still the same restless and swaggering cavalry leader prone to risky moves. He was also eager to play his own role in the unfolding drama. On March 30, while the attentions of the Vienna Congress were focused on events in France, Murat had called for nothing less than the unification of Italy, and launched a surprise attack against the Papal States.

This had been rash, and many of his advisers had argued against it. Murat's wife, Caroline, was one who strongly opposed any action that could be seen as breaking his agreements with Austria. "What need have I of alliances," Murat had said, "since the Italians salute me as their sovereign?"

Even Napoleon had also been against such an invasion. In fact, he had ordered Murat *not* to attack, at least not yet. Timing was everything, and, at the moment, he needed Murat to stay in the south and keep Austria anxious about its Italian holdings. But Murat had been thrilled by Napoleon's successes and wanted to undertake his own. He would succeed, he was confident, just as he had at Marengo, Austerlitz, Jena, Eylau, and many other battles where, with his bold strikes, he had played a key role in Napoleon's victories.

Fortunately for Talleyrand, who had tried to warn diplomats about the dangers of this man for months, Murat's move was now making his job much easier. As Talleyrand put it, this attack "has at last opened the eyes of Austria, and made an end of all her hesitations."

Actually, it was not that Austria suddenly realized the dangers of Murat, but rather that the king of Naples had finally made the fatal error of judgment that Metternich had long expected. Austria declared war. One hundred thousand Austrian troops were ordered to march and restore order in Italy. The whole Naples affair, Talleyrand predicted confidently, "will very soon be definitely settled."

Once this matter was resolved, the remaining issues would most likely fall into place. "All that will then remain for us to do," Talleyrand elaborated, "will be to collect all the articles already agreed upon, and form them into the act which is to terminate the Congress."

As far as France was concerned, the sooner the congress was finished, the better. The embassy was virtually bankrupt. Fortunately, Talleyrand had managed to secure some emergency financial assistance from Great Britain, though this barely covered the embassy's most basic expenses, never mind the stack of unpaid bills. Talleyrand had to send many of his staff home, including his chef and several assistants. While Talleyrand struggled with the new financial realities, Napoleon went one step further and revoked his authority as a French diplomat.

Indeed, messengers were already on their way from Paris with papers officially dissolving the mission of Talleyrand, Dalberg, and the whole "diplomatic phalanx" at Kaunitz Palace. The French embassy had suddenly found itself without anyone to represent—that is, besides a dethroned king who had fled the country.

Opinion in Vienna was becoming increasingly hostile to the Bourbon dynasty, who had abandoned the country without much of a fight. The king's supporters had certainly seemed lackluster; Castlereagh had labeled them "Criers of *Vive le Roi!* Doers of nothing." This was a problem because, as Talleyrand rightly urged, the king needed to show that he maintained the support of his people. The king should, moreover, return to France as soon as possible, and in all events he should not remain anywhere near the coast. This only gave the impression that the king would soon once again flee to Britain.

Frustratingly, days now passed without any news from King Louis

XVIII or anyone in the exiled French Foreign Ministry, which had recently moved from Brussels to Ghent. Talleyrand was used to a fair amount of discretionary power, but at this late stage of the conference, the lack of information was exasperating, and he was forced to wait for every morsel with "extreme impatience."

As SPRING CAME early to Vienna, dinners and salons had been reenergized, though with less of a stellar cast in attendance than before. Many headed out to enjoy the Prater in bloom, or found themselves caught up in the long conferences that had become the rule. A new martial air had also come over the congress. In a series of conferences, with military matters now assuming top priority, Vienna's peacemakers sat down to appoint commanders, assign troops, persuade other powers to join its alliance, and, in short, devise a general strategy to face Napoleon.

"If we are to undertake the job," Castlereagh wrote from London to advise the British delegation, "we must leave nothing to chance. It must be done upon the largest scale." The Allies must amass an enormous force, strike hard, and, as he put it, "inundate France from all directions."

But to do that would be expensive, and, after the last war, few states had the resources for such an undertaking. Indeed, for many plenipotentiaries, the negotiations at the war council were taken as an invitation to barter for financial support from Great Britain. The London government was viewed as an inexhaustible bank freely dispensing its gifts. Such subsidies would help ensure a well-supplied army, and, at the same time, many hoped that they would help prevent the worst cases of pillaging sure to result when the large armies took to the field. The Prussians, in particular, were feared as a modern "Praetorian Guard" drunk with revenge.

Some of the smaller German states also set a price for their participation, promising to cooperate with the Allies in the war in return for a guarantee that the conference would establish a German *Bund,* or union of the German states. This loosely unified Germany should, moreover, be guaranteed a "liberal constitution" with many rights for the people, ranging from a free press to freedom of religion.

In addition, while all these demands were being championed with unexpected intensity, the Great Powers had to wrestle with startling signs of disloyalty among their own troops. Many Saxons, for instance, were manifestly upset about joining the Kingdom of Prussia. The king of Saxony had never agreed to relinquish any part of his country, nor had he freed the troops from their personal oath to him. Many Saxon soldiers plainly preferred to fight their new rulers, the Prussians, rather than Napoleon.

In the unstable environment of Napoleon's return, Bavaria also seemed to be showing just how to profit from the tension. Bavaria was planning to send twice the troops Vienna requested, and this enthusiastic support worried Metternich. As Austria and Bavaria had still not agreed over who should own Salzburg or the surrounding Alpine regions, Metternich feared that Bavaria was cynically exploiting the threat of Napoleon to mobilize a huge force, and then maneuver it, under the pretext of defense, into a strategic offensive position. That way, with the increased leverage, Bavaria could be assured of its gains, either from diplomacy in Vienna or outright seizure on the battlefield.

WITH HIS RETURN to Paris, Napoleon was claiming to be a new man who had learned from his mistakes. He promised to be more moderate in his actions, guaranteeing a liberal constitution with a freedom of the press. He would establish "an empire of liberty," honoring all existing treaties, including the ones that parceled out his previous conquests. All he wanted, in return, was recognition of his authority as the legitimate ruler of France.

Leaders at Vienna had learned from experience to be wary of Napoleon's appeals to peace. This new pledge to respect all existing agreements, many were sure, was as credible as the string of broken treaties he had previously left behind.

Realizing the dangers of Napoleon's usual "divide and conquer" diplomacy, the delegates at the Vienna Congress went to work on another declaration that would reaffirm the aims of their coalition and the basis for the war against Napoleon, "the tiger that had escaped from his cage":

> [Europe] is arming, not against France, but as much for the welfare of France as for her own security. She acknowledges no other enemy than Napoleon Bonaparte, and all who fight in his cause.

The Vienna Congress would not recognize Napoleon's authority, and the many ambassadors he sent to Vienna would be treated merely as "messengers," and then promptly ignored.

But despite the virtual unanimity, ignoring Napoleon's representatives was becoming increasingly difficult. Was not the fact that they had signed a second declaration reaffirming their position a sign that they might not be as unified as they wished to appear?

There was a betting chance, Napoleon gambled, that Austria might be persuaded to accept peace with him as the ruler of France. After all, he had a Habsburg wife and son, and Metternich was known to be the least antagonistic of the Allies. And many at the congress did fear that Metternich was secretly scheming to accept Napoleon as ruler of France.

The Russian tsar was another one who might be lured away from the coalition. Alexander had personally been kind to many Bonaparte family members in Vienna, often visiting Marie Louise at Schönbrunn and spending a great deal of time with Napoleon's stepson, Prince Eugène. In addition, Napoleon now had a copy of the secret treaty that would reveal what the tsar's so-called allies really thought of him.

As for Britain, Napoleon knew that he had virtually no chance at winning over Castlereagh and the Tory Party that controlled Parliament. What he could do, however, was undermine their government. Indeed, on assuming power in France, Napoleon immediately abolished the slave trade, accomplishing at one stroke what the congress had only managed to condemn after endless discussion and countless concessions. Whig opposition leaders, very much impressed, seized the opportunity to denounce the British government for wanting to wage war against such an enlightened ruler.

Napoleon certainly knew how to target his appeals with great skill, and he had a plan for winning over Talleyrand as well. The emperor promised to be forgiving—for he, too, had made mistakes, he admitted. Despite their differences in the past, Napoleon wanted Talleyrand back: "He is still the man, who knows the most about the century, the cabinets, and the peoples." The person he chose to convey this message, Count Auguste-Charles-Joseph Flahaut de la Billarderie, was none other than Talleyrand's son, from an affair back in Paris thirty years before.

When Flahaut had difficulty reaching Vienna, arrested on the way at Stuttgart by officials of the king of Württemberg, Napoleon sent another courier, Count François-Casimir Mouret de Montrond, the charming adventurer known in Paris salons as the "beautiful Montrond" or the "most devilish man in France." He had long been one of Talleyrand's close friends. Montrond's relationship would guarantee an opportunity to present his appeal to the foreign minister. His charm, Napoleon hoped, would do the rest.

Count Montrond made his way to Vienna, arriving successfully by using the false name of Abbé Altieri. On the first evening at the Kaunitz Palace, Montrond asked Talleyrand, point-blank, if he, as French foreign minister, could really support a war against France.

"Read the declaration," Talleyrand responded, pointing to the Vienna papers that outlawed Bonaparte; "it does not contain a single word with which I do not agree." Besides, the French foreign minister continued, "The question, too, is not of a war against France, but of a war against the man of Elba."

This was a firm response, without the equivocation that often shrouded the comments of his gifted colleague Metternich. Or was it, as some of Talleyrand's enemies feared, merely a ploy to raise the price of his cooperation? Almost certainly, Talleyrand had no intention of joining Napoleon, though his former boss continued to raise the stakes.

By the end of the month, another messenger would convey an additional offer intended to appeal to Talleyrand's notorious mercurial streak. All his extensive properties in France, which had been impounded on Napoleon's return, would be restored, along with a salary of some 200,000 livres, if Talleyrand "behaves like a Frenchman and renders me a few services." Refusal to comply, of course, would be interpreted by Napoleon as an insult and a sign of hostility.

WHEN KING LOUIS XVIII fled Paris in March, he risked appearing as a cowardly and unpopular ruler desperate only to protect himself. The king, however, clung to the belief that he maintained the support of the vast majority of Frenchmen. It was only a matter of time before his faithful subjects would rise up against the outlaw. All they needed was a spark to ignite the explosion of support. Perhaps the Vienna Congress could assist in providing that spark.

Yet, as Talleyrand knew, it was going to be a difficult task to convince

Vienna's leaders to restore the Bourbons on the throne for a second time. The king had, among other things, purged the Senate, imposed a strict censorship, and made a mockery of the freedoms that had been promised to the French on the Bourbons' return. Their blunders seemed endless: "They had learned nothing, forgotten nothing," as was commonly said of the Bourbon family.

The Russian tsar, for one, regretted putting them on the throne the last time, and did not wish to repeat that mistake. Metternich, too, was secretly looking into other options. As he confided that spring to the Duchess of Sagan, the Bourbons looked "morally sick" and unable to cope. Opposition to the Bourbons, then, was bringing Metternich and Alexander almost into agreement.

The most prominent spokesmen for the Bourbons, on the other hand, were the British delegates. It was Britain, after all, who had supported Louis' restoration the first time, just as they did before, when he spent many years in exile at Hartwell House in Buckinghamshire. They had, in a sense, invested heavily in him, and presumably did not want to abandon him now. Louis was the best bet, Castlereagh gambled, for a friendly France and a more stable peace.

But imposing the Bourbons over the wishes of Alexander, Metternich, and clearly many Frenchmen would not be easy. Many Englishmen back at home were also opposed to war for this purpose. English debt was already of substantial proportions, amassed in the recent war against the United States and the long, drawn-out struggle against Napoleon. In February, it had passed the £700 million mark, and payments on this debt alone consumed about one-third of the state's annual budget.

In the last war, Britain had paid Russia, Prussia, Austria, Spain, Portugal, Sweden, Sicily, Bavaria, and many German states to fight Napoleon. Was Britain, again, to "subsidize all the world"? Was restoring the Bourbons again really worth risking so much loss in life, not to mention the wartime threats to English commerce and the continued hated income tax, the first in the world?

Members of the opposition Whig Party certainly did not think so. Sir Francis Burdett, for one, did not wish "to plunge this country into a sea of blood to reinstate the Bourbon line in France." This dynasty did not have a good track record. One wit, Richard Sheridan, expressed the discontent rather well, summing up British foreign policy over the previous

150 years: half of it trying to remove the Bourbons, and the other half trying to restore them.

Besides, the Whigs argued, look how easily Napoleon had returned. "No man can doubt that this Napoleon stands as Emperor of France by the will of the French people." Burdett spoke for many when he concluded, "Let then the French settle their own affairs." It was not for Britain or Europe to intervene in their domestic disputes.

While these matters were debated in Parliament, newspapers, and clubs around the country, the Duke of Wellington made a fateful decision: He decided to pledge Britain's full support to the war effort. It was a risky move even in a time of considerable ministerial discretion. Yet he pushed ahead and guaranteed British participation. By the time the Allied troops were marching, none of the opposition—or anyone else in the country, for that matter—had time to realize what had happened. Britain was going to war.

As MATTERS LOOKED grim for the Bourbons in their exiled court at Ghent, Belgium, Talleyrand was praised as their best hope for the future. Arnail François, Comte de Jaucourt, his colleague in the Foreign Ministry, wrote, pleading with him to finish his affairs in Vienna, hurry back to the king, and accept a position of power.

At the same time, many of the other exiled ministers around the king also wanted Talleyrand recalled—but certainly not to offer him any more influence. For many, Talleyrand was to be lured out of Vienna and then sacked. Extreme royalists around the king had never forgiven him for his past; he was an aristocrat who joined the Revolution and then helped bring Bonaparte to power. There was no amount of evidence that would convince them that Talleyrand was not intriguing. The viper would soon again shed his skin.

By late April, King Louis XVIII would, in fact, summon Talleyrand back to his headquarters in Ghent. Talleyrand, however, stalled, and with good reason. He had to be cautious, as he suspected, quite rightly, the motives of many of the king's closest advisers. What's more, he knew that the business in Vienna was about to be wrapped up, and he did not want to leave as the congress approached its climax.

"My anxiety to find myself at Your Majesty's side would make me start tomorrow," Talleyrand answered, "if affairs were sufficiently advanced to render only my signature necessary, or if the termination of the Congress were still in the distance." In another excuse, he argued that as others were preparing to depart, he could leave shortly, so as not to injure the king's interests by being one of the first to leave town.

Two weeks later, Talleyrand was still making excuses for his delay. It was clear that those who wanted his recall, supporters and enemies alike, would have to think of something more powerful than a direct order from the king.

Chapter 29

FAREWELLS

The demon is not far from us, and the Gates of Hell are always open.

— CARDINAL CONSALVI

etermined to strike a deal, Napoleon kept on dispatching messengers to Vienna, and they kept on being stopped. Even his most recent courier, a former chamberlain to Emperor Francis, Monsieur de Stassart, had not succeeded. Arrested in Bavaria, his letters were seized and sent to the congress. Metternich promised to open these confiscated papers in front of his colleagues.

On May 3, Napoleon's secret letters, seals seemingly unbroken, were brought into the conference room and set down on the familiar green table. Did Metternich know their contents already, with the help of the Austrian Cabinet Noir? It was hard to imagine that he did not.

Before he opened the letters, though, Metternich first wanted all nonessential diplomats "politely eased" out of the room. At that particular moment, this included only one person, Prussia's minister of war, General Hermann von Boyen, who had arrived in town the previous month. Ambassador Humboldt was asked to escort his colleague out of the room, which he did, and then rushed back in for the show. The minister of war was left outside, upset and insulted.

With great flair, Metternich broke the seals, unfolded the letters, and began deciphering Napoleon's monstrous scrawl. Sure enough, the emperor was emphasizing his pacific intentions and hoping to persuade Austria to accept peace with him. Metternich promptly affirmed his commitment to the Allies and announced that he would not even dignify Napoleon's request with a response. This scene was exploited for all it was worth as a show of solidarity. He might as well have bowed and blown kisses after his performance.

Later that night, while dining in Chancellor Hardenberg's rooms, Humboldt had the misfortune of running into Boyen again. The Prussian war minister was quite upset with Humboldt—enraged is more accurate. By the end of the tense conversation, on a second-floor balcony, the Prussian minister of war had challenged the ambassador to a duel.

Humboldt, to be sure, was no fighter. Count Carl Axel Löwenhielm, the Swedish delegate, earlier summed up this fact well, when he remarked ironically that if the issues of the Congress of Vienna ended up being decided by physical combat of the participants, then he hoped to draw the Prussian ambassador.

When Humboldt tried to apologize, the proud minister of war refused to listen. The challenge had been issued, and the duel would take place as planned, he insisted. They would meet that Friday, May 5, at three in the afternoon, and drive out to a lonely spot, just outside Vienna.

At the appointed time, after Humboldt had spent the morning in conference and then dined, as he put it, like "Homeric heroes always did before battle," he went to his duel. The location was actually moved to a more secluded place, "a pretty meadow near a wood" in the wine-growing region at Spitz. The minister of war, who had the first shot, aimed his pistol and, at the last second, deliberately shot wide. Humboldt's pistol then also "misfired." As Humboldt wrote home afterward, the two duelists realized the "pure foolishness" of the quarrel, had a good laugh, and walked back to town like old friends. Humboldt said that he had learned a lesson, namely, that it was much braver to reject a duel than it was to fight one.

Meanwhile, with most police resources concentrated on providing information and security in Vienna, the surrounding countryside was left more exposed and preyed upon, as one person complained, by many "plunderers, deserters and discharged soldiers averse to honest labor." Among them was a young veteran, Captain Johann Georg Grasel, who had become so thoroughly disgusted with the prevailing "unequal distribution of wealth" in evidence that he had taken matters into his own hands. Young Grasel had become an outlaw: He would be the Robin Hood of the Vienna Congress.

Legends were quickly developing around this rogue and his gang of robbers, hiding out in a secret lair somewhere in the Vienna Woods. His followers were growing, and sometimes said to number in the fifties, sixties, or even the hundreds. Crimes were traced back to him all throughout the spring, and magnified into mythic proportions. They had a team of horses for quick strikes, always limited, as the story went, to "castles and public offices." As the tradition developed, under the influence of Romanticism, Grasel was celebrated as a people's bandit who would "rob the State and the rich in order to give to those he believed to be unjustly poor and oppressed."

Grasel and his band of forest robbers did not penetrate any of the major delegations, or attack the main figures, but he aroused great interest. Critics of Napoleon saw Grasel as the outlaw emperor in miniature, while others compared the bandits to Prussians seizing territory at will from the Saxons and other Germans. Critics who accused the congress, as a whole, of "robbing the have-nots for the benefit of the haves" found the popular bandit alluring, turning the tables on the rich and powerful. It would not last for long, however. Captain Grasel was arrested later that year, and eventually executed.

NAPOLEON, MEANWHILE, WAS hoping to show the true feelings of the tsar's so-called allies, Britain and Austria, and sent him a copy of the secret treaty that they had signed, with Bourbon France, back in January. Alexander was furious. He threw a fit, stomping around his suites in the palace and glowering so much that, in the words of his adviser Kapodistrias, his face turned bright red and his ears purple. He called for Metternich at once. "Do you know this document?" the tsar demanded.

As Metternich stumbled through his excuses, Alexander interrupted him brusquely—he could be as forgiving as he could be petty. "While we live, there must be no mention of this between us again!" Alexander said, allegedly throwing the paper into the fire. "There are better things for us to do. We must think of nothing but our alliance against Napoleon." The tsar was enjoying the chance to be magnanimous, and in all likelihood, he had suspected this agreement long before.

The Prussian generals also read the secret treaty, which Napoleon had published in newspapers. They were likewise disgusted, though ultimately this had little effect on their already low estimate of Prince Metternich.

Besides, they had already discovered the treaty themselves, when searching a captured French official at Liège. What disturbed them most, however, was the participation of Great Britain. The secret treaty had confirmed their fears about this "Perfidious Albion," as Napoleon had called them.

Back in London, Castlereagh was having difficulty defending his actions in Vienna. He was criticized for abandoning Poland, carving up Saxony, destroying Genoa, and generally making a mockery of diplomacy. His colleague, the Duke of Wellington, was likewise rebuked for his signature on the document that branded Napoleon an outlaw, and his adherence to this so-called doctrine of assassination. Worse still, the Duke of Wellington's pledge that Great Britain would enter the war against Napoleon reached Parliament, and the opposition was outraged.

Britain had been tricked into accepting a war that, essentially, had already been decided upon, opposition party leaders fumed. Castlereagh, Wellington, and the war hawks of the Tory Party were senselessly trying to drown the continent in blood "in order to put down one man," and, moreover, they had guaranteed British funds to pay for it all. "You have deceived us shamefully," declared one member, who spoke for many that spring.

Castlereagh responded by going through a litany of reasons for the war: the impossibility of trusting Napoleon's word—an ironic beginning perhaps, given the critiques against himself. He continued to warn about the dangers of having Bonaparte back in power, and the sheer uncertainty it meant for the future. In this speech, there were many reasons for the war, but, noticeably, no outright denial of any of the charges.

Britain was standing by its commitment to fight and subsidize the Allies in the war. And so the world's first income tax, which had been imposed in Great Britain as "a temporary measure" in the war crisis of the 1790s and was supposed to be repealed in peacetime, would now not be abolished after all.

But even with this tax, the Duke of Wellington was frustrated with the military situation. The British army, gathering in Belgium, was not in the best of shape. Most of the hardened veterans of the Spanish campaign were not available, as many had been released from service at the end of the war and others were now making their way home after service in the American war. In fact, the army Wellington found was only about twelve thousand men, adequate enough perhaps for enforcing the handover of

Belgium to Dutch control. But they were hardly in a position to face Napoleon.

Ever since the duke had arrived in Brussels back on April 4, and moved into the hotel on rue Montagne du Parc, he had worked to whip the troops into shape. Besides the small size of the army, the soldiers were young, poorly trained, and appallingly "ill-equipped," not to mention being encumbered by a "very inexperienced Staff." The commander in chief of the Allied armies in Belgium at this time was the Prince of Orange, a twenty-three-year-old who had been given command as a token of British support for the Dutch royal family. His nickname was "Slender Billy," and the soldiers were not exactly impressed by his leadership abilities.

Indeed, many things had rankled the duke on his arrival. Besides the fact that most of the army spoke German and he did not, Wellington had to worry about the loyalty of some troops. There were Saxons who resented the treatment of their kingdom and refused to be commanded by the Prussians, and Belgians who likewise did not like the prospects of Dutch rule and were reluctant to fight their idol, Napoleon. Wellington had been voicing these complaints and many others, but he was increasingly frustrated by the slow response of the British government. "In my opinion," he wrote to Lord Stewart in Vienna, "they are doing nothing in England."

While the Austrians were mainly on the Rhine, or in Italy facing Murat, and the Russians were farther back as a reserve force, Wellington was to be assisted primarily by the Prussians. Their commander was officially Field Marshal von Blücher, a seventy-two-year-old with silver hair, a pinkish face, and a bushy white mustache. He was rather large—one person who saw him the previous summer thought he was "the stoutest man that ever did live." Blücher may not have been the best general of the Prussian staff, but he certainly was brave. His no-nonsense aggressive approach verged on recklessness, and his usual order, "Attack," earned him the nickname "Old Marshal Vorwärts!"

Blücher's chief of staff, General August von Gneisenau, had considerable authority and actually helped counter this rashness. The king of Prussia had even given Gneisenau authority to assume control, should Blücher again fall sick. The field marshal was prone to some strange delusions, including one belief that he had become pregnant and would soon give birth to an elephant!

Wellington was prepared to shrug aside such beliefs as the harmless idiosyncrasies of an exceptional soldier. The Prussian field marshal, he insisted, was eager for battle—"if anything too eager." At any rate, Wellington preferred Blücher to his assistant, Gneisenau, who had some marked suspicions of the British that would soon be even more pronounced.

Amid the public attempts to display German unity, Vienna learned of trouble in the Prussian army. In early May, the Saxon army had rioted, and in fact almost captured its Prussian commander. Both Blücher and Gneisenau had to "slip out" their back door and flee to safety. Worse still, the rigorous suppression of the mutiny confirmed the worst fears of Prussian brutality.

Allied troops were in the meantime waiting—waiting for orders from their officers, waiting for what Napoleon would do, waiting for what would happen next in the remarkable year of 1815. They passed the time as best they could. The First Regiment of Foot Guards, for instance, played a friendly game of cricket: The soldiers with last names beginning with the letters *A* through *G* faced all the rest, and, reportedly, to use a popular phrase of the day, "beat the others hollow."

ALL THROUGHOUT MAY, as dignitaries and guests prepared to leave, awarding jeweled snuffboxes and portraits freely all around, Vienna looked more beautiful than ever. The green expanse of the Prater seemed ideal for a leisurely carriage ride down the boulevard under chestnut trees exploding in brilliant pink. It was "divine weather," and as Gentz noted in his diary, "the most beautiful spring I've ever seen."

With feelings no doubt of excitement, fear, sadness, and exhaustion all at once, the delegates and guests alike made their plans to depart. The tsar of Russia and the king of Prussia, having entered town together, planned to leave together. On May 26, 1815, eight months and a day after their entrance into town, the two sovereigns departed for the new Allied headquarters at Heilbronn. The king of Prussia would stop off first, briefly, in his capital of Berlin.

After some difficult moments, the tsar was nevertheless leaving with Poland, smaller than he liked, though still large enough for him to feel that he had accomplished something. This was, of course, in addition to his previous gains in the war, including Finland and Bessarabia, which were confirmed. Some of his last known appearances were actually in taverns. One person claimed to have seen His Majesty, the Tsar of All the Russias, engaging challengers in a contest to see who "could make the most horrible face." And according to an anonymous informant, Alexander had said, in the end, that if he had not been tsar, he would desire "nothing more than being a general in Austria."

Metternich was also leaving town for his summer villa on the Rennweg. He would spend a couple of weeks there with his wife, his children, and the most recent addition to the family, the pet parrot Polly. This parrot had been given to Metternich by an old English sea captain, though the bird had by now, he joked, "lost his English accent." Metternich would celebrate his forty-second birthday with fellow diplomats at his summer residence on May 15, and return to the Chancellery office periodically in the last month to wrap up the congress.

His assistant, Gentz, was bagging a number of sundry gifts for his many services: honors, payments, snuffboxes, and even a new carriage, which had been dropped off at his apartment by an unnamed benefactor. So many were happy with and grateful to the man who would write the official treaty of the Vienna Congress. One historian called Gentz the most bribed man in history. Although certainly an overstatement, the secretary of the congress did, in fact, pocket a fortune, and as soon as he finished working on the draft, he went house hunting. He found a large, eighteenth-century manor outside town, in the Weinhaus, and felt "as happy as a child" looking forward to moving in there, "as soon as this wretched Congress is over."

Princess Bagration, by contrast, was spending the last days at the congress in deep financial trouble. Already that spring, her chef, Monsieur Bretton, had been forced to stop advancing the princess money for the food and dinners that he prepared himself. He could no longer continue this way until his wages, back wages, and all the other reimbursements were paid. Of all her friends in Vienna the last several months, few were willing or able to help. She wrote her stepfather back in St. Petersburg to send more money.

Ironically, while many had earlier urged the police to remove Princess Bagration from the city, there were a great number in late May trying to make sure that she did not leave, at least before she repaid her enormous debts. According to her close friend Aurora de Marassé, the princess owed a staggering 21,801 ducats, another 18,121 florins, and some 7,860 in promissory notes. There were other outstanding debts to various bankers around town. It was feared that the princess might move straight from the gilded salon to the debtor's prison.

Another matter that bothered the princess was the departure of a new lover she had taken, the Crown Prince of Württemberg. She accompanied the handsome prince out of town, all the way to the first postal stop, Purkersdorf, where they said good-byes so tender that one police agent noted ironically that it might lead to the birth of another "illegitimate child for the virtuous princess."

The Duchess of Sagan was one of the last to leave town. She would, however, vacate the Palm Palace first, leaving Princess Bagration there reigning, though besieged less by admirers than creditors. The duchess's lover, Prince Alfred von Windischgrätz, had left Vienna in April to join his regiment as it prepared to fight Napoleon. The duchess moved into his mansion, the nearby Windischgrätz Palace. The parties were tapering off back in Vienna, she said, and she was "dying of boredom."

In truth, though, the duchess was losing interest in Prince Alfred, and their relationship would soon be over, though Alfred would fight for its continuation, just as Metternich had done before him. While he was away, the duchess had been seeing more and more of the British ambassador, Lord Stewart.

They dined together and rode through the city's many parks, Wilhelmine on a prized horse that she had earlier purchased from Stewart. They took several excursions into the countryside, just as she had done with Alfred. Stewart was like him in many ways, though more wild and unpredictable. "Lord Pumpernickel" had taken advantage of the absence of Castlereagh, Wellington, and Clancarty and, according to one disapproving critic, turned the British embassy into a gambling den and brothel.

Clearly, the Duchess of Sagan and Lord Stewart were struggling to adjust to a city that no longer hosted a spectacular royal carnival. By the end of May, most of the guests had left town, either to face Napoleon, return home, or head off elsewhere in search of the next adventure. "Vienna is becoming a desert," the Duchess of Sagan said with sadness.

Chapter 30

ONQUERING THE PEACE

I have spent the whole day cutting Europe into bits like a piece of cheese.

— PRINCE METTERNICH

On the first of June, Napoleon celebrated his triumphant return with a massive public ceremony, arguably the most grandiose since his coronation as emperor in Notre Dame eleven years before. It was held on the Champs de Mars, a wide parade ground in central Paris that would later hold the Eiffel Tower. A pyramid-like platform and amphitheater had been constructed there for the occasion, outside the officer cadet academy, the École Militaire.

At the center was Napoleon, sitting on a purple throne, wearing a black hat with white ostrich feather and a purple coronation mantle tossed over his shoulders. He was surrounded by his brothers, his marshals, his eagles on columns, and many war trophies. Only his wife and son were missing.

Shouts of *"Vive l'Empereur!"* were heard in the throngs below, estimated at two hundred thousand. After the cannon boomed and Mass was celebrated, a spokesman for the new legislature addressed the crowd, at least those at the very front who could hear:

> What do these monarchs desire, Sire, who are advancing against us with such warlike preparations? What have we done to justify their aggressive proceedings? Have we violated any of the treaties of peace?

Posing the question to the crowd, he then promptly answered it. The enemies of France "do not like the ruler we have chosen, and we do not like him, they would impose on us."

After the speech and the applause, the emperor's arch-chancellor introduced the new constitution, the Acte Additional, which the people of France had affirmed in a recent vote. The margin had been large. About 1.3 million approved the constitution, and only 4,206 cast their vote against it—voting under Napoleon always revealed more about his manipulation of the procedures than it evidenced any real freedom of expression. The constitution was then dropped at the foot of the throne for Napoleon's signature.

Napoleon was very good at creating grandiose spectacles to demonstrate, symbolize, and enhance his power. "A government must dazzle and astonish," he had long known, and this was never truer than with a new government. Napoleon needed to fire imaginations, just as he had done in other crucial moments, such as when he first seized power, launched a risky endeavor, or experienced a major setback.

The whole event had originally been planned as a large democratic forum inaugurating the proclaimed new reign of liberty. But only a fraction of the eligible voters had participated, the turnout in Paris estimated at one in ten, indicating that neither Napoleon nor his constitution was as popular as he wished. So he changed his plans and, instead, staged an event with every detail tightly controlled to present a picture of a country rallying around its enlightened emperor.

Tsar Alexander, meanwhile, had arrived at the southern German town of Heilbronn, literally meaning "holy spring," which then temporarily served as Allied headquarters. He was happy about the outcome in Poland, but he agonized over other matters. Why had the French welcomed Napoleon so enthusiastically, and why had the power of the Bourbon king collapsed so easily? Was it really worth shedding more blood just to restore this dynasty?

Even assuming for the moment that this was a worthwhile war aim, the tsar was troubled by the fact that his Russian army, stationed mainly on the other side of the Vistula in the new Kingdom of Poland, was far away from the likely center of action, and would likely be relegated to reserve functions. He had lost his bid to be supreme commander as well. All these concerns nagged at the tsar as he sat alone late one night in early June at his study in the Rauch'sche Palais. It was perfectly clear, at least to him, that he was being punished for all the decadence of the Vienna Congress.

Suddenly, about two that morning, there was a knock on his door, and his aide-de-camp, Prince Volkonski, entered, visibly troubled and apologetic for disturbing the tsar at that hour. He had a message, admittedly strange, to relay to the tsar. There was a woman who insisted on seeing the tsar. It was Julie von Krüdener.

"You can imagine my surprise," Alexander later said. He had just then been thinking about Baroness Krüdener as he contemplated a passage in the book of Revelation: "And there appeared a great wonder in heaven: a woman clothed with the sun." Now the woman who he believed could help him most was standing at the door.

> I thought I was dreaming. I received her immediately, and as if she had read my soul, she spoke strong consoling words which calmed the inner turmoil which had obsessed me for so long.

It was an extraordinary three-hour visit in the middle of the night. The prophetess could illuminate certain passages in the Holy Scriptures that baffled the tsar, and then explain their meaning in the context of the difficulties that he faced. Above all, she assured him that the "white angel" (the tsar) would "conquer the Dragon" (Napoleon). She had a mystic faith in an upcoming apocalypse that, with the tsar's help, would envelop the world with "a great explosion of love."

In the meantime, she explained why inner peace had been so elusive to the Tsar of All the Russias: "You have not renounced your sins and have not humbled yourself before Christ," she said. You must approach God, she further instructed the tsar, "like a criminal begging for mercy."

Few had spoken to the tsar with such blunt criticism of his sins and mistakes before (his favorite sister, Grand Duchess Catherine, was one who did). But Baroness Krüdener knew exactly what she was doing, and Alexander was entranced. She moved into a nearby hut, and during the tense summer, on the eve of hostilities, she came over to visit the tsar virtually every night for study, usually beginning about six and continuing until two in the morning. The tsar's main advisers, on the other hand, were not invited to take part in this spiritual quest.

BY JUNE, EVERYONE knew that war might begin at any moment. There was a flurry of activity among those remaining in Vienna to complete the negotiations as soon as possible. The king of Saxony had finally accepted the congress's solution about the fate of his country, and thereby removed one of the last obstacles that the German Committee faced in its deliberations. Its members now went forward in finalizing their decisions, and their series of meetings behind closed doors, seven in all from late May to early June, were among the stormiest of the entire congress.

In discussing the future of the states of Germany, the committee wrangled over everything from writing a constitution to establishing an army. The delegates wrestled with difficult questions about the exact nature of the freedoms that should be granted in the new constitution. Freedom of press, freedom of worship, and freedom of movement, including the right to attend a university, figured prominently on the list for many on the committee. At one point, the Austrian representative noted that he had no fewer than forty-six different drafts of a constitution on his desk.

One of the hotly debated topics in these sessions was the treatment of Jewish minorities in the new German Confederation. The relations varied widely from state to state, but generally, in places the French conquered, occupied, or exerted considerable influence, conditions were better for the Jewish communities. In many places, old laws discriminating against Jews had been repealed, and new laws guaranteeing equality enacted. But now that the French had been defeated, many cities and states wanted the new laws tossed out, along with the unpopular French. Some of the most progressive places, like Westphalia, Frankfurt, and the Hanseatic towns, were now at risk of a vehement backlash.

The Jewish delegations had worked the last eight months behind the scenes in salons like Fanny von Arnstein's to rally support for their cause. Humboldt was a staunch supporter of Jewish rights, joined by the Prussian chancellor Hardenberg. The two had, of course, cooperated well before on this question. Humboldt penned a remarkable treatise calling for full civic equality in 1809, and Hardenberg enacted the law in 1812 that emancipated Prussian Jews. The king of Prussia, less committed personally, had gone along with the reforms.

On January 4, 1815, Chancellor Hardenberg had taken time away from the impending Saxon crisis to appeal for the full equality of Jews. He argued the case well, citing every reason from the humane to the self-seeking; the Jews had made "sacrifices of every kind" in the war, showing "true courage and vaunted disregard of the perils of war." The Jews, he added, had also played a valuable role in the "system of credit and commerce of the various German states." A return to repression would only encourage them to move away, bringing their talents and assets with them.

Another source of support was Prince Metternich and the Austrian team. Friedrich von Gentz was a particularly valuable asset to the Jewish delegates; his diary shows his regular meetings with them that spring. Unlike Metternich and Humboldt, who refused to accept gifts for their support, including fine rings and silver plate, Gentz had no qualms. At meetings with Simon Edler von Lämel of Prague, for instance, Gentz accepted first an unnamed "beautiful present," then another 1,000 ducats, and then another 2,000 ducats, which prompted him to marvel about how all his "financial affairs are working out wonderfully." The Rothschilds had also made appeals on behalf of Jewish rights, both at the Congress of Vienna as well as in London, where the family had played a large role managing the British war effort and financing the huge subsidies that the British government dispensed to enemies of Napoleon.

Opposition, however, came from many circles, including the delegates of Bavaria, Württemberg, Frankfurt, and the former Hanseatic towns of Hamburg, Bremen, and Lübeck. Jacob Grimm's boss, Count Dorotheus Ludwig Keller of Hesse-Cassel, was another opponent. Indeed, when the question of Jewish rights was first officially proposed in the German Committee in late May, the Bavarian delegate, Count Aloys von Rechberg, had started laughing, and, as one eyewitness described it, the laughter ominously became infectious, spreading through the many hostile men in the room.

After many long sessions, however, Humboldt, Hardenberg, Metternich, and their allies had prevailed, and an article guaranteeing Jewish rights would be inserted into the new German constitution. Article XVI specifically instructed the future confederation to find ways to protect its Jewish minorities. In the meantime, all the privileges already granted in the states were to be safeguarded. The Vienna Congress was again launching into a pioneering discussion of human rights at a peace conference. Unfortunately, however, there was a problem that passed unnoticed and soon undermined this victory.

The representative of Bremen, Senator Johann Smidt, had managed to insert a small change in the actual wording of the article. At the last minute, he changed the phrase "[all the rights] granted *in* the several states" to "[all the rights] granted *by* the several states" (italics added). This single preposition would have dire consequences. German states would soon be able to argue that this constitutional guarantee specifically excluded laws passed by outside authorities, like the French. Within one year of the congress, some states were ignoring the rights supposedly guaranteed, and other towns, such as Bremen and Lübeck, even expelled their Jewish populations.

The delegates for the publishing houses and booksellers would also soon be disappointed. After the initial success in October, there had been a long spell without any action. Carl Bertuch's memorandum of April 14 had not restored any momentum. Now, too, as the German Committee deliberated on the constitution, there was a call to postpone a decision about the press and intellectual property rights until the new diet of the German Confederation met later in Frankfurt. This was barely defeated, and discussions continued for several meetings.

On the third of June, another last-minute change was inserted to the draft of Article XVIII, which was to safeguard freedom of the press and literary copyrights. Authors and publishers were still to be protected against forgeries of their works, but the stipulation guaranteeing freedom of the press was quietly dropped, and replaced by a pledge of uniform governmental regulation that would at least level the playing field. The minutes of the meeting do not reveal who initiated this change.

WHILE THE GERMAN Committee labored, leaders of the congress had decided to write one general treaty that would include every decision of the Vienna Congress. This was important, it was believed, to increase the stability of the agreement. Future aggressors were seen as less likely to break a single treaty signed by all the powers than several dozen separate agreements, each contracted by only a couple of interested powers.

Three people were placed in charge of assembling the document: Friedrich von Gentz, the Duke of Dalberg, and Lord Clancarty. The latter two had been added at the last minute after two other delegates declined: Russia's Count Anstett was suffering too much from his gout to focus completely on writing this important treaty, and Talleyrand's assistant, Comte de la Besnardière, was too preoccupied by Napoleon's seizure of his personal property.

The task of this three-man committee was colossal. They were supposed to incorporate the endless committee meetings, negotiations, and resolutions of eight months into one coherent document. And given Napoleon's stunning successes, this was indeed a race against time.

Recently, too, Gentz and his colleagues had encountered another unexpected obstacle. Critics and opponents of a general treaty were coming out en masse. Would not attempting to write such a single document, some asked, give rise to endless dissension among a group of powers that, in wartime, should be united? Even if unity were somehow preserved, would not the war—always full of unexpected consequences—likely end up creating a whole new set of conditions that would make the agreements irrelevant, or worse? The peace treaty could be outdated the very day it was signed.

In the end, the plenipotentiaries decided to take this risk, reasoning that this general treaty would indeed be better for the future security of Europe. Twenty-six secretaries, with scratching quills, labored around the clock on completing the 121-article treaty.

The favorite name for this encompassing document was not at first settled. Some called it simply the Treaty, the "European Treaty," or the "Grand European Treaty," though these were not the most appropriate names for a treaty that not all of Europe had participated in, and many states had only a vague idea of its contents. Others proposed the "New Charter for Europe." Eventually, the name that gained the most acceptance was the "Final Act," which was, as Gentz explained, conceived of as the final act of the victorious coalition against Napoleon.

On June 9, 1815, the delegates to the Vienna Congress gathered in the reception hall of the imperial palace to sign the Final Act—the closest, in fact, that the congress ever came to convening. Even then, it was not exactly a congress, and not everyone was invited to sign. Only the powers on the Committee of Eight would sign, and the rest would be asked to "accede separately." This decision had again insulted and infuriated the many excluded powers, who were once more denied a voice.

Ironically, many of the key figures at the congress were not even present. The host himself, Emperor Francis, had already left for the field of battle. Tsar Alexander and King Frederick William of Prussia were not there, either, having left about two weeks before. As for the British team, Castlereagh was long gone and the Duke of Wellington was somewhere outside Brussels. With the exception of Metternich and Talleyrand, two genuine survivors, none of the main leaders actually signed the treaty that concluded the Vienna Congress. And Talleyrand had only been able to stay for the signature by deliberately and repeatedly disobeying the king's orders.

Cardinal Consalvi had criticized the congress earlier as a Tower of Babel. The diplomats had begun with grand aspirations, but, in the end, they literally could not speak the same language. Consalvi would now issue a formal protest against the Congress of Vienna for its treatment of the pope. Although the Papal States had been restored, the pope had not received his due—either Avignon or Ferrara—Consalvi argued.

Another person who was upset was the Spanish delegate Pedro de Labrador, and he refused to sign the treaty. His government could not sanction the transfer of the Spanish royal territory of Parma to the wife of the detested usurper Bonaparte, nor agree to hand over the town of Olivenza to Portugal, as the congress had demanded. At this point, the delegates refused to make any more changes, either removing articles or adding in qualifications. Labrador would not budge, either. Each of the representatives of the other seven powers, in the meantime, took plume in hand, dipped the tip of the quill in the silver inkwell, and signed one of the most influential documents of the century. Spain would only accept the terms two years later, in May 1817.

The dancing congress ended without a great celebration to mark the occasion of the signing. The remaining participants simply drifted away. Metternich had a last dinner Monday night with Gentz, and then left Vienna at one o'clock the next morning, June 13, for Allied headquarters.

Talleyrand, too, was not to remain in Vienna for long after signing the Final Act. Having bid his farewells and exchanged snuffboxes, Talleyrand made a last tour of Kaunitz Palace, the site of so many parties, dinners, and intrigues the last nine months. As for that "great mass of papers" produced by the embassy, Talleyrand was not about to leave them for the maids, many of whom would surely be employed by the Austrian police. "I have, therefore, burnt the greater portion of these papers, and left the remainder in Vienna in safe hands." He was now ready to return to the king.

Chapter 31

To Conquer or Die

*My dear, with what refinement men go about destroying all the
good things which Providence has showered on them.*

— Prince Metternich

Murat had achieved a number of stunning successes in
rapid succession. He had conquered Rome, Florence,
and Bologna in two weeks, but he could not consoli-
date his victories. On May 3, the Austrian army caught up with him at
Tolentino in the Apennines and defeated him soundly. Murat's forces dis-
integrated. The Austrians recaptured the territory and, on the twenty-
third, even seized his capital, Naples. Murat fled to France in the disguise
of a sailor, hoping to join Napoleon. After only one month, Murat's rash
adventure had come to an abrupt end.

Napoleon was furious at Murat for his lack of foresight, and he
feared that this defeat would have unpleasant consequences for his own
campaign. The French emperor had lost a potential ally that could have
tied up some one hundred thousand Austrian troops in the Italian peninsula for an undetermined period of time, but now, instead, the Austrians
were firmly in control of the region and free to concentrate on him.
Worse still, Napoleon had started to fear that fortune was abandoning
him, something hard to swallow, with his superstitious reverence for a
force that he believed governed his destiny.

Indeed, troubles were popping up for Napoleon everywhere with a
great deal more frequency. The emperor still suffered serious financial
problems, arising from years of revolution, war, and, most recently, mis-
management. When King Louis XVIII and his royal court left Paris, they

had run off with as much treasure as they could quickly carry away. The state's annual income at the time of Napoleon's return to Paris was barely one-third of the total he had enjoyed back in 1812. He would be forced to take desperate measures to raise money, everything from levying new emergency taxes to selling all state-owned forestlands.

In addition, the army Napoleon inherited was not the one he had left at his abdication one year before. The king's supposed 200,000 soldiers were at best about 120,000, and poorly equipped. Most of Napoleon's talented officers had been removed, and replaced by royalist cronies, many of whom had little or no experience on the battlefield. Veterans had also been dismissed from service or reduced to half pay. Ammunition was in short supply. Muskets, gun carriages, bayonets, and other weapons had been sold as "army surplus," and the money had disappeared.

But during the previous three months, Napoleon had scrambled to turn this unwieldy mass of men into an efficient army. All soldiers officially on leave, some 32,800, had been ordered to report to duty immediately, and the 82,000 known deserters also recalled. Press gangs roamed the capital and the countryside, rounding up even more "recruits." The National Guard was called, gaining an additional 234,000 men between the ages of twenty and sixty. Students at the École Polytechnique and the military academy at Saint-Cyr-l'École were pulled out of classrooms to man fortifications, and sailors lifted from the navy. Napoleon figured he wouldn't need a fleet in the upcoming struggle.

As for equipping the troops, who would have to cover some six hundred miles of exposed frontier in the east alone, Napoleon launched another monumental effort. He placed orders for some 235,000 muskets and some 15,000 pistols for his cavalry. He ordered new cartridges, uniforms, boots, and everything else he needed for his campaign, though it was by no means clear where the money would come from to pay for all these supplies.

Overwhelmed with these demands, ordered at breakneck speed with challenging timetables, many provincial authorities resisted Napoleon's decrees. The new sacrifices and hardships only reminded many Frenchmen of what they had disliked last time about his reign, and the grumbling was getting worse. Even many who had welcomed Napoleon a few months ago were now growing disillusioned.

Supporters of the exiled King Louis XVIII, meanwhile, had been stirring in the west, particularly in the old Bourbon strongholds of Brittany and Vendée, and soon some thirty thousand royalists had rallied under the Marquis de la Rochejacquelin. From the other political extreme, some Jacobins and former revolutionaries were already plotting Napoleon's downfall. Clearly, most radicals had only accepted Napoleon as a temporary ally who could help sweep out the detested Bourbons. Now that this was accomplished, many felt, it was time to remove Napoleon and restore real freedom to France.

As the Allied forces prepared their armies for war, some of Napoleon's advisers suggested that he consolidate his strength and adopt a defensive campaign. His minister of the interior, Carnot, was one who argued for this approach. Britain and Prussia would probably not be in a position to attack for some time, and, moreover, they would likely await the arrival of the other allies. This would mean that the first battle would probably not take place until July at the earliest. Napoleon could use the next few weeks to strengthen his situation at home, both politically and militarily. Let the Allies enter the country as invaders, and discontent with Napoleon would quickly disappear as Frenchmen rallied to his side.

This was certainly an interesting suggestion, but anyone who had studied Napoleon's behavior in critical situations would know that he was inclined to attack. After all, the Allies were only getting stronger. They would soon have as many as seven or eight hundred thousand soldiers marching into France. As for the domestic unrest, Napoleon would address that the best way he knew how: He would fight, and he would win. He knew the stakes. One major defeat could end his reign and his dynasty. A big victory, on the other hand, could cause the fledgling alliance forged at Vienna to collapse from its own internal weakness.

In the early morning of June 12, Napoleon quietly left Paris to launch his invasion of Belgium. Two days later, on the anniversary of his victories at Marengo and Friedland, Napoleon issued a stirring proclamation from Beaumont in northeastern France: Soldiers, he said, "the time has come to conquer or die."

NAPOLEON'S GOAL WAS to make a quick devastating strike and knock out either the Duke of Wellington or Field Marshal Blücher before they could combine their forces. After this first victory, he would then wheel over and defeat the other army. Napoleon had used this general strategy, again and again, in vanquishing larger enemy armies. This time, too, Napoleon actually had a slight advantage in the strength of his troops and fire-power over either Wellington or Blücher, but if they combined their forces, he would be significantly outnumbered.

While the armies were positioning themselves for the upcoming battle, one of the most famous parties in history, the Duchess of Rich-mond's ball, took place on the rue de Blanchisserie in Brussels. Lord Byron celebrated it memorably in *Childe Harold's Pilgrimage,* and William Makepeace Thackeray used it for a scene in *Vanity Fair.* Actually, the his-torical ball was slightly different from the one of literature with its "high halls" of marble: It took place in a carriage house, or rather a coachman's workshop.

Some 224 people appeared on the guest list: Wellington, the Prince of Orange, the Duke of Brunswick, and many other British and Allied offi-cers, including twenty-two colonels. The duke was later criticized for attending such a frivolous event during the time of crisis, though this view fails to appreciate Wellington's intentions that evening. He had come to the ball as a way to dispel fears, and, as he put it, "reassure our friends." He would attend, calm as usual, and show that despite Napoleon's invasion of Belgium, everything was perfectly under control.

During the ball, however, a messenger arrived with the news that Napoleon was again on the march and apparently headed straight for the capital, Brussels. He was also taking an unexpected route (through Charleroi and not, as Wellington had suspected, through Mons). Welling-ton casually stayed on another twenty minutes, as if nothing were amiss, and then departed, pretending to be leaving for a good night's sleep. As he thanked the Duke of Richmond for the evening, he asked if his host happened to have "a good map in the house." The two men retired to a side room. Peering over a map on the table, Wellington confessed that he had misjudged the situation. "Napoleon has humbugged me, by God," Wellington said. "He has gained twenty-four hours' march of me."

The Allies would have to move quickly to protect the capital, the exiled royal court, and, of course, the coastal towns that formed their supply lines back to Great Britain. Wellington would engage the French at Quatre Bras, a strategic crossroads on the main road north, though he well knew that the Allied troops would probably not have enough time to arrive in strong enough forces to win decisively. At this point, Wellington allegedly ran his finger over the map and said, "I must fight him here." He pointed to a small village called Waterloo.

A few hours later, on the sixteenth of June, the soldiers were marching, some officers still in silk stockings from the ball. Two battles in fact would take place almost simultaneously that day. In one of them, at Quatre Bras, the Duke of Wellington and the Anglo-Allied troops drove back a French detachment under Marshal Ney. The other battle, about seven miles to the east, at Ligny, was a different matter. Napoleon, in command, won an impressive victory. The Prussians lost some 16,000 troops and a further 8,000 soldiers deserted. The French, by contrast, suffered 11,500 losses. Field Marshal Blücher had nearly been killed. His horse had been shot, and its fall had pinned down the seventy-two-year-old, who was then trampled by two French cavalrymen.

As the Prussians fled the scene in disarray, the French emperor, confident in his success, did not order an energetic pursuit of the defeated. He was already planning the next stage of his campaign. It was some twelve hours later—about eleven the next morning—when Napoleon finally sent away two corps and a force of some thirty-three thousand men under his most recent marshal, Emmanuel de Grouchy, to catch the Prussian army and finish them off. By then, the Prussians had managed to escape the worst danger.

The Prussian military staff, still stunned from the heavy defeat, was upset, and some blamed Wellington. The chief of staff, General August von Gneisenau, in particular, felt betrayed. He had had the distinct impression that Wellington would send several regiments over to aid them at Ligny. Wellington had, in fact, promised to help the Prussians in a meeting on the morning of the sixteenth, though he had added an important qualification that he would only be in a position to send troops if he were not attacked himself. The ferocity of the French attack at Quatre Bras prevented him from sending any assistance.

Wellington, meanwhile, learned of the disaster that struck his Prussian allies and realized that he, too, was now in a very exposed position. He could not remain at Quatre Bras, as a sitting duck, for the armies of Napoleon and Ney to fall upon him, but would have to march quickly. Wellington sent a messenger over to his Prussian allies, informing them that he would retreat north to a place called Mont-Saint-Jean just south of the village of Waterloo, where he would set up his headquarters. He hoped to engage the French there, and requested that the Prussians send over a corps if they could spare one.

Napoleon's campaign was certainly off to a good start. Having hammered the Prussians, he would now bring the bulk of his troops together, defeat the Duke of Wellington, and watch the alliance unravel.

THIS WOULD ACTUALLY be the first time that the French would fight an army with so many British troops since the Egyptian campaign some sixteen years before, and it was the first and only time that Napoleon and Wellington would face each other on the battlefield. Both were forty-six years old, with outstanding reputations—Napoleon, the bold strategist, inclined to quick surprise strikes, and Wellington, the brilliant tactician who preferred a more cautious and balanced approach. Napoleon was as feared as Alexander the Great and Genghis Khan; Wellington had never lost a battle.

Napoleon, it must be said, had many advantages. Thanks to his zealous efforts rebuilding the army, he had more soldiers, seventy-two thousand to Wellington's sixty-eight thousand, and more artillery, 246 cannons to Wellington's 156. He also had more veterans, compared to Wellington's many raw recruits and troops of uncertain loyalty (some two-thirds of his troops were non-British, mainly Dutch, Belgian, or German; many of them had either served the French in the past or were suspected of having French loyalties, or both). Napoleon, moreover, had a number of marshals who had fought Wellington in Spain and knew his tactics well.

Remarkably, as Wellington marched north on the seventeenth, neither Napoleon nor Ney seized the opportunity to attack. Orders had not been clear or timely, and Ney had hesitated more than usual. Some historians have wondered if Ney suffered from a form of "battle fatigue," or perhaps feared that Wellington's march was another one of his tricks. At any rate, Wellington had advanced his troops unharmed, and when the French realized that a good opportunity of striking the enemy was slipping away, they started marching. They were soon obstructed, however, by a violent storm, with heavy rain and then heavy mud bogging down their movement. By the evening, Napoleon decided to rest his army. "Have all the troops take up positions and we will see what happens tomorrow," he said, moving on to his headquarters a mile away, at a white stone farmhouse called Le Caillou, on the road to Brussels.

Wellington had managed to move into position, and chose the field of battle. It was a classical Wellington selection—a deceptively flat plain with "dips and folds" where he could place his troops on the inverse slope, better to conceal their numbers and protect them from enemy fire. Behind him was the Soignies Forest. Wellington was confident that this would cover his back and, should it be necessary, aid his retreat while also hindering the French cavalry pursuit. Napoleon, on the other hand, thought that Wellington had made a mistake and that the Anglo-Allied troops would end up trapped in the forest. The French emperor wanted to make sure that he did not miss this excellent opportunity to eliminate the British-led army.

In the early hours of June 18, the day of the fateful Battle of Waterloo, the Duke of Wellington was uncharacteristically having trouble sleeping. He got out of bed at three in the morning and wrote a few letters, mainly last-minute orders, though one letter was more personal, to a friend, Lady Frances Wedderburn Webster. Wellington suggested that she prepare to leave Brussels, just in case the battle that day went poorly.

At some point that morning (the time is disputed), a courier arrived at Wellington's headquarters with a message from Field Marshal Blücher. Wellington ripped open the dispatch and read. It was good news: The First and Second Corps of the Prussian army were on their way to join the Allies in battle. This was twice the number of soldiers that Wellington had hoped, but, problematically, the Prussians were not ready to leave for a couple of hours. "The exhaustion of the troops," Blücher explained, "did not allow my commencing my movement earlier."

Would the Prussians really be able to march as Blücher promised? Blücher was notoriously overoptimistic with his predictions, and the slow speed of the courier arriving with the message did not enhance Wellington's confidence. "Blücher picked the fattest man in his army to ride with an express to me," Wellington complained, "and he took thirty hours to go thirty miles." If the Prussian army had any hope of arriving that day, they would have to move faster than that.

About six o'clock that chilly and damp morning, the duke put on his blue coat, his blue cloak, and his boots, high up on the leg. With his hat in hand, which he typically wore front-back as opposed to Napoleon, who wore it side to side, Wellington walked over to his small charger, the chestnut Copenhagen, stepped into the iron stirrup, and vaulted into the stiff hussar saddle with the high pommel in front. He rode off to be everywhere at once.

Allied soldiers arrived exhausted onto the plateau around Mont-Saint-Jean. Many regiments had marched forty to fifty miles in the previous two days, each soldier carrying some fifty to sixty pounds of equipment. They slept in fields, soaked by the continuous hard rains, and not everyone had a tent. Water had poured down that night like "buckets emptying from the heavens," and "ran in streams from the cuffs of jackets." Many awoke with wet clothes still clinging to their body, and "petrified with cold." The lucky ones had breakfast, even if it was only the "half mouthful of broth and a biscuit" given to the soldiers of the Fifty-second Light Infantry.

Meanwhile, about eight o'clock that morning, at a small whitewashed farmhouse two miles south on the Charleroi-Brussels road, Napoleon was eating breakfast with several senior commanders. After the meal, the imperial silver was removed and maps were spread out on the table.

"We have . . . ninety chances in our favor, and not ten against us," Napoleon said, calculating the odds of success that day.

Marshal Ney, however, was troubled, fearing that Wellington would sneak away in a retreat and the French would miss the opportunity for a decisive victory. Napoleon rejected the possibility outright. Britain could no longer leave the scene, he said. "Wellington has rolled the dice, and they are in our favor."

Marshal Soult, the recently appointed chief of staff, was also concerned, though for a different reason. Soult had fought Wellington in Spain several times, without success—the British infantry was the devil himself, as he had once put it. Perhaps Napoleon should recall Marshall Grouchy and the thirty-three thousand men whom he had dispatched the previous day to pursue the Prussians. Napoleon bluntly dismissed the suggestion: "Because you have been beaten by Wellington, you consider him a great general."

"Wellington is a bad general," Napoleon continued, "the English are bad troops, and this will be like eating breakfast."

"I earnestly hope so," Soult replied.

In truth, Napoleon probably did not believe his harsh indictment of

Wellington's ability as a commander; the emperor often spoke with such dash on the eve of battle, mainly as a tactic to bolster morale, and morale in war, Napoleon said, was everything. Still, the French emperor was probably not too impressed with Wellington so far in the campaign. In the last three days, the British general had been caught by surprise by Napoleon's invasion route, been forced to retreat from Quatre Bas, and now found himself trapped like prey.

All morning, generals, staff officers, and couriers kept coming and going from French headquarters. General Honoré Reille, who would command the Second Corps on the far left or western flank, had just arrived, and on account of his experience fighting in Spain, fielded Napoleon's follow-up question about the British infantry. Reille's answer was not reassuring. The British infantry was fierce, he said, and if they were attacked from the front, "I consider the English infantry to be impregnable." At the same time, Reille noted that the British could be defeated by striking at their flanks. Their infantry was "less agile, less supple, less expert in maneuvering than ours."

Other generals at French headquarters emphasized the importance of attacking on either flank, rather than launching a direct frontal assault on the Allied center. General Maximilien Sébastien Foy, another veteran of the Spanish campaign, pointed out an additional reason why the British were so difficult to defeat: The crafty Duke of Wellington "never shows his troops." Indeed, Wellington had defeated no fewer than eight of Napoleon's marshals in Spain, and many other generals, including several who would take the field later that day.

Prince Jérôme, Napoleon's youngest brother and once widely castigated as the spoiled brat of the Bonaparte family, informed the emperor of a rumor he had heard the previous night at the inn Roi d'Espagne in Genappe. According to a waiter, one of Wellington's aides-de-camp had been boasting, indiscreetly, that the Prussians would return to the field later that day and join the British-led Allies.

"Nonsense," Napoleon snapped, remembering how soundly he had defeated the Prussians two days before. They would require at least two days of hard marching, he added, naturally assuming that the Prussians had retreated north to their supply lines at Wavre. Besides, "the Prussians have Grouchy on their heels."

It was at this morning strategy session that Napoleon's former governor of Elba, Marshal Drouot, advised the emperor to delay the attack a few hours to allow the soggy ground to dry so that they could move and fire artillery more effectively. The emperor agreed. He also knew that his army, which had camped over a large area, needed more time to be in a position for the attack.

By the end of the morning, Napoleon had decided on a general strategy. The French would not concentrate on turning one of the weaker flanks, as several generals plainly hoped, but instead launch a direct frontal assault on the Allied center. The emperor would rely on power, not finesse—a quick strike at the enemy defenses without elaborate feints or maneuvers, which he probably figured would have been useless anyway given the wet ground. Besides that, the small size of the battlefield, barely three miles in width, was not conducive to such grand sweeping maneuvers (Austerlitz, by contrast, was seven miles; Wagram, twelve; and Leipzig, twenty-one). As the emperor's valet Louis Marchand remembered the scene, Napoleon then suddenly rose from the table. "Gentlemen," he concluded confidently, "if my orders are carried out well, tonight we shall sleep in Brussels."

Chapter 32

La Belle Alliance

The ball is at my foot, and I hope I shall have strength to give it a good kick.

— ARTHUR WELLESLEY, THE FUTURE DUKE OF
WELLINGTON, BEFORE THE BATTLE OF TALAVERA

Nobody knows for certain when the Battle of Waterloo began, but it was probably a little after 11:30 a.m., when Napoleon's youngest brother, Prince Jérôme, leading a division of Comte Reille's Second Corps, launched an attack on the Hougoumont manor on the extreme western flank of the battlefield. Hougoumont commanded the narrow roadway that passed through the rye fields and protected Wellington's right flank against any wide enveloping movements. Napoleon had no intention of concentrating on this outpost, but only wanted to deceive Wellington into thinking that this would be the main thrust of his attack. Then, when Wellington began to shift troops away from the center, Napoleon would slam into his real target with his full strength.

Wellington had selected a Highlander, Lieutenant Colonel James Macdonnell, and five companies of Scots Guards and Coldstream Guards to hold the position at Hougoumont. In addition to the manor with its thick surrounding walls, there was a garden, an orchard, and a forest, as well as nearby hedges and fields. Granaries, storehouses, barns, sheds, stables, cattle pens, two small cottages, and other structures shielded the defenders. The inhabitants of the manor had fled long ago, except for a lone gardener, Willem van Kylsom, who hid in the cellar.

As Prince Jérôme's division of about sixty-five hundred infantrymen attempted to storm the manor, three-quarter-inch iron balls whizzed by from rye fields, woods, and soon also from the manor itself with its windows, loopholes, and makeshift scaffolds. Britain's musket, "Brown Bess," which had only slightly been altered since its introduction in 1745, wreaked a heavy toll on the advancing division. The German light infantry in the forests—*Jäger*, or "hunters"—were deadly accurate, too. Prince Jérôme, however, refused to yield. He had his orders, and he would seize the manor. His reputation was at stake, as was the family name.

Very soon, the fighting became intense hand-to-hand combat in and around the manor, where shots seemed to come from "every crack in the stone," as Victor Hugo put it. The French troops tried to force their way through a gate in the back of the manor, which had been used for supplying the troops. Eventually, a large Frenchman nicknamed L'Enforceur knocked a hole in the defenses and some one hundred Frenchmen streamed into a courtyard. Macdonnell and some fellow Scotsmen managed to close the gate again. The French intruders, trapped on the inside, were slaughtered. The only exception was a young drummer boy.

Undeterred by the lack of success, Prince Jérôme ordered a second attack on the manor, adding another four battalions, despite the protests of General Foy. Prince Jérôme would seize it "at all costs," an order, he later claimed improbably, that came from Napoleon himself. Progress was slow and brief. The French only managed to capture the forest and the orchard for a time. Even the fire that began to rage on the manor roof in the early afternoon, and soon spread throughout the many structures, did not obliterate the defense. A small, exhausted contingent of twenty-six hundred Allied troops was pinning down a force several times their size.

Indeed, rather than diverting troops from Wellington's center, the French assault was proving a drain on Napoleon's main attack. Years later, Wellington attributed the victory at Waterloo to the early action here on the periphery, or, as he put it, "the closing of the gates at Hougoumont."

One of many mysteries about the Battle of Waterloo was why Napoleon did not begin the attack by firing not only cannons but also howitzers, whose high-arced explosive shells would have likely devastated the walls of the manor. Such a bombardment was routine for this type of action, and would have paved the way for Jérôme's brave but ultimately ineffective assaults. Was the strange absence of the howitzers due to the fact that the French simply could not see the terrain and did not know how well the manor would be defended? Perhaps they did not even know the manor was there, as the historian Alessandro Barbero suggested. Orders already seemed confused, and miscommunication was rife; individual commanders were taking major decisions into their own hands, with great repercussions.

Meanwhile, just over fourteen miles away near the village of Walhain, Marshal Emmanuel de Grouchy, commander of the thirty-three thousand men of the Third and Fourth Corps, was eating strawberries in a requisitioned summerhouse when one of his soldiers rushed in with news that the rumble of the guns could be heard from the west. Grouchy's assistant, General Gérard, urged that they immediately turn around the armies and march them in the direction of the cannons.

The firing might well be a "rear-guard affair," Grouchy said. His orders were to advance to Wavre and finish off the Prussians. True, he had written Napoleon earlier that morning, about four o'clock, to ask for further instructions, but no reply had yet arrived. Grouchy reasoned:

> The Emperor told me yesterday that it was his intention to attack the English army if Wellington accepted battle . . . If the Emperor had wanted me to take part in it, he would not have detached my army just when he was preparing to attack the English.

Besides, marching on the muddy, soggy roads, he said, would make it difficult to reach the battlefield "in time to be of any use." He insisted on obeying the order precisely.

So over the spirited protests of his assistant and several other officers, Grouchy ordered the army to march away from the guns and away from Napoleon, who would very soon need the thirty-three thousand soldiers of the Third and Fourth Corps, who seemed destined to spend the day vainly roaming the countryside in search of the Prussian troops.

ABOUT ONE O'CLOCK that afternoon, Napoleon was on the hill near the Rossomme farm, sweeping the plain with his telescope. To the northeast, he saw an object that looked like a dark cloud. Was it an approaching army? Some officers near him claimed it was just a cloud, a cluster of trees, or really nothing at all. Napoleon had seen this sight many times before and knew otherwise.

But was it the French corps under Grouchy returning from their mission of finishing off the Prussians? Or was it the Prussians somehow nearing the scene? Napoleon sent scouts out to investigate. A courier was captured and interrogated, removing the last trace of doubt. It was the Prussians, and it was not just a minor detachment. It was the main Prussian army.

Remarkably, after the Prussian loss at Ligny two days before, Blücher's chief of staff, Gneisenau, had made a snap decision to retreat north—one of the fateful orders of the entire campaign. Had he retreated in any other direction, which was more obvious given their supply lines, the location of their headquarters, or the vicinity of strategic fortresses, the Prussians would never have been able to arrive on the scene. That morning, when the Prussians were debating whether to link up with the Allies, Gneisenau had argued against it. Blücher, however, overruled him. Having recuperated from his wounds, he was determined that the Prussians would reach the battlefield in time and fight the French.

When Napoleon first learned of the approaching Prussian army, said to be about six to eight miles away, he was not too concerned. "Even now, we have a sixty percent chance of winning," he said. Napoleon sent messengers to order Grouchy (wherever he was) to return at once. He sent two cavalry divisions, or some two thousand troops, east to distract or lure away the vanguard of the Prussians. In the meantime, he would attack Wellington and win quickly. "A more careful man," Clausewitz judged, "would have broken off the engagement and retreated."

Minutes later, however, some eighty-four French guns thundered onto Mont-Saint-Jean, where Wellington had positioned his troops. After the cannons plowed through the defense, Napoleon planned to order Lieutenant General Jean-Baptiste Drouet, Count d'Erlon, and the First Corps onto the weakened center. Then he would unleash his superior cavalry and complete his victory before the Prussians had time to arrive. Parade uniforms were already in knapsacks waiting for the triumphant march into Brussels.

At 1:30 p.m., Count d'Erlon and the sixteen thousand soldiers of the First Corps began to advance, slowly, through the muddy rye fields to attack the Allies. The columns were enormous, spanning some two hundred men or files across, and twenty-four to twenty-seven deep. This was an intimidating formation that showcased the strength of the attackers, and elevated morale, but it was hardly practical. Packing the soldiers so closely together limited movement, flexibility, and visibility, not to mention restricting firepower to the first two or three ranks. The rest of the soldiers—the vast majority—had virtually no offensive potential. Equally problematic, the deep columns presented a frightfully exposed target to British cannons. Napoleon had not chosen this formation for the assault, but neither had he overruled it. The French infantry would pay terribly for this poor choice.

But as the colossal columns marched forward, twenty-seven steps a minute to keep pace with the roll of the drums, some Allied troops, under the Dutch general Willem Frederik Graf van Bijlandt, fled in terror. British veterans hissed, hooted, and nearly fired at their allies as they raced by, calling them cowards and worse. Actually, many of the Dutch and Belgian soldiers in this brigade were suspected of identifying with Napoleon and hardly relished the thought of fighting their beloved emperor. They were also young troops fighting their first battle. Placed out front, too, they had also been more exposed to Napoleon's cannon salvos than any other troops on the Allied side.

As in all large battles, once it began in earnest, chaos seemed to reign. The thick black smoke of cannons obscured, from many angles, what little coherence might be imposed on the scene, and the low clouds of that overcast morning did not help visibility. In fact, the clouds were so near the ground that they seemed to magnify the roar of the cannons.

That day, some 150,000 men and 30,000 horses would charge, shoot, and hack their way through a muddy plain, not quite three miles long and barely one and a half miles wide. Musket balls struck swords or breastplates like a "violent hailstorm beating upon panes of glass." Sabers, lances, and grapeshot did their worst. Cannons wreaked even more damage. After the first thirty minutes, there were probably more than 10,000 dead and wounded. There were also the awful sights and sounds of the crying horses. It is no surprise that this battle would inspire one of the first modern efforts to protect animals from cruelty.

During the melee, which soon seemed to shift in favor of France, partly out of sheer force, the commander of the Allied cavalry and horse artillery, Lord Henry William Paget Uxbridge, ordered an attack. Outnumbered by perhaps five to one, the Household Brigade and the Union Brigade charged. It was a resounding success, at least initially. The horsemen sabered many Frenchmen, who turned and fled. Advancing quickly, they seized artillery guns, took some three thousand prisoners, and captured two Napoleonic eagles. The French attack had been repulsed.

True to form, the impetuous cavalrymen had difficulty restraining themselves in their triumph. Soon the brigades had overreached, riding deep into enemy ranks. Napoleon, who saw their vulnerability, ordered fresh lancers and dragoons into the fray. The result was devastating, and the "charge of the heavy brigade" came to an abrupt end. No fewer than a thousand of the twenty-five hundred horsemen perished.

As THE DIVERSION at Hougoumont turned into a quagmire and Count d'Erlon's attack had been repulsed, Napoleon had to launch his next big offensive against a center that had not been weakened.

Marshal Ney ordered a massive cavalry charge, comprising two brigades of the First Corps, or a total of about five thousand troops. William Gronow, a nineteen-year-old Etonian who fought with the First Foot Guards, described the approach of Ney's horsemen.

> Not a man present who survived could have forgotten in after life the awful grandeur of that charge. You perceived at a distance what appeared to be an overwhelming, long moving line, which, ever advancing, glittered like a stormy wave of the sea when it catches the sunlight . . . [as they approached] the very earth seemed to vibrate beneath their thundering tramp. One might have supposed that nothing could have resisted the shock of this terrible moving mass.

British commanders gave the famous order to form a square: "Prepare to receive cavalry." The soldiers in the front knelt down, readied their bayonets, and formed a human wall, or, as one veteran described it, "a wall bristling with steel, held together by steady hands." Behind this line, two rows of infantry bit off cartridges, loaded, rammed, and prepared to fire their muskets at the attackers.

Britain's infantry squares were actually often closer to rectangles, being larger on the front and the rear than on the sides. The formation was based on the assumption that a horse simply will not ride into a wall of bayonets. Indeed, despite contemporary paintings that depict gory cavalry charges, the horses generally stopped at about twenty yards' distance, no matter how much the riders cursed, or shouted "*Vive l'Empereur.*"

The best approach was to fire artillery into the infantry squares first. Cannon fire was, of course, the infantryman's nightmare. Unlike the saber, the lance, or the musket ball, the heavy eight- and twelve-pounders mangled bodies, smashed bones, and lopped off heads. Napoleon had planned to open with them, "his beautiful daughters," as he referred to the twelve-pounders. The problem was that many cannonballs had sunk in the mud rather than richochet through the ranks, and Wellington had protected them well, anyway, on the reverse side of the slopes. The French guns had done much less damage than Napoleon had hoped or expected.

As Wellington issued orders under an elm tree at a crossroads north of the farm of La Haye-Sainte, or riding down the lines encouraging the troops, Napoleon launched attack after attack on the center. The British infantry held firm. Wellington marveled at Napoleon's lack of finesse in varying his tactics: "Damn that fellow! He is a mere pounder after all."

One soldier compared the repeated charges of the French cavalry against the British infantry to "a heavy surf breaking on a coast beset with isolated rocks"; the massive wave crashes "with furious uproar, breaks, divides, and runs, hissing and boiling." Losses were heavy on all sides. One British regiment at the center, the Twenty-seventh Inniskillings, lost 450 of its 750 men, and only an estimated 1 in 18 made it through the grueling day without a wound.

The first cavalry charge, as the historian J. Holland Rose noted, came too soon. It was also plagued by the lack of coordination with artillery and infantry—an unsupported cavalry charge against an unbroken infantry square was recklessly ineffective. In fairness to Ney, it is likely that he misjudged the movements behind the Allied line, thinking that the repositioning of the squares a hundred yards back (to avoid the cannons) and the evacuation of wounded and prisoners was actually Wellington in retreat. Ney had suspected that Wellington would attempt to flee since the beginning of battle, and he was sensitive to any sign that indicated it was taking place. He thought he was cutting off the retreat.

But Wellington was not retreating. The infantry, locked into approximately twenty squares, held firm and the slaughter continued.

DETERMINED TO WIN before the Prussians arrived, Napoleon ordered Ney, about 3:30 p.m., to seize the strategic farm, La Haye-Sainte, on Wellington's left, or eastern, flank that was vital to his center. As at Hougoumont, the result was another intense fight. Against great odds, the King's German Legion on the inside, and the Ninety-fifth Rifles in the nearby gravel pit, held out for hours. But the KGL soon ran out of ammunition, and the standard reinforcements did not fit the Baker rifles used by the specialist sharpshooters. This proved to be another battle within a battle, ending just after six o'clock that evening, when the French captured the farm.

This was certainly a blow to Wellington and the Allies. This eastern flank was one of Wellington's weaknesses—he had deliberately under-defended it because he expected the Prussians to arrive that day and cover his flank. Now that Napoleon had captured La Haye-Sainte, he could place his own artillery and sharpshooters closer in range and apply much more pressure on the Allies.

Soon Wellington was in serious trouble and the center was about to break. Wellington's men were taking a beating, and more Allied regiments had already fled. Basil Jackson, a young staff officer, reported that the forests near the battlefield were full of defectors, entire companies with "fires blazing under cooking kettles, while the men lay about smoking." Most famously, the Cumberland Hussars, a volunteer regiment of Hanoverian gentlemen in splendid uniforms, galloped straight from the battlefield to Brussels with the alarming news that defeat was imminent and the French would soon march through the capital in triumph.

Sensing an imminent Allied defeat, Marshal Ney pleaded with the emperor for more troops to deliver the knockout blow. As military historian David Chandler argued, the situation was critical for Wellington, and with fresh reinforcements, Ney probably would have shattered the Allied center. Napoleon, however, failed to seize the opportunity, answering only in frustration about the impossibility of sending more soldiers: "Where the devil do you expect me to find them! Do you want me to make them?"

Napoleon could have sent in six battalions of the Middle Guard and eight battalions of the Old Guard—the elite troops that he held in reserve. As Chandler further pointed out, had the emperor sent in half of them, Napoleon would probably have won the Battle of Waterloo. Wellington was taking a severe beating, and two brigades had already been destroyed. Others seemed on the verge of breaking.

Napoleon, of course, had no way of knowing just how close Wellington's center was to collapsing—that is the advantage of hindsight. In fairness, too, Ney's record thus far in the campaign could hardly have inclined the emperor to comply with the request. Again and again, Ney had made brave, though ultimately untimely and disorganized, attacks that had proved costly. It would have been easy to see this request in that light. Moreover, Napoleon never liked to use his reserves until the enemy had first committed his, and this was not the case yet.

So, rather than sending in some additional troops for Ney's attack on Wellington's center, Napoleon ordered some eleven battalions of the Guard to take Plancenoit, the largest village in the region, which would hold their position and lines of communication, in preparation for the Prussian arrival. Twenty minutes later, the French had succeeded here as well. Wellington was powerless to help. The British Fifth Division, defending, lost some 3,500 of 4,000 soldiers. "Let us pray to God," Wellington allegedly said on hearing the news, "for the coming of night—or of Blücher."

By THE LATE afternoon, the army in the distance was unmistakably drawing nearer, and Napoleon was racing against time. A small detachment of Prussians, under General Bülow, was already active on the eastern flank. The French were holding them off, but Blücher, commanding thirty thousand men, was quickly approaching from the east. Wellington, in the meantime, was shuffling troops quickly to shut the hole in his center.

A gambler by nature, Napoleon decided to risk everything, and the French attacks increased in intensity. Marshal Ney, leading charge after charge against the British infantry, had four horses shot from under him. As the vanguard of the Prussian army neared the battlefield, Napoleon told his French soldiers, untruthfully, that the army in the distance was actually Grouchy's.

In the end, Napoleon, desperate, ordered his elite Imperial Guard, "Les Invincibles," to attack. The feared veterans were never used unless the battle was almost over and victory secure, and they had never failed.

So, to drums, "La Marseillaise," and the famous cry *"Vive l'Empereur!"* they started marching. But this time, it was a suicide mission.

Napoleon personally took the lead of some twelve battalions and sixty-five hundred famous veterans of the Grande Armée (fifteen thousand total were in the assault) and marched off in what was to be the warlord's final charge. About six hundred yards out, Napoleon turned aside, handing over responsibility for the attack to Marshal Ney. The Guards marched straight ahead, without any cavalry support, right into the fields where Wellington's troops suddenly rose up from concealed positions and fired with devastating accuracy. Three hundred of Napoleon's veterans died in a minute, according to Captain Siborne's estimate.

Later that evening, when the sun shone brightly for the first time in days and now penetrated the clouds of smoke hovering over the plain, the French were in full retreat. Wellington, standing in his stirrups and waving his hat, urged his men forward to finish the victory. The French flight lost all sense of order. It was "a panic-stricken rabble," as Napoleon called it.

The Prussian leader Blücher, said to have a personal grudge against the French, was determined to catch the French emperor himself. The Imperial Guard, having been repulsed for the first time, had regrouped and now covered the retreat of the French well. Napoleon himself was able to escape, riding away in his bulletproof carriage and then switching to his white charger, Marengo.

The Prussians followed in hot pursuit, continuing the chase long into the night. In the end, the Prussians nearly captured Napoleon himself. They had his carriage, still with his ceremonial sword, a bottle of rum, a bottle of old Malaga, a toothbrush, and a million francs' worth of diamonds, which his sister had given him on Elba. Napoleon's carriage was presented as a gift to the Prince Regent, who put it on show in London and later sold it to Madame Tussaud for her museum, where it remained until it was destroyed in the fire of 1925.

Napoleon himself blamed this defeat—"the horrible piece of bad luck"—on everything from the rain to the mistakes of his subordinates. Marshal Soult had struggled in his new position as chief of staff, sending too few messengers; as a result, many orders never reached their target or arrived too late. Marshal Ney, likewise, had made numerous errors, ranging from unfortunate delays at the opening of the campaign to reckless and untimely attacks that lost many lives. Still "in spite of all," Napoleon added, "I should have won that battle."

For a long time afterward, historians debated the actual causes of this Allied victory. Had Wellington essentially won the battle, or did the arrival of the Prussians prove decisive? Actually, the question is absurd, as the historian Andrew Roberts rightly remarked. Wellington would never have waited on the plain that day for a battle if he had not expected the Prussians to arrive and defend his left flank. At the same time, he would probably not have won without the timely assistance of the Prussians. Both armies deserve the credit.

Wellington's tactics and strategic choice of terrain had been crucial. He had used his information sources effectively and had a sound knowledge of Napoleon's strengths and movements through his spies, including in-depth reports from Napoleon's treacherous minister of police, Joseph Fouché. Moreover, he knew of the Old Guard attack in advance from a defector. The English could also thank the formidable infantry, which withstood Napoleon's increasingly desperate charges. The English, of course, had new weapons such as Congreve rockets, but they were far less important than the human factors.

Napoleon, for his part, had made a number of mistakes that day, some of them bizarre. Besides the large detachment he sent away on the eve of the battle to fight the Prussians, and which might have proven decisive, Napoleon had not used the talents of many of his marshals to the fullest. Davout, an excellent commander, was still in Paris as minister of war. Murat, the greatest cavalry leader of the day, was disdained and not allowed to fight. Another, Louis Gabriel Suchet, was placed in a secondary position defending the eastern approach to France. David Chandler wondered if Napoleon had deliberately "fielded a second team" to preserve the glory for himself.

Napoleon, further, broke many of his own military maxims. Some have claimed that the emperor was suffering from any number of ailments: acromegaly, inflammation of the bladder and urinary tract, or even hemorrhoids. At any rate, Napoleon was not at his best that day. "Everything failed me just when everything had succeeded," he later said.

During that short campaign, there were confusing orders, vague, contradictory, and slow to arrive; personality clashes among his subordinates further hurt their efforts, as did some well-known examples of treachery, such as General Louis August Victor Bourmont's defection to the Prussians. Significantly, too, Napoleon delayed his initial attack almost four hours in the morning to allow the wet ground to dry, a crucial fact that allowed Wellington to dry his weapons and the Prussians to arrive on the scene. And so on. There were countless "ifs" that might have tipped the balance.

The battle was over, and now it was time to name it. Blücher suggested that it should be called "the Battle of La Belle-Alliance," punning on the name of an inn in the Forest of Soignies where the two victors met that evening after the battle. Wellington preferred Waterloo.

SOMETIME AFTER MIDNIGHT, Wellington started drafting the famous Waterloo dispatch. Finishing it the next day at Brussels, he folded it up into the small purple velvet sachet that he had received at the Duchess of Richmond ball and sent it off with a courier to his government back in London. "It is a glorious victory," Wellington announced, though unfortunately "the loss of life had been fearful, and I have lost many friends."

About 40,000 men had been killed that day, and many more wounded. Wellington suffered between 13,000 and 15,000 casualties, and Napoleon's losses are usually estimated between 25,000 and 30,000. Blücher lost about 7,000 men. Total casualties of the four-day campaign were perhaps 115,000 (some 60,000 French and 55,000 Allies).

Nearby Brussels seemed one giant hospital. Carts of mangled, bloodied, and bandaged soldiers rattled through the streets and dropped off the wounded onto beds of straw around the city. Citizens cared for as many in their homes as possible, and carried water to the thirsty. One surgeon described the ordeal of continually operating on the wounded for thirteen hours straight, until, as he put it, his clothes were "stiff with blood, and [his] arms powerless with the exertion of using the knife!" Unfortunately for the soldiers, it was a dreadful experience: The rushed and overworked surgeons labored without the benefit of anesthesia or sophisticated instruments.

Metternich wrote to congratulate the Duke of Wellington for his victory at Waterloo, or, as he put it, "the brilliant opening of the campaign." Wellington, though, was more optimistic about its significance. "I may be wrong," he said shortly afterward, "but my opinion is that we have given Napoleon his death blow." Nine days after completing the historic Final Act in Vienna, the Duke of Wellington, Field Marshal Blücher, and their combined armies had indeed defeated the French emperor.

Napoleon, however, was not ready to concede. He arrived back in Paris three days after the battle, ready to raise another army. He would use Grouchy's troops as a core, combine them with his National Guard reserves, and impose another conscription. He would take the field again with some three hundred thousand men and avenge Waterloo.

But a powerful group within his own government was disturbed at the thought of another awful fight to the death under a desperate Bonaparte, and worked to undermine his plan. Among the many plotters were Napoleon's minister of police, Fouché, "a Trojan horse within the city walls" of Paris. Fouché worked closely with several leaders in the French legislature, including the former Bonapartist who had also been an assistant to George Washington and a French revolutionary hero, the Marquis de Lafayette. Now, years later, the fifty-seven-year-old was using his influence to denounce Napoleon in the chambers.

"The Emperor must abdicate without delay," Lafayette said, as the legislature debated its course of action following Waterloo. "If we rid ourselves of him, peace will be ours for the asking!" One of Napoleon's advisers, Carnot, took the podium to defend the emperor, as did Napoleon's brother Lucien and the former revolutionary Emmanuel Sièyes. True, "Napoleon has lost a battle," another said, but the French must rally to his side and "drive the barbarians from our country." Napoleon was their best chance for victory.

"Have you forgotten where the bones of our sons and brothers whiten?" Lafayette asked. The deserts of Egypt, the snows of Russia, and now the plains of Belgium—Will it also be the streets of Paris? France had already sacrificed a few million, all victims "of this one man who wanted to fight all Europe! Enough!" he concluded, tired of the bloodshed.

As the chambers debated whether to demand Napoleon's abdication, Napoleon's own advisers were encouraging him to send in the army and seize emergency power. Napoleon's brother Lucien strongly urged this response. Napoleon thought it over in a hot bath, and then later that day in a walk through the palace gardens, while a small crowd outside the gates still shouted, *"Vive l'Empereur!"*

On June 22, the French legislature demanded that Napoleon step down from the throne voluntarily or he would be removed. He had one hour to decide. Napoleon's advisers did not agree on the response, though several still wanted him to march the army over to the legislature. Napoleon, this time, refused. "I have not returned to drench Paris in blood," he said. At three o'clock that afternoon, Napoleon abdicated for a second time.

Chapter 33

SHIFTING SAND

Finita la commedia.

— GENTZ, WRITING IN HIS DIARY THE LAST
NIGHT OF THE PEACE CONFERENCE

ews of the victory at Waterloo traveled across Europe by courier, carriage, and pigeon. Souvenir hunters almost immediately descended onto the grim site. One was Lord Byron, who openly mourned the French emperor's defeat—"damned sorry for it," he was. Another curious visitor was Sir Walter Scott, who described what he saw:

> The ground is still torn with the shot and shells, and covered with cartridges, old hats, and shoes, and various relics of the fray which the peasants have not thought worth removing.

There was everything from flowers for the slain to enterprising peasants claiming to have been with Napoleon and now offering guided tours. Swords, decorations, and other mementos were hawked at a nearby market. Sir Walter Scott bought two cuirasses.

As the leading powers behind the victory at Waterloo, the British and the Prussians were, no surprise, the first to reach Paris, and they would also play the most decisive role in determining the adjustments that would be made to Vienna's Final Act. Napoleon's escape from Elba had forced a revision of the terms of peace, at least for France, though the Allies were by no means agreed on what those changes would be. Napoleon's return to power had lasted roughly a hundred days; the peace negotiations afterward would drag on for 133.

Paris during these four months would sometimes seem like a sedate reunion of the Vienna Congress. Most of the cast was back. Cafés, theaters, and the opera flourished, along with a new popular ballet about Waterloo. There were dinners at restaurants such as Beauvilliers, Robert's, or Massinot's, and gambling in the gilded halls of Frascati's and Salon des Étrangers. One English captain in Paris that summer advised all players looking to make a fortune at the fashionable roulette tables to imagine that the entrance to these gambling chambers bore the inscription atop the gates of Dante's hell: "Abandon hope all ye who enter here."

With some 150,000 soldiers in town, the elegant capital looked like a military camp. White tents of the British army lined the Champs-Élysées, stretching all the way to Napoleon's still-unfinished Arc de Triomphe. Other contingents camped out in the grasses in the shadow of Notre Dame Cathedral, or in the Bois de Boulogne.

This army was needed for many functions, not least the supervision of the return of King Louis XVIII. Despite the widespread resistance, Britain had gotten its way, and the Bourbon king was restored a second time to the throne. This was done quickly, before any rival candidates had time to organize support and lobby effectively. Louis XVIII was returning with the Allied army, or, as critics said, "behind the scarlet uniforms freshly dyed in the crimson blood of Frenchmen."

King Louis may have had a crown, a throne, and a guard again, but he did not yet rule. The capital was in a volatile state. French and Allied soldiers dueled and clashed, as did returning royalists and Bonapartists who refused to abandon their idol.

Castlereagh had returned from London for the diplomatic discussions, joining the Duke of Wellington to work closely again, as they had briefly in Vienna and more generally the previous several years. Both men would push for moderation, not wishing to saddle France with a vindictive peace that would only make matters worse for Louis XVIII and the future stability of the Continent.

The Prussians, on the other hand, disagreed. France was a "criminal country," as Blücher put it, and should be punished accordingly. Some Prussian generals, swept up in a victory that had come so suddenly and completely, demanded a partition of France, claiming for themselves Alsace, Lorraine, Saarland, Savoy, Luxembourg, Franche-Comté, Flanders, and Burgundy, along with a reparations bill of 1.2 billion francs. Such excessive demands once again worried Hardenberg. "I find myself," he sighed, "in the midst of Praetorian bands."

On the way to the capital, the Prussian army had laid waste to the countryside, eager to avenge "the cruelties, the extortion, insults, and hard usage their own capital has suffered." Reports of Prussian looting appalled the Allies: "The work of devastation I have no language to describe," one said. They had stormed a château, and "not one article of furniture, from the costly pier-glass down to the common coffee-cup . . . was not smashed to atoms." A mad dog in France was, for a long time, called a Blücher.

When the Prussian troops reached Paris, they showed no signs of mellowing. Blücher wanted to blow up the bridge Pont d'Iéna in central Paris, because the name commemorated one of Napoleon's major victories over the Prussians in 1806. The field marshal had, in fact, mined the base and was about to order its detonation, when Talleyrand, in protest, threatened to come and sit on the bridge. Fine, Blücher said, remembering the French minister's opposition in Vienna. He would hold off the detonation until Talleyrand had time to arrive.

The Duke of Wellington, however, intervened, calmed Blücher down, and, just to make sure, posted a British sentry on the bridge. Talleyrand, in the end, also helped diffuse the crisis, proposing to rename it Pont de l'École Militaire, and the bridge was saved (and later renamed Pont d'Iéna).

But Talleyrand was not exactly comforted by what he had seen so far. Arrogance, greed, abuse of power—hopefully, the behavior of the Great Powers was not an indication of how unsuccessful the congress had been. As Talleyrand knew, if the peacemakers had not established a just peace, Europe could count on "revolutions for the rest of our life."

As the Allies settled into Paris for the negotiations, the question immediately arose about what to do with Napoleon. For the Prussians, the answer was simple: Send him to a firing squad. No doubt, had the Prussians captured Napoleon after Waterloo, he would have met such a demise. No doubt, too, they had not abandoned their hunt. Blücher's orders were to capture Napoleon "dead or alive."

There was still a chance that the former French emperor would rally his remaining supporters among the army and the people. The last remnants of the Waterloo army, under Marshal Grouchy, were reportedly on their way back from Belgium, and there was another force heading for the capital, after squashing a royalist rebellion in the west. The total strength was unknown, though some feared that it could be as high as 150,000 to 200,000 men. This was exaggerated, of course, but Napoleon could very well field a large enough army to make a final, bloody stand.

None of Napoleon's enemies wanted to take any chances. A few days after the emperor's abdication, the new leader of the provisional government, Joseph Fouché, had ordered Napoleon to leave the capital. Many historians believe that Fouché hoped that the Prussians would capture and dispose of him. At any rate, the former emperor duly headed out to Malmaison, the three-story château on the banks of the Seine where he had lived with his first wife, Joséphine, and spent some of his happiest days in his rise to power. Josephine died shortly after he had left for Elba. "Poor Joséphine," he said, reminded of his early career, "I feel as if I ought to meet her at every turn."

The Prussians, meanwhile, were closing in, and, by late June, they were reportedly in the vicinity of Malmaison. As the French government claimed it could no longer guarantee his safety, Napoleon was ordered out of France. He did, however, have one final request. Napoleon wanted to resume his position as general, rally the army, and defeat the invaders, who were then spread out thin and vulnerable to attack. He promised not to interfere anymore with politics. The offer was declined.

So Napoleon secretly left for the port of Rochefort on the west coast of France, hoping to find transport to the United States or, failing that, Mexico or South America. Two French frigates were waiting on him, he was told, and by the time he arrived, so were two British warships that had no intention of allowing Napoleon to escape.

Surrounded by his last loyal friends, many of them from Elba, Napoleon debated what to do. Should he attempt to race past the English warships? But even if he broke out initially, it would be difficult to outrun the Royal Navy and evade capture. Perhaps he could slip away undetected on board an American merchant ship like the one his brother

Joseph had chartered, or under the flag of a neutral power. What about first leaving shore on a small, inconspicuous whale or fishing boat, and then, once at sea, switching over to a larger, friendly vessel? Many other possibilities were suggested, including smuggling Napoleon on board a ship in a barrel.

None of this, Napoleon concluded, was befitting the dignity of a man who once ruled the largest empire that Europe had ever known. Napoleon would instead appeal directly to British honor. Referring to the ancient Athenian general who beseeched King Artaxerxes after the Persian Wars, Napoleon wrote to the Prince Regent that he came, like Themistocles, to trust his fate to the hands of his most committed enemy. On the morning of July 15, Napoleon boarded the HMS *Bellerophon* and surrendered.

For months, politicians and the people alike had debated what to do with Napoleon, and now, all of a sudden, Britain had him. Many clamored for vengeance. Editors of the London *Times* had wanted Napoleon hanged; the Prussians preferred a firing squad. Some thought that the "Corsican ogre" should be locked up in the Tower of London or the Fort St. George, or even shuffled off with other criminals to Botany Bay. Yet another suggestion was simply turning him over to the French government for trial, though many rightly feared that the new government would be far too shaky to pull that off.

By the end of July, Britain had made its decision—and it was Britain's decision, as the Allies had recently agreed to hand over the entire responsibility to it. Napoleon would not be executed or imprisoned on the British Isles. Nor would he be given asylum, as he clearly had hoped; that was far too risky. The prime minister, Lord Liverpool, had concluded that Napoleon, already an object of curiosity, might soon be popular and dangerous, a source of unrest and rallying point for the Continent's disillusioned. No one wanted to fight another Waterloo.

Napoleon was furious when the British undersecretary of state announced his fate on July 31: He was to be banished to St. Helena in the South Atlantic. He had been tricked, he protested. He accused (probably unjustly) Captain Frederick Maitland of the HMS *Bellerophon* of promising him asylum in Britain, and denounced the treachery, but there was nothing he could do. The former emperor was transferred to the HMS *Northumberland*, a seventy-four-gun ship that would carry him into exile. It would be a ten-week voyage to the tiny volcanic island some 1,800 miles east of Brazil and 1,200 miles west of Angola. Its nearest neighbor, 700 miles away, was not even a dot on the map.

WHILE BONAPARTE WAS being removed, and the Bourbon dynasty restored, the Allies debated the future of France. It would take the rest of the summer and most of the autumn. One of the most high-profile controversies raged over the artwork stolen during the French Revolutionary and Napoleonic Wars.

Frustrated with the slow process of negotiation, however, the Prussians were not waiting on the diplomats to decide on the matter. Only days after arriving in the capital, some troops stormed into the Louvre and started removing the works of art that Napoleon had stolen, or that they claimed had been stolen. Were all those Raphaels and Titians being yanked down from the walls really from Prussian collections? What about the portraits of Napoleon and the Bonaparte family that Marshal Blücher personally requested?

Parisians were furious at this sacking of the Louvre by modern vandals. The museum director, Baron Dominique-Vivant Denon, tried to resist, and cited the exact terms of the capitulation of Paris that guaranteed French property (Article XI), but the Prussian officer in charge, von Ribbentrop (an ancestor of the Nazi ambassador and foreign minister), threatened to have him arrested and sent to a prison in Berlin. One British officer defended the Prussian action as just "plundering the plunderer." Allied soldiers, meanwhile, had to hold back angry mobs who threatened violence over the desecration of their museum.

Pope Pius VII worked more legally to regain his lost treasures. On Cardinal Consalvi's advice, the pope sent the renowned sculptor Antonio Canova to examine the Louvre carefully for the paintings, sculptures, and gems that belonged to the Vatican. The pope had arguments of legitimacy on his side. His treasures had been stolen, and the treaty that sanctioned that theft was invalidated, as it had been made under duress. The French countered that this treaty was a legal contract, and, moreover, the art better served scholars and students in the Louvre, where the museum was better lit, and the works categorized into galleries according to their style and carefully preserved in one place.

On September 20, the Allies decided that the art should be returned to its earlier and proper owners. The restoration began immediately. Soldiers carried the Venus de Medici, armless and feet first, out of the Louvre, to protests and cries of "Shame!" The four bronze horses that had been on the Arc de Triomphe du Carrousel for the last seventeen years were now taken down and returned to St. Mark's Basilica in Venice, where they remain today. Metternich wanted the four bronze horses as a goodwill gesture to celebrate the return of Venice to Austrian rule.

The Vatican received the vast majority of its treasures, including the Apollo Belvedere and *Laocoön and His Sons*. Documents, too, were returned to other collections. Leonardo da Vinci's secret notebooks, the Codex Atlanticus, and the manuscripts in the Ambrosiana Library, which Napoleon had stolen in 1796 and donated to the Institut de France, were now returned to Milan. For many of the transfers, such as the large statues and paintings going back to the Vatican, Britain magnanimously paid the expenses.

But Britain would gain a great deal of unpopularity in the process. Many Englishmen were booed in the streets or challenged to duels. Even the Duke of Wellington had to leave the theater one night because of the zeal of his hecklers. The official chosen to oversee the art restoration hardly helped matters. He was William Richard Hamilton, the career diplomat who had previously played a role in bringing several treasures to the British Museum, including no less than the Elgin Marbles and the Rosetta Stone. What was he going to seize now? Nothing, actually, but many officials at the Louvre feared the worst.

The French protested to the end. "All the best statues are gone," one observer complained, "and half the rest" were as well. Officially, some 2,065 paintings, 289 bronzes, and 317 statues, busts, and wooden sculptures had been removed, along with another 2,432 miscellaneous works of art, as one of the Louvre's founders tallied. The great museum now seemed only "full of dust, ropes, triangles, and pulleys." It might as well close, another said. The museum curator, and chief looter during the wars, Baron Dominique-Vivant Denon, resigned in anger, having seen his beloved museum emptied of numerous treasures in a matter of weeks.

It was, at that time, history's most comprehensive restoration of art. This was not, however, without some accidents and mishaps. Some of the works looted in the war, like Paul Veronese's *Marriage at Cana,* were too big to transport safely and remained in the Louvre. (It had been ripped in two when the French removed it from Venice). Other paintings disappeared in transit, including Rubens' *Diogenes.* Rumors that the original masterpieces had been replaced with imitations would proliferate for years. One painting, Raphael's *Virgin of Loreto,* was an obvious copy. Another one, Correggio's *Leda with the Swan,* came back to its owners with the figure of Leda having a different head.

Several art collections already dispersed from the capital were overlooked in the sweeping restoration. There were also difficulties with the archives, and one of the many people looking for treasures stolen by the French was Jacob Grimm. Vatican files before AD 900, which Napoleon had stolen in 1810, were particularly difficult to retrieve. Many had been destroyed or sold to cardboard manufacturers, and authorities tried everything to resist. The documents surrounding Galileo's trial in 1633 were also a problem. None of these were returned by the time the Allies left Paris; heated disputes continued for years. By 1817, the Vatican had recovered many files, though some estimate as much as two-thirds had been destroyed in the ordeal. Records continued to trickle in for years, including one Galileo Codex kept by the Duke of Blacas and returned after his death in 1843.

MEANWHILE, IN A dark salon near the Élysée Palace, Tsar Alexander was enjoying nightly discussions with Baroness Krüdener, the mystic adviser whom someone dubbed the "Ambassadress of Heaven." They were working on one of the tsar's cherished projects, which he had apparently begun back in Vienna during December 1814 and would now officially propose. It was to be "a pact of love," as he put it. Historians call it the Holy Alliance.

This was an attempt to create a new style of diplomacy that would end war, revolution, and the old diplomatic practices, such as secret treaties and balance-of-power politics, that strained relations between states. The tsar now called on the leaders of the world to commit themselves to guiding their actions by "the precepts of that Holy Religion; namely, the precepts of Justice, Christian Charity, and Peace." The Russian tsar, the Austrian emperor, and the king of Prussia all signed on September 26, 1815.

The three monarchs—Roman Catholic, Protestant, and Russian

Orthodox—would cooperate as "three branches of the One family" under the Sovereign of Heaven, the source of all "love, science and infinite wisdom," and they would view all the peoples of their kingdoms as citizens of this international brotherhood. The leaders would protect "Religion, Peace, and Justice" and other powers would be welcome to join this league if they accepted these "sacred principles." As Henry Kissinger noted, the occasion of the Holy Alliance was, in fact, the first time that Europe's leaders had signed an international treaty binding themselves to "a common mission."

In 1919, some historians already saw hints of Woodrow Wilson's Covenant in this condemnation of old diplomacy, in the emphasis on the family of states, and in the attempt to end war and replace it with a permanent system of international cooperation. There were many hints, but the Holy Alliance was very much in the spirit of the early nineteenth-century Romantic revival, that is, as interpreted by the tsar and his prophetess, who was undoubtedly influencing him heavily at this time.

Winning over the king of Prussia was not difficult, but Emperor Francis had been skeptical, and consulted Metternich, who called the tsar "a madman to be humored" and advised that they accept. Britain, however, refused to sign the treaty. The government did not trust Russia or its tsar. Castlereagh dismissed the document as "a piece of sublime mysticism and nonsense." The pope, Pius VII, was also skeptical of the activities, and the sultan of Turkey, of course, was not invited.

The tsar had hoped that the Holy Alliance would be his crowning achievement of peacemaking that year, but it was to be overshadowed by a second treaty, completed in Paris in November 1815, that included the same three eastern powers, in addition to Great Britain. This was the Quadruple Alliance—consisting of the Big Four who signed the military pact at the end of the Napoleonic Wars and organized the committees at the Vienna Congress. The hope was to maintain the vigilance, cohesion, and strength of the wartime alliance that defeated Napoleon as a way to guard the peace in the postwar world.

Most significantly, Article VI of the Quadruple Alliance treaty specifically called for periodic meetings of the great powers to manage international relations. This "diplomacy by conference" would examine policies "most salutary for the repose and prosperity of the peoples and for the peace of Europe." The goal was to prevent any potential threat from erupting into a full-scale crisis, and then respond by consensus, using force only when necessary. This "great experiment" was attempting to establish an institutional framework for managing international anarchy. There was even talk of creating an "office of Europe" and appointing Friedrich von Gentz the first "Secretary-General of Europe," though this idea was soon abandoned.

But with the Quadruple Alliance, the powers had guaranteed the peace settlement. No act of aggression was to be tolerated, unless the Great Powers collectively gave their assent. This was one of the most significant achievements. By this treaty, the veterans of the Vienna Congress had launched what diplomatic historian Sir Charles Webster rightly called the first ever attempt "to regulate international affairs during a time of peace."

AFTER HER EXPERIENCES at the Vienna Congress, Dorothée returned to Paris in early July as a new woman, "a sort of queen of the diplomatic world." She was determined, more than ever, to take a new direction in her life. For one thing, this meant the end of her marriage. Although she could not divorce, as a Catholic, she managed to obtain a legal separation from Edmond and continued her love affair with Count Clam-Martinitz.

Despite the cool reserve that he presented to the world, Talleyrand also seemed in love—deeply in love—and the object of his affections, many of his friends agreed, was Dorothée. Indeed, few had seen Talleyrand act this way in years. "It was a frantic passion," his young friend Charles de Rémusat wrote. Another friend, the minister of justice, Pasquier, agreed that this "all-devouring ardor" had "entirely deprived him of all presence of mind."

But Talleyrand was now experiencing the unusual sensation of not having his affections returned. Dorothée clearly preferred Count Clam-Martinitz. At the end of the autumn, when the count joined the Austrian army in Italy, Dorothée followed him, leaving a despondent Talleyrand back in Paris. The French foreign minister began to resemble Metternich the previous autumn, when he had been shattered by the rejection of Dorothée's older sister. Now Talleyrand lost his famous composure, "devoured by a slow fever caused by the absence of his mistress, and began to die, quite literally, of disappointed love."

As if that were not difficult enough, Talleyrand was also concerned about the future of France. The Prussians and many others were demanding many changes to the map, and many leading diplomats were listening. Even the Allied declaration, back in March, that specifically named Napoleon as the enemy, not France, was being ignored. The Prussian delegation now shrugged it aside, arguing that the French had rallied to Napoleon's side, thus proving that they were his collaborators, not his victims. It was time for punishment, many argued, and for making demands also in the interests of security, so France would not disturb the peace again. The terms for France, in other words, would be much harsher this time.

As the treaty was hammered out, France would lose territory that had been awarded in the spring of 1814 (its borders would no longer be what they had been in 1792, but rather what they were in 1790). Alsace and Lorraine remained French, but not the Saar valley, and much of the Rhine was sliced off and given to its neighbors. France was effectively ringed by the enlarged states of the Kingdom of Netherlands, Prussia, Piedmont-Sardinia, Bavaria, and the neutral Switzerland. France was also forced to surrender key fortresses guarding the entrances to its kingdom, and pay 700 million francs' indemnity, along with the expenses of a large occupation army for five years. According to the treaty, 150,000 Allied soldiers were garrisoned in fortresses around the country, at an expense already estimated at some 1.75 million francs a day. This was to last until 1820, though it ended in 1818.

Napoleon's flight from Elba and the Hundred Days had cost France dearly, and many were upset at how harsh the terms had become. Gentz looked on with disillusionment, blaming the Prussians first, and then the English for not standing up to the Prussians more effectively. The peace treaty was, as Russia's Pozzo di Borgo summed it up, "a masterpiece of destruction."

The terms made no sense, Talleyrand also protested. "To demand concessions," he said, "there has to be a conquest. To have a conquest there has to be a state of war," and the Great Powers were *not* in a state of war with France. As the Vienna Congress had declared, the war was only against Napoleon, and he was gone. The king had been an ally. Why now were they treating France this way? The Allies were only making matters more difficult for the king.

"I refuse to sign," Talleyrand said of the document. Such an unjust treaty, he added, "would leave us neither France nor a king!" Talleyrand was so appalled with the way events were developing that on September 24 he offered his resignation. He had hoped that this gesture would alarm everyone to the folly of this treaty. But instead, much to his surprise, the king accepted his resignation.

Talleyrand had played a crucial role in returning Louis XVIII to his throne in 1814, advancing the king's interests at the Congress of Vienna and then helping restore him a second time that summer. Now his dismissal was painfully abrupt. There was no formal ceremony, not even a few words of thanks. The king's ingratitude, Talleyrand said, was "not disguised enough."

Metternich, who stayed on to complete the signing, was also feeling melancholy about this so-called triumphant return to Paris, a city he had known and loved years before as a young man serving as a diplomat. So much had changed since then. He stepped out of his room, onto the balcony, and stared at the Paris skyline. "This city and this sun," Metternich observed in a letter to his daughter, "will still greet one another when there are no longer any traditions of Napoleon and Blücher, and least of all of myself." So important it had all once seemed. All they were really doing, he concluded, was "dabbling in the mud, or in the shifting sand."

EPILOGUE

On October 17, after a seventy-one-day voyage, the frigate HMS *Northumberland* reached the small harbor of Jamestown, St. Helena. Unlike at Elba seventeen months before, there were no cheering crowds or celebrations waiting Napoleon's arrival. He was no longer emperor, even of this island, "a black wart rising out of the ocean." This time, Napoleon was a prisoner, and there would be no escape.

Just as she had never come to Elba, Marie Louise would not go to St. Helena—actually, she could not have come even if she had wanted to do so, as all Napoleon's family members had been prohibited from accompanying him in his exile. Marie Louise moved instead to the Duchy of Parma, which she had secured with the help of the Russian tsar. She was joined by her lover, Count Neipperg, and later they secretly married. At the time of Napoleon's death, in May 1821, Marie Louise revealed her marriage to her family, and it was quickly legalized. The couple eventually had three children, and when Neipperg died, she married a third time. Her son by Napoleon, on the other hand, never left Vienna, remaining a virtual prisoner of the palace, where he died of tuberculosis in 1832, only twenty-one years old.

Both the Duchess of Sagan and Princess Bagration would also later marry again. After breaking up with Prince Alfred and, not long afterward, with Lord Stewart, the Duchess of Sagan married a major in the Austrian army named Count Karl Schulenburg. She tried for a long time to regain her daughter, Adelaide-Gustava, though without success, and her spirits rapidly declined. "She was so sad, so disheartened, so troubled by everything," one of her foster daughters claimed of her later years. "She seemed to have attacks of sheer despair." The duchess moved back to Vienna, where she died in 1839. She never saw her daughter again.

Her rival, Princess Bagration, was fortunate to have escaped the clutches of her creditors. One member of the Sicilian embassy, the Duke of Serra Capriola, came to her aid, guaranteeing that her bills would be paid. The princess would later marry a rich Englishman, John Hobard Caradoc, and continue her now legendary extravagance. She moved into a lavish residence, Hôtel de Brunoy, in central Paris, where she would again host a fashionable salon. Metternich's granddaughter saw her in her sixties. "Who has not seen her has seen nothing remarkable," she said.

She has forgotten to grow old and thinks that she still lives in that magical time when Isabey painted her crowned with roses, enveloped in veils and surrounded with clouds. Only the veils and roses remain. The mass of curly blond ringlets has been reduced to four or five thin yellow hairs. Her skin is the color of a lemon; her body, yes—her body, one could see it—is a crackling skeleton.

She died in 1857, on a trip to Venice.

Both Princess Bagration and the Duchess of Sagan would always cling to their memories of their salons at the Vienna Congress, when, as each claimed, two great empires had fought over them. Both women, in fact, also ended up in literature: Princess Bagration in Balzac's *La Peau de Chagrin,* the Duchess of Sagan in Němcová's story "Babička" ("Granny"), about a princess who befriends a peasant. As for the Palm Palace, site of intrigue at the congress, it was torn down in the 1880s to make room for the Burgtheater.

The president of the Congress, Metternich, would remain Austria's foreign minister for another thirty years, enjoying many diplomatic successes and weathering many controversies in an unusually long career. Older histories called the period the "Age of Metternich." He was rewarded for his work at the Vienna Congress with a castle, Johannisberg, on the Rhine. Metternich's power only ended with the revolution of 1848, when the seventy-five-year-old dignitary was forced to escape a riotous mob. After a year in exile, Metternich returned to Vienna, though he felt increasingly like a "phantasm" or an "imaginary being." This was indeed different from the days when, as he vainly put it, he had "ruled Europe." Fortunately for him, he would not live to see the many Austrian defeats and losses of territory that occurred in the 1860s and afterward.

Later immortalized as the tsar of Tolstoy's *War and Peace,* Alexander would have the most ambiguous fate. According to the official account, he died in 1825 while vacationing in the Crimea. The cause of death was never determined, though it was speculated to be everything from malaria and typhus to syphilis and poisoning. Rumors would long circulate that the tsar had actually faked his death and retreated to live as a monk in the mountains. According to this view, still championed by some historians, Alexander lived until 1864 as the rather extroverted Siberian hermit named Feodor Kusmitch. Another theory, emerging later in the nineteenth century, suggested that he died in the Holy Land on a pilgrimage. At any rate, despite the probability that Alexander died of typhus, the persistence of the rumors testifies to the enduring image of this most puzzling tsar. As Pushkin put it, Alexander was "a Sphinx who carried his riddle with him to the tomb."

One of the last survivors of the Vienna Congress was Prince Talleyrand. After his retirement from the foreign ministry, he stayed in Paris, at his estate on rue Saint-Florentin, where he wrote, or rather dictated, his memoirs. Looking back, historians might well see Talleyrand as a representative of the peaceful and nonmilitaristic France, and his strategy of positioning his country as the leader of a coalition of smaller powers would be adopted repeatedly by later French leaders, from Napoleon III to Charles de Gaulle.

If Louis XVIII continued to shun Talleyrand for the rest of his reign, others appreciated his services at the congress. The king of Saxony had rewarded him liberally for his role in saving the kingdom, and the king of Naples gave Talleyrand another title, the Duke of Dino, for restoring the kingdom. Talleyrand, however, declined the latter, and asked that the title, with its properties, be given to his nephew and his niece Dorothée.

Dorothée—the new Duchess of Dino—returned to Paris in February 1816, after breaking up with Count Clam-Martinitz, and moved back in with Talleyrand. In December 1820, she gave birth to a daughter, Pauline, and many suspected that the seventy-four-year-old Talleyrand was the father. Very possibly having become lovers during the congress, Talleyrand and his niece-by-marriage certainly remained intimate over the years. They were still living together in 1830, when Talleyrand helped another king to the throne, Louis Philippe. He would spend his last working years as ambassador to England, the country with which he had worked hard to establish more friendly relations after some 150 years of hostility. Dorothée joined him in England as well. Talleyrand died in 1838, at age eighty-four, with Dorothée at his bedside.

"Vienna, Vienna," Dorothée wrote. "The whole of my destiny is contained in the name of this city." She looked back with fond memories of that period of her life, though she was always vague about the precise details. "If I ever did more than lick stamps," she said of her time at the French embassy, "I never had the bad taste to brag about it." She would host a fashionable salon for years until her death in September 1862 at age sixty-nine.

The most tragic fate, however, was Britain's Castlereagh. Oddly, the most rational figure at the congress ended up consumed by paranoia and madness. His internationalism was soon out of step with Britain, which was gripped by an isolationist impulse and eager to shun long-term foreign commitments. Castlereagh refused to make policy based on public opinion, and he became very unpopular. Convinced that the world was in a conspiracy against him, Castlereagh would never leave his house without a couple of loaded pistols. He felt stalked, and he collapsed into a severe "mental delirium." Friends feared for his safety, shocked by his increasingly strange and erratic behavior. Pistols, knives, and razors were carefully removed from his room. But the efforts to protect Castlereagh from himself were in vain. On the morning of August 12, 1822, Castlereagh slit his throat with a penknife he had smuggled into his study.

IN THE EARLY months of 1919, diplomats gathered in Paris to make peace after World War I. One of their main goals was to avoid the shocking decadence of the Congress of Vienna, or as Woodrow Wilson put it, "the odour of Vienna."

Indeed, the Vienna Congress has been subjected to many critiques, not least for the many quarrels and celebrations that distracted the peacemakers and dragged out the negotiations endlessly. At the same time, however, there was one unintended consequence: All the saber rattling at the congress meant that no Great Power felt secure enough to demobilize its army after the war ended; hence, each Great Power could field a large army quickly when Napoleon decided to leave Elba. The slow pace of the negotiations, moreover, meant that all the powers would be in one place at the same time to plan Napoleon's final defeat. Had the congress wrapped up its affairs earlier, the leaders would have dispersed across the Continent and the challenges of coordinating a campaign, let alone a war, would have been much more difficult.

Of course, this does not lessen the sting or the validity of the criticism that could be hurled at the leaders. Their secret diplomacy did sow much distrust and suspicion, and their sheer exclusiveness alienated many smaller states left outside as mere spectators. The principles for reconstructing Europe were applied selectively and inconsistently. Despite the talk of legitimacy, for example, old republics such as Genoa and Venice would not be re-created, and disappeared forever. Likewise, the Holy Roman Empire was not restored, nor were the Knights of Malta to their properties.

The congress delegates certainly looked after their own interests. As frequently pointed out, the interests of the people were often sacrificed to the interests of the dynasties. "The Big fish devour the small," Spain's Labrador had protested. Russia was one of the main winners, walking away with Finland and Bessarabia, both of which it had seized in the Napoleonic Wars. With the addition of the nominally independent Kingdom of Poland, Russia would now be in a position to influence not only central Asia and the Middle East, but also a large part of northern, southeastern, and central Europe. Russia had become more of a European power than at any time in its history.

The Austrians took advantage of their position as hosts of the congress to regain the Tyrol, as well as Dalmatia and Istria, which brought them deeper into the Balkans, where they would be embroiled until World War I and the end of the Habsburg monarchy. Austria also extended its rule over northern Italy, gaining Lombardy and Venetia, while Tuscany, Parma, and Modena were given to members of the Habsburg family. Even the restored Bourbon dynasty in Naples was dependent on policy making in Vienna. Austria's dominance would survive until Italy's unification later that century.

The Kingdom of Piedmont-Sardinia, for that matter, left the peace conference with Genoa, French Savoy, Nice on the Riviera, the suzerainty of Monaco, and other territorial gains that would significantly increase the kingdom's power, wealth, and status. The additions at Vienna would play no small role in helping Piedmont-Sardinia, only fifty years later, to drive the Austrians out and complete the unification of Italy.

Certainly, the congress left many disgruntled peoples around the continent. Just as its leaders ignored Spanish America and most of the non-European world, they also largely ignored national passions and oppressed nations. But this latter criticism, at least, is partly anachronistic, stemming from later nineteenth-century historians writing at a time when nationalism was a much more powerful force than in 1815. Nationalism at the congress was still primarily regarded as a potentially dangerous force, and the peacemakers in Vienna subordinated it, when drawing maps, to other concerns—whether they were legitimacy, balance of power, or simply, as Gentz said, "dividing the spoils."

The Great Powers are also often accused of arbitrarily intervening in the domestic politics of smaller sovereign states. There is considerable substance to this claim. In four major meetings of the "concert of Europe" (Aix-la-Chapelle 1818, Troppau 1820, Laibach 1821, Verona 1822), the Great Powers redefined the basis of their alliance from resisting any attempt to upset the peace settlement to asserting a more general right to intervene in the affairs of states to preserve law and order. In the process, the Great Powers became what Castlereagh called "a general European police."

In 1820, for example, when the leaders met at Troppau in what is now Opava, the peace seemed threatened in a number of ways. The year had witnessed a conspiracy to blow up London's House of Parliament, the assassination of the heir to the French throne, and revolutions in Spain, Portugal, Piedmont, and Naples. In response, the Great Powers declared that they would not recognize revolutionary or illegal changes to the peace settlement and pledged to use force, if necessary, to defeat any such challenge. In practice, this would mean propping up many unpopular, autocratic rulers. The Congress of Vienna did not, of course, cause or carry out these policies, but it had set the machinery in place that the Great Powers exploited.

It is clear that many loose ends remained when the last princes and plenipotentiaries left Vienna in June 1815. One community was left without a state for one hundred years. Tiny Moresnet, centered around a lucrative zinc mine four miles south of Aix-la-Chapelle, was claimed by both Prussia and the Netherlands, and no one had been able to broker a solution. A compromise was reached the following year, whereby the territory was split between the two kingdoms, with a third part, consisting of just over one square mile of land around the mine, declared "Neutral Moresnet," which would remain in existence until World War I (when it was seized by Germany, and in 1919 granted to Belgium). Other omissions were more serious. Castlereagh would not be the only person regretting that the congress had not established a more satisfactory arrangement between Russia and Turkey over the Balkans, the Black Sea, and the East Mediterranean.

Not long after the congress, many of its decisions had already collapsed. In 1830, only five years after the end of Tsar Alexander's reign, the Poles revolted, and the Russians squashed the uprising brutally. The Kingdom of Poland, or "Congress Poland," was fully incorporated into the Russian empire, and it would not gain its independence again until the end of World War I. Also that year, France once again erupted in revolution, removing a Bourbon king from the throne for a third time. In 1831, Belgium broke away from the newfangled Kingdom of the Netherlands, and a young man at the congress, the Prince of Saxe-Coburg-Saalfeld, became Belgium's first king. Greece, too, had become a nation-state, and a member of the tsar's Vienna delegation, Iōannēs Antōniou Kapodistrias, was named its first president.

Other decisions of the Vienna Congress would have a more lasting impact. With the exception of the Republic of Kraków, which was conquered by Russia in 1846, borders in eastern Europe remained largely as they were drawn in Vienna for one hundred years. In northern Europe too, the Scandinavian map was set, with a few exceptions, until the twentieth century. Sweden lost the Baltic island of Rügen and its piece of Pomerania in northern Germany, the last vestige of its former empire. "Swedish Pomerania" went to Prussia, which, in a triangular trade, then ceded the Principality of Lauenberg to Denmark, which in turn handed over Norway to Sweden, where it remained until its independence in 1905. Denmark, however, was not forced to surrender its former Norwegian colonies of Iceland, Greenland, and the Faroe Isles—or, for that matter, Holstein, which it had received from the Holy Roman Empire (and later lost, along with Schleswig, to Prussia in the 1860s). Iceland would gain its independence in 1944, Greenland home rule in 1979, and the autonomous Faroe Isles are still aligned with the Danish crown.

In central Europe, Germany was created as a loosely organized confederation of independent states that remained largely intact until 1866. Originally there were thirty-nine members, which gave the confederation more states, in fact, than the rest of Europe combined. The most powerful members were Austria and Prussia, followed by the former Napoleonic kingdoms of Bavaria, Württemberg, and Saxony. Hanover, which had been elevated to a kingdom in Vienna, also joined, along with several principalities; grand duchies; duchies; the four "free cities" of Lübeck, Frankfurt, Bremen, and Hamburg; and tiny Liechtenstein. Foreign states were designated as nonvoting participants on the basis of their holdings in the confederation: King of England (Hanover), King of Denmark (Holstein), and King of Netherlands (Luxembourg).

The German Confederation undoubtedly had many drawbacks, with no common army, currency, court system, or customs union. It did, however, have greater success internationally. As Henry Kissinger noted, the confederation came the closest to solving the fundamental "German problem" of modern European history; that is, it created a Germany that was neither too weak nor too strong, a Germany that would be neither a temptation for outside powers nor a threat to the security of its neighbors. After 1815, Germany would enjoy a period of relative peace, which was so desperately needed after the destruction of the Napoleonic Wars.

The biggest effect the congress had on central Europe was on Prussia. Even though members of its delegation were dissatisfied because they gained only a fraction of what they felt their country deserved, Prussia was granted valuable territory that laid the basis for its spectacular economic growth in the nineteenth century and its leadership role in the unification of Germany. As a result of the congress, Prussia now commanded the Rhine, in addition to the Oder, the Elbe, and the Vistula; it gained many historic cities like Cologne and Trier, not to mention the Saar, where Europe's richest coal and iron deposits would soon be discovered. "A better defense has been provided for Germany than has existed at any period of our history," Castlereagh said. As the late nineteenth and early twentieth centuries would show, Castlereagh and his fellow peacemakers in Vienna had succeeded on this point even more than they had realized.

Britain had also been successful at strengthening its own position.

Many strategic islands, scooped up in the Napoleonic Wars, were retained, including Malta, the Cape of Good Hope, Ceylon, Mauritius, and the Ionian isles. The British Royal Navy now had vital bases in the Mediterranean, south Atlantic, and Indian Ocean, securing the route to India, which would soon be the unrivaled "jewel in the crown" of the British empire. Castlereagh had also built a ring around France, with a stronger Netherlands and Piedmont-Sardinia, and a neutral Switzerland, and had helped create a more powerful Prussia to balance the Continent. Castlereagh's emphasis on establishing a "just equilibrium" was very much in line with British interests—that is, keeping the Continent locked in a rough balance of power while the Royal Navy was busy elsewhere, creating the largest empire the world had ever seen.

The Congress of Vienna would have many other indirect and unexpected results. In the early 1820s, as several countries in South America revolted from Spanish rule, the Great Powers refused to recognize the new revolutionary governments and threatened to send a military expedition across the Atlantic to restore Spanish authority. This was highly unlikely, though Tsar Alexander seemed eager to intervene, as did some influential factions in Bourbon France. On December 2, 1823, President James Monroe announced that he would view any attempt to interfere in South America as "the manifestation of an unfriendly disposition toward the United States." This announcement from the young republic was bold, to say the least—Metternich thought it was as revolutionary as the Declaration of Independence.

The United States could not, of course, have made such a challenge to the Great Powers, at this point, without the help of Britain (which had its own commercial designs on the region and wanted to block the ambitions of rival European powers). Still, the "Monroe Doctrine" was a major step in the long process whereby isolationist America would gradually take a more active role in international affairs. Over time, this doctrine would come to define American foreign policy as the union expanded westward to the Pacific and extended its influence in the western hemisphere.

Until Napoleon's escape, the Congress of Vienna might have been seen as a model for its generous treatment of the vanquished. France was not shunned by the international community or even severely punished for its repeated invasions. Such vindictiveness, Castlereagh had warned, would only lead to more bloodshed and warfare, an insight that was unfortunately forgotten in Paris in the autumn of 1815. The much harsher terms succeeded mainly in isolating France from international affairs, to the detriment of everyone. In 1818, when France paid off the bulk of its indemnity, Allied occupation troops were evacuated and France joined the Quadruple Alliance, which was later renamed the Quintuple Alliance.

But despite all the scandals, controversies, and mistakes of this swirling vanity fair, the Congress of Vienna did achieve some surprising successes. The delegates fixed borders, ranging from the establishment of the Grand Duchy of Luxembourg to the reorganization of Switzerland as a confederation of cantons with a written constitution and a formal guarantee of its "perpetual neutrality." The papacy regained its territories, the Legations and the Marches, though Avignon was lost forever. Significantly, too, Article LXXIII of the Final Act, concerning Belgium, contained the world's first complete and unqualified guarantee of religious toleration.

Among many other things, the Vienna Congress was the first international peace conference to discuss humanitarian issues. The leaders affirmed the civil rights of Jews, condemned the slave trade, combated literary piracy, and created many diplomatic procedures that have persisted until the present day. The four grades of representatives—ambassadors and papal legates, ministers plenipotentiary, ministers resident, and *chargés d'affaires*—have their origins with the congress, along with the tradition of determining precedence by rank and length of service, rather than by the prestige of the state. To reduce economic conflict, rivers that crossed national borders were placed under international control and the right of navigation was proclaimed. There was also a massive restoration of stolen art—one of the greatest in history.

Finally, and most important, the congress established peace—a genuine peace that lasted much longer than any of the delegates would have imagined. Indeed, despite the many tensions and hatreds that would long simmer in the age of nationalism and would result in numerous riots, rebellions, and civil wars, it is significant that no conflict would actually explode and drag all the Great Powers to war for a full one hundred years. The next major conflict was the Crimean War, followed by the

Italian and German unifications, but none of these flared up on the scale of the Napoleonic Wars or World War I.

But even if the Vienna Congress was not the only factor in this success, it certainly played an indispensable role. Its peacemakers had established a system of collective security, a development rightly heralded by Castlereagh as the "great machine of European safety." They had also created a forum where leaders came together for periodic meetings to work out their differences—the first time, in fact, that leaders of the world would meet, in a time of peace, for the purpose of maintaining peace. And when the regular meetings ended in 1822, occasional meetings continued, and consultation at a congress would remain the preferred means of conflict resolution for almost a century. The Congress of Vienna would, indeed, foster a spirit of cooperation that, in some ways, has still not been surpassed. No other peace conference in history can claim such success.

LIST OF ABBREVIATIONS OF WORKS FREQUENTLY CITED

BD   C. K. Webster, ed. *British Diplomacy, 1813–1815: Select Documents Dealing with the Reconstruction of Europe.* London, 1921.

CC   Robert Stewart, Viscount Castlereagh. *Correspondence, Despatches and Other Papers of Viscount Castlereagh, Second Marquess of Londonderry.* X–XI. London, 1853.

DCV   Commandant Maurice Henri Weil, ed. *Les Dessous du Congrès de Vienne d'après des documents originaux des archives du Ministère impérial et royal de l'intérieur à Vienne.* I–II. Paris, 1917.

GE   *Guide des étrangers à Vienne pendant le congrès contenant les noms des souverains présents dans cette capitale ainsi que ceux des ministres et chargés d'affaires des differentes cours auprès de celle de Vienne au mois d'octobre 1814.* Vienna, 1814.

GPWK   August Fournier, ed. *Die Geheimpolizei auf dem Wiener Kongress: Eine Auswahl aus ihren Papieren.* Vienna, 1913.

HHSA   *Haus-, Hof- und StaatsArchiv,* Vienna.

MSB   Maria Ullrichová, ed. *Clemens Metternich—Wilhelmine von Sagan: Ein Briefwechsel 1813–1815.* Graz-Köln, 1966.

NP   Prince Richard Metternich, ed. *Aus Metternich's nachgelassenen Papieren.* I-II, Vienna, 1880–1884.

SG   *Supplement du Guide des étrangers au quel on a joint La Liste Générale des cavaliers employés par sa Majesté l'Empereur et Roi en qualité du grand maitres, aides de camp generaux, adjudants, chambellans et pages auprès des augustes étrangers a Vienne 1814.* Vienna, 1814.

TLC   M.G. Pallain, ed. *The Correspondence of Prince Talleyrand and King Louis XVIII during the Congress of Vienna.* New York, 1973.

TLI   Gaston Palewski, ed. *Le Miroir de Talleyrand: Lettres inédites à la duchesse de Courlande pendant le Congrès de Vienne.* Paris, 1976.

WD   Colonel Gurwood, ed. *The Dispatches of Field Marshal the Duke of Wellington.* VIII–IX, London, 1844–1847.

WSD   *Supplementary Despatches and Memoranda of Field Marshal Arthur, Duke of Wellington.* IX, X, and XI. London, 1858–1872.

WZ   *Wiener Zeitung.*

NOTES AND SOURCES

For historians and enthusiasts alike, there is a wonderful collection of primary sources about the Congress of Vienna. First, there are the protocols, memoranda, treaties, minutes of meetings, and other documents of the conference itself, published by E. J. B. Chodzko, the Comte d'Angeberg, *Le Congrès de Vienne et les traités de 1815*, I–IV (1864), as well as in older editions such as Johann Ludwig Klüber's *Acten des Wiener Congresses in den Jahren 1814 und 1815*, I–IX (1815–1835). The notes and drafts for many of these records are housed at Vienna's Haus-, Hof- und Staatsarchiv St.K. Kongressakten Kart.1-16.

Many leading diplomats and foreign ministers also wrote memoirs, reminiscences, or other reflections on their experience at Vienna, including Metternich's *Aus Metternich's nachgelassenen Papieren*, edited by his son, Prince Richard Metternich (1880–1884), especially vols. I–II, and Talleyrand's *Mémories Complets et Authentiques de Charles-Maurice de Talleyrand, 1754–1815*, vols. II and III. Both memoirs, originally published posthumously in the late nineteenth century, have been heavily edited for posterity. These valuable though one-sided accounts can be supplemented by many other sources. Talleyrand's letters to King Louis XVIII during the Vienna Congress, *Correspondance inédite du Prince de Talleyrand et du roi Louis XVIII pendant le Congrès de Vienne*, ed. G. Pallain (1881), is indispensable, as is his correspondence with the acting foreign ministry in Paris, Arnail-François de Jaucourt, *Correspondance du Comte du Jaucourt avec le Prince de Talleyrand pendant le Congrès de Vienne* (1905), which includes some letters that do not appear in the official correspondence of the French embassy in Vienna with the Foreign Ministry in Paris, published in his memoirs.

Essential, too, are Talleyrand's letters to the Duchess of Courland, published in *Talleyrand Intime, d'après sa correspondance inédite avec la duchesse de Courlande* (1891), and Gaston Palewski, ed., *Le Miroir de Talleyrand: Lettres inédites à la duchesse de Courlande pendant le Congrès de Vienne* (1976). One helpful source that has not been fully used is an early history of the congress, penned actually by one of Talleyrand's friends, Abbé de Pradt, and published already in 1815: *Congrès de Vienne*, I–II. Another interesting early chronicle that deserves more attention is from Gaëtan de Raxis de Flassan, a historian who attended the Vienna Congress with the hope of writing its history, which he did in his *Histoire du Congrès de Vienne* (1829). See also the second volume of *Mein Antheil an der Politik*, which was written by a delegate who represented Holland and Nassau, Hans Christoph Gagern, *Nach Napoleons Fall: Der Congress zu Wien* (1826).

Some 616 new letters from Metternich to the Duchess of Sagan between 1812 and 1818 have been made available, thanks to the Czech scholar Maria Ullrichová's discovery in 1949, and her publication of the correspondence during the end of the war and the peace conference, *Clemens Metternich—Wilhelmine von Sagan: Ein Briefwechsel, 1813–1815* (1966). Some of Metternich's later correspondence also makes occasional reference to the people or events of our period—for example, with Dorothea de Lieven: *The Private Letters of Princess Lieven to Prince Metternich, 1820–1826*. Among the many other sources, there is another one, almost never used in writing the history of the congress: a memoir of the Vienna Congress from one of Metternich's assistants, Baron Binder, unpublished, and housed in Vienna's Haus-, Hof- und Staats Archiv St.K. Kongressakten Kart. 16.

Another one of Metternich's assistants, Friedrich von Gentz, who had been named secretary of the Vienna Congress, had allegedly written a history of the conference, but seeing how critical the manuscript had become, he later destroyed it. This was unfortunate, because Gentz was an exceptional writer, with a sharp critical mind honed by his studies under Immanuel Kant, and he had an intimate knowledge of many aspects of the congress. Yet some of his many insights, however, can be found in his extensive correspondence. A good place to begin is *Oesterreichs Theilnahme an den Befreiungskriegen: Ein Beitrag zur Geschichte der Jahre 1813 bis 1815*, edited by Klinkowström (1887). His letters to Bucharest, for example, were published by the Comte Prokesch-Osten, *Dépêches inédites du chevalier de Gentz aux hospodars de Valachie pour servir a l'histoire la politique européene*, I (1876), *Briefe von Friedrich von Gentz an Pilat*, I–II, by Karl Mendelssohn-Bartholdy (1868), and a few other letters from this time can be found in the third volume of *Briefe von und an Friedrich von Gentz*, edited by Friedrich Carl Wittichen and Ernst Salzer (1913), and some also with his friend Adam Müller, who also came to Vienna in April 1815, in the first volume of *Adam Müllers Lebenszeugnisse*, ed. Jakob Baxa (1966). There is also a surviving fragmentary memoir of the Vienna Congress, *Denkschrift von Friedrich von Gentz*, written in February 1815, *NP* II 473ff, as well as Gentz's personal diary, *Tagebücher*, I–IV, published by Varnhagen's von Ense (1873).

One deservedly well-known source for the congress is the correspondence of Britain's plenipotentiary, Robert Stewart, Viscount Castlereagh, *Correspondence, Despatches and other Papers of Viscount Castlereagh, Second Marquess of Londonderry* (1853), X and XI; the Duke of Wellington's *The Dispatches of Field Marshal the Duke of Wellington, during His Various Campaigns* VII–VIII (1844–1847), and his *Supplementary Dispatches*, and *Memoranda of Field Marshal Arthur, Duke of Wellington* (1858–1872), variously numbered, though, most commonly, IX and X are also valuable. Among the many other publications of British foreign policy documents from this period, C. K. Webster has an excellent selection in *British Diplomacy, 1813–1815: Select Documents Dealing with the*

Reconstruction of Europe (1921). Occasional help has come from the many published accounts of people who knew Castlereagh and Wellington, which swelled into a veritable cottage industry in the nineteenth century, including Countess Granville, Countess Bronow, Lady Shelley, Captain R. H. Gronow, John Cam Hobhouse, Stanhope, Farrington, John Wilson Croker, and Thomas Creevey, to name a few, as well as generally interested observers such as Countess Potocka, Countess Rosalie Rzewuska, Princess Radziwill, and Marquise de La Tour du Pin, wife of a French delegate. Also interesting are Landamman Monod's *Mémoires du Landamman Monod pour servir a l'histoire de la Suisse en 1815* (1975), the Bavarian Graf Montgelas's *Denkwürdigkeiten des Bayerischen Staatsministers Maximilian Grafen Von Montgelas (1799–1817)* (1887), and Sweden's Elisabeth Charlottes Hedvig, particularly the ninth volume of her *Dagbok.*

Among the writings of many other leading delegates, Chancellor Karl von Hardenberg's diary, *Tagebücher und Autobiographische Aufzeichnungen*, was published in a good scholarly edition by Thomas Stamm-Kuhlmann in 2000. Prussian ambassador Wilhelm von Humboldt's letters to his wife, *Wilhelm und Caroline von Humboldt in ihren Briefen*, IV–V, ed. Anna von Sydow (1910), with many of his protocols and memoranda published in Humboldt's *Gesammelte Schriften*, XI–XII, and other places such as Angeberg, and appendices 4, 5 and 6 of Webster's *The Congress of Vienna 1814–1815* (1919). Tsar Alexander I's letters to the Grand Duchess Catherine, mostly shorter notes from the peace conference, printed in *Scenes of Russian Court Life: Being the Correspondence of Alexander I with his Sister Catherine* (undated). Adam Czartoryski's *The Memoirs of Prince Adam Czartoryski and his Correspondence with Alexander I*, I–II, ed. Adam Gielgud (1888, 1968). See also his collection of letters, *Alexandre 1er et le Prince Czartoryski: correspondance particulière et conversations 1801–1823* (1865). Baron vom Stein fragementary autobiography, *Die Autobiographie des Freiherrn vom Stein*, ed. Kurt von Raumer (1960), unfortunately ends without much discussion on the congress, but his diary published in the fifth volume of Erich Botzenhart and Walter Hubatsch's edition of *Briefe und amtliche Schriften* (1957–1974) is revealing. Russia's Count Nesselrode's *Autobiographie*, which was published posthumously by his grandson, can be found in vol. II of *Lettres et papiers du chancelier comte de Nesselrode, 1760–1850*, and some letters from the congress in vol. V. See also the correspondence between Count Pozzo di Borgo and Count Nesselrode, published by Pozzo di Borgo's grandson, *Correspondance Diplomatique du Comte Pozzo di Borgo, ambassadeur de Russie en France et du Comte du Nesselrode depuis la restauration des Bourbons jusqu'au Congrès d' Aix-la-Chapelle, 1814–1818* (1890), and the second volume of the *Correspondance de Frédéric-César La Harpe et Alexander 1er*, published by Jean Charles Biaudeet and Françoise Nicod (1978–1979), and occasionally some comments in works such as Count Ouvaroff's *Esquisses politiques et littéraires* (1848).

In addition to the memoirs, correspondence, and writings of leading participants or delegates of the Big Four, I have used the works of many lesser-known figures or leaders of less-prominent delegations that have often been overshadowed by their more famous counterparts, both at the congress and later in historical accounts of it. In addition to the representative of Nassau and Holland cited above, there is also Spain's Don Pedro Labrador, *Mélanges sur la vie privée et publique du marquis de Labrador* (1849), Sweden's Löwenhielm's pithy but interesting document *Berättelse om händelserna, 1814–1815,* Piedmont's Marchese di San Marzano's diary, *Diario,* which has been published in Ilario Rinieri, ed., *Corrispondenza inedita dei Cardinali Consalvi e Pacca nel tempo del Congresso di Vienna* (1903). Geneva's Pictet de Rochemont's correspondence with selections from his diary, published by Edmond Pictet in *Biographie, travaux et correspondance diplomatique* (1892), and more fully in Cramer, ed., *Correspondance diplomatique de Charles Pictet de Rochemont et François d'Yvernois 1814–1816* (1914). The correspondence of the pope's delegate and secretary of state, Cardinal Consalvi, with Cardinal Bartolomeo Pacca back at the Vatican, cited above, in addition to a few documents printed in the edition of Consalvi's *Mémoires,* I–II (1864). Hanover's Count Münster dispatches published by his son, Count George Herbert Münster, in *Political Sketches of the State of Europe, 1814–1867: Containing Count Ernst Münster's Despatches to the Prince Regent from the Congress of Vienna* (1868), and the Duke of Weimar (soon to be Grand Duke) has correspondence in the third volume of *Politischer Briefwechsel des Herzogs und Grossherzogs Carl August von Weimar: Von der Rheinbundzeit bis zum Ende der Regierung, 1808–1828,* ed. Willy Andreas and Hans Tümmler (1973); Denmark's Niels Rosenkrantz *Journal du Congrès de Vienne, 1814–1815* (1953), published by Georg Nørregaard, who has also written a helpful study of Denmark's work at the congress, *Danmark og Wienerkongressen, 1814–1815* (1954).

There are also many fascinating eyewitness accounts of the social life at the congress that, like the minor delegations, have been surprisingly underused. A good place to start are the collections by Hilde Spiel, *Der Wiener Kongress in Augenzeugeberichten* (1965), and Frederick Freksa's *Der Wiener Kongress: Nach Aufzeichnungen von Teilnehmern und Mittarbeitern* (1914), the first translated by Richard H. Weber in 1968, and the second by Harry Hansen in 1919. These are valuable, though the works sampled have now been published in full. The most famous account of the social scene is Comte Auguste de La Garde-Chambonas's *Souvenirs du congrès de Vienne,* which has been translated into English as *Anecdotal Recollections of the Congress of Vienna* (1902), though this omits a few passages that the editor found unsuitable. La Garde-Chambonas, of course, makes many mistakes in his account, but that does not mean that everything in the memoir is worthless, and he can be used with caution, particularly when his observations are supported by other reliable sources. The German publisher Carl Bertuch has a valuable diary, *Tagebuch vom Wiener Kongress,* edited by Hermann Freiherrn von Egloffstein (1916). Friedrich Anton von Schönholz's *Traditionen zur Charakteristik Österreichs, seines Staats- und Volkslebens unter Franz I* (1914) are acerbic but absorbing, as are the accounts of socialites such as Countess Lulu Thürheim's *Mein Leben: Erinnerungen aus Österreichs Grosser Welt 1788–1819,* II (1913) and Countess Bernstorff's *Ein Bild aus der Zeit von 1789 bis 1835: Aus ihren Aufzeichnungen,* I (1896), whose reflections were published by her granddaughter. The antiquarian bookseller Franz Gräffer's anecdotal *Kleine Wiener Memoiren und Wiener Dosenstucke,* I–II, published in 1845 and again by Gustav Gugitz (1918), contains many reflections about the city and its personalities. The English physician Dr. Richard Bright visited Vienna during the congress, from November to March, and published his impressions from his stay, *Travels from Vienna through Lower Hungary with Some Remarks on the State of Vienna During the Congress in the year 1814* (1818). Some letters and documents from Sir Sidney Smith's stay are in the second volume of *The Memoirs of Admiral Sir Sidney Smith* (1839), written by Edward Howard with Smith's sanction, and John Barrow's ed. *The Life and Correspondence of Admiral Sir William Sidney Smith* (1848), II. See also the soldier Karl von Nostitz's *Leben und Briefwechsel: Auch ein Lebensbild aus den Befreiungskriegen* (1848), and the Russian "army historiographer" Alexander Ivanovich Mikhailovsky-Danilevsky, whose diary was recently found and selections published by Alexander Sapojnikov in Ole Villumsen Krog, ed., *Danmark og Den Dansende Wienerkongres: Spillet om Danmark* (2002). Among many other soldiers, there are some letters in Field Marshal Prince Schwarzenberg's correspondence with his wife, published by Johann Friedrich Novák, *Briefe des Feldmarschalls Fürsten Schwarzenberg an seine Frau, 1799–1816* (1913), and the reflections of the Bonapartist aide-de-camp Anatole Montesquiou, published as part of his *Souvenirs sur la révolution, l'empire, la restauration et le règne de Louis-Philippe* (1961). Of the many other sources on the festive side, noted below, see Archduke Johann's *Aus dem Tagebuche Erzherzog Johanns von Oesterreich 1810–1815* (1891), Caroline Pichler's *Denkwürdigkeiten aus meinem Leben* (1914), Anna Potocka's memoir, and the intriguing *Mémoires* of Tsarina Elizabeth's lady-in-waiting Roxanne Stourdza, who was later known as the Countess Edling (1888).

Henrich Graf zu Stolberg-Wernigerode's *Tagebuch über meinen Aufenthalt in Wien zur Zeit des Congresses* (2004) is also essential, as is the diary of a government official, Matthias Franz Perth's *Wiener Kongresstagebuch, 1814–1815* (1981). Karl August Varnhagen von Ense, who had planned to write a history of the congress, has many valuable comments in his *Denkwürdigkeiten des Eignen Lebens,* II (1987), as well as Rahel Varnhagen's *Briefwechsel,* Volumes 1–4, ed. Friedhelm Kemp (1979), and most recently in Karl August's *Varnhagen von Ense und Cotta: Briefwechsel, 1810–1818,* I–II, ed. Konrad Feilchenfeldt, Bernhard Fischer, and Dietmar Pravida (2006). The Swiss banker who represented Geneva, Jean-Gabriel Eynard, wrote a two-volume journal of his stay in Vienna during the congress, *Au Congrès de Vienne: journal de Jean-Gabriel Eynard* I–II (1914–1924), and his wife, Anna Eynard-Lullin, a diary, many passages of which can be found in Alville's *Anna Eynard-Lullin et l'époque des congrès et des révolutions* (1955). Baronne du Montet, a French émigré living in Vienna who attended many of the congress celebrations, which she described in *Souvenirs, 1785–1866* (1904), and Baron Méneval, named secretary to Marie Louise by Napoleon in 1812, was present with the former empress at Schönbrunn, leaving a valuable memoir of the time. Another enjoyable source is from the delegate of Hesse, the philologist Jacob Grimm. As usual, Grimm stayed in close touch with his brother Wilhelm, and their correspondence reveals more than his *Selbstbiographie: Briefwechsel zwischen Jacob und Wilhelm Grimm aus der Jugendzeit* (1963).

The semiofficial court newspaper *Wiener Zeitung* was also valuable for understanding the setting of the Congress of Vienna, as was the rare *Guide des étrangers à Vienne pendant le Congrès contenant les noms des souverains présents dans cette capitale ainsi que ceux des ministres et chargés d' affaires des differentes cours auprès de celle de Vienne au mois d' octobre 1814* (1814), and its supplement, *Supplement du Guide des étrangers au quel on a joint La Liste Générale des cavaliers employés par sa Majesté l'Empereur et Roi en qualité du grand maitres, aides de camp generaux, adjudants, chambellans et pages auprès des augustes étrangers a Vienne 1814* (1814).

One of the most pleasant discoveries was the richness of the records of the Vienna police and censorship office, led by Baron Franz von Hager. The existence of this collection is well-known among scholars, but for a variety of reasons, they have been underused as a historical source. All the documents of this police ministry were, of course, destroyed in the early twentieth century, but fortunately, there were two historians, almost one hundred years ago, who combed the archives and managed to publish their research before their destruction: August Fournier, ed., *Die Geheimpolizei auf dem Wiener Kongress: Eine Auswahl aus ihren Papieren* (1913), and Commandat Maurice Henri Weil, ed., *Les Dessous du Congrès de Vienne d'après des documents originaux des archives du ministère impérial et royal de l'intérieur à Vienne, I–II* (1917).

Of course much gossip, rumor, innuendo, and sometimes outrageous misinterpretations can be found in these some two thousand pages of police dossiers, but they are a gold mine for understanding the daily life of the Vienna Congress. After all, it is not only confirmed facts that influence the actions of statesmen and decision makers. To overlook the rumors, gossip, and intrigue that circulated because they might clash with what we now know, or think we know, is in many ways to underestimate the uncertainties of the time and risk simplifying the past. Besides that, the police reports are not as bad as often claimed (as an examination of both their reputation and their actual contents in these collections will show, on the whole, how unfairly they have been dismissed). Sure, the quality varies from time to time, and some agents are clearly better than others. But many of the agents were keen observers who immersed themselves in the swirl of the congress, took advantage of an extensive network of social contacts, and often show many insights into the conference. Especially valuable in these dossiers, too, are the hundreds of confidential letters that the police agents intercepted from the British, French, Prussian, Russian, and indeed just about every major delegation in town, and several of the minor ones as well.

It was a pleasure, too, to read the historians and diplomats who have previously studied this peace conference. Enno E. Kraehe's *Metternich's German Policy,*

I–II (1963–1983), is outstanding, and Charles Webster's *The Foreign Policy of Castlereagh, 1812–1815: Britain and the Reconstruction of Europe* (1931) is like wise a model of scholarship. Henry Kissinger's *A World Restored* (1957), deriving from his PhD dissertation, is an insightful analysis that covers the ten-year period with the conference at its middle. Another valuable dissertation is Hannah Alice Straus's *The Attitude of the Congress of Vienna Toward Nationalism in Germany, Italy and Poland* (1949). The congress has attracted many statesmen to its study, including in France, for example, Gaston Palewski, who edited Talleyrand's letters to the Duchess of Courland, Dominque de Villepin's *Les Cent Jours* (2001), and diplomats like Jacques-Alain de Sédouy, *Le Congrès de Vienne: L'Europe contre la France, 1812–1815* (2003).

Karl Griewank's *Der Wiener Kongress und Die Neuordnung Europas, 1814–15* was long viewed as perhaps the best researched history of the conference itself, particularly the 1954 edition, which was retitled *Der Wiener Kongress und die europäische Restauration*, and happily discards the early 1940s agenda that accompanied the first edition (1942). Gregor Dallas's *The Final Act: The Roads to Waterloo* (1997) is a well-written scholarly work, with many valuable insights, and contributions to the understanding of the period. Susan Mary Alsop's *The Congress Dances* (1984) is another good read and one of the best on the social life, though at just over two hundred pages, some one hundred of which are in Vienna, it is brief. Webster's *The Congress of Vienna 1814–1815* (1919) is likewise helpful, though also short and written with an emphasis on helping guide the British delegation at Versailles.

Adam Zamoyski's *The Rites of Peace: The Fall of Napoleon and the Congress of Vienna* (2007) is a good, recent study that surveys European diplomacy in the decade between December 1812 and the Congress of Verona in the autumn of 1822. Edward Vose Gulick's *Europe's Classical Balance of Power: A Case History of the Theory and Practice of One of the Great Concepts of European Statecraft* (1955) also analyzes coalition diplomacy, arguing that the balance of power served as the most important strategy in guiding the statesmen—a well-researched thesis, though by no means the only way to interpret the proceedings. Freiherr von Bourgoing's *Vom Wiener Kongress: Zeit- und Sittenbilder* (1943) has more on the social events than most histories, and remains a valuable contribution. The most widely known book on the congress is Harold Nicolson's *The Congress of Vienna: A Study in Allied Unity, 1812–1822* (1946), commissioned to coincide with the end of World War II. Despite its many factual errors and its reliance on only a fraction of the primary sources, this book has many good insights from an erudite former diplomat.

Vienna, 1814 also draws on the work of many other scholars who have written biographies of the statesmen at this conference, studied its diplomacy, or examined international relations or some aspects of early nineteenth-century Europe, as will be clear from the notes below. Paul Schroeder's eight-hundred-page study of the eighty-five-year period from 1763 to 1848, *The Transformation of European*

Politics, is magisterial. For the lives of some of the women at this conference, too often ignored in accounts of the congress, Dorothy Guis McGuigan has written an excellent study of the Duchess of Sagan, and Philip Zeigler, Françoise de Bernardy, and Micheline Dupuy have written biographies of her younger sister, Dorothée. Rosalynd Pflaum has an account of that remarkable family, *By Influence and Desire: The True Story of Three Extraordinary Women—The Grand Duchess of Courland and Her Daughters* (1984). These have also aided greatly, as have museums all over Vienna that have helped me reimagine the setting for this pageant. Catalogs of previous museum exhibits on the congress have also been valuable in this regard, particularly the spring 2002 exhibit at Christiansborg Palace in Copenhagen, Denmark, edited by Ole Villumsen Krog (cited above) and enriched with many excellent scholarly articles. This is also true of the 150th anniversary exhibit at the Hofburg, *Der Wiener Kongress Ausstellung, 1 Juni bis 15 Oktober 1965* (1966), and the 1896 exhibit at the Hofburg, *Der Wiener Congress: Culturgeschichte die Bildenden Künste und das Kunstgewerbe Theater—Musik in der Zeit von 1800 bis 1825,* ed. Eduard Leisching (1898). The British historian Alan Palmer has the distinction of writing the biographies of Prince Metternich, Tsar Alexander I, Empress Marie Louise, Bernadotte, as well as histories of the Habsburg dynasty and of Russia during the time of the Napoleonic invasion.

Historians sometimes use the term *Congress of Vienna* to refer to a number of negotiations that took place between 1812 and 1822. The Congress of Vienna, however, was much more specific than that. It had no existence before May 30, 1814, when Article XXXII of the Treaty of Paris stipulated that a "general congress" should be held in Vienna. Its opening date was scheduled for July 1814, though this would be postponed again and again—in fact, the congress never really met, at least not in the way most people had expected. On June 9, 1815, the European Treaty, or "Final Act," was signed, and nine days later Napoleon was defeated at Waterloo. By then, the Congress of Vienna was well on its way to becoming a legend.

Perhaps the most widely recognized feature of the Congress of Vienna is its extravagant social life, and this, ironically, is one of the least understood. This is unfortunate, because it is difficult to understand the peace conference without setting it in the context of the ballrooms, bedrooms, and palaces in which much diplomacy, and many of the intrigues, took place. The Congress of Vienna was a spectacular nine-month drama that unfolded when the world came to town.

PREFACE

The HMS *Undaunted* making entrance into harbor and the cheering crowds come from the memoir of the ship's captain, Thomas Ussher, "Napoleon's Deportation to Elba" published in *Napoleon's Last Voyages, Being the Diaries of Admiral Sir Thomas Ussher, R.N., K.C.B. (on board the "Undaunted") and John R. Glover, Secretary to Rear Admiral Kockburn (on board the "Northumberland"),* (1895), 50–51, and Neil Campbell, *Napoleon at Fontainebleau and Elba; Being a Journal of Occurrences in 1814–1815* (1869), 216; the number of rowers are in Gregor Dallas, *The Final Act: The Roads to Waterloo* (1997), 263. The excitement is also in Norman Mackenzie, *The Escape from Elba: The Fall and Flight of Napoleon, 1814–1815* (1982), 74, and Robert Christophe, *Napoleon on Elba*, trans. Len Ortzen (1964), 36. Napoleon on deck and his well-known uniform are from Campbell (1869), 215. The emperor's rapid pacing and snuff habits were described by Campbell (1869), 157, as well as by three of Napoleon's secretaries, Bourrienne, Méneval, and Fain. Napoleon's suicide attempt, once controversial, is now widely accepted by scholars and can be found in many sources, including General Armand Augustin Louis Caulaincourt's *Mémoires* (1933), III, 357–377; Baron Claude-François de Méneval's *Memoirs Illustrating the History of Napoleon I from 1802 to 1815*, edited by Baron Napoleon Joseph Méneval (1894), III, 255–257; and Baron Agathon Jean François Fain's *Souvenirs de la campagne de France (Manuscrit de 1814)* (1914), 240ff.

One list of representatives, though incomplete, can be found in Angeberg, *Le Congrès de Vienne et les traités de 1815* (1864), I, 255–256, and II, 257–264. The sense of a new era with high expectations and hope for avoiding a flawed peace, is in Abbé de Pradt, *Du Congrès de Vienne* (1815) I, iv–vi, 6ff, 11. Metternich's prediction of the congress lasting three weeks is from his letter to Duchess of Sagan, April 23, 1814, *MSB*, 252, and the prediction of six weeks from his letter, September 19, 1814, 264. Castlereagh also thought the congress would be finished by the autumn, with the embassy home for Christmas, Castlereagh to Liverpool, September 3, 1814, *BD* 191, and the tsar thought six weeks at most, Report to Hager, September 18, 1814, no. 106, and Agent Schmidt, October 1, 1814, *DCV*, I, No. 222. Many others shared these assumptions; for example, Steinlein to King of Bavaria, August 6, 1814, *DCV*, I, no. 58, and Baron Braun, September 14, 1814, *DCV*, I, no. 98. The phrase "sparkling chaos" comes from Henri Troyat's *Alexander of Russia: Napoleon's Conqueror*, trans. Joan Pinkham (1982), 215. That making peace was proving more difficult than defeating Napoleon, Princess Bagration had told Metternich himself, Agent Nota [Carpani] to Hager, February 5, 1815, *DCV*, II, no.1513.

Metternich's account of how the news of Napoleon's flight reached Vienna and his actions immediately afterward come from his *NP* I, 209–210 and 328. Writing many years after the event, Metternich mistakenly traced the dispatch back to Genoa, and this has long been repeated in Metternich biographies as well as histories of the congress. The correct sender was Livorno, as reported at the time in several sources, from the semiofficial *Wiener Zeitung* to the correspondence of the secretary of the Vienna Congress, Friedrich von Gentz, in a dispatch written that day to Karadja, March 7, 1815, in the first volume of *Dépêches inédites du chevalier de Gentz aux hospodars de Valachie pour servir a l'histoire la politique européene (1813–1828)*, ed. Le Comte Prokesch-Osten fils (1876), 144. This is also confirmed by the officer named in the dispatch, Sir Neil Campbell, whose journal records that he first landed at Tuscany, as he believed that Napoleon was on the way to Naples.

Dressed "in a flash" comes from *NP* I, 210, and "Happy, unfettered" in Comte Auguste de La Garde-Chambonas, *Anecdotal Recollections of the Congress of Vienna* (1902), 35. The phrase "the most feared warlord" from Alastair Horne, *The Age of Napoleon* (2004), xxx. Words on Talleyrand's charm are in the *Memoirs of Madame de la Tour du Pin* (1971), trans. Felice Harcourt, 246. Napoleon's words "shit in silk stockings" ("*Merde dans un bas de soie!*") come from a tirade against Talleyrand in late January 1809, Georges Lacour-Gayet, *Talleyrand, 1754–1838* (1928–1934), II, 272. Prussia as "too strong to be a minor power and not strong enough to be in the front rank" comes from Count Molé, *The Life and Memoirs of Count Molé (1781–1855)* (1924) I, 322–323. One impression of the king of Prussia's appearance at the congress, "looking like a thundercloud," is in Karl von Nostitz's diary entry, January 23, 1815, *Leben und Briefwechsel: Auch ein Lebensbild aus den Befreiungskriegen* (1848), 155. The Prussian delegation was second largest in town, after the Russians, *GE*, 16–21.

Napoleon on Alexander, expressed in a letter to Josephine in 1808, can be found in many sources, for example, J. Christopher Herold, ed., *The Mind of Napoleon* (1955), 173, Alan Schom, *Napoleon Bonaparte* (1997), 477, and Steven Englund, *Napoleon: A Political Life* (2004), 293. "A Kingdom was cut into bits" is in Comte Auguste de La Garde-Chambonas, *Anecdotal Recollections of the Congress of Vienna* (1902), 1–2. Kissinger's words on the congress are in *Diplomacy* (1994), 79, and more fully elaborated in his *A World Restored: Metternich, Castlereagh and the Problems of Peace, 1812–1822* (1957). Albert Sorel called the result also the most fruitful period of peace the continent had known, *L'Europe et La Révolution Française*, VIII, 502.

CHAPTER 1. BREAD AND CIRCUSES

Prince de Ligne's words at the opening of the chapter come from Comte Auguste de La Garde-Chambonas, *Anecdotal Recollections of the Congress of Vienna* (1902), 14. Castlereagh describes the poor roadways, undated letter to his wife, probably January 1814, printed in C. K. Webster's *The Foreign Policy of Castlereagh, 1812–1815: Britain and the Reconstruction of Europe* (1931), 503–504. Talleyrand's troubles on the road, and his near accident, Talleyrand to the Duchess of Courlande, September 18, 1814, in *TLI* 31. Paul Johnson succinctly summarizes the difficulties of travel at this time in *The Birth of the Modern: World Society, 1815–1830* (1991), 169ff. Reference to "murderer's den" is found in Gregor Dallas, *The Final Act: The Roads to Waterloo* (1997), 136. This was, of course, in part, due to the many veterans the war turned out, without pension and with little chance of pay as the economy deteriorated in the immediate aftermath of the war. The torched towns and the devastation is also in Henrich Graf zu Stolberg-Wernigerode, September 11–15, 1814, *Tagebuch über meinen Aufenthalt in Wien zur Zeit des Congresses* (2004), 6ff. The words "fearless foolish or suicidal" are in Lesley Adkins and Roy Adkins, *The Keys of Egypt: The Obsession to Decipher Egyptian Hieroglyphics* (2000), 7. The figure of one hundred thousand is a well-known estimate of the number of people arriving during the congress, and although still unverified, it is not unreasonable. Announcing the congress, Webster (1931), 327; Enno E. Kraehe, *Metternich's German Policy* (1963–1983), II, 125. The order for the *Wiener Hofzeitung* and the early planning can be found at HHSA St.K. Kongressakten Kart. 16.

The French and Napoleonic Wars as the first "total war," T. C. W. Blanning, *The French Revolutionary Wars, 1787–1802* (1996), 101, and the August 1793 law, often called the *levée en masse*, along with the translation, 100–101, as well as Simon Schama, *Citizens: A Chronicle of the French Revolution* (1989), 762. The number of deaths is in Paul W. Schroeder, *The Transformation of European Politics 1763–1848* (1994), 580. Carl von Clausewitz has a fascinating discussion of this warfare, of course, in *On War*, trans. and with notes by Bernard Brodie, in Michael Howard and Peter Paret's *Clausewitz: On War* (1976), and more on the exhaustion that followed in *Correspondance Diplomatique du comte Pozzo di Borgo, ambassadeur de Russie en France et du comte du Nesselrode depuis la restauration des Bourbons jusqu'au Congrès d' Aix-la-Chapelle, 1814–1818*, by Comte Charles Pozzo di Borgo (1890)—for example, Pozzo di Borgo to Nesselrode, September 14–26, 1814, 73.

The fact that almost nothing was settled, besides the drawing of French borders, comes from C. K. Webster, *The Foreign Policy of Castlereagh, 1812–1815: Britain and the Reconstruction of Europe* (1931), 327–328, and this is seen by looking at the treaty itself, printed *Le Congrès de Vienne et les traités de 1815* (1864), I, 161–170, with secret articles, 171ff. On Poland as the greatest challenge at the beginning, see Bernstorff intercepted letter, July 13, 1814, *DCV*, I, no. 28, and Report to Baron Hager, September 27, 1814, I, no. 171, and Bernstorff to Rosencrantz, July 7, 1814, August Fournier, ed., *GPWK* 94–95, Gentz to Karadja, *Dépêches inédites*, June 21, 1814, 79–82, Bernstorff's letter to Rosencrantz, July 20, 1814, *GPWK*, 100–101, and agent, September 28, 1814, *GPWK*, 133–134.

Napoleon's words on Poland come from Las Casas, *Mémorial de Saint-Hélène* (1823; repr. 1961), II, 458ff, and his words to the Poles come from an address given after seizing Vienna in 1805. For more on this period and its partitions, see Norman Davies's *God's Playground: A History of Poland* (1982), I, 510–527, and Paul Schroeder (1994), 11–19, 122–124, 144–150. The carve-up of Poland blamed as cause of many problems that later plagued Europe, Talleyrand to Metternich, December 19, 1814, printed in *Le Congrès de Vienne et les traités de 1815* (1864), II, 540–544, and for many, too, its re-creation would mean "the safety of Europe," as Chateaubriand put it, *Mémoires d'outre-tombe* (1951), I, 997.

Napoleon on Paris, cited in Alaistair Horne, *The Age of Napoleon* (2004), comes from the year 1798. Rumors of the art being restored, after the lack of success in Paris, intercepted letter of Gentz, June 7, 1814, *DCV*, I, no. 4. One person already pressing for the restoration of the art was Pope Pius VII's delegate, Cardinal Consalvi, soon to be joined by others, including some Benedictine monks who appealed to the British embassy, Duke of Wellington to Comte de Jaucourt, November 21, 1814, *WD*, VIII, 604. One area that was successful was restoring art in the Louvre not yet unpacked from the crates.

Dr. Justus Bollmann's activities at the congress are discussed in Paul Sweet's "Erich Bollmann at Vienna in 1815," *AHR* (1941): 580–587. One good study, in English, of the Jewish delegation at the congress in English is Max J. Kohler's *Jewish Rights at the Congresses of Vienna (1814–1815), and Aix-la-Chapelle (1818)* (1918). For publishing agent Johann Georg Cotta's wishes for intellectual property and freedom of the press, see Agent H to Hager, October 11, 1814, *DCV*, I, no. 342. Cotta has been studied recently in Daniel Moran's *Towards the Century of Words: Johann Cotta and the Politics of the Public Realm in Germany, 1795–1832* (1990).

The end of Holy Roman Empire was, of course, an involved process, which can be followed in any number of good histories, such as Friedrich Heer, *The Holy Roman Empire* (1968), or C. A. Macartney, *The Habsburg Empire, 1790–1918* (1969). One important factor in the dissolution was the *Reichsdeputationshauptschluss*, or the Imperial Recess of 1803, which not only removed ecclesiastic states like Salzburg from the empire, but also meant that the Habsburgs would likely lose their majority to Protestant electors in the College of Electors. Emperor Francis was thus the last Holy Roman Emperor (Francis II) and, by his proclamation in 1804, the first emperor of Austria (Francis I).

Travelers comparing Vienna to a "royal palace," for example, are noted in Marcel Brion, *Daily Life in the Vienna of Mozart and Schubert*, trans. Jean Stewart (1962), 23, and descriptions of the palaces on the narrow streets, Jean-Gabriel Eynard, October 5, 1814, *Au Congrès de Vienne: journal de Jean-Gabriel Eynard* (1914–1924), I, 4. Joseph's decree on planting trees comes from Raymond F. Betts, *Vienna: A City Apart*, printed privately, unpaginated. Of the many French émigrés in Vienna, Baronne du Montet's *Souvenirs, 1785–1866* (1904) is a good read, and many of the exiles gathered at the Prince de Ligne's salon, Potocka, *Memoirs of the Countess Potocka*, ed. Casimir Stryienski, trans. Lionel Strachey (1900), 112. Vienna as a counterrevolutionary center comes from Eugen Guglia, "Der Wiener Congress, seine Fürsten und Staatsmänner," in Eduard Leisching, ed., *Der Wiener Congress: Culturgeschichte die Bildenden Künste und das Kunstgewerbe Theater—Musik in der Zeit von 1800 bis 1825* (1898), 21–22, and the phrase "lunched until dinner" with more on the context in relation to the violence in France, Philip Mansel's *Prince of Europe: The Life of Charles-Joseph de Ligne, 1735–1814* (2003), 150–151. The city walls and King Richard: Richard Bright, *Travels from Vienna through Lower Hungary with Some Remarks on the State of Vienna During the Congress in the Year 1814* (1818), 33, and rumored financing of the walls appears in several places, as well as John P. Spielman, *The City and the Crown: Vienna and the Imperial Court, 1600–1740* (1993), 29. Travelers often noted the fortress, for instance, Jacob Grimm to Wilhelm Grimm, October 2, 1814, *Briefwechsel zwischen Jacob und Wilhelm Grimm aus der Jugendzeit* (1963), 350. Population figures at this time are often difficult to gauge, and estimates vary. The figure 250,000 is also accepted by Enno Kraehe (1963–1983), II, 118, and size of the capital, Waltraud Heindl's "People, Class, Structure and Society," in Raymond Erickson, ed., *Schubert's Vienna* (1997), 38. Vienna's population increased by a third during the congress: Stella Musulin's *Vienna in the Age of Metternich: From Napoleon to Revolution, 1805–1848* (1975), 140–141. "Vienna is the city" is from Baronne du Montet (1904), 24, "homeland of happiness," La Garde-Chambonas (1902), 35, and the Viennese as not being excessively polite, for example, Friedrich Anton von Schönholz, *Traditionen zur Charakteristik Österreichs, seines Staats-und Volkslebens unter Franz I* (1914), II, 104.

The popularity of Emperor Francis is attested by many accounts, including, for example, Frederick Lamb to Castlereagh, June 18, 1814, 57; Bright, (1818), 89; Rzewuska (1939), I, 64–65; and the appendix to the first volume of Eynard's (1914–1924), 334. Haydn, of course, wrote the music to "Gott erhalte Franz der Kaiser" ("God preserve Francis the Emperor") and the text was by Haschka. "If you blow hard" comes from Alville's *Anna Eynard-Lullin et l'époque des Congrès et des Révolutions* (1955), 157. Emperor Franz as Venus can be seen, for example, in Princess Therese to Princess Amalie von Sachsen, January 14, 1815, *GPWK*, 363; letter to Prince Maximilian von Sachsen, the next day, 364; and others, including, for example, "the goddess of love," May 6, 1815, 476. A. J. P. Taylor calls the Habsburgs, frankly, "the greatest dynasty of modern history" in *The Habsburg Monarchy, 1809–1918: A History of the Austrian Empire and Austria-Hungary* (1966), 10. Francis's family orchestra, in Walter Consuelo Langsam's *Francis the Good: The Education of an Emperor, 1768–1792* (1949), 162. The housing is in many contemporary sources, though the residence of the king of Denmark, less often cited, can be found in Nørregaard, *Danmark og Wiener Kongress* (1948), n. 29, 16.

Description of the coffee kettles come from Countess Bernstorff, *Ein Bild aus der Zeit von 1789 bis 1835: Aus ihren Aufzeichnungen* (1896), I, 148, and the kitchens at the Hofburg, with the words "the poor animals," in Hilde Spiel's *The Congress of Vienna: An Eyewitness Account*, trans. Richard H. Weber (1968), 87–88. The Hofburg's Silberkammer has a collection of items used at banquets, and my discussion of standard wine and entrée combinations draws on the excellent commentary of Dr. Ingrid Haslinger. For more on the culinary arts at the time, see her article in Ole Villumsen Krog, ed., *Danmark og Den Dansende Wienerkongres: Spillet om Danmark* (2002), 223. Vienna wits' description of the sovereigns was reported to Hager in late October, 1814, *DCV*, I, no. 502, and also, in alternative form, no. 503 and Perth's *Wiener Kongresstagebuch 1814–1815*, 62. The popularity of sovereigns in Vienna at first can be seen, for example, in Agent Nota to Hager, October 28, 1814, *DCV*, I, no. 253.

Chapter 2. Two Princes

Count François-Casimir Mouret de Montrond's words on Talleyrand are cited in J. F. Bernard, *Talleyrand: A Biography* (1973), 209. The age of the Tokay comes from Constantin de Grunwald, *Metternich* (1953), 122–123, and the number of carriages on loan in many sources, including Richard Bright, *Travels from Vienna Through Lower Hungary with Some Remarks on the State of Vienna During the Congress in the Year 1814* (1818), 13. Their description, Pictet de Richemont, *Biographie, travaux et correspondance diplomatique* (1892), 153; Jean-Gabriel

Eynard, *Au Congrès de Vienne: journal de Jean-Gabriel Eynard* (1914–1924), October 5, 1814, I, 2, and the comparison to maid chambers in Signor Castelli, Dallas, *The Final Act: The Roads to Waterloo* (1997), 135.

Metternich's personality is in Nesselrode, *Lettres et papiers du chancelier comte de Nesselrode, 1760–1850,* III, 132. His background draws on his comments in the first and second volumes of *Aus Metternich's nachgelassenen Papieren,* ed. Prince Richard Metternich (1880–1884), as well as Heinrich Ritter von Srbik's *Metternich Der Staatsmann und Der Mensch* (1925), I, 53ff, and Constantin de Grunwald *Metternich* (1953), 7–14. Metternich's reputation for grace and tact are in Helen du Coudray's *Metternich* (1936), 17–18. "I cannot understand" and "if I had not been" are in Dorothy Guis McGuigan, *Metternich and the Duchess* (1975), 18. For more on Metternich's other affairs, see Egon Cäsar Corti's *Metternich und die Frauen* (1948), I–II, and Raoul Auernheimer's *Prince Metternich: Statesman and Lover* (1940), though both of these appeared before the discovery of Metternich's correspondence with the Duchess of Sagan, *MSB.* "Secret dashes" comes from Paul Johnson's *The Birth of the Modern: World Society, 1815–1830* (1991), 91.

Loss of family estates on the Rhine and his first visit to Vienna come from *NP,* I, 21. Criticisms of Metternich were well known by the congress, and were soon multiplied, as seen in the police reports, where Agent ** followed the changing fortunes closely—for example, his reports to Hager: October 10, 1814, *DCV,* I, no. 324, and October 15, 1814, no. 384. "Butterfly minister" comes from Karl von Nostitz, in his diary, January 16, 1815, *Leben und Briefwechsel* (1848), 151. Another nickname, for example, was Le Comte de la Balance, Agent Freddi to Hager, undated report from September 1814, *DCV,* I, no. 83. "Hateful invention" is in McGuigan (1975), 119; "haughtiness for dignity," Alan Palmer, *Metternich* (1972), 32; and "tacking, evasion, and flattery," *NP,* II, 311. The historian praising the success of Metternich's diplomacy was du Coudray (1936), 83, and his maneuvers are analyzed in Henry Kissinger's *A World Restored: Metternich, Castlereagh, and the Problems of Peace 1812–1822* (1957), 62–84.

Metternich on the Battle of Leipzig, *MSB,* 81. Tracing the conference back to Tsar Alexander and the Battle of Leipzig is attributed to the historian August Fournier, who apparently draws on an article in the *Berliner Zeitung* after the battle, October 26, 1813, and also in the *Wiener Zeitung* on November 5, Spiel, *Der Wiener Kongress in Augenzeugen berichtet* (1965), 31. Article XXXII of the Treaty of Paris, signed May 30, 1814, is in *Le Congrès de Vienne et les traités de 1815* (1864), I, 170. Castlereagh's impact on the invitation comes from Gregor Dallas, *The Final Act: The Roads to Waterloo* (1997), 135. The delay of the conference first until August 15 and then October 1, on the tsar's insistence, Edward Vose Gulick, *Europe's Classical Balance of Power* (1955), 181. Francis's army and its losses, pun on Julius Caesar, G. R. Marek, *Beethoven: Biography of a Genius* (1970), 106. Austria had fought Napoleon for 108 months, longer than any other power besides Britain (240), Prussia for 58, Russia for 55, not to mention having "the largest contingent" of soldiers in the battles of 1813–1814, Gunther

Rothenurg, *Napoleon's Great Adversaries: The Archduke Charles and the Austrian Army, 1792–1814* (198?), 14.

My account of Talleyrand's arrival in Vienna and Kaunitz Palace draws upon his *Memoirs*, II, 199, 201, and letters to Louis XVIII, September 25, 1814, *TLC*, 1; Talleyrand to the Duchess of Courland, September 25, 1814, *TLI*, 35; and Gentz to Karadja, September 27, 1814, *Dépêches inédites*, 99. His address on Johannesgasse comes from a report to Hager, September 27, 1814, *DCV*, I, no. 161, as well as the *Wiener Zeitung*, September 25, 1814, though the street address is no longer that today. The French embassy headquarters, and prominent staff there, *GE*, 11. Length of journey from Paris is in Rosalynd Pflaum's *By Influence and Desire: The True Story of Three Extraordinary Women—the Grand Duchess of Courland and Her Daughters* (1984), 213. Some reported that he traveled eight days, but Talleyrand set off from Paris on September 16 and arrived Friday night around midnight on the twenty-third. The earlier arrival of French staff noted by many diarists, for example, Matthias Franz Perth, *Wiener Kongresstagebuch, 1814–1815* (1981), August 30, 1814, 32. Reference to the moths in the mattresses, see surveillance report to Hager, September 20, *DCV*, I, no. 111.

"I shall probably play a wretched role," Talleyrand said two or three days before leaving Paris to Pasquier, III, 69. Difficulties France faced and the phrase "singularly difficult" come from his *Memoirs* (1891), II, 151. See also his summary of the congress, including his isolation, *TLC*, 519–522. Many in Vienna agreed— for example, Baron Méneval, *Memoirs*, III, 384. Talleyrand's background draws on the biographies by Emmanuel de Waresquiel, Georges Lacour-Gayet, Emile Dard, J. F. Bernard, Jean Orieux, Duff Cooper, Crane Brinton, and Louis Madelin. Talleyrand and the Louisiana Purchase comes from Dallas (1997), 113, and the reference to Talleyrand's conversational skills is from Germaine de Staël, cited by Jean Orieux, *Talleyrand: The Art of Survival* (1974), 159 and Bernard (1973), 104. Manners, seeming "thoroughly satiated and bored with everything," Potocka (1900), 79. The dangers of the Napoleonic system, as opposed to international relations based on justice, *TLC*, 525–526. Talleyrand's break with Napoleon is often dated to 1805, though this is debatable. Messenger with invisible ink, coded message, and advice, Nesselrode *Autobiographie*, in Le Comte A. de Nesselrode, ed., *Lettres et papiers du chancelier comte de Nesselrode, 1760–1850*, II, 113, Baron de Vitrolles, *Mémoires et relations politiques* (1884), I, 66ff, and Chateaubriand *Mémoires d' outre-tombe* (1951), I, 854–855. Dalberg, who joined Talleyrand in Vienna, played a crucial role in this transaction, as discussed by one of his descendants, Lord Acton (or Dalberg-Acton), in his "Essay on the Mémoires of Talleyrand," in *Historical Essays and Studies* (1926), 412. Metternich on Talleyrand as a double-edged sword, J. F. Bernard (1973), 291.

Chapter 3. Illustrious Strangers

"A holiday for kings" appears in several variants, for example, Count Auguste de La Garde-Chambonas's *Anecdotal Recollections of the Congress of Vienna* (1902), 105, or Baronne du Montet's *Souvenirs 1785–1866* (1904), 112 and 115. The reference to the burning of Moscow lighting the tsar's soul comes from Carolly Erickson's *Our Tempestuous Day: A History of Regency England* (1986), 118. The early morning cannon shots are in Henrich Graf zu Stolberg-Wernigerode's *Tagebuch über meinen Aufenthalt in Wien zur Zeit des Congresses* (2004), 28; and Metternich's comments are in Dorothy Gies McGuigan's *Metternich and the Duchess* (1975), 330. His letter to the duchess is in *MSB*, 265.

This account of the tsar's entry into Vienna draws upon Baron Hager's report to the emperor, September 25–26, 1814, *DCV*, I, no. 124; and Agent Siber, September 27, 1814, I, no. 155. The crowds are in Baronne du Montet (1904), 112; the procession, La Garde-Chambonas (1904), 7—both of which also appear in the description in the *Wiener Zeitung*, September 26, 1814. The appearance of the tsar and the king of Prussia are in, among others, Lulu Thürheim's *Mein Leben: Erinnerungen aus Österreichs Grosser Welt 1788–1819* (1913), II, 92–97; Jean-Gabriel Eynard's *Au Congrès de Vienne: journal de Jean-Gabriel Eynard* (1914–1924), I, 327–332; and Countess Bernstorff's *Ein Bild aus der Zeit von 1789 bis 1835: Aus ihren Aufzeichnungen* (1896), I, 154. The riding arrangements are in Archduke Johann's diary, September 25, 1814: *Aus dem Tagebuche Erzherzog Johanns von Oesterreich 1810–1815*, ed. Franz Ritter von Krones (1891), 172; Niels Rosenkrantz's entry that day in his *Journal du Congrès de Vienne 1814–1815* (1953), 27; and Perth (1981), 38–39. The words "perfect order" and "no incident" are by Agent Siber, September 27, 1814, *DCV*, I, no. 155. The breakfast that morning is in Hardenberg, *Tagebücher und autobiographische Aufzeichnungen*, ed. Thomas Stamm-Kuhlmann (2000), 797–798. Lively first evening is in Gentz *Tagebücher*, September 25, 1814 (1873), I, 310.

Thomas Jefferson's words on Alexander come from Alan Palmer's *Alexander: Tsar of War and Peace* (1974), xvi. The tsar's education even included the sacred right of resisting tyrants: *Correspondance de Frédéric-César La Harpe et Alexander 1er*, eds. Jean Charles Biaudeet and Françoise Nicod (1978–9), II, 14. The tsar's relationship with his sister is controversial, though Sir Charles Webster thought Alexander's correspondence "breathes more than a brother's tenderness," *The Foreign Policy of Castlereagh 1812–1815: Britain and the Reconstruction of Europe* (1931), 288. Some of the tsar's correspondence with his sister, including some notes from the Vienna Congress, can be found in Grand Duke Nicholas Mikhailovitch's fascinating *Scenes of Russian Court Life: Being the Correspondence of Alexander I with his Sister Catherine*, an undated publication, though before 1917. The relationship between Alexander and Elizabeth is also in the memoir of a lady-in-waiting, Countess Edling, *Mémoires* (1888), 33ff. Alexander was not concerned about Elizabeth-Czartoryski affair, Henri Troyat, *Alexander of Russia: Napoleon's Conqueror*, trans. Joan Pinkham (1982), 43–44, and its lack of negative impact on the tsar's view of Czartoryski, Webster (1931), 334, as well as Marian Kukiel's *Czartoryski and European Unity 1770–1861* (1955), 22. For more on Czartoryski, see also Zawadzki's *A Man of Honour: Adam Czartoryski as a Statesman of Russia and Poland, 1795–1831* (1993), and Patricia Kennedy Grimsted's *The Foreign*

Ministers of Alexander I: Political Attitudes and the Conduct of Russian Diplomacy, 1801–1825 (1969), 110–113, 147–150, and 221–224.

Early impressions of the tsar's stance on Poland, Count Münster, September 19, 1814, *Political Sketches of the State of Europe, 1814–1867: Containing Count Ernst Münster's Despatches to the Prince Regent from the Congress of Vienna* (1868), 187, and the cooperation with Prussia, Archduke Johann, September 23, 1814, *Aus dem Tagebuche Erzherzog Johanns von Oesterreich, 1810–1815*, ed. Franz Ritter von Krones (1891), 170. Castlereagh had some idea of the tsar's intentions for Poland from the British ambassador in St. Petersburg, Lord Walpole to Castlereagh, August 9, 1814, CC X, 83, and the tsar also aware of opposition, and likely Metternich-Castlereagh cooperation, La Harpe to Alexander, August 10, 1814, no. 257, II, 566–567. La Harpe advised him to pretend that he did not know of this intrigue, and more on Poland in late September, *Annexe I* to La Harpe to Alexander, September 26, 1814, II, no. 259, 576–577. Gentz reported the risks of Poland to Karadja, *Dépêches inédites du chevalier de Gentz aux hospodars de Valachie pour servir a l'histoire la politique européene (1813–1828)*, ed. Le Comte Prokesch-Osten (1876), I, 93–94. For some background on the tsar's views of Poland from the perspective of Prince Adam Czartoryski, see *Memoirs of Prince Adam Czartoryski and His Correspondence with Alexander*, ed. Adam Gielgud (1968), II, for example, 11, 53, 165ff, 191ff, and 201ff. Talleyrand's summary of the dispute from May 1815, *TLC*, 509–510.

Metternich, "You cannot" comes from Seward, *Metternich: The First European* (1991), 194. Description of the people in his waiting room, Metternich to Duchess of Sagan, September 19, 1814, *MSB*, 263–264. Gentz also noted the crowds that morning, *Tagebücher*, September 19, 1814 (1873), 307. Metternich's office decorations, Pflaum, *By Influence and Desire: The True Story of Three Extraordinary Women—the Grand Duchess of Courland and Her Daughters* (1984), 204, and furniture that summer, McGuigan, *Metternich and the Duchess* (1975), 287. It is sometimes said that Metternich was not named president of the Congress, but that is not what the protocol of the Conference of the Eight for October 30 records, HHSA St.K Kongressakten Kart. 2.

Hardenberg's arrival was on the seventeenth and not, as sometimes said, the fifteenth (Hardenberg was then at Prague), *Tagebücher* (2000), September 17, 1814, 796. Hardenberg describing Metternich as "invisible" comes from Helen du Coudray's *Metternich* (1936), 119. The Knights of Malta representatives are in *Le Congrès de Vienne et les traités de 1815* (1864), II, 264, and their memorandum that day, Klüber (1815–1835), I, 85, with more on their efforts at this time can be found in an intercepted letter, September 14, 1814, *DCV* I no. 98. Plight is seen, too, in history of order, H. J. A. Sire, *The Knights of Malta* (1994), and some of the hopes for the congress, such as gaining the idea of Minorca, Marquis de Labrador, *Mélanges sur la vie privée et publique* (1849), 37–39. Desire for restoration of Holy Roman Empire, Gentz to Karadja, September 27, 1814 (1876), 102–103, Stein's *Tagebuch* is another good source for this question, found in *Briefe und amtliche*

Schriften (1957–1974), V, as well as many police reports, for example, the offer of the crown, Siber surveillance report to Hager, September 20, 1814, *DCV*, I, no. 109. Hopes grew over time, particularly after the elevation of the Electorate of Hanover to a kingdom, and then again, in March, after Napoleon's flight from Elba. "Four to six weeks of hell," Kraehe's *Metternich's German Policy* (1963–1983), II, 124.

My account of Duchess of Sagan builds on several sources, most important being Dorothy Guis McGuigan's outstanding study (1975), cited above, and the correspondence itself, in *MSB*. Metternich turning to the duchess in that time of crisis well illustrated by McGuigan (1975), 45–46. Sagan's background here as well, including hospital (146–147), midwife (153–154). Metternich's first love letter, Metternich to the Duchess of Sagan, July 12, 1813, though printed incorrectly as June 12 in *MSB* 23, as McGuigan shows, n. 14, 525. Correspondence cited here between Metternich and Sagan draws on McGuigan's translations, 102, and the following "I am writing," 108. "I do not know how I love you," Duchess of Sagan to Metternich, September 8, 1813, *MSB*, 58, and McGuigan (1975), 136. "Transported" and "you have made" are also here. Descriptions of salon, Pflaum (1984), 165, and Duchess of Sagan's claims about ruining herself with husbands, said to Comtesse Fuchs, Agent ** to Hager, November 19, 1814, *DCV*, I, no. 818. Description of Princess Bagration comes from Comte Auguste de La Garde-Chambonas (1902), 95, with more background in Hastier's "Les Bagration" in *Vieilles histoire, étranges enigmes,* sixième série (1962). Princess Bagration as beautiful, competitive, and half Viennese given her stay in the city, Karl August Varnhagen von Ense's *Denkwürdigkeiten des Eignen Lebens* (1987), II, 573. The queen bees comparison was made by Raoul Auernheimer in *Prince Metternich: Statesman and Lover* (1940), 141. Hager's spies filled a dossier on this rivalry; see, for example, October 2, 1814, *DCV*, I, no. 232, including annexe II, 809–811, and Sagan, annexe XIII, 811–812. "Cleopatra of Courland," Agent Nota, October 2, 1814, *DCV*, I, no. 232. Another nickname for Bagration was the "Russian Andromeda."

CHAPTER 4. DOROTHÉE'S CHOICE

Castlereagh's arrival in Vienna comes from Castlereagh to Liverpool, September 24, 1814, *BD*, CIX 193, confirmed by Gentz, *Tagebücher,* September 14, 1814, 305, Count Münster's dispatch on the seventeenth in *Political Sketches of the State of Europe, 1814–1867: Containing Count Ernst Münster's Despatches to the Prince Regent from the Congress of Vienna* (1868), 185, and the September 15 edition of the *Wiener Zeitung.* The reference to his clothes and demeanor comes from *The Private Letters of Princess Lieven to Prince Metternich, 1820–1826,* ed. Peter Quennell and Dilys Powell (1938), 12. Many sources in Vienna soon agreed, for example, Jean-Gabriel Eynard, October 8, 1814, *Au Congrès de Vienne: journal de Jean-Gabriel Eynard* (1914–1924), I, 9, Pictet de Rochemont, *Biographie, travaux et correspondance diplomatique* (Geneva, 1892), 168–169, and Countess Edling, *Mémoirs* (1898), 179.

Some accounts of the congress report that Castlereagh stayed in the street *Im Auge Gottes,* but this was actually the building, located on the current Milchgasse and now a bank. Mozart's earlier residence there, and working on the pieces there, Volkmar Braunbehrens, *Mozart in Vienna, 1781–1791*, trans. Timothy Bell (1989), 48, 63–64. It is not certain that he finished the works there, and the case has been made that Mozart moved into an apartment belonging to Fanny von Arnstein, where he lived until his marriage, Hilde Spiel, *Fanny von Arnstein: A Daughter of the Enlightenment, 1758–1818*, trans. Christine Shuttleworth (1991), 77. The reference to the harmonium is from Harold Nicholson, *The Congress of Vienna: A Study in Allied Unity, 1812–1822* (1946), 127. Castlereagh's house and move to Minoritenplatz, September 27, 1814, *DCV*, I, no. 158. The address is in *GE*, 5. The delegation was spread out, among other places, on the Gondelholf, Mölker Bastei, Juden Platz, and am Hof, as well as in hotels the Roman Emperor, the Austrian Empress, and the Hungarian Crown. Castlereagh, Cooke, Planta, and a few others were on the Minoritenplatz, the square that today houses the Haus-, Hof- und Staat Archiv, where many documents of the congress can be read.

Castlereagh's objectives at this time are analyzed in C. K. Webster's *The Foreign Policy of Castlereagh, 1812–1815: Britain and the Reconstruction of Europe* (1931), 328, and Edward Vose Gulick's *Europe's Classical Balance of Power: A Case History of the Theory and Practice of One of the Great Concepts of European Statecraft* (1955), 205–211. Castlereagh's "just equilibrium" identified as his "first object," Castlereagh to Liverpool, November 11, 1814, *BD*, CXXVIII, 232. Castlereagh's instructions for his first visit to the continent, in early 1814, can be found in *BD*, LXX, 123–126, and the "Memorandum on the Maritime Peace," 126–128.

Britain's priority of the Netherlands can be seen in many reports of the time, for example, Wellington's assessment of the location in a letter to Bathurst, September 22, 1814, 563, and his "Memorandum on the defense of the frontier of the Netherlands," same day, 564–567. See G. J. Renier's *Great Britain and the Establishment of the Kingdom of the Netherlands: A Study in British Foreign Policy* (1930), 273–276. Castlereagh described the importance of keeping Antwerp out of French hands, Castlereagh to Aberdeen, November 13, 1813, *BD*, LXIII 112, CC, IX, 73. See also a decoded though undated spy report, *DCV*, I, no. 524. The reference to the "loaded pistol" is from Lockhart, *The Peacemakers, 1814–1815* (1934), 254. The agreement had been worked out at Paris and confirmed at London, August 13, 1814, in Angeberg (1864), I, 209–213. Belgian resentment at Dutch rule was already detected, Fouché to Talleyrand, September 25, 1814, appendix, 587.

Castlereagh as a "stubborn mule," Princess Therese to Amalie von Sachsen, January 26, 1815, *GPWK*, 371. Castlereagh's role in appointing the diplomatic service comes from Webster (1931), 44–48; and the British staff in Vienna, Webster (1931), 329–330, as well as Harold Nicholson, *The Congress of Vienna: A Study in Allied Unity, 1812–1822* (1946), 129–130. Lord Stewart arrived later, as noted by the *Wiener Zeitung*, October 8, 1814, and his influence on Castlereagh noted in many sources, for example, John Wilson Croker, *The Croker Papers: The Correspondence and Diaries of the Late Right Honourable John Wilson Croker* (1884), I, 347. "Out to kick" is found in Hilde Spiel, *The Congress of Vienna: An Eyewitness*

Account, trans. Richard H. Weber (1968), 221. The words are from Karl von Nostitz, who elaborates on Stewart's aggression, January 15, 1815, *Leben und Briefwechsel* (1848), 148. The nickname "Lord Pumpernickel" was noted, for example, in a report by Agent **, December 18, 1814, *GPWK*, 305, and this in light of a popular comedy, *Rochus Pumpernickel*, that played that autumn and sporadically through early June at the Theater an der Wien.

Talleyrand's visits, *Memoirs*, II (1891), 199, the phrase "would weary," September 25, 1814, *TLI*, 35, and continuation of the visits, Talleyrand to Louis XVIII, September 29, 1814, *TLC*, 6. His new title from the king of France, Lacour-Gayet, *Talleyrand, 1754–1838*, II (1930), 429. For more on the challenges of the French embassy, see notes to chapter 2. Talleyrand's instructions are in *Le Congrès de Vienne et les traités de 1815* (1864) I, 215–238, as well as *Memoirs* (1891), II, 157–184. Instructions celebrated, by Lacour-Gayet (1930), II, 425, as well as diplomatic historian Duff Cooper in *Talleyrand: A Biography* (1932), 240–241. Talleyrand's selection of staff including assistants Challeye, Perrey, and M de Formond, in his *Memoirs*, II, 152–154, as well as Lacour-Gayet (1930), II, 427–428, and other members of staff such as La Martinière, Rouen, and Jean-Baptiste Bresson, Emmanuel de Waresquiel, *Talleyrand: le prince immobile* (2003), 476–478, 708. La Tour du Pin's selection, Le comte de la Tour du Pin, Pozzo di Borgo to Count Nesselrode, June 24–July 6, 1814, *Correspondance Diplomatique du comte Pozzo di Borgo, ambassadeur de Russie en France et du comte du Nesselrode depuis la restauration des Bourbons jusqu'au Congrès d' Aix-la-Chapelle, 1814–1818*, Comte Charles Pozzo di Borgo (1890), 22, and, of course, his wife's memoirs, Marquise de La Tour du Pin, *Journal d'une femme de cinquante ans* (1989). Dalberg's character is also in Méneval, *Baron Claude-François de Méneval's Memoirs Illustrating the History of Napoleon I from 1802 to 1815*, ed. Baron Napoleon Joseph de Méneval (1894), III, 182, and Nesselrode to Pozzo di Borgo, September 24, 1814 (1890), 77. Dalberg as a talented man with a breadth of knowledge, though frivolous, report to Hager, September 27, 1814, *DCV*, I, no. 187, and "the premier spy," report to Hager, September 27, 1814, *DCV*, I, no. 188. That he was an excellent worker was noted by many, including Varnhagen von Ense, *Denkwürdigkeiten des Eignen Lebens* (1987), II, 626. His role in writing Talleyrand's letters already suspected, Méneval (1894), III, 378. Alexis de Noailles, well known for his beliefs, and praised, no surprise, by Baronne du Montet, *Souvenirs 1785–1866* (1904), 138. Noailles "still too young to be a minister," Eynard, *Journal* (1914–1924), I, 95, November 7, 1814. None of Talleyrand's appointments would "be in his way," or hinder his actions, Pasquier thought, III, 76.

Dorothée's background, including upbringing, relationship with sister, and education, comes from her *Souvenirs de la duchesse de Dino* (1900), 127–140, and the study by Philip Ziegler, *The Duchess of Dino: Chatelaine of Europe* (1962), 22 and 31. Batowski as her father, Gaston Palewski noted in his introduction to *TLI*, 12–13, and Ziegler also thought probable (1962), 14. The Czartoryski episode, including the deceit: Pflaum (1984), 79–101 and Ziegler (1962), 49–67, though Czartoryski's memoirs, no surprise, neglected the episode. Dorothée tells the story herself (1900), 159–165, 201–203, and 224–253. "Small, skinny, yellow" is in Ziegler (1962), 23. Edmond as a husband, Ziegler (1962), 51; Bernard (1973), 296–298; and Orieux (1974), 367–377. The death of Dorothée's daughter and the appointment to Vienna, Ziegler (1962), 102–104 and Bernardy (1966), 104–107; Talleyrand's concern for her health surfaces in several letters, for example, a letter to the Duchess of Courland, May 10, 1814, *Talleyrand intime, d'après sa Correspondance Inédite avec la duchesse de Courlande* (1891), 247–248. Talleyrand's view of Dorothée is in *Memoirs* (1891), II, 208.

Chapter 5. The Big Four

The monkey, the owl, and the shark come from Carl Bertuch's *Tagebuch vom Wiener Kongress* (1916), x, the optical theater exhibitions, Matthias Franz Perth, September 5, 1814, *Wiener Kongresstagebuch, 1814–1815* (1981) 33, and other exhibits in Stolberg-Wernigerode, October 9, 1814, *Tagebuch über meinen Aufenthalt in Wien zur Zeit des Congresses* (2004), 54. The reference to the "green carpet" comes from Cadet de Gassicourt, in Gaston Palewski, ed., *TLI,* 164. Shops in Richard Bright, *Travels from Vienna through Lower Hungary with Some Remarks on the State of Vienna During the Congress in the Year 1814* (1818), 5, and Castlereagh's wife's comments are in McGuigan, *Metternich and the Duchess* (1975), 325.

Everyone complained of the rents, for example, Piedmont's San Marzan, October 10, 1814, *Diario,* lviii, and Eynard thought the prices were worse than Paris, *Journal,* October 5, 1814, I, 3. Humboldt's words on "no hole in the wall" come from a letter to his wife, August 10, 1814, in Sydow, ed., *Wilhelm und Caroline von Humboldt in ihren Briefen,* IV, 373. Housing crunch was notoriously bad in Vienna, indeed already a problem at the time of its first census, John P. Spielman, *The City and the Crown: Vienna and the Imperial Court, 1600–1740* (1993), 31–32. The rising prices for necessities were noted by many, for example, Perth, September 1, 1814, *Wiener Kongresstagebuch, 1814–1815,* 32. "Cartage, sawing and splitting," the congress roll, and "the congress is going to have" are in Hilde Spiel's *The Congress of Vienna: An Eyewitness Account,* trans. Richard H. Weber (1968), 85–87. Members of the House of Reuss are in several memoirs, for example, by the nephew of Henry LII, Henrich Graf zu Stolberg-Wernigerode's *Tagebuch über meinen Aufenthalt in Wien zur Zeit des Congresses* (2004), and the tradition of naming sons in the Reuss family is in Jerome Blum, *In the Beginning: The Advent of the Modern Age: Europe in the 1840s* (1994), 273–274. "Whenever a scaffold" and "don servants' garb" come from Friedrich Anton von Schönholz memoirs *Traditionen zur Charakteristik Österreichs, seines Staats-und Volkslebens unter Franz I* (1914), II, 68, and the translation from Hilde Spiel (1968), 79–80. Jakob Grimm's attempts to visit the library whenever possible, along with other varied literary pursuits at this time, letter to Wilhelm Grimm, October 21, 1814, *Briefwechsel zwischen Jacob und Wilhelm Grimm aus der Jugendzeit* (1963), 360. Prince de Ligne's words on not missing the congress, Philip Mansel *Prince of Europe: The Life of Charles-Joseph de Ligne, 1735–1814* (2003), 250.

On the origins of the police and its role in the reforms of Joseph II, Fournier, *Die Geheimpolizei auf dem Wiener Kongress* (1913) xviii, Weil, *Dessous du Congrès de Vienne* (1917), xviiff. My account also draws on August Fournier's overview in *GPWK* (1–90), along with the monograph by Donald Eugene Emerson, *Metternich and the Political Police: Security and Subversion in the Hapsburg Monarchy* (1815–1830), and Paul P. Bernard's study of Baron Hager's predecessor, *From the Enlightenment to the Police State: The Public Life of Johann Anton Pergen* (1991). Francis's role in enhancing the service, spies working "day and night without respite," *DCV*, I, xxii, the expansion of services, no. 13, and the increase in budget, Dallas, *The Final Act: The Roads to Waterloo* (1997), 147. People likely to be employed, Hager to von Leurs, July 1, *DCV*, I, no. 15. Some additional insight into the structure and functions of the police force can be found in the annexes to the police dossiers cited above.

The plot to kill the emperor is in McGuigan, *Metternich and the Duchess* (1975), 333–334. Fear of Italian secret societies dedicated to removing Austrians from Italy, as German societies had set up against the French, Agent Nota to Hager, October 17, 1814, *GPWK*, 188–189, though not appearing in the same entry in *DCV*, I, no. 413. Police chief instructions, Hager to Siber, August 29, 1814, *DCV*, I, no. 77, Hager to Agent **, September 24, 1814, no. 125. See also Hager to Siber, July 1, 1814, no. 13. One secret staircase, already suspected for example, N N to Hager, September 29, 1814, no. 186, and Schmidt, October 1, 1814, no. 222.

The protocol for the meeting, September 22, 1814, in *Le Congrès de Vienne et les traités de 1815* (1864), I, 249–251. Helpful discussions on these lengthy early sessions are Enno E. Kraehe, *Metternich's German Policy*, II (1963–1983), 123–125, C. K. Webster, *The Foreign Policy of Castlereagh, 1812–1815: Britain and the Reconstruction of Europe* (1931), 337–338, Guglielmo Ferrero, *The Reconstruction of Europe: Talleyrand and the Congress of Vienna, 1814–1815*, trans. Theodore R. Jaeckel (1941), 144–146, and Gregor Dallas (1997), 171–172, which shows the contrast between Castlereagh's "open Congress diplomacy" and Metternich's "closed cabinet diplomacy." Nicolson's *The Congress of Vienna: A Study in Allied Unity, 1812–1822* (1946) has helpful insights in his discussion (133–140), though there are some errors. "General congress" and "all the powers" come from Talleyrand's *Memoirs* II (1891), 144–146. Objections to opening the congress are reported by Gentz to Karadja, *Dépêches inédites*, October 6, 1814, 109. Metternich stopped using the word *congress*, Kraehe, II (1963–1983), 125. Words on the "deliberative assembly" come from Paul Sweet's *Wilhelm von Humboldt: A Biography*, II (1980), 179, and "the core of the congress," 180. Talleyrand's words on the secret meetings, *Memoirs*, II (1891), 201, and his *TLC*, 519–520. Castlereagh to Liverpool, September 24, 1814, *BD*, CIX, 193–195. The first conference lasting five hours, Metternich to the Duchess of Sagan, September 19, 1814, *MSB*, 264, and Binder in *Anhang 5* of Griewank, *Der Wiener Kongress und Die Neuordnung Europas, 1814–15* (1942), 311. Binder was still attending the meetings at this point, rather than Gentz, and Binder's unpublished memoir is at HHSA St.K Kongressakten Kart. 16.

Nesselrode's background in the navy, by appointment of Catherine the Great just before her death in 1796. Nesselrode, *Autobiographie du Comte Charles-Robert de Nesselrode*, in le Comte A. de Nesselrode, ed., *Lettres et papiers du chancelier comte de Nesselrode, 1760–1850* (1904–1912), II, 21. Some success of French intrigue, Agent ** to Hager, October 2, 1814, *DCV*, I, no. 229, and not behaving as many had expected, with more outspoken or "open opposition," Nesselrode to Pozzo di Borgo, September 27, 1814 (15th), *Correspondance Diplomatique du comte Pozzo di Borgo, ambassadeur de Russie en France et du comte du Nesselrode depuis la restauration des Bourbons jusqu'au Congrès d' Aix-la-Chapelle, 1814–1818* (1890), 81–82, along with other statements on Talleyrand's likely willingness to go along that summer, for example, his letters to Nesselrode, III and XXIV. The words "That this congress was not a congress . . ." was one way Talleyrand described it, for instance, King's Ambassadors, no. 11A, November 6, 1814, in his *Memoirs* (1891), II, 295. Gentz letter on Talleyrand's imminent participation in meeting, September 29, 1814, *DCV*, I, no. 215; report to Hager, October 1, *DCV*, I, no. 217. More on the background to Talleyrand's invitation to the Big Four meeting, Gentz to Karadja, September 27, 1814, *Dépêches inédites* (1876), I, 97ff, and Labrador's version, Marquis de Labrador, *Mélanges sur la vie privée et publique* (1849), 34ff. Metternich and others realizing necessity of coming together against Talleyrand influence, Stein's *Tagebuch*, in an undated entry before the second of October 1814, *Briefe und amtliche Schriften*, V (1964), 319.

Chapter 6. Bartering Destiny

The epigraph comes from a letter Talleyrand wrote to the Duchess of Courland, May 5, 1814, *Talleyrand intime* (1891), 246. Talleyrand as a late riser is a well-known fact, confirmed not least by many at the time who report arriving only to find him still in bed, or dressing in his ritual. My account draws on a number of people who witnessed the ceremony, such as Count Molé, who saw him "practically every morning" (1924), 208, and Comte Auguste de La Garde-Chambonas, who saw it at the congress, *Anecdotal Recollections of the Congress of Vienna* (1904), 375–376. The comparison to the elephant trunk in Charles Comte de Rémusat, who witnessed it in 1815, *Mémoires de ma vie . . . présentés et annotés par Charles-H. Pouthas* (1958–1967), II, 271. "Drawers," "Combing" and "such in" are in Orieux, *Talleyrand: The Art of Survival* (1974), 495.

Talleyrand worked closely with Spain on eve of congress, Pozzo di Borgo noted in *Correspondance Diplomatique du comte Pozzo di Borgo* (1890), Pozzo di Borgo to Count Nesselrode, June 1/13, 1814, 8. Their relationship, he added, was "inevitable." But actually it was rather strained from early on, Labrador, *Mélanges sur la vie privée et publique* (1849), 33. The two had met back in Paris when Talleyrand was foreign minister and Labrador Spain's emissary about to depart for the papal conclave in Venice that would select Pope Pius VII, *Mélanges* (1849), 6–7. For a strong view of Spain's reliance on France at this time, see Abbé de Pradt, *Congrès de Vienne* (1815), I, 70–71. Labrador's words on not playing role of marionettes comes from a discussion with an agent on his arrival in Vienna, Freddi, September 18, 1814, *DCV*, I, no. 122.

The meeting on September 30 did not take place at the Chancellery as often reported, Nicolson, *The Congress of Vienna: A Study in Allied Unity, 1812–1822* (1946), 141, but rather at Metternich's summer villa. On this meeting, see HHSA St.K Kongressakten Kart. 2, Talleyrand's report to King Louis XVIII, October 4, 1814, *TLC*, 12–19; *Memoirs*, II (1891), 202–204 and 227–228, Gentz's review, *Dépêches inédites*, October 6, 1814 (1876), I, 108, and his diary, *Tagebücher*, I, 312. See also Duff Cooper's *Talleyrand: A Biography* (1932) (1986 ed.), 249–250; Agent Nota's account to Hager, October 2, 1814, *DCV*, I, no. 231; and an intercepted letter from Prince Bellio to the Prince de Valachia, October 3, 1814, no. 269. Some effects, Nota to Hager, October 3, 1814, no. 249. Hardenberg's silence on the meeting, other than merely noting the presence of Labrador and Talleyrand, with a comment on the latter's limp, is revealing, *Tagebücher* (2000), September 30, 1814, 799.

The letter of protest from the Portuguese minister that Castlereagh read is at Vienna's HHSA, St.K Kongressakten 2. Dialogue from Talleyrand's letter to the king, cited above, and words "absolute masters," October 4, 1814, *TLC*, 17. "It was necessary to annul all that had been done without France," Talleyrand, *Memoirs*, II, 200. Metternich and Gentz stroll in garden afterward, Gentz, *Tagebücher*, I, September 30, 1814, 312. "Furiously upset" comes from here, as well as the description of the critical state of their position. Prussian headquarters were on the Graben, but like other delegations, they were spread out around Vienna on the Johannesgasse, Kärtnerstrasse, Herrengasse, Freyung, Wollzeile, Hoher Markt, Naglerstrasse, Judenplatz, and elsewhere. Humboldt was then at 620 Münzerstrasse, *GE* 16–18, and *SG* 11–12. Humboldt's arrival in Vienna, analysis of an intercepted letter, Bernstorff to Rosencrantz, August 10, 1814, *DCV*, I, no. 61, and Gentz, *Tagebücher*, I, August 8, 1814, 291. Humboldt to his wife, August 8, 1814, Sydow, ed., *Wilhelm und Caroline von Humboldt in ihren Briefen* (1910), IV, 372. Bagration salon as "gathering place of the beau monde," Hardenberg, noted in his diary, September 21, 1814 (2000), 797.

Description of Humboldt comes from Paul Sweet's *Wilhelm von Humboldt: A Biography*, II (1980), his work on the translation of Aeschylus, tour of the battlefield, 151, and "Wars and treaties of peace fade away, but a good verse lives forever" in Humboldt's letter to his wife, Caroline, December 14, 1813 in *Briefe*, IV (1910), 197. By the end of December, he had reached the chorus introduction of *Agamemnon*, letter to his wife, December 20, 1814 *Briefe*, IV (1910), 442. Humboldt's "subtleties and paradoxes" and "toying with the world," Sweet (1980), II, 160–161, and also Gentz to Karadja, March 8, 1815, *Dépêches inédites*, 62–63. Awarding an Iron Cross, Sweet, 165, and "lions," Talleyrand to Louis XVIII, October 13, 1814, *TLC*, 46. Talleyrand's strong opinion on the delegation, Prussians as a nasty people and none more than Humboldt, Talleyrand to the Duchess, October 13, 1814, *TLI*, 55. Prussia the most suffering "in proportion to its size," F. M. Kircheisen, *Napoleon*, trans. Henry St. Lawrence (1932), 686, and the kingdom, of course, much more exposed in the west and east than the south, as Brendan Simms shows well in his *The Struggle for the Mastery of Germany, 1779–1850* (1998).

More of the background can be found in, among others, James J. Sheehan, *German History, 1770–1866* (1994), and Hajo Holborn, *A History of Modern Germany, 1648–1840* (1968). The Copenhagen-Rome-Warsaw-Paris illustration is in Joachim Menzhausen, former director of the Green Vault, in his essay "Five Centuries of Art Collecting in Dresden" in *The Splendor of Dresden: Five Centuries of Art Collecting* (1978), 15. The king of Saxony's still refusing to surrender any territory, King of Saxony to King Louis XVIII, September 19, 1814, printed in appendix, 582, and protest in *Le Congrès de Vienne et les traités de 1815* (1864), II, 401–403. Castlereagh's poor knowledge of geography, including "military topography," Talleyrand to King Louis XVIII, January 19, 1815, *TLC*, 270–271. King of Saxony captured and made prisoner, though unfortunately with few details, Nesselrode, *Autobiographie*, in Nesselrode, ed., *Lettres et papiers du Chancelier Comte de Nesselrode, 1760–1850*, II, 106.

Chapter 7. "Europe, Unhappy Europe"

Chapter title comes from Talleyrand to King Louis XVIII, October 4, 1814, *TLC*, 23. My account of Metternich and Duchess of Sagan builds on Ullrichová's edition of their correspondence, *MSB*; Pflaum's *By Influence and Desire: The True Story of Three Extraordinary Women—the Grand Duchess of Courland and Her Daughters* (1984); and especially Dorothy Guis McGuigan's *Metternich and the Duchess* (1975). Emperor Francis words on regarding the Duchess of Sagan as most necessary ingredient, Metternich to Duchess of Sagan, August 14, 1814, *MSB*, 260.

The discovery consisted of some 327 letters from Prince Metternich and 278 from Duchess of Sagan, and other supplements, from February 1812 to December 1818 *MSB*, 11. The Duchess's "bitterest regret," migraines, and depression are in McGuigan (1975), 26–27, Sagan to Metternich, January 21, 1814, *MSB*, 187, and more on Vava, Pflaum (1984), 166–167. Armfelt's wit was recognized by many, including Princess Radziwill, *Forty-Five Years of My Life (1770–1815)*, trans. A. R. Allinson (1912), 187. Description of the Duchess of Sagan's salon, Pflaum (1984), 165. The Russians gathering at Bagration's salon, report to Hager, October 14, 1814, *DCV*, I, no. 368, and the file, annexe XII, 809–811. La Garde-Chambonas called it "the Russian drawing room par excellence" while also making the comparison to St. Petersburg about 1810, *Anecdotal Recollections of the Congress of Vienna* (1902), 94. Her salon had long been known for being popular with Russians, *Lettres et papiers du chancelier comte de Nesselrode, 1760–1850*, III (1904), 174. The Metternich and Bagration affair is in Egon Cäsar Corti's *Metternich und die Frauen* (1948), I, 70–72. Metternich asked ministers if they wanted to discuss in Baden, Gentz, *Tagebücher*, September 15, 1814 (1873), 306. Humboldt had been in favor of this move for a while, Humboldt to Hardenberg, September 3, 1814, *GPWK*, 116, and apparently agents were looking for places to rent for Castlereagh and Hardenberg, Gentz to Pilat, September 3, 1814, *Briefe von Friedrich von Gentz an Pilat*, ed. Karl Mendelssohn-Bartholdy, I–II (1868), I, 152. Metternich was visiting Bagration less frequently, as Agent ** summarized it, November 4, 1814, *DCV*, I, no. 674, and again on November 22, 1814, no. 849.

The tsar and Bagration conversation, "Metternich has never loved you," Agent Nota to Hager, October 3, 1814, *DCV*, I, no. 252.

Talleyrand's interview with the tsar, Talleyrand to King Louis XVIII, October 4, 1814, *TLC*, 21–24, 1814, *Memoirs*, II (1891), 228–229. According to Talleyrand, the tsar was supposed to have returned afterward a little more amiable, 24. Many other accounts circulated, Gentz to Karadja, October 6, 1814, *Dépêches inédites* (1876), 113. Castlereagh to Liverpool, October 24, 1814, *BD*, CXIX, 213, Rosenkrantz, *Journal*, October 23, 1814, 50, and Nota to Hager, October 6, 1814, *DCV*, I, no. 293. Pasquier criticized Talleyrand for his antics, *Histoire de mon temps: mémoires du chancelier Pasquier* (1893–1894), III, 77, and the tsar's *froideur* on eve of interview, Pozzo di Borgo to Nesselrode, September 14–26, 1814, *Correspondance Diplomatique du comte Pozzo di Borgo, ambassadeur de Russie en France et du comte du Nesselrode depuis la restauration des Bourbons jusqu'au Congrès d' Aix-la-Chapelle, 1814–1818* (1890), 80. Tsar with his 200,000 and challenge, Nota, October 3, 1814, *DCV*, I, no. 252. An army of 230,000 was ready to march on Vienna, according to a report to Hager, September 29, 1814, I, no. 195.

CHAPTER 8. SPIES ARE EVERYWHERE!

Hager's attempt to gain access to domestic staff at the palace, Hager to Emperor Francis, September 28, 1814, *DCV*, I, no. 151, and Hager to Trauttmansdorff, September 27, 1814, no. 152. The importance of finding agents active in society, for instance, appears in the *Rapport du ministre de la police Sumeraw sur l'organisation du service de la police secrète, Annexe*, II, 785. Instructions to them and more on the Cabinet Noir and Bureau de Déchiffrement in *Annexe*, III, 787–788. The use of steam and smokeless candle is in Freiherr von Bourgoing's *Vom Wiener Kongress: Zeit- und Sittenbilder* (1943), 13–14. Some agents can be identified: Agent Nota was Carpani, Herr H was Heibenstreit, and Agent ∞ was probably the Hungarian-born official Neustädter. For more on the general background of the espionage, see notes to chapter 5.

My account of early successes is drawn from a number of reports in the police files: Infiltration of Stein, as a valet, Siber to Hager, October 3, 1814, *DCV*, I, no. 244, and Agent Göhausen, no. 246. The words "we have enough proofs" come from Wilhelm von Humboldt's letter to his wife Caroline, August 1, 1814, in Anna von Sydow, ed., *Wilhelm und Caroline von Humboldt in ihren Briefen* (1910), IV, 368, and Humboldt later describing how some letters, clumsily treated in the post, raised suspicions, November 4, 1814, IV, 406. Occasionally, despite their efforts, not all of the letters were decoded. See Marescalchi to Dalberg, September 16, 1814, *DCV*, I, no. 149. The king of Denmark's cape and appearance are in Schön-holz, *Traditionen zur Charakteristik Österreichs, seines Staats-und Volkslebens unter Franz I* (1914), II, 76, and the affair with the lady calling herself the "Queen of Denmark" comes from Baronne du Montet, *Souvenirs, 1785–1866* (1904), 116. The king's mistress was later the Danish widow after his departure, *GPWK* 63, 148, 473; for more on the affair, Rosenkrantz, *Journal du Congrès de Vienne*,

1814–1815 (1953), March 28, 1814, 202, and Nørregaard, *Danmark og Wienerkongressen, 1814–1815* (1948), 17.

Prince de Ligne background comes from his *Memoirs*, I–II; of the several biographies, see particularly Philip Mansel, *Prince of Europe: The Life of Charles-Joseph de Ligne, 1735–1814* (2003). The "Prince Charming" reference is from Henri Troyat, *Catherine the Great*, trans. Joan Pinkham (1981), 283, and his "roguish wit," Countess Anna Potocka, *Memoirs of the Countess Potocka*, ed. Casimir Stryiens, trans. Lionel Strachey (1900), 111. Prince de Ligne and Casanova in Gilbert, *The Prince de Ligne: A Gay Marshal of the Old Regime*, trans. Joseph McCabe (1923), 153–157, 157–159. Prince de Ligne's old carriage, with the two horses, Gilbert (1923), 206, and the words on his preferences are in Franz Gräffer, *Kleine Wiener Memoiren und Wiener Dosenstucke* (1918), I, 187, noted as well by Rosalie Rzewuska, *Mémoires de la comtesse Rosalie Rzewuska* (1788–1865) I, 238, and as color of House of Ligne, Mansel (2003), 198. "Pink as" comes from Spiel (1968), 193. Another nickname for Prince de Ligne's house was the "l'hôtel de Ligne," Ouvaroff, *Esquisses politiques et littéraires* (1848), 121. Prince de Ligne's words on the congress dances, Comte Auguste de La Garde-Chambonas, 14 (1904), as well as anonymous to Princess Bagration, intercepted, December 17–18, 1814, *DCV*, I, no. 1155, and again anonymous to Gagern intercept, December 26, 1814, no. 1161. See also Jacob Grimm to his brother, November 23, 1814, *Briefwechsel zwischen Jacob und Wilhelm Grimm aus der Jugendzeit* (1963), 379. Tsar Alexander, in particular, was offended at hearing Prince de Ligne's words because he took it personally, Agent L to Hager, November 27, 1814, *DCV*, I, no. 914. "On her head" is in Spiel (1968), 289, and Countess Protassoff is in Ludwig Hevesi's "Die Wiener Gesellschaft zur Zeit des Congresses" in Eduard Leisching, ed., *Der Wiener Congress: Culturgeschichte die Bildenden Künste und das Kunstgewerbe Theater—Musik in der Zeit von 1800 bis 1825* (1898), 68.

France was at first "completely isolated," as Talleyrand put it in his summary of the Vienna Congress, May 1815, *TLC*, 509, and intentional isolation, Talleyrand to Louis XVIII, October 19, 1814, *TLC*, 69, intercepted letter from Dalberg, October 20, 1814, *DCV*, I, no. 472, among others. Ill will against them, Pasquier (1893–1894), III, 76. "No one dared to visit its members . . . ," Labrador reproached for visiting French embassy often, called a "turncoat," Talleyrand to Louis XVIII, October 19, 1814, *TLC*, 68–69, and the king of Bavaria's apparent difficulty, Ambassadors of the King to the Foreign Minister, October 20, 1814, *Memoirs* (1891), II, 270.

On Dorothée's success, Talleyrand to the Duchess, October 13, 1814, *TLI*, 52, again October 15, 1814, *TLI*, 56, and how she pleases Vienna, on the nineteenth, 58. Dalberg to his uncle, intercepted, November 24, 1814, *DCV*, I, no. 872. Sagan's request on behalf of her sister and Metternich's invitation, Metternich to the Duchess of Sagan, undated, *MSB*, 266. "Stroke of bad luck" comes from Baronne du Montet (1904), 114. Dorothée's success is in La Garde-Chambonas (1902), 64–65; Talleyrand dictating his dispatches to Dorothée, McGuigan, *Metternich and the Duchess* (1975), 405, their "battle of the words," Pflaum, *By Influence and*

Desire: The True Story of Three Extraordinary Women—the Grand Duchess of Courland and Her Daughters (1984), 239. The Metternich-Sagan love affair was not on October 8, as sometimes presented [Dallas, *The Final Act* (1997), 201], but actually on the first. Their relationship was very different by the eighth. "Greatest happiness of my life" comes from a letter to Sagan, cited in McGuigan (1975), 341. Some historians suggest that Metternich was not officially named president, but this contradicts the protocol for the meeting on the thirtieth of October, HHSA St.K Kongressakten Kart. 2. Alexander's visit to Princess Bagration on the night of September 30–October 1, 1814, Agent Nota to Hager, October 1, 1814, *DCV*, I, no. 233. Everyone talking about Alexander's meeting with Bagration, Nota to Hager, October 2, 1814, no. 232.

CHAPTER 9. DANCING WITH THE WORLD IN THEIR HANDS

The words "truly magnificent" come from Countess Bernstorff's *Ein Bild aus der Zeit von 1789 bis 1835: Aus ihren Aufzeichnungen* (1896), I, 155. The number of candles in the ballroom was estimated at everything from 4,000 (Montebello) to 16,000 (Bertuch), including 5,000–6,000 (Stolberg-Wernigerode), 8,000 (Schön-holz), and 12,000 (San Marzan). Description of the palace decorations and the crowds come from Friedrich von Schönholz's *Traditionen zur Charakteristik Öster-reichs, seines Staats-und Volkslebens unter Franz I* (1914), II, 106; more on the colors and the orange grove is in Carl Bertuch's diary that night, *Tagebuch vom Wiener Kongress* (1916), 20–21; and Henrich Graf zu Stolberg-Wernigerode's Stolberg-Wernigerode, *Tagebuch über meinen Aufenthalt in Wien zur Zeit des Congresses* (2004), 40. The abuse of the invitations is in Matthias Franz Perth's *Wiener Kongresstagebuch, 1814–1815* (1981), 45–46. Schönholz describes one of the methods as well in his memoir (1914), II, 106. The words "murderous crush" are in Hilde Spiel's *The Congress of Vienna: An Eyewitness Account*, trans. Richard H. Weber (1968), 93. The catering record is in Ole Villumsen Krog, ed., *Danmark og Den Dansende Wienerkongres: Spillet om Danmark* (2002), 464.

Humboldt's plans to avoid the ball, along with his words "stand without stir-ring," come from a letter to his wife, *Wilhelm und Caroline von Humboldt in ihren Briefen* (1910), IV, 391–392, and Münster's carriage accident and broken rib are also in Hardenberg's *Tagebücher und autobiographische Aufzeichnungen* (2000), 799. Comte Auguste de La Garde-Chambonas's descriptions that evening, along with his words on the waltz and the flirting in the ballroom, are in his *Anecdotal Recollections of the Congress of Vienna* (1902), 37–40 and 193. The popularity of white dresses that evening comes from Henrich Graf zu Stolberg-Wernigerode's *Tage-buch*, October 2, 1814 (2004), 43. On popular dresses at the time, see Regina Karner's excellent "Fashion During the Congress of Vienna" in Ole Villumsen Krog, ed. (2002), 264, as well as Carl Masner "*Das Costüm der Empirezeit*" in Eduard Leisching, ed., *Der Wiener Kongress: Culturgeschichte die Bildenden Kün-ste und das Kunstgewerbe Theater—Musik in der Zeit von 1800 bis 1825* (1898), 233–245.

The waltz as the "revolving dance" with background on its development in

Hans Fantel's *The Waltz Kings: Johan Strauss, Father and Son, and their Romantic Age* (1972), 31; Elizabeth Aldrich's "Social Dancing in Schubert's World" in Raymond Erickson, ed., *Schubert's Vienna* (1997), 131–138; and Otto Biba's "The Congress of Vienna and Music" in Krog, ed. (2002), 201. The importance of masked balls at the congress, Baronne du Montet, *Souvenirs 1785–1866* (1904), 113; and excitement and intrigues in this environment, Stolberg-Wernigerode's diary (2004), 100. The "living image of a society" is in La Garde-Chambonas (1902), 193, and the words "you should," "shimmering silks," and "the continuous music," Dorothy Guis McGuigan's *Metternich and the Duchess* (1975), 342–343. The frenzy of the waltz at the congress appears in many other sources, such as Karl von Nostitz, in his diary, *Leben und Briefwechsel* (1848), 149. The loss of the silver spoons comes from Friedrich von Schönholz's memoir (1914), II, 106.

"Sparkling" comes from Baronne du Montet (1904), 114. Antonio Salieri's rumored poisoning, although difficult to trace its origins, was circulating in Vienna long before the congress, as seen by Volkmar Braunbehren's *Maligned Master: The Real Story of Antonio Salieri*, trans. Eveline L. Kanes (1992), 4. Interestingly, one of Baron Franz von Hager's agents at the Congress of Vienna, Giuseppe Antonio Carpani (or "Nota," as he signed his reports), wrote a defense of Salieri in September 1824, *Lettera del sig. G. Carpani in difesa del Mo Salieri calunniato dell'avvelenamento del M' Mozard*.

Tuesday evening soirees at the British embassy, Agent ** to Hager, October 15, 1814, *DCV*, I, 384, *GPWK*, 181–182, and Jean-Gabriel Eynard, who regularly attended them, *Au Congrès de Vienne: Journal de Jean-Gabriel Eynard* (1914–1924), I, 38–40, 67–68. Impressions of English pride and the isolation, Eynard, (1914–1924), I, 136, November 18, 1814, eccentricities and odd fashions noted by many, including among others Baronne du Montet (1904), 137, Rosalie Rzewuska, *Mémoires de la Comtesse Rosalie Rzewuska* (1788–1865) (1939) I, 253, Dr. Richard Bright, *Travels from Vienna Through Lower Hungary with Some Remarks on the State of Vienna During the Congress in the Year 1814* (1818), 10, Karl von Nostitz, January 15, 1815, in *Leben und Briefwechsel* (1848), 146–147, and Pictet de Rochemont to family, November 19, 1814, *Biographie, travaux et correspondance diplomatique* (1892), 176. On Stewart and the coachman, Hager to the Emperor, November 1, 1814, *DCV*, I, no. 620; San Marzan's diary, October 26, 1814, in Ilario Rinieri ed., *Corrispondenza inedita dei Cardinali Consalvi e Pacca nel tempo del Congresso di Vienna* (1903), lx; and Karl August Varnhagen von Ense's *Denkwürdigkeiten des Eignen Lebens* (1987), II, 602. This was a topic of conversation around town, Stolberg-Wernigerode, October 29, 1814 (2004), 82; Karl von Nostitz also realized that the coachman did more damage than the ambassador, as noted in his diary, January 15, 1815, *in Leben und Briefwechsel* (1848), 148. Phrase "emptied some bottles" comes from Jean-Gabriel Eynard, November 6, 1814 (1914–1924), I, 89. Physician Carro confirmed the bruises, and Stewart not pressing charges, November 8, 1814, 97.

Speculation of Marie Louise's arrival in Vienna, for example, is in Agent Göhausen to Hager, October 6, 1814, *DCV*, I, no. 291, and Marie Louise's dilemma well-presented in Alan Palmer's *Napoleon and Marie Louise: The Emperor's Second Wife* (2001), 175–176. Her letters, which she numbered after reaching Rambouillet, nos.186–205, published by the king of Sweden, Gustav VI Adolf's private secretary, C. F. Palmstierna, and translated by E. M. Wilkinson, *My Dearest Louise: Marie-Louise and Napoleon 1813–1814* (1958), 194–224.

Talleyrand's October 1 Note addressed to the powers, HHSA St.K Kongressakten Kart.2, the King's Ambassadors at the Congress, October 4, 1814, no. 3A, *Memoirs* (1891), II, 228, letter to King Louis XVIII, October 4, 1814, *TLC*, 20–21, and letter to King Louis XVIII, October 9, 1814, 28–29, with repeated phrase on their league to "make themselves masters of everything." This note was essentially repeating his position, Gentz to Karadja, October 6, 1814, *Dépêches inédites de chevalier de Gentz aux hospodars de Valachie pour servir a l'histoire la politique européene,* ed. Le Comte Prokesch-Osten fils (1876), I, 109; its impact on many small German princes and powers, Castlereagh to Liverpool, October 9, 1814, *BD*, CXIV, 203. The French ploy is in an intercepted letter, too, Dalberg to Jaucourt, October 8, 1814, *GPWK*, 222–223. Spain's support, including Labrador's boast of cracking the cabal, Freddi to Hager, October 2, *GPWK*, 150. "Supreme arbiters," Humboldt "a firebrand flung into our midst," and the Prussian rumors about the French, Talleyrand to Louis XVIII, October 9, 1814, *TLC*, 28–29. Castlereagh's words on "entirely confidential," 29, and Castlereagh's words "rather excited apprehension" from his letter to Liverpool, October 9, 1814, *BD*, CXIII, 202. Additional critiques of Talleyrand, who was provoking "distrust and alarm," come from Castlereagh to Liverpool, the same *BD*, CXV, 204–205, and also in *WSD*, IX, 323.

Talleyrand's note on October 3 appears in *Le Congrès de Vienne et les traités de 1815* (1864), II, 264. Gentz's background is traced in the biographies by Paul Sweet, *Friedrich von Gentz: Defender of the Old Order* (1941), and Golo Mann, *Secretary of Europe: The Life of Friedrich Gentz, Enemy of Napoleon* (1946). Gentz "took pleasure in himself"—"*sich selbst zu geniessen,*" Hannah Arendt, *Rahel Varnhagen: The Life of a Jewess,* ed. Liliane Weissberg and trans. Richard and Clara Winston (1997), 146. Kant allowed the student to proof his writings, Mann (1946), 8. On the fourth, it was not Castlereagh who handed the note as sometimes claimed, but rather Metternich. See King's Ambassadors at the Congress, no. 4A, October 8, 1814, in Talleyrand *Memoirs* (1891), II, 238, letter to King Louis XVIII, October 9, 1814, *TLC*, 30. October 5 meeting as "very stormy and very memorable," Gentz, *Tagebücher,* October 5, 1814 (1873), 314, and Metternich's threats to call off the congress at once, *Dépêches inédites,* October 6, 1814 (1876), I, 110. The end of the meeting on October 5 that "evaporated rather than ended" comes from Talleyrand's letter dated October 9, 1814, in *TLC*, 33–34.

CHAPTER 10. THE PEOPLE'S FESTIVAL

Castlereagh's goals, including his plans for a strong Prussia, are analyzed in C. K. Webster, *The Foreign Policy of Castlereagh, 1812–1815: Britain and the Reconstruction of Europe* (1931). Lord Stewart's image as friendly to the Prussians, or "entirely Prussian" in Talleyrand's words, comes from a letter to Louis XVIII, October 19, 1814, *TLC*, 71. Castlereagh hopes for a closer Prussian Austrian cooperation, Castlereagh to Liverpool, October 9, 1814, *BD*, CXIII, 201. Hardenberg and Humboldt shared Castlereagh's concerns about Russia, as can be seen in many places, such as Humboldt's comments in a letter to his wife, November 2, 1814, 399, or report to Hager, October 20, 1814, *DCV*, I, no. 462, or Gentz to Karadja, *Dépêches inédites*, June 21, 1814, 81–82. Humboldt pressing for "close union" with Austria, in intercepted letter to King of Prussia, September 14, 1814, *GPWK*, 118, and I, no. 100. Hardenberg disagreeing with the king, already from his first meeting at the Hofburg, *Tagebücher und autobiographische Aufzeichnungen* (2000), September 26, 1814, 798. The unpopularity of the Russians with many Prussians also noted by many police agents, Nota to Hager, October 1, 1814, *DCV*, I, no. 210. The difficulties to surmount for an Austria and Prussia combination against Russia were considerable, given the risks inherent in traditional alliance systems, as explained well by Schroeder, *The Transformation of European Politics, 1763–1848* (1994), 14–15. Tensions were surfacing, too, over dividing the spoils, as noted in an earlier intercepted letter from Danish embassy, Rosencrantz to Bernstorff, August 16, 1814, *GPWK*, 111.

Castlereagh and Talleyrand had their differences, especially on priorities, for instance, Talleyrand to Louis XVIII, October 31, 1814, *TLC*, 103–104. Arguments on behalf of Saxony and suspicions of Castlereagh's fears also in this letter, 104–107. The People's Festival at Augarten, Eynard, "un fête superbe," *Au Congrès de Vienne: journal de Jean-Gabriel* (1914–1924) I, 5, October 6, and Countess Bernstorff's *Ein Bild aus der Zeit von 1789 bis 1835: Aus ihren Aufzeichnungen*, I (1896), 156. Comte Auguste de La Garde-Chambonas, *Anecdotal Recollections of the Congress of Vienna* (1902), 83–86, and balloonist that day, Spiel (1968), 95. Other activities, including the riding, the acrobatics, and the fireworks, are in Matthias Franz Perth, October 6, 1814, *Wiener Kongresstagebuch, 1814–1815* (1981), 48, and Stolberg-Wernigerode, the same day, *Tagebuch über meinen Aufenthalt in Wien zur Zeit des Congresses* (2004), 51–52, who thought it all seemed a big confusion.

Talleyrand and Metternich preconference conversation on October 8, and the public law debate, King's Ambassadors at the Congress, no. 4A, October 8, 1814, 240. The meeting itself, Talleyrand to King Louis XVIIII, October 9, 1814, *TLC*, 31–34 and 36–42, and McGuigan (1975), 347–348. Nesselrode on tsar's intentions to leave also in Nesselrode to Pozzo di Borgo, September 27, 1814 (the fifteenth in the Russian calendar), *Correspondance Diplomatique du comte Pozzo di Borgo* (1890), 82. The Great Powers had met earlier that afternoon, before Talleyrand, and then again in the evening, Gentz, *Tagebücher*, October 8, 1814 (1873), I, 316. The public law insertion, King's Ambassadors at the Congress, no. 5A, October 12, 1814, *Memoirs* (1891), II, 249. Hardenberg noted without comment, *Tagebücher und autobiographische Aufzeichnungen* (2000), October 8, 1814, 801. The new Committee of Eight meeting with the postponement of the congress is in *Le Congrès de Vienne et les traités de 1815*, ed. Comte d' Angeberg (1864) II, 272–273, as well as the *Wiener Zeitung*, October 13, 1814, and its purpose as supposedly to represent the congress itself, Gaëtan de Raxis de Flassan, *Histoire du Congrès de Vienne* (1829), I, 26. The delay, of course, would be highly beneficial to the French delegation, as noted by many, including Karl August Varnhagen von Ense, *Denkwürdigkeiten des Eignen Lebens* (1987), II, 597.

Dinner with Duchess of Sagan on Wednesday, October 5, Gentz, *Tagebücher* (1873) I, 314–315, though he did not mention the incident with Windischgrätz. Sagan's relationship with Windischgrätz, the story of the ring, are in Pflaum, *By Influence and Desire: The True Story of Three Extraordinary Women—the Grand Duchess of Courland and Her Daughters* (1984), 118–119, and more background, particularly, McGuigan, *Metternich and the Duchess* (1975), 60. Rzewuska elaborates on the help of the apothecary and the perfume after the ring's "adventurous journey," *Mémoires de la comtesse Rosalie Rzewuska* (1788–1865) (1939), I, 262. Windischgrätz's role in promoting the cigar, see Pflaum, 118. Metternich was not present, hosting his own reception the same day, San Marzan, *Diario*, October 5, 1814, lviii. Metternich and the duchess relationship at this time, and the rivalry, Rzewuska (1939) I, 259, and Metternich writing to her in a meeting, October 9, 1814, *MSB*, 267. His "tears of joy" also comes from this letter. The costume of the Four Elements comes from many sources, including Eynard, October 10, 1814 (1914–1924), I, 15, Countess Edling, *Mémoires* (1888), 183, Schönholz, *Traditionen zur Charakteristik Österreichs, seines Staats-und Volkslebens unter Franz I* (1914), II, 108, Countess Bernstorff, (1896), I, 155–156, Perth (1981), 52, and San Marzan, *Diario*, October 9, 1814, lviii.

CHAPTER II. A LAWLESS SCRAMBLE?

The wait in Metternich's office, including the description of the tired foreign minister, Eynard, October 11, 1815, *Journal* (1914–1924), I, 17–21. Pictet de Rochemont, who joined Eynard at that meeting, agreed that Metternich was "all smiles," though he also felt that Metternich seemed ignorant of the issues, *Biographie, travaux et correspondance diplomatique* (1892), 168–169. Consalvi's sophistication was also noted by Archduke Johann, September 23, 1814, *Aus dem Tagebuche Erzherzog Johanns von Oesterreich 1810–1815*, ed. Franz, Ritter von Krones (1891), 171. Consalvi's background in *Mémoires* (1864) and John Martin Robinson's *Cardinal Consalvi, 1757–1824* (1987), E. E. Y. Hales, *Revolution and Papacy, 1769–1846* (1960), 229–230. Consalvi on Napoleon in *Mémoires* (1864), II, 397; Cardinal Consalvi's work with the monuments and streets, Robinson (1987), 60–61, and Consalvi as the only papal-vicar, 76–77. Consalvi's objectives noted in police report to Hager, September 18, 1814, *DCV*, I, no. 106, and determination, for example, Nota to Hager, October 3, 1814, I, no. 254.

Napoleon's plundering of the Vatican is in Dorothy Mackay Quynn's "The Art Confiscations of the Napoleonic Wars," *AHR*, 50, no. 3. (April 1945), 437–460, Owen Chadwick, *The Popes and European Revolution* (1981), 462. One reason for Austria's interests in the Legations was perhaps as an exchange with Marie Louise that would keep her out of Parma with its proximity to Elba, or perhaps as compensation for the king of Saxony for losing his territory, Humboldt to King of Prussia, intercepted, September 14, 1814, *DCV*, I, no. 100.

Metternich and Bagration relationship, including their daughter Clementine, is in Hastier's *"Les Bagration": Vieilles histoire, étranges enigmes* (1962), McGuigan, *Metternich and the Duchess* (1975), 16, and Corti, *Metternich und die Frauen* (1948), I, 70–72. Tsar Alexander's regular visits to Princess Bagration salon, Siber to Hager, October 3, 1814, *DCV*, I, no. 247, and Agent Göhausen to Hager, October 6, 1814, no. 291. The tsar's interest particularly in her relationship with Metternich, Nota to Hager, October 3, *DCV*, I, no. 252, and suspicion that she was complying, Report to Hager, October 14, no. 415.

Many of Marie Louise's letters have been discovered in the twentieth century. In addition to 243 of her letters to Duchesse de Montebello, published in Edouard Gachot's *Marie-Louise Intime* (1912), there was another collection of 318 letters between Marie Louise and Napoleon that was found inside a desk by her children with Adam Neipperg. The collection remained private, but passed through various owners until 1934, when one of Marie Louise's great-grandsons put them at auction in London, and the French government purchased them. Another 127 of Marie Louise's letters, many of them replies to Napoleon, were uncovered eleven years later in Sweden, by the archivist Nils Holm (Napoleon had given the letters to his older brother Joseph for safekeeping; but when Joseph fled to America after Waterloo, he believed that they would be more secure with his sister-in-law, Désirée, wife of former marshal and then Swedish Crown Prince Bernadotte). She preserved the packet in Sweden, where she died in 1860. The king of Sweden, Gustav VI Adolf's private secretary, C. F. Palmstierna, published a number of the letters, along with others from the Bernadotte files, translated into English by E. M. Wilkinson, *My Dearest Louise: Marie-Louise and Napoleon 1813–1814* (1958), 194–224. Marie Louise's secretary, Baron Claude-François de Méneval's *Memoirs Illustrating the History of Napoleon I from 1802 to 1815*, ed. Baron Napoleon Joseph de Méneval (1894), are also engrossing, and the episode in this chapter is discussed in III, 162–311. A valuable recent study is Alan Palmer's *Napoleon and Marie Louise* (2001), 150–190. Palmer (p. 188), like Palmstierna (p. 223) and many others, dates the empress's arrival in Vienna on the fourth of October, but I have preferred the seventh because of a number of references in Vienna itself, ranging from diarists like Matthias Franz Perth's *Wiener Kongresstagebuch, 1814–1815* (1981) to the *Wiener Zeitung*, which, on October 8, 1814, reported her arrival at Schönbrunn the previous day. "Peaches and cream" and "turner's workshop" are in Hilde Spiel, ed., *The Congress of Vienna: An Eyewitness Account*, trans. Richard H. Weber (1968), 251. Napoleon's wishes that his wife and son do not "fall into the hands of the enemy, in any case whatever," Napoleon to his brother Joseph, March 16, 1814, Méneval (1894), III 195; and Marie Louise's unhappiness about returning to Vienna appears in several letters, for example, Marie Louise to Méneval, August 15, 1814, Méneval (1894), III, 298.

My discussion of the book dealers in Vienna draws on Enno E. Kraehe's *Metternich's German Policy* (1963–1983), II, 188–189. Kraehe, like virtually every historian who discusses the bookseller delegation in Vienna, identifies the publishing delegate as Friedrich Bertuch. This is incorrect. It was not Friedrich who came, but his son, Carl. Friedrich had backed out at the last minute and was home, ill. The censorship edict of 1810 is in Donald E. Emerson's *Metternich and the Political Police: Security and Subversion in the Hapsburg Monarch (1815–1839)* (1968), 29. The book dealers are shadowed by several spies, Agent Schmidt, October 7, 1814, *GPWK*, 160, as well as *DCV*, I, no. 301. Cotta's contacts worried Agent H, September 29, 1814, *GPWK*, 136, and *DCV*, I, no. 201. Agent H's reports following Cotta, for example, in *GPWK*, 171, as well as *DCV*, I, no. 342, and the audience on the fourteenth of October with Metternich, *GPWK*, 180–181. Cotta and Bertuch feared to be associated with the Tugendbund, R to Hager, October 11, 1814, *DCV*, I, no. 582. Cotta and Bertuch meeting with Metternich, along with his positive impression of the Austrian foreign minister, Carl Bertuch, October 8, 1814, *Tagebuch vom Wiener Kongress* (1916), 27–28.

For more on the Jewish delegations at this time, see Kraehe (1963–1983), II, 190, where he notes Metternich's help and previous relationship with Jakob Baruch. Additional background on the delegations is in Max J. Kohler's *Jewish Rights at the Congresses of Vienna (1814–1815), and Aix-la-Chapelle (1818)*, (1918), 4–5, and Salo Baron's *Die Judenfrage auf dem Wiener Kongress, auf Grund von zum Teil ungedruckten Quellen dargestellt* (1920). Government instructions are in Hager to La Roze, July 1, 1814, *DCV*, I, no. 14, and surveillance, for instance, Goehausen report, October 27, 1814, *GPWK*, 207, and note to Hager, October 21, 1814, *DCV*, I, no. 467. The arrival of the Grand Duke of Baden, Prince Thurn und Taxis, and Prince Nassau-Weilburg was reported in the *Wiener Zeitung*, October 3, 1814. Alexander Ivanovich Mikhailovsky-Danilevsky's words on Prince of Nassau-Weilburg come from Dr. Alexandre Sapojnikov's "The Congress of Vienna in the Memoirs of a Russian Officer" in Ole Villumsen Krog's, ed., *Danmark og Den Dansende Wienerkongres: Spillet om Danmark* (2002), 148. O'Bearn as a whist player is in Ludwig Hevesi, "Die Wiener Gesellschaft zur Zeit des Congresses," in *Der Wiener Congress: Culturgeschichte die Bildenden Künste und das Kunstgewerbe Theater—Musik in der Zeit von 1800 bis 1825*, ed. Eduard Leisching (1898), 68. The socialite describing the gambling tables in Madame Frazer's salon was Anna Eynard-Lullin, Alville's *Anna Eynard-Lullin et l'époque des Congrès et des Révolutions* (1955), 177–178.

The tour of the battlefield is in *Wiener Zeitung*, October 11, along with many diaries, such as Matthias Franz Perth's *Wiener Kongresstagebuch, 1814–1815* (1981), October 11, 1814, 52. Castlereagh interview with tsar comes from his letter to Liverpool, October 14, 1814 *BD*, CXVI, 206–208. Memorandum attached, and printed, is in *Le Congrès de Vienne et les traités de 1815* (1864), II, 291–293. Phrases "moral duty" and "happiness of the Poles" come from his letter to Liverpool that day just cited, 207. Castlereagh had first learned that his information was correct, and the tsar demanded the Duchy of Warsaw, with only a few exceptions, in his first audience with the tsar, Castlereagh to Liverpool, October 2, 1814, *BD*, CXI, 197. Differences in rank troubled Castlereagh, a follow-up letter that same day, *BD*, CXII, 199–200. The memorandum: Viscount Castlereagh to the Emperor of All the Russias, 208–209, also *WSD*, IX, 329; for more on his view of Poland, see also Castlereagh to Liverpool, October 2, 1814, *BD*, CXI, 197–199, as well as Castlereagh's "First Memorandum on the Polish Question," *BD*, 209–210, and *WSD*, IX, 332. The interview made the rounds, Gentz, *Tagebücher*, 318, and Talleyrand's overview, Talleyrand to Louis XVIII, October 17, 1814, *TLC*, 56–60. The tsar over to Princess Bagration on the thirteenth, Siber to Hager, October 14, 1814, *DCV*, I, no. 361, and report to Hager, the same day, no. 368.

Many sources, including Stein's *Tagebuch*, describe the Polish question as paralyzing the conference, undated entry from early November 1814, *Briefe und amtliche Schriften*, V (1964), 333–334. The description of Poland as the "aching tooth" comes from Maurice Paléologue's *The Enigmatic Tsar* (1938), 222. For more on background of this question, see notes to chapter 1. Talleyrand's views on Saxony can be found in many of his letters from the congress: Saxony as significant for both legitimacy and balance of power, Talleyrand to Louis XVIII, January 6, 1815, *TLC*, 250–251; the threat of a strong Prussia: "who can foresee the consequences . . . ," *TLC*, October 17, 1814, 63. Talleyrand's allies in Germany, including Count Münster, who defended Saxony as it would preserve "the balance, perhaps even the existence of Germany," (1868) 61, and Count Münster's dispatches show that he generally agreed. Fear of rising Prussia shared by many others, from the king of Bavaria to Archduke Johann, who often commented on the question in his diary. Russia and Prussia would be less bold in front of a congress, for example, Talleyrand to Louis XVIII, September 29, 1814, 9. Saxe-Coburg defense is in Kraehe, *Metternich's German Policy* (1963–1983), II, 266, along with Talleyrand's letters to king Louis XVIII, December 7 and 15, 1814, and *Memoirs*, II (1891), 355 and 363–365.

Castlereagh working with Metternich and Hardenberg to oppose Russia, Castlereagh to Liverpool, October 9, 1814 *BD*, CXIII, 201. Hardenberg's letter of October 10 is in HHSA, StK, Kongressakten Kart 7, and Castlereagh's response the following day in Angeberg (1864), II, 274–276, with Hardenberg's comments in turn from his diary also on the eleventh, *Tagebücher und autobiographische Aufzeichnungen* (2000), 801. Gentz translated Castlereagh's letter into French, and his critique of its "miserable reasoning" *(Armseligkeiten)* is in his *Tagebücher*, October 12, 1814, (1873), 317–318, as well as his account to Prince Metternich the next day, *Briefe von und ab Friedrich von Gentz*, ed. Friedrich Carl Wittichen and Ernst Salzer (1913), III, 303. Danish member Rosenkrantz, who also saw the letter, was not impressed, November 16, 1814, *Journal du Congrès de Vienne 1814–1815* (1953), 80–81. "Metternich is in love," Talleyrand to the Duchess of Courland, October 2, 1814, *TLI*, 40. Gentz's frustrations in trying to discuss crisis over Saxony and words on Metternich's liaison, *Tagebücher*, October 14, 1814, 319.

Chapter 12. Six Weeks of Hell

Chapter title comes from Metternich's letter to his wife, September 19, 1814, Enno E. Kraehe, *Metternich's German Policy* (1963–1983), II, 124, and Karl von Nostitz's words from an undated diary entry in December 1814, *Leben und Briefwechsel* (1848), 131. Description of the weather on the day of the festival comes from Jean-Gabriel Eynard, October 18, 1814, *Au Congrès de Vienne: journal de Jean-Gabriel Eynard* (1914–1924), I, 41; Carl Bertuch's *Tagebuch vom Wiener Kongress* (1916), 35; and Caroline Pichler, *Denkwürdigkeiten aus meinem Leben* (1914), III, 33. My reference to the summer holding out refers to late September through October 21, and does not include August, which had many rainy days; gray, overcast skies; and frequent thunderstorms. This information comes from a number of diarists who regularly reported the weather.

The words on the hat shops come from Hilde Spiel's *The Congress of Vienna: An Eyewitness Account*, trans. Richard H. Weber (1968), 96. Metternich's intentions and the emperor's orders are in McGuigan, *Metternich and the Duchess* (1975), 365–367. Schwarzenberg's complaints on last-minute change, letter to his wife, October 15, 1814, is in Johann Friedrich Novák, ed. *Briefe des Feldmarschalls Fürsten Schwarzenberg an seine Frau, 1799–1816* (1913), 408. The celebration was described as "military celebration" Hardenberg, October 18, 1814, *Tagebücher und autobiographische Aufzeichnungen* (2000), 802, and Stein, who watched from the balcony of the pavilion, noted how it left the tsar annoyed and somewhat disturbed, October 18, 1814, *Briefe und amtliche Schriften*, V (1964), 324.

The handrailings are in Heinrich Graf zu Stolberg-Wernigerode's *Tagebuch über meinen Aufenthalt in Wien zur Zeit des Congresses*, October 18, 1814 (2004), 64. The pyramid is in Carl Bertuch, *Tagebuch vom Wiener Kongress* (1916), 35, and the "*waffenobelisken*" and trophies are also in Schönholz's *Traditionen zur Charakteristik Österreichs, seines Staats-und Volkslebens unter Franz I* (1914), II, 105–106. The carpets, the flowers, and the celebration of High Mass are in Comte Auguste de La Garde-Chambonas, *Anecdotal Recollections of the Congress of Vienna* (1902), 25–28. The setting for the Festival of Peace can be found in many other sources, for example, Countess Bernstorff's *Ein Bild aus der Zeit von 1789 bis 1835: Aus ihren Aufzeichnungen* (1896), I, 158–159, Countess Lulu Thürheim's *Mein Leben: Erinnerungen aus Österreichs Grosser Welt 1788–1819* (1913), II, 107–109. Stolberg-Wernigerode was not impressed with the trophies, though he praised the food (2004), 63–64. The menu appears, for example, in Matthias Franz Perth's *Wiener Kongresstagebuch 1814–1815* (1981), 58–60 and, with some variation, in the *Wiener Zeitung* the following day, with more description of the event following in its edition for October 21. The toast and the sergeants serving the food are in Gregor Dallas's *The Final Act: The Roads to Waterloo* (1997), 206. Countess Edling's praise of the tsar's toast is in *Mémoires* (1888), 182. The size of the Vienna garrison at celebration is in Enno E. Kraehe's *Metternich's German Policy* (1963–1983), II, 196.

The setting for Metternich's party, including balloon ascent and temples to Apollo, Athena, and Mars, are in *Programme de la fête de la paix pour être exécuté dans les jardins de son excellence le prince Metternich auprès de Vienne*, which can be found in *NP*, I, 266–268. Other views of the illumination and the tents at the party are in Eynard's journal, October 19, 1814 (1914–1924), I, 42, as well as Bernstorff (1896), I, 158–159. Reference to palace in *1,001 Nights* was made by Anna Eynard, Alville *Anna Eynard-Lullin et l'époque des congrès et des révolutions* (1955), 181; and Karl August Varnhagen von Ense likewise praised its magnificence, *Denkwürdigkeiten des Eignen Lebens* (1987), II, 599. Talleyrand did not attend the commemoration of the Battle of Leipzig, of course, because it celebrated a victory over France, even if Napoleonic France, but he did not miss Metternich's Peace Ball. Nor did Gentz, who noted the magnificence and his late departure in his diary, October 18, 1814, in *Tagebücher* (1873), I, 320–321. That Metternich's festival surpassed everything one guest had seen in France, including under Napoleon, is from Jean-Gabriel Eynard's journal, October 19, 1814 (1914–1924), I, 43. A different view of the party is in Countess Edling *Mémoires* (1888), 181–182. Metternich's garden at the time of the congress was much larger than today, stretching all the way to today's Russian embassy. His home is now the Italian embassy in Vienna, and special thanks to H. E. Raffaele Berlenghi, Ambassador, Patrizia Fusco, and Cristina Morrone for the wonderful tour.

Breakfast with Metternich the morning after the Festival comes from Gentz's *Tagebücher*, October 19, 1814 (1873), 321. Alexander at Metternich's Peace Ball, with comments on too many diplomats present, report to Hager, October 20, 1814, *DCV*, I, no. 457. Repeating the words, too, when he noticed that Archduke Johann was in the vicinity, Archduke Johann observed, October 18, 1814, *Aus dem Tagebuche Erzherzog Johanns von Oesterreich, 1810–1815*, ed. Franz, Ritter von Krones (1891), 178–179. Metternich's "our child," for example, *MSB*, January 21, 1814, 185, and six days later, 196. Armfelt as "a scoundrel," March 25, 1814, 237–238, and his death reported by the *Wiener Zeitung*, September 25, 1814. Troubles that autumn are in McGuigan, *Metternich and the Duchess* (1975), 359–361. Gentz still working hard on this case, as made clear by his reference to Wratislaw, who served as the attorney recruited for the case, October 20, 1814, *MSB*, 321. The Talleyrand-Metternich conversation, with the question "How have you the courage to put Russia like a belt?" is not from September 23 [Nicolson, *The Congress of Vienna: A Study in Allied Unity, 1812–1822* (1946), 156], the day Talleyrand arrived in Vienna, but October, and his words advising Austria to resist the Prussian takeover of Saxony, "justice, propriety, even safety," Talleyrand to Louis XVIII, October 19, 1814, *TLC*, 72.

Dallas is one of the few historians of the congress to deal with the Duchess of Sagan in his valuable book, but there is some confusion in his account: Sagan did not receive Metternich's letter on the twentieth and then invite the tsar over for breakfast [*The Final Act: The Roads to Waterloo* (1997), 209]. That breakfast had been set up two days before she received the note, when she encountered the tsar at the Russian ambassador Stackelberg's ball. It was the duchess's request for an audience with the tsar at that ball that in part prompted Metternich to write his letter. The duchess did not receive that letter on the twentieth, either (209); Metternich wrote it in the early-morning hours after the ball, or the twenty-first, and she received it on the twenty-second at Count Zichy's ball. On the tsar-duchess of

Sagan's breakfast that morning, there is an anonymous report to Hager, November 1, 1814, no. 635, and no. 476. Metternich's letter, dated four in the morning, October 21, 1814, was published *MSB*, 267–269. Metternich's other difficult letter on Saxony is in Angeberg (1864), II, 316–320.

Metternich spoke to Gentz that day, October 22, of his "permanent breaking" with the duchess, *Tagebücher* (1873), I, 322. Gentz does not mention Saxon letter, and despite what some historians have asserted, it is probably because he did not know of it. Gentz was against this policy. For Gentz's view of this letter, see his *Denkschrift* written in February 1815, *NP*, II, 489. For more on background of Austria and Russia, see Gentz's *Denkschrift* in *NP*, II, 474–476, and the dispute over Switzerland, Nesselrode, *Autobiographie* in *Lettres et papiers du chancelier comte de Nesselrode, 1760–1850*, II, 108–109, Helen du Coudray's *Metternich* (1936), 139–141. The tsar's pledges to honor Swiss neutrality and assurances from Austria, Tsar Alexander I to La Harpe, January 3, 1814–December 22, 1813, La Harpe to Tsar Alexander, *Correspondance de Frédéric-César La Harpe et Alexander 1er* (1978–1979), II, 505. Tsar Alexander was said to have had an instant reaction or dislike to anything Metternich said, Archduke Johann, October 21, 1814, *Aus dem Tagebuche Erzherzog Johanns von Oesterreich, 1810–1815*, ed. Franz, Ritter von Krones (1891), 180. Talleyrand and Gentz speaking more and then dining together is clear from Gentz's diary, and many spy reports, such as unnamed agent to Hager, December 31, 1814, *DCV*, I, no. 1215. Later Gentz notes many gifts he received from delegates, including some 24,000 florins, on behalf of the king of France, *Tagebücher* (1873), I, 343. Gentz and Talleyrand were in agreement on many things, including Saxony.

My account of the plan to present the tsar with the opening of the congress draws on a series of letters in Castlereagh's correspondence, particularly the "First Memorandum on the Polish Question," *BD*, 209–210, Castlereagh to Liverpool, October 20, 1814, *BD*, CXVIII 211, and his follow-up on the twenty-fourth, XXIX, 212–213, along with the "The Memorandum on the Best Method of Handling the Polish Question," 213–215. Czartoryski's *The Memoirs of Prince Adam Czartoryski and His Correspondence with Alexander I*, ed. Adam Gielgud, I–II (1968), II, 284, along with the discussions in Webster, *The Foreign Policy of Castlereagh, 1812–1815: Britain and the Reconstruction of Europe* (1931), 347ff, and Kraehe, *Metternich's German Policy* (1982), II, 207ff. Talleyrand's critique of his colleagues, as well as the reference to tortoises, comes from a letter to the Duchess of Courland, October 31, 1814, *TLI*, 60. The dialogue between the tsar and Talleyrand, the evening of October 23, Talleyrand to Louis XVIII, October 25, 1814, *TLC*, 84–89, and the King's Ambassadors at the Congress to the Minister of Foreign Affairs, No. 8A, October 24, 1814, 274. Agent ** to Hager, October 26, 1814, *DCV*, I, no. 559. The tsar's threat about the king of Saxony was also related by a member of the Russian delegation, Stein, for example, in an undated entry before October 2, 1814, *Tagebuch*, in *Briefe und amtliche Schriften*, V (1964), 319. Talleyrand's thoughts on Poland and Saxony before meeting the tsar appear in Talleyrand to Louis XVIII, October 19, 1814, *TLC*, 75–76.

Metternich's words on the context for his interview with the tsar are in his *NP*, I, 326ff, and Gentz's view in *NP*, II, 482–483, as well as Castlereagh to Liverpool, November 11, 1814, *BD*, CXXVIII, 229, Talleyrand to Louis XVIII, October 31, 1814, *TLC*, 99–100, the latter reporting Tsar Alexander's shocking language, Metternich's "tone of revolt," and his state afterward. Metternich's comparison of the tsar to Napoleon is in Archduke Johann's diary, October 25, 1814, *Aus dem Tagebuche Erzherzog Johanns von Oesterreich 1810–1815*, ed. Franz, Ritter von Krones (1891), 181, and Metternich's declaration not to meet with him again in private, Gentz's memoir on the Congress, *Denkschrift*, *NP*, II, 483. Police agents reported Tsar Alexander wish for Metternich being sacked, Agent ** to Hager, October 28, 1814, *DCV*, I, no. 598. That Metternich sometimes seemed to treat the sovereigns frivolously was also a complaint of the king of Denmark, Nota to Hager, January 3, 1815, *DCV*, I, no. 1230. The tsar's threat to throw Metternich out the window, Eynard, October 28, 1814, *Journal* (1914), I, 73. Many Metternich biographers place the rumored Metternich-Alexander duel here, but this is not correct. The challenge to the duel, if it did happen, came later in December; see notes to chapter 19. The trip to Hungary, often misdated, began on the morning of the twenty-fourth. The tsar left no one in charge, Talleyrand to Louis XVIII, October 25, 1814, *TLC*, 93.

Chapter 13. Robinson Crusoe

The reference to *Clisson and Eugénie* comes from Andy Martin's *Napoleon the Novelist* (2000), 118–120, and Steven Englund's recent biography, *Napoleon: A Political Life* (2004). Englund was given access to some other parts of the work that previous Napoleonic scholars have not been able to see. The tsar's role in the selection of Elba and his offer to Napoleon after his abdication is in Norman Mackenzie, *The Escape from Elba: The Fall and Flight of Napoleon, 1814–1815* (1982), 14–15, 22, which is an invaluable resource for Napoleon's days on Elba. See also J. M. Thompson, *Napoleon Bonaparte* (1952), 391, August Fournier, *Napoleon the First: A Biography*, trans. Margaret Bacon Corwin and Arthur Dart Bissell (1903), 675–677 and F. M. Kircheisen *Napoleon* (1932), 674ff. Many, of course, saw Elba as a humiliation, for example, Princess Radziwill, *Forty-five Years of My Life (1770–1815)*, trans. A. R. Allinson (1912), 390. Metternich at Dijon, his opposition to the choice of Elba, and his prediction of war again within two years, *NP*, I, 198–201. For more on this situation, see also two of his letters to Emperor Francis, both dated April 11, 1814, and the emperor's responses, including his opposition to the tsar's plans, *NP*, II 469–472. On the Allied entry into Paris, with Emperor Francis remaining behind at Dijon, Palmer notes that the emperor preferred it that way, *Napoleon and Marie Louise: The Emperor's Second Wife* (2001), 170. The tsar's "theatrical generosity" is from Lord Stewart, Castlereagh's late arrival and refusal to sign, Mackenzie (1982), 25, as well as Norwood Young, *Napoleon in Exile: Elba* (1914), 49.

Elba as Napoleon's principality, and "full sovereignty and property" with two million annual revenue, are from Article III, and the money for his family in Article

VI. Napoleon also, importantly, renounced the French empire in the first article. *Le Congrès de Vienne et les traités de 1815* (1864), I, 148–151. Population, legends, and reference to the seedy port come from Mackenzie, *The Escape from Elba* (1982), 66–68. The population figures were also accepted at the time of the congress, as noted in the minutes of the second meeting of the Evaulations Committee, December 25, 1814, in Angeberg (1864), II, 566. The committee reached this number, actually, by a compromise estimate between two authorities (11,385 and 13,750). Café Buono Gusto and the wine are in Robert Christophe, *Napoleon on Elba*, trans. Len Ortzen (1964), 91. Resources of Elba are in Sir Neil Campbell journal, published in *Napoleon at Fontainebleau and Elba; Being a Journal of Occurrences in 1814–1815* (1869), 254. Richness of iron ore, with center at Rio, Mackenzie (1982), 65, Christophe (1964), 30 and 44, and salt warehouse, 21, and mines as the island's most profitable enterprise, Kircheisen (1932), 681. See also André Pons de l'Hérault, *Souvenirs et anecdotes de l'île d'Elba* (1897).

Turmoil on Elba, including the revolt and change in government, Captain Ussher, "Napoleon's Deportation to Elba," in *Napoleon's Last Voyages, being the Diaries of Admiral Sir Thomas Ussher, R.N., K.C.B. (on board the "Undaunted") and John R. Glover, Secretary to Rear Admiral Kockburn (on board the "Northumberland")* (1895), 48–49, Campbell (1869), 214. Firing at the *Undaunted* as it arrived, Mackenzie (1982), 63, Christophe (1964), 16–17, 26–27. French General Dalesme in charge, the Bourbon flag up for forty-eight hours, and narrowly escaped being British property, which would have made for an interesting development, Thompson (1952), 396. Napoleon's palace and throne, Mackenzie (1982), 73, and other similar references, found, for example, in Abbé de Pradt, *Congrès de Vienne* (1815), I, 216, or Count Molé, *The Life and Memoirs of Count Molé* (1781–1855), ed. Marquis de Noailles (1924), I, 205, as a throne without a nation as "simply four pieces of wood covered with a piece of velvet." The Prince de Ligne's words on Robinson Crusoe are in many sources, including Comte Auguste de La Garde-Chambonas, *Anecdotal Recollections of the Congress of Vienna* (1902), 14, and Pictet de Rochemont, *Biographie, travaux et correspondance diplomatique* (1892), 211. Palffy and Bigottini come from report to Hager, October 14, *DCV*, I, no. 415, and Karl von Nostitz, in an undated entry from the end of December, *Leben und Briefwechsel* (1848), 140, while the ballerina's confinement some nine months later in Paris, *The Diary of Frances Lady Shelley (1787–1817)* (1912), 109. The offending busts of Tsar Alexander, Agent O to Hager, October 19, 1814, DCV, I, no. 450. Count Anstett, rumored to be fond of his drink, Niels Rosenkrantz, October 6, 1814, *Journal du Congrès de Vienne, 1814–1815* (1953), 40, was another good source, and he was followed closely by the spies. Josephine Wolters in the Burg, report to Hager, October 12, 1814, *DCV*, I, no. 346. She was coming "almost every evening" to Wolkonsky, Goehausen to Hager, October 16, 1814, DCV, I, no. 396, and still observed sneaking into the palace, report, October 22, 1814, no. 477. Emperor on Wolters, Hager's report, October 25, 1814, no. 498.

The story of the game of blindman's buff in the salon and the following trouble almost ending in a duel, October 11, 1814, *DCV*, I, no. 337, Rzewuska, *Mémoires de la comtesse Rosalie Rzewuska (1788–1865)* (1939) I, 254–255, and Archduke Johann's diary, October 9, 1814, *Aus dem Tagebuche Erzherzog Johanns von Oesterreich, 1810-1815*, ed. *Franz, Ritter von Krones* (1891), 176. More background on the "personal rivalry" of the crown princes is in Countess Bernstorff's *Ein Bild aus der Zeit von 1789 bis 1835: Aus ihren Aufzeichnungen* (1896), I, 151. The duel stopped, Rechbert to his father, undated, Le Comte de Goerz, no. 343, and Field Marshal Prince Schwarzenberg to his wife, October 8, 1814, Johann Friedrich Novák, ed., *Briefe des Feldmarschalls Fürsten Schwarzenberg an seine Frau, 1799–1816* (1913), 408. The Bellio affair is in many spy reports around the time of seizure: *DCV*, I, nos. 443–446. See also intercepted letter from Mavrojény, October 22, 1814, no. 487. Gentz learned of Prince Bellio's expulsion for copying his letters at the Peace Ball, *Tagebücher*, October 18, 1814 (1873), 320–321. Abduction rumor, Mackenzie (1982), 163. Hints of abduction were found in the French embassy, for example, Marioti to Dalberg, October 5, 1814, *GPWK*, 219–220, and appearing also in *DCV*, I, no. 563. The emperor ordered closer surveillance. See notes to chapter 18.

Carl Bertuch noted that cooler "November weather" had finally arrived, *Tagebuch vom Wiener Kongress*, October 25, 1814, 38, and Stolberg-Wernigerode noted the pouring rain that day, *Tagebuch über meinen Aufenthalt in Wien zur Zeit des Congresses* (2004), 78—this supported, too, by others who regularly noted the weather, for instance, Gentz, *Tagebuch*, and San Marzan, *Diario*. "I am no longer the man I was the day before yesterday," McGuigan (1975), 381. Rumors of the tsar's pressure on the duchess made their rounds, for example, Rosenkrantz, October 27, 1814 (1953), 54. Metternich asked her not to speak about him to the tsar, *MSB*, October 31, 1814, 269. "I am no longer astonished" comes from his letter, November 1, 1814, *MSB*, 270.

Date for the departure to Hungary often confused, though should be October 24 as many diaries confirm. Just before leaving, Emperor Francis ordered all spy reports to be sent to Prince Metternich, Emperor to Hager, October 23, 1814, *DCV*, I, no. 475. One Hungarian newspaper account of the stay was excerpted by the *Wiener Zeitung*, November 1, and again November 4, 1814. The volatile trip is clear from many sources, for instance, King's Ambassadors at the Congress to the Minister of Foreign Affairs, no. 9A, October 31, 1814, 285, Alexander's words on Metternich, and Emperor Francis on leaving work to the ministers, Talleyrand to King Louis XVIII, October 31, 1814, *TLC*, 100–101, and Stein also reported the tsar's criticisms of the Austrian foreign minister in his diary, October 29–November 7, 1814, *Briefe und amtliche Schriften*, V (1964), 330. The trouble between the sovereigns noted by Stein, as well as the report to Hager, the same day, *DCV*, I, no. 626. Tsar Alexander blaming the ministers, and hoping to settle matters among sovereigns themselves, Castlereagh to Liverpool, November 11, 1814, *BD*, CXXVIII, 230. Bavaria's Wrede also informed Rosenkrantz, October 30, 1814, *Journal*, 56. The tsar's time with beautiful ladies in Hungary, Agent ** to Hager, November 6, 1814, *DCV*, I, no. 692. Buda and Pest are described in contemporary travel account of the same year, published in 1818, by Bright, *Travels from Vienna through Lower*

Hungary with some remarks on the state of Vienna during the congress in the year 1814, 207ff.

Tsar Alexander and Emperor Francis exchange on Metternich and their deteriorating relations, that made some fear that the tsar would soon leave Vienna, Eynard (1914–1924), I, 86–87. Tsar Alexander wanted Metternich to be sacked, and his plans for taking the matter up with Francis, Agent ** to Hager, October 28, 1814, *DCV*, I, no. 598. Rosenkrantz also heard of the tsar's attempts to overthrow Metternich, his information coming from one of Metternich's assistants, Hudelist, *Journal*, November 6, 1814 (1953), 67. Castlereagh also denounced the tsar's diplomacy and "his habit to be his own minister" comes from a letter to Liverpool, November 5, 1814, *BD*, CXXV, 222. Many agreed, including Count Münster in his dispatch, November 27, 1814, *Political Sketches of the State of Europe, 1814–1867: Containing Count Ernst Münster's Despatches to the Prince Regent from the Congress of Vienna* (1868), 190. King of Prussia's "blind attachment" to the tsar, and the Prussian officials hoping for another approach, even if it meant yielding on Saxony, Talleyrand rightly suspected in a letter to Louis XVIII, October 31, 1814, *TLC*, 103. King of Prussia nickname as tsar's "valet de chambre," Agent ** to Hager, November 14, 1814, *DCV*, I, no. 768.

CHAPTER 14. DINNER WITH THE TSAR

Public opinion about the congress was falling low for many reasons: Frustration and confusion about its ending and beginning, report to Hager, October 15, *DCV*, I, no. 387, and slow progress, Piquot to X, intercepted, October 19, 1814, no. 452, just one of many reports expressing this sentiment. Agent B on criticism of too many parties and preference for different city, October 25, 1814, no. 533. The king of Prussia's displeasure at the congress, and words "we seem only to be here . . ." cited by San Marzan, *Diario*, October 22, 1814, lix. The French plenipotentiary Dalberg, for one, blamed both Metternich and the tsar, Agent **, October 7, 1814, no. 304. Metternich's fall was predicted, and desired by many, Agent ** reported to Hager October 15, 1814, no. 384. Agent ** was particularly interested in this question, and filed many reports on the fluctuations in public opinion.

On the imminent disintegration of congress and fear of war, report to Hager, October 20, 1814, *DCV*, I, no. 459. Departures of sovereigns already rumored, intercepted letter from Bellio, October 15, 1814, no. 446, and the fear of no congress at all, Eynard, October 29, 1814, *Journal*, 75. Conditions worsening, Eynard, November 3, 1814 (1914–1924), 86, Rosenkrantz, November 2, 1814, *Journal*, 61. "No one knows what to believe, or who to believe," Agent Nota to Hager, October 23, 1814, no. 496. Talleyrand's frustration with Castlereagh can be seen in many letters at this time, such as Talleyrand to King Louis XVIII, October 17, 1814, *TLC*, 60–61, Metternich, Castlereagh and Prussia in his letter to the Duchess of Courland, October 19, 1814, *TLI*, 58.

Castlereagh claimed to be aware of the risks of his Prussian policy, Castlereagh to Wellington, October 25, 1814, *BD*, CXXII, 218–219, though he placed confidence in the Prussian cabinet, Castlereagh to Wellington, October 25, 1814, *BD*, CXXII, 218, and also *WSD*, IX, 372. He also brushed aside the risks of a strong Prussia as a "secondary danger" relative to the threat of renewed French aggression, Castlereagh to Wellington, October 1, 1814, *CC*, X, 144–145, and whole letter, 142–145. The words "France need never dread a German league . . ." came from Castlereagh's letter to Wellington, October 25, 1814, *CC*, X, 175.

Talleyrand urging Castlereagh to open the congress, and how that would stop the tsar, comes from Talleyrand to Louis XVIII, October 25, 1814, *TLC*, 91. Metternich's conference with Talleyrand, and the meeting of the Committee of Eight on the thirtieth of October, Talleyrand to Louis XVIII, October 31, 1814, *TLC*, 108; its duration, Gentz, *Tagebücher*, October 30, 1814 (1873), I, 325. See also *Le Congrès de Vienne et les traités de 1815* (1864), II, 358ff, with Nesselrode's objection on 362, and a discussion of this meeting in Kraehe's *Metternich's German Policy* (1963–1983), II, 227–228. Intrigues hatched at masked ball, and not all romantic affairs, Baronne du Montet (1904), noted under the entry November 6, 1814, 113. The bribery scene is discussed by McGuigan, *Metternich and the Duchess* (1975), 391. The attempt is, of course, like many intrigues, debatable. The English delegate Cooke is our best source for it, *WSD*, IX, 473. Other tantalizing though by no means conclusive references are found here and there, including Stein, who was then working for the Russian delegation and noted the tsar's attempt to use the Duchess of Sagan to influence Metternich, in his entry in his *Tagebuch* for the period October 29–November 7, 1814, *Briefe und amtliche Schriften*, V (1964), 331.

Talleyrand voiced suspicions that Castlereagh was not following the goals of Britain's prince regent, Talleyrand to Louis XVIII, October 25, 1814, 91–92. Confirmation from the Duke of Wellington, Louis XVIII sent back in a dispatch dated two days later, 96, and a longer report, November 9, 1814, 122–126. He was correct, as seen in the later correspondence between Liverpool and Castlereagh. Webster called Castlereagh's move "direct defiance," *The Foreign Policy of Castlereagh, 1812–1815: Britain and the Reconstruction of Europe* (1931), 371, and Rory Muir, *Britain and the Defeat of Napoleon, 1807–1815* (1996), 337–338.

The early-November dinner was described by Talleyrand, who received his information from the tsar's adviser Czartoryski, November 12, 1814, 127–128, Rosenkrantz, November 11, 1814 (1953), 73–74, noting the tsar's treatment of Hardenberg in the "most violent manner" with reference, here, to the fears for the chancellor's health. His information came from members of both Russian delegation (Razumovsky) and the Austrian (Hudelist), November 6, 1814, 66–67. Stein likewise reported how the tsar had hurt Hardenberg, *Tagebuch*, in an undated entry between October 29, and November 7, 1814, *Briefe und amtliche Schriften*, V (1964), 332. "It is not enough" is in McGuigan (1975), 394. Hardenberg's words on the king being wrong, November 6, 1814, *Tagebücher und autobiographische Aufzeichnungen* (2000), 804, and his usual "charming conversation" at dinner, Countess Bernstorff, who admired her uncle, *Ein Bild aus der Zeit von 1789 bis 1835: Aus ihren Aufzeichnungen* (1896), I, 163. Metternich's denial of the tsar's accusation and the scene are also McGuigan, *Metternich and the Duchess* (1975), 393–394, and 395. Gentz learned of the result, a Prussian move, or what he called "treachery" on the stairway at Lord Stewart's ball on Monday, November 7, *Tagebücher*, 327–328. The story was confirmed by Metternich two days later, November 9, 328.

CHAPTER 15. PURSUING PHANTOMS

Baron Franz von Gärtner's intercepted letter to Count Erbach is in *DCV*, II, no. 2396. Napoleon's first night at the town hall, and hunt for a house, along with the smells, Robert Christophe, *Napoleon on Elba*, trans. Len Ortzen (1964), 38. Il Mulini, and the motives for selection, Norman Mackenzie, *The Escape from Elba: The Fall and Flight of Napoleon, 1814–1815* (1982), 77–78, and Christophe (1964), 42–43, 53–55. Impatience to move in, during the renovations, Christophe, 55. Wet paint and other surroundings, André Pons de l'Hérault, *Souvenirs et anecdotes de l'île d'Elbe* (1897), 147; Paul Gruyer, *Napoleon King of Elba* (1906), 63. The heat, or "natural sun-traps," is in J. M. Thompson, *Napoleon Bonaparte* (1952), 397. Napoleon's feelings of insecurity on the island, August Fournier, *Napoleon the First: A Biography*, trans. Margaret Bacon Corwin and Arthur Dart Bissell (1903), 680, and Mackenzie (1982), 77.

Napoleon's fear of pirates was noted by Captain Thomas Ussher, "Napoleon's Deportation to Elba," published in *Napoleon's Last Voyages, being the Diaries of Admiral Sir Thomas Ussher, R.N., K.C.B. (on board the "Undaunted") and John R. Glover, Secretary to Rear Admiral Kockburn (on board the "Northumberland")* (1895), 84, and the journal of Neil Campbell, published in *Napoleon at Fontainebleau and Elba; Being a Journal of Occurrences in 1814–1815* (1869), 156. The Allied powers had, of course, also pledged to use "good offices" to make sure pirates respected Napoleon's flag and territory, in Article V of the Treaty of Fontainebleau, but Napoleon was skeptical of their intent to honor it. Napoleon's fear, too, was that pirates might be paid by enemies to abduct him, Mackenzie (1982), 164. Napoleon's Guard arrive Campbell (1869), 241. Ussher (1895), 76–78. Mackenzie (1982), 93–94, 97, and also Christophe, who interviewed an old woman who heard the story of their arrival from her grandfather (1964), 76–77.

Drouot, Cambronne, and Bertrand's views on Elba, Mackenzie (1982), 137, Drouot as "the Wise Man of the Grand Army," Christophe (1964), 15, and more on character, 70–71, along with Bertrand and Cambronne here as well as on 77–78. Cambronne as "a desperate uneducated ruffian," Campbell (1869), 370. The Elban navy is in Mackenzie (1982), 98–99. Napoleon's letters to Marie Louise at Vienna, and also use of General Bertrand and Méneval, III, 285–289. "Each day there was a fresh story" comes from Méneval (1894), III, 319, with the empress's writing habits and views expressed in five selected letters to Méneval, III, 294–300. More on Napoleon and Marie Louise at this time, 217ff, her love for him, 220; daily life at Schönbrunn can be followed in many police reports that autumn until the surveillance was suspended in early December, Agent ** to Hager, December 2,

1814, I, no. 958 (see also Hager to Emperor, November 30, 1814, I, no. 927), though they soon resumed again. Marie Louise's riding, learning Italian, and drawing, among other things, in Méneval (1894), III, 279–283, and 314ff. Neipperg chosen as her escort, Méneval (1894), III, 282, and police agents noting Neipperg as an excellent choice, Agent ** to Hager, October 24, 1814, *DCV*, I, no. 499. Neipperg's instructions, Castelot, 513, and "any means" clearly included physical, Mackenzie (1982), 131. Neipperg and Marie Louise affair by late August, Mackenzie, 133–134, or late September, Palmer (2001), 188. Description of the general, including black eye patch and Hungarian uniform, 291–292. "Prince Metternich's great agent in seduction" Méneval, (1894), III, 398. On Count Neipperg, an article on the occasion of his death appeared in *Revue Britannique*, February 1829, reprinted in the appendix to Méneval (1894), III, 509ff. The Prince de Ligne as one of the most frequent visitors, Baron Méneval (1894), III, 313. Description of the former king of Rome is in many sources, including Carl Bertuch's *Tagebuch*, November 19, 1814 (1916), 57. Little Napoleon as a stubborn child, reported by Dr. Frank, Agent ** to Hager, December 24, 1814, no. 1141.

Metternich's masked ball on November 8, *MSB*, November 8, 1814, 328. Description of the décor and the switch of masks, McGuigan (1975), 397, the Venetian coats in San Marzan, November 8, 1814, lxi, and the dresses, the ornaments in hair, and Lady Castlereagh's costume are in Thürheim, *Mein Leben: Erinnerungen aus Österreichs Grosser Welt, 1788–1819* (1913), II, 109. Other costumes, including an English jockey, Stolberg-Wernigerode heard from friends who had been invited, *Tagebuch über meinen Aufenthalt in Wien zur Zeit des Congresses* (2004), 91. The evening seemed magical to Carl Bertuch (1916), 50. Humboldt missing the ball, letter to Caroline, November 9, 1814, Anna von Sydow, ed., *Wilhelm und Caroline von Humboldt in ihren Briefen* (1910), IV, 411. "Everything is still so completely changed . . ." *MSB*, 258, though not in July as listed, but rather the autumn, as McGuigan correctly pointed out (1975), no. 70, 546 and translated, 381. "My health: there is no question of it," Metternich to the Duchess of Sagan, November 1, 1814, *MSB*, 270, and McGuigan (1975), 388–389.

Italy under Napoleon, see Michael Broers, *The Napoleonic Empire in Italy, 1796–1814* (2005), as well as Rath's *The Fall of the Napoleonic Kingdom of Italy (1814)* (1941), and Murat, *Jean Tulard* (1999). Napoleon's looting is in Dorothy Mackay Quynn's "The Art Confiscations of the Napoleonic Wars," *AHR*, vol. 50, no. 3 (April, 1945), 450; Paul Schroeder's "Napoleon's Foreign Policy: A Criminal Enterprise," *Journal of Military History*, vol. 54 (199), 147–161; and Charles Saunier's *Les Conquêtes Artistiques de la révolution et de l'empire: reprises et abandons des alliés en 1815* (1902). My account of the Prussian occupation is based on several sources: Saxon minister waiting at French embassy with news, Talleyrand to Louis XVIII, November 17, 1814, 149. Prince Repnin's declaration, November 8, 1814, *Le Congrès de Vienne et les traités de 1815*, II, 413–414. Prussian seizure as a "scandalous transaction," King's Ambassadors at the Congress to the Minister of Foreign Affairs, no. 13A, November 17, 1814, *TLC*, 317–318.

Talleyrand on the "last excrement" is in Georg Nørregaard's *Danmark og den Wienerkongressen 1814–1815* (1948), 118. Rumors of this surfaced in Vienna, in many spy reports and intercepted letters from late October, particularly from the Swedish delegation (468, 486, 546–548, 506). The king of Saxony had declared his intention not to yield any of his territory, November 4, 1814, *Le Congrès de Vienne et les traités de 1815*, II, 401–403. Wrede on Saxony loss as "precursor to the inevitable ruin of Bavaria," report to Hager, November 26, 1814, *DCV*, I, no. 900. Effects of Prussian march into Saxony on Metternich and Castlereagh, including the absolute wording when "purely conditional," Talleyrand to Louis XVIII, November 17, 1814, *TLC*, 150.

CHAPTER 16. THE LAST JOUST

"The Congress seemed" comes from Countess Bernstorff's *Ein Bild aus der Zeit von 1789 bis 1835: Aus ihren Aufzeichnungen* I (1896), 178. Beethoven's personality, walking habits, and rushing to piano come from G. R. Marek's *Beethoven: Biography of a Genius* (1970), 160, and more on his personality in Lewis Lockwood, *Beethoven: The Music and the Life* (2003), 333–335. Frida Knight, *Beethoven and the Age of Revolution* (1973), and Groves, II, 354–394, esp. 389–392. Some valuable studies on Beethoven's music at the congress are Ingrid Fuch's "The Glorious Moment—Beethoven and the Congress of Vienna" in Villumsen Krog, ed., *Danmark og Den Dansende Wienerkongres: Spillet om Danmark*/ Denmark and the Dancing Congress of Vienna (Copenhagen, 2002), as well as Otto Biba's article in the same collection, and Wilhelm Freiherrn von Weckbecker, "Die Musik zur Zeit des Wiener Congresses," in Leisching (1898), 273–287. Beethoven's "From the Emperor to the bootblack," and the changing concept of genius is in Paul Johnson, *The Birth of the Modern: World Society, 1815–1830* (1991), 106, and 117–118. Visitors already having to shout can be seen, for example, when Wenzel Tomascheck visited Beethoven that fall, the account printed in Hamburger, ed., *Beethoven: Letters, Journals and Conversations* (1960), 120. His notorious untidiness is illustrated by the fact that just a few months before, Beethoven was writing to ask to borrow a copy of the *Fidelio* because he wanted to revise it for a performance at the Court Theater in May. He could not locate his own copy. Letter to Count Moritz Lichnowksy, January or February 1814, in Emily Anderson, ed., *The Letters of Beethoven*, I (1961), 444. Reference to congress breaking down is rampant. Agent ** predicted that the Vienna Congress would likely end in war, report to Hager, November 24, 1814, *DCV*, I, no. 870.

Baronne du Montet's words on the kings in Vienna come from her *Souvenirs 1785–1866* (1904), 114, and the popularity of hunts that autumn is clear from the diary of Matthias Franz Perth, a young official on the Forestry Commission, *Wiener Kongresstagebuch, 1814–1815* (1981). "Barbarity of a bullfight" comes from Richard Bright's *Travels from Vienna through Lower Hungary with some remarks on the state of Vienna during the congress in the year 1814* (1818), 19. The hunt and the dimensions of the "hunting arena" are in Freiherr von Bourgoing's *Vom Wiener Kongress: Zeit- und Sittenbilder* (1943), 177. Henrich Graf zu Stolberg-Wernigerode elaborated on the animals at the hunt, though the numbers vary somewhat, *Tagebuch über meinen Aufenthalt in Wien zur Zeit des Congresses* (2004), November 10, 1814, 92. *Wiener Zeitung* noted the court outing on November 11, 1814, and Agent ** reported back to Hager, November 12, 1814, *DCV*, I, no.748. Jean-Gabriel Eynard's description and assessment is from *Au Congrès de Vienne: journal de Jean-Gabriel Eynard* (1914–1924), I, 115–116.

Tolstoy on Genoa, *War and Peace*, trans. Rosemary Edmonds (1982), 3, and Hannah Alice Straus, *The Attitude of the Congress of Vienna Toward Nationalism in Germany, Italy and Poland* (1949), 89 and 92, and Guglielmo Ferrero, *The Reconstruction of Europe: Talleyrand and the Congress of Vienna, 1814–1815* (1941), 206–207. Bentinck's claim against orders, John Rosselli, *Lord William Bentinck: The Making of a Liberal Imperialist, 1774–1839* (1974), 67, 176ff. The Protocol for the meeting on Genoa is in Angeberg (1864), II, 424–427, as well as Gentz, *Tagebücher*, November 13, 1814, 330, San Marzan, *Diario*, same day, lxi, or Labrador, *Mélanges sur la vie privée et publique* (1849), 46–47, and more background, La Harpe to Alexander, November 15, 1814, II, 602. Castlereagh's views are in his letter to Liverpool, November 21, 1814, *BD*, CXXXI, 237–238. Frustration that the Republic of Genoa had "finally perished at the murderous thrusts of ambition and shocking injustices of the monarchs," report to Hager, November 15, *DCV*, no. 774. The Marquis de Brignoles's formal protest, December 10, is in Angeberg (1864), II, 510–511.

The first meeting of the Swiss Committee, November 14, 1814, is in Angeberg (1864), II, 430, and the breakup of the German Committee two days later, II, 438–339. Humboldt's words on the chaos, letter to his wife Caroline, November 9, 1814, *Wilhelm und Caroline von Humboldt in ihren Briefen*, ed. Anna von Sydow (1910), IV, 412–413. Importance of Saxony at time of Carousel is seen in Comte Auguste de La Garde-Chambonas, *Anecdotal Recollections of the Congress of Vienna* (1902), 44, as well as Count Münster, who at that point regarded Saxon affairs as having "more importance to the peace of Europe than those of Poland," November 27, 1814, Count George Herbert Münster, ed., *Political Sketches of the State of Europe, 1814–1867: Containing Count Ernst Münster's Despatches to the Prince Regent from the Congress of Vienna* (1868), 191.

Carl Bertuch's comments on the tournament are in his diary entry, November 23, 1814, *Tagebuch vom Wiener Kongress* (1916), 58–59, and the anticipation is reported, for example, by Agent ** to Hager, November 14, 1814, *DCV*, I, no. 768. Decorations also in Countess Edling, *Mémoires* (1888), 183–184, and Alexander Ivanovich Mikhailovsky-Danilevsky called it the most beautiful riding hall on the continent, Alexander Sapojnikov's "The Congress of Vienna in the Memoirs of a Russian Officer" in Ole Villumsen Krog (2002), 142. The Carousel tickets are in Comte Auguste de La Garde-Chambonas, *Anecdotal Recollections of the Congress of Vienna* (1902), 120; and Matthias Franz Perth's diary entry for November 22, 1814, *Wiener Kongresstagebuch, 1814–1815* (1981), 69. Talleyrand's conversation with Humboldt on the way to the Carousel is in Talleyrand to the Duchess of Courland, 24 November 1814, *TLI*, 74. Bright estimated audience at not over one thousand, *Travels from Vienna through Lower Hungary with Some Remarks on the State of Vienna During the Congress in the Year 1814* (1818), 14, but it should be remembered that he was describing one of the repeat performances in early December.

Descriptions of dresses, champions, the events, and audience, including papal and Turkish delegates, are also in La Garde-Chambonas, *Anecdotal Recollections* (1904), 162–173. Lady Castlereagh was often seen wearing the order of the garter, for example, in Baronne du Montet, *Souvenirs 1785–1866* (1904), 137; Rosalie Rzewuska, *Mémoires de la comtesse Rosalie Rzewuska (1788–1865)*, I, 253; and Edling, *Mémoires* (1888), 179. The list of ladies at the tournament is in the *Wiener Zeitung*, November 25, 1814. Dorothée's success that night was noted by Talleyrand to the Duchess of Courland, November 24, 1814, *TLI*, 74. Prussian words on the campaign come from an unnamed agent to Hager, November 24, 1814, *DCV*, I, no. 869. The Florentine banker estimate is also here, and comments on the mixture of the diamonds after the Carousel, Jean-Gabriel Eynard, *Au Congrès de Vienne: journal de Jean-Gabriel Eynard* (1914–1924), November 28, 1814, I, 161. "Storm of applause" is in Thürheim's *Mein Leben: Erinnerungen aus Österreichs Grosser Welt 1788–1819* (1913), II, 113.

The tsar was not there because he was in his suite, Agent L to Hager, November 27, 1814, *DCV*, I, no. 914. Alexander's sickness is in Agent Nota to Hager, November 20, 1814, *DCV*, I, no. 826; as well as Carl Bertuch's *Tagebuch* (1916), 54; and Pictet de Rochemont, November 19, 1814, *Biographie, travaux et correspondance diplomatique* (1892), 176. A poisoning rumor was noted already, too, by Niels Rosenkrantz, *Journal du Congrès de Vienne 1814–1815* (1953), November 10, 1814, 72. Eynard reported what he heard about the tsar's illness, dancing, and fatigue at a Castlereagh soiree, November 16, 1814 (1914–1924), I, 130, and according to Field Marshal Prince Schwarzenberg, Alexander had looked pale that night at the Palffy Ball, and some feared that he might pass out: letter to his wife, November 17, 1814, Johann Friedrich Novák, ed., *Briefe des Feldmarschalls Fürsten Schwarzenberg an seine Frau, 1799–1816* (1913), 411. The tsar was consumed by a "dance mania," Agent ** reported to Hager, November 14, 1814, *DCV*, I, no. 768.

The list of knights is in *Wiener Zeitung*, November 25, 1814. "Tantamount to a diploma" is in Hilde Spiel's *The Congress of Vienna: An Eyewitness Account*, trans. Richard H. Weber (1968), 105. The plume is in La Garde-Chambonas (1902), 167. The games are also in Rosalynd Pflaum's *By Influence and Desire: The True Story of Three Extraordinary Women—The Grand Duchess of Courland and Her Daughters* (1984), 232–235, and Dorothy Guis McGuigan's *Metternich and the Duchess* (1975), 407–409. Other maneuvers, such as dipping the lances, are in Thürheim, *Mein Leben: Erinnerungen aus Österreichs Grosser Welt 1788–1819* (1913), II, 113. King of Württemberg as "five feet of height and six of girth" is in Eynard's journal entry for October 19, 1814 (1914–1924), I, 46 and his table, for example, Thürheim (1913), II, 114. The number of guests at the masked ball afterward was also estimated at twenty-five hundred, *Wiener Zeitung*, November 25,

1814. The Festivals Committee gave repeat performances of the Carousel for the tsar on first of December, and again on the fifth.

CHAPTER 17. "THE GLORIOUS MOMENT"

Resentment at congress and phrase "eat your enemy" come from unnamed agent to Hager, December 27, 1814, *DCV* I no. 1172. Disputes over precedence are in countless sources, for example, Gaëtan de Raxis de Flassan's *Histoire du Congrès de Vienne* (1829), I, 295ff. The Spanish and French carriage incident is in Harold Nicolson's *The Congress of Vienna: A Study in Allied Unity, 1812–1822* (1946), 216–217, as well as his *Diplomacy* (1955), 179–180. Questions of the Precedents Committee are in Angeberg (1864), III, 934–935 and 939–940 and discussion, too, from the chair of the commission, Labrador, *Mélanges sur la vie privée et publique* (1849), 50–51.

"To meet three or four kings" comes from Talleyrand to Louis XVIII, November 6, 1814, *TLC*, 119, and others agreed, like San Marzan, January 28, 1815, *Diario*, lxx, and Edling, *Mémoires* (1888), 166–167. The reference to almost confusing the king of Prussia is in Eynard, *Journal*, January 10, 1815, I, 251. The meetings at the Empress of Austria are in Comte Auguste de La Garde-Chambonas, *Anecdotal Recollections of the Congress of Vienna* (1902), 92, and Hager to Emperor, December 10, 1814, *DCV*, I, no. 1013, with more on the members in a report by Agent B . . . to Hager, December 9, 1814, no. 1015.

Werner's popularity at this time can be seen in many sources, for example, Caroline Pichler, *Denkwürdigkeiten aus meinem Leben* (1914), III, 65, and Carl Bertuch, who called him a sensation, December 8, 1814, *Tagebuch vom Wiener Kongress*, 65. He was also described by Agent Schmidt, February 21, 1815, *GPWK*, 400, the poet as a "great preacher," Méneval, *Memoirs* III, 331, his long thick shoulder-length hair, and thin, even haggard *(hâve)* appearance, Baronne du Montet, *Souvenirs*, 117–118. The audience was inclined to weep or laugh during his emotional, sometimes boisterous sermons, Rzewuska (1939), I, 267, and his coarse language, Karl von Nostitz, *Leben und Briefwechsel* (1848), 176. Bertuch noted his amusing style, often with "thundering eloquence," October 9, 1814, *Tagebuch vom Wiener Kongress*, 29. Werner dined at Metternich's, Gentz *Tagebücher*, November 16, 1814, 331, and Gentz encountered Werner over at Metternich's again, reading an act from one of his tragedies, December 15, 1814, 340. "Ladies and gentlemen" and "shall" are in Rosalynd Pflaum, *By Influence and Desire: The True Story of Three Extraordinary Women—The Grand Duchess of Courland and Her Daughters* (1984), 252. The sermon and audience reactions are in Friedrich Anton von Schönholz's *Traditionen zur Charakteristik Österreichs, seines Staats- und Volkslebens unter Franz I* (1914) II, 127, and Karl August Varnhagen von Ense's *Denkwürdigkeiten des Eignen Lebens* (1987), II, 659.

Emperor Francis' sickness is in Agent L to Hager, November 17, 1814, *DCV*, I, no. 812, Pictet de Rochemont, November 19, 1814, *Biographie, travaux et correspondance diplomatique* (1892), 176. Metternich now bedridden, Talleyrand to Louis XVIII, November 30, 1814, *TLC*, 180, same day to Minister of Foreign Affairs, no. 16A, 344, and Gentz on his visit on the twenty-ninth, *Tagebücher*

(1873), 335. Hardenberg also feeling sick, Talleyrand reported, King's Ambassadors at the Congress to the Minister of Foreign Affairs, no. 16A, November 30, 1814, 344. Dorothée ill, Talleyrand to the Duchess of Courland, November 30, 1814, *TLI*, 76, Bagration sick in November, report to Hager, November 16, 1814, *DCV*, I, no. 786. Many others, too, fell ill at this time from Prince Eugène to the little Prince of Parma.

The delays are clear from the announcement of the concert, first for November 20, and the following postponements, until the twenty-second for "unforeseen circumstances," then to the twenty-seventh, and finally again at "high request" for the twenty-ninth. Announcements and postponements are in *Wiener Zeitung*, November 18 and 27, 1814, as well as *New Beethoven Letters*, ed. Donald W. MacArdle and Ludwig Misch (1957), 129–130. The reason as falling on a Sunday comes from Agent ** to Hager, November 30, 1814, *DCV*, I, no. 938. Beethoven also claimed that the postponement was due to faulty copying of the scores, as reported by Wenzel Tomascheck, in Hamburger, ed., *Beethoven: Letters, Journals and Conversations* (1960), 123. Beethoven had requested the University Hall for his concerts at the congress, but received instead the larger Redoutensaal, letter to George Friedrich Treitschke, undated though probably early September 1814, *New Beethoven Letters*, ed. Donald W. MacArdle and Ludwig Misch (1957), 122–123.

The "wholly new cantata" and the "new symphony," according to the Concert Announcement, November 16, 1814, *New Beethoven Letters*, ed. Donald W. MacArdle and Ludwig Misch (1957), 128–129. "The Battle Symphony" for the panharmonicon, Beethoven to Dr. Carl, Edler von Adlersburg, July 1814, *The Letters of Beethoven*, ed. Emily Anderson, vol. I (1961), 459–460. Mälzel's contributions to Beethoven, Marek (1970), 457–458. Beethoven's collaborator, the physician and poet Alois Weissenbach, *Kleine Wiener Memoiren und Wiener Dosenstucke* (1918), vol. I, 249–250. Weissenbach also wrote an account of his stay in Vienna, the rare *Meine Reise zum Congress*, published by Wallishauser in 1816. Descriptions of Beethoven's performance are cited in Spiel (1968), 123–124, 242–243, and McGuigan (1975), 418, though this was not as they wrote, the premiere, which occurred the previous year.

For more on the symphony, see Lockwood (2003), 230–234, and a discussion of Beethoven at the congress, G. R. Marek, *Beethoven: Biography of a Genius* (1970), 475–487, and especially Ingrid Fuchs's "The Glorious Moment— Beethoven and the Congress of Vienna" in Krog (2002). Spohr, the rehearsal and "badly out of tune" are in Fuchs, 194. Divisions noted at other parties about this time as well: Russia's Stackelberg's ball, Austrian emperor not there, and no English, November 25, 1814, 157. Division into factions supporting or opposing Beethoven, and the fact that the "overwhelming majority" no longer wanted to listen to his works, Agent ** to Hager, November 30, 1814, *DCV*, I, no. 938. Beethoven's music as too heavy, "like Hercules using his club to kill flies," Mayek (1970), 443. Stolberg-Wernigerode was one who thought it was too heavy, November 29, 1814, *Tagebuch über meinen Aufenthalt in Wien zur Zeit des Congresses* (2004) 103, Rosenbaum was just bored. Beethoven complained of the tips here,

Marek (1970), 480. That Beethoven was exhausted, or still exhausted from the concert, along with his complaint about the "fatiguing affairs" comes from a letter to Archduke Rudolph, November 30, 1814, Anderson (1961), 476.

References to congress breaking down are numerous, including, for example, Agent **'s prediction of a "recourse to arms," November 24, 1814, *DCV*, I, no. 870. Gentz's words "language of Justice" are from a letter to Karadja, November 7, 1814 (1876) 120. Countess Széchenyi-Guilford's response to Tsar Alexander comes from Agent ** to Hager, November 21, 1814, no. 834. Alexander was seen dancing with her a lot before, report to Hager October 16, 1814, no. 416, though the story was repeated by some members of the Russian delegation with the king of Prussia inserted instead, for example, Alexander Ivanovich Mikhailovsky-Danilevsky, December 1, 1814 (Russian calendar), Alexander Sapojnikov in Ole Villumsen Krog (2002), 140. The German protest statement is in M. G. Pallain, *Correspondance inédite du prince de Talleyrand et du roi Louis XVIII pendant le Congrès de Vienne* (1881), n. 1, 176–177, Talleyrand to Louis XVIII, December 7, 1814, *TLC*, 193, Count Münster, December 17, 1814, George Herbert Münster, ed., *Political Sketches of the State of Europe, 1814–1867: Containing Count Ernst Münster's Despatches to the Prince Regent from the Congress of Vienna* (1868), 205, Gentz to Karadja, December 20, 1814 (1876), 126. Bavaria and all of Germany supporting the defense of Saxony, Gentz to Karadja, December 20, 1814 (1876), 126, as well as Archduke Johann, December 20, 1814, *Aus dem Tagebuche Erzherzog Johanns von Oesterreich, 1810–1815*, ed. Franz, Ritter von Krones (1891), 192. The fate of that document, Talleyrand to Louis XVIII, December 15, 1814, *TLC*, 202–205. Talleyrand's letter to Metternich, December 19, 1814, is printed in Angeberg (1864), II, 540–544, as well as *NP*, 509–514, with Castlereagh's reaction noted in Talleyrand to Louis XVIII, December 28, 1814, *TLC*, 228. "That everywhere," "every ambition," and selected passages are in Ferrero (1941), 268–272. Louis XVIII was also pleased, Louis XVIII to Talleyrand, December 30, 1814, *TLC*, 238 (same letter with the alternative date of December 28, appears in his *Memoirs*, II, 383–384).

It had long been reported that the French army had been in a state of agitation requiring the greatest care, Pozzo di Borgo to Nesselrode, June 1/13, 1814, *Correspondance Diplomatique du comte Pozzo di Borgo, ambassadeur de Russie en France et du comte du Nesselrode depuis la restauration des Bourbons jusqu'au Congrès d'Aix-la-Chapelle, 1814–1818* (1890), 7. Soldiers' attachment to Napoleon, Pozzo di Borgo to Nesselrode, July 13/25, 1814, 39, popularity of Napoleon with the soldiers met everywhere in Pasquier's journey through Champagne, Picardy, Flanders, and Normandy to inspect bridges and roads, Pasquier, III, 43. The soldiers drinking, D'Hauterive to Talleyrand, dated November 14, 1814, *TLC*, n. 3, 190. Minister of war was heavily critiqued, and army "in a state difficult to describe," Pozzo di Borgo to Nesselrode, September 14/26, 1814, 71. "Nothing but conspiracies, secret discontent, and murmuring," the "storm about to burst," and the frustration in counteracting rumors, Talleyrand's words to Louis XVIII, November 25, 1814, *TLC*, 160–161.

CHAPTER 18. THE COOK, THE PAINTER, THE BALLERINA,
AND THE DIPLOMAT

Epigraph is in Metternich's *NP*, I, 12. Designing and sewing the Elban flag, Sir Neil Campbell's "Journal," published in *Napoleon at Fontainebleau and Elba; Being a Journal of Occurrences in 1814–1815* (1869), 216, and Thomas Ussher, "Napoleon's Deportation to Elba," published in *Napoleon's Last Voyages, being the Diaries of Admiral Sir Thomas Ussher, R.N., K.C.B. (on board the "Undaunted") and John R. Glover, Secretary to Rear Admiral Kockburn (on board the "Northumberland")* (1895), 50–51. Napoleon's impatience to move into *Il Mulini*, and the environment, Christophe, *Napoleon on Elba*, trans. Len Ortzen (1964), 55, and Gruyer, *Napoleon King of Elba* (1906), 63. Description of Napoleon's couch is found in Peyrusse, appendix 51. Suites prepared for Marie Louise and King of Rome, seizing furniture from Élisa, and his hires, Norman Mackenzie, *The Escape from Elba: The Fall and Flight of Napoleon, 1814–1815* (1982), 86–88. The staff in the kitchens and the grounds, Mackenzie (1982), 90, and Gruyer (1906), 72. Napoleon's hairdresser, Christophe (1964), 70, and the description of Napoleon's hair comes from an English visitor that autumn, J. B. Scott, cited in Mackenzie (1982), 139. Campbell's background, the difficulty of finding someone, and knowledge from newspapers, Mackenzie (1982), 40–41, and Campbell (1869), 153, 161. He never saw treaty until late, right before escorting Napoleon to Elba, and this partly because Britain had not signed the treaty. The uncertainty of his mission, and the British government's expectations, 58. His functions, Gruyer (1906), 99, though not exactly jailer, as he claimed.

Castlereagh's offer is in Campbell's "Journal" (1869), 153, and references from instructions from here, printed, 154–155. Another letter from Castlereagh, though no clearer, asked Campbell to continue to "pursue the same line of conduct and communication with this department" and work "without assuming any further official character than that in which you are already received," July 15, 1814 (1869), 273. Campbell's wounds in battle at end of war, on eve of the march to Paris, Campbell (1869), 153, and Captain Ussher (1895), 25. Bandages and sling, Campbell, 158. Conversations about Scotland, the poet Ossian, and, of course, especially military, *Journal of Sir Neil Campbell* (1869), 158–159, Ussher (1895), 85. Napoleon pronunciation of name, 222.

Gruyer believes that the congress's attempts to remove him to another island were only "empty rumours" and "highly improbable" (147), but this was not the case. Many were in fact working on this plan. Talleyrand's proposal for the Azores, Talleyrand to King Louis XVIII, October 13, 1814, *TLC*, 48. Bourbon supporters wanting this accomplished, Wellington reported to Earl of Liverpool, August 28, 1814, *WD*, 541. Intrigues against Napoleon on Elba at Vienna, Méneval, III, 334. Nota to Hager, November 22, 1814, *DCV*, I, no. 853, and the rumor that Napoleon would be "carried off elsewhere," Nota to Hager, December 1, 1814 no. 945. Napoleon's removal, rumored to have been decided by November 8, 1814, Eynard (1914–1924), I, 97. News of stirrings on Elba, Mariotti to Talleyrand,

November 15, 1814, and forwarded to Louis XVIII with his December 7 letter, *TLC*, 198–199. San Marzan and Metternich had heard similar news, *Diario*, 195–196. Plots acknowledged too by Alan Schom, *Napoleon Bonaparte* (1997), 707, Mackenzie (1982), 146, with Mariotti and "oil merchant" Mackenzie (1982), 149–152, 163. For one likely theory linking this "oil merchant" to Alessandro Forli, see Christophe (1964), 153. Olive Oil Merchant arrived the thirtieth of November. Mackenzie identifies other plotters including the Comte d'Artois, the Comte Chavigny de Blot, and the military governor on Corsica, Louis Guerin de Bruslart.

Advent at the Congress, Metternich to Duchess of Sagan, November 27, 1814, *MSB*, 273. Dinner with Bollmann at Gentz's flat, *Tagebücher*, December 12, 1814, 339, and references to Gentz looking crushed *(zerschmettert)*, and as if a murder attempted in his presence, Varnhagen von Ense, *Denkwürdigkeiten des Eignen Lebens* (1987), II, 644–645. Bollmann's arrival recently from America, Gentz noted, *Tagebücher*, November 29, 1814, 335. Bollmann's plans for a new currency and national bank, letter to La Fayette, January 3, 1815, *DCV*, I, no. 1232, and for more on his background, see Paul Sweet's "Erich Bollmann at Vienna in 1815," *AHR*, 1941, 580–587. Gentz's cramped apartment was described by Countess Bernstorff, *Ein Bild aus der Zeit von 1789 bis 1835: Aus ihren Aufzeichnungen* (1896), I, 164, and more fully in Franz Gräffer's *Kleine Wiener Memoiren und Wiener Dosenstucke* (1918), II, 1–4. The ghost story is in Dorothy Guis McGuigan, *Metternich and the Duchess* (1975), 419, and others were told, for example, at Julie Zichy's salon, Alville, *Anna Eynard-Lullin et l'époque des Congrès et des Révolutions* (1955), 176. Baronne du Montet's description of the whimsical chess is in her *Souvenirs 1785–1866* (1904), 115, and more on the entertainment during Advent can be found in Karl von Nostitz's *Leben und Briefwechsel: Auch ein Lebensbild aus den Befreiungskriegen* (1848), 131. Count Clam-Martinitz already confiding about his interest in Dorothée, "his new passion" Gentz *Tagebücher* ed. Varnhagen's von Ense, November 6, 1814, (1873), I, 327. Hager's spies did not miss her other interests, for example, Agent ** to Hager, November 28, 1814, *DCV*, I, no. 918. French desserts and Dorothée's growing attachment to Clam-Martinitz, are in Pflaum (1984), 236–8. Many historians place chef Antonin Carême in Vienna during the congress, and while this is not impossible, it is open to question. Carême's latest biographer, Ian Kelley, doubted his presence altogether: *Cooking for Kings: The Life of Antonin Carême the first celebrity chef* (2004). Philippe Alexandre and Béatrix de l'Aulnoit, *Le roi Carême* (2003), did not make him attend either. Carême's memoirs [published in *Classiques de table* (1843)] do not convince me that he was present during the congress. Whether Carême was in Vienna or not, there was certainly a highly talented chef at the French embassy who knew many of his dishes. Even Metternich had sent his chef to study under Carême earlier in 1814 to prepare for the congress.

The painter Isabey's arrival in Vienna, Report to Hager, October 1, 1814, *DCV*, I, no. 224, and for more on his residence, see Basily-Callimaki, *J.B. Isabey: Sa Vie—Son temps, 1767–1855* (1909), 160ff, as well as Marion W. Osmond's *Jean*

Baptiste Isabey: The Fortunate Painter 1767–1855 (1947), 134–139. Painting the sovereigns, Méneval, *Memoirs*, III, 327. Isabey's work during December on the congress painting, Freddi to Hager, December 30, 1814, *DCV*, I, no. 1203. Portraits and designs in his studio, and his flattery from Baronne du Montet, who visited there in December 1814 (1904), 133. Isabey's words on his salon are in Basily-Callimaki (1909), 164, and the Monday salons noted by many, for example, Bertuch's *Tagebuch vom Wiener Kongress*, December 19, 1814, 75. Bigottini success, Talleyrand to the Duchess of Courland, November 17, 1814, *TLI*, 71, La Comtesse Charles de Nesselrode to la Comtesse Hélène Gourief, October 30, 1814, *Nesselrode Lettres et papiers*, V, 196, and Karl August Varnhagen von Ense, *Denkwürdigkeiten des Eignen Lebens* (1987), II, 599. A great change since their arrival, by early December, out in society, Talleyrand to Louis XVIII, December 7, 1814, *TLC*, 197. Talleyrand's feat in breaking the isolation, admired by colleague La Tour du Pin, in an intercepted letter to Marquis de Bonnay, December 8, 1814, *DCV*, I, no. 1010. Tableaux at court, San Marzan, December 9, 1814, *Diario*, lxiv, Bright's *Travels from Vienna through Lower Hungary with Some Remarks on the State of Vienna During the Congress in the Year 1814* (1818), 28–29, and on the Olympus scene, Méneval, *Memoirs*, III, 345–346, Comte Auguste de La Garde-Chambonas, *Anecdotal Recollections of the Congress of Vienna* (1902), 139–149, and Ludwig Hevesi, "Wien Stadtbild, Festlichkeiten, Volksleben," in Eduard Leisching, ed., *Der Wiener Congress: Culturgeschichte die Bildenden Künste und das Kunstgewerbe Theater—Musik in der Zeit von 1800 bis 1825* (1898), 87. "Mount Olympus" was repeated several times during the congress. The late evening, along with the meeting with Prince de Ligne and Count Z, comes from La Garde-Chambonas (1902), 218–226, and the possible identification also noted by the editor Fleury (1902), n. 1, 222.

Chapter 19. Indiscretion

Castlereagh compared to "a traveler who has lost his way," Talleyrand to Louis XVIII, December 20, 1814, *TLC*, 220. The words "impossibility of H.R.H. consenting to involve this country in hostilities at this time for any of the objects . . . ," Bathurst to Castlereagh, November 27, 1814 *BD*, CXXXVIII, 248. Castlereagh's new orders are also noted by Talleyrand in a letter to King Louis XVIII, December 7, 1814, *TLC*, 191. Rosenkrantz view was removed, as he heard it from the king of Denmark, who in turn learned it from Emperor Francis, December 9, 1814, *Journal* (1953), 106. Views about the effects of Castlereagh's new instructions, Rosenkrantz on December 9–12, 1814, *Journal*, 106–108. Many had passed the information about Castlereagh back to London, including Hanover, Saxe-Coburg, Wellington, and Talleyrand. Instructions on Saxony, including the words "it would certainly be very desirable that a *noyau* of it at least should be preserved," Liverpool to Castlereagh, November 18, 1814, *BD*, CXXX, 236.

Hardenberg's poem, "Away discord," sent over December 3, Strauss, *The Attitude of the Congress of Vienna Toward Nationalism in Germany, Italy and Poland* (1949), 31, and Kraehe (1963–1983), II, 261. Metternich's letter of December 10 with population figures is in Angeberg (1864), II, 505–510, and Hardenberg calling it "unexpected" in his diary the same day, *Tagebücher und autobiographische Aufzeichnungen* (2000), 807. Hardenberg showed confidential letters, and words on the indiscretion, "an act of treachery," Münster, December 17, 1814, George Herbert Münster, *Political Sketches of the State of Europe, 1814–1867: Containing Count Ernst Münster's Despatches to the Prince Regent from the Congress of Vienna* (1868), 202. Hardenberg did not mention in his *Tagebücher*, though many others did like Stein, *Tagebuch*, V, 343–346, Archduke Johann, December 21, 1814, *Aus dem Tagebuche Erzherzog Johanns von Oesterreich 1810–1815*, ed. Franz, Ritter von Krones (1891), 194–195, and Rosenkrantz, *Journal*, December 13, 1814, 109. Metternich had his own letters and some advised him to retaliate.

The challenge of a duel appears in many Alexander biographies, though many of these, if they offer a date, place it in October. If it took place, it was clearly December. Metternich always claimed that the tsar did make the challenge, *NP*, I, 326–327. More rain, cold, and melted snow that week, San Marzan, *Diario*, December 6, 7, 10–12, 1814, lxiv. Gentz visited Prince de Ligne on December 8, and noted he was very sick, December 8, 1814, *Tagebücher*, 337, and a few days later, the prince was described as "dangerously sick," Bertuch, *Tagebuch vom Wiener Kongress*, 67. The prince's tendency to dress more for show rather than the weather, Franz Gräffer, *Kleine Wiener Memoiren und Wiener Dosenstucke* (1918), I, 186. Conversations Eynard had at that time with Prince de Ligne's doctor, December 12, 1814 (1914–1924), I, 204. Prince de Ligne's death, for example, Agent Freddi to Hager, December 14, 1814, no. 1049 and Agent ** to Hager, December 14, 1814, no. 1050; almost every memoir or diary of the time refers to this event, for example, Talleyrand to the Duchess of Courland, December 15, 1814, *TLI*, 82; La Garde-Chambonas, 244–255, Bright, 44, Eynard, *Journal*, December 13, 1814, 206–207, and Lulu Thürheim's *Mein Leben: Erinnerungen aus Österreichs Grosser Welt, 1788–1819*, II, 105, who incorrectly listed the time of his death. "I know" is in Spiel (1968), 136. Many quips cited in the sources, from the field marshal (Rzewuska, I, 238, and Thürheim, II, 104, for example) to those who denied that he said it, like La Garde-Chambonas. The cancellation of tableaux and comedy at court that night, San Marzan, *Diario*, December 13, 1814, lxiv, though other activities around town continued, like Arnstein's salon, Bertuch's *Tagebuch*, 68. Prince de Ligne "finished off by the festivities," Méneval, *Memoirs*, III, 323, and his death marking the passing of a whole epoch, Varnhagen von Ense, *Denkwürdigkeiten des Eignen Lebens* (1987), II, 604. The funeral procession is in Bright (1818), 45, Alville, *Anna Eynard-Lullin et l'époque des Congrès et des Révolutions* (1955), 190, and Stolberg-Wernigerode's *Tagebuch über meinen Aufenthalt in Wien zur Zeit des Congresses* (2004), 118–119, as well as Bertuch, who watched it at the corner of the Kohlmarkt, *Tagebuch vom Wiener Kongress*, 70–71, and Countess Bernstorff, who watched from her window (1896) 168. The route of the procession is in Perth, *Wiener Kongresstagebuch, 1814–1815* (1981), 77–78. For more on the prince and the symbolism of the black knight, see Mansel's

Prince of Europe: The Life of Charles-Joseph de Ligne, 1735–1814 (2003), 261–262. Rain that day, on December 15, "complete springtime," Gentz, *Tagebücher,* December 15, 1814, 339–340.

Snowing on Christmas Eve, San Marzan, *Diario,* December 24, 1814, lxv, and Stolberg-Wernigerode, *Tagebuch über meinen Aufenthalt in Wien zur Zeit des Congresses* (2004), 131. Christmas tree, *l'arbre de Noël,* Agent ** to Hager, December 26, 1814, *DCV,* I, no. 1160, as well as Stolberg-Wernigerode, who was also present, December 24, 1814, *Tagebuch,* 131. First Christmas tree to Vienna is cited in Musulin, *Vienna in the Age of Metternich* (1975), 169–170, as well as Spiel, *Fanny von Arnstein: A Daughter of the Enlightenment, 1758–1818,* trans. Christine Shuttleworth (1991), 292. Christmas at French embassy, Pflaum (1984), 240–241, and Metternich and the duchess at this time, McGuigan (1975), 424–428, along with her wondering, too, if Metternich really attended the Zichy ball as La Garde-Chambonas claimed.

Beethoven's work on the Polonaise in C Major (op. 89), his attempt to rededicate the violin sonatas (op. 30), and his last public concert as a pianist are in Ingrid Fuchs's "The Glorious Moment—Beethoven and the Congress of Vienna" in Krog (2002), 184. Carl Bertuch attended Salieri's mass at the palace chapel, December 25, 1814: *Tagebuch vom Wiener Kongress* (1916), 80. Castlereagh's dinner at the British embassy was reported by Agent ** to Hager, December 26, 1814, *DCV,* I, no. 1160. Talk with the tsar's physician increasing, for example, Agent P to Hager, December 4, 1814, *DCV,* I, no. 978, and another anonymous one, December 7, 1814, no. 1002.

The king of Württemberg's departure on the morning of December 26 is in Carl Bertuch, *Tagebuch* (1916), 81–82, Matthias Franz Perth's *Wiener Kongresstagebuch, 1814–1815* (1981), same day, 79, and the following day in the *Wiener Zeitung.* The king's personality was widely described, for example, in Nesselrode's *Autobiographie* in *Lettres et papiers du chancelier comte de Nesselrode, 1760–1850,* II, 27, and his rudeness noted, for instance, by Archduke Johann, September 22, 1814, *Aus dem Tagebuche Erzherzog Johanns von Oesterreich 1810–1815,* ed. Franz, Ritter von Krones (1891), 170. The kings' refusal to raise his hat comes from Schönholz (1914), II, 25, and also Agent Schmidt to Hager, October 5, 1814, *DCV,* I, no. 274. Württemberg as a monster, Schmidt to Hager, October 7, 1814, *DCV,* I, no. 301. Spies also had hints of his love affair, for example, September 27, 1814, *DCV,* I, no. 172—more would soon follow. The king of Württemberg's gifts are noted by Agent ** to Hager, December 25, 1814, no. 1147; Bertuch in his diary December 26, 1814 (1916), 82; Count Münster, December 29, 1814, *Political Sketches of the State of Europe 1814–1867: Containing Count Ernst Münster's Despatches to the Prince Regent from the Congress of Vienna* (1868), 219–220; and *Wiener Zeitung,* December 31, 1814. Generosity had improved his image, and a list of gifts compiled by Goehausen to Hager, nos. 1172 and 1183.

Dalberg's papers lying around, and spy notes Sidney Smith plan for clearing Mediterranean waters of pirates, report to Hager, October 25, 1814, *DCV,* I, no.

511. Sidney Smith's Wednesday evening soirees, for instance, Agent ** to Hager, December 22, 1814, no. 1119. His conversation, for example, Jean-Gabriel Eynard (1914–1924), October 17, 1814, 37–38, and his "wit and gaiety," Radziwill, who had known him for a long time, *Forty-five Years of My Life (1770–1815)*, trans. A. R. Allinson (1912), 92.

For more on Smith and his diplomatic work on behalf of Sweden, see Johan Feuk, *Sverige på Kongressen i Wien* (1915) and Tom Pocock's *Thirst for Glory: The Life of Admiral Sir Sidney Smith* (1966). Some letters he wrote at the time in the second volume of *The Memoirs of Admiral Sir Sidney Smith* (1839) by Edward Howard and John Barrows, ed., *The Life and Correspondence of Admiral Sir Sidney Smith* (1848). Smith's wearing of orders and one of his picnics in Countess Bernstorff's *Ein Bild aus der Zeit von 1789 bis 1835: Aus ihren Aufzeichnungen* (1896), I, 156–158, Baronne du Montet, *Souvenirs*, 136–137, as well as Saint-Marzan, *Diario*, December 29, 1814, lxvi. The words "three ducats," "the bill collector," and the laughter afterward are in La Garde-Chambonas's *Anecdotal Recollections of the Congress of Vienna* (1902), 268–278. The event is also described by Dr. Richard Bright in Travels (1818), 20–21, Archduke Johann, *Aus dem Tagebuche Erzherzog Johanns von Oesterreich, 1810–1815*, ed. Franz, Ritter von Krones (1891), 197–198, Carl Bertuch, *Tagebuch vom Wiener Kongress*, 85, among many others. Agent ** also covers the picnic at the Augarten, Agent ** to Hager, December 29, 1814, *DCV*, I, no. 1186, and again on the thirty-first, no. 1217, though others such as Rzewuska, I, 253–254, described the event secondhand.

CHAPTER 20. KING OF THE SUBURBS

Nickname for Count Razumovsky is in, for example, Baronne du Montet's *Souvenirs, 1785–1866* (1904), 180. Talleyrand's words at the opening of the chapter come from Alan Palmer, *Metternich* (1972), 139. Saxony "eclipsed" the other questions, Gentz to Karadja, December 13, 1814, *Dépêches inédites*, 123, and its importance in unlocking other difficult questions, in a letter on the twentieth, 128. The Prussian plan for placing the king of Saxony on the Rhine reported, Münster, December 18, 1814, George Herbert Münster, *Political Sketches of the State of Europe, 1814–1867: Containing Count Ernst Münster's Despatches to the Prince Regent from the Congress of Vienna* (1868), 207–208, and December 24, 1814, 214–215. Metternich sent over statistical tables to show that Prussia could have its 1805 population by gaining only 330,000 Saxons, Talleyrand to Louis XVIII, December 15, 1814, *TLC*, 205, and more on the disagreements over numbers, 209.

Historians of the congress usually follow Webster's lead and credit Castlereagh with the creation of the Evaluations Committee, and there are some documents that suggest that. I have inclined to Metternich as an initiator behind Castlereagh's proposal because of his relationship with the Prussians at this time, the importance of a statistical argument to his position, and his work prior to the existence of the committee trying to gather statistics, as noted in many places, including an attempt to seek assistance from Archduke Johann, December 5–7, 1814, *Aus dem Tagebuche Erzherzog Johanns von Oesterreich, 1810–1815*, ed. Franz, Ritter von Krones

(1891), 187–188. The instructions to the new committee, given by Metternich, are in Angeberg (1864), vol. II, 561–562. Enno Kraehe is one scholar who believes that Metternich proposed the committee [*Metternich's German Policy* (1963–1983), II, 285]. Talleyrand and Castlereagh's discussion on the Evaluations Committee, Talleyrand to Louis XVIII, December 28, 1814, *TLC*, 228–230, as well as the King's Ambassadors at the Congress to the Minister of Foreign Affairs, no. 21A, December 27, 1814, 375. Stewart's visit to Talleyrand and their conversation, Talleyrand to Louis XVIII, December 28, 1814, *TLC*, 230–231, and Talleyrand's threat to leave Vienna also appears here, and the words "calling for his horses," *BD*, xxx. The first meeting on December 24, 1814, and the minutes recording Dalberg's presence in *Le Congrès de Vienne et les traités de 1815* (1864), II, 562–565.

The meeting of December 30, the last of the year, is in Angeberg (1864), IV, 1869–1874. Some historians refer to a meeting on the thirty-first, apparently relying on Castlereagh's description, in his letter of January 1, 1815, in *BD*, CLV, 277–278, which almost certainly was a mistake, as Kraehe rightly points out, in n. 76, 291 of II (1963–1983). Prussia's insistence on "total incorporation" comes from a letter, Castlereagh to Liverpool, January 1, 1815, *BD*, CLIV, 276, and Hardenberg's words "tantamount to a declaration of war," and his own response on how "better to break up the Congress," related by Castlereagh, in a letter to Liverpool, January 1, 1815, *BD*, CLV, 278. Politics at end of year "dismal" and "enormous weight suspended over our heads" appear in Gentz's end-of-year reflections 1814, *Tagebücher*, 344.

Razumovsky palace described in Eynard *Journal*, October 25, 1814, 65–66, November 20, 1814, 145, and Nota to Hager, October 12, 1814, *DCV*, I, no. 354, and Agent ** to Hager, October 13, 1814, no. 352. Nickname "King of the Suburbs" is in Baronne du Montet, *Souvenirs*, 180. The early-morning fire drums are in Carl Bertuch, December 31, 1814, *Tagebuch vom Wiener Kongress*, 88, and Perth's diary from same day, *Wiener Kongresstagebuch, 1814–1815* (1981), 79. The descriptions of the wasteland, its transformation into a "princely Eden," the fuses, the activities to save the belongings, the roof, and the tsar-Razumovsky conversation are in Friedrich Anton von Schönholz's *Traditionen zur Charakteristik Österreichs, seines Staats- und Volkslebens unter Franz I* (1914), II, 120–125. "Vesuvius" and the crowds come from Comte Auguste de La Garde-Chambonas, *Anecdotal Recollections of the Congress of Vienna* (1902), 256–258. "A piece of wasteland," "Eden," and "temple of art" are in Spiel (1968), 132–134. The fire is also in Gentz, *Tagebücher*, December 31, 1814, 343, and San Marzan, *Diario*, December 31, 1814, lxvi, among others. The description of furniture, mirrors, paintings, statues, and other items in the garden is in Stolberg-Wernigerode, December 31, 1814, *Tagebuch über meinen Aufenthalt in Wien zur Zeit des Congresses* (2004), 141. The cause of the fire was reported by many, and speculations of its origins in the bakery and the stalls are in Perth (1981), 80. Both Perth and Schönholz deliberately note that the heating system was French, Perth, January 1, 1815, 80, and Schönholz (1914), II, 121. The tsar's description of Metternich as unreliable, Stein, *Tagebuch* V, 346. Metternich refusing to attend Razumovsky ball, his attempts to see Duchess of Sagan on New Year's Eve, and likely spending night in office, McGuigan (1975), 424–428. Gentz visiting the Duchess of Sagan that evening, and encountering Dorothée, Count Clam-Martinitz, Windischgrätz, and others, *Tagebücher*, December 31, 1814, 344. "I had hoped to say" comes from Pflaum (1984), 243. La Garde-Chambonas's claim to have seen Metternich at the Zichy ball is in *Anecdotal Recollections* (1902) 265.

CHAPTER 21. REQUIEM

The first masked ball and the opening of the carnival season is in Perth, January 2, 1815, *Wiener Kongresstagebuch, 1814–1815* (1981), 80. News of the peace at Ghent arrives and its effects, Castlereagh to Liverpool, January 5, 1815, CC, CLX, 283; *WSD*, IX, 527, and Archduke Johann, in his diary, January 1, 1815, *Aus dem Tagebuche Erzherzog Johanns von Oesterreich, 1810–1815*, ed. Franz, Ritter von Krones (1891), 199, along with a few intercepted letters: Hager to Emperor, January 1, 1815, *DCV*, I, no. 1210, II, no. 1281, and II, no. 1288. Snow on the ground in Vienna that day, Bertuch's *Tagebuch vom Wiener Kongress*, January 1, 1815, 88, and Stolberg-Wernigerode, *Tagebuch über meinen Aufenthalt in Wien zur Zeit des Congresses* (2004), 142. News of the Ghent peace, and "only the precursor of a still more fortunate event," Talleyrand to Louis XVIII, January 4, 1815, *TLC*, 241, along with Talleyrand's perspective on the secret treaty, 242–244. The "joy of the English ministers" afterward, and those of Talleyrand, as he shared a carriage with them, San Marzan, *Diario*, January 1, 1815, lxvi. Prussian language "very warlike," and its influence on him, Castlereagh to Liverpool, January 1, 1815, *BD*, CLV, 277–278. Talleyrand was, of course, not unaware of this help: Austria, and Britain would only approach France "in a case of extreme necessity," he had long known, Talleyrand to Louis XVIII, November 25, 1814, *TLC*, 166, and Prussian arrogance in meetings as one major factor influencing Castlereagh to sign the secret treaty, Talleyrand to Louis XVIII, January 4, 1815, *TLC*, 243. See also Talleyrand's assessment, in the Report Presented to the King During His Journey from Ghent to Paris, June 1815, 529. Castlereagh's defiance of British government is in Webster (1931), 371. January 3 souper at Castlereagh's, Eynard, *Journal*, January 4, 1815, 241–243, and the violin music, San Marzan, *Diario*, January 3, 1815, lxvii. The terms of the secret treaty are in *Le Congrès de Vienne et les traités de 1815* (1864), II, 589–592.

Rumors of secret treaty circulated, Agent Br to Hager, January 29, 1815, *DCV* II, no. 1437. Dalberg was speaking of it to agents, report to Hager, February 1, 1815, *DCV* II, no. 1461. Hardenberg warned of possible secret agreement between Britain, Austria, and France, as he noted in his diary, December 16, 1814, *Tagebücher und autobiographische Aufzeichnungen* (2000), 808. Rumors of Metternich's sacking abound, as did those of Nesselrode being out of favor. Talleyrand's entry onto the Big Four committees, noted in advance, Wintzingerode and Linden to the King of Württemberg, intercepted, January 5, 1815, II, no. 1249. Castlereagh's proposal for French joining in Saxon discussions, Castlereagh to Liverpool, January 1, 1815, *BD*, CLIV, 276–277, and Castlereagh and Metternich refusing to negotiate on Saxony without including Talleyrand, Castlereagh's summary, letter to Liverpool, January 3, 1815, *BD*, CLVIII, 280–281. On proposing that France be admitted, Gentz to Karadja, January 4, 1815, *Dépêches inédites*, 138–140. The meeting included France, as noted in the protocol, *Le Congrès de Vienne et les traités de 1815* (1864), II, 594.

"Periodic evolutions of his mind," *NP*, I, 317, and Palmer, *Metternich* (1972), 141. Signs of the tsar changing, and less inclined to support Prussia, were noted even earlier by the observant Talleyrand, his letter to Louis XVIII, November 17, 1814, *TLC*, 146–147, Gentz, *Tagebücher*, November 21, 1814, 332, Archduke Johann, November 24, 1814, *Aus dem Tagebuche Erzherzog Johanns von Oesterreich, 1810–1815*, ed. Franz, Ritter von Krones (1891), 184, and report to Hager, December 20, 1814, *DCV*, I, no. 1098. Tsar's shift, of course, was not with Metternich, Nota to Hager, January 5, 1815, II, no. 1239. Alexander was still preferring to deal with Metternich with pistols, Rosenkrantz, *Journal*, January 10, 1815, 123.

Krüdener in her letters, and lady-in-waiting Stourdza's memoirs, "meanly lodged," at the Hofburg, Countess Edling, *Mémoires* (1883), 163, and "do you suppose" from Paléologue, *The Enigmatic Czar* (1938), 228. The tsar's visits and the letters in Edling (1888), 163–164, 217, and 197ff. Krüdener's correspondence to Stourdza from October, Clarence Ford's *Life and Letters of Madame de Krudener* (1893), 153ff, though it had begun before Vienna, back in April that year, Ernest John Knapton, *The Lady of the Holy Alliance* (1939), 139. White angel-black angel, Paléologue, 228–229, "the Dragon," Paléologue, 246, and more on the relationship between the tsar and Krüdener, Palmer, *Alexander I: Tsar of War and Peace* (1974), 318–319. Spies note his religious turn, and rumored desire to unify Orthodox and Roman Catholic Churches, report of unidentified agent to Hager, November 7, 1814, *DCV*, I, no. 703. Palmer points out how the tsar's affairs start to slip, and in fact abruptly disappear after the second week of December or even the fifth of December (317ff), but this is not strictly the case. For example, Schwarz, said to be "Alexander's mistress," still arriving to see him in secret, Goehausen to Hager, January 8, 1815, II, no. 1319. Other sources besides the spies also continue to report his affairs, for example, Baronne du Montet, *Souvenirs*, February 1, 1815, on tsar always with Gabrielle Auersperg.

It is clear that the tsar must have known, or at least suspected the secret treaty. He had even discussed the "rumor" with Castlereagh himself, as the British minister noted in a letter to Liverpool, January 8, 1815, *CC*, CLXI, 284. Others in the Russian suite did not fail to notice the cooperation of the three powers, for example, Karl von Nostitz, in his diary, January 7, 1815, in *Leben und Briefwechsel* (1848), 141. Other priorities and a possible attack into Turkey, and reference La Harpe and Pozzo di Borgo, July 7, 1814, Kraehe, *Metternich's German Policy* (1963–1983), II, 134–135. Many Russian advisers supported a war against Turkey, Gentz noted, to Karadja, October 15, 1815, *Dépêches inédites*, 184. The tsar's confusion on what or whom to believe, Talleyrand to Louis XVIII, December 15, 1814, *TLC*, 208–209. Talleyrand's success in early 1815 pointed out, with king of

Denmark to Emperor Francis, Marquis de Bonnay to Talleyrand, January 10, 1815, II, no. 1415.

Metternich and the Duchess at this time, including "I was your lover" and "called to lead," are in McGuigan (1975), 438, and *MSB*, 275. For Talleyrand's account of the Requiem, see his letter to King Louis XVIII, January 21, 1815, *TLC*, 273–275, *Memoirs*, II, 205, Ambassadors of the King at the Congress to the Minister of Foreign Affairs, No. 25, January 19, 1815, 14 (incorrectly dated March 19), along with the Ambassadors of the King at the Congress to the Minister of Foreign Affairs, no. 26, January 24, 1815, 20–21, Talleyrand to Jaucourt, January 21, 1815, *Correspondance du comte du Jaucourt avec le prince de Talleyrand pendant le Congrès de Vienne* (1905), 163. The symbols of the four statues are in Comte Auguste de La Garde-Chambonas, *Anecdotal Recollections of the Congress of Vienna* (1902), 309–312, Bright, *Travels from Vienna through Lower Hungary with some remarks on the state of Vienna during the congress in the year 1814* (1818), 37, and many others. This date as "the anniversary of a day of horror and eternal mourning" and "solemn expiatory service" Talleyrand to Louis XVIII, January 4, 1815, *TLC*, 240. Gaining St. Stephen's and the Archbishop of Vienna, and words "nothing shall be neglected that can render the ceremony imposing," Talleyrand to Louis XVIII, January 6, 1815, 252, Talleyrand to Louis XVIII, January 10, 1815, 259–260. Neukomm working on the music, Talleyrand to the Duchess of Courland, January 11, 1815, *TLI*, 99. Requiem for Louis XVI, note to Hager, January 21, 1815, *DCV* II, no. 1360, and intercepted letter Wintzingerode to king of Württemberg, January 22, 1815, II, no. 1369. The fur-lined coats inside, San Marzan, *Diario*, January 21, 1815, lxix. Baronne du Montet, *Souvenirs*, 133–134. Not everyone was impressed by the ceremony, as seen by the critiques of Karl von Nostitz, January 24, 1815, in *Leben und Briefwechsel* (1848), 159, or Carl Bertuch, *Tagebuch vom Wiener Kongress*, 102–103. Varnhagen von Ense also critiqued it for many reasons, at least for being unnecessary and commemorating a deed better left in obscurity, *Denkwürdigkeiten des Eignen Lebens* (1987), II, 649–650. Gentz was at the "solemn dinner" at the French embassy, and saw many of the congress figures there, January 21, 1815, *Tagebücher*, 351. Other entertainments not necessary canceled, as rumored, San Marzan went over to gamble at Zichys. Princess Bagration held an evening soiree with theater and a ball that night, Agent ** to Hager, January 24, 1815, *DCV*, II, no. 1390. Many accounts report that the emperor of Austria picked up the tab, but this was not the case, Talleyrand noted in his letter to Jaucourt, February 9, 1815, *Correspondance du comte du Jaucourt* (1905), 184.

CHAPTER 22. THE GREAT SLEIGH RIDE

My account of the weather is based on several descriptions of the time, particularly Bright's *Travels from Vienna through Lower Hungary with Some Remarks on the State of Vienna During the Congress in the Year 1814* (1818), 33–35, and San Marzan, January 8–22, 1815, *Diario*, lxviiiff. Descriptions of the sleighs from La Garde-Chambonas, *Anecdotal Recollections of the Congress of Vienna* (1902),

317–318. Eynard, *Au Congrès de Vienne: journal de Jean-Gabriel Eynard* (1914–1924), who looked down from a window in the imperial palace, January 22, 1815, I, 290–294, and Rahel Varnhagen to Moritz und Ernestine Robert, January 23, 1815, *Briefwechsel*, ed. Friedhelm Kemp (1979) IV, 70. Talleyrand to the Duchess of Courland, January 24, 1815, *TLI*, 108, and Gentz *Tagebücher* (1873), I, 22, 351. Description of bells around horses shoulders, Bright (1818), 34, and the pairings of the sovereigns, Perth, January 22, 1815, *Wiener Kongresstagebuch, 1814–1815*, 86, with a more complete one in *Wiener Zeitung*, January 24, 1815. "Heavy snowfall," "biting frost," and "taste" are in Spiel (1968), 115. The delay at the opening along with the snowing on the return are in Eynard (1914–1924), January 22, 1815, 291–292 and 294–295. Stewart's behavior is also in Alexander Ivanovich Mikhailovsky-Danilevsky journal, Alexander Sapojnikov in Ole Villumsen Krog (2002), 146. Marie Louise looking through a "window let into the attic," Baron Claude-François de Méneval's *Memoirs Illustrating the History of Napoleon I from 1802 to 1805*, ed. Baron Napoleon Joseph de Méneval (1894), III, 312. The inflation was noted by many, including Thürheim, *Mein Leben: Erinnerungen aus Österreichs Grosser Welt, 1788–1819* (1913), II, 106, and "they ride" is in Spiel (1968), 119. The state of affairs, and tensions in the French-English-Austrian alliance, Mavrojény to his brother, January 25, 1815, *GPWK*, 370–371. Britain and Austria differences after the defensive treaty, Castlereagh to Liverpool, January 22, 1815 *BD*, CLXVIII, 292–294, and his letter the following week, when he makes his appeal to the tsar, Castlereagh to Liverpool, January 29, 1815 *BD*, CLXIX, 297–298. Talleyrand, of course, sided with Metternich, as seen in this last letter, as well as Talleyrand's dispatches. Castlereagh's ultimatum, January 19, 1815, *Le Congrès de Vienne et les traités de 1815* (1864), II, 795–797. Castlereagh's chagrin at Metternich made rounds, Eynard heard it, January 24, 1815 (1914–1924), 299.

Germaine de Staël's work *De l'Allemagne* had been printed, censored, and suppressed in 1810, and appeared fully in 1813. Gentz's words on the people "who hold the world" are from his diary, January 12, 1815, *Tagebücher* (1873), I, 348. "I enjoy," which comes from Gentz's end-of-the-year summary, and "foibles of the world" are in Golo Mann's *Secretary of Europe: The Life of Friedrich Gentz, Enemy of Napoleon*, trans. William H. Woglom (1946), 212–213. Fanny von Arnstein's hospitality is in Karl August Varnhagen von Ense's *Denkwürdigkeiten des Eignen Lebens* (1987), II, 573–574. "Tall, slim" and the Hoher Markt setting are from Hilde Spiel's *Fanny von Arnstein: A Daughter of the Enlightenment 1758–1818*, trans. Christine Shuttleworth (1991), 190–191. The description of Jean Carro is in Rosalie Rzewuska's *Mémoires de la comtesse Rosalie Rzewuska* (1788–1865), I, 98. The drinks and pastries served are from Carl Bertuch's diary entry for November 1, 1814, *Tagebuch vom Wiener Kongress* (1916), 45. The wax figures celebration appears in many sources, including Bertuch diary entry for January 10, 1815 (1916), 96; Marchese di San Marzano's diary in Ilario Rinieri, ed., *Corrispondenza inedita dei Cardinali Consalvi e Pacca nel tempo del Congresso di Vienna* (1903), lxviii; and Henrich Graf zu Stolberg-Wernigerode's entry the same day in his diary, *Tagebuch über meinen Aufenthalt in Wien zur Zeit des Congresses* (2004), 150. Humboldt did not attend that particular night, because he was busy working on his arguments for Jewish equality, he noted in a letter to his wife, Caroline, January 17, 1815, *Wilhelm und Caroline von Humboldt in ihren Briefen*, ed. Anna von Sydow (1910), IV, 458.

Jacob Grimm's critiques of the congress can be read in several letters to his brother Wilhelm, for example, *Briefwechsel zwischen Jacob und Wilhelm Grimm aus der Jugendzeit* (1963), October 8, 1814, 354—the source for his description of it as a maze, 355. Grimm was at the library whenever he could slip away from the embassy, and his varied literary pursuits come, for example, from his letter to Wilhelm, October 21, 1814 (1963), 360. Grimm's work with Serbian and Czech folklore, and some manuscripts is also in Murray B. Peppard's *Paths Through the Forest: A Biography of the Brothers Grimm* (1971), 88. Grimm's dinner at the tavern, his words about "children's tales," and contacts with other scholars at the congress is in Ruth Michaelis-Jena's *The Brothers Grimm* (1970), 73–74. Grimm's address at the congress, first with the head of the delegation at Alleegasse Nr. 79, and later at Pannikelgasse Nr. 80. Grimm was not in GE, but he did make the supplement, *SG*, 9.

Napoleon's mother arrives at Elba, Sir Neil Campbell, "Journal," published in *Napoleon at Fontainebleau and Elba; Being a Journal of Occurrences in 1814–1815* (1869), 278–279, and Napoleon cheating at cards, Christophe, *Napoleon on Elba*, trans. Len Ortzen (1964), 138. Rumored arrival of Marie Louise and visit of Marie Walewska are in Norman Mackenzie, *The Escape from Elba: The Fall and Flight of Napoleon, 1814–1815* (1982), 128–130, and Christophe (1964), 109–127. Jaucourt informs Talleyrand, September 27, 1814, *Correspondance du comte du Jaucourt avec le prince de Talleyrand pendant le Congrès de Vienne* (1905), 10. Marie Walewska's background is in Potocka, who claimed to have sat between them at the ball where their affair began, *Countess Anna Potocka's Memoirs of the Countess Potocka*, ed. Casimir Stryienski, trans. Lionel Strachey (1900), 79–80. Napoleon planned to seize Pianosa almost from the beginning, Captain Thomas Ussher, "Napoleon's Deportation to Elba," in *Napoleon's Last Voyages, Being the Diaries of Admiral Sir Thomas Ussher, R.N., K.C.B. (on Board the "Undaunted")* and *John R. Glover, Secretary to Rear Admiral Kockburn (on Board the "Northumberland")* (1895), 54, Campbell (1869), 217, Mackenzie (1982), 85. Napoleon's plans for Pianosa are in Campbell's "Journal" (1869), 244.

CHAPTER 23. "ODIOUS AND CRIMINAL TRAFFICK IN HUMAN FLESH"

The epigraph comes from Castlereagh's letter to Liverpool, *CC*, X, 490. "Six weeks" is from Sir Robert Keith, (1849), 456. "Magnificent weather" is from Gentz, February 19, 1815, *Tagebücher* (1873), I, 359, and cited in McGuigan, *Metternich and the Duchess* (1975), 441, and also San Marzan's diary entry, February 26, 1815, in Ilario Rinieri, ed., *Corrispondenza inedita dei Cardinali Consalvi e Pacca nel tempo del Congresso di Vienna* (1903), lxxii. A "swarm of idlers and newsmongers" is in Comte Auguste de La Garde-Chambonas, *Anecdotal Recollections of the*

Congress of Vienna (1902), 379. On the dinners in early February, Talleyrand to the Duchess of Courland, February 8–9, 1815, *TLI*, 114. The accounts of Tsar Alexander and Countess Flora Wrbna-Kageneck's wager at Princess Bagration's salon, and subsequent competiton certainly made the rounds, though the sources do not agree on key elements, such as the length of time, the margin of victory, and the prize awarded. See the descriptions, for example, in Countess Thürheim's *Mein Leben* (1913), II, 117–118, Méneval, *Memoirs*, III, 345, San Marzan, *Diario*, February 20, 1815, lxxii; Rzewuska *Mémoires de la comtesse Rosalie Rzewuska 1788–1865* (1939), I, 265, Bernstorff, *Ein Bild aus der Zeit von 1789 bis 1835: Aus ihren Aufzeichnungen* (1896), I, 175, Humboldt to Caroline, February 23, 1815, *Briefe*, IV, 485, Agent ** to Hager, February 16, 1815, *DCV*, II, no. 1636. Rosenkrantz's *Journal du Congrès de Vienne 1814–1815* (1953), February 23, 1815, 159. Castlereagh wondering if Wellington might consider replacing him in Vienna, Castlereagh to Wellington, December 17, 1814, *CC*, X, 217–220. Castlereagh now wanting to delay his departure: the day after the secret treaty, Castlereagh to Liverpool, January 4, 1815, *CC*, X, 235–236, and a letter to Wellington, *CC*, X, 236.

Many historians write that Wellington arrived in Vienna on February 3, as did Castlereagh, Castlereagh to Liverpool, draft, February 6, 1815, *CC*, X, 248. But that does not bear out, according to references in diaries of other people who saw Wellington or dined with him prior to that date. Talleyrand, who hosted an early dinner for Wellington, reported that he arrived on the first, Talleyrand to King Louis XVIII, February 8, 1815, *TLC*, 303. San Marzan also noted his arrival that day, February 1, 1815, *Diario*, lxx, as did Rosenkrantz, who saw him, February 1, 1815, 136. A police report also noted it for the first, report to Hager, February 2, 1815, *DCV*, II, no. 1467. Talleyrand's dinner for Duke of Wellington on the fourth of February was, of course, not the first in Vienna held in his honor. The reference to the great gathering in the homes of bankers is in Karl von Nostitz, undated entry from the beginning of February 1815, *Leben und Briefwechsel* (1848), 166.

The enthusiasm surrounding Wellington's arrival in Vienna is in Comte Auguste de La Garde-Chambonas, *Anecdotal Recollections of the Congress of Vienna* (1902), 381–382, and the duke breathing life into celebrations, Méneval, *Memoirs*, III, 349. Wellington and escort Grassini, Karl von Nostitz, undated entry from the beginning of February 1815, in *Leben und Briefwechsel* (1848), 168, as well as note to Hager, February 3, 1815, *DCV*, II, no. 1483, and Agent Nota to Hager, who added the words of Grassini as "belle of the universe," same day, II, no. 1499. Wellington's mannerisms are in Elizabeth Longford, *Wellington: Years of the Sword* (1969), 352–368, Andrew Roberts, *Napoleon and Wellington: The Battle of Waterloo and the Great Commanders Who Fought It* (2001), and Richard Holmes *Wellington* (2002). The phrase "stern monosyllables" and the laugh are in Longford (1969), 353. Wellington had been a field marshal since Battle of Vitoria 1813, and duke since 1814, resolved in House of Commons, May 13, 1814, and also in House of Lords, June 27, 1814, text printed in *WD*, VII, 522–525. Castlereagh sent his dispatches to London through Wellington's embassy in Paris, Castlereagh to Liverpool, as seen, for example, October 25, 1814, *BD*, CXXI, 216.

Before leaving for Vienna, Talleyrand had promised assistance on the slave trade issue at the congress, Wellington to Castlereagh, October 4, 1814, *WD*, VII, 574. Talleyrand's proposal for a commission on the slave trade, Talleyrand to Louis XVIII, December 15, 1814, *TLC*, 211. Slave trade, Ambassadors of the King at the Congress to the Minister of Foreign Affairs, no. 26, January 24, 1815, *Memoirs* III (1891), 18–19. Challenges and frustrations of the many vested interests in France also in a letter to William Wilberforce, September 15, 1814, *WD*, VII, 558–559. He adds here in this letter that the abolition was unfairly associated with the turmoil of the French Revolution, and suffered accordingly. The influence of the press and particularly the difficulty of getting anything published in favor of abolition, Wellington to Wilberforce, October 8, 1814, *WD*, VII, 576. Another objection was that Britain had an ulterior motive—using the former slaves as soldiers to fight their war with the United States: Wellington to Wilberforce, December 14, 1814, *WD*, VII, 620. France did not respond to Britain's offer of an island in exchange for France's support on the question of slave trade, for example, is in Castlereagh to Liverpool, October 25, 1814, *BD*, CXX, 215. Description of life on board the slave ship and the words "a scene of horror" come from Olaudah Equiano (Gustavus Vasa), which, as Adam Hochschild noted, remains one of a few from a slave, *Bury the Chains: Prophets and Rebels in the Fight to Free an Empire's Slaves* (2005), 32. See Hochschild, and for more on this question at the congress, see Jerome Reich, "The Slave Trade at the Congress of Vienna—a Study in English Public Opinion," *Journal of Negro History*, 53, April 1968, 129–43. There is a large collection of documents on this matter at HHStA, StK Kongressakten 13. The protocol and the declaration are published in *Le Congrès de Vienne et les traités de 1815* (1864), II, 724–727.

Castlereagh on the fervor of the issue and "the popular impatience which has been excited" hindering his negotiations, Castlereagh to Liverpool, October 25, 1814, *BD*, CXX, 215–216. British view that all merchant vessels offer "permission to visit" and that all vessels with slaves on board "should be liable to be seized," Wellington to Talleyrand, August 26, 1814 *WD*, VII, 540. The proposal of a mutual right to search ships had not been favorably received by the French government, Wellington to Castlereagh, November 5, 1814 *WD*, VII, 595. Castlereagh's idea of "a sort of permanent European Congress in existence" working on the slave trade, Castlereagh to Liverpool, November 21, 1814 *BD*, CXXIX, 233. Castlereagh's idea of peacetime economic sanctions, Castlereagh to Liverpool, October 25, 1814, *BD*, CXX, 216, and discussion in Webster, *The Foreign Policy of Castlereagh, 1812–1815: Britain and the Reconstruction of Europe* (1931), 415ff. Slave trade example for many sacrifices, and others skeptical, Webster, *The Art and Practice of Diplomacy* (1961), 2–3. The Slavery Commission Conference is in C. K. Webster, *The Congress of Vienna 1814–1867* (1919) (1937 ed.), 89, and Jerome Reich's "The Slave Trade at the Congress or Vienna," April 1969,

109–143. The first meeting of Slavery Commission, January 20, 1815, II, 660–670, *Le Congrès de Vienne et les traités de 1815*, ed. Comte d'Angeberg (1864), and the opposition from Portuguese and Spanish are seen in many places, for example, the meeting on the sixteenth, in II, 612–614. Some of Castlereagh's letters on slave trade intercepted, such as one to Portuguese minister Palmella, January 30, 1815, *DCV*, II, no. 1354, also to Gentz, Hager to Emperor, January 25, 1815, II, no. 1378. Agreement with Portugal is in Angeberg (1864), II, 670–673. Additional information on the slave trade negotiations, as Castlereagh saw it, or rather wished to present it before parliament, Castlereagh in speech in the House of Commons, March 20, 1815, *BD*, appendix, II, 395–396. See also Talleyrand to King Louis XVIII, February 8, 1815, *TLC*, 309–310, and his letter on the fifteenth, 322. "Odious and criminal traffick . . ." and the progress report comes from Castlereagh to Liverpool, January 1, 1815, *BD*, CLIII, 274, and another variation in Memorandum as to the Mode of Conducting the Negotiations in Congress for the Final Abolition of the Slave Trade, *BD*, 235. The condemnation of the slave trade itself, dated February 8, 1815, is in Angeberg (1864), II, 726–727, with the phrase "desolated Africa, degraded Europe, and grieved humanity" on 726.

Chapter 24. Before the Cake Was Cut

Isabey working on the painting of the congress was noted by Agent Freddi to Hager, December 30, 1814, *DCV*, I, no. 1203, and, on the eve of Wellington's arrival, he had just painted Hardenberg, as the Prussian noted in his diary, January 17, 1815, *Tagebücher und autobiographische Aufzeichnungen* (2000), 812. For Isabey's stay in Vienna, see Basily-Callimaki, *J. B. Isabey: sa vie—son temps, 1767–1855* (1909), 159–197. Isabey's solution to the dilemma, and conversation with Humboldt, are also in Marion W. Osmond's *Jean Baptiste Isabey: The Fortunate Painter, 1767–1855* (1947), 135–136. The outcome on Poland and Saxony, Webster, *The Foreign Policy of Castlereagh, 1812–1815: Britain and the Reconstruction of Europe* (1931), 384–385. The signing on February 11 was, of course, followed by several other agreements between Russia and Austria, Russia and Prussia, working out the details—Czartoryski's disillusionment, with comments on the problems of the Grand Duke Constantine's administration and a rash of suicides in the army, for example, come from *Adam Czartoryski's Memoirs and His Correspondence with Alexander I*, ed. Adam Gielgud (1968), II, 306ff, with additional information in Patricia Kennedy Grimsted's *The Foreign Ministers of Alexander I: Political Attitudes and the Conduct of Russian Diplomacy, 1801–1825* (1969), 224; Kukiel's *Czartoryski and European Unity, 1770–1861* (1955), 131–133; and Zawadzki's *A Man of Honour: Adam Czartoryski as a Statesman of Russia and Poland, 1795–1831* (1993). Talleyrand's perspective on the Saxon dispute is in his letter to King Louis XVIII, February 1, 1815, *TLC*, 294–297, with more on the dispute over Leipzig, and the tsar's offer of Thorn, Talleyrand to King Louis XVIII, February 8, 1815, *TLC*, 305–306, Castlereagh to Liverpool, February 6, 1815, *BD*, CLXXII, 301. Hardenberg and Prussian insistence on Leipzig, and the claims of not being able to return to Berlin without it, Castlereagh to Liverpool, January 29,

1815, *BD*, CLXIX, 296–297. For more on the reasons behind the Prussian state, opinion, military strategy, and commerce, see Gaëtan de Raxis de Flassan's *Histoire du Congrès de Vienne* (1829), I, 185–186. The king of Saxony being freed, and the settlement, *TLC*, 307, 316–317, and 526–530. The tsar's role was also acknowledged by Castlereagh, February 13, 1815, *BD*, CLXXIV, 304.

The success of the Evaluations Committee was noted in the letter by the French Ambassadors of the King at the Congress to the Minister of Foreign Affairs, no. 23, January 6, 1815, 5, and the value of the secret treaty, Castlereagh to Liverpool, February 13, 1815, *BD*, CLXXIV, 303. Unpopularity of agreements in Berlin is in Nota to Hager, February 24, 1815, *DCV* II, no. 1713, and also Berlin unhappy with Prussian performance at Congress of Vienna, Zerboni di Sposetti to Leipziger, February 25, 1815, *DCV*, II, no. 1736. See also Castelalfer to Saint-Marsan, intercepted February 18, 1815, no. 1715. Rosenkrantz also heard of Hardenberg's windows being broken over his perceived failure to secure Saxony, March 11, 1815, *Journal*, 181, and more on the unpopularity in the Rhineland, note to Hager, February 15, 1815, II, no. 1622. Blücher's words on not being able to wear the Prussian uniform, Flassan, *Histoire du Congrès de Vienne* (1829), I, 225. "Where is Germany," "Prussia," and "with the first" are in Sweet (1980), II, 193–195. For more on Prussia's traditional focus on the east, rather than the west, see Brendan Simms, *The Struggle for Mastery in Germany, 1779–1850* (1998), 61. Another excellent overview can be found in James J. Sheehan's *German History, 1770–1866* (1994).

The activities of one of Baron Hager's informers on the night cited in the narrative, including the carriage ride back with Dalberg and early morning return, come from the reports of Agent ** for February 7, 1815, *DCV*, II, nos. 1533 and 1534. The Jean de Paris was described by Friedrich Anton von Schönholz, *Traditionen zur Charakteristik Österreichs, seines Staats-und Volkslebens unter Franz I* (1914), II, 129–130. "I am the victim" comes from Baron Claude-Francois de Méneval, *Memoirs Illustrating the History of Napoleon I from 1802 to 1815*, ed. Baron Napoleon Joseph de Méneval (1894), III, 387. Jomini's advice comes from one of his intercepted letters to his brother, January 30, 1815, *DCV*, II, no. 1471.

The words "every one contributes, and every one wins" come from Talleyrand's letter to Louis XVIII, March 3, 1815, *TLC*, 365. Castlereagh finalizing his work and planning on his handover of the embassy to the Duke of Wellington, Castlereagh to Liverpool, February 6, 1815, *BD*, CLXXII, 300. Castlereagh pressing for an extension of his stay, Castlereagh to Liverpool, January 4, 1815, *BD*, CLIX, 281; *WSD*, IX, 525. Castlereagh leaves Vienna, February 14, according to Webster, 396, who relied upon Castlereagh, 396. It was, however, more likely the fifteenth, as noted by many around him, for example, Talleyrand to King Louis XVIII, February 15, 1815, *TLC*, 316, San Marzan, *Diario*, lxxi, Hardenberg, February 15, 1815, *Tagebücher*, 816, and Perth, *Wiener Kongresstagebuch, 1814–1815*, 91. Some of Castlereagh's last discussions, before leaving Vienna, were about Turkey, *GPWK*, 411–413, and Gentz to Karadja, February 24, 1815, Castlereagh working on Russian tsar and the guarantee of status quo, Gentz to Karadja, February 24, 1815, 143. Castlereagh's negotiations with Turkish minister,

Castlereagh to Robert Liston, February 14, 1815, *BD*, CLXXV, 306. Enclosure along with Wellington letter, announcing that he would replace Castlereagh, Wellington to Liston, February 16, 1815, also printed in *DCV*, II, no. 1672, though without the insert on the Castlereagh-Mavrojény discussions. Castlereagh trying to ensure that the great powers protected Turkey is also in Webster, *The Art and Practice of Diplomacy* (1961), 21. Like Castlereagh, Metternich was interested in obtaining a guarantee of Ottoman territory, Gentz to Karadja, January 14, 1815, *Dépêches inédites* (1876), 141–142. My discussion of the Austrian-Bavarian dispute over Salzburg and other territories draws on many sources, particularly Enno E. Kraehe (1963–1983), II, 313ff. Talleyrand and the tsar conversation on the thirteenth of February, Talleyrand to King Louis XVIII, February 15, 1815, *TLC*, 325–330.

It is, of course, disputed when exactly Napoleon decided to leave Elba, ranging from the first day of arrival or even before his arrival, to mid-February, when he clearly began his plans. Some, like J. M. Thompson, believe that it began as soon as he left France, if not at Fontainebleau, *Napoleon Bonaparte* (1952), 401, while others, like F. M. Kircheisen, suggest a later date, probably January 1815 (*Napoleon*, trans. Henry St. Lawrence (1932), 685), and certainly by February, August Fournier, *Napoleon the First: A Biography* (1903), 687, and John Holland Rose, *The Life of Napoleon I* (1916), II, 405. Fleury de Chaboulon wrote his fascinating if controversial account, *Mémoires pour servir a l'histoire de la vie privée, du retour et du règne de Napoleon en 1815* (1820), I–II. The importance of Fleury de Chaboulon visit in early February, John Holland Rose (1916), II, 405–406, and Thompson (1952), 401–402, which likely only confirmed what Napoleon had already intended by early February; Norman Mackenzie agrees, *The Escape from Elba: The Fall and Flight of Napoleon, 1814–1815* (1982), 201. Troubles of the Bourbon dynasty in France, Grote to Münster, February 27, 1815, *DCV*, II, no. 1843, Goltz to Hardenberg, same day, no. 1845. Napoleon apparently knew of the attempts at Vienna to send him off to St. Helena, and one Englishman reported a conversation on Elba in January to that effect, Agent ** to Hager, May 9, 1815, no. 2353. Napoleon had the impression that the congress was ending, and Murat had written him to that effect, in February 1815, Thompson (1952), 401. Many had fed him that information, including Count Colonna, Fleury de Chaboulon, Kircheisen (1932), 685, and Rose, II, 403–404. Napoleon never accepting defeat and seeing betrayal all around him, Thompson (1954), 390–391, and developed by David Hamilton-Williams in *The Fall of Napoleon: The Final Betrayal* (1994). Napoleon's men gardening, before departure in Campbell's journal, *Napoleon at Fontainebleau and Elba; Being a Journal of Occurrences in 1814–1815* (1869), 380. Departure from the island, Fleury de Chaboulon (1820), I, 152–154, Houssaye *1815* (1904), I, 193–196. André Castelot, *Napoleon*, trans. Guy Daniels (1971), 520–521, Mackenzie (1982), 214–215, Lefebvre, *Napoleon* II (1969), 360, Napoleon's words "without striking a blow" are in Felix Markham, *Napoleon* (1963), 226, as well as Austrian police report, Freddi to Hager, March 10, 1815,

DCV, II, no. 1855. Napoleon's orders for the day of departure, including his address to the soldiers, are in *Ordres et Apostilles de Napoléon* (1911–1912), IV, nos. 6515–6520.

CHAPTER 25. TIME TO SAVE THE WORLD AGAIN

Jean-Gabriel Eynard's words come from his journal entry, March 14, 1815, in *Au Congrès de Vienne: journal de Jean-Gabriel Eynard* (1914–1924), II, 21. The meeting the previous night is in Comte d'Angeberg, *Le Congrès de Vienne et les traités de 1815*, II, 896–898. The arrival of the dispatch, Metternich's reactions, the meeting with the emperor, conversation with Talleyrand, and the conference with the other powers are in *NP,* I, 209-211. Dorothée and Talleyrand that morning is in Philip Ziegler's *The Duchess of Dino: Chatelaine of Europe* (1962), 124–125 and Micheline Dupuy, *La Duchesse de Dino* (2002), 189. Talleyrand's opinion on Napoleon's destination is in *NP,* 210, and also Nota to Hager, March 8, 1815, *DCV* (1917), II, no. 1831, San Marzan, Ilario Rinieri, ed., *Corrispondenza inedita dei Cardinali Consalvie Pacca nel tenpo del Congresso di Vienna* (1903), March 8, 1815, lxxiii, Talleyrand to King Louis XVIII, March 7, 1815, *TLC,* 374. Wellington also recounts the unity of the courts at the meetings that morning, March 7, Wellington to Castlereagh, March 12, 1815, *WD,* VIII, 1. Pozzo di Borgo's words are also cited in Maurice Paléologue, *The Enigmatic Czar* (1938), 231. The uncertainty of his destination is clear, but many believed he would land at Naples, note to Hager, March 8, 1815, *DCV,* II, no. 1827. Reports of Napoleon arriving in Naples, anonymous note to Hager, March 10, 1815, II, no. 1856, and the opinion that Napoleon was going to France was held by "a great minority," Méneval, *Memoirs,* III, 350. Gentz learned of the escape, in *Tagebucher* (1873), I, 363.

Spies also learned of Napoleon's departure, March 7, Agent Freddi reported to Hager, II, no. 1819. They also had intercepted a letter on Napoleon's departure that contained a reasonably accurate account of the number of soldiers with him, II, no. 1820. Warnings of Napoleon's likely flight preceded his departure, for instance, Weyland to Hager, February 13, 1815, II, no. 1604, and premature reports of his departure, Agent Nota to Hager, February 25, 1815, *DCV,* II, no. 1728, and another one, February 24, 1815, no. 1875. The evening at the theater, when news spread, is in, for example, Thürheim, *Mein Leben: Erinnerungen aus Österreichs Grosser Welt, 1788–1819* (1913), II, 121ff, and the attempt to remain focused on the performance, 122. Countess Bernstorff also heard the news at the theater, *Ein Bild aus der Zeit von 1789 bis 1835: Aus ihren Aufzeichnungen* (1896), I, 178. Both note the fear on the faces of the congress dignitaries. Other sources note the arrival of the news at the theater, from Bertuch's *Tagebuch vom Wiener Kongress* that day (141) to Archduke Johann, *Aus dem Tagebuche Erzherzog Johanns von Oesterreich, 1810–1815,* ed. Franz, Ritter von Krones (1891), 208-209. On the performance of the Kotzebue play that night, see also Hugo Wittmann's "Wiener Theater zur Zeit des Congresses" in Eduard Leisching's *Der Wiener Congress: Culturgeschichte die Bildenden Künste und das Kunstgewerbe*

Theater—Musik in der Zeit von 1800 bis 1825 (1898), 271. A number of other ballets and tableaux were also scheduled, including a pantomime called "The Caliph of Baghdad," as Hardenberg recorded in his diary, March 6–7, 1815, *Tagebücher und autobiographische Aufzeichnungen* (2000), 818.

Response of many Poles to Napoleon's flight, note to Hager, March 8, 1815, *DCV*, II, no. 1828, and the Polish enthusiasm still strong, Agent N.N. to Hager, May 10, 1815, no. 2361. Rzewuska agreed (I, 271). English as "guilty of a negligence," Talleyrand to King Louis XVIII, March 7, 1815, *TLC*, 374. Blaming Britain, Agent ** to Hager, March 8, 1815, *DCV*, II, no. 1826, and an interception from the same day, no. 1825, along with speculation, note to Hager, same day, 1827. Lord Stewart asking, "Are we Napoleon's keepers?" N.N. to Hager, March 12, 1815, no. 1864.

Dalberg blaming Austria and Russia, and comments on France overheard by Agent Devay, Agent ** to Hager, March 24, 1815, *DCV*, II, no. 2005. Humboldt's opinion on Napoleon's escape, Agent ** to Hager, March 18, 1815, no. 1938. Humboldt wondering about the source of Napoleon's money, Agent L to Hager, undated report, though written sometime in mid-March, editor puts it reasonably on the nineteenth or the twentieth, II, no. 1950. On General Koller's trip to Elba, see, for example, the report of an anonymous agent to Hager, November 27, 1814, *DCV* I no. 911, Goehausen to Hager, November 23, 1814, no. 854 and Agent P . . . to Hager, December 4, 1814, no. 978. Méneval discusses the atmosphere of blame, for example, in *Memoirs*, III (1894), 351. The comparison to the dangerous man in prison refused bread comes from Denmark's Minister of Foreign Affairs Niels Rosenkrantz, March 7, 1815, *Journal de Congrès de Vienne 1814–1815* (1953), 176. Hanover's Count Münster agreed about "the almost criminal carelessness" in facing Bonaparte, March 18, 1815, 227. "It was not difficult to perceive" comes from Clancarty to Castlereagh, March 11, 1815, *CC*, X, 264–265, and many others confirm the sense of fear, such as Archduke Johann in his diary, March 17, 1815, *Aus dem Tagebuche Erzherzog Johanns von Oesterreich, 1810–1815*, ed. Franz, Ritter von Krones (1891), 211. "Set the world" from Bernstorff (1896), I, 178.

CHAPTER 26. HIS MAJESTY, THE OUTLAW

King Louis XVIII's response is in Henri Houssaye's *1815: La première restauration, le retour de l'île d'Elbe, les cent jours* (1904), 22, and Alan Schom, *One Hundred Days: Napoleon's Road to Waterloo* (1992), 34–35. "Act of a madman" comes from a supplement to Comte de Blacas d'Aulps letter to Prince Talleyrand, April 10, 1815, in Talleyrand, *Memoirs*, III, 99, as well as Noailles and king of Prussia discussion at Zichy's salon, Note to Hager, 8 March 1815, *DCV*, II, no. 1828.

The king of Saxony would be freed, and his kingdom saved, Talleyrand wrote to the Duchess of Courland, February 8–9, 1815, *TLI*, 114. King of Saxony moved from Friedrichsfeld, Princess Radziwill, February 21, 1815, *DCV*, II, no. 1752, and Castelalfter, the same day, no. 1753. Talleyrand, Metternich, and Wellington visited with the king of Saxony, Talleyrand, *Memoirs* (1891), II, 209–211, Talleyrand to King Louis XVIII, March 7, 1815, *TLC*, 376–377, and his account of the audience, including the words "nothing but objections" and "they seemed to nourish a hope," Talleyrand to King Louis XVIII, March 12, 1815, *TLC*, 380–381. Documents from the visit in *DCV*, II, 900–904. On the king of Saxony's refusal to sign, Freddi to Hager, March 18, 1815, no. 1925, and more on its lack of success an anonymous note to Hager, that same day, *DCV*, II, no. 1943, and Méneval, *Memoirs*, III, 352. King of Saxony treatment "a stain on the history of the Congress," Gentz wrote in *Denkschrift*, *NP*, II, 494, Rosenkrantz, March 8, 1815, *Journal*, 177–178.

"A pretext" comes from an anonymous report to Hager, March 8, 1815, *DCV*, II, 1827. "If not the only topic of conversation," "walks, at gatherings," and the king of Bavaria as "deranged," Alexander Ivanovich Mikhailovsky-Danilevsky, February 26, 1815 (Russian calendar), trans. Alexander Sapojnikov in Ole Villumsen Krog, ed., *Danmark og Den Dansende Wienerkongres: Spillet om Danmark* (2002), 146. Police agents also noted the king of Bavaria's unease, for example, in a report to Hager, March 10, 1815, *DCV*, II, no. 1856, and bets are in several reports. Baronne du Montet's words are in *Souvenirs* (1904), 137. The description of the make-believe scene at Metternich's is in La Garde-Chambonas, *Anecdotal Recollections* (1904), 414–415. Vienna had been in Lent for weeks; Ash Wednesday was February 8. "Quivering violins" comes from Countess Lulu Thürheim's *Mein Leben: Erinnerungen aus Österreichs Grosser Welt, 1788–1819* (1913), II, 91. Emperor Francis's letter to the lord chamberlain about cutting back on expenses, dated March 21, 1815, is in HHSTA, OmeA Nr 237 ext 1815, in Krog, ed., *Danmark og den dansende Kongress* (2002), 458.

Napoleon's progress eluding ships is in Houssaye (1904), I, 203–209, and Mackenzie (1982), 217–223. The pace through the snow-covered Alps is in Fournier, *Napoleon the First*, trans. Margaret Bacon Corwin and Arthur Dart Bissell (1903), 689, and Thiers, *History of the Consulate and the Empire of France Under Napoleon*, XI (1894), 186, Napoleon's proclamations to soldiers and the people, Fournier (1903), 689–690, Englund (2004), 427–428, Castelot (1971), 527–528, Kircheisen (1932), 689, Fisher (1912), 218, "delirious enthusiasm," Johnston, 215–216. Marchand at Grenoble had orders to "stop . . . Buonaparte's brigands," Castelot (1971), 527, and more on the encounter at Laffrey, Chandler, *The Campaigns of Napoleon* (1966), 1011. "The inhabitants of Grenoble" is in Alan Schom's *One Hundred Days: Napoleon's Road to Waterloo* (1992), 26, and the strength of the Bourbon armies, David Hamilton-Williams's *The Fall of Napoleon: The Final Betrayal* (1994), 174. Additional problems of the Bourbon government, particularly regarding the loyalty of Napoleon's former marshals, is in Arnail-François de Jaucourt's letter to Talleyrand, March 11, 1815, *Correspondance du comte du Jaucourt avec le prince de Talleyrand pendant le Congrès de Vienne* (1905), 230–231. Napoleon's flight and the market, for example, is recorded by the banker Jean-Gabriel Eynard, March 15, 1815, *Au Congrès de Vienne: journal de Jean-Gabriel Eynard* (1914–1924), II, 23. The happiness of the

Prussians was noted already by Humboldt in a letter to his wife, Caroline, March 7, 1815, *Wilhelm und Caroline von Humboldt in ihren Briefen*, Anna von Sydow, ed. (1910), IV, 491. The increased warlike attitudes of the Prussians appears in many sources at this time, for instance, an intercepted letter from the king of Prussia, March 14, 1815, *DCV*, II, no. 1913. The scoundrels in Vienna were for Napoleon, the tsar observed, note to Hager, April 8, 1815, no. 2149.

The Committee of Eight signs the declaration against Napoleon: Talleyrand discussed it in many places, Talleyrand to King Louis XVIII, March 12, 1815, *TLC*, 382–383; Talleyrand to King Louis XVIII, March 14, 1815, *TLC*, 387 (dated the thirteenth in his memoirs), and letter to the Duchess of Courland, March 15, 1815, *TLI*, 138, as well as Talleyrand to Labrador, intercepted, April 15, 1815, no. 2210 (though the date was misprinted), and Labrador, *Mélanges sur la vie privée et publique* (1849), 40–41. Talleyrand's words "if I succeed" come from Jean Orieux's *Talleyrand: The Art of Survival*, trans. Patricia Wolf (1974), 481. The declaration against the outlaw, which was published on the front page of the *Wiener Zeitung* in French and German on March 15, can be read in *Le Congrès de Vienne et les traités de 1815* (1864), III, 912–913. Talleyrand was referring to Napoleon as a bandit already, in a letter, on March 8, 1815, *TLI*, 135, and being outside the law, Talleyrand to King Louis XVIII, March 7, 1815, *TLC*, 374, as were others in the French embassy, March 9, 1815, *DCV*, II, no. 1836.

Work on the declaration, note to Hager, March 12, 1815, no. 1872, and the meeting, Agent ** March 13, 1815, no. 1887; its duration and signing at midnight, Gentz, *Tagebücher*, March 13, 1815 (1873), I, 364. Several smaller powers were upset at not being included in the declaration, for example, Münster, March 18, 1815, George Herbert Münster, *Political Sketches of the State of Europe, 1814–1867: Containing Count Ernst Münster's Despatches to the Prince Regent from the Congress of Vienna* (1868), 228. March 13 statement seen as "an incitement to murder, worthy of the days of barbarism," Méneval (1894), III, 357, 491. "Dagger of the assassin," Wellington to Wellesley Pole, May 5, 1815, *WD*, VIII, 61. Other criticisms of the declaration are in Archduke Johann's diary, March 14–18, 1815, *Aus dem Tagebuche Erzherzog Johanns von Oesterreich, 1810–1815*, ed. Franz, Ritter von Krones (1891), 211.

News of Napoleon's flight reaches Schönbrunn Palace and Empress Marie Louise, Méneval (1894), III, 349–351, her confusion, 355, and her dejection, 358. Weeping in her room, Goehausen to Hager, March 9, 1815, *DCV*, II, no. 1837, and the court around her, Nota to Hager, same day, no. 1838. Other reports of her sadness overheard by Agent **, March 13, 1815, no. 1887, and rumors that she might end up in Salzburg, then disputed heavily between Austria and Bavaria, were noted by Agent ** to Hager, February 14, 1815, II, no. 1624. Archduke John feeling sorry for Marie Louise, Méneval (1894), III, 435, and entourage still Bonapartist, Agent ** to Hager, March 16, 1815, *DCV*, II, no. 1910. Marie Louise change of livery is in a report to Hager, March 15, 1815, no. 1900.

Some historians are quick to dismiss rumors of a plot to kidnap young Napoleon as unfounded, or just an excuse to fire his Bonapartist staff, now that Napoleon had escaped, but this is not necessarily so easy a conclusion. It is possible that the police had the wrong person. Montesquiou's defense, Premier Récit de "Mamman Quiou," and, more important, the Second Récit de "Mamman Quiou," are printed by her son, Anatole Montesquiou, *Souvenirs sur la révolution, L'empire, la restauration et le règne de Louis-Philippe* (1961), 356–383. Talleyrand's advice for Anatole de Montesquiou to leave Vienna at once, Talleyrand to Louis XVIII, March 17, 1815, 413, and more on him, Münster (1868), April 8, 1815, 240. Little Napoleon's sadness at the abrupt loss of his governess is clear from many intercepted letters, including, among others, nos. 2225, 2246, 2299, 2324, and 2388. Fouché's words on the attempt and near success are in *Mémoires de Joseph Fouché* (1967), II, 191.

Chapter 27. With the Spring Violets

Ney's words on the "iron cage" come from the supplement to Comte de Blacas d'Aulps letter to Prince Talleyrand, April 10, 1815, Talleyrand, *Memoirs*, III, 100. French securities dropped from 83 in early March to 51 in early April, Fournier, *Napoleon the First*, trans. Margaret Bacon Corwin and Arthur Dart Bissell (1903), 700. King Louis' words on dying in defense of his country come from a speech before the chambers, Henri Houssaye, *1815: La première restauration, le retour de l'ile d'Elbe, les cent jours* (1904), I, 335–336. Description of Paris deserted came from the Royal Horse Artillery officer, Captain Edmund Walcot, in Antony Brett-James, *The Hundred Days: Napoleon's Last Campaign from Eye-witness Accounts* (1964), 11–12, who also reported that Paris, on Napoleon's return, resembled a fair. Paris and royal court on the eve of departure also in Thiers (1894), XI, 255–264. The flight of King Louis XVIII rumored, and reported beforehand, report to Hager, March 18, 1815, *DCV*, II, no. 1922. Crown diamonds and several millions with the king at his departure, Jaucourt to Talleyrand, April 10, 1815, *TLC*, 435. On the series of military meetings, Talleyrand to King Louis XVIII, March 19, 1815, *TLC*, 419–420, and another letter on the twenty-third, 422–423. The conference and treaty signed on March 25 are in *Le Congrès de Vienne et les traités de 1815* (1864), III, 969–976. Wellington on the difficulties of renewing the Treaty of Chaumont, and his support of the Allies in obtaining British subsidies, Wellington to Castlereagh, March 25, 1815, *BD*, CLXXXIV, 316, and also in *WD*, VIII, 9. "Nothing can be done with a small or inefficient force . . ." also comes from this dispatch.

"Debauched, dissolute" come from Agent Nota's description of the Duchess of Sagan's salon, March 2, 1815, *DCV*, II, no. 1776. The Duchess of Sagan's financial troubles, McGuigan, *Metternich and the Duchess* (1975), 451, and Metternich selling the duchess's sapphires here, as well. See also Metternich's letter to the Duchess of Sagan, March 21, 1815, *MSB*, 279, and Montesquiou's "*Second Récit de 'Mamman Quiou,'*" in Anatole Montesquiou's *Souvenirs sur la révolution, L'empire, la restauration et le règne de louis-philippe* (1961), 359–360. Many French émigrés reached Vienna that spring, Baronne du Montet, *Souvenirs*, 138.

Dorothée's mother, the Duchess of Courland, arrived in Vienna, report to Hager, March 25, 1815, no. 2014, and Gentz, *Tagebücher*, March 25, 1815 (1873), 367. A number of short notes between Talleyrand and the Duchess of Courland after she arrived in late March are preserved and can be read in *TLI*, 143–210. Spies had reason to believe of Napoleon's return to Paris, note to Hager, March 21, 1815, no. 1977, and also from an intercepted letter, March 29, 1815, no. 2068. The king's flight from another intercept, March 28, 1815, no. 2043, and Napoleon's entrance, report to Hager, same day, no. 2044. "Paris had the characteristic air" comes from Antony Brett-James (1964), 13, and more on the setting, in *The Memoirs of Queen Hortense*, published by arrangement with Prince Napoleon, trans. Arthur K. Griggs (1927), II, 188, and Fleury de Chaboulon's *Mémoires pour servir a l'histoire de la vie privée, du retour et du règne de Napoleon en 1815* (1820), I, 260–261. Napoleon carried up, John Holland Rose, *The Life of Napoleon I* (1916), II, 409, ascending, Fournier, *Napoleon the First*, trans. Margaret Bacon Corwin and Arthur Dart Bissell (1903), 693; "It's you! It's you!" André Castelot, *Napoleon*, trans. Guy Daniels (1971), 534. Napoleon on the happiest time of his life, said at St. Helena, Steven Englund, *Napoleon: A Political Life* (2004), 429, and Felix Markham, *Napoleon* (1963), 227. The Napoleonic bee under the Bourbon fleur-de-lis is in Comte de Lavalette's *Mémoires et souvenirs du comte de Lavalette* (1905), 345.

Metternich's return to the salon of the Duchess of Sagan and words "at last broken" are in McGuigan (1975), 449–450. On Wellington's departure from Vienna on the morning of March 29, see Wellington to Castlereagh, April 5, 1815, *WD*, VIII, 15, Clancarty to Castlereagh letter that day, *BD*, CLXXXVII, 318, Talleyrand to King Louis XIV, March 29, 1815, *TLC*, 433. Stewart to Rose, March 30, 1815, no. 2079, report to Hager, March 29, 1815, *DCV*, II, no. 2052, and confirmation, report to Hager, April 2, 1815, *DCV*, II, no. 2090. See also report to Hager, March 19, 1815, no. 1939. The kissing was noted, later in Paris, to Lady Shelley, *The Diary of Frances Lady Shelley, 1787–1817*, ed. Richard Edgcumbe (1914), 112, and also in Elizabeth Longford, *Wellington: Years of the Sword* (1969), 396. Wellington was often surrounded by women in salons, and some asked for a kiss also, in Countess Bernstorff, *Ein Bild aus der Zeit von 1789 bis 1835: Aus ihren Aufzeichnungen* (1896), I, 182. Earl of Clancarty to succeed Wellington after his departure, Wellington to Castlereagh, March 18, 1815, *WD*, VIII, 6. Metternich's April Fools' prank is in Gentz's *Tagebücher*, April 1, 1815, 369, and Gentz's insomnia, again, March 27, 1815, 367, with his reputation for "unreasonable cowardice," Rzewuska, I, 103. The text of the fake paper and "both shaking hands" are Pflaum (1984), 257, and the words "nearly paralyzed" are in Bernstorff, *Ein Bild aus der Zeit von 1789 bis 1835: Aus ihren Aufzeichnungen* (1896), I, 180.

Dalberg on the desperate embassy is in a note to Hager, April 10, 1815, *DCV*, II, no. 2168, and France losing its position at congress after Napoleon, Dalberg to his wife, April 11, 1815, no. 2209. Credit problems, learned from banker Geymüller, Rosenkrantz, March 24, 1815, *Journal*, 199, and Talleyrand's attempts to deal with new realities, as a result of Napoleon cutting off funds the day of his arrival at Paris, Talleyrand to Jaucourt, April 23, 1815, *Correspondance du comte du Jaucourt avec le prince de Talleyrand pendant le Congrès de Vienne* (1905), 287. French credit at the Bank of France stopped as of March 21, and the inability to pay staff, given the lack of money from Paris, Talleyrand to King Louis XVIII, May 5, 1815, *TLC,* 498. Four secretaries at French embassy, report to Hager, undated, *DCV,* II, no. 1934, and more on staff, report to Hager, April 16, 1815, no. 2215. Rosenkrantz, March 25, 1815, *Journal,* 201, Talleyrand's possessions impounded, Talleyrand to the Duchess of Courland, April 5, 1815, *TLI,* 160. Order of Elephant to Talleyrand, Rosenkrantz, March 30, 1815, *Journal* (1953), 204. Talleyrand's inquiry about the state of his correspondence with the king and foreign ministry, and words cited on that subject, Talleyrand to King Louis XIV, March 29, 1815, *TLC,* 434. "I did not take with me," Reinhardt to Talleyrand, March 28, 1815, n. 4, 435, and the burning of a few, particularly from Mariotti, Jaucourt to Talleyrand, March 27, 1815, 436, and more fully in *Correspondance du comte du Jaucourt* (1905), 246–248. Fear of the secret treaty being found by Bonaparte, Castlereagh to Wellington, March 27, 1815, *CC,* X, 286–287, and fear confirmed a few days later, April 8, 1815, 300–301.

CHAPTER 28. CRIERS OF *VIVE LE ROI!* DOERS OF NOTHING

"Let us embrace and let everything be forgotten" comes from Metternich, *NP,* I, 329. News of Murat's attack on the Papal States, and its effects on Austria, Talleyrand to King Louis XVIII, April 3, 1815, *TLC,* 437–438. Murat's attack as a "declaration of war," Metternich told Clancarty, Clancarty to Castlereagh, April 8, 1815, *BD,* CXC, 322. Caroline Murat's opposition to Murat's attack is in Albert Espitalier's *Napoleon and King Murat* (1912), 478–480. Murat acted like he had justification, even approval, from Napoleon, but this was not the case, A. Hilliard Atteridge's *Joachim Murat: Marshal of France and King of Naples* (1911), 279–280. Britain subsidized the French embassy, Talleyrand repeated to King Louis XIV, March 29, 1815, *TLC,* 433–434, and Dalberg to Stewart, March 29, 1815, no. 2058. The limits of the funding, Talleyrand to King Louis XVIII, May 5, 1815, *TLC,* 498. For more on the challenges the French embassy faced, see notes to chapter 27. "Diplomatic phalanx" comes from one of Jaucourt's undated letters to Talleyrand, *TLC,* 485. The words "Criers of *Vive le Roi!*" and "if we are to undertake the job" come from Castlereagh's letter to Wellington, March 26, 1815, in *CC,* X, 285–286. The other powers wanting British subsidies, Wellington to Castlereagh, March 18, 1815, *WD,* VIII (1844–1847), 4–6, and more on their demands, Wellington to Castlereagh, March 25, 1815, 9. Hardenberg described the officers near the king as "praetorian bands," Castlereagh reported in a letter to Liverpool, August 24, 1815, *BD,* 370. German princes and their demands for a confederation, Rosenkrantz, March 23, 1815, *Journal,* 197. Fear of Saxon troops, Pozzo di Borgo to Nesselrode, April 30/May 12, 1815, Comte Charles Pozzo di Borgo (1890), *Correspondance Diplomatique du comte Pozzo di Borgo, ambassadeur de Russie en*

France et du comte du Nesselrode depuis la restauration des Bourbons jusqu'au Congrès d' Aix-la-Chapelle, 1814–1818, 115. The dispute between Austria and Bavaria is in Enno E. Kraehe, *Metternich's German Policy* (1963–1983), II, 308–314 and 336–342.

Napoleon's appeals to the Great Powers, Fisher (1912), 221–223, and appeals to "peace and liberty," Fournier, *Napoleon the First,* trans. Margaret Bacon Corwin and Arthur Dart Bissell (1903), 694. Napoleon's attempts to send emissaries to the Vienna Congress (Flahaut, Stassart, and Montrond), Méneval, *Memoirs,* III, 380–382, and Talleyrand to King Louis XVIII, April 13, 1815, *TLC,* 446–448, among many others. Dalberg reported the orders not to receive any negotiator from Napoleon, March 31, 1815, *DCV,* II, no. 2080. Napoleon's protest against the obstruction of his courier, intercepted, April 4, 1815, no. 2183. Montrond's arrival comes from Talleyrand to the Duchess of Courland, April 5, 1815, *TLI,* 160. His stay at French embassy, report to Hager, April 7, 1815, no. 2135, and Hager to Emperor, same day, no. 2117. See also Nesselrode to Pozzo di Borgo, April 22, 1815, *Correspondance Diplomatique du comte Pozzo di Borgo* (1890), 105, among other references at this time. Talleyrand's conversation with Montrond, including words "Read the Declaration," *TLC,* 447, and May 9, 1815, n. 2, 450. For Metternich's negotiations with Fouché at this time, see Ray Ellisworth Cubberly's *The Role of Fouché During the Hundred Days* (1969), 54–70.

Alexander's "open war" on Metternich, Münster, April 12, 1815, George Herbert Münster, *Political Sketches of the State of Europe, 1814–1867: Containing Count Ernst Münster's Despatches to the Prince Regent from the Congress of Vienna* (1868), 242. King Louis XVIII's claim of support and appeal for Allied help, King Louis XVIII to Talleyrand, April 9, 1815, *TLC,* 442–443. Talleyrand made many requests for information that spring, and the words "extreme impatience" come from his letter to King Louis XIV, March 30, 1815, *TLC,* 437. "I am most anxious to have you with me," King Louis XVIII to Talleyrand, April 22, 1815, *TLC,* 465. Jaucourt's appeal, Jaucourt to Talleyrand, April 28, 1815. Belief that King Louis XVIII would make Talleyrand his first minister, Grote to Münster, May 8, 1815, *DCV,* II, no. 2416. Talleyrand viewed as leading figure of the king's future cabinet, Pozzo di Borgo to Nesselrode, May 11/23, 1815, *Correspondance Diplomatique* (1890), 140, and his presence as vital, Pozzo di Borgo to Nesselrode, April 28, 1815, 111, and again a few days later, May 6, 1815, 114. Talleyrand's stalling is seen, for example, in Talleyrand to Jaucourt, May 13, 1815, as well as a letter the following day to the king, May 14, 1815, *TLC,* 499–500, and *Memoirs,* III, 124, and again later, May 23, 1815, 504, dated May 25 in his memoirs.

CHAPTER 29. FAREWELLS

May 3 letter, and Metternich at meeting, Kraehe, *Metternich's German Policy* (1963–1983), II, 354–355, and Humboldt's letter to his wife, May 5, 1815, *Wilhelm und Caroline von Humboldt in ihren Briefen* (1910), IV, 541–546, along with June 1, 1815, 562–564. Varnhagen von Ense also notes the quarrel in his memoir,

Denkwürdigkeiten des eignen Lebens (1987), II, 652–653. See also Angeberg, *Le Congrès de Vienne et les traités de 1815* (1864), IV, 1902–1905. Boyen had only recently arrived in Vienna, report to Hager, April 6, 1815, *DCV* II, no. 2113, and Hardenberg, *Tagebücher und autobiographische Aufzeichnungen*, February 26, 1815 (2000), 817. Reference to the Swedish minister and combat preference, Löwenhielm to his brother, intercepted, October 18, 1814, *DCV*, I, no. 453. "Homeric heroes" and "pretty meadow" come from Humboldt's letter to his wife, Caroline, May 5, 1815, 544–545, and "pure foolishness," June 1, 1815, 564. Fear of Metternich's leniency toward Napoleon, note to Hager, May 25, 1815, *DCV*, II, no. 2440, and Metternich opening Napoleon's letters, Clancarty to Castlereagh, May 6, 1815, *BD*, CXCV, 331. "Plunders," "castles," and "to rob the state" are in Hilde Spiel's *The Congress of Vienna: An Eyewitness Account*, trans. Richard H. Webes (1968), 307, 309. Grasel is in Friedrich Anton von Schönholz's memoirs, *Traditionen zur Charakteristik Österreichs, seines Staats- und Volkslebens unter Franz I* (1914), II, 156–158, as well as Caroline Pichler, who heard some details at a souper with an indiscreet official from the police administration, *Denkwürdigkeiten aus meinem Leben* (1914), III, 100–101. "Utterly annihilated," Clancarty to Castlereagh, May 13, 1815, *BD*, CXCVI, 333.

Napoleon sending the treaty to the tsar can be read in many sources, for example, Castlereagh's letter to Wellington, April 8, 1815, *CC*, X, 300–301. Alexander's reaction is in Baron vom Stein's diary entry the same day, *Briefe und amtliche Schriften*, eds. Erich Botzenhart and Walter Hubatsch (1957–1974), V, 380–381. "While we live" and "better things" are in Maurice Paléologue's *The Enigmatic Tsar: The Life of Alexander I of Russia*, trans. Edwin and Willa Muir (1938), 234. The scene is also in Alan Palmer's *Metternich* (1972), 145, and his *Alexander I: Tsar of War and Peace* (1974), 322. The tsar throwing the document into the fire is in Allen McConnell's *Tsar Alexander I: Paternalistic Reformer* (1970), 132; Leonid I. Strakhovsky's *Alexander I of Russia: The Man Who Defeated Napoleon* (1949), 162; and Henri Troyat's *Alexander of Russia: Napoleon's Conqueror* (1980), 221. The Prussians already knew of the secret treaty, as can be seen in, among other places, an intercepted letter, *DCV*, II, no. 2232.

Wellington's concerns for the number and quality of troops in the Netherlands were voiced before he left Vienna, Wellington to Castlereagh, March 26, 1815, *WD*, VIII, 12, and confirmed upon arrival, Wellington to Bathurst, April 6, 1815, VIII, 18. Many other complaints followed that month, and for more, see Rory Muir's *Britain and the Defeat of Napoleon, 1807–1815* (1996), 351, and Elizabeth Longford, *Wellington: Years of the Sword* (1969), 401–403. "Ill-equipped," "very inexperienced Staff," and the frustrations that "they are doing nothing in England" come from Wellington to Lord Stewart, May 8, 1815, *WD*, VIII, 66. King of Holland as the Frog, for instance, Hon. H. G. Bennet to Mr. Creevey, June 13, 1815, *The Creevey Papers* (1904), I, 217. Wellington blamed the difficulty of raising troops in Belgium on the French and Bonapartist sympathies of many soldiers, Wellington to Torrens, May 22, 1815, *WD*, VIII, 102.

Blücher as "Vorwärts" is in many sources, such as Karl von Nostitz, January 27, 1815, in *Leben und Briefwechsel* (1848), 161. "The stoutest old fellow" comes from Lady Shelley, *The Diary of Frances Lady Shelley 1787–1817*, ed. Richard Edgcumbe (1914), 60. Wellington called Blücher "a fine fellow," but added that he was "a very rough diamond with the manner of a common soldier," R. H. Gronow, *The Reminiscences and Recollections of Captain Gronow, Being Anecdotes of the Camp, Court, Clubs, and Society 1810–1860* (1900), 129. Blücher's belief that he was pregnant, Longford (1969), 406, and Andrew Roberts's *Waterloo: June 18, 1815: The Battle for Modern Europe* (2005), 24. Fear of Saxon troops can be seen in many sources, such as Pozzo di Borgo to Nesselrode, 30 April/12 May 1815, *Correspondance Diplomatique* (1890), 115, and the mutiny, Wellington to Clancarty, May 3, 1815, *WD*, VIII, 57, and a letter he wrote two days later, on page 60. See also letters intercepted in Vienna, such as *DCV*, II, no. 2395 and no. 2436, as well as Agent **, who reports the broken windows, May 13, 1815, no. 2381. "Slip out" is from Wilhelm von Humboldt's letter to his wife, Caroline, May 12, 1815, *Wilhelm und Caroline von Humboldt in ihren Briefen*, Anna von Sydow, ed. (1910), IV, 548. Wellington tireless in his organization of the coalition forces, Pozzo di Borgo observed from Brussels, Pozzo di Borgo to Nesselrode, April 28, 1815, *Correspondance Diplomatique* (1890), 111. The cricket match is from Lieutenant-Colonel Alexander Lord Saltoun's letter to his wife, in Antony Brett-James, ed., *The Hundred Days: Napoleon's Last Campaign from Eyewitness Accounts* (1964), 26.

The weather is in Gentz, May 1, 1815, *Tagebüch*er, 375, and San Marzan same day, *Diario*, lxxix. Chestnut trees blooming is in Bertuch, May 7–11, 1815, *Tagebuch vom Wiener Kongress*, 184–185, as well as McGuigan, *Metternich and the Duchess* (1975), 471. "The most beautiful spring," Gentz, May 16, 1815, *Tagebüch*er, 379. Tsar Alexander leaving Vienna, Stein, *Briefe und amtliche Schriften*, eds. (1957–1974), V, 386, eds. Erich Botzenhart and Walter Hubatsch, and report to Hager, May 26, 1815, *DCV*, II, no. 2493. This agent also informs of the departures of the king of Prussia and Emperor Francis, and Münster, June 3, 1815, George Herbert Münster, *Political Sketches of the State of Europe, 1814–1867: Containing Count Ernst Münster's Despatches to the Prince Regent from the Congress of Vienna* (1868), 268. Alexander's words on being, if not a tsar, then a general in Austrian army, reported to Hager, April 15, 1815, II, no. 2206. Gifts of Tsar Alexander and king of Prussia, note to Hager, May 26, 1815, II, no. 2461. King of Prussia, too, Agent ** to Hager, May 29, 1815, no. 2472. "Lost his English accent" is in McGuigan (1975), 475, and Metternich's birthday party, Gentz, May 15, 1815, *Tagebücher*, 378. English carriage from London, Gentz, noted April 16, 1815, 372. Gentz as "most bribed man in history," Helen du Coudray, *Metternich* (1936), 25. Gentz's house hunting, his carriage, and discussion of late May, Golo Mann's *Secretary of Europe; The Life of Friedrich Gentz, Enemy of Napoleon*, trans. William H. Woglem (1946), 237–240, and McGuigan (1975), 467–471. Gentz signed for his new place, April 20, 1815, *Tagebücher*, 373, and more on May 16, 1815, 379. Nesselrode on Gentz, noting the accusations against his helpful colleague, "not without foundation," though his defense of Gentz, who "only took money from those who thought like him," *Autobiographie* in A. de Nesselrode, ed., *Lettres et papiers du chancelier comte de Nesselrode, 1760–1850*, II, 35.

Bagration's financial distress is chronicled in many police reports: Nota to Hager, June 8, 1815, no. 2536; Agent ** to Hager, June 11, 1815, no. 2570. Agent Nota trying to find out about Princess Bagration's debts, and planning to go through intermediary, Nota to Hager, June 13, 1815, no. 2574, and Nota to Hager, June 14, 1815, no. 2584. The creditors besieging her salon is also in Gentz to Metternich, June 20, 1815, *Briefe von und ab Friedrich von Gentz*, III, 308–309, and the resolution of Bagration's financial crisis, Agent Nota to Hager, June 22, 1815, no. 2614, and Agent**, June 25, 1815, no. 2624. Prison risk for Bagration is also discussed in Hastier's *"Les Bagration": Vieilles histoire, étranges enigmes* (1962), 174, and Susan Mary Alsop, *The Congress Dances: Vienna, 1814–1815* (1984), 204. Princess Bagration's tender good-byes to Crown Prince of Württemberg, Agent ** to Hager, April 11, 1815, *DCV*, II, no. 2173, as well as in McGuigan (1975), n. 51, 553. Stewart and Duchess of Sagan affair discovered by police, note to Hager, May 19, 1815, no. 2411, and Stewart still spending every night with her, report to Hager, May 28, 1815, no. 2470. Stewart and Duchess of Sagan were still having their affair, as seen by a series of reports to Hager intermittently in the first week of June, no. 2500–2524. Life at their inn, and the embassy, intercepted letter from Jean de Carro, June 7, 1815, no. 2528, along with reports to Hager, June 7, 1815, no. 2531, and June 11, no. 2563.

Chapter 30. Conquering the Peace

Intentions for Champ de Mars ceremony, Fournier, *Napoleon the First*, trans. Margaret Bacon Corwin and Arthur Dart Bissell (1903), 692; comparison with coronation, J. M. Thompson, *Napoleon Bonaparte* (1952), 409, and the lack of enthusiasm in the cheers, Ludwig, *Napoleon*, trans. Eden Paul and Cedar Paul (1926), 520, who in turn drew from Coignet's *Memoirs*. Schom also shows this well in his depiction of the ceremony, *Napoleon Bonaparte* (1997), 731–734. See also Steven Englund, *Napoleon: A Political Life* (2004), 436–437, Fournier, *Napoleon the First*, trans. Margaret Becon Corwin and Arthur Dart Bissell (1903), 705–707, and Méneval, *Memoirs*, III, 449. Pozzo saw this planned Champ de Mars ceremony as a "ridiculous parody," Pozzo di Borgo to Nesselrode, April 17, 1815, *Correspondance Diplomatique du comte Pozzo di Borgo, ambassadeur de Russie en France et du comte du Nesselrode depuis la restauration des Bourbons jusqu'au Congrès d' Aix-la-Chapelle, 1814–1818* (1890), 89. For more on the changes, and Napoleon's use of power, see also Pozzo di Borgo to Nesselrode, May 30/June 11 1815, 156. Some thought the Champ de Mars fete would be "fatal to Bonaparte" and his reign would end that day, Creevey, *The Creevey Papers: A Selection from the Correspondence and Diaries of the Late Thomas Creevey, M.P.* (1904), I, 227. The number of affirmatives is sometimes higher, calculating votes from the soldiers as well.

The tsar's words of June 4 come from a letter of Krüdener to Mme. Stourdza, Clarence Ford, *Life and Letters of Madame de Krudener* (1893), 165, and "you can imagine" are in Countess Edling, *Mémoires* (1888), 232. Additional parts of the conversation, such as "you have not humbled" and "like a criminal," are in Troyat, *Alexander of Russia*, trans. Joan Pinkham (1982), 225, and Edling (1888), 231–233. "A great explosion of love" comes from Gregor Dallas's *The Final Act: The Roads to Waterloo* (1997), 410. For more, see also Walter Alison Phillips's *The Confederation of Europe: A Study of the European Alliance 1813–1823 as an Experiment in the International Organization of Peace* (1966), 125–126; W. P. Cresson's *The Holy Alliance: The European Background of the Monroe Doctrine* (1922), 32–35; and Ernest John Knapton's *The Lady of the Holy Alliance* (1939).

The German Congress, or committee as it now called itself in its enlarged version, faced many challenges, and they can be followed in detail in Enno E. Kraehe's *Metternich's German Policy* (1963–1983), II, 366–399, Paul Sweet's *Wilhelm von Humboldt: A Biography* (1980), II, 195–208, and Guglielmo Ferrero's *The Reconstruction of Europe: Talleyrand and the Congress of Vienna, 1814–1815* (1941), 314–323. Humboldt expressed the frustration succinctly, calling the German conference "un-German," letter to Caroline Humboldt, May 21, 1815, *Wilhelm und Caroline von Humboldt in ihren Briefen*, Anna von Sydow, ed. (1910), IV, 556. Count Münster elaborates on the difficulties in a letter, June 3, 1815, *Political Sketches of the State of Europe, 1814–1867: Containing Count Ernst Münster's Despatches to the Prince Regent from the Congress of Vienna* (1868), 269–271, and another letter of the same date, 271–275. Minutes of the meeting can be read in Angeberg's *Le Congrès de Vienne et les traités de 1815* (1864), III, 1227ff.

Hardenberg and Humboldt's cooperation on the protection of Jewish minorities is in Max J Kohler's *Jewish Rights at the Congresses of Vienna (1814–1815), and Aix-la-Chapelle (1818)*, (1918), 9–11. Hardenberg's letter on behalf of the Jewish communities in Hamburg, Lübeck, and Bremen, January 4, 1815, is in Kohler (1918), 11–12, as is Humboldt's report on Jewish rights, which can be found in *Gesammelte Schriten*, X, 97–115. Gentz received many gifts as seen in his diary, and the "beautiful present" appeared, for instance, April 13, 1815, *Tagebücher* (1873), I, 371. Humboldt declines the gifts, for example, in a letter to Caroline, June 4, 1815, *Wilhelm und Caroline von Humboldt in ihren Briefen*, ed. Anna von Sydow (1910), IV, 566–567. Opposition in the meetings reported here as well, 565–567. Rechberg's laughing is in Kohler (1918), 23, and the change to the text in Kohler (1918), 27, and Kraehe (1963–1983), II, 382. Carl Bertuch's memorandum is housed at HHStA Kongressakten Kart 8. The minutes do not identify the source of the change to Article XVIII, Kraehe (1963–1983), II, 383.

Plans for a *traité général*, Gentz to Karadja, April 22, 1815, *Dépêches inédites*, 151. Uncertainty of the treaty, Spaen to Nagell, May 25, 1815, *DCV* II, no. 2445, and the magnitude of the challenge, Münster, May 15, 1815, George Herbert Münster, *Political Sketches of the State of Europe, 1814–1867: Containing Count Ernst Münster's Despatches to the Prince Regent from the Congress of Vienna* (1868), 263. The question of a general treaty, or several separate ones, Gentz to Karadja, June 26, 1815, *Dépêches inédites*, 162 and 164–165, and Talleyrand's report to the king, *TLC*, 536–537. The commission for writing the treaty, Münster, June 3, 1815

(1868), 268. First suggestions were Gentz, Anstedt, and Besnardière, though the latter two declined to participate, Gentz to Karadja, June 26, 1815, *Dépêches inédites*, 162.

The eight powers who signed at Paris to sign at Vienna and the others "accede separately," Münster, June 3, 1815 (1868), 274–275. Signing the final act, Gentz, June 9, 1815, *Tagebücher*, 385, Gentz to Karadja, June 26, 1815, *Dépêches inédites*, 166–167. The twenty-six hands copying "morning to night" is in Gentz letter to Metternich, June 20, 1815, *Briefe von und ab Friedrich von Gentz*, (1913), III, 307. Signing of the act and some additional agreements added on the tenth, Hesse-Darmstadt on "cession of the duchy of Westphalia" and German treaty, Münster, June 11, 1815, 278, and the backdating, or retaining the eighth, Münster, letters June 11 through June 14, 278, 281, 283. Consalvi's protest, Angeberg (1864), IV, 1450–1453, and again on behalf of the pope, June 14, 1815, IV, 1922–1929. After the second signing, "definite closure of the congress," Gentz, June 19, 1815, *Tagebücher* (1873), 386. Spain's refusal to sign, given the "serious mistakes" of the congress, Labrador, *Mélanges sur la vie privée et publique du marquis de Labrador* (1849), 52–53, and his several protests in Angeberg (1864), III, 1018–1020, 1341–1342, and again, 1456–1458. Spain had not technically signed Treaty of Paris, at least as of May 30—it signed almost two months later, July 20. The Final Act is in Angeberg (1864), III, 1386–1433.

Metternich and Gentz dining in the garden, Gentz, June 12, 1815, *Tagebücher*, 385. Münster met with Metternich before the Austrian foreign minister left on night June 12–13, June 14, 1815 (1868), 284, Gentz, June 12, 1815, *Tagebücher*, 385. Talleyrand burning papers before leaving Vienna, comes from a report to the king, June 1815, *TLC*, 554.

Chapter 31. To Conquer or Die

Murat's defeats are in Jean Tulard, *Murat* (1999), as well as Albert Espitalier, *Napoleon and King Murat* (1912), and A. Hilliard Atteridge, *Joachim Murat: Marshal of France and King of Naples* (1911). Talleyrand to King Louis XVIII, May 1, 1815, *TLC*, 491. Napoleon's troubles and its rigorous efforts to overcome them are in Hamilton-Williams, *The Fall of Napoleon: The Final Betrayal* (1994), 206–208. Napoleon's dilemma, attack or defend, Chandler, *Waterloo: The Hundred Days* (1980), 25, and more on his challenges in Chandler's *The Campaigns of Napoleon* (1966), 1014ff. Carnot's advice to Napoleon, Ludwig, *Napoleon*, trans. Eden Paul and Cedar Paul (1926), 521. "To conquer or die" comes from John Holland Rose, *The Life of Napoleon I* (1916), II, 419.

The ball, Andrew Roberts, *Waterloo: June 18, 1815: The Battle for Modern Europe* (2005), 27–29, Antony Brett-James, ed., *The Hundred Days: Napoleon's Last Campaign from Eyewitness Accounts* (1964), 39–44, the *Vanity Fair* depiction, particularly chapters 28 and 32, along with John Hagan's "A Note on the Napoleonic Background of *Vanity Fair,*" *Nineteenth-Century Fiction*, 15, no. 4 (March 1961), 358–361. The coachhouse location comes from the daughter of the Duke and Duchess of Richmond, Lady Georgiana Lennox, Brett-James (1964), 41.

Proclamation to the citizens of Brussels already printed, Fournier, *Napoleon the First*, trans. Margaret Bacon Corwin and Arthur Dart Bissell (1903), 716. Wellington receiving news of the French move at the ball is also in *The Creevey Papers: A Selection from the Correspondence and Diaries of the Late Thomas Creevey, M.P.* (1904), I, 229, and Wellington present, "as composed as ever," 223. "A good map," "Napoleon has humbugged," and "I must fight" are in Longford (1969), 419 and 421. One of many critiques that Wellington received for attending the ball, J. M. Thompson, *Napoleon Bonaparte* (1952), 411, and Wellington and the Duke of Richmond looking over maps, Lady Shelley, *The Diary of Frances Lady Shelley, 1787–1817*, ed. Richard Edgcumbe (1914), I, 171, among many others. Richmond "marked the map with a pencil, and that mark I saw," Lady Shelley, who visited the Richmonds shortly afterward, 171.

Quatre Bras was described by Captain R. H. Gronow in *The Reminiscences and Recollections of Captain Gronow, Being Anecdotes of the Camp, Court, Clubs, and Society 1810–1860* (1900), I, 66–67. Ligny and the significance of the Prussian retreat north are in David G. Chandler, *The Campaigns of Napoleon* (1966), 1034–1047, and also his *Waterloo: The Hundred Days* (1980), 102–103 and 106. Prussian bitterness toward British allies, Colonel E. Kaulbach's "The Prussians" in Alun Chalfont, ed., *Waterloo: Battle of Three Armies* (1980), 64. News of Bonaparte's victory over the Prussians and Wellington's falling back were magnified even more at the time, Creevey (1904), 231–232. Actions on the seventeenth are in Owen Connelly's *Blundering to Glory: Napoleon's Military Campaigns* (1987), 210; Roberts's *Waterloo: June 18, 1815: The Battle for Modern Europe* (2005), 34–37; and Kircheisen (1932), 699, with Napoleon's fear of Wellington's escape.

The deceptively flat ground was described as "a great undulating plain," Croker to his wife, July 27, 1815, *The Croker Papers: The Correspondence and Diaries of the late Right Honourable John Wilson Croker*, ed., Louis J. Jennings (1884), I, 72; and a "vast undulating ground," Victor Hugo's *The Battle of Waterloo*, trans. Lascelles Wraxall (1907), 29. Wellington's activities on the morning of the eighteenth, including the letter to Lady Frances Wedderburn Webster, are in Gregor Dallas's *The Final Act: The Roads to Waterloo* (1997), 372. The "exhaustion of the troops" is in John Sutherland's *Men of Waterloo* (1966), 186, and "Blücher picked the fattest man" is in Barbero (2005), 45. A "torrent of rain" is in R. H. Gronow, *The Reminiscences and Recollections of Captain Gronow, Being Anecdotes of the Camp, Court, Clubs, and Society 1810–1860* (1900), I, 67. The conditions that night are well presented in Roberts (2005), 36–37, and the sleeping, lack of breakfast, and "petrified with cold" are in John Keegan's *The Face of Battle* (1976), 134–136.

My account of Napoleon's breakfast that morning draws on Andrew Roberts's *Napoleon and Wellington: The Battle of Waterloo—and the Great Commanders Who Fought It* (2001), xxix–xxxi; Alessandro Barbero's *The Battle: A New History of Waterloo*, trans. John Cullen (2005), 57; and John Holland Rose (1916), II, 451–452. The words "in war, morale" come from Roberts (2001), 163. General Drouot's suggestion is in David G. Chandler's *Waterloo: The Hundred Days* (1980), 126, and the small size of the battlefield in his *The Campaigns of Napoleon* (1966), 1064.

CHAPTER 32. LA BELLE ALLIANCE

The manor of Hougoumont was described by Robert Southey in *Journal of a Tour in the Netherlands in the Autumn of 1815* (1902), 89–90, and Colonel Alexander Woodford of Coldstream Guards, in Antony Brett-James, ed., *The Hundred Days: Napoleon's Last Campaign from Eye-Witness Accounts* (1964), 108–109. The attack is presented well in David Howarth's *Waterloo: Day of Battle* (1968), 71–80, and William Seymour in Alun Chalfont, ed., *Waterloo: Battle of Three Armies* (1980), 73–76, 85–90. Prince Jérôme's desperation, hurt pride, and the significance of the failed diversion are shown in Alan Schom's *One Hundred Days: Napoleon's Road to Waterloo* (1992), 280; John Sutherland's *Men of Waterloo* (1966), 197; and David G. Chandler's *The Campaigns of Napoleon* (1966), 1072–1073. The lone gardener hiding in the manor, Willem van Kylsom, and the words "every crack in the stone" come from Victor Hugo, *Battle of Waterloo*, trans. Lascelles Wraxall (1907), 14, 16–17. Wellington's words on "the closing of the gates" are in Elizabeth Longford's *Wellington: The Years of the Sword* (1969), I, 459, and Wellington repeated its importance to several other people, for example, to Lady Shelley, as she noted in her diary, September 1815, *The Diary of Frances Lady Shelley 1787–1817*, ed. Richard Edgcumbe (1914), 172. Alessandro Barbero's interpretation of the inability of the French to see the manor comes from *The Battle: A New History of Waterloo*, trans. John Cullen (2005), 76.

Grouchy and Gérard's conversation comes from Henry Houssaye, *1815: Waterloo* (1904), 293–296, and background on the commanders is told succinctly by Jacques Champagne in Chalfont, ed. (1980), 41 and 44–45, and Owen Connelly's *Blundering to Glory: Napoleon's Military Campaigns* (1987), 215. Napoleon at Rossomme and the sight of the Prussians as a cloud, Sutherland (1966), 198, and Longford (1969), I, 460. "Even now, we have" and "a more careful man" are in Schom (1992), 281 and discussed also in Chandler (1966), 1076. The guns are in Brett-James, ed. (1964), 113. The problems of Count d'Erlon formation are in Roberts (2001), 175, Roberts (2005), 63–65, and Howarth (1968), 88–89. Bijlandt's brigades are in Barbero (2005), 126–127, 130 and 134, and the low clouds are in Gregor Dallas's *The Final Act: The Roads to Waterloo* (1997), 373. Bullets on the breastplates and "a violent hailstorm" are from R. H. Gronow's *The Reminiscences and Recollections of Captain Gronow, Being Anecdotes of the Camp, Court, Clubs, and Society 1810–1860* (1900), I, 190–191. The animal-rights campaign was noted by Paul Johnson, *The Birth of the Modern: World Society 1815–1830* (1991), 85.

Uxbridge and the charge are from Roberts (2005), 68–71, and Barbero (2005), 139–168. Corporal John Dickson's account of the Union Brigade charge reveals the enthusiasm of such a charge, "a strange thrill run through me, and I am sure my noble beast felt the same," Brett-James, ed. (1964), 116–119. "Not a man present" and "walls bristling with steel" are in Gronow (1900), I, 69–71. The actual shape of the squares, and the actions of the horses as they charged a square, Roberts (2005), 78 and 85, and John Keegan, *The Face of Battle* (1976), 157–159. "Damn that fellow!" comes from Longford (1969), I, 468. Wellington called Waterloo a "pounding match," Wellington to Beresford, July 2, 1815, *WD*, VIII, 185–186. "Heavy surf" is in Captain C. Mercer's *Journal of the Waterloo Campaign* (1870), 110, and often cited in accounts, Keegan (1976), 158. Ney's first cavalry charge too early, John Holland Rose's *The Life of Napoleon I Including New Materials from the British Official Records* (1916), II, 461 and 463. Wellington's crisis, with center about to collapse, Longford (1969), I, 473, and Commandant Henry Lachouque's *Waterloo* (1975), 177. Napoleon's opportunities to win are in Chandler (1966), 1085–1087. Basil Jackson on deserters, *Notes and Reminiscences of a Staff Officer* (1903), 447. "Where do you want," John Holland Rose, *The Life of Napoleon I* (1916), II, 465, and Wellington's alleged "Let us pray," Barbero (2005), 242. The Prussians advanced despite many obstacles, in many sources, for instance, Colonel E. Kaulbach in Chalfont, ed. (1980), 92–93. Napoleon sending Guard into battle, Barbero (2005), 261–269, and Lachouque (1975), 182, and Wellington rallying his men, Longford (1969), I, 476–478.

The French fleeing "in utmost confusion," and the capture of approximately 150 cannon along with ammunition, Wellington to Earl Balhurst, June 19, 1815, *WD*, VIII, 149. Napoleon's words on the panic are in Gaëtan de Raxis de Flassan's *Histoire du Congrès de Vienne* (1829), II, 353. "Panic-stricken rabble" is in David Hamilton-Williams, *The Fall of Napoleon: The Final Betrayal* (1994), 239. "Everything failed me," David Chandler, *Waterloo: The Hundred Days* (1980), 10. Marshals on the sidelines are in Chandler (1966), 1022–1023, and Roberts (2005), 38. Roberts's words on the absurdity of the debate whether Wellington could have won without the Prussians (2005), 104.

Ney's actions at opening are discussed, for example, in Chandler (1980), 87–89, 92, and generally, 127, 187–190, and also in Chandler (1966), 1047–1057, 1061, 1092. Wellington's letter to Earl Balhurst, written at Waterloo, June 19, 1815, *WD*, 146–151, and a later one of the same date, from Brussels, 152. Wellington's words "death blow" come from a letter to Earl of Uxbridge, June 23, 1815, *WD*, VIII, 162. Varnhagen, like many, had difficulty at first believing the extent of the victory, Varnhagen to Cotta, June 30, 1815, *Varnhagen von Ense und Cotta: Briefwechsel 1810–1818*, eds. Konrad Feilchenfeldt, Bernhard Fischer and Dietmar Pravida (2006), I, 51. Some Prussians were already referring to La Belle Alliance, Hardenberg, June 18–24, 1815, *Tagebücher und autobiographische Aufzeichnungen* (2000), 822. Casualty estimates appear in David Chandler (1966), 1093–1094. Brussels as "vast hospital" comes from Eynard, June 30, 1815, *Au Congrès de Vienne: Journal de Jean-Gabriel Eynard* (1914–1924), II, 202. One of the overworked surgeons is in Brett-James (1964), 202–203. This surgeon, Charles Bell, made many sketches of the wounds, some of which were published in his pioneering study of neurology *The Nervous System of the Human Body* (1830). Napoleon's captured spurs comes from Wellington to Prince Regent, July 8, 1815,

WD, VIII, 202–203. "A Trojan horse" is in Hamilton-Williams (1994), 221. The secrecy surrounding Napoleon's return to Paris is in Pozzo di Borgo to Nesselrode, June 15/27, 1815 (1890), 175. Napoleon considering a dictatorship, and his abdication, August Fournier, *Napoleon the First: A Biography* (1903), 722–724, and F. M. Kircheisen, *Napoleon*, trans. Henry St. Lawrence (1932), 703, and more on his troubles 706–707. The legislative debate after Waterloo and Napoleon's early responses, Steven Englund, *Napoleon: A Political Life* (2004), 443–445. Lafayette's version is in his *Mémoires, correspondance et manuscrits* (1837–38), V, 86. Napoleon's last orders as emperor were making some final appointments and awarding pensions, *Ordres et apostilles de Napoléon* (1911–1912), IV, nos. 6869–6876.

CHAPTER 33. SHIFTING SAND

"Finita" comes from Gentz, *Tagebücher* (1873), 433. Pigeons often used in relaying messages, and even in World War II, as Reuters's Charlie Lynch did at Normandy in 1944, Walter Cronkite, *A Reporter's Life* (1996), 104. Sir Walter Scott's words on Waterloo come from *Private Correspondence*, II, 381, and also Carolly Erickson, *Our Tempestuous Day: A History of Regency England* (1986), 182. Lady Shelley toured the site three months later, staying with the Duke and Duchess of Richmond, and also noted the peasants selling items, *The Diary of Frances Lady Shelley, 1787–1817*, ed. Richard Edgcumbe (1914), 168. Croker to his wife, July 27, 1815, *The Croker Papers: The Correspondence and Diaries of the late Right Honourable John Wilson Croker* (1884), I, 72. Hats, caps, and other items were still on the battlefield that autumn, *Reminiscences and Recollections of Captain Gronow, Being Anecdotes of the Camp, Court, Clubs, and Society, 1810–1860* (1900), Robert Southey, *Journal of a Tour in the Netherlands in the Autumn of 1815*, the manuscript purchased at a Southey sale in the 1860s and published in 1902, 93.

Peace negotiations for 133 days, Palmer, *Metternich* (1972), 151, and gambling in Paris in 1815, with the games, Gronow (1900), 87–88, and more on the setting, 299–305. The military atmosphere is clear, the soldiers, for example, tying horses to trees on the Champs-Élysées, G.O., August 12, 1815, *WD*, VIIII, 240. Wellington's support of another Bourbon restoration, Wellington to Bathurst, July 2, 1815, *WD*, VIII, 188–193, and reference to the return of the Bourbons and the "foreign bayonets," in Count Molé, *The Life and Memoirs of Count Molé (1781–1855)*, ed. Marquis de Noailles (1924), I, 240. Clashes between Bonapartists and royalists, Eynard noted (1914–1924), July 27, 1815, II, 251, Croker to his wife, July 17, 1815, (1884), 65, and, of course, between the former and Allied soldiers, for example, Gentz to Pilat, September 12, 1815, *Briefe von Friedrich von Gentz an Pilat*, by Karl Mendelssohn-Bartholdy (1868), I, 182–183. King Louis XVIII's unpopularity, however, soon growing again, the view of the advisers, and fear of returning the country to the seventeenth century, Gentz to Karadja, October 23, 1815, *Dépêches inédites*, (1876), I, 187.

Blücher wanted Napoleon killed, Duke of Wellington reported to Sir Charles Stuart, June 28, 1815, the comments enclosed in a letter from Sir Charles Stuart to

Castlereagh, June 30, 1815, *CC*, X, 386–387. Castlereagh had written in support of sending Napoleon to Fort St. George in Scotland, letter to Lord Liverpool, July 17, 1815, *BD*, 350. Wellington agreed, Lady Shelley noted, *The Diary of Frances Lady Shelley 1787–1817*, ed. Richard Edgcumbe (1914), 105. Two frigates to take Napoleon to America, French delegation informed Allied leaders, Pozzo di Borgo to Nesselrode, June 20/July 2, 1815, *Correspondance Diplomatique du comte Pozzo di Borgo* (1890), 183.

Napoleon's readiness to fight, and strength of French forces still after Waterloo, are in David G. Chandler (1966), 1093–1094. Napoleon at Malmaison is in Henry Lachouque, *The Last Days of Napoleon's Empire: From Waterloo to St. Helena*, trans. Lovett F. Edwards (1966), 119–138, and *The Memoirs of Queen Hortense*, trans. Arthur K. Griggs (1927), II, 237–250. Napoleon weighing his options also in Gilbert Martineau, *Napoleon Surrenders*, trans. Frances Partridge (1971), 79–83, and more too, along with his time on the *Bellerophon*, in David Cordingly's fascinating *The Billy Ruffian: The Bellerophon and the Downfall of Napoleon: The Biography of a Ship of the Line, 1782–1836* (2003), 228–278. Liverpool's words on Napoleon becoming "an object of curiosity" are from his letter to Castlereagh, July 21, 1815, *CC*, X, 434. Napoleon boarding the Northumberland is from John R. Glover, Secretary to Rear Admiral George Cockburn on the Northumberland, August 7, 1815, *Taking Napoleon to St. Helena* (1895), 93.

While Prussia pressed for a dismemberment, England supported the "integrity of French territory," particularly as it existed in 1790, Gentz to Karadja, September 5, 1815, *Dépêches inédites*, 176–177. Russia supported moderation. Gneisenau had a hardness that approached vengeance (especially for France's role in keeping Saxony from Prussian hands), Pozzo di Borgo to Nesselrode, July 2, 1815 (1890), 187 (the June 20 date is in the Russian calendar). "Considerable difficulty with the Prussians," Castlereagh to Liverpool, July 12, 1815, *BD*, 342. The destruction of the manor comes from Gronow (1900), 201, and more violence, 201–203, and their occupation in passing, for example, 98–99, 130–131, 206–207. Complaints of Prussian excess and its many negative consequences, in many letters, Castlereagh to Liverpool, July 24, 1815, *BD*, CCVII, 351, and *WSD*, XI, 122. Hardenberg feeling "in the midst of Praetorian bands," Castlereagh to Liverpool, August 24, 1815, *BD*, 370; as well as *WSD*, XI, 137. Hardenberg exasperated with Blücher, noting in diary that he had "thousand bickerings," August 31 1815, *Tagebücher und autobiographische Aufzeichnungen* (2000), 825. Prussians worrying about influence of army on their cabinet, Pozzo di Borgo to Nesselrode, October 17, 1815 (1890), 220–221. On mad dogs in France, Gregor Dallas, *The Final Act: The Roads to Waterloo* (1997), 402. Blücher was also the name of the Duke of Richmond's Newfoundland, Johnson (1991), 717. Fears of the Prussians, including their demand for payments of enormous sums, and the mining of the bridge, Castlereagh to Liverpool, July 8, 1815, *CC*, X, 419–420, Croker to his wife, July 13, 1815, Croker (1884), 62. Pozzo di Borgo to Nesselrode, July 9, 1815, *Correspondance Diplomatique* (1890), 203. Prussians and blowing up Pont d'Iena, Count Molé 317, who was in charge of bridges and repairing them, noted damage to some 12,000 francs. Wellington's intervention on behalf of the bridge, Wellington to Blücher, July 8, 1815, *WD*, VIII, 201, and the next day, 203–204, including his arguments against the 100-million-franc levy. Wellington's protection, too, is in Lady Shelley's *Diary* (1914), 107, and Pozzo di Borgo (1890), 203. Croker claimed he saw the "marks of explosion," letter to his wife, July 13, 1815 (1884), 62, Gronow (1900), 129.

Prussia "animated by hatred and spirit of vengeance" was noted in context of how some in England were won over by this Prussian attitude, Gentz to Karadja, September 5, 1815, *Dépêches inédites* (1876), 173, and more demands, Gentz to Karadja, September 5, 1815, 174–175, Castlereagh to Liverpool, September 21, 1815, *BD*, CCXXVI, 378–379, and *WSD*, XI, 165. "Revolutions for the rest of our life," Talleyrand to the Duchess of Courland, June 1, 1815, *TLI*, 199. Vivant Denon's *Précis de ce qui s'est passé au musée royal depuis l'entrée des alliés à Paris*, and several letters describing the scenes, such as to le duc de Richelieu, July 10, 1815, are in Marie-Ann Dupuy, Isabelle le Masne de Chermont, Elaine Williamson, eds., *Vivant Denon: directeur des musées sous le consulat et l'empire correspondance (1802–1815)* (1999). Denon's efforts to protect art in the Louvre are in Judith Nowinski's *Baron Dominique Vivant Denon (1747–1825): Hedonist and Scholar in a Period of Transition* (1977), 102–104. More on the Prussians storming the museum that July is in Dorothy Mackay Quynn's "The Art Confiscations of the Napoleonic Wars," *AHR*, vol. 50, no. 3 (April, 1945), 450, and Charles Saunier's *Les Conquêtes Artistiques de la révolution et de l'empire: reprises et abandons des alliés en 1815* (1902), 101–111.

Wellington describes the efforts of the king of Prussia and the king of the Netherlands to restore their art, Wellington to Castlereagh, September 23, 1815, *WD*, VIII, 267–270. Wellington's words on loot are in Elizabeth Longford's *Wellington: Pillar of State* (1972), 27. Canova's mission to inspect the looted treasures, September 15, 1815, Ercole Consalvi, *Mémoires* (1864), 85–87, and October 2, 1815, 87–89. "Fear and hope," the difficulties arising from Treaty of Tolentino, and the arguments encountered in favor of retaining the art and manuscripts in Paris, Canova to Pope Pius VII, September 15, 1815, Consalvi (1864), 85–86. For more on the art looted from papacy, John Martin Robinson's *Cardinal Consalvi 1757–1824* (1987), 35; Owen Chadwick, *The Popes and European Revolution* (1981), 462; and E. E. Y. Hales, *Revolution and the Papacy* (1960), 113–115. Carrying out *Venus*, the bronze horses, and the art controversy are in Dorothy Mackay Quynn (April 1945), 451–460. Denon as "very low-spirited," Croker to his wife, July 14, 1815, John Wilson Croker, *The Croker Papers: The Correspondence and Diaries of the Late Right Honourable John Wilson Croker 1809 to 1830*, ed. Louis J. Jennings (1884), I, 62. Wellington being booed in the theater is in Rorry Muir, *Britain and the Defeat of Napoleon 1807–1815* (1996), 372. The tally of art removed comes from Louis-Antoine Lavallée, printed in Charles Saunier (1902), 161. Grimm's searching for manuscripts can be seen in a letter to Wilhelm, September 23, 1815, *Briefwechsel zwischen Jacob und Wilhelm Grimm aus der Jugendzeit* (1963), 453–454. Soldiers protecting the workers at the Arc de Triomphe, and the inability to return the Veronese, Schwarzenberg to his wife, September 29, 1815, Johann Friedrich Novák,

ed., *Briefe des Feldmarschalls Fürsten Schwarzenberg an seine Frau, 1799–1816*
(1913), 422. Basil Jackson witnessed the soldiers there, and the removal, *Notes and
Reminiscences of a Staff Officer* (1903), 106–110.

Tsar under influence of Krüdener, Clarence Ford, *Life and Letters of Madame
de Krudener* (1893), 176ff, Ernest John Knapton, *The Lady of the Holy Alliance*
(1939), 147ff, Countess Edling, *Mémoires* (1888), 241–242. The signing of the
Holy Alliance, Hardenberg, September 26, 1815, *Tagebücher und autobiographische Aufzeichnungen* (2000), 826. The terms are in *Le Congrès de Vienne et les
traités de 1815* (1864), IV, 1547–1549. The "great explosion of love" and hints of
Wilson's covenant in this alliance, Dallas (1997), 410 and 442. Cited passages
from the Act of the Holy Alliance come from the full text of the act, which appears
in the appendix of Walter Alison Phillips's *The Confederation of Europe: A Study
of the European Alliance, 1813–1823 as an Experiment in the International Organization of Peace* (1966), 305–306. Tsar Alexander told Castlereagh "nothing had
given him so much satisfaction as to fix his signature to this bond of peace,"
Castlereagh to Liverpool, September 28, 1815, *BD*, 384. Many other powers did
join the three original signatories of the Holy Alliance, including the king of Württemberg, king of Saxony, king of Sardinia, king of the Netherlands, as well as the
Republic of Switzerland and some former Hanseatic cities. The United States
remained aloof, though some, like the Massachusetts Peace Society, hoped it would
join, and wrote to the tsar about their intent to "disseminate the very principles
avowed in the wonderful Alliance." For more on the Holy Alliance and the United
States, William Penn Cresson's *The Holy Alliance: The European Background of
the Monroe Doctrine* (1922), 48. Henry Kissinger's words on the Holy Alliance are
in his *Diplomacy* (1994), 83. Consalvi's protests against the Holy Alliance, Hales,
Revolution and Papacy, 1769–1846 (1960), 237. Metternich's views are in *NP*, I,
214–216, and Castlereagh's "sublime mysticism and nonsense" comes from a letter
to Liverpool, September 28, 1815, *BD*, CCXXVIII, 383; *WSD*, XI, 175.

"Diplomacy by conference" is in Edward Vose Gulick's *Europe's Classical Balance of Power: A Case History of the Theory and Practice of One of the Great
Concepts of European Statecraft* (1967), 289–290. The significance of Article VI is in
Kissinger, *A World Restored: Metternich, Castlereagh, and the Problems of Peace
1812–1822* (1957), 221, and also his *Diplomacy* (1994), 83. Gentz as a possible Secretary General of Europe, October 21, 1815, *Tagebücher* (1873), I, 421. The words
"to regulate" come from Webster's *The Foreign Policy of Castlereagh, 1815–1822*
(1929), 121.

"A sort of queen in the diplomatic world" is from R. H. Gronow's *The Reminiscences and Recollections of Captain Gronow, Being Anecdotes of the Camp,
Court, Clubs, and Society 1810–1860* (1900), I, 300, and "A frantic passion" is in
Charles Rémusat, *Mémoires de ma vie* (1958–1967), I, 274–275. Dorothée was
viewed as Talleyrand's favorite also by Agent Nota to Hager, November 5, 1815,
DCV, II, no. 2768, and others, too, like Pasquier, *Histoire de mon temps: Mémoires
du chancelier Pasquier* (1893–1894), III, 369. Philip Ziegler agreed that "Talleyrand loved Dorothea deeply" and critiques the sources well, *The Duchess of*

Dino: Chatelaine of Europe (1962), 127–134, 141–142, as does Françoise de Berardy's *Talleyrand's Last Duchess* (1966), 126–131, and Emmanuel de Waresquiel's *Talleyrand: le prince immobile* (2003), 481–482. "Devoured by a slow fever" is in Count Mathieu Molé, ed., *The Life and Memoirs of Count Molé (1781–1855)*, (1924), III, 343–344.

Desires of French neighbors Netherlands, Prussia, Bavaria, and Württemberg on gaining more territory, Castlereagh to Liverpool, July 24, 1815, *BD*, CCVII, 350; *WSD*, XI, 122. Claims for indemnity and security, rather than a right from conquest, is in Castlereagh to Liverpool, September 25, 1815, *BD*, CCXXVII, 380. Loss of French territory predicted, including Alsace and Lorraine, Nota to Hager, August 10, 1815, *DCV* II, no. 2698. Gentz denied the rumored interference of the Great Powers in the dismissal of Talleyrand, Gentz to Karadja, September 25, 1815, *Dépêches inédites*, 179–180. Hardenberg, though, noted Alexander lobbied for Pozzo di Borgo, who was apparently offered the position with French government, September 21, 1815, *Tagebücher und autobiographische Aufzeichnungen*, 825. Letter King Louis XVIII to Tsar Alexander, September 11/23, 1815, reprinted in *Correspondance Diplomatique* (1890), 209–211. Pozzo did not think the king of France could accept such terms, August 15/27, 1815, 207. Expenses, single round of ammunition cost soldier's daily ration, Gunther E. Rothenberg, "The Austrian Army in the Age of Metternich," *Journal of Modern History* 40, no. 2 (June 1968), 165. Second Peace of Paris, Kircheisen, 705, and signing of the treaty, Gentz, November 20, 1815, *Tagebücher*, 430, Gentz to Karadja, November 25, 1815, *Dépêches inédites*, 192. Richelieu reading the treaty, as Molé saw him, "tears filled his eyes," and Talleyrand preferring to lose his hands than sign the treaty, Molé, II, 78 and 89. Edling also thought it was an "abuse of victory" (1888), 244. A "masterpiece of destruction," or *"un chef-d'oeuvre de destruction,"* in Pozzo di Borgo to Emperor Alexander, August 15/27, 1815, *Correspondance Diplomatique* (1890), 207. The treaty is in Angeberg (1864), IV, 1595ff. "This city and this sun . . ." comes from a letter, Metternich to his daughter Marie, July 13, 1815, and the translation of these lines is by Mrs. Alexander Napier, *Memoirs of Prince Metternich 1773–1815* (1880), II, 612.

EPILOGUE

Napoleon reached the harbor on the fifteenth, but he did not step onto the island until the seventeenth. "Black wart" is from naval surgeon Henry, cited by Alan Schom, *Napoleon Bonaparte* (1997), 767, and John Holland Rose, *The Life of Napoleon I* (1916), II, 497. Alexander had helped Marie-Louise gain Parma, as he had promised, and a secret treaty had been signed guaranteeing her son's succession to the duchy. Marie-Louise's gift to Metternich, Agent Freddi to Hager, July 13, 1815, *DCV*, II, no. 2657. The Duchess of Sagan's later marriage, depression, and words "she was so sad" come from Dorothy Guis McGuigan's *Metternich and the Duchess* (1975), 506–507, 513. The resolution of Princess Bagration's affairs and her later marriage are in Louis Hastier's "Les Bagration" in *Vieilles histoire, étranges enigmes* (1962), 175 and 182. Bagration and Feodora in Balzac's *La Peau de chagrin "avec une étonnante précision,"* Hastier (1962), 184–185, and Susan Mary Alsop, *The Congress Dances: Vienna 1814–1815* (1984), 208. "She has forgotten" and "only the veils" are also in Alsop (1984), 209. The Duchess in Czech literature is in McGuigan (1975), 516. "Phantasm" and "imaginary being" are in Harold Nicolson's *The Congress of Vienna: A Study in Allied Unity: 1812–1822* (1946), 274.

A vague death certificate is one reason for the controversy surrounding the tsar's death, Allen McConnell, *Tsar Alexander I: Paternalistic Reformer* (1970), 185. Henri Troyat agreed, *Alexander of Russia: Napoleon's Conqueror,* trans. Joan Pinkham (1980), note 293, and he surveyed some additional problems with the certificate, 302–303. The theory that the tsar fled to a monastery in Palestine was examined in Maurice Paléologue, *The Enigmatic Czar* (1938), 317–318. One proponent of the tsar as Feodor Kusmitch was Prince Vladimir Bariatinsky, *Le Mystère d'Alexandre Ier* (1929). Russian history, of course, has many legends of previous rulers, from false Dimitris to several Peter IIIs. "A sphinx who carried his secret with him into the tomb" is in Alan Palmer's *Alexander I: Tsar of War and Peace* (1974), xvii. See also Grand duc Nicolas Mikahaïlovitch, *Le Tsar Alexandre* (1931), I, 343–344.

The king of Saxony's money coming to Talleyrand appears in many sources, including Lord Acton's "Essay on the *Mémoires* of Talleyrand" in his *Historical Essays and Studies* (1926), 397. Acton, or John Emerich Edward Dalberg-Acton, was a grandson of the duke of Dalberg who served with Talleyrand at Vienna. Acton cited a conversation with Count Senfft, a former Saxon minister, who knew Talleyrand and reported Saxon money coming to him, to the tune of £40,000. For Talleyrand and Dorothée's likely love affair in Vienna, see notes to previous chapter. "Vienna, Vienna" and "If I ever did more" are in Ziegler, *The Duchess of Dino: Chatelaine of Europe* (1962), 127 and 121. Castlereagh's death is in Montgomery Hyde's *Strange Death of Lord Castlereagh* (1959).

Woodrow Wilson's comment on not wanting "any odour of the Congress of Vienna" into the Paris proceedings was prompted by a comment from the prime minister of New Zealand, who was about to pose a question in the Council of Ten after reading Webster's *Congress of Vienna* (1919), and that was the last anyone said about the congress at that conference, Webster later wrote, *The Art and Practice of Diplomacy* (1961), 28. "The Big fish" comes from Marquis de Labrador's *Mélanges sur la vie privée et publique* (1849), 33. For more on the question of nationalism at the Congress of Vienna, see Hannah Strauss's *The Attitude of the Congress of Vienna Toward Nationalism in Germany, Italy, and Poland* (1949). "Dividing the spoils" is in Gentz's memoir of the congress, *NP*, II, 474. Kissinger's words on the German Confederation is in his *Diplomacy* (1994), 80–81, and the legacy of the congress in Germany until 1866, James Sheehan, *German History, 1770–1866* (1994), 401. "Just equilibrium" is from Castlereagh's letter to Liverpool, November 11, 1814, in *BD*, 232. For more on the relationship between the Great Powers and the Monroe Doctrine, see William Penn Cresson's *The Holy Alliance: The European Background of the Monroe Doctrine* (1922). The declaration of Swiss neutrality is in Angeberg (1864), IV, 1640–1641. Diplomatic precedence from the chair of the commission on diplomatic rank, Labrador, *Mélanges sur la vie privée et publique* (1849), 50–51 as well as Annexe XVII of the Final Act, which was dated March 19, 1815 (1864), III, 934–935 and 939–940. Castlereagh on the "machine" in a speech before the House of Commons, March 20, 1815, printed in Appendix II to *BD*, 395. The Final Act is in *Le Congrès de Vienne et les traités de 1815* (1864), III, 1386–1433.

ILLUSTRATION CREDITS

1. *The Congress of Vienna/Meeting of the Plenipotentiaries of the Committee of Eight*, by Jean Baptiste Isabey, engraving by Jean Godefroy. (Wienmuseum)

2. *Promenade in the Prater* (Anonymous engraving from *Der Wiener Congress: Culturgeschichte die Bildenden Künste und das Kunstgewerbe Theater—Musik in der Zeit von 1800 bis 1825*, by Eduard Leisching, 1898)

3. *Austrian Foreign Minister, Prince Metternich.* (Castle Kynzvart)

4. *French Foreign Minister, Charles Maurice de Talleyrand, Prince de Bénévent*, by Tony Goutière, drawing by Leopold Massard, from a painting by François Gérard. Private Collection. (AKG Images)

5. *Emperor Francis I*, by Friedrich von Amerling. (Kunsthistorisches Museum, Wien)

6. *Alexander I, Emperor of Russia*, by Sir Thomas Lawrence. (The Royal Collection © 2006, Her Majesty Queen Elizabeth II)

7. *Frederick William III, King of Prussia*, by Sir Thomas Lawrence. (The Royal Collection © 2006, Her Majesty Queen Elizabeth II)

8. *Britain's Foreign Secretary Robert Stewart, Viscount Castlereagh*, by Sir Thomas Lawrence. (The Royal Collection © 2006, Her Majesty Queen Elizabeth II)

9. *Chancellor Prince Karl August von Hardenberg*, by Sir Thomas Lawrence. (The Royal Collection © 2006, Her Majesty Queen Elizabeth II)

10. *Prussian Ambassador and Scholar, Wilhelm von Humboldt*, by Sir Thomas Lawrence. (The Royal Collection © 2006, Her Majesty Queen Elizabeth II)

11. *Arthur Wellesley, First Duke of Wellington*, by Sir Thomas Lawrence. (The Royal Collection © 2006, Her Majesty Queen Elizabeth II)

12. *Princess Bagration*, by Jean-Baptiste Isabey. (© Louvre [*Cabinet de dessins*], Paris, France/Giraudon/The Bridgeman Art Library)

13. *Duchess of Sagan* (from *Freiherr von Bourgoing, Vom Wiener Kongress*, 1943)

14. *Dorothée, Comtesse de Périgord*, anonymous engraving based on *Prud'hon* (from *Der Wiener Congress: Culturgeschichte die Bildenden Künste und das Kunstgewerbe Theater—Musik in der Zeit von 1800 bis 1825* by Eduard Leisching, 1898)

15. *Vienna in 1814* (Hendes Majestæt Dronningens Håndbibliotek, Copenhagen/ Her Majesty The Queen's Reference Library, Copenhagen)

16. *View of Vienna Skyline* (Hendes Majestæt Dronningens Håndbibliotek, Copenhagen/Her Majesty The Queen's Reference Library, Copenhagen)

17. *Emperor Francis I of Austria Greets Tsar Alexander I of Russia and Frederick William III of Prussia, on 25 September 1814, Before Their Entrance to the Congress*, by Johann Nepomuk Hoechle. (AKG Images)

18. The Hofburg Palace in Vienna. (Hendes Majestæt Dronningens Håndbibliotek, Copenhagen/Her Majesty The Queen's Reference Library, Copenhagen)

19. *Peace Festival at the Prater, Held on 18 October, 1814, the First Anniversary of the Victory at the Battle of Leipzig*, by Balthasar Wigand. (Wienmuseum)

20. *Ball at Prince Metternich's During the Congress of Vienna*, wood engraving c. 1880 after Joseph Weiser. (AKG Images)

21. *View of the Imperial and Royal Redoutensaal in the Hofburg During a Masked Ball*, colored engraving by Joseph Schütz. (Wienmuseum)

22. *Grand Carousel Held on November 23, 1814, in the Winter Riding School*, by Carl Beyer. (Archiv, Bibliothek und Sammlungen der Gesellschaft der Musikfreunde in Wien)

23. A page from the score of Beethoven's unfinished celebration of the Vienna Congress, "The Choir of the Allied Princes." (Archiv, Bibliothek und Sammlungen der Gesellschaft der Musikfreunde in Wien)

24. Twelfth Night, or What You Will! *at the Theatre Royal Europe*, by George Cruickshank. (Anne S. K. Brown Military Collection, Brown University Library)

25. Klosterneuberg on the Danube. (Hendes Majestæt Dronningens Håndbibliotek, Copenhagen/Her Majesty The Queen's Reference Library, Copenhagen)

26. Gardens at Belvedere with a view of Vienna. (Hendes Majestæt Dronningens Håndbibliotek, Copenhagen/Her Majesty The Queen's Reference Library, Copenhagen)

27. *Razumovsky Palace*, by Maria Geisler 1812. (Archiv, Bibliothek und Sammlungen der Gesellschaft der Musikfreunde in Wien)

28. Portrait of Marshal Charles-Joseph (1735–1814), Prince de Ligne (litho) (b/w photo) Grevedon, Henri (1776–1860) (after). (© Bibliotheque Nationale, Paris France/The Bridgeman Art Library)

29. *Sleigh Ride to Schönbrunn, 22 January 1815*, by Friedrich Philipp Reinhold. (Wienmuseum)

30. *Napoleon at Elba*, by W. Morgan. (Anne S. K. Brown Military Collection, Brown University Library)

31. Napoleon camps outside Antibes after his arrival in France. (Anne S. K. Brown Military Collection, Brown University Library)

32. *Napoleon Returning from Elba*, by Vasily Ivanovich Sternberg (Wilhelm) (1818–45). (© Private Collection/Photo © Christie's Images/The Bridgeman Art Library)

33. Louis XVIII leaving the Tuileries. (Anne S. K. Brown Military Collection, Brown University Library)

34. *Duchess of Richmond Ball*, oil on canvas, by Robert Alexander Hillingford. (© Goodwood House, West Sussex, UK/The Bridgeman Art Library)

35. *The Aftermath of Waterloo* (Anne S. K. Brown Military Collection, Brown University Library)

36. Satire on the Congress in session, copperplate engraving by J. Zutz. (Wien-museum)

37. Satirical cartoon depicting the key protagonists in a dance at the Congress of Vienna in 1815 (engraving) by French School (19th century). (© Musée de la Ville de Paris, Musée Carnavalet, Paris, France/Lauros/Giraudon/ The Bridgeman Art Library)

Acknowledgments

It is a pleasure to thank the many people who have helped over the years I spent researching and writing this book. First, I would like to thank my agent, Suzanne Gluck at the William Morris Agency, for being the greatest and most wonderful agent anyone could ever possibly have. My editor, John A. Glusman, an award-winning historian himself, also deserves the highest awards for his editing. He was always supportive and encouraging, and his insightful comments have enormously improved the narrative.

Among many scholars, historians, experts, archivists, and librarians who have helped in the project, I would like to thank the friendly and professional staffs at Vienna's Haus-, Hof-, und StaatsArchiv; the Hofburg Palace; Schönbrunn Palace; the Schloß Schönbrunn Kultur- und BetriebsgesmbH; and many other museums and sites around town associated with the congress. Thanks to H. E. Raffaele Berlenghi, Ambassador; Patrizia Fusco; and Cristina Morrone for a superb private tour of Metternich's summer mansion, now the Italian embassy, and then site of many congress festivities and meetings. Dr. Elisabeth Hassmann at the Wagenburg Museum let me know of surviving sleigh harnesses in Vienna built for the congress. I would like to thank John Heath of the University of Vienna—I got to know John during the years we played on the baseball team at Cambridge and he became a great friend (I will never forget how he taught me to play cricket to the sounds of Johnny Cash). John's intimate knowledge of Vienna and his lively wit made my stay a pure delight. I also want to thank Ilir Ferra, a fellow writer, who also went out of his way to make me feel most welcome. Indeed in writing a book centering on Viennese hospitality, I was fortunate to experience its lavishness firsthand.

I would like to thank the Gaines Center for the Humanities for a fellowship that brought me to Vienna for a summer some seventeen years ago. This, really, instilled my love of the city, and for this I am most indebted to Professor Raymond F. Betts. Dr. Betts was not only one of the foremost European historians of our time, but also an adviser, mentor, and friend who helped in a million ways over the years until his death in 2007. It is Professor Betts who comes to mind when I think of what a historian really can become, and it is also Professor Betts who comes to mind when I think of what a profoundly positive impact someone can have on the lives of other people. I will always be thankful for the opportunity to have known such a wonderful human being.

Thanks to Dr. Christian Gottlieb at the Queen's Reference Library in Copenhagen for kindly tracking down a number of souvenirs that the king of Denmark, Frederick VI, brought back from the Congress of Vienna, including the very rare poster from the Beethoven concert on November 29, 1814, and the Christmas concert. I would also like to thank Greger Bergvall in the Kart- och bildsamlingen at the Royal Library in Stockholm; Milos Riha and Ladislav Novotny at Castle Kynzvart; Peter Harrington at the Anne S. K. Brown Military Collection at Brown University Library. Special thanks, too, to Kim Kanner Meisner for all her help and warm support of this project. I was fortunate to have my first class in diplomatic history many years ago from Professor George Herring, past Chair of the Patterson School of Diplomacy and Commerce, whose expertise in the field has been inspiring. Special thanks to Professors David Olster, Jane Gentry Vance, and Ulla Järlfors, who have generously given their time and expertise over the course of many years, and to my great benefit. I would also like to thank Professor Jeremy Popkin for magisterially fielding my complicated questions on French history, and Jake Morrissey for sharing his knowledge of sculpture, particularly explaining Canova's techniques, as well as all his support in the past. Professor Ellen Furlough and Sarah Beth Childers helped me understand spa culture in the early nineteenth century. I would also like to thank a number of old friends and fellow *Diplomacy* enthusiasts at Cambridge who made sure that we almost always had a lively evening in our weekly marathon forays into that masterpiece game of intrigue. Thanks to photographer Danielle Pousette, her husband Gustav, my brother Brent, and Chef Donnie Justice for helping me visualize some popular Viennese pastries served at congress festivities, and of course, any errors remaining in the text are mine alone. Special thanks also goes to the librarians at the Young library, Fine Arts library, and the interlibrary loan team at the University of Kentucky for all their help in obtaining countless rare books, many of them 150 to 175 years old, and coming from dozens of research libraries all over the United States and the world.

My wife, Sara, as always, makes everything so much more enjoyable. Your encouragement, support, and sense of humor are deeply appreciated, and your reading of the narrative was wildly valuable. Thanks, and I love you! A big I-love-you also goes to Julia, almost three years old, and Max, now eleven weeks, for being their adorable selves. I also want to thank my parents, Van and Cheryl King, for all their love and support, not only of this project, but of everything else, and it is a pleasure to dedicate this book to you, with all my love and gratitude.

INDEX

About the Author

DAVID KING is the author of *Finding Atlantis,* which was a Main Selection of the Book-of-the-Month Club and has been translated into several foreign languages. A Fulbright Scholar with a master's degree from Cambridge University, he taught European history at the University of Kentucky for several years. He lives in Lexington, Kentucky with his wife and their two children.

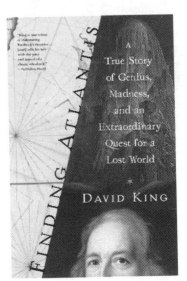

Printed in the United States
by Baker & Taylor Publisher Services